The π-calculus: a Theory of Mobile Processes

Davide Sangiorgi
INRIA Sophia Antipolis

David Walker
University of Oxford

CAMBRIDGE
UNIVERSITY PRESS

PUBLISHED BY THE PRESS SYNDICATE OF THE UNIVERSITY OF CAMBRIDGE
The Pitt Building, Trumpington Street, Cambridge, United Kingdom

CAMBRIDGE UNIVERSITY PRESS
The Edinburgh Building, Cambridge CB2 2RU, UK
40 West 20th Street, New York NY 10011–4211, USA
477 Williamstown Road, Port Melbourne, VIC 3207, Australia
Ruiz de Alarcón 13, 28014 Madrid, Spain
Dock House, The Waterfront, Cape Town 8001, South Africa

http://www.cambridge.org

First published 2001
First paperback edition 2003

A catalogue record for this book is available from the British Library

ISBN 0 521 78177 9 hardback
ISBN 0521 54327 4 paperback

Quelli che s'innamoran di pratica sanza scientia
son come 'l nocchiere ch'entra in navilio sanza timone o bussola,
che mai ha certezza dove si vada.

– Leonardo da Vinci

Contents

Foreword

Computer science aims to explain the way computational systems behave for us. The notion of calculational process, or algorithm, is a lot older than computing technology; so, oddly enough, a lot of computer science existed before modern computers. But the invention of real stored-program computers presented enormous challenges; these tools can do a lot for us if we describe properly what we want done. So computer science has made immense strides in ways of *presenting* data and algorithms, in ways of manipulating those presentations themselves as data, in matching algorithm description to task description, and so on. Technology has been the catalyst in the growth of modern computer science.

The first large phase of this growth was in free-standing computer systems. Such a system might have been a single computer program, or a multi-computer serving a community by executing several single programs successively or simultaneously. Computing theorists have built many mathematical models of these systems, in relation to their purposes. One very basic such model – the λ-calculus – is remarkably useful in this role, even if it was designed by Alonzo Church around 1940.

The second phase of the growth of computer science is in response to the advent of computer networks. No longer are systems freestanding; they interact, collaborate and interrupt each other. This has an enormous effect on the way we think about our systems. We can no longer get away with considering each system as sequential, goal-directed, deterministic or hierarchical; networks are none of these. So if we confine ourselves to such concepts then we remain dumb if asked to predict whether a network will behave in a proper – or an improper – way; for example, whether someone logging in to his bank may (as happened recently) find himself scanning someone else's account instead of his own.

The present book is a rigorous account of a basic calculus which aims to underpin our theories of interactive systems, in the same way that the λ-calculus did for freestanding computation. The authors are two of the original researchers on the π-calculus, which is now over ten years old and has served as a focus for much theoretical and practical experiment. It cannot claim to be definitive; in fact, since it was designed it has become common to express ideas about interaction and mobility in variants of the calculus. So it has become a kind of workshop of ideas.

That's the spirit in which the book is written. Half the book analyses the constructions of the calculus, searching out its meaning and exploring its expressivity by looking at weaker variants, or by looking at various type disciplines. Enthusiasts about types in programming will be struck to find that π-calculus types don't just classify *values*; they classify *patterns of behaviour*. This reflects the fact that what matters most in mobile interactive systems is not values, but connectivity and mobility of processes. With or without types, the unifying feature is *behaviour*, and what it means to say that two different processes behave the same.

The later part of the book deals with two generic applications. One of these is classical; how the π-calculus can actually do the old job which the λ-calculus does in underpinning conventional programming. The other is modern; how the calculus informs one of the most important models of interaction, the *object-oriented* model. These applications bring together much of the theory developed earlier; together, they show that a small set of constructs, provided that they emphasize *interaction* rather than calculation, can still bring some conceptual unity to the greatly extended scope of modern computing.

This book has been a labour of love for the authors over several years. Their scholarship is immense, and their organisation of ideas meticulous. As one privileged to have worked closely with them both, it's a great pleasure to be able to recommend the result as a storehouse of ideas and techniques which is unlikely to be equalled in the next decade or two.

Robin Milner
Cambridge
February 2001

Preface

Mobile systems, whose components communicate and change their structure, now pervade the informational world and the wider world of which it is a part. But the science of mobile systems is yet immature. This science must be developed if we are properly to understand mobile systems, and if we are to design systems so that they do what they are intended to do. This book presents the π-calculus, a theory of mobile systems, and shows how to use it to express systems precisely and reason about their behaviour rigorously.

The book is intended to serve both as a reference for the theory and as an extended demonstration of how to use the π-calculus to express systems and analyse their properties. The book therefore presents the theory in detail, with emphasis on proof techniques. How to use the techniques is shown both in proofs of results that form part of the theory and in example applications of it.

The book is in seven Parts. Part I introduces the π-calculus and develops its basic theory. Part II presents variations of the basic theory and important subcalculi of the π-calculus. A distinctive feature of the calculus is its rich theory of types for mobile systems. Part III introduces this theory, and Part IV shows how it is useful for understanding and reasoning about systems. Part V examines the relationship between the π-calculus and higher-order process calculi. Part VI analyses the relationship between the π-calculus and the λ-calculus. Part VII shows how ideas from π-calculus can be useful in object-oriented design and programming.

The book is written at the graduate level and is intended for computer scientists interested in mobile systems. It assumes no prior acquaintance with the π-calculus: both the theory and the viewpoint that underlies it are explained from the beginning.

Although the book covers quite a lot of ground, several topics, notably logics for mobility, and denotational and non-interleaving semantics, are not treated at all. The book contains detailed accounts of a selection of topics, chosen for their interest and because they allow us to explore concepts and techniques that can also be used elsewhere. Each Part ends with some references to sources and additional notes on related topics. We have not attempted the arduous task of referring to all relevant published work. The references given provide starting points for a reader who wishes to go more deeply into particular topics. Sometimes, an element of arbitrariness in the choice of references was inevitable.

Many exercises are suggested to help appreciation of the material; the more difficult of them are marked with an asterisk. We intend to maintain a Web page for general information and auxiliary material about the book. At the time of writing, this page is located at

`http://www-sop.inria.fr/mimosa/personnel/Davide.Sangiorgi/Book_pi.html`

Acknowledgements Our greatest debt is to Robin Milner. The field that is the subject of this book was shaped by his fundamental work on CCS and in creating and developing the π-calculus. Further, we have both been privileged to have worked with Milner, and his influence on our approach to the subject and how to write about it are profound.

We thank the many colleagues – too many to mention here – with whom we have worked on or discussed π-calculus and related topics, and whose insights and comments have contributed to our understanding.

We are grateful to the following people for reading parts of a draft of the book and offering comments that helped us improve it: Michael Baldamus, Silvia Crafa, Cédric Fournet, Daniel Hirshkoff, Kohei Honda, Naoki Kobayashi, Giovanni Lagorio, Cédric Lhoussaine, Huimin Lin, Barbara König, Robin Milner, Julian Rathke, Vasco Vasconcelos, Nobuko Yoshida, and especially Marco Pistore.

We record our appreciation of the work of David Tranah and his colleagues at Cambridge University Press in guiding the book into print.

Finally, we thank Laurence Sangiorgi and Katharine Grevling for their encouragement, assistance, and patience during the seemingly interminable process of writing.

General Introduction

Mobile systems are everywhere. Palpable examples are mobile communication devices and the networks that span the Earth and reach out into Space. And less tangibly, there is mobile code and the wondrous weaving within the World Wide Web. An accepted science of mobile systems is not yet established, however. The development of this science is both necessary and challenging. It is likely that it will consist of theories offering explanations at many different levels. But there should be something basic that underlies the various theories.

This book presents the π-calculus, a theory of mobile systems. The π-calculus provides a conceptual framework for understanding mobility, and mathematical tools for expressing mobile systems and reasoning about their behaviours. We believe it is an important stepping-stone on the path to the science of mobile systems.

But what is mobility? When we talk about mobile systems, what are the entities that move, and in what space do they move? Our broad answer is based on distinguishing two kinds of mobility. In one kind, it is *links* that move in an abstract space of *linked processes*. For example: hypertext links can be created, can be passed around, and can disappear; the connections between cellular telephones and a network of base stations can change as the telephones are carried around; and references can be passed as arguments of method invocations in object-oriented systems. In the second kind of mobility, it is *processes* that move in an abstract space of linked processes. For instance: code can be sent over a network and put to work at its destination; mobile devices can acquire new functionality using, for instance, the Jini technology [AWO$^+$99]; and procedures can be passed as arguments of method invocations in object-oriented systems.

The π-calculus treats the first kind of mobility: it directly expresses movement of links in a space of linked processes. There are two kinds of basic entity in the (untyped) π-calculus: names and processes. Names are names of links. Processes can interact by using names that they share. The crux is that the data that processes communicate in interactions are themselves names, and a name received in one interaction can be used to participate in another. By receiving a name, a process can acquire a capability to interact with processes that were unknown to it. The structure of a system – the connections among its component processes – can thus change over time, in arbitrary ways. The source of the π-calculus's strength is how it treats scoping of names and extrusion of names from their scopes.

The second kind of mobility, where it is processes (or, more generally, computational entities built from processes) that move, can be made precise in several ways. We will examine a theory based on process-passing, the Higher-Order π-calculus, in Part V. In the book, calculi based on process-passing mobility are called *higher-order* calculi, and those, such as the π-calculus, that are based on name-passing mobility are called *first-order* calculi.

What can be said by way of comparison between name-passing and process-passing, and in particular for the precedence given in this book to first-order calculi? First, naming and name-passing are ubiquitous: think of addresses, identifiers, links, pointers, references. Secondly, as we will see, name-passing as embodied in the π-calculus is extremely expressive. In particular, Part V shows how process-passing calculi can be modelled in π-calculus. But name-passing is also more refined than process-passing. For by passing a name, one can pass partial access to a process, an ability to interact with it only in a certain way. Similarly, with name-passing one can easily model sharing, for instance of a resource that can be used by different sets of clients at different times. It can be complicated to model these things when processes are the only transmissible values. Thirdly, it was possible to work out the theory of π-calculus, and the theory is tractable. The theory of process-passing is harder, and important parts of it are not yet well understood. Its advancement has been, and can continue to be, greatly helped by the existence of the simpler theory of the π-calculus, in much the same way that the development of π-calculus was made much easier by prior work on theories of non-mobile processes.

The π-calculus does not explicitly mention location or distribution of mobile processes. The issue of location and distribution is orthogonal to the question of name-passing or process-passing. One can envisage worlds in which processes reside at locations and exchange links, worlds in which they exchange processes, and worlds in which they exchange both links and processes. It is too early to be able to distil the right concepts for treating distributed mobile systems and all the associated phenomena. We may hope, however, that ideas from π-calculus will continue to contribute to the search for these concepts and the development of theories based on them. At the time of writing, many theories treating location or distribution are being investigated. Some of them are extensions or close relatives of the π-calculus, for instance the Distributed Join Calculus [FGL+96] and the Distributed π-calculus [HR98b], while others are influenced by it, such as the Ambient Calculus [CG98] and Oz [Smo95]. All of these calculi and languages benefit from the theory of π-calculus.

In π-calculus, names are names of links. But what is a link? The calculus is not prescriptive on this point: *link* is construed very broadly, and names can be put to very many uses. This point is important and deserves some attention. For example, names can be thought of as channels that processes use to communicate. Also, by syntactic means and using type systems, π-calculus names can be used to represent names of processes or names of objects in the sense of object-oriented programming. (Part VII is about objects and π-calculus.) Further, although the π-calculus does not mention locations explicitly, often when describing systems in π-calculus, some names are naturally thought of as locations. Finally, some names can be thought of as encryption keys as, for instance, in the Spi calculus [AG97], which applies ideas from π-calculus to computer security.

The π-calculus has two aspects. First, it is a theory of mobile systems. The π-calculus has a rich blend of techniques for reasoning about the behaviour of systems, as we will see in the book. There has been some initial work on development of (semi-) automatic tools to assist in reasoning, but substantial challenges, both theoretical and practical, remain. Second, the π-calculus is a general model of computation, which takes interaction as primitive. The relationship between the π-calculus and the λ-calculus, which is a general model of computation that takes function application as primitive, is studied in depth in Part VI. Just as the λ-calculus underlies functional programming languages, so the π-calculus, or a variant of it, is the basis for several experimental programming languages, for instance Pict [PT00], Join [INR], and TyCO [VB98].

Of central concern in concurrency theory is when two terms express processes that have the same observable behaviour. The technical basis for the account of behavioural equivalence in the book is the notion of *bisimulation*. Bisimulation is one of the most stable and mathematically natural concepts developed in concurrency theory. It is at the heart of a successful theory of behavioural equivalence for non-mobile processes [Mil89], and it has important connections with non-well-founded sets [Acz88], domain theory [Abr91], modal logic [HM85], and final coalgebras [RT94]. Two π-calculus terms will be deemed to express the same behaviour if they are *barbed congruent*, that is, if no difference can be observed when the terms are put into an arbitrary π-calculus context and compared using the appropriate bisimulation game. Although the book concentrates on barbed congruence and other equivalences based on bisimulation, almost all of the results presented hold for other contextually-defined equivalences. The basic theory of the π-calculus is presented in Part I and Part II.

When employing π-calculus to describe a system, one normally follows a discipline that governs how names can be used. Such disciplines can be made explicit using *types*. This brings several benefits, notably the possibility of statically detecting many programming errors. Using types also has important consequences for the behaviour of processes and the techniques for reasoning about behaviour. Types are one of the most important differences between π-calculus and non-mobile process calculi. They are studied in Part III and Part IV.

A technical theme that recurs throughout the book is interpreting one calculus or language in another. There are several reasons for presenting and studying interpretations. First, in many cases, doing so addresses fundamental concerns relating to the expressiveness of calculi, and gives insight into how to use them for modelling systems. Secondly, showing how to express terms of one language or calculus in another often demonstrates effective use of important programming idioms. And thirdly, by studying properties of encodings, we show various proof techniques in action and illustrate ideas that are useful for analysing systems.

Robin Milner's invention of the Calculus of Communicating Systems (CCS) in the late 1970s was a watershed in the theory of concurrency [Mil80]. CCS inspired the field of process calculus, which continues to flourish some twenty years later. The π-calculus was created in the late 1980s by Milner, Joachim Parrow, and the second author [MPW89]. It evolved from CCS via an Extended Calculus of Communicating Systems introduced by Mogens Nielsen and Uffe Engberg [EN86].

The first book treating π-calculus was written by Milner [Mil99]. Based on an undergraduate course, it recapitulates CCS and then introduces π-calculus, with emphasis on examples and using the calculus to express systems. [Mil99] is an excellent introduction to concurrency theory in general and to CCS and the π-calculus in particular, and a reader unfamiliar with the field may find it easier to start with it. The present book covers more of the basic theory and in greater depth, and takes the reader further into the subject. We hope that it forms a natural complement to Milner's book.

Part I

The π-calculus

Introduction to Part I

Part I introduces the π-calculus. It explains how the terms of the calculus describe the structure and the behaviour of mobile systems. It also develops the basic theory of behavioural equivalence, and introduces basic techniques for reasoning about systems.

How system behaviour is expressed is fundamental to the theory. Two accounts of behaviour will be given. The first explains how a system represented by a π-calculus term can evolve independently of its environment. At the heart of this first account is a binary relation on terms called *reduction*. The second account explains not only activity within a system but also how the system can interact with its environment. Central to it is a *labelled transition system* on terms.

Why are there two accounts of behaviour? The reason is that each has useful qualities that the other lacks. Reduction explains activity within systems in a way that overcomes the rigidity of linear syntax. This makes the account based on reduction easy to grasp, something that is helpful when the π-calculus is encountered for the first time. Reduction has two related limitations, however. First, it does not say how a system can interact with its environment. And second, the free treatment of syntax, which helps to make the account simple, also makes it difficult to prove things about behaviours. The account based on transition overcomes both of these limitations, but at the unavoidable cost of a little increase in complexity. It explains both activity within a system and interaction between a system and its environment by describing the *actions* that processes can perform. And it explains action in a way that is guided by the syntax of terms, so that, in particular, the structure of proofs can follow the syntax.

Reduction is a relation of a kind familiar from term-rewriting systems, while labelled transition systems are well known from process calculi. In term-rewriting systems, the definition of the reduction relation is relatively straightforward because a redex of a term must be a *subterm*. For example, in the λ-calculus –

perhaps the best-known term-rewriting system – in order for a function to be applied to an argument, the two must be contiguous. It is less straightforward to define reduction on terms of π-calculus (or indeed of any process calculus), because two subterms of a process-term may interact even though they are not contiguous. To define reduction on process-terms, a relation, called *structural congruence*, that allows manipulation of term-structure is needed. On the other hand, the labelled transition system is standard, albeit with some elaboration to treat name-passing properly.

Structural congruence and reduction on π-terms are defined by rules whose simplicity helps in making clear the meanings of the π-calculus operators. Some of the rules defining the labelled transition system on π-terms are a little more subtle. The two accounts of behaviour are in harmony, however: the internal transitions of a term are the same as the term's reductions, up to structural congruence.

The relation we adopt as behavioural equivalence on π-terms is *barbed congruence*. Its definition is couched in terms of internal transition and a notion of *observation* of processes. Two π-terms are deemed barbed congruent if no difference can be observed between the processes obtained by placing them into an arbitrary π-context. The notion of observation has the flavour of the report of the successful outcome of an experiment, as in a theory of *testing* equivalence [DH84]. The definition of barbed congruence is simple and robust in that it can be applied to different calculi, as we will see, for instance, in Part IV when we consider typed processes and in Part V when we consider higher-order processes.

This method of defining equivalence of behaviour, involving quantification over contexts, is natural and properly sensitive to the calculus under consideration. The definitions it yields are, however, difficult to work with. This fact motivates the study of auxiliary behavioural equivalences that afford tractable techniques. These *labelled* equivalences are based on direct comparison of the actions that processes can perform, rather than on observation of arbitrary systems containing them. There are in fact several labelled equivalences, each of which has characteristics that make it useful in some way. It turns out, however, that one of them (arguably the most natural) leads to a characterization of barbed congruence. This fact leads us to concentrate on that particular labelled equivalence, which we call *bisimilarity*. The labelled equivalences are not as robust as barbed congruence. Indeed, we will see in Part IV and Part V that bisimilarity can be much too discriminating on extensions of the π-calculus.

The actions that π-calculus processes perform fall into two categories. First, there are the *internal* actions. An internal action of a process is typically the result of an interaction between two of its components. The *visible* actions comprise the second category. They describe a process's potential for interaction with its environment. When the π-calculus is applied, it is invariably the visible actions that are of interest. For this reason, barbed congruence (and the labelled equivalences) must abstract from internal action. Rather than introducing both aspects of equivalence (the bisimulation game and abstraction from internal action) together, however, it is better to study first simpler, and more demanding, variants of the equivalences that treat internal action and visible action on a par.

An equivalence that abstracts from internal action is sometimes called a *weak* equivalence, and one that does not a *strong* equivalence. Introducing strong equivalence before weak equivalence has three benefits. First, in many respects weak equivalence differs from strong equivalence only in details, and there is advantage in working out the simpler case first. Secondly, in some respects the difference between weak equivalence and strong equivalence is *not* just a matter of detail, and it is valuable to expose this fact and to see where and why more complex technical machinery is needed. Thirdly, strong equivalence can be helpful when working with weak equivalence, because the strong version of an equivalence implies the weak version and strong equivalences are often useful as auxiliary relations in proof techniques. It is important to bear in mind, however, that the goal is weak equivalence, and that strong equivalence is just a useful stepping-stone on the route to it.

Structure of the Part Part I is composed of two chapters. Chapter 1 introduces the language of the π-calculus, and explains how its terms, the processes, express mobile systems. Chapter 2 presents the basic theory of behavioural equivalence of processes.

Chapter 1 is in four sections. Section 1.1 presents the processes of the π-calculus, together with an informal account of their meanings. Binding and substitution, which are central to the modelling of changing connectivity, are also explained. Section 1.2 begins the formal account of behaviour by defining structural congruence and reduction. It also gives several examples to illustrate mobility in the π-calculus. Section 1.3 introduces the labelled transition system. The rules defining the transition relations are discussed and illustrated in detail. Basic properties of the transition system are presented in Section 1.4. In particular, the relationship between the two accounts of process activity, via the reduction relation and via the transition relations, is shown.

Chapter 2 is also in four sections. Section 2.1 begins the development of the theory of strong equivalence. The principal relation is strong barbed congruence. Strong barbed equivalence is also introduced. This is defined like strong barbed congruence, but using only some of the contexts; precisely, processes are compared by running them in parallel with other processes that play the role of testers. Section 2.2 introduces the main strong labelled equivalences, strong bisimilarity and strong full bisimilarity, and establishes their basic properties, in particular that they coincide with strong barbed equivalence and strong barbed congruence, respectively. In addition, many results useful in reasoning about processes are presented, including the Expansion Lemma for unfolding process behaviour and results concerning the replication operator, the operator that makes it possible to express infinite behaviour. Further techniques for showing processes to be strong barbed congruent, up-to techniques, are developed in Section 2.3. In Section 2.4 (weak) barbed congruence is finally defined, and basic results about barbed congruence and the main labelled equivalences are presented.

1

Processes

1.1 Syntax

This section introduces the language of the π-calculus. Its terms, the processes, express mobile systems. The meanings of processes are discussed informally, and name-binding and name-substitution, two notions needed for the formal account, are explained.

The simplest entities of the π-calculus are *names*. They can be thought of as names of communication links. Processes use names to interact, and pass names to one another by mentioning them in interactions. Names received by a process can be used and mentioned by it in further interactions. A countably-infinite set of names is presupposed, ranged over by lower-case letters.

Processes evolve by performing actions. The capabilities for action are expressed via the *prefixes*, of which there are four kinds:

$$\pi \quad ::= \quad \overline{x}y \mid x(z) \mid \tau \mid [x=y]\pi \ .$$

The first capability is to send the name y via the name x, and the second to receive any name via x – the role of z will be explained shortly. The third is a capability for unobservable action – this will also be explained soon. The fourth is a conditional capability: the capability π if x and y are the same name.

We now define the processes and a particular subclass of them.

Definition 1.1.1 (π-calculus) The *processes* and the *summations* of the π-calculus are given respectively by

$$\begin{array}{lcl} P & ::= & M \mid P \mid P' \mid \nu z\, P \mid\ !P \\ M & ::= & \mathbf{0} \mid \pi . P \mid M + M' \ . \end{array}$$

□

We give a brief, informal account of the intended interpretation of processes, beginning with the summations.

(1) $\mathbf{0}$ is *inaction*; it is a process that can do nothing.

(2) The *prefix* $\pi.P$ has a single capability, expressed by π; the process P cannot proceed until that capability has been exercised.

The *output prefix* $\overline{x}y.P$ can send the name y via the name x and continue as P.

The *input prefix* $x(z).P$ can receive any name via x and continue as P with the received name substituted for z. For instance, $x(z).\overline{y}z.\mathbf{0}$ can receive any name via x, send the name received via y, and become inactive, while $x(z).\overline{z}y.\mathbf{0}$ can receive any name via x, send y via the name received, and become inactive.

The *unobservable prefix* $\tau.P$ can evolve invisibly to P. As in CCS, τ can be thought of as expressing an internal action of a process.

The *match prefix* $[x=y]\pi.P$ can evolve as $\pi.P$ if x and y are the same name, and can do nothing otherwise. For instance, $x(z).[z=y]\overline{z}w.\mathbf{0}$, on receiving a name via x, can send w via that name just if that name is y; if it is not, the process can do nothing further. A second example: as its third action, $x(z).y(w).[z=w]\overline{v}u.\mathbf{0}$ can send u via v just if it receives the same name via x and y in its first two actions.

(3) The capabilities of the *sum* $P+P'$ are those of P together with those of P'. When a sum exercises one of its capabilities, the others are rendered void. For instance, $x(z).\overline{z}y.\mathbf{0}+\overline{w}v.\mathbf{0}$ has two capabilities: to receive a name via x, and to send v via w. If the first capability is exercised and u is the name received via x, then the continuation is $\overline{u}y.\mathbf{0}$; the capability to send v via w is lost. If, on the other hand, the second capability is exercised, then the continuation is $\mathbf{0}$, and the capability to receive via x is lost.

(4) In the *composition* $P \mid P'$, the components P and P' can proceed independently and can interact via shared names. For instance, $(x(z).\overline{z}y.\mathbf{0}+\overline{w}v.\mathbf{0}) \mid \overline{x}u.\mathbf{0}$ has four capabilities: to receive a name via x, to send v via w, to send u via x, and to evolve invisibly as an effect of an interaction between its components via the shared name x.

(5) In the *restriction* $\boldsymbol{\nu} z\, P$, the scope of the name z is restricted to P. Components of P can use z to interact with one another but not with other processes. For instance, $\boldsymbol{\nu} x\,((x(z).\overline{z}y.\mathbf{0}+\overline{w}v.\mathbf{0}) \mid \overline{x}u.\mathbf{0})$ has only two capabilities: to send v via w, and to evolve invisibly as an effect of an interaction between its components via x. The scope of a restriction may change as a result of interaction between processes. This important feature of the calculus will be explained in detail later.

(6) Finally, the *replication* $!P$ can be thought of as an infinite composition $P \mid P \mid \cdots$ or, equivalently, a process satisfying the equation $!P = P \mid !P$. Replication is the operator that makes it possible to express infinite behaviours. For example, $!x(z).\, !\overline{y}z.\mathbf{0}$ can receive names via x repeatedly, and can repeatedly send via y any name it does receive.

It is worth making three observations about processes at this point. First, the operands in a sum must themselves be summations. Allowing the operands in a sum to be arbitrary processes complicates the theory and is seldom useful. Secondly, an alternative to replication as a means of expressing infinite behaviour is recursive definition of processes. Replication is technically simpler than recursion, but recursion is often convenient. We will examine the relationship between the two in Section 3.2. Thirdly, the language has no *mismatch* prefix form $[x \neq y]\pi$, with the interpretation that $[x \neq y]\pi.\, P$ can evolve as $\pi.\, P$ just if x and y are different. Match, and especially mismatch, prefixes are seldom useful for describing systems. Match prefixes are needed, however, to formulate the Expansion Lemma for strong full bisimilarity (see Section 2.2.2). The inclusion of mismatch prefixes, on the other hand, would violate the following monotonicity property of processes: that application of a name-substitution to a process does not diminish its capabilities for action (Lemma 1.4.8). We will see a place where this property is useful for reasoning about the behaviour of processes in Section 4.6.

The π-calculus has two name-binding operators:

Definition 1.1.2 (Binding) In each of $x(z).\, P$ and $\nu z\, P$, the displayed occurrence of z is *binding* with *scope* P. An occurrence of a name in a process is *bound* if it is, or it lies within the scope of, a binding occurrence of the name. An occurrence of a name in a process is *free* if it is not bound. □

We write $\mathsf{fn}(P)$ for the set of names that have a free occurrence in P. For instance,

$$\mathsf{fn}((\overline{z}y.\mathbf{0} + \overline{w}v.\mathbf{0}) \mid \overline{x}u.\mathbf{0}) = \{z, y, w, v, x, u\}$$

and

$$\mathsf{fn}(\nu x\, ((x(z).\, \overline{z}y.\mathbf{0} + \overline{w}v.\mathbf{0}) \mid \nu u\, \overline{x}u.\mathbf{0})) = \{y, w, v\}\ .$$

It is straightforward to show by induction that $\mathsf{fn}(P)$ is finite for every P.

The free names of a process circumscribe its capabilities for action: for a name x, in order for P to send x, to send via x, or to receive via x, it must be that $x \in \mathsf{fn}(P)$. Thus in order for two processes to interact via a name, that name must occur free in both of them, in one case expressing a capability to send, and in the other a capability to receive. Much can be understood about the behaviour of processes by looking closely at how names occur in them.

The binding of a name z in a process $x(z).P$ is analogous to the binding of a variable z in a λ-calculus term $\lambda z.N$: the free occurrences of z in N indicate the places where the argument will be substituted when the λ-term is applied; the free occurrences of z in P indicate the places where the name received via x will be substituted when the process acts. It is by means of such substitutions of names for names that change of connectivity among the components of a system is expressed.

The second binding operator, restriction, is related to the CCS restriction operator: in $\boldsymbol{\nu} z\, P$, components of P can use z to interact with one another but not with other processes. Restriction in π-calculus has other aspects, however: in $\boldsymbol{\nu} z\, P$, components of P can also pass z to one another, and they can extrude the scope of z by sending z via some other name. This will be explained when we examine reduction and transition formally.

To illustrate some of the points made above, consider the process

$$(x(z).\,\overline{z}a.\,\mathbf{0} \mid \overline{x}w.\,\overline{y}w.\,\mathbf{0}) \mid y(v).\,v(u).\,\mathbf{0}\ .$$

The first and second components share the name x, that is, x occurs free in both of them. Similarly, the second and third components share y. The first and third components, however, share no name. This last fact guarantees that the first and third components cannot interact immediately. Moreover, the second and third components cannot interact immediately as the name y that they share is underneath a prefix in the second component. The first two components can interact, however, via x, and the resulting process is

$$(\overline{w}a.\,\mathbf{0} \mid \overline{y}w.\,\mathbf{0}) \mid y(v).\,v(u).\,\mathbf{0}\ .$$

The second component can now send the name w to the third component via y, resulting in

$$(\overline{w}a.\,\mathbf{0} \mid \mathbf{0}) \mid w(u).\,\mathbf{0}\ .$$

As an effect of these two interactions, the first and third components, which initially shared no names, now share w. Indeed, the first can send the third the name a via w.

To express that a process can use names it receives, syntactic substitution of names for names is employed.

Definition 1.1.3 (Substitution) A *substitution* is a function on names that is the identity except on a finite set. □

Notation 1.1.4 (Substitution) We use σ to range over substitutions, and write $x\sigma$, or sometimes $\sigma(x)$, for σ applied to x. The *support* of σ, $\mathsf{supp}(\sigma)$, is $\{x \mid x\sigma \neq x\}$, and the *co-support* of σ, $\mathsf{cosupp}(\sigma)$, is $\{x\sigma \mid x \in \mathsf{supp}(\sigma)\}$. We write $\mathsf{n}(\sigma)$ for $\mathsf{supp}(\sigma) \cup \mathsf{cosupp}(\sigma)$, and refer to it as the set of *names* of σ. We write $\{y_1,\ldots,y_n/x_1,\ldots,x_n\}$ for the substitution σ such that $x_i\sigma = y_i$ for each i and $x\sigma = x$ for $x \notin \{x_1,\ldots,x_n\}$. If X is a set of names, we write $X\sigma$ for $\{x\sigma \mid x \in X\}$. □

We wish to define the effect of applying a substitution σ to a process P. This is essentially to replace each free occurrence of each name x in P by $x\sigma$. The replacement must, however, be done in such a way that unintended capture of names by binders is avoided, just as in λ-calculus the substitution of a term for a variable in a term must not result in unintended capture of variables by binders. For instance, the result of substituting the name z for the name x in the process $y(z).\,\overline{z}x.\,\mathbf{0}$ should be $y(w).\,\overline{w}z.\,\mathbf{0}$ for some name $w \neq z$, just as the result of substituting the λ-term zz for the variable x in the λ-term $\lambda z.\,zx$ is $\lambda w.\,w(zz)$ for some variable $w \neq z$. The following definitions are useful, as in λ-calculus.

Definition 1.1.5 (α-convertibility)

(1) If the name w does not occur in the process P, then $P\{w/z\}$ is the process obtained by replacing each free occurrence of z in P by w.
(2) A *change of bound names* in a process P is the replacement of a subterm $x(z).\,Q$ of P by $x(w).\,Q\{w/z\}$, or the replacement of a subterm $\boldsymbol{\nu}z\,Q$ of P by $\boldsymbol{\nu}w\,Q\{w/z\}$, where in each case w does not occur in Q.
(3) Processes P and Q are *α-convertible*, $P = Q$, if Q can be obtained from P by a finite number of changes of bound names. □

For example,

$$y(z).\,\overline{z}x.\,\mathbf{0} = y(w).\,\overline{w}x.\,\mathbf{0}$$

and

$$\boldsymbol{\nu}y\,(y(z).\,\overline{z}x.\,\mathbf{0} \mid \boldsymbol{\nu}w\,\overline{y}w.\,w(v).\,\overline{x}v.\,\mathbf{0}) = \boldsymbol{\nu}u\,(u(y).\,\overline{y}x.\,\mathbf{0} \mid \boldsymbol{\nu}w\,\overline{u}w.\,w(z).\,\overline{x}z.\,\mathbf{0})\,.$$

We have used the symbol '=' for α-convertibility because we intend to identify α-convertible processes. In π-calculus, the entities of interest are the equivalence classes of processes modulo α-convertibility, in the same sense that in λ-calculus the entities of interest are the equivalence classes of λ-terms modulo α-convertibility. α-convertibility in π-calculus is essentially the same as α-convertibility in λ-calculus. One feature of π-calculus gives rise to a point about α-convertibility not found in λ-calculus, however. This is the possibility of extrusion of the scope of a name; see Section 1.3.

Having noted all of this we adopt two conventions:

Convention 1.1.6 Processes that are α-convertible are identified. □

Convention 1.1.7 When considering a collection of processes and substitutions, we assume that the bound names of the processes are chosen to be different from their free names and from the names of the substitutions. □

Convention 1.1.7 will be extended in a natural way to encompass other kinds of entity when we consider scope extrusion (Convention 1.4.10).

To define the effect of applying a substitution to a process, we first define the effect of applying a substitution σ to a prefix π. This is simply to replace each occurrence of each name x in π by $x\sigma$. In the clauses for input prefix $[x_1 = y_1] \cdots [x_n = y_n] x(z).\, P$ and restriction $\boldsymbol{\nu} z\, P$ below, the bound name z is assumed by Convention 1.1.7 not to be in $\mathsf{fn}(P)\sigma \cup \mathsf{n}(\sigma)$. Consequently the definition is straightforward. We write $\stackrel{\text{def}}{=}$ for definitional equality.

Definition 1.1.8 (Application of substitution) The process, $P\sigma$, obtained by applying σ to P is defined as follows:

$$\begin{aligned}
\mathbf{0}\sigma &\stackrel{\text{def}}{=} \mathbf{0} \\
(\pi.\, P)\sigma &\stackrel{\text{def}}{=} \pi\sigma.\, P\sigma \\
(P + P')\sigma &\stackrel{\text{def}}{=} P\sigma + P'\sigma \\
(P \mid P')\sigma &\stackrel{\text{def}}{=} P\sigma \mid P'\sigma \\
(\boldsymbol{\nu} z\, P)\sigma &\stackrel{\text{def}}{=} \boldsymbol{\nu} z\, P\sigma \\
(!P)\sigma &\stackrel{\text{def}}{=} !P\sigma\,.
\end{aligned}$$

□

By the definition we have, for example,

$$(y(w).\, \overline{w}x.\, \mathbf{0})\{z/x\} = y(w).\, \overline{w}z.\, \mathbf{0}$$

and

$$(\,!\boldsymbol{\nu} z\, \overline{x}z.\, \mathbf{0} \mid y(w).\, \mathbf{0})\{v,v/x,y\} = !\boldsymbol{\nu} z\, \overline{v}z.\, \mathbf{0} \mid v(w).\, \mathbf{0}\,.$$

Notation 1.1.9 (Operator precedence) When writing processes as linear expressions, we use parentheses to resolve ambiguity, and observe the conventions that prefixing, restriction, and replication bind more tightly than composition, and prefixing more tightly than sum. Thus $\pi.\, P \mid Q$ is $(\pi.\, P) \mid Q$, $\boldsymbol{\nu} z\, P \mid Q$

is $(\nu z\, P) \mid Q$, $!P \mid Q$ is $(!P) \mid Q$, and $\pi.\, P + Q$ is $(\pi.\, P) + Q$. Further, when writing expressions involving substitutions, we regard a substitution as binding more tightly than a process operator. So, for example, $\pi.\, P\sigma$ is $\pi.\,(P\sigma)$. We also sometimes insert parentheses to aid reading, for instance writing $(\nu x)\, P$. □

1.2 Reduction

This section begins to make the informal account of behaviour precise by defining the *reduction* relation, $\longrightarrow$, on processes. The assertion $P \longrightarrow P'$ expresses that process P can evolve to process P' as a result of an intraaction, that is, an action *within* P. Reduction is defined by a family of inference rules, and a relation of structural congruence plays a key role in the definition by allowing manipulation of term-structure to bring potential interactors together.

The section comprises three subsections. The first discusses the rules defining reduction informally. The second defines structural congruence and reduction, and gives several small examples. The last subsection contains an extended example.

1.2.1 Discussion

The essence of reduction is captured in the axiom:

$$(\overline{x}y.\, P_1 + M_1) \mid (x(z).\, P_2 + M_2) \longrightarrow P_1 \mid P_2\{y/z\}\ . \tag{1.1}$$

The process, P, on the left of the arrow consists of two components. Among their capabilities are in the one case to send y via x, and in the other to receive a name via x. The axiom expresses that P has a reduction arising from an interaction between its components via x, and that as effects of this reduction: y is passed from the first component to the second and is substituted for the placeholder z in P_2, the two prefixes are consumed, and the other capabilities of the two components, expressed by M_1 and M_2, are rendered void; in summary, P evolves to $P_1 \mid P_2\{y/z\}$.

One might immediately envisage a second, variant, axiom:

$$(x(z).\, P_2 + M_2) \mid (\overline{x}y.\, P_1 + M_1) \longrightarrow P_2\{y/z\} \mid P_1\ . \tag{1.2}$$

It will not be necessary to adopt (1.2) as an axiom, however, because of the presence of a general structural rule that will make it possible to infer reduction (1.2) from reduction (1.1). The structural rule is:

$$\text{from } P_1 \equiv P_2 \text{ and } P_2 \longrightarrow P_2' \text{ and } P_2' \equiv P_1', \text{ infer } P_1 \longrightarrow P_1'\,, \tag{1.3}$$

where $\equiv$ is the structural-congruence relation, defined below. It is possible to infer reduction (1.2) from reduction (1.1) using the structural rule because $P \mid P' \equiv P' \mid P$ for any processes P and P'.

There will be a second axiom,

$$\tau.\, P + M \longrightarrow P\,, \tag{1.4}$$

where we think of the τ prefix as expressing an intraaction whose origin is not made explicit. The other capabilities are again rendered void by the reduction; and again the variant axiom-candidate

$$M + \tau.\, P \longrightarrow P$$

will be unnecessary, this time because $M_1 + M_2 \equiv M_2 + M_1$ for any summations M_1 and M_2.

To complete the inference system defining $\longrightarrow$, the axioms (1.1) and (1.4) and the structural rule (1.3) are joined by two further rules. The first is:

$$\text{from } P_1 \longrightarrow P_1' \text{ infer } P_1 \mid P_2 \longrightarrow P_1' \mid P_2\,. \tag{1.5}$$

It expresses that if the component P_1 of the process $P_1 \mid P_2$ has a reduction, then $P_1 \mid P_2$ itself has a reduction, the effect of which is just the effect on P_1: the other component P_2 is unaffected by the action within P_1. Note that by (1.5) and the structural rule (1.3) we have also that

$$\text{if } P_1 \longrightarrow P_1' \text{ then } P_2 \mid P_1 \longrightarrow P_2 \mid P_1'\,.$$

The second further rule expresses that restriction of a name does not inhibit a reduction:

$$\text{from } P \longrightarrow P' \text{ infer } \boldsymbol{\nu} z\, P \longrightarrow \boldsymbol{\nu} z\, P'\,. \tag{1.6}$$

The reduction is not inhibited even if it arises from a communication via the name that is restricted. For instance, by (1.1) and (1.6),

$$\boldsymbol{\nu} x\, ((\overline{x}y.\, P_1 + M_1) \mid (x(z).\, P_2 + M_2)) \longrightarrow \boldsymbol{\nu} x\, (P_1 \mid P_2\{y/z\})\,.$$

This approach to defining reduction – the two axioms (1.1) and (1.4), the two rules (1.5) and (1.6), and the structural rule (1.3) – is beautifully simple. It is clear, however, that for the approach to capture the richness of process behaviour, much of the action must be in the structural-congruence relation, which features so prominently in the crucial structural rule.

1.2.2 Structural congruence and reduction

The basis for the definition of structural congruence is a small collection of axioms that allow manipulation of term-structure. The particular axioms are chosen because they allow just the desired manipulations, and because each of them expresses something intrinsic to the meanings of π-operators.

To define structural congruence, we need the notions of context and congruence. First, a minor auxiliary definition, needed because only summations can be operands in sums: an occurrence of $\mathbf{0}$ in a process is *degenerate* if it is the left or right term in a sum $M_1 + M_2$, and *non-degenerate* otherwise. For instance in $\mathbf{0} + \overline{x}y.\,\mathbf{0}$, the first occurrence is degenerate but the second is non-degenerate.

Informally, a context differs from a process only in having the *hole* $[\cdot]$ in place of a non-degenerate occurrence of $\mathbf{0}$. Contexts that are α-convertible are not identified, however: a context is regarded as a syntactic entity that transforms processes to processes. Formally, therefore, we have:

Definition 1.2.1 (Context) A *context* is obtained when the hole $[\cdot]$ replaces a non-degenerate occurrence of $\mathbf{0}$ in a process-term given by the grammar in Definition 1.1.1. □

Example contexts are

$$\boldsymbol{\nu} z\,([\cdot] \mid !z(w).\,\overline{w}a.\,\mathbf{0})$$

and

$$x(z).\; !\boldsymbol{\nu} w\,(\overline{z}w.\,[\cdot] + y(v).\,\mathbf{0})\;.$$

If C is a context and P a process, we write $C[P]$ for the process obtained by replacing the $[\cdot]$ in C by P. The replacement is literal, so names free in P may be bound in $C[P]$. For example, writing C_0 for the first example context above,

$$C_0[!\overline{z}b.\,\mathbf{0}] = \boldsymbol{\nu} z\,(!\overline{z}b.\,\mathbf{0} \mid !z(w).\,\overline{w}a.\,\mathbf{0})\;.$$

The notion of congruence is very important in the theory of processes. It provides the technical underpinning for a compositional account of behavioural equivalence.

Definition 1.2.2 (Congruence) An equivalence relation $\mathcal{S}$ on processes is a *congruence* if $(P, Q) \in \mathcal{S}$ implies $(C[P], C[Q]) \in \mathcal{S}$ for every context C. □

We can now define structural congruence.

Definition 1.2.3 (Structural congruence) *Structural congruence*, $\equiv$, is the smallest congruence on processes that satisfies the axioms in Table 1.1. □

In other words, processes P and Q are structurally congruent if $P \equiv Q$ can be inferred from the axioms listed in Table 1.1 together with the rules of equational reasoning, that is, the rules in Table 1.2 (where $=$ is read as $\equiv$).

SC-MAT	$[x=x]\pi.P$	$\equiv$	$\pi.P$
SC-SUM-ASSOC	$M_1 + (M_2 + M_3)$	$\equiv$	$(M_1 + M_2) + M_3$
SC-SUM-COMM	$M_1 + M_2$	$\equiv$	$M_2 + M_1$
SC-SUM-INACT	$M + \mathbf{0}$	$\equiv$	M
SC-COMP-ASSOC	$P_1 \mid (P_2 \mid P_3)$	$\equiv$	$(P_1 \mid P_2) \mid P_3$
SC-COMP-COMM	$P_1 \mid P_2$	$\equiv$	$P_2 \mid P_1$
SC-COMP-INACT	$P \mid \mathbf{0}$	$\equiv$	P
SC-RES	$\boldsymbol{\nu} z\, \boldsymbol{\nu} w\, P$	$\equiv$	$\boldsymbol{\nu} w\, \boldsymbol{\nu} z\, P$
SC-RES-INACT	$\boldsymbol{\nu} z\, \mathbf{0}$	$\equiv$	$\mathbf{0}$
SC-RES-COMP	$\boldsymbol{\nu} z\, (P_1 \mid P_2)$	$\equiv$	$P_1 \mid \boldsymbol{\nu} z\, P_2$, if $z \notin \mathsf{fn}(P_1)$
SC-REP	$!P$	$\equiv$	$P \mid !P$

Table 1.1. *The axioms of structural congruence*

REFL	$P = P$
SYMM	$P = Q$ implies $Q = P$
TRANS	$P = Q$ and $Q = R$ implies $P = R$
CONG	$P = Q$ implies $C[P] = C[Q]$

Table 1.2. *The rules of equational reasoning*

The axioms of structural congruence allow manipulation of term-structure. Axiom SC-RES-COMP expresses that a restriction can be moved so as to include in or exclude from its scope a process in which the restricted name is not free. It shows clearly that $\boldsymbol{\nu}$ is a static binder.

For instance, suppose $M \stackrel{\text{def}}{=} \overline{x}z.\mathbf{0}$, $N \stackrel{\text{def}}{=} \overline{y}w.\mathbf{0}$, and $N' \stackrel{\text{def}}{=} x(v).\mathbf{0}$. Then

$$(N + N') \mid \boldsymbol{\nu} z\, M \equiv \boldsymbol{\nu} z\, ((N + N') \mid M)$$

using SC-RES-COMP; and using the axioms SC-COMP-COMM, SC-SUM-COMM, and SC-SUM-INACT, we have

$$\begin{aligned} \boldsymbol{\nu} z\, ((N + N') \mid M) &\equiv \boldsymbol{\nu} z\, (M \mid (N + N')) \\ &\equiv \boldsymbol{\nu} z\, (M \mid (N' + N)) \\ &\equiv \boldsymbol{\nu} z\, ((M + \mathbf{0}) \mid (N' + N)), \end{aligned}$$

where in the last process, the term underneath the restriction,

$$(\overline{x}z.\mathbf{0} + \mathbf{0}) \mid (x(v).\mathbf{0} + N),$$

is of the form appearing in the first axiom of reduction (1.1).

Axiom SC-REP succinctly expresses that $!P$ can be thought of as an infinite composition $P \mid P \mid \cdots$, for by the axiom and associativity of composition,

$$!P \equiv P \mid !P \equiv P \mid P \mid !P \equiv \cdots .$$

In general, by means of the axioms SC-COMP-ASSOC, SC-COMP-COMM, SC-RES, SC-RES-COMP, and SC-REP, any restriction not underneath a prefix can be brought to the top of a term. For instance with M, N, and N' as above:

$$\begin{array}{rcl} \boldsymbol{\nu}x\,((N+N') \mid !\boldsymbol{\nu}z\,M) & \equiv & \boldsymbol{\nu}x\,((N+N') \mid (\boldsymbol{\nu}z\,M \mid !\boldsymbol{\nu}z\,M)) \\ & \equiv & \boldsymbol{\nu}x\,(((N+N') \mid \boldsymbol{\nu}z\,M) \mid !\boldsymbol{\nu}z\,M) \\ & \equiv & \boldsymbol{\nu}x\,(\boldsymbol{\nu}z\,((N+N') \mid M) \mid !\boldsymbol{\nu}z\,M) \\ & \equiv & \boldsymbol{\nu}x\,(!\boldsymbol{\nu}z\,M \mid \boldsymbol{\nu}z\,((N+N') \mid M)) \\ & \equiv & \boldsymbol{\nu}x\,\boldsymbol{\nu}z\,(!\boldsymbol{\nu}u\,M\{^u\!/\!_z\} \mid ((N+N') \mid M)) \\ & \equiv & \boldsymbol{\nu}z\,\boldsymbol{\nu}x\,(!\boldsymbol{\nu}u\,M\{^u\!/\!_z\} \mid ((N+N') \mid M)) . \end{array}$$

Further, using the SC-COMP-INACT, SC-RES-COMP, and SC-RES-INACT axioms, we can prove that restricting a name not free in a process has no effect, that is, if $z \notin \mathsf{fn}(P)$ then $\boldsymbol{\nu}z\,P \equiv P$. The proof is:

$$\boldsymbol{\nu}z\,P \equiv \boldsymbol{\nu}z\,(P \mid \mathbf{0}) \equiv P \mid \boldsymbol{\nu}z\,\mathbf{0} \equiv P \mid \mathbf{0} \equiv P .$$

SC-MAT is the only axiom whose application can change the free names of a process:

Exercise 1.2.4 Show that if $P \equiv Q$ can be inferred without using SC-MAT, then $\mathsf{fn}(P) = \mathsf{fn}(Q)$. □

Here are four more examples to illustrate structural congruence. We will return to them later to illustrate reduction.

Example 1.2.5 Suppose

$$P \stackrel{\text{def}}{=} \boldsymbol{\nu}x\,(x(z).\,\overline{z}y.\,\mathbf{0} \mid (\overline{x}a.\,\mathbf{0} \mid \overline{x}b.\,\mathbf{0})) .$$

Then by associativity and commutativity of composition, and introduction of $\mathbf{0}$ as a summand,

$$P \equiv P_1 \stackrel{\text{def}}{=} \boldsymbol{\nu}x\,(((\overline{x}a.\,\mathbf{0} + \mathbf{0}) \mid (x(z).\,\overline{z}y.\,\mathbf{0} + \mathbf{0})) \mid \overline{x}b.\,\mathbf{0}) .$$

In the transformation from P to P_1, two potential interactors have been brought together, and in the form required for axiom (1.1) of reduction to be applied. Equally,

$$P \equiv P_2 \stackrel{\text{def}}{=} \boldsymbol{\nu}x\,(((\overline{x}b.\,\mathbf{0} + \mathbf{0}) \mid (x(z).\,\overline{z}y.\,\mathbf{0} + \mathbf{0})) \mid \overline{x}a.\,\mathbf{0}) ,$$

where the other potential sender has been brought into contact with the potential receiver. □

Example 1.2.6 Suppose

$$Q \stackrel{\text{def}}{=} \boldsymbol{\nu} x\,((x(y).\,x(z).\,\overline{y}z.\,\mathbf{0} \mid x(w).\,x(v).\,\overline{v}w.\,\mathbf{0}) \mid \overline{x}a.\,\overline{x}b.\,\mathbf{0})\;.$$

Then

$$Q \equiv Q_1 \stackrel{\text{def}}{=} \boldsymbol{\nu} x\,(((\overline{x}a.\,\overline{x}b.\,\mathbf{0}+\mathbf{0}) \mid (x(y).\,x(z).\,\overline{y}z.\,\mathbf{0}+\mathbf{0})) \mid x(w).\,x(v).\,\overline{v}w.\,\mathbf{0})$$

and

$$Q \equiv Q_2 \stackrel{\text{def}}{=} \boldsymbol{\nu} x\,(((\overline{x}a.\,\overline{x}b.\,\mathbf{0}+\mathbf{0}) \mid (x(w).\,x(v).\,\overline{v}w.\,\mathbf{0}+\mathbf{0})) \mid x(y).\,x(z).\,\overline{y}z.\,\mathbf{0})\,,$$

where as before the potential interactors have been brought together. □

Example 1.2.7 Suppose

$$R \stackrel{\text{def}}{=} \boldsymbol{\nu} x\,((x(u).\,u(y).\,u(z).\,\overline{y}z.\,\mathbf{0} \mid x(t).\,t(w).\,t(v).\,\overline{v}w.\,\mathbf{0}) \mid \boldsymbol{\nu} s\,\overline{x}s.\,\overline{s}a.\,\overline{s}b.\,\mathbf{0})\;.$$

Then using also axiom SC-RES-COMP,

$$\begin{aligned} R \equiv R_1 \stackrel{\text{def}}{=} \boldsymbol{\nu} x\;\; (\; & \boldsymbol{\nu} s\,((\overline{x}s.\,\overline{s}a.\,\overline{s}b.\,\mathbf{0}+\mathbf{0}) \mid (x(u).\,u(y).\,u(z).\,\overline{y}z.\,\mathbf{0}+\mathbf{0})) \\ \mid\; & x(t).\,t(w).\,t(v).\,\overline{v}w.\,\mathbf{0}) \end{aligned}$$

and

$$\begin{aligned} R \equiv R_2 \stackrel{\text{def}}{=} \boldsymbol{\nu} x\;\; (\; & \boldsymbol{\nu} s\,((\overline{x}s.\,\overline{s}a.\,\overline{s}b.\,\mathbf{0}+\mathbf{0}) \mid (x(t).\,t(w).\,t(v).\,\overline{v}w.\,\mathbf{0}+\mathbf{0})) \\ \mid\; & x(u).\,u(y).\,u(z).\,\overline{y}z.\,\mathbf{0})\;. \end{aligned}$$

□

Example 1.2.8 Suppose

$$S \stackrel{\text{def}}{=} \boldsymbol{\nu} x\,((x(u).\,u(y).\,u(z).\,\overline{y}z.\,\mathbf{0} \mid x(t).\,t(w).\,t(v).\,\overline{v}w.\,\mathbf{0}) \mid !\boldsymbol{\nu} s\,\overline{x}s.\,\overline{s}a.\,\overline{s}b.\,\mathbf{0})\;.$$

Then using also SC-REP,

$$\begin{aligned} S \equiv S_1 \stackrel{\text{def}}{=} \boldsymbol{\nu} x\;\; (\; & \boldsymbol{\nu} s\,((\overline{x}s.\,\overline{s}a.\,\overline{s}b.\,\mathbf{0}+\mathbf{0}) \mid (x(u).\,u(y).\,u(z).\,\overline{y}z.\,\mathbf{0}+\mathbf{0})) \\ \mid\; & (x(t).\,t(w).\,t(v).\,\overline{v}w.\,\mathbf{0} \mid !\boldsymbol{\nu} s\,\overline{x}s.\,\overline{s}a.\,\overline{s}b.\,\mathbf{0})) \end{aligned}$$

and

$$\begin{aligned} S \equiv S_2 \stackrel{\text{def}}{=} \boldsymbol{\nu} x\;\; (\; & (\boldsymbol{\nu} s\,((\overline{x}s.\,\overline{s}a.\,\overline{s}b.\,\mathbf{0}+\mathbf{0}) \mid (x(u).\,u(y).\,u(z).\,\overline{y}z.\,\mathbf{0}+\mathbf{0}))) \\ \mid\; & (\boldsymbol{\nu} s\,((\overline{x}s.\,\overline{s}a.\,\overline{s}b.\,\mathbf{0}+\mathbf{0}) \mid (x(t).\,t(w).\,t(v).\,\overline{v}w.\,\mathbf{0}+\mathbf{0}))) \\ \mid\; & !\boldsymbol{\nu} s\,\overline{x}s.\,\overline{s}a.\,\overline{s}b.\,\mathbf{0})\;. \end{aligned}$$

□

Notation 1.2.9 (Tuples)

(1) We abbreviate a tuple of entities $E_1, \ldots, E_n$ to $\widetilde{E}$. When the entities are names $x_1, \ldots, x_n$, we write $\widetilde{x}$ also for the set of names occurring in the tuple, relying on the context of the discussion to resolve any ambiguity.

(2) We abbreviate $\boldsymbol{\nu} x_1 \ldots \boldsymbol{\nu} x_n$ to $(\boldsymbol{\nu} x_1, \ldots, x_n)$. □

Exercise 1.2.10 Show that each process is structurally congruent to a process of the form

$$(\boldsymbol{\nu}\widetilde{x})\,(M_1 \mid \ldots \mid M_n \mid !R_1 \mid \ldots \mid !R_k)$$

where each M_i is a summation. □

We say that an occurrence of a process Q in a process P is *guarded* if the occurrence is underneath a prefix in P, and *unguarded* otherwise. We also say that Q *has* an (un)guarded occurrence in P if some occurrence of Q in P is (un)guarded.

The following exercise will be useful for showing properties of the reduction relation.

Exercise 1.2.11

(1) Show that if P has an unguarded occurrence of a prefix $\pi.\, R$, then $P \equiv (\boldsymbol{\nu}\widetilde{z})\,((\pi.\, R + M) \mid Q)$ for some M, Q, and $\widetilde{z} \subseteq \mathsf{fn}(\pi.\, R + M)$.

(2) Suppose that P has an unguarded occurrence of a summation M that has an unguarded occurrence of a prefix $\pi.\, R$. Show that if $P' \equiv P$ then P' has an unguarded occurrence of a summation M' such that $M' \equiv M$ and M' has an unguarded occurrence of a prefix $\pi'.\, R'$ such that $\pi'.\, R' \equiv \pi.\, R$.

(3) Show that $\boldsymbol{\nu} z\, P \equiv \boldsymbol{\nu} z\, P'$ does not imply $P \equiv P'$. (Hint: consider the possibility of α-converting z in transforming $\boldsymbol{\nu} z\, P$ into $\boldsymbol{\nu} z\, P'$, and consider rules SC-RES and SC-MAT.) □

We now define reduction.

Definition 1.2.12 (Reduction) The *reduction relation*, $\longrightarrow$, is defined by the rules in Table 1.3. □

In other words, processes P and Q stand in the reduction relation just if the assertion $P \longrightarrow Q$ can be inferred via the rules. The assertion expresses that P can evolve to Q in a single autonomous step. We sometimes refer to a proof of a reduction as a *reduction derivation*. We view a reduction derivation as a tree whose root is the reduction that is inferred. Thus the leaves are instances of the rules R-INTER and R-TAU. We refer to the rule whose application yields

$$\text{R-INTER} \quad \overline{(\overline{x}y.\, P_1 + M_1) \mid (x(z).\, P_2 + M_2) \longrightarrow P_1 \mid P_2\{y/z\}}$$

$$\text{R-TAU} \quad \overline{\tau.\, P + M \longrightarrow P}$$

$$\text{R-PAR} \quad \frac{P_1 \longrightarrow P_1'}{P_1 \mid P_2 \longrightarrow P_1' \mid P_2} \qquad \text{R-RES} \quad \frac{P \longrightarrow P'}{\nu z\, P \longrightarrow \nu z\, P'}$$

$$\text{R-STRUCT} \quad \frac{P_1 \equiv P_2 \longrightarrow P_2' \equiv P_1'}{P_1 \longrightarrow P_1'}$$

Table 1.3. *The reduction rules*

the root as *the last rule* applied in the derivation. (We think of the root as being at the base of the tree.) We use similar terminology later for derivations from other sets of rules.

Note that the structural rule R-STRUCT allows restructuring both before and after a reduction. The use of R-STRUCT *after* the reduction ensures that the reduction relation is closed under structural congruence, in the sense that if $P \longrightarrow Q$ and $R \equiv Q$, then $P \longrightarrow R$. We illustrate reduction by continuing Examples 1.2.5–1.2.8 above.

Example 1.2.13 (Example 1.2.5 ctd.) Recall that

$$\begin{aligned} P &\stackrel{\text{def}}{=} \nu x\, (x(z).\, \overline{z}y.\, \mathbf{0} \mid (\overline{x}a.\, \mathbf{0} \mid \overline{x}b.\, \mathbf{0})) \\ P_1 &\stackrel{\text{def}}{=} \nu x\, (((\overline{x}a.\, \mathbf{0} + \mathbf{0}) \mid (x(z).\, \overline{z}y.\, \mathbf{0} + \mathbf{0})) \mid \overline{x}b.\, \mathbf{0})\,. \end{aligned}$$

Since, by R-INTER,

$$(\overline{x}a.\, \mathbf{0} + \mathbf{0}) \mid (x(z).\, \overline{z}y.\, \mathbf{0} + \mathbf{0}) \longrightarrow \mathbf{0} \mid \overline{a}y.\, \mathbf{0}\,,$$

by R-PAR and R-RES,

$$P_1 \longrightarrow P_3 \stackrel{\text{def}}{=} \nu x\, ((\mathbf{0} \mid \overline{a}y.\, \mathbf{0}) \mid \overline{x}b.\, \mathbf{0})\,.$$

Further, as $P_3 \equiv P_4 \stackrel{\text{def}}{=} \nu x(\overline{a}y.\, \mathbf{0} \mid \overline{x}b.\, \mathbf{0})$, by R-STRUCT, also $P \longrightarrow P_4$. Similarly,

$$P \longrightarrow P_5 \stackrel{\text{def}}{=} \overline{b}y.\, \mathbf{0} \mid \nu x\, \overline{x}a.\, \mathbf{0}\,.$$

This shows that reduction is not confluent since neither P_4 nor P_5 has any reductions. □

Example 1.2.14 (Example 1.2.6 ctd.) Recall that

$$\begin{aligned} Q &\stackrel{\text{def}}{=} \nu x\,((x(y).\,x(z).\,\overline{y}z.\,\mathbf{0} \mid x(w).\,x(v).\,\overline{v}w.\,\mathbf{0}) \mid \overline{x}a.\,\overline{x}b.\,\mathbf{0}) \\ Q_1 &\stackrel{\text{def}}{=} \nu x\,(((\overline{x}a.\,\overline{x}b.\,\mathbf{0} + \mathbf{0}) \mid (x(y).\,x(z).\,\overline{y}z.\,\mathbf{0} + \mathbf{0})) \mid x(w).\,x(v).\,\overline{v}w.\,\mathbf{0})\,. \end{aligned}$$

Since, by R-INTER, R-PAR and R-RES,

$$Q_1 \longrightarrow Q_3 \stackrel{\text{def}}{=} \nu x\,((\overline{x}b.\,\mathbf{0} \mid x(z).\,\overline{a}z.\,\mathbf{0}) \mid x(w).\,x(v).\,\overline{v}w.\,\mathbf{0})\,,$$

again by R-STRUCT, $Q \longrightarrow Q_3$. Also

$$Q \longrightarrow Q_4 \stackrel{\text{def}}{=} \nu x\,((\overline{x}b.\,\mathbf{0} \mid x(v).\,\overline{v}a.\,\mathbf{0}) \mid x(y).\,x(z).\,\overline{y}z.\,\mathbf{0})\,.$$

Note further that

$$Q_3 \longrightarrow Q_5 \stackrel{\text{def}}{=} \nu x\,(x(z).\,\overline{a}z.\,\mathbf{0} \mid x(v).\,\overline{v}b.\,\mathbf{0})$$

and also that

$$Q_3 \longrightarrow Q_6 \stackrel{\text{def}}{=} \nu x\,(\overline{a}b.\,\mathbf{0} \mid x(w).\,x(v).\,\overline{v}w.\,\mathbf{0})\,.$$

In the evolution $Q \longrightarrow Q_3 \longrightarrow Q_5$, one of the pair a, b is passed to one component and the other to the other component, while in $Q \longrightarrow Q_3 \longrightarrow Q_6$ both are passed to the same component. □

Example 1.2.15 (Example 1.2.7 ctd.) Recall that

$$R \stackrel{\text{def}}{=} \nu x\,((x(u).\,u(y).\,u(z).\,\overline{y}z.\,\mathbf{0} \mid x(t).\,t(w).\,t(v).\,\overline{v}w.\,\mathbf{0}) \mid \nu s\,\overline{x}s.\,\overline{s}a.\,\overline{s}b.\,\mathbf{0})\,.$$

This example illustrates how the second of the outcomes in the previous example can be ensured, even though x is shared among the components. The combination $\nu s\,\overline{x}s$ expresses a capability simultaneously to create and send via x a *fresh* name, that is, one not free in any other process. After the reduction, this name will be private to the sending and receiving processes; the names a and b can therefore be sent via it without danger of their being misdirected:

$$\begin{aligned} R &\longrightarrow \nu x\,(\nu s\,(\overline{s}a.\,\overline{s}b.\,\mathbf{0} \mid s(y).\,s(z).\,\overline{y}z.\,\mathbf{0}) \mid x(t).\,t(w).\,t(v).\,\overline{v}w.\,\mathbf{0}) \\ &\longrightarrow \nu x\,(\nu s\,(\overline{s}b.\,\mathbf{0} \mid s(z).\,\overline{a}z.\,\mathbf{0}) \mid x(t).\,t(w).\,t(v).\,\overline{v}w.\,\mathbf{0}) \\ &\longrightarrow \nu x\,(\overline{a}b.\,\mathbf{0} \mid x(t).\,t(w).\,t(v).\,\overline{v}w.\,\mathbf{0}) \end{aligned}$$

using also the fact that $\nu s\,\overline{a}b.\,\mathbf{0} \equiv \overline{a}b.\,\mathbf{0}$ as $s \notin \mathsf{fn}(\overline{a}b.\,\mathbf{0})$. Also,

$$\begin{aligned} R &\longrightarrow \nu x\,(\nu t\,(\overline{t}a.\,\overline{t}b.\,\mathbf{0} \mid t(w).\,t(v).\,\overline{v}w.\,\mathbf{0}) \mid x(u).\,u(y).\,u(z).\,\overline{y}z.\,\mathbf{0}) \\ &\longrightarrow \nu x\,(\nu t\,(\overline{t}b.\,\mathbf{0} \mid t(v).\,\overline{v}a.\,\mathbf{0}) \mid x(u).\,u(y).\,u(z).\,\overline{y}z.\,\mathbf{0}) \\ &\longrightarrow \nu x\,(\overline{b}a.\,\mathbf{0} \mid x(u).\,u(y).\,u(z).\,\overline{y}z.\,\mathbf{0})\,. \end{aligned}$$

□

Example 1.2.16 (Example 1.2.8 ctd.) Recall that

$$S \stackrel{\text{def}}{=} \boldsymbol{\nu} x\,((x(u).\,u(y).\,u(z).\,\overline{y}z.\,\mathbf{0} \mid x(t).\,t(w).\,t(v).\,\overline{v}w.\,\mathbf{0}) \mid !\boldsymbol{\nu} s\,\overline{x}s.\,\overline{s}a.\,\overline{s}b.\,\mathbf{0})\,.$$

This example illustrates also the treatment of replication. In the following evolution from S, the pair of names a, b is passed safely to each of the receivers. The prefixes giving rise to the reductions are highlighted by underlining.

$$\begin{array}{rl}
S \;\equiv & \boldsymbol{\nu} x\;(\boldsymbol{\nu} s\,((\underline{\overline{x}s}.\,\overline{s}a.\,\overline{s}b.\,\mathbf{0}+\mathbf{0}) \mid (\underline{x(u)}.\,u(y).\,u(z).\,\overline{y}z.\,\mathbf{0}+\mathbf{0}))\\
& \quad \mid (x(t).\,t(w).\,t(v).\,\overline{v}w.\,\mathbf{0} \mid !\boldsymbol{\nu} s\,\overline{x}s.\,\overline{s}a.\,\overline{s}b.\,\mathbf{0}))\\
\longrightarrow & \boldsymbol{\nu} x\;(\boldsymbol{\nu} s\,(\underline{\overline{s}a}.\,\overline{s}b.\,\mathbf{0} \mid \underline{s(y)}.\,s(z).\,\overline{y}z.\,\mathbf{0})\\
& \quad \mid (x(t).\,t(w).\,t(v).\,\overline{v}w.\,\mathbf{0} \mid !\boldsymbol{\nu} s\,\overline{x}s.\,\overline{s}a.\,\overline{s}b.\,\mathbf{0}))\\
\longrightarrow & \boldsymbol{\nu} x\,(\boldsymbol{\nu} s\,(\underline{\overline{s}b}.\,\mathbf{0} \mid \underline{s(z)}.\,\overline{a}z.\,\mathbf{0}) \mid (x(t).\,t(w).\,t(v).\,\overline{v}w.\,\mathbf{0} \mid !\boldsymbol{\nu} s\,\overline{x}s.\,\overline{s}a.\,\overline{s}b.\,\mathbf{0}))\\
\longrightarrow & \boldsymbol{\nu} x\,(\overline{a}b.\,\mathbf{0} \mid (x(t).\,t(w).\,t(v).\,\overline{v}w.\,\mathbf{0} \mid !\boldsymbol{\nu} s\,\overline{x}s.\,\overline{s}a.\,\overline{s}b.\,\mathbf{0}))\\
\equiv & \boldsymbol{\nu} x\,((\overline{a}b.\,\mathbf{0} \mid \boldsymbol{\nu} s\,(\underline{\overline{x}s}.\,\overline{s}a.\,\overline{s}b.\,\mathbf{0} \mid \underline{x(t)}.\,t(w).\,t(v).\,\overline{v}w.\,\mathbf{0})) \mid !\boldsymbol{\nu} s\,\overline{x}s.\,\overline{s}a.\,\overline{s}b.\,\mathbf{0})\\
\longrightarrow^3 & \boldsymbol{\nu} x\,((\overline{a}b.\,\mathbf{0} \mid \overline{b}a.\,\mathbf{0}) \mid !\boldsymbol{\nu} s\,\overline{x}s.\,\overline{s}a.\,\overline{s}b.\,\mathbf{0})\\
\equiv & (\overline{a}b.\,\mathbf{0} \mid \overline{b}a.\,\mathbf{0}) \mid \boldsymbol{\nu} x\; !\boldsymbol{\nu} s\,\overline{x}s.\,\overline{s}a.\,\overline{s}b.\,\mathbf{0}\,.
\end{array}$$

□

Note that the pair a, b is passed safely to each receiver also in reduction sequences in which the evolutions of the receivers are interleaved (rather than being one after the other as in the example).

Axiom SC-RES-COMP of structural congruence (allowing movement of a restriction) plays a vital role in the definition of reduction: without it, R-INTER would be inadequate – it would not be possible to infer the reduction of the process $(\boldsymbol{\nu} w\,\overline{x}w.\,\mathbf{0}) \mid x(z).\,\mathbf{0}$, for instance. It is worth emphasizing, however, that the axiom is applicable only if the restricted name is not free in the neighbouring component. For instance,

$$\overline{x}a.\,\mathbf{0} \mid \boldsymbol{\nu} x\,(\overline{x}b.\,\mathbf{0} \mid x(z).\,\mathbf{0}) \not\equiv \boldsymbol{\nu} x\,(\overline{x}a.\,\mathbf{0} \mid \overline{x}b.\,\mathbf{0} \mid x(z).\,\mathbf{0})\,.$$

Note that an interaction in which a is sent via x is possible in the second of these processes but not in the first. Rather,

$$\overline{x}a.\,\mathbf{0} \mid \boldsymbol{\nu} x\,(\overline{x}b.\,\mathbf{0} \mid x(z).\,\mathbf{0}) \equiv \boldsymbol{\nu} w\,(\overline{x}a.\,\mathbf{0} \mid \overline{w}b.\,\mathbf{0} \mid w(z).\,\mathbf{0})$$

and there is, correctly, no new reduction as a result of the movement of the restriction.

A further noteworthy point is that although $P \longrightarrow P'$ implies $P \mid Q \longrightarrow P' \mid Q$ and $\boldsymbol{\nu} z\, P \longrightarrow \boldsymbol{\nu} z\, P'$, it is not the case that $P \longrightarrow P'$ implies $!P \longrightarrow !P'$. Again this accords with the intended interpretation of $!P$ as $P \mid P \mid \cdots$, for allowing $!P \longrightarrow !P'$ to be inferred from $P \longrightarrow P'$ would be tantamount to permitting infinite progress in a single reduction.

Exercise 1.2.17 Give an example to show why $\nu z\,!P \equiv !\nu z\,P$ is not an axiom of structural congruence. That is, give a process P and argue informally that $\nu z\,!P$ and $!\nu z\,P$ have different behaviours. □

Actions within a process P have two sources: pairs of subterms of the form $\overline{x}y.\,R_1 + N_1$ and $x(z).\,R_2 + N_2$, and subterms of the form $\tau.\,R + N$. In each case, however, the relevant subterm(s) must be unguarded. This accords with the intended interpretation of prefix given earlier: the process Q in $\pi.\,Q$ cannot proceed until the capability expressed by π has been exercised. Thus, for instance,

$$\overline{x}a.\,\overline{y}b.\,\mathbf{0} \mid y(z).\,\mathbf{0}$$

has no reductions. To justify these assertions formally, we establish some properties of the reduction relation.

First, although the rule R-STRUCT can be applied many times in inferring reductions of processes, any reduction has a derivation of a particular form.

Lemma 1.2.18 If $P \longrightarrow Q$ then there is a derivation of the reduction in which R-STRUCT is applied, if at all, only as the last rule.

Proof The proof involves checking that each of the rules R-PAR and R-RES commutes with R-STRUCT, and that two applications of R-STRUCT can be condensed to one. For instance, suppose $\nu z\,P \longrightarrow \nu z\,Q$ is inferred by R-RES from $P \longrightarrow Q$, which is in turn inferred from $P \equiv P' \longrightarrow Q' \equiv Q$ by R-STRUCT. Then from $P' \longrightarrow Q'$ one can infer $\nu z\,P' \longrightarrow \nu z\,Q'$ by R-RES; and from this and $\nu P \equiv \nu z\,P'$ and $\nu Q' \equiv \nu z\,Q$ one can infer $\nu z\,P \longrightarrow \nu z\,Q$ by R-STRUCT. The reader may care to check the other two assertions. □

By refining the observation in Lemma 1.2.18, we can give a precise characterization of the reductions of processes.

Definition 1.2.19 (Normalized derivation) A *normalized derivation* of the reduction $P \longrightarrow Q$ is of the following form. The first rule applied is an instance

$$(\overline{x}y.\,R_1 + N_1) \mid (x(z).\,R_2 + N_2) \longrightarrow R_1 \mid R_2\{y/z\}$$

of R-INTER or an instance

$$\tau.\,R + N \longrightarrow R$$

of R-TAU. The derivation continues (in the first case: the second is similar) with an application of R-PAR, yielding

$$((\overline{x}y.\,R_1 + N_1) \mid (x(z).\,R_2 + N_2)) \mid S \longrightarrow (R_1 \mid R_2\{y/z\}) \mid S\,,$$

followed by zero or more applications of R-RES involving names $\widetilde{z} \subseteq \mathsf{fn}(\overline{x}y.\, R_1 + N_1, x(z).\, R_2 + N_2)$, yielding

$$(\boldsymbol{\nu}\widetilde{z})\,(((\overline{x}y.\, R_1 + N_1) \mid (x(z).\, R_2 + N_2)) \mid S) \longrightarrow (\boldsymbol{\nu}\widetilde{z})\,((R_1 \mid R_2\{y/z\}) \mid S)\ .$$

The last rule applied in the derivation is R-STRUCT, so that

$$P \equiv (\boldsymbol{\nu}\widetilde{z})\,(((\overline{x}y.\, R_1 + N_1) \mid (x(z).\, R_2 + N_2)) \mid S)$$

and

$$Q \equiv (\boldsymbol{\nu}\widetilde{z})\,((R_1 \mid R_2\{y/z\}) \mid S)\ .$$

□

Lemma 1.2.20 If $P \longrightarrow Q$ then one of the following holds:

(1) there are x, y, z, $\widetilde{z}$, R_1, N_1, R_2, N_2, and S such that

$$\begin{array}{rcl} P & \equiv & (\boldsymbol{\nu}\widetilde{z})\,(((\overline{x}y.\, R_1 + N_1) \mid (x(z).\, R_2 + N_2)) \mid S) \\ Q & \equiv & (\boldsymbol{\nu}\widetilde{z})\,((R_1 \mid R_2\{y/z\}) \mid S) \end{array}$$

(2) there are $\widetilde{z}$, R, N, and S such that

$$\begin{array}{rcl} P & \equiv & (\boldsymbol{\nu}\widetilde{z})\,((\tau.\, R + N) \mid S) \\ Q & \equiv & (\boldsymbol{\nu}\widetilde{z})\,(R \mid S)\ . \end{array}$$

□

Exercise 1.2.21

(1) Show that every reduction has a normalized derivation. (Hint: extend the proof of Lemma 1.2.18.)
(2) Hence prove Lemma 1.2.20. □

To gain further insight into structural congruence and reduction, we look more deeply into how reductions of processes can be inferred.

We write $P \Rrightarrow_1 Q$ if P can be transformed to Q by applying to a subterm of P an axiom of structural congruence other than SC-REP from right to left, and we write $\Rrightarrow$ for the reflexive and transitive closure of $\Rrightarrow_1$. Thus if $P \Rrightarrow Q$ then P can be transformed to Q without 'folding' any subterm under a replication, that is, without replacing any subterm $R \mid !R$ by $!R$.

Definition 1.2.22 (Well-normalized derivation) A reduction derivation is *well normalized* if it is normalized and the last step in it is of the form

$$\frac{P \Rrightarrow P' \longrightarrow Q' \equiv Q}{P \longrightarrow Q}$$

□

Thus a well-normalized derivation of $P \longrightarrow Q$ consists of an instance of R-INTER or of R-TAU, followed by an application of R-PAR and then zero or more applications of R-RES to yield $P' \longrightarrow Q'$, followed by an application of R-STRUCT in which P is transformed to P' without folding any subterm under a replication, and Q' is transformed to Q.

Lemma 1.2.25 strengthens the result in Exercise 1.2.21(1) by showing that every reduction has a well-normalized derivation. To prove it we need another result, Lemma 1.2.24, and to state that result we need to introduce contexts with several holes. We will use multi-hole contexts several times in the book, and will introduce them formally in Definition 2.3.18. The definition below introduces a simpler form of multi-hole context that is used only for Lemmas 1.2.24 and 1.2.25.

Definition 1.2.23 (n-hole context) For $n \geq 1$, an *n-hole context* is obtained when n non-degenerate occurrences of $\mathbf{0}$ in a process-term given by the grammar in Definition 1.1.1 are replaced by the *holes* $[\cdot]_1, \ldots, [\cdot]_n$. If C is an n-hole context then we write $C[P_1, \ldots, P_n]$ for the process obtained by replacing $[\cdot]_i$ in C by P_i for each i. □

Lemma 1.2.24 Suppose that C is a (1-hole) context, R is a process, and $C[\,!R] \Rrightarrow A$.

(1) There are $n \geq 1$, an n-hole context D, and processes $R_1, \ldots, R_n$ with $R \Rrightarrow R_i$ for each i such that $A = D[\,!R_1, \ldots, !R_n]$. Also, $C[R \mid !R] \Rrightarrow B \stackrel{\text{def}}{=} D[R \mid !R_1, \ldots, R \mid !R_n]$.

(2) Further, if there is a reduction derivation of $A \longrightarrow P$ in which the rule R-STRUCT is not used, then there are k and m with $k \leq m \leq n$, an m-hole context E, and a substitution σ such that

$$P = E[\,!R_1\sigma, \ldots, !R_k\sigma, !R_{k+1}, \ldots, !R_m]$$

and moreover

$$B \longrightarrow E[R\sigma \mid !R_1\sigma, \ldots, R\sigma \mid !R_k\sigma, R \mid !R_{k+1}, \ldots, R \mid !R_m]\,.$$

Proof We first prove (1) by induction on the number of steps in the transformation $C[\,!R] \Rrightarrow A$. If that number is 0 then (1) holds with $n = 1$ and $D \stackrel{\text{def}}{=} C$ and $R_1 \stackrel{\text{def}}{=} R$. So suppose the number is not 0 and the transformation is

$$C[\,!R] \Rrightarrow A' \Rrightarrow_1 A\,.$$

By induction hypothesis there are $n' \geq 1$, an n'-hole context D', and processes

$R'_1, \ldots, R'_{n'}$ with $R \Rrightarrow R'_i$ for each i such that

$$A' = D'[!R'_1, \ldots, !R'_{n'}] \quad \text{and} \quad C[R \mid !R] \Rrightarrow B' \stackrel{\text{def}}{=} D'[R \mid !R'_1, \ldots, R \mid !R'_{n'}] \, .$$

For some context D^* and processes Q' and Q such that $Q' = Q$ is an instance of an axiom of structural congruence other than SC-REP from right to left we have $A' = D^*[Q']$ and $A = D^*[Q]$. We argue by case analysis on the axiom in question and the position of Q' in relation to $R'_1, \ldots, R'_{n'}$ in A'. We consider just the three most interesting cases and invite the reader to check the others.

Case 1 Suppose Q' is a proper subterm of some R'_i. By renaming holes if necessary we may assume that $i = 1$. We take $n = n'$ and $D \stackrel{\text{def}}{=} D'$ and $R_j \stackrel{\text{def}}{=} R'_j$ for $j \neq 1$, and we take R_1 to be R'_1 with Q' replaced by Q. Then we have $A = D[!R_1, \ldots, !R_n]$ and also $B' \Rrightarrow_1 B$ as required.

Case 2 Suppose $Q' = !R'_1$ (again renaming holes if necessary) and $Q = R'_1 \mid !R'_1$, so the axiom is SC-REP from left to right. We take $n = n'$ and $R_i \stackrel{\text{def}}{=} R'_i$ for each i and we have

$$A = D'[R_1 \mid !R_1, \ldots, !R_n] = D[!R_1, \ldots, !R_n]$$

for the appropriate D, and moreover

$$\begin{array}{ll} & D'[R \mid !R'_1, \ldots, R \mid !R'_n] \\ \Rrightarrow_1 & D'[R \mid (R_1 \mid !R_1), \ldots, R \mid !R_n] \\ \Rrightarrow_1 & D'[R_1 \mid (R \mid !R_1), \ldots, R \mid !R_n] \\ = & D[R \mid !R_1, \ldots, R \mid !R_n] \end{array}$$

so $B' \Rrightarrow B$ as required.

Case 3 Suppose $Q' = !S$ and $Q = S \mid !S$ where S is not R'_i for any i. Let (again renaming holes if necessary) $R'_1, \ldots, R'_k$ be the R'_i that are subterms of S. We take $n = n' + k$ and $R_i \stackrel{\text{def}}{=} R'_i$ for each $i \leq n'$, and then for the appropriate context D we have

$$A = D[!R_1, \ldots, !R_k, !R_1, \ldots, !R_{n'}] \, ,$$

and moreover

$$\begin{array}{ll} & D'[R \mid !R'_1, \ldots, R \mid !R_{n'}] \\ \Rrightarrow_1 & D[R \mid !R_1, \ldots, R \mid !R_k, R \mid !R_1, \ldots, R \mid !R_{n'}] \end{array}$$

so $B' \Rrightarrow B$ as required.

We now prove (2) by induction on the reduction derivation of $A \longrightarrow P$. We consider in turn each of the four possibilities for the last rule applied in the derivation.

(R-INTER) Then $A = (\overline{x}y.\,S + M) \mid (x(z).\,S' + M')$ and $P = S \mid S'\sigma$ where $\sigma = \{y/z\}$ for some x, y, z, S, M, S', and M'. Assume (renaming holes is necessary) that $R_1, \ldots, R_k$ are the R_i that are subterms of S' and that $R_{k+1}, \ldots, R_m$ are the R_i that are subterms of S. Then

$$P = E[\,!R_1\sigma, \ldots, \,!R_k\sigma, \,!R_{k+1}, \ldots, \,!R_m]$$

for the appropriate context E, and moreover

$$B \longrightarrow E[R\sigma \mid !R_1\sigma, \ldots, R\sigma \mid !R_k\sigma, R \mid !R_{k+1}, \ldots, R \mid !R_m]\,.$$

(R-TAU) This case is similar to (and simpler than) the previous case.

(R-PAR) Then $A = A_1 \mid A_2$ and $P = P_1 \mid A_2$ where $A_1 \longrightarrow P_1$. We have (renaming holes if necessary) that

$$A_1 = D_1[\,!R_1, \ldots, \,!R_p] \quad \text{and} \quad A_2 = D_2[\,!R_{p+1}, \ldots, \,!R_n]$$

for some D_1, D_2, and p, and by induction hypothesis

$$P_1 = E_1[\,!R_1\sigma, \ldots, \,!R_k\sigma, \,!R_{k+1}, \ldots, \,!R_m]$$

for some E_1, σ, k, and m with $k < m < p$. Also, if $B_1 \stackrel{\text{def}}{=} D_1[R \mid !R_1, \ldots, R \mid !R_p]$ then

$$B_1 \longrightarrow E_1[R\sigma \mid !R_1\sigma, \ldots, R\sigma \mid !R_k\sigma, R \mid !R_{k+1}, \ldots, R \mid !R_m]\,.$$

Hence with $E \stackrel{\text{def}}{=} E_1 \mid D_2$ we have

$$P = E[\,!R_1\sigma, \ldots, \,!R_k\sigma, \,!R_{k+1}, \ldots, \,!R_m, \,!R_{p+1}, \ldots, \,!R_n]$$

and by R-PAR,

$$B \longrightarrow$$
$$E[R\sigma \mid !R_1\sigma, \ldots, R\sigma \mid !R_k\sigma, R \mid !R_{k+1}, \ldots, R \mid !R_m, R \mid !R_{p+1}, \ldots, R \mid !R_n]\,.$$

(R-RES) This case is similar to (and simpler than) the previous case. □

Lemma 1.2.25 Every reduction has a well-normalized derivation.

Proof By the result in Exercise 1.2.21(1) it suffices to show that given a normalized derivation of $P \longrightarrow Q$, we can find a well-normalized derivation of $P \longrightarrow Q$. Fix a normalized derivation and let its last step be

$$\frac{P \equiv P' \longrightarrow Q' \equiv Q}{P \longrightarrow Q}$$

We argue by induction on the number of applications of SC-REP from right to left in the transformation of P to P'. If that number is 0 then $P \Rrightarrow P'$ and the result is immediate. So suppose the number is not 0 and consider the last application of SC-REP from right to left. The transformation $P \equiv P'$ must be of the form

$$P \equiv C[R \mid !R] \rightsquigarrow C[!R] \Rrightarrow P'$$

for some C and R, where $\rightsquigarrow$ indicates that the only change is the replacement of $R \mid !R$ by $!R$.

By Lemma 1.2.24 there are $n \geq 1$, an n-hole context D, and processes $R_1, \ldots, R_n$ with $R \Rrightarrow R_i$ for each i such that $P' = D[!R_1, \ldots, !R_n]$, and $C[R \mid !R] \Rrightarrow P'' \stackrel{\text{def}}{=} D[R \mid !R_1, \ldots, R \mid !R_n]$. Further, since $P' \longrightarrow Q'$ does not involve R-STRUCT, there are k and m with $k \leq m \leq n$, an m-hole context E, and a substitution σ such that

$$Q' = E[!R_1\sigma, \ldots, !R_k\sigma, !R_{k+1}, \ldots, !R_m]$$

and moreover

$$P'' \longrightarrow Q'' \stackrel{\text{def}}{=} E[R\sigma \mid !R_1\sigma, \ldots, R\sigma \mid !R_k\sigma, R \mid !R_{k+1}, \ldots, R \mid !R_m] \,.$$

Now $Q'' \equiv Q'$ since $R \equiv R_i$ for each i, and so $Q'' \equiv Q$ Hence since $P \equiv P''$ contains one fewer application of SC-REP from right to left than $P \equiv P'$, by the induction hypothesis there is a well-normalized derivation of $P \longrightarrow Q$. □

1.2.3 An extended example

This subsection contains an extended example to illustrate mobility in the π-calculus. It concerns a system in which a pair of processes cooperate to build two unbounded chains of storage cells. Other processes can navigate the chains by retrieving and following links stored in the cells that comprise them. The system is expressed by P where

$$\begin{array}{rcl}
P & \stackrel{\text{def}}{=} & (\nu n, s)\,(H \mid I \mid G \mid U \mid L) \\
H & \stackrel{\text{def}}{=} & h(z).\, !\overline{h}z.\mathbf{0} \\
L & \stackrel{\text{def}}{=} & \ell(z).\, !\overline{\ell}z.\mathbf{0} \\
G & \stackrel{\text{def}}{=} & !\nu p\, \overline{n}p.\, p(z).\, !\overline{p}z.\mathbf{0} \\
I & \stackrel{\text{def}}{=} & \nu i\, (\overline{i}h.\mathbf{0} \mid !i(z).\, n(a).\, \overline{z}a.\, \overline{s}a.\, s(c).\, \overline{i}c.\mathbf{0}) \\
U & \stackrel{\text{def}}{=} & \nu u\, (\overline{u}\ell.\mathbf{0} \mid !u(z).\, n(b).\, \overline{z}b.\, n(c).\, \overline{b}c.\, s(a).\, \overline{s}c.\, \overline{u}a.\mathbf{0}) \,.
\end{array}$$

The process H can be thought of as a storage cell named h: on receiving a name via h, it repeatedly sends that name via h. The process L is a similar cell named

ℓ. The process G is a generator of cells: the combination $!\nu p\, \overline{n}p$ expresses that it can repeatedly send fresh names via n; on sending a name, it continues as the composition of a cell bearing that name and the generator. The process P is composed from the two cells, the generator, and the processes I and U, which are responsible for building the chains of cells. As we will see, the processes I and U are similar to one another except that U performs two building steps for every one step of I. The two processes swap places periodically so that each gets to work on both chains and the chains grow at more or less the same rate.

The system in its initial state, expressed by P, is pictured in Figure 1.1, where the nodes represent the components, and the connections between them show the sharing of names. For instance, h, which is free in P, is shared by H and I, while n, which is restricted, indicated in the picture by the parentheses around n, is shared by I, G and U. (The restricted names are indicated in this figure only for clarity; it is more common to omit such annotations.) Other processes can navigate the chains of cells beginning at h and ℓ.

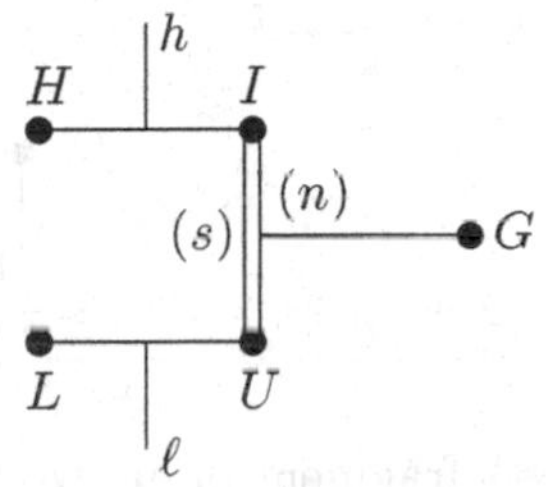

Fig. 1.1. The structure of P

Below we work out in detail one possible evolution of P, consisting of 10 reduction steps. The evolution is summarized in Figure 1.2, which shows the states reached after two, three, and 10 steps. In the last state shown, I_5 and U_7 are the same as I and U, except that they are connected to different cells and hence are slightly different terms. The evolution can therefore continue from the last state shown for another 10 steps, and then another 10, and so on. The system has many other evolutions, because many of the reduction steps can occur in different orders. All evolution paths reach the same state (up to $\equiv$) after 10 steps, however, and the same is true after 20 steps, and so on.

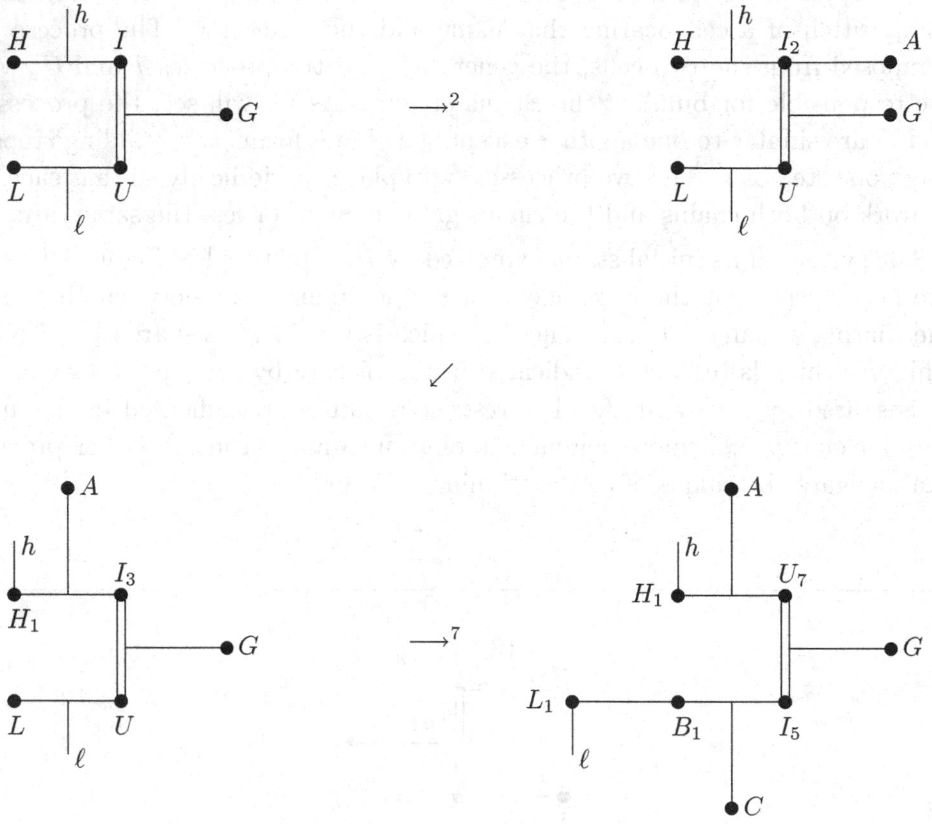

Fig. 1.2. A fragment of an evolution of P

In detail, the evolution begins with an interaction between the components of I via the restricted name i,

$$P \longrightarrow P_1 \stackrel{\text{def}}{=} (\boldsymbol{\nu} n, s)\,(H \mid I_1 \mid G \mid U \mid L)$$

where

$$I_1 \stackrel{\text{def}}{=} \boldsymbol{\nu} i\,(n(a).\,\overline{h}a.\,\overline{s}a.\,s(c).\,\overline{i}c.\,\mathbf{0} \mid !i(z).\,n(a).\,\overline{z}a.\,\overline{s}a.\,s(c).\,\overline{i}c.\,\mathbf{0})\;.$$

It is the replication in I that allows the process to carry out its construction task repeatedly. The first component in I_1 will do one construction step, then, as we will see, swap places with U, and then activate another copy of the replicated process, which will carry out another construction step, and so on.

The evolution continues with an interaction between G and I_1 via n:

$$P_1 \longrightarrow P_2 \stackrel{\text{def}}{=} (\boldsymbol{\nu} n, s, a)\,(H \mid I_2 \mid A \mid G \mid U \mid L)$$

where

$$\begin{aligned} I_2 &\stackrel{\text{def}}{=} \boldsymbol{\nu} i\,(\overline{h}a.\,\overline{s}a.\,s(c).\,\overline{i}c.\,\mathbf{0} \mid !i(z).\,n(a).\,\overline{z}a.\,\overline{s}a.\,s(c).\,\overline{i}c.\,\mathbf{0}) \\ A &\stackrel{\text{def}}{=} a(z).\,!\overline{a}z.\,\mathbf{0}\,. \end{aligned}$$

This second step expresses the simultaneous creation and transmission from G to I_1 via n of a fresh name a. The name a is borne by the new storage cell A. Note that

$$P_2 \equiv (\boldsymbol{\nu} n, s)\,(H \mid \boldsymbol{\nu} a\,(I_2 \mid A) \mid G \mid U \mid L)$$

as only I_2 and A have a free, that is, a is private to them.

From P_2 the evolution continues with

$$P_2 \longrightarrow P_3 \stackrel{\text{def}}{=} (\boldsymbol{\nu} n, s, a)\,(H_1 \mid A \mid I_3 \mid G \mid U \mid L)$$

where

$$\begin{aligned} H_1 &\stackrel{\text{def}}{=} !\overline{h}a.\,\mathbf{0} \\ I_3 &\stackrel{\text{def}}{=} \boldsymbol{\nu} i\,(\overline{s}a.\,s(c).\,\overline{i}c.\,\mathbf{0} \mid !i(z).\,n(a).\,\overline{z}a.\,\overline{s}a.\,s(c).\,\overline{i}c.\,\mathbf{0})\,. \end{aligned}$$

This expresses that I_2 stores a in H, which becomes H_1. This completes a construction step by the I-process, one new cell having been added to the chain. The I-process must now wait to communicate with the U-process, because I_3, the continuation of the I-process, can proceed only by sending via s, which is restricted.

The next three reductions are similar to the first three but involve U carrying out a construction step rather than I. The configuration reached is

$$P_6 \stackrel{\text{def}}{=} (\boldsymbol{\nu} n, s, a, b)\,(H_1 \mid A \mid I_3 \mid G \mid U_3 \mid B \mid L_1)$$

where

$$\begin{aligned} U_3 &\stackrel{\text{def}}{=} \boldsymbol{\nu} u\,(n(c).\,\overline{b}c.\,s(a).\,\overline{s}c.\,\overline{u}a.\,\mathbf{0} \mid !u(z).\,n(b).\,\overline{z}b.\,n(c).\,\overline{b}c.\,s(a).\,\overline{s}c.\,\overline{u}a.\,\mathbf{0}) \\ B &\stackrel{\text{def}}{=} b(z).\,!\overline{b}z.\,\mathbf{0} \\ L_1 &\stackrel{\text{def}}{=} !\overline{\ell}b.\,\mathbf{0}\,. \end{aligned}$$

In the next two reductions, the U-process carries out another construction step, resulting in

$$P_8 \stackrel{\text{def}}{=} (\boldsymbol{\nu} n, s, a, b, c)\,(H_1 \mid A \mid I_3 \mid G \mid U_5 \mid C \mid B_1 \mid L_1)$$

where

$$
\begin{aligned}
U_5 &\stackrel{\text{def}}{=} \nu u\,(s(a).\,\overline{s}c.\,\overline{u}a.\,\mathbf{0} \mid !u(z).\,n(b).\,\overline{z}b.\,n(c).\,\overline{b}c.\,s(a).\,\overline{s}c.\,\overline{u}a.\,\mathbf{0})\\
C &\stackrel{\text{def}}{=} c(z).\,!\overline{c}z.\,\mathbf{0}\\
B_1 &\stackrel{\text{def}}{=} !\overline{b}c.\,\mathbf{0}\,.
\end{aligned}
$$

Now the I-process and the U-process swap places, that is, each moves to work on the other chain. This is achieved by I_3 sending a to U_5 via s, and the continuation of U_5 then sending c to the continuation of I_3 also via s, leading to

$$P_{10} \stackrel{\text{def}}{=} (\nu n, s, a, b, c)\,(H_1 \mid A \mid U_7 \mid G \mid I_5 \mid C \mid B_1 \mid L_1)$$

where

$$
\begin{aligned}
U_7 &\stackrel{\text{def}}{=} \nu u\,(\overline{u}a.\,\mathbf{0} \mid !u(z).\,n(b).\,\overline{z}b.\,n(c).\,\overline{b}c.\,s(a).\,\overline{s}c.\,\overline{u}a.\,\mathbf{0})\\
I_5 &\stackrel{\text{def}}{=} \nu i\,(\overline{i}c.\,\mathbf{0} \mid !i(z).\,n(a).\,\overline{z}a.\,\overline{s}a.\,s(c).\,\overline{i}c.\,\mathbf{0})\,.
\end{aligned}
$$

This completes a cycle in the evolution of P: three construction steps have been performed, one on the chain accessible via h, and two on the chain accessible via ℓ, and the processes I and U have resumed their initial states, though they are now connected to different cells.

In summary, I and U go on a journey, constructing the paths as they go with the help of G. The process U takes two steps for every one taken by I, and they periodically swap places to keep roughly in step. Initially, I is up above and U down below; from P_{10}, for a while, U'll take the high road and I'll take the low road.

1.3 Action

Activity within a system is described by the reduction relation. Reduction does not explain how a system can interact with its environment, however. And in order to understand the behaviour of a system by analysing it into parts, it is necessary to talk about the actions that the parts can perform. This section supplies an account of action in π-calculus by defining a family of labelled transition relations on processes. The transition relations are defined by inference rules. This section presents and discusses the rules; Section 1.4 establishes basic properties of the relations.

The transition relations are labelled by the *actions*, of which there are four kinds.

Definition 1.3.1 (Actions) The *actions* are given by

$$\alpha \ ::= \ \overline{x}y \ \mid \ xy \ \mid \ \overline{x}(z) \ \mid \ \tau\,.$$

We write *Act* for the set of actions. □

The first action is sending the name y via the name x, the second is receiving y via x, the third is sending a fresh name via x (the role of z will be explained shortly), and the last is internal action.

The transition relation labelled by α will be written $\xrightarrow{\alpha}$. Thus, $P \xrightarrow{\overline{x}y} Q$ will express that P can send y via x and evolve to Q; $P \xrightarrow{xy} Q$ that P can receive y via x and become Q; $P \xrightarrow{\overline{x}(z)} Q$ that P can become Q by sending via x a fresh name, which it calls z (we will see below exactly what is meant by this); and $P \xrightarrow{\tau} Q$ that P can evolve invisibly to Q.

Table 1.4 displays terminology and notation pertaining to actions. Its columns list, respectively, the *kind* of the action, its *subject*, its *object*, its set of *free names*, its set of *bound names*, its set of *names*, and the effect of applying a substitution to it. Thus for example in the free-output action $\overline{x}y$, the subject is x, the object is y, and both names are free; in the bound-output action $\overline{x}(z)$, x is free and z is bound. In every case, the set of names, $\mathsf{n}(\alpha)$, of α is $\mathsf{fn}(\alpha) \cup \mathsf{bn}(\alpha)$. The input and output actions are collectively referred to as *visible* actions.

α	kind	$\mathsf{subj}(\alpha)$	$\mathsf{obj}(\alpha)$	$\mathsf{fn}(\alpha)$	$\mathsf{bn}(\alpha)$	$\mathsf{n}(\alpha)$	$\alpha\sigma$
$\overline{x}y$	free output	x	y	$\{x, y\}$	$\emptyset$	$\{x, y\}$	$\overline{x\sigma}y\sigma$
xy	input	x	y	$\{x, y\}$	$\emptyset$	$\{x, y\}$	$x\sigma y\sigma$
$\overline{x}(z)$	bound output	x	z	$\{x\}$	$\{z\}$	$\{x, z\}$	$\overline{x\sigma}(z)$
τ	internal	—	—	$\emptyset$	$\emptyset$	$\emptyset$	τ

Table 1.4. *Terminology and notation for actions*

We now define the transition relations.

Definition 1.3.2 (Transition relations) The *transition relations*, $\{\xrightarrow{\alpha} \mid \alpha \in \mathit{Act}\}$, are defined by the rules in Table 1.5. Elided from the table are four rules: the symmetric form SUM-R of SUM-L, which has $Q + P$ in place of $P + Q$, and the symmetric forms PAR-R, COMM-R, and CLOSE-R of PAR-L, COMM-L, and CLOSE-L, in which the roles of the left and right components are swapped. □

We sometimes refer to an inference of a transition as a *transition derivation*. We discuss and illustrate the rules, using examples from the informal account of action given in Section 1.1.

The rules OUT, INP, TAU, MAT, SUM-L, and SUM-R determine the actions of summations, in a way that corresponds straightforwardly to the informal explanation of the operators in Section 1.1. Note that there is no rule for inferring transitions of $\mathbf{0}$, and that there is no rule for inferring an action of $\pi . P$ other

$$\text{OUT}\quad \frac{}{\overline{x}y.\,P \xrightarrow{\overline{x}y} P} \qquad\qquad \text{INP}\quad \frac{}{x(z).\,P \xrightarrow{xy} P\{y/z\}}$$

$$\text{TAU}\quad \frac{}{\tau.\,P \xrightarrow{\tau} P} \qquad\qquad \text{MAT}\quad \frac{\pi.\,P \xrightarrow{\alpha} P'}{[x=x]\pi.\,P \xrightarrow{\alpha} P'}$$

$$\text{SUM-L}\quad \frac{P \xrightarrow{\alpha} P'}{P+Q \xrightarrow{\alpha} P'}$$

$$\text{PAR-L}\quad \frac{P \xrightarrow{\alpha} P'}{P \mid Q \xrightarrow{\alpha} P' \mid Q} \quad \mathsf{bn}(\alpha) \cap \mathsf{fn}(Q) = \emptyset$$

$$\text{COMM-L}\quad \frac{P \xrightarrow{\overline{x}y} P' \quad Q \xrightarrow{xy} Q'}{P \mid Q \xrightarrow{\tau} P' \mid Q'}$$

$$\text{CLOSE-L}\quad \frac{P \xrightarrow{\overline{x}(z)} P' \quad Q \xrightarrow{xz} Q'}{P \mid Q \xrightarrow{\tau} \boldsymbol{\nu} z\,(P' \mid Q')} \quad z \notin \mathsf{fn}(Q)$$

$$\text{RES}\quad \frac{P \xrightarrow{\alpha} P'}{\boldsymbol{\nu} z\, P \xrightarrow{\alpha} \boldsymbol{\nu} z\, P'} \quad z \notin \mathsf{n}(\alpha) \qquad\qquad \text{OPEN}\quad \frac{P \xrightarrow{\overline{x}z} P'}{\boldsymbol{\nu} z\, P \xrightarrow{\overline{x}(z)} P'} \quad z \neq x$$

$$\text{REP-ACT}\quad \frac{P \xrightarrow{\alpha} P'}{!P \xrightarrow{\alpha} P' \mid !P}$$

$$\text{REP-COMM}\quad \frac{P \xrightarrow{\overline{x}y} P' \quad P \xrightarrow{xy} P''}{!P \xrightarrow{\tau} (P' \mid P'') \mid !P}$$

$$\text{REP-CLOSE}\quad \frac{P \xrightarrow{\overline{x}(z)} P' \quad P \xrightarrow{xz} P''}{!P \xrightarrow{\tau} (\boldsymbol{\nu} z\,(P' \mid P'')) \mid !P} \quad z \notin \mathsf{fn}(P)$$

Table 1.5. *The transition rules*

than one arising from exercise of the capability expressed by π. Note especially that $x(z).P$ can receive *any* name via x, and that when a name is received, it is substituted for the placeholder z in P. Further, when a sum exercises one of its capabilities, the others are rendered void.

For example, for any name a, by INP and OUT,

$$x(z).\,\overline{z}y.\mathbf{0} \xrightarrow{xa} \overline{a}y.\mathbf{0} \xrightarrow{\overline{a}y} \mathbf{0}$$

and

$$x(z).\,\overline{y}z.\mathbf{0} \xrightarrow{xa} \overline{y}a.\mathbf{0} \xrightarrow{\overline{y}a} \mathbf{0}\,.$$

Also,

$$x(z).\,[z = y]\overline{z}w.\mathbf{0} \xrightarrow{xy} [y = y]\overline{y}w.\mathbf{0}$$

and since $\overline{y}w.\mathbf{0} \xrightarrow{\overline{y}w} \mathbf{0}$, by MAT,

$$[y = y]\overline{y}w.\mathbf{0} \xrightarrow{\overline{y}w} \mathbf{0}\,.$$

Further, by INP and SUM-L,

$$x(z).\,\overline{z}y.\mathbf{0} + \overline{w}v.\mathbf{0} \xrightarrow{xa} \overline{a}y.\mathbf{0}$$

and by OUT and SUM-R,

$$x(z).\,\overline{z}y.\mathbf{0} + \overline{w}v.\mathbf{0} \xrightarrow{\overline{w}v} \mathbf{0}\,.$$

Let us consider next the rules for restriction, RES and OPEN. The first ensures that an action of P is also an action of $\boldsymbol{\nu} z\, P$, provided the restricted name z is not in the action. In particular, restriction of z does not inhibit use or mention of other names. For instance,

$$\boldsymbol{\nu} z\, \overline{x}y.\,\overline{z}w.\mathbf{0} \xrightarrow{\overline{x}y} \boldsymbol{\nu} z\, \overline{z}w.\mathbf{0}\,.$$

Restriction of z does inhibit use of z, however: the process $\boldsymbol{\nu} z\, \overline{z}w.\mathbf{0}$ has no transitions.

There is a small point to note about α-conversion here. It is that identifying α-convertible processes, as we have done, amounts to having a transition rule:

$$\frac{P \xrightarrow{\alpha} P'}{Q \xrightarrow{\alpha} P'} \quad Q = P\,.$$

For example, consider $Q \stackrel{\text{def}}{=} \boldsymbol{\nu} z\, x(w).\,R$ where $R \stackrel{\text{def}}{=} \overline{w}z.\mathbf{0}$. For $a \neq z$, we have

$$Q \xrightarrow{xa} \boldsymbol{\nu} z\, R\{a/w\} = \boldsymbol{\nu} z\, \overline{a}z.\mathbf{0}\,.$$

Moreover, Q can also receive z via x, with suitable change of bound names:

$$Q = \boldsymbol{\nu} u\, x(w).\, R\{^{u}\!/\!_{z}\} \xrightarrow{xz} \boldsymbol{\nu} u\, R\{^{u}\!/\!_{z}\}\{^{z}\!/\!_{w}\} = \boldsymbol{\nu} u\, \overline{z}u.\mathbf{0}\,.$$

Now consider OPEN. Using it we can infer a transition of $\boldsymbol{\nu} z\, P$ labelled by the bound-output action $\overline{x}(z)$ from a transition of P labelled by the free-output action $\overline{x}z$, provided $z \neq x$. The rule expresses extrusion of the scope of a name. The side-condition $z \neq x$ is necessary as the restriction of z is intended to inhibit $\boldsymbol{\nu} z\, P$ from using z to interact with other processes (though components of P can use it to interact with one another and can pass it to one another). Note, however, that z is not restricted in the process to which $\boldsymbol{\nu} z\, P$ evolves.

What happens to this restriction? The answer is found in the CLOSE-L and CLOSE-R rules. These express that a process capable of performing a bound output $\overline{x}(z)$ can interact with a process that can receive z via x and in which z is not free. The interaction is represented by a τ transition, and in the derivative the two components are within the scope of a restriction $\boldsymbol{\nu} z$. Thus the restriction reappears encompassing the composite process. We may say that the scope of the name z is opened via OPEN and closed again via a CLOSE rule. The scope of the restricted name is extended to include just the process that receives it.

Compare this with the axiom of structural congruence allowing a restriction to be moved,

$$\boldsymbol{\nu} z\, (P_1 \mid P_2) \equiv P_1 \mid \boldsymbol{\nu} z\, P_2\,, \quad \text{if } z \notin \mathsf{fn}(P_1)\,,$$

and recall the purpose of the side condition on z. The side condition in the CLOSE rules has the same purpose. As an illustration, consider the process

$$P \stackrel{\text{def}}{=} (\boldsymbol{\nu} s\, \overline{x}s.\, \overline{s}a.\, \overline{s}b.\, \mathbf{0}) \mid x(w).\, (w(v).\, w(u).\, \overline{v}u.\, \mathbf{0} \mid z(t).\, \mathbf{0})\,.$$

The intention here is that the pair of names a, b is passed via a private connection that is established as a result of an interaction via x. By OUT and OPEN,

$$\boldsymbol{\nu} s\, \overline{x}s.\, \overline{s}a.\, \overline{s}b.\, \mathbf{0} \xrightarrow{\overline{x}(s)} \overline{s}a.\, \overline{s}b.\, \mathbf{0}\,,$$

and by INP,

$$x(w).\, (w(v).\, w(u).\, \overline{v}u.\, \mathbf{0} \mid z(t).\, \mathbf{0}) \xrightarrow{xs} s(v).\, s(u).\, \overline{v}u.\, \mathbf{0} \mid z(t).\, \mathbf{0}\,.$$

Hence, as the side condition of CLOSE-L is met by s,

$$P \xrightarrow{\tau} \boldsymbol{\nu} s\, (\overline{s}a.\, \overline{s}b.\, \mathbf{0} \mid (s(v).\, s(u).\, \overline{v}u.\, \mathbf{0} \mid z(t).\, \mathbf{0}))\,,$$

as desired. By change of bound name, however,

$$\boldsymbol{\nu} s\, \overline{x}s.\, \overline{s}a.\, \overline{s}b.\, \mathbf{0} \xrightarrow{\overline{x}(z)} \overline{z}a.\, \overline{z}b.\, \mathbf{0}\,,$$

and without the side condition on CLOSE-L it would be possible to infer also the unintended transition

$$(?)\quad P \xrightarrow{\tau} P' \stackrel{\text{def}}{=} \nu z\,(\overline{z}a.\,\overline{z}b.\,\mathbf{0} \mid (z(v).\,z(u).\,\overline{v}u.\,\mathbf{0} \mid z(t).\,\mathbf{0}))\,,$$

and thence, by OUT, INP, COMM-L, and RES, the misdirection of a:

$$P' \xrightarrow{\tau} \nu z\,(\overline{z}b.\,\mathbf{0} \mid (z(v).\,z(u).\,\overline{v}u.\,\mathbf{0} \mid \mathbf{0}))\,.$$

As we will confirm in Lemma 1.4.9, because of Convention 1.1.7 on bound names, the object of a bound-output action can always be chosen in such a way that the side condition of the CLOSE rules is satisfied.

The side condition in PAR-L and PAR-R has a similar purpose. Consider this time

$$Q \stackrel{\text{def}}{=} ((\nu s\,\overline{x}s.\,\overline{s}a.\,\overline{s}b.\,\mathbf{0}) \mid z(t).\,\mathbf{0}) \mid x(w).\,w(v).\,w(u).\,\overline{v}u.\,\mathbf{0}\,.$$

By OUT and OPEN and change of bound name we have

$$\nu s\,\overline{x}s.\,\overline{s}a.\,\overline{s}b.\,\mathbf{0} \xrightarrow{\overline{x}(z)} \overline{z}a.\,\overline{z}b.\,\mathbf{0}\,,$$

but because of the side condition in PAR-L we correctly do not have

$$(?)\quad (\nu s\,\overline{x}s.\overline{s}a.\overline{s}b.\,\mathbf{0}) \mid z(t).\,\mathbf{0} \xrightarrow{\overline{x}(z)} \overline{z}a.\overline{z}b.\,\mathbf{0} \mid z(t).\,\mathbf{0}\,.$$

We have rather

$$(\nu s\,\overline{x}s.\,\overline{s}a.\,\overline{s}b.\,\mathbf{0}) \mid z(t).\,\mathbf{0} \xrightarrow{\overline{x}(s)} \overline{s}a.\,\overline{s}b.\,\mathbf{0} \mid z(t).\,\mathbf{0}$$

and hence

$$Q \xrightarrow{\tau} \nu s\,((\overline{s}a.\,\overline{s}b.\,\mathbf{0} \mid z(t).\,\mathbf{0}) \mid s(v).\,s(u).\,\overline{v}u.\,\mathbf{0})\,.$$

The third pair of communication rules, COMM-L and COMM-R, are straightforward: they ensure that one process can pass a free name to another process. For instance, using OUT we have

$$\overline{s}a.\,\overline{s}b.\,\mathbf{0} \xrightarrow{\overline{s}a} \overline{s}b.\,\mathbf{0}$$

so by PAR-L,

$$\overline{s}a.\,\overline{s}b.\,\mathbf{0} \mid z(t).\,\mathbf{0} \xrightarrow{\overline{s}a} \overline{s}b.\,\mathbf{0} \mid z(t).\,\mathbf{0}\,.$$

Also, using INP we have

$$s(v).\,s(u).\,\overline{v}u.\,\mathbf{0} \xrightarrow{sa} s(u).\,\overline{a}u.\,\mathbf{0}\,,$$

so by COMM-L,

$$(\overline{s}a.\,\overline{s}b.\,\mathbf{0} \mid z(t).\,\mathbf{0}) \mid s(v).\,s(u).\,\overline{v}u.\,\mathbf{0} \xrightarrow{\tau} (\overline{s}b.\,\mathbf{0} \mid z(t).\,\mathbf{0}) \mid s(u).\,\overline{a}u.\,\mathbf{0}\,.$$

Hence by Res,

$$P \xrightarrow{\tau} \boldsymbol{\nu} s\,((\overline{s}b.\,\mathbf{0} \mid z(t).\,\mathbf{0}) \mid s(u).\,\overline{a}u.\,\mathbf{0})\,.$$

Finally, consider the rules Rep-act, Rep-comm, and Rep-close that determine the transitions of replications. They capture formally that $!P$ is to be thought of as an infinite composition $P \mid P \mid \cdots$. A transition of $!P$ arises either via Rep-act from an action of one copy of P, or via Rep-comm or Rep-close from an interaction between two copies of P. For instance, using Inp and Rep-act, and then Out, Rep-act, and Par-l, we have

$$\begin{array}{rcl} !x(z).\,!\overline{y}z.\,\mathbf{0} & \xrightarrow{xa} & !\overline{y}a.\,\mathbf{0} \mid !x(z).\,!\overline{y}z.\,\mathbf{0} \\ & \xrightarrow{\overline{y}a} & (\mathbf{0} \mid !\overline{y}a.\,\mathbf{0}) \mid !x(z).\,!\overline{y}z.\,\mathbf{0}\,. \end{array}$$

Moreover if $P \stackrel{\text{def}}{=} \boldsymbol{\nu} w\,(\overline{x}w.\,\mathbf{0} + x(z).\,!\overline{y}z.\,\mathbf{0})$ then using Out, Sum-l, Open, Inp, Sum-r, Res, and Rep-close, we have

$$!P \xrightarrow{\tau} (\boldsymbol{\nu} w\,(\mathbf{0} \mid \boldsymbol{\nu} v\ !\overline{y}w.\,\mathbf{0})) \mid !P\,.$$

Note that just as there is no rule of reduction of the form: from $P \longrightarrow P'$ infer $!P \longrightarrow !P'$; so, and for the same reason, there is no transition rule of the form: from $P \xrightarrow{\alpha} P'$ infer $!P \xrightarrow{\alpha} !P'$.

In some works on π-calculus, a slightly different family of transition relations is used, here called $\{\xrightarrow{\alpha}_! \mid \alpha \in \mathit{Act}\}$. These relations are defined by decorating all the arrows in Table 1.5 with a subscript '!', and replacing the three replication rules Rep-act, Rep-comm, and Rep-close by the rule

$$\text{Rep}\quad \frac{P \mid !P \xrightarrow{\alpha}_! P'}{!P \xrightarrow{\alpha}_! P'}$$

This way of proceeding has the immediate advantage that there is one rule for replication rather than three, and consequently some proofs, notably those by transition induction, may be shorter. There are several drawbacks to using Rep to define the transitions of replications, however. First, adopting Rep forces one to work up to structural congruence (or up to some relation that includes structural congruence) in making and proving assertions about the behaviour of replications. The reason is that the relations $\xrightarrow{\alpha}_!$ are *not* image-finite; see Definition 1.4.3. Indeed for any process P and action α, if P has one α transition, then $!P$ has $\xrightarrow{\alpha}_!$ transitions to infinitely many different processes. For instance, if $P \stackrel{\text{def}}{=} \overline{x}y.\,\overline{y}z.\,\mathbf{0}$ then there are infinitely many P' such that $!P \xrightarrow{\overline{x}y}_! P'$, among them $\overline{y}z.\,\mathbf{0} \mid !P$ and $P \mid (\overline{y}z.\,\mathbf{0} \mid !P)$; and if $Q \stackrel{\text{def}}{=} \overline{x}y.\,\mathbf{0} + x(z).\,\mathbf{0}$ then there are infinitely many Q' such that $!Q \xrightarrow{\tau}_! Q'$, among them $\mathbf{0} \mid (\mathbf{0} \mid !Q)$ and $\mathbf{0} \mid (Q \mid (Q \mid (\mathbf{0} \mid !Q)))$. In contrast, using the relations $\{\xrightarrow{\alpha} \mid \alpha \in \mathit{Act}\}$, one is not forced to work up to structural congruence, and, as we will see in Section 1.4, each $\xrightarrow{\alpha}$ is image-finite. As we will also see, however, each relation $\xrightarrow{\alpha}_!$ is image-finite up to $\equiv$, and agrees with $\xrightarrow{\alpha}$ up to structural congruence. Consequently, one may use the $\xrightarrow{\alpha}_!$ relations to prove properties of the $\xrightarrow{\alpha}$ relations, should this be convenient.

There are three further points of contrast between the two sets of replication rules. First, the rules REP-ACT, REP-COMM, and REP-CLOSE seem more in the spirit of structural operational semantics than REP, in that for a given prefix in a given process P, there is at most one inference of a transition of P that consumes just that prefix, and the syntax guides the construction of that inference. Second, the three rules are more suited to implementation (for instance, for carrying out proofs with the aid of a machine) as the $\xrightarrow{\alpha}$ relations are image-finite. Third, and this is a minor point, the three rules allow proofs about $\xrightarrow{\alpha}$ by structural induction on terms while REP does not. (Although this technique is rarely used, we will see an example where it is in the proofs of Corollary 1.4.6 and the two lemmas that precede it.)

Exercise 1.3.3

(1) By considering a process of the form $!(Q \mid R)$, show that it is not the case in general that for a given pair of prefixes in a given process P, there is at most one inference of a transition of P that consumes the pair.
(2) Show that on the subcalculus each of whose replications is of the form $!\pi.P$ or $!\nu z\,\overline{x}z.P$, the rules REP-COMM and REP-CLOSE can be omitted without changing the transition relations. □

A final point is that REP-ACT is by far the most frequently used of the three rules in practice, as many of the replications that arise are of the form $!\pi.P$ or $!\nu z\,\overline{x}z.P$, and, as we saw in Exercise 1.3.3, REP-COMM and REP-CLOSE cannot be applied to such terms. Indeed as we will see at the end of Section 2.2, any term can be transformed to an equivalent term in which every replication is of one of these forms.

Exercise 1.3.4 Let $P \stackrel{\text{def}}{=} !\nu y\, Q$ where $Q \stackrel{\text{def}}{=} \overline{x}y.\,\overline{y}y.\,\mathbf{0} + x(z).\,z(w).\,\mathbf{0}$. Work out and then compare and contrast an inference of the reduction

$$P \longrightarrow \nu y\,(\overline{y}y.\,\mathbf{0} \mid \nu v\; y(w).\,\mathbf{0}) \mid P$$

and an inference of the transition

$$P \xrightarrow{\tau} \nu y\,(\overline{y}y.\,\mathbf{0} \mid \nu v\; y(w).\,\mathbf{0}) \mid P\,.$$

□

Doing this exercise gives some feel for the nature of the intimate relationship between the reduction relation and the τ-transition relation. In order to show this relationship it is necessary to develop some basic properties of the transition system. This we now do.

1.4 Basic properties of the transition system

This section presents basic results about the transition relations on π-calculus processes that are fundamental to the theory. It is organized into five subsections, dealing with free names, image-finiteness, substitution, reduction, and replication, respectively.

1.4.1 Transition and free names

The first result describes how in a transition $P \xrightarrow{\alpha} P'$, the free names of P' are delimited by the free names of P and the names of α. We abbreviate $\mathsf{fn}(P_1) \cup \ldots \cup \mathsf{fn}(P_n) \cup \{x_1, \ldots, x_m\}$ to $\mathsf{fn}(P_1, \ldots, P_n, x_1, \ldots, x_m)$.

Lemma 1.4.1 Suppose $P \xrightarrow{\alpha} P'$.

(1) If $\alpha = \overline{x}y$ then $x, y \in \mathsf{fn}(P)$ and $\mathsf{fn}(P') \subseteq \mathsf{fn}(P)$.
(2) If $\alpha = xy$ then $x \in \mathsf{fn}(P)$ and $\mathsf{fn}(P') \subseteq \mathsf{fn}(P, y)$.
(3) If $\alpha = \overline{x}(z)$ then $x \in \mathsf{fn}(P)$ and $\mathsf{fn}(P') \subseteq \mathsf{fn}(P, z)$.
(4) If $\alpha = \tau$ then $\mathsf{fn}(P') \subseteq \mathsf{fn}(P)$.

Proof The proof is by induction on the inference of $P \xrightarrow{\alpha} P'$. The first assertion is needed to prove the third, and the first three are needed to prove the last. The proof is a long but routine case analysis on the last rule applied in the inference. We give just two sample cases.

In the proof of the third part, suppose $P = \boldsymbol{\nu} z\, Q$ and $P \xrightarrow{\overline{x}(z)} P'$ is inferred by Open from $Q \xrightarrow{\overline{x}z} P'$. By the first part, $x, z \in \mathsf{fn}(Q)$ and $\mathsf{fn}(P') \subseteq \mathsf{fn}(Q)$. By the side condition of Open, $x \neq z$. Hence $x \in \mathsf{fn}(P)$, and $\mathsf{fn}(P') \subseteq \mathsf{fn}(P, z)$.

In the proof of the last part, suppose $P = Q \mid R$ and $P \xrightarrow{\tau} P'$ is inferred by Close-l from $Q \xrightarrow{\overline{x}(z)} Q'$ and $R \xrightarrow{xz} R'$ where $z \notin \mathsf{fn}(R)$, so $P' = \boldsymbol{\nu} z\, (Q' \mid R')$. By the third part, $\mathsf{fn}(Q') \subseteq \mathsf{fn}(Q, z)$, and by the second part, $\mathsf{fn}(R') \subseteq \mathsf{fn}(R, z)$. Hence $\mathsf{fn}(P') = \mathsf{fn}(Q' \mid R') - \{z\} \subseteq \mathsf{fn}(Q \mid R) = \mathsf{fn}(P)$. □

Exercise 1.4.2 Show that if $P \xrightarrow{\overline{x}(z)} P'$ and the transition derivation does not contain an application of Sum-l, Sum-r, or Mat, then $z \notin \mathsf{fn}(P)$. □

1.4.2 Image-finiteness

For any process P and action α there are only finitely many processes Q such that $P \xrightarrow{\alpha} Q$; see Corollary 1.4.6. Image-finiteness properties of this kind are important both in the theory and in its applications.

Definition 1.4.3 (Image-finiteness) Let $\mathcal{R}$ be a relation on processes.

(1) If $\mathcal{S}$ is a relation on processes then $\mathcal{R}$ is *image-finite up to* $\mathcal{S}$ if for any P there are $n \geq 0$ and $P_1, \ldots, P_n$ such that if $(P, Q) \in \mathcal{R}$ then $(Q, P_i) \in \mathcal{S}$ for some i.

(2) $\mathcal{R}$ is *image-finite* if it is image-finite up to $=$. □

To prove that the transition relations are image-finite we need two lemmas. The first is about input actions. If a process can perform one input action then it can perform infinitely many input actions. Only finitely many names can be the subject of an input action of a given process, however.

Lemma 1.4.4

(1) If $P \xrightarrow{xz} P'$ and $z \notin \mathsf{fn}(P)$, then $P \xrightarrow{xy} P'\{y/z\}$ for any y.

(2) If $P \xrightarrow{xy} P'$ and $z \notin \mathsf{fn}(P)$, then there is P'' such that $P \xrightarrow{xz} P''$ and $P''\{y/z\} = P'$.

(3) For any P and x there are $n \geq 0$ and $P_1, \ldots, P_n$ and $z \notin \mathsf{fn}(P)$ such that if $P \xrightarrow{xy} P'$ then $P' = P_i\{y/z\}$ for some i.

(4) For any P there are only finitely many x such that $P \xrightarrow{xz} P'$ for some z and P'.

Proof The first two parts are proved by induction on inference, and the last two by induction on P. The reader may care to check a few cases. □

The second lemma is a similar result about output actions.

Lemma 1.4.5

(1) For any P there are only finitely many triples x, y, P' such that $P \xrightarrow{\overline{x}y} P'$.

(2) For any P and x there are $n \geq 0$ and $P_1, \ldots, P_n$ and $z \notin \mathsf{fn}(P)$ such that if $P \xrightarrow{\overline{x}(y)} P'$ then $P' = P_i\{y/z\}$ for some i.

(3) For any P there are only finitely many x such that $P \xrightarrow{\overline{x}(z)} P'$ for some z and P'.

Proof All three assertions are proved by induction on P. The proofs of the second and third use the first. □

From these lemmas we have:

Corollary 1.4.6 (Image-finiteness of transition relations) For every $\alpha \in$ *Act*, the relation $\xrightarrow{\alpha}$ is image-finite. □

Exercise 1.4.7 Prove Corollary 1.4.6. (Hint: argue by induction on processes, using Lemma 1.4.4 and Lemma 1.4.5.) □

1.4.3 Transition and substitution

As substitution is central to the description of behaviour in the π-calculus, it is important to understand precisely the relationship between it and transition. Consider first the process

$$P \stackrel{\text{def}}{=} \overline{x}y.\, y(z).\, \mathbf{0} \mid x(w).\, \overline{w}v.\, \mathbf{0}$$

and two of its transitions:

$$P \xrightarrow{\overline{x}y} P' \stackrel{\text{def}}{=} y(z).\, \mathbf{0} \mid x(w).\, \overline{w}v.\, \mathbf{0}$$

and

$$P \xrightarrow{\tau} P'' \stackrel{\text{def}}{=} y(z).\, \mathbf{0} \mid \overline{y}v.\, \mathbf{0}\ .$$

Applying the substitution $\sigma = \{a, a/x, y\}$ we have $P\sigma \xrightarrow{(\overline{x}y)\sigma} P'\sigma$, that is,

$$P\sigma \xrightarrow{\overline{a}a} a(z).\, \mathbf{0} \mid a(w).\, \overline{w}v.\, \mathbf{0}\ .$$

Further, since application of σ does not destroy the identity of the subjects of the complementary prefixes, $P\sigma \xrightarrow{\tau\sigma} P''\sigma$, that is,

$$P\sigma \xrightarrow{\tau} a(z).\, \mathbf{0} \mid \overline{a}v.\, \mathbf{0}\ .$$

These are instances of the general fact that application of a substitution to a process does not diminish its capabilities for action.

Lemma 1.4.8 If $P \xrightarrow{\alpha} P'$ then $P\sigma \xrightarrow{\alpha\sigma} P'\sigma$, provided if $\alpha = \overline{x}(z)$ then $z \notin \mathsf{fn}(P\sigma) \cup \mathsf{n}(\sigma)$.

Proof The proof is by induction on the inference of $P \xrightarrow{\alpha} P'$. Like the proofs of earlier lemmas it is a routine case analysis. It is worth noting, however, that the identification of α-convertible processes and Convention 1.1.7 on bound names simplify the task considerably. We give just one sample case.

Suppose $P \xrightarrow{\tau} P'$ is inferred by COMM-L from $Q \xrightarrow{\overline{x}y} Q'$ and $R \xrightarrow{xy} R'$, so $P' = Q' \mid R'$. By induction hypothesis, $Q\sigma \xrightarrow{\overline{x\sigma}y\sigma} Q'\sigma$ and $R\sigma \xrightarrow{x\sigma y\sigma} R'\sigma$. Hence by COMM-L, $P\sigma \xrightarrow{\tau} (Q'\sigma \mid R'\sigma) = P'\sigma$. $\square$

The proviso in Lemma 1.4.8 is necessary. For instance if $P \stackrel{\text{def}}{=} \boldsymbol{\nu} z\, \overline{x}z.\overline{z}y.\mathbf{0}$ and $\alpha = \overline{x}(z)$, then $P \xrightarrow{\alpha} P' \stackrel{\text{def}}{=} \overline{z}y.\mathbf{0}$; but if σ is $\{z/y\}$ then it is not the case that $P\sigma \xrightarrow{\alpha\sigma} P'\sigma$, because z cannot be the object of a bound output of $P\sigma$; and if σ is $\{y/z\}$, then again there is no transition $P\sigma \xrightarrow{\alpha\sigma} P'\sigma$, this time because $z \in \mathsf{fn}(P')$.

Note in passing that Lemma 1.4.8 would fail if the mismatch prefix form were added to the calculus. For instance if $Q \stackrel{\text{def}}{=} [x \neq y]\overline{x}y.\mathbf{0}$ then Q has a transition but $Q\{y/x\}$ does not.

Since α-convertible processes are identified, the object of a bound-output action can be α-converted. For example if

$$P \stackrel{\text{def}}{=} \boldsymbol{\nu} z\,(\overline{x}z.\overline{z}y.\mathbf{0} \mid \overline{u}v.\mathbf{0})$$

then

$$P \xrightarrow{\overline{x}(z)} \overline{z}y.\mathbf{0} \mid \overline{u}v.\mathbf{0}$$

and provided $w \notin \mathsf{fn}(P)$,

$$P \xrightarrow{\overline{x}(w)} \overline{w}y.\mathbf{0} \mid \overline{u}v.\mathbf{0}\,.$$

The general result is:

Lemma 1.4.9 If $P \xrightarrow{\overline{x}(z)} P'$ and $w \notin \mathsf{fn}(\boldsymbol{\nu} z\, P)$, then $P \xrightarrow{\overline{x}(w)} P'\{w/z\}$.

Proof The proof is by induction on the inference of $P \xrightarrow{\overline{x}(z)} P'$. Again it is a routine case analysis. We consider just the most crucial case.

Suppose $P = \boldsymbol{\nu} z\, Q$ and $P \xrightarrow{\overline{x}(z)} P'$ is inferred by OPEN from $Q \xrightarrow{\overline{x}z} P'$, so $z \neq x$. Suppose $w \notin \mathsf{fn}(P)$. Then $w \neq x$ since $x \in \mathsf{fn}(P)$ by Lemma 1.4.1. Moreover, $P = \boldsymbol{\nu} w\, Q\{w/z\}$, and by the previous lemma, $Q\{w/z\} \xrightarrow{\overline{x}w} P'\{w/z\}$. Hence by OPEN, $P \xrightarrow{\overline{x}(w)} P'\{w/z\}$. $\square$

Lemma 1.4.9 justifies the obvious extension to actions of Convention 1.1.7 on bound names. We assume that the bound names of actions, like the bound names of processes, are fresh:

Convention 1.4.10 (Bound Names) In any discussion, we assume that the bound names of any processes or actions under consideration are chosen to be different from the names free in any other entities under consideration, such as processes, actions, substitutions, and sets of names. This convention is subject to the limitation that in considering a transition $P \xrightarrow{\overline{x}(z)} Q$, the name z that is bound in $\overline{x}(z)$ and in P may occur free in Q. This limitation is necessary for expressing scope extrusion. □

As an illustration of Convention 1.4.10, note that, according to it, the side condition in Lemma 1.4.8 is not harmful, and indeed can be omitted.

A partial converse of Lemma 1.4.8 holds. An example of it is that if

$$P \stackrel{\text{def}}{=} \overline{x}a.\, x(w).\, \mathbf{0} \mid y(z).\, \overline{z}a.\, \mathbf{0}$$

and $\sigma = \{y/x\}$, then the transition

$$P\sigma \xrightarrow{\overline{y}a} Q \stackrel{\text{def}}{=} y(w).\, \mathbf{0} \mid y(z).\, \overline{z}a.\, \mathbf{0}$$

of $P\sigma$ has as counterpart the transition

$$P \xrightarrow{\overline{x}a} P' \stackrel{\text{def}}{=} x(w).\, \mathbf{0} \mid y(z).\, \overline{z}a.\, \mathbf{0}$$

of P. That is, to the transition $P\sigma \xrightarrow{\beta} Q$ where $\beta = \overline{y}a$ corresponds the transition $P \xrightarrow{\alpha} P'$ where $\alpha = \overline{x}a$; note that $\alpha\sigma = \beta$ and $P'\sigma = Q$.

The full converse of Lemma 1.4.8 does not hold, however. One reason is that the application of a substitution to a process may allow new liaisons among its components. For instance if again

$$P \stackrel{\text{def}}{=} \overline{x}a.\, x(w).\, \mathbf{0} \mid y(z).\, \overline{z}a.\, \mathbf{0}$$

and $\sigma = \{y/x\}$, then

$$P\sigma \xrightarrow{\tau} y(w).\, \mathbf{0} \mid \overline{a}a.\, \mathbf{0}\ ;$$

but P has no τ transition. Another reason why the full converse fails is that if $P\sigma$ receives a name that is in $\mathsf{supp}(\sigma) - \mathsf{cosupp}(\sigma)$ then P has no corresponding transition. For instance for the same P and σ as above we have

$$P\sigma \xrightarrow{yx} R \stackrel{\text{def}}{=} \overline{y}a.\, y(w).\, \mathbf{0} \mid \overline{x}a.\, \mathbf{0}\, ;$$

but there are no α and P' such that $P \xrightarrow{\alpha} P'$ and $\alpha\sigma = yx$ and $P'\sigma = R$.

To express the partial converse of Lemma 1.4.8 we say that a substitution σ is *injective on* a set X if $x \neq y$ implies $x\sigma \neq y\sigma$ whenever $x, y \in X$; and we say that two substitutions σ and ρ *agree on* X if $x\sigma = x\rho$ for all $x \in X$. An auxiliary observation:

Lemma 1.4.11 If σ is injective on a finite set X then there is a bijective substitution θ such that σ and θ agree on X.

Proof Since X is finite and σ is injective on X, there is a bijection $\rho : (X\sigma - X) \to (X - X\sigma)$. Define θ by

$$x\theta = \begin{cases} x\sigma & \text{if } x \in X \\ x\rho & \text{if } x \in X\sigma - X \\ x & \text{if } x \notin X \cup X\sigma \,. \end{cases}$$

□

Now we have the partial converse of Lemma 1.4.8.

Lemma 1.4.12 If σ is injective on $\mathsf{fn}(P)$ then there is a bijective substitution θ such that σ and θ agree on $\mathsf{fn}(P)$, so $P\sigma = P\theta$; and for any such θ, if $P\theta \xrightarrow{\beta} Q$ then $P \xrightarrow{\alpha} P'$ with $\alpha\theta = \beta$ and $P'\theta = Q$.

Proof The existence of θ follows from Lemma 1.4.11. The proof of the second assertion is a straightforward induction on the inference of $P\theta \xrightarrow{\beta} Q$. The reader may care to check a few cases. □

The last lemma relating substitution and action describes how transitions of a process $P\sigma$ arise from transitions of P for an arbitrary substitution σ. The result is for processes that contain no match prefixes. The first part shows how an output action or an input action whose object is a fresh name arises. The second part shows how a τ action of $P\sigma$ arises either from a τ action of P or from a pair of actions that the application of σ makes complementary. We write the juxtaposition of two transition relations to indicate their composition; thus $Q \xrightarrow{\alpha}\xrightarrow{\alpha'} Q'$ means that there is Q'' such that $Q \xrightarrow{\alpha} Q''$ and $Q'' \xrightarrow{\alpha'} Q'$.

Lemma 1.4.13 Suppose that P contains no match prefixes.

(1) If $P\sigma \xrightarrow{\beta} P'$ where β is $\overline{x}y$ or $\overline{x}(z)$ or xw where w is fresh, then $P \xrightarrow{\alpha} P''$ for some P'', α with $\alpha\sigma = \beta$ and $P''\sigma = P'$.

(2) If $P\sigma \xrightarrow{\tau} P'$ then

  (a) $P \xrightarrow{\tau} P''$ for some P'' with $P''\sigma = P'$, or

  (b) $P \xrightarrow{\overline{x}y}\xrightarrow{zy} P''$ for some P'', x, y, z with $x\sigma = z\sigma$ and $P''\sigma \equiv P'$, or

  (c) $P \xrightarrow{\overline{x}(y)}\xrightarrow{zy} P''$ for some P'', x, y, z with $x\sigma = z\sigma$ and $\boldsymbol{\nu} y\, P''\sigma \equiv P'$.

Proof Again the proof is by induction on inference. We consider just two cases in the proof of the second part.

(1) Suppose $P \stackrel{\text{def}}{=} P_1 \mid P_2$ and $P\sigma \xrightarrow{\tau} P' \stackrel{\text{def}}{=} P'_1 \mid P'_2$ is inferred by COMM-L from $P_1\sigma \xrightarrow{\overline{a}b} P'_1$ and $P_2\sigma \xrightarrow{ab} P'_2$. Choose a fresh w. Then $P_2\sigma \xrightarrow{aw} P''_2$ with $P''_2\{b/w\} = P'_2$, by Lemma 1.4.4(2).

By the first part of the lemma, $P_1 \xrightarrow{\overline{x}y} Q_1$ and $P_2 \xrightarrow{zw} Q_2$ with $x\sigma = z\sigma = a$ and $y\sigma = b$ and $Q_1\sigma = P'_1$ and $Q_2\sigma = P''_2$. Then, $P_2 \xrightarrow{zy} Q'_2 \stackrel{\text{def}}{=} Q_2\{y/w\}$, by Lemma 1.4.4(1).

If $x = z$ then $P \xrightarrow{\tau} Q \stackrel{\text{def}}{=} Q_1 \mid Q'_2$ and

$$Q\sigma = Q_1\sigma \mid Q_2\{y/w\}\sigma = Q_1\sigma \mid Q_2\sigma\{b/w\} = P'_1 \mid P''_2\{b/w\} = P'_1 \mid P'_2 = P' \,,$$

so (2a) holds.

If $x \neq z$ then $P \xrightarrow{\overline{x}y} Q_1 \mid P_2 \xrightarrow{zy} P'' \stackrel{\text{def}}{=} Q_1 \mid Q'_2$ and

$$P''\sigma = Q_1\sigma \mid Q_2\{y/w\}\sigma = P'_1 \mid P''_2\{b/w\} = P' \,,$$

so (2b) holds.

(2) Suppose $P \stackrel{\text{def}}{=} P_1 \mid P_2$ and $P\sigma \xrightarrow{\tau} P' \stackrel{\text{def}}{=} P'_1 \mid P_2\sigma$ is inferred by PAR-L from $P_1\sigma \xrightarrow{\tau} P'_1$. By induction hypothesis there are three cases.

(a) If $P'_1 = P''_1\sigma$ where $P_1 \xrightarrow{\tau} P''_1$, then $P \xrightarrow{\tau} P'' \stackrel{\text{def}}{=} P''_1 \mid P_2$ and $P''\sigma = P'$, so (2a) holds.

(b) If $P_1 \xrightarrow{\overline{x}y}\xrightarrow{zy} P''_1$ and $x\sigma = z\sigma$ and $P''_1\sigma \equiv P'_1$, then we have $P \xrightarrow{\overline{x}y}\xrightarrow{zy} P'' \stackrel{\text{def}}{=} P''_1 \mid P_2$ and

$$P''\sigma = P''_1\sigma \mid P_2\sigma \equiv P'_1 \mid P_2\sigma = P'$$

since $\equiv$ is preserved by composition, so (2b) holds.

(c) If $P_1 \xrightarrow{\overline{x}(y)}\xrightarrow{zy} P''_1$ and $x\sigma = z\sigma$ and $\boldsymbol{\nu} y\, P''_1\sigma \equiv P'_1$, then we have $P \xrightarrow{\overline{x}(y)}\xrightarrow{zy} P'' \stackrel{\text{def}}{=} P''_1 \mid P_2$ and

$$\boldsymbol{\nu} y\, P''\sigma = \boldsymbol{\nu} y\,(P''_1\sigma \mid P_2\sigma) \equiv (\boldsymbol{\nu} y\, P''_1\sigma) \mid P_2\sigma \equiv P'$$

since $y \notin \mathsf{fn}(P_2\sigma)$ and $\equiv$ is preserved by composition, so (2c) holds.

This completes the sketch of the proof. □

Exercise 1.4.14 Show that the assumption in Lemma 1.4.13 that P contains no match prefixes cannot be removed. □

1.4.4 Transition and reduction

We now have the assertion of the intimate relationship between reduction and transition. First, the composition $\equiv\xrightarrow{\alpha}$ is included in $\xrightarrow{\alpha}\equiv$; and secondly, the reduction relation and the τ-transition relation agree, up to structural congruence.

Lemma 1.4.15 (Harmony Lemma)

(1) $P \equiv\xrightarrow{\alpha} P'$ implies $P \xrightarrow{\alpha}\equiv P'$.
(2) $P \longrightarrow P'$ iff $P \xrightarrow{\tau}\equiv P'$.

Proof (1) Rather than giving the whole (long) proof, we explain the strategy and invite the reader to check some of the details. The main result needed is:

> **Fact 1.4.16** If $Q \equiv R$ and $Q \xrightarrow{\alpha} Q'$, then for some R' we have $R \xrightarrow{\alpha} R'$ and $Q' \equiv R'$.
>
> This can be proved by first showing the result for the case when Q can be rewritten to R by a single application of an axiom of structural congruence to a subterm of Q, and then arguing by induction on the number of such rewriting steps. □

The assertion in (1) follows from Fact 1.4.16.

(2) The proof is in two parts. First, if $P \longrightarrow P'$ then by Lemma 1.2.20 either $P = Q \stackrel{\text{def}}{=} (\boldsymbol{\nu}\widetilde{z})\,(((\overline{x}y.\,R_1 + N_1) \mid (x(z).\,R_2 + N_2)) \mid S)$ and $P' \equiv Q' \stackrel{\text{def}}{=} (\boldsymbol{\nu}\widetilde{z})\,((R_1 \mid R_2\{y/z\}) \mid S)$, or $P \equiv Q \stackrel{\text{def}}{=} (\boldsymbol{\nu}\widetilde{z})\,((\tau.\,R + N) \mid S)$ and $P' \equiv Q' \stackrel{\text{def}}{=} (\boldsymbol{\nu}\widetilde{z})\,(R \mid S)$. In either case $Q \xrightarrow{\tau} Q'$ and so by Fact 1.4.16, $P \xrightarrow{\tau}\equiv Q' \equiv P'$.

Secondly, one shows that $P \xrightarrow{\tau} P'$ implies $P \longrightarrow P'$, from which it follows that $P \xrightarrow{\tau}\equiv P'$ implies $P \longrightarrow P'$. To show that $P \xrightarrow{\tau} P'$ implies $P \longrightarrow P'$ one argues by induction on the inference of $P \xrightarrow{\tau} P'$ using:

(1) if $Q \xrightarrow{\overline{x}y} Q'$ then $Q \equiv (\boldsymbol{\nu}\widetilde{w})\,((\overline{x}y.\,R + M) \mid S)$ and $Q' \equiv (\boldsymbol{\nu}\widetilde{w})\,(R \mid S)$ where $x, y, \notin \widetilde{w}$
(2) if $Q \xrightarrow{\overline{x}(z)} Q'$ then $Q \equiv (\boldsymbol{\nu}z, \widetilde{w})\,((\overline{x}z.\,R + M) \mid S)$ and $Q' \equiv (\boldsymbol{\nu}\widetilde{w})\,(R \mid S)$ where $x \notin z, \widetilde{w}$
(3) if $Q \xrightarrow{xy} Q'$ then $Q \equiv (\boldsymbol{\nu}\widetilde{w})\,((x(z).\,R + M) \mid S)$ and $Q' \equiv (\boldsymbol{\nu}\widetilde{w})\,(R\{y/z\} \mid S)$ where $x \notin \widetilde{w}$.

This completes the sketch of the proof. □

This result reinforces the definitions of structural congruence, reduction, and transition. Some of the axioms of structural congruence are not needed to prove it, however, for example $P \mid \mathbf{0} \equiv P$ and $\boldsymbol{\nu}z\,\mathbf{0} \equiv \mathbf{0}$. These axioms are justified by other considerations, for instance their role in proving that $\boldsymbol{\nu} z\, P \equiv P$ if $z \notin \mathsf{fn}(P)$, which makes sense as a structural equality because if z is not free, then the restriction of z has no effect.

In view of Lemma 1.4.15 we can use whichever of reduction or τ transition is more convenient, provided we remember to work up to $\equiv$.

The converse of Lemma 1.4.15(1) does not hold.

Exercise 1.4.17 Show that $P \xrightarrow{\alpha}\equiv P'$ does not imply $P \equiv\xrightarrow{\alpha} P'$. (Hint: consider a process of the form $Q \mid \overline{x}y.\, \boldsymbol{\nu} z\, Q'$ where $z \notin \mathsf{fn}(Q)$, or a process of the form $x(w).\, (R \mid !R')$ where $w \in \mathsf{fn}(R) - \mathsf{fn}(R')$.) □

The final exercise in this section concerns the reduction relation.

Exercise 1.4.18

(1) Show that $\longrightarrow$ is image-finite up to $\equiv$. (Hint: use some results in this section.)
(2) Show that $\longrightarrow$ is not image-finite. □

1.4.5 Transition and replication

The next lemma gives a useful description of transitions of processes involving replication.

Lemma 1.4.19

(1) If $!P \xrightarrow{\alpha} R$ where $\alpha \neq \tau$, then there is P' such that $P \xrightarrow{\alpha} P'$ and $R = P' \mid !P$.
(2) If $!P \xrightarrow{\tau} R$ then there is Q such that $P \mid P \xrightarrow{\tau} Q$ and $R \equiv Q \mid !P$.
(3) If $S \mid !P \xrightarrow{\tau} R$ then there is Q such that $S \mid (P \mid P) \xrightarrow{\tau} Q$ and $R \equiv Q \mid !P$.

Proof The first part is immediate from the fact that the last rule applied in inferring the transition must be REP-ACT.

The second part is shown by a case analysis on the last rule applied in the inference of the transition. This rule must be REP-ACT, REP-COMM, or REP-CLOSE.

The third part is also shown by a case analysis on the last rule applied in the inference of the transition. This must be one of the PAR, COMM, or CLOSE rules.

It is instructive to carry out these two case analyses, to see exactly the forms that the process R can take, and which axioms of structural congruence are needed. □

Finally, an exercise about the alternative way of treating replication discussed in Section 1.3.

Exercise 1.4.20 Recall the family of relations $\{\xrightarrow{\alpha}_! \mid \alpha \in Act\}$ discussed towards the end of Section 1.3. Prove that:

(1) Each $\xrightarrow{\alpha}_!$ is image-finite up to $\equiv$ but is not image-finite.
(2) $P \xrightarrow{\alpha} P'$ does not imply $P \xrightarrow{\alpha}_! P'$, and $P \xrightarrow{\alpha}_! P'$ does not imply $P \xrightarrow{\alpha} P'$.
(3) $P \xrightarrow{\alpha} P'$ implies $P \xrightarrow{\alpha}_! \equiv P'$, and $P \xrightarrow{\alpha}_! P'$ implies $P \xrightarrow{\alpha}\equiv P'$.
(4) $P \xrightarrow{\alpha}\equiv P'$ iff $P \xrightarrow{\alpha}_! \equiv P'$. □

2

Behavioural Equivalence

2.1 Strong barbed congruence

This section begins to develop the theory of behavioural equivalence by introducing strong barbed bisimilarity and strong barbed congruence. The former is defined via a kind of bisimulation involving internal action and a notion of observation. Two terms are strong barbed congruent if the processes obtained by placing them into an arbitrary context are strong barbed bisimilar. The barbed bisimilarity and congruence are *strong* in that they take processes to evolve only in *single* τ transitions: there is no provision for abstraction from the number of τ transitions that comprise an evolution. When such provision is made, we obtain (weak) barbed bisimilarity and barbed congruence, the latter being the relation we adopt as the principal behavioural equivalence for π-terms throughout the book. These relations will be introduced in Section 2.4.

We begin by introducing strong barbed bisimilarity. Consider first the following two-player game on the directed graph whose nodes are the processes and whose arrows are given by the τ-transition relation. The players move alternately. A play either is infinite, or in its final position the player whose turn it is cannot move. A play begins with two nodes occupied by tokens. The first player can move either of the tokens from the node it is on along an outgoing edge to a neighbouring node. The second player can respond only by moving the other token from the node it is on along an outgoing edge to a neighbouring node. If a play is infinite then the second player wins. If after some finite number of moves the player whose turn it is cannot move, then that player loses.

For given starting processes, the second player has a winning strategy for the game iff the processes are *reduction bisimilar*, that is, they are related by a bisimulation on the graph.

Definition 2.1.1 (Reduction bisimilarity) A relation $\mathcal{S}$ is a *reduction bisimulation* if whenever $(P, Q) \in \mathcal{S}$,

(1) $P \xrightarrow{\tau} P'$ implies $Q \xrightarrow{\tau} Q'$ for some Q' with $(P', Q') \in \mathcal{S}$
(2) $Q \xrightarrow{\tau} Q'$ implies $P \xrightarrow{\tau} P'$ for some P' with $(P', Q') \in \mathcal{S}$.

Reduction bisimilarity is the union of all reduction bisimulations. In other words, P and Q are *reduction bisimilar* if $(P, Q) \in \mathcal{S}$ for some reduction bisimulation $\mathcal{S}$. □

As a process equivalence, reduction bisimilarity is seriously defective: for instance, it relates any two processes that have no τ transitions, such as $\overline{x}y.\mathbf{0}$ and $\mathbf{0}$. A more interesting relation is reduction congruence, where P and Q are *reduction congruent* if $C[P]$ and $C[Q]$ are reduction bisimilar for any context C. Reduction congruence distinguishes, for instance, between $\overline{x}a.\mathbf{0}$ and $\overline{y}a.\mathbf{0}$: a context that distinguishes them is $C \stackrel{\text{def}}{=} [\cdot] \mid x(z).\mathbf{0}$. It also distinguishes between $\overline{a}x.\mathbf{0}$ and $\overline{a}y.\mathbf{0}$, a distinguishing context being $C \stackrel{\text{def}}{=} [\cdot] \mid a(z).(\overline{z}b.\mathbf{0} \mid y(w).\mathbf{0})$. If $R \stackrel{\text{def}}{=} !\tau.\mathbf{0}$, however, reduction congruence does not distinguish between R and $R \mid \overline{a}x.\mathbf{0}$. Indeed since $R \xrightarrow{\tau}\equiv R$, for any P the process $R \mid P$ is reduction congruent to R. Moreover, in the weak case, when we abstract from internal activity by allowing a τ transition of one process to be matched by any number (even 0) of τ transitions of another, reduction congruence makes no distinctions among processes: it is the universal relation.

To obtain a satisfactory notion in this vein it is therefore necessary to allow more to be observed of processes. The observables of a process are deemed to be the names it can use for receiving and the names it can use for sending. For instance, $x(z).\overline{z}b.\mathbf{0} + y(w).\mathbf{0}$ has observables x and y – it is capable of receiving via x and via y – while $\overline{x}a.\mathbf{0}$ has observable $\overline{x}$ – it can send via x. The restricted composition $\boldsymbol{\nu}x\,((x(z).\overline{z}b.\mathbf{0} + y(w).\mathbf{0}) \mid \overline{x}a.\mathbf{0})$ of these processes has only observable y, and its continuation $\overline{a}b.\mathbf{0}$ after reduction has only observable $\overline{a}$.

This notion of observation is reminiscent of the report of the successful outcome of an experiment in a theory of *testing* equivalence. In such a theory (see the references at the end of the Part), the basis for comparing processes is the results of experiments in which the processes are tested by composing them with special terms. The notion also brings to mind observation of λ-terms, where λ-abstractions, and in typed calculi also constants, are deemed observable: a λ-abstraction can be thought of as capable of accepting an argument, and a constant as capable of emitting the value it stands for. The notion can also be applied to concurrent calculi other than the π-calculus, and to imperative and object-oriented programming languages.

To express observability formally, we say that if x is a name then $\overline{x}$ is a *co-name*, and we use μ to range over names and co-names.

Definition 2.1.2 (Observability predicates) For each name or co-name μ, the *observability predicate* $\downarrow_\mu$ is defined by

(1) $P \downarrow_x$ if P can perform an input action with subject x
(2) $P \downarrow_{\overline{x}}$ if P can perform an output action with subject x. □

For example, if

$$P \stackrel{\text{def}}{=} \boldsymbol{\nu} z\,(![x=x]\overline{x}z.\,\mathbf{0} \mid \boldsymbol{\nu} w\,(\overline{w}a.\,\mathbf{0} \mid (w(v).\,\mathbf{0} + y(u).\,\mathbf{0})))$$

then $P \downarrow_y$ and $P \downarrow_{\overline{x}}$, and these are the only observables of P.

It is possible to recast the definitions of the observability predicates so as not to involve the transition relations.

Exercise 2.1.3

(1) Show that the following are equivalent:
 (a) $P \downarrow_x$
 (b) $P \equiv (\boldsymbol{\nu}\widetilde{w})\,((x(z).\,Q + M) \mid R)$, where $x \notin \widetilde{w}$
 (c) P has an occurrence that is unguarded and is not underneath $\boldsymbol{\nu}x$ of a process of the form $[y_1 = y_1] \ldots [y_n = y_n]x(z).\,Q$.
(2) Show that the following are equivalent:
 (a) $P \downarrow_{\overline{x}}$
 (b) $P \equiv (\boldsymbol{\nu}\widetilde{w})\,((\overline{x}y.\,Q + M) \mid R)$, where $x \notin \widetilde{w}$
 (c) P has an occurrence that is unguarded and is not underneath $\boldsymbol{\nu}x$ of a process of the form $[y_1 = y_1] \ldots [y_n = y_n]\overline{x}y.\,Q$. □

We modify reduction bisimilarity to take observability into account in the following definition.

Definition 2.1.4 (Strong barbed bisimilarity) A relation $\mathcal{S}$ is a *strong barbed bisimulation* if whenever $(P, Q) \in \mathcal{S}$,

(1) $P \downarrow_\mu$ implies $Q \downarrow_\mu$
(2) $P \xrightarrow{\tau} P'$ implies $Q \xrightarrow{\tau} Q'$ for some Q' with $(P', Q') \in \mathcal{S}$
(3) $Q \downarrow_\mu$ implies $P \downarrow_\mu$
(4) $Q \xrightarrow{\tau} Q'$ implies $P \xrightarrow{\tau} P'$ for some P' with $(P', Q') \in \mathcal{S}$.

Strong barbed bisimilarity is the union of all strong barbed bisimulations. In other words, P and Q are *strong barbed bisimilar*, $P \stackrel{\cdot}{\sim} Q$, if $(P, Q) \in \mathcal{S}$ for some strong barbed bisimulation $\mathcal{S}$. □

Lemma 2.1.5 $\dot{\sim}$ is the largest strong barbed bisimulation.

Proof It follows from the definition that a union of strong barbed bisimulations is a strong barbed bisimulation. □

Note that a relation is a strong barbed bisimulation just if it is a reduction bisimulation that respects observability. Thus $P \dot{\sim} Q$ just if P and Q have the same observables, and to each τ transition of one there corresponds a τ transition of the other to a strong-barbed-bisimilar process. For example,

$$\nu z\,(\overline{z}a.\,\mathbf{0} \mid z(w).\,\overline{x}w.\,\mathbf{0}) \,\dot{\sim}\, \tau.\,\overline{x}b.\,\mathbf{0}$$

as

$$\{(\nu z\,(\overline{z}a.\,\mathbf{0} \mid z(w).\,\overline{x}w.\,\mathbf{0}), \tau.\,\overline{x}b.\,\mathbf{0}),\ (\nu z\,(\mathbf{0} \mid \overline{x}a.\,\mathbf{0}), \overline{x}b.\,\mathbf{0})\}$$

is a strong barbed bisimulation. As a second example,

$$\nu z\,(\nu w\ !\overline{z}w.\,\mathbf{0} \mid !z(v).\,\overline{x}v.\,v(u).\,\mathbf{0}) \,\dot{\sim}\, !\tau.\,\overline{x}a.\,\mathbf{0}\,.$$

Like reduction bisimilarity, strong barbed bisimilarity is unsatisfactory as a process equivalence. For instance, $\nu z\,(\overline{z}z.\,\overline{y}a.\,\mathbf{0} \mid z(w).\,\mathbf{0}) \,\dot{\sim}\, \tau.\,\overline{y}b.\,\mathbf{0}$, and $\overline{x}a.\,P \,\dot{\sim}\, \nu z\,\overline{x}z.\,Q$ for any P, Q. In neither case, however, would the two processes be considered to have the same observable behaviour, because they send different names via y and x, respectively. Strong barbed bisimilarity will, however, underpin strong barbed congruence, which is a satisfactory equivalence. We therefore show some of the properties of the bisimilarity, beginning with Lemma 2.1.8. But first, we pause to consider how to abbreviate Definition 2.1.4.

We will consider many forms of bisimilarity in the book. Each form will be the union of all bisimulations of the appropriate kind. To help draw attention to the distinctive features of each form, and to make the definitions more compact, we will adopt the following convention. It is justified by the fact that for each form, the union of a set of bisimulations will be a bisimulation; in particular, the union of all bisimulations will be the bisimilarity.

Convention 2.1.6 (Defining bisimilarities) A definition of a kind of *bisimilarity* will state that it is the largest symmetric relation satisfying some appropriate condition; the definition of the corresponding kind of *bisimulation* is to be understood as implicit in the definition of the bisimilarity. □

For instance, following this convention, Definition 2.1.4 becomes:

Definition 2.1.7 *Strong barbed bisimilarity* is the largest symmetric relation, $\dot{\sim}$, such that whenever $P \dot{\sim} Q$,

(1) $P \downarrow_\mu$ implies $Q \downarrow_\mu$
(2) $P \xrightarrow{\tau} P'$ implies $Q \xrightarrow{\tau}\dot{\sim} P'$,

and the definition of *strong barbed bisimulation* given in Definition 2.1.4 is understood to be implicit in Definition 2.1.7. The stipulation that $\dot{\sim}$ is *symmetric* obviates the need to write essentially the same clauses twice. (A barbed bisimulation need not be symmetric, however.) Note that the existential quantification in the second clause of Definition 2.1.4 is absorbed in the composition of relations $\xrightarrow{\tau}\dot{\sim}$ in the second clause of Definition 2.1.7. Similar remarks apply to all later definitions following Convention 2.1.6. Note also that Definition 2.1.7 is justified by Lemma 2.1.5.

Lemma 2.1.8 $\dot{\sim}$ is an equivalence relation.

Proof This follows easily from the definitions. □

We will use the following proof technique for strong barbed bisimilarity in the proof of Lemma 2.1.19 below.

Exercise 2.1.9 Suppose $\mathcal{S}$ is such that whenever $(P, Q) \in \mathcal{S}$,

(1) $P \downarrow_\mu$ iff $Q \downarrow_\mu$
(2) if $P \xrightarrow{\tau} P'$ then $Q \xrightarrow{\tau} Q'$ for some Q' with $P' \dot{\sim}\mathcal{S}\dot{\sim} Q'$.
(3) if $Q \xrightarrow{\tau} Q'$ then $P \xrightarrow{\tau} P'$ for some P' with $P' \dot{\sim}\mathcal{S}\dot{\sim} Q'$.

Show that $(P, Q) \in \mathcal{S}$ implies $P \dot{\sim} Q$. (Hint: show that $\dot{\sim}\mathcal{S}\dot{\sim}$ is a strong barbed bisimulation.) □

A relation $\mathcal{S}$ as in Exercise 2.1.9 is called a *strong barbed bisimulation up to* $\dot{\sim}$. In Sections 2.3 and 2.4 we will study in depth related techniques for showing bisimilarity.

Exercise 2.1.10 Show that $P \equiv Q$ implies $P \dot{\sim} Q$. □

We have defined strong barbed bisimilarity using the τ-transition relation as this yields the most convenient definition. In Lemma 1.4.15, however, we saw the intimate relationship between reduction, structural congruence, and transition. Using this it is straightforward to recast the definition.

Exercise 2.1.11 Show that strong barbed bisimilarity is the largest symmetric relation, $\doteq$, such that whenever $P \doteq Q$,

(1) $P \downarrow_\mu$ implies $Q \downarrow_\mu$
(2) $P \longrightarrow P'$ implies $Q \longrightarrow\doteq P'$. □

As a tiny illustration of the convenience of using τ transition rather than reduction in the definition of strong barbed bisimilarity, consider again the assertion

$$\boldsymbol{\nu} z\,(\overline{z}a.\mathbf{0} \mid z(w).\overline{x}w.\mathbf{0}) \stackrel{\centerdot}{\sim} \tau.\overline{x}b.\mathbf{0}\,,$$

which was established above on the basis of Definition 2.1.7 by exhibiting the strong barbed bisimulation

$$\{(\boldsymbol{\nu} z\,(\overline{z}a.\mathbf{0} \mid z(w).\overline{x}w.\mathbf{0}), \tau.\overline{x}b.\mathbf{0}),\ (\boldsymbol{\nu} z\,(\mathbf{0} \mid \overline{x}a.\mathbf{0}), \overline{x}b.\mathbf{0})\}\ .$$

Exercise 2.1.12 Show that if strong barbed bisimilarity were defined as in Exercise 2.1.11, then the above relation would not be a strong barbed bisimulation, and the smallest strong barbed bisimulation relating the two processes in question would be infinite. □

The fact that strong barbed bisimilarity is preserved by injective substitution will be useful.

Lemma 2.1.13 If $P \stackrel{\centerdot}{\sim} Q$ and σ is injective on $\mathsf{fn}(P, Q)$, then $P\sigma \stackrel{\centerdot}{\sim} Q\sigma$. □

Exercise 2.1.14 Prove Lemma 2.1.13. (Hint: use Lemma 1.4.12.) □

Notation 2.1.15 (Prefixes) We write $x.P$ for $x(z).P$ where $z \notin \mathsf{fn}(P)$, and $\overline{x}.P$ for $\boldsymbol{\nu} z\,\overline{x}z.P$ where $z \notin \mathsf{fn}(P)$. These notations are helpful when considering processes where the names passed in communications are unimportant. Two further convenient abbreviations are: π for $\pi.\mathbf{0}$, and μ for $\mu.\mathbf{0}$. So for instance, x and $x(z)$ are short for $x(z).\mathbf{0}$, while $\overline{x}$ abbreviates $\overline{x}.\mathbf{0}$ which in turn is short for $\boldsymbol{\nu} z\,\overline{x}z.\mathbf{0}$. □

Exercise 2.1.16 Show that $\stackrel{\centerdot}{\sim}$ is preserved by prefixing, sum, and restriction. □

Although strong barbed bisimilarity is preserved by prefixing, sum, and restriction, it is very far from being a congruence. For instance, if $P \stackrel{\text{def}}{=} \overline{x}y.\overline{a}$ and $Q \stackrel{\text{def}}{=} \overline{x}y$ then $P \stackrel{\centerdot}{\sim} Q$, but if $R \stackrel{\text{def}}{=} x(z)$ then $P \mid R \stackrel{\centerdot}{\not\sim} Q \mid R$ as $P \mid R \stackrel{\tau}{\longrightarrow}\downarrow_{\overline{a}}$. We therefore make the following definition.

Definition 2.1.17 (Strong barbed congruence) Processes P and Q are *strong barbed congruent*, $P \simeq^{\mathrm{c}} Q$, if $C[P] \stackrel{\centerdot}{\sim} C[Q]$ for every context C. □

Directly from the definition:

Lemma 2.1.18 $\simeq^{\mathrm{c}}$ is the largest congruence included in $\stackrel{\centerdot}{\sim}$. □

Hence, since structural congruence is a congruence and is included in strong barbed bisimilarity, $P \equiv Q$ implies $P \simeq^{\mathrm{c}} Q$. Thus the axioms of structural congruence express equivalences of behaviour as well as of structure.

Here are a couple of examples to illustrate how strong barbed congruence discriminates among processes. First, if $P \stackrel{\text{def}}{=} \boldsymbol{\nu} z\,(\overline{z}.\,\overline{y}a \mid z)$ and $Q \stackrel{\text{def}}{=} \tau.\,\overline{y}b$, then $P \not\simeq^{\mathrm{c}} Q$. For if $R \stackrel{\text{def}}{=} y(w).\,w$ then $P \mid R \not\sim Q \mid R$ as $P \mid R \stackrel{\tau}{\longrightarrow}\stackrel{\tau}{\longrightarrow}\downarrow_a$ while $Q \mid R \stackrel{\tau}{\longrightarrow}\stackrel{\tau}{\longrightarrow}\downarrow_b$. Secondly, $\overline{x}a \not\simeq^{\mathrm{c}} \boldsymbol{\nu} z\,\overline{x}z$ as if $S \stackrel{\text{def}}{=} x(w).\,(\overline{w} \mid a)$ then $\overline{x}a \mid S \stackrel{\tau}{\longrightarrow}\stackrel{\tau}{\longrightarrow}$ but only $\boldsymbol{\nu} z\,\overline{x}z \mid S \stackrel{\tau}{\longrightarrow} \boldsymbol{\nu} z\,(\mathbf{0} \mid (\overline{z} \mid a))$.

The definition of strong barbed congruence is often difficult to apply directly, because it involves universal quantification over contexts. The following Context Lemma enables us to show that processes are strong barbed congruent by considering only a subclass of the contexts (and applying substitutions). It asserts that two processes are strong barbed congruent iff the systems obtained by applying an arbitrary substitution to them and then composing with an arbitrary process are strong barbed bisimilar.

Lemma 2.1.19 (Context Lemma for $\simeq^{\mathrm{c}}$) $P \simeq^{\mathrm{c}} Q$ iff $P\sigma \mid R \stackrel{\centerdot}{\sim} Q\sigma \mid R$ for any R and σ.

Proof First suppose that $P \simeq^{\mathrm{c}} Q$, and that $\sigma = \{\widetilde{y}/\widetilde{z}\}$ where $\widetilde{y} = y_1, \ldots, y_n$ and $\widetilde{z} = z_1, \ldots, z_n$. Fix R, choose a fresh name x, and set

$$C \stackrel{\text{def}}{=} \overline{x}y_1.\,\ldots.\,\overline{x}y_n.\,\mathbf{0} \mid x(z_1).\,\ldots.\,x(z_n).\,[\cdot] \mid R\,.$$

Then $C[P] \stackrel{\centerdot}{\sim} C[Q]$. Hence since $C[P]$ reduces in n steps to $P\sigma \mid R$, and (up to $\equiv$) the only process S such that $C[Q]$ reduces in n steps to S and not $S \downarrow_{\overline{x}}$ is $Q\sigma \mid R$, it follows by Exercises 2.1.10 and 2.1.11 that $P\sigma \mid R \stackrel{\centerdot}{\sim} Q\sigma \mid R$.

Conversely, since $\simeq^{\mathrm{c}}$ is the largest congruence included in $\stackrel{\centerdot}{\sim}$, it suffices to show that if $P\sigma \mid R \stackrel{\centerdot}{\sim} Q\sigma \mid R$ for any R and σ, then $C[P]\sigma \mid R \stackrel{\centerdot}{\sim} C[Q]\sigma \mid R$ for any C and R and σ. This is done by induction on C. We consider four cases and invite the reader to check the remainder.

Suppose $C \stackrel{\text{def}}{=} x(z).\,C'$. Set

$$\mathcal{S} \stackrel{\text{def}}{=} \{(C[P]\sigma \mid R, C[Q]\sigma \mid R) \mid \; R \text{ and } \sigma \text{ arbitrary }\} \cup \stackrel{\centerdot}{\sim}\,.$$

Then $\mathcal{S}$ is a strong barbed bisimulation. We check just one case. Suppose

$$C[P]\sigma \mid R \stackrel{\tau}{\longrightarrow} \boldsymbol{\nu} y\,(C'[P]\sigma\{y/z\} \mid R')$$

where $y \notin \mathsf{fn}(C[P]\sigma)$. Then also

$$C[Q]\sigma \mid R \stackrel{\tau}{\longrightarrow} \boldsymbol{\nu} y\,(C'[Q]\sigma\{y/z\} \mid R')\,.$$

By the induction hypothesis,

$$C'[P]\sigma\{y/z\} \mid R' \stackrel{\cdot}{\sim} C'[Q]\sigma\{y/z\} \mid R',$$

from which the required closure follows since $\stackrel{\cdot}{\sim}$ is preserved by restriction (Exercise 2.1.16), and $\stackrel{\cdot}{\sim}$ is included in $\mathcal{S}$.

Suppose $C \stackrel{\text{def}}{=} C' \mid S$. Then for any R and σ,

$$C[P]\sigma \mid R \equiv C'[P]\sigma \mid (S\sigma \mid R) \stackrel{\cdot}{\sim} C'[Q]\sigma \mid (S\sigma \mid R) \equiv C[Q]\sigma \mid R,$$

using the induction hypothesis.

Suppose $C \stackrel{\text{def}}{=} \nu z\, C'$. Then for any R and σ we have $C'[P]\sigma \mid R \stackrel{\cdot}{\sim} C'[Q]\sigma \mid R$ by the induction hypothesis, and hence, assuming as usual that $z \notin \mathsf{fn}(R) \cup \mathsf{n}(\sigma)$, since $\stackrel{\cdot}{\sim}$ is preserved by restriction we have

$$C[P]\sigma \mid R \equiv \nu z\,(C'[P]\sigma \mid R) \stackrel{\cdot}{\sim} \nu z\,(C'[Q]\sigma \mid R) \equiv C[Q]\sigma \mid R\,.$$

Finally, suppose $C \stackrel{\text{def}}{=} !C'$. Set

$$\mathcal{S} \stackrel{\text{def}}{=} \{(C[P]\sigma \mid R, C[Q]\sigma \mid R) \mid R \text{ and } \sigma \text{ arbitrary}\}\,.$$

We show that $\mathcal{S}$ is a strong barbed bisimulation up to $\stackrel{\cdot}{\sim}$ (see Exercise 2.1.9).

Set $A = C'[P]\sigma$ and $A^* = C[P]\sigma$, so that $A^* = !A$. Similarly, set $B = C'[Q]\sigma$ and $B^* = C[Q]\sigma$, so that $B^* = !B$.

Suppose $R \mid A^* \xrightarrow{\tau} S$. Then by Lemma 1.4.19(3) there is T such that $R \mid (A \mid A) \xrightarrow{\tau} T$ and $S \equiv T \mid A^*$. Now

$$\begin{array}{rcll} R \mid B^* & \equiv & (R \mid B^*) \mid B & (\text{by } B^* = B \mid B^*) \\ & \stackrel{\cdot}{\sim} & (R \mid B^*) \mid A & (\text{by induction hypothesis}) \\ & \equiv & (R \mid B^* \mid A) \mid B & (\text{by } B^* \equiv B \mid B^*) \\ & \stackrel{\cdot}{\sim} & (R \mid B^* \mid A) \mid A & (\text{by induction hypothesis}) \\ & \equiv & R \mid (A \mid A) \mid B^*\,. & \end{array}$$

Hence since $R \mid (A \mid A) \mid B^* \xrightarrow{\tau} T \mid B^*$, there is U such that $R \mid B^* \xrightarrow{\tau} U$ and $U \stackrel{\cdot}{\sim} T \mid B^*$.

So in summary, if $R \mid A^* \xrightarrow{\tau} S$ then there is U such that $R \mid B^* \xrightarrow{\tau} U$ and $S \equiv \mathcal{S} \stackrel{\cdot}{\sim} U$, as required.

The argument is dual for $R \mid B^* \xrightarrow{\tau} S$. □

An analogue of the Context Lemma holds for all of the subcalculi of the π-calculus considered in the book. (The proof of the implication from left to right just given makes use of the input and output prefixes. What is really required, however, is the ability to express substitutions, and this can be done in other ways in subcalculi that lack the full input and output prefixes.)

By definition, two processes are strong barbed congruent if they are strong barbed bisimilar in every context. Strong barbed equivalence, which demands bisimilarity only in certain contexts, will also be important. It equates two processes just if no difference can be observed when each is composed with an arbitrary term. This regime is similar to the characterization of strong barbed congruence given by the Context Lemma, but with the difference that no substitution is applied to the two processes. It turns out that this difference makes strong barbed equivalence less discriminating than strong barbed congruence. It also turns out that strong barbed equivalence is the largest *non-input congruence* included in strong barbed bisimilarity, in the sense that two processes equated by strong barbed equivalence are indistinguishable in all contexts in which the hole does not occur under an input prefix. The regime also brings to mind testing equivalence described earlier, whose basis is composing processes with a test term and observing what happens.

Definition 2.1.20 (Strong barbed equivalence) Processes P and Q are *strong barbed equivalent*, $P \simeq Q$, if $P \mid R \stackrel{\centerdot}{\sim} Q \mid R$ for any R. □

Clearly, strong barbed congruence is included in strong barbed equivalence. The following exercise shows that the inclusion is proper.

Exercise 2.1.21 Let $P \stackrel{\text{def}}{=} \overline{z} \mid a$ and $Q \stackrel{\text{def}}{=} \overline{z}.\, a + a.\, \overline{z}$.

(1) Show that $P \simeq Q$.
(2) Show that $P \not\simeq^{c} Q$. □

Strong barbed equivalence can equivalently be defined, on the π-calculus, by requiring that $(\boldsymbol{\nu}\widetilde{z})\,(P \mid R) \stackrel{\centerdot}{\sim} (\boldsymbol{\nu}\widetilde{z})\,(Q \mid R)$ for any process R and names $\widetilde{z}$.

Definition 2.1.22 (Non-input context) A *non-input context* is a context in which $[\cdot]$ does not occur under an input prefix. □

For instance, $[\cdot] \mid R$ and $\boldsymbol{\nu} z\,([\cdot] \mid R)$ are non-input contexts, while $x(z).\,([\cdot] \mid R)$ is not. If C is non-input then a name z free in P is bound in $C[P]$ only if $[\cdot]$ is under some $\boldsymbol{\nu} z$ in C.

Definition 2.1.23 (Non-input congruence) An equivalence relation $\mathcal{S}$ on processes is a *non-input congruence* if $(C[P], C[Q]) \in \mathcal{S}$ whenever $(P, Q) \in \mathcal{S}$ and C is a non-input context. □

The following lemma substantiates an assertion made above about strong barbed equivalence.

Lemma 2.1.24 $\simeq$ is the largest non-input congruence included in $\dot{\sim}$.

Proof This is a consequence of Theorem 2.2.8(1) and Theorem 2.2.9(1) below. Alternatively, it suffices to show that $\simeq$ is a non-input congruence, and this can be proved by an argument similar to the proof of the Context Lemma for $\simeq^{\mathrm{c}}$ (Lemma 2.1.19).

Suppose that $P \simeq Q$. One shows that $C[P] \simeq C[Q]$ by induction on the non-input context C. For instance, it is easy to show from the definition and the fact that structural congruence is included in strong barbed bisimilarity that $P \mid R \simeq Q \mid R$ and $\boldsymbol{\nu} z\, P \simeq \boldsymbol{\nu} z\, Q$ for any R and z. It is straightforward to handle (non-input) prefixing and sum.

We outline as a series of exercises an argument for replication that is slightly different from the one given in the proof of Lemma 2.1.19. This argument depends on the fact that the transition relations are image-finite. Although the technique cannot therefore be used to prove the analogous result in the weak case (Lemma 2.4.9), we give it as it is interesting and can be applied in other circumstances.

For a process R, set $R^n \stackrel{\text{def}}{=} R \mid \ldots \mid R$ (n copies), where $R^0 \stackrel{\text{def}}{=} \mathbf{0}$.

Exercise 2.1.25 Show that if $P \simeq Q$ then $P^n \simeq Q^n$ for each n. □

Now define relations $\dot{\sim}_n$ $(n < \omega)$ by setting $\dot{\sim}_0$ to be the universal relation, and stipulating that $P \mathrel{\dot{\sim}_{n+1}} Q$ if

(1) $P \downarrow_\mu$ implies $Q \downarrow_\mu$
(2) $P \xrightarrow{\tau} P'$ implies $Q \xrightarrow{\tau} \dot{\sim}_n P'$

and vice versa. Then define relations $\simeq_n$ $(n < \omega)$ by setting $P \simeq_n Q$ if $(\boldsymbol{\nu}\tilde{z})\,(P \mid R) \mathrel{\dot{\sim}_n} (\boldsymbol{\nu}\tilde{z})\,(Q \mid R)$ for any process R and names $\tilde{z}$.

Exercise 2.1.26

(1) Show that $P \mathrel{\dot{\sim}} Q$ iff $P \mathrel{\dot{\sim}_n} Q$ for all n. (Hint: for the implication from left to right, argue by induction on n. For the converse, show that the intersection of the relations $\dot{\sim}_n$ for $n < \omega$ is a strong barbed bisimulation. Image-finiteness is important here.)
(2) Deduce that $P \simeq Q$ iff $P \simeq_n Q$ for all n. □

Exercise 2.1.27 Show that if $k \geq 2n$ then $R^k \simeq_n {!R}$. □

Exercise 2.1.28 Hence show that if $P \simeq Q$ then $!P \simeq {!Q}$. □

This completes the proof of the lemma. □

Let us briefly take stock. We have defined strong barbed bisimilarity in terms of τ transition and observability, and stipulated that two processes are strong barbed congruent if the processes formed by placing them into any given context are strong barbed bisimilar. We have thus given a simple account of behavioural equivalence. Moreover, we have presented the Context Lemma, which is sometimes helpful for showing that processes are strong barbed congruent. It will be essential, however, to have more powerful techniques. We now turn to a form of bisimilarity that meets this need.

2.2 Strong bisimilarity

There are several plausible bisimilarities on π-terms based on direct comparison of the actions that they can perform. Each of them has qualities that make it useful for showing barbed congruence in some circumstances. This section introduces what is arguably the most natural of these bisimilarities, in its strong version, and begins to show how it provides a tractable technique for proving strong barbed congruence.

The section is in three subsections. The first defines strong bisimilarity and the associated congruence, strong full bisimilarity. It also establishes some basic results about these relations, among them that they in fact coincide with strong barbed equivalence and strong barbed congruence, respectively. The second subsection studies the important technique of unfolding of process behaviour and gives expansion lemmas for π-terms. The third subsection collects useful results involving replication.

2.2.1 Strong bisimilarity and full bisimilarity

Strong bisimilarity on π-terms is similar to strong bisimilarity on CCS-terms, but modified to take name-passing properly into account. Consider the directed graph whose nodes are the processes and whose arrows are given by the transition relations. The bisimulation game on this graph is similar to the game described in Section 2.1 in connection with the definition of reduction bisimilarity. The difference is that if the first player moves a token from one node to another along an edge labelled with an *arbitrary* action α, the second player must respond by moving the other token from the node it is on along an edge also labelled α.

There is one small caveat. It stems from Convention 1.4.10 that bound names in actions are fresh, and indeed illustrates the importance of freshness. Consider the processes $P \stackrel{\text{def}}{=} \boldsymbol{\nu} z\, \overline{x}z.\mathbf{0}$ and $Q \stackrel{\text{def}}{=} \boldsymbol{\nu} z\, \overline{x}z.\mathbf{0} \mid \boldsymbol{\nu} w\, \overline{w}y.\mathbf{0}$. On the basis of their transitions, the only difference between P and Q is that P can perform the action $\overline{x}(y)$ but Q cannot: the side condition of the transition rule PAR-L prevents it as y is free in the inert second component of Q. We would not wish, however, to distinguish between P and Q, as the behaviour of each is simply to send a fresh name via x and become inactive. In the definition of bisimilarity, therefore, a bound-output action of one process need be matched by the other only if the bound name of the action is not free in either process. This is not a harmful restriction, since by Lemma 1.4.9 the bound name can be chosen to be almost any name. Indeed as noted above, by Convention 1.4.10, the object of a bound-output action is tacitly assumed not to be free in any processes under consideration. Thus implicit in the following definition, and later definitions like it, is the assumption that $\mathsf{bn}(\alpha) \cap \mathsf{fn}(P, Q) = \emptyset$.

Definition 2.2.1 (Strong bisimilarity) *Strong bisimilarity* is the largest symmetric relation, $\sim$, such that whenever $P \sim Q$, if $P \xrightarrow{\alpha} P'$ then $Q \xrightarrow{\alpha} \sim P'$. □

For example,

$$\boldsymbol{\nu} z\, (\overline{z}a \mid z(w).\, \overline{x}w) \sim \tau.\, \overline{x}a$$

since

$$\{(\boldsymbol{\nu} z\, (\overline{z}a \mid z(w).\, \overline{x}w), \tau.\, \overline{x}a),\ (\boldsymbol{\nu} z\, (\mathbf{0} \mid \overline{x}a), \overline{x}a),\ (\boldsymbol{\nu} z\, (\mathbf{0} \mid \mathbf{0}), \mathbf{0})\}$$

is a strong bisimulation.

As an easy consequence of the definitions and Lemma 1.4.15, structural congruence is a strong bisimulation, and so $P \equiv Q$ implies $P \sim Q$. Further, as we will see shortly, $P \sim Q$ implies $P \stackrel{\cdot}{\sim} Q$. Strong bisimilarity is much more discriminating than strong barbed bisimilarity, however. For instance, $\overline{x}a$ and $\overline{x}b$ are strong barbed bisimilar, but they are not strong bisimilar because they can perform only different free-output actions. Similarly, $\overline{x}a \stackrel{\cdot}{\sim} \boldsymbol{\nu} z \overline{x}z$ but $\overline{x}a \not\sim \boldsymbol{\nu} z \overline{x}z$.

We will see below that strong bisimilarity is a non-input congruence. It is not, however, preserved by input prefix. For instance, we have that

$$\overline{z} \mid a \sim \overline{z}.\, a + a.\, \overline{z}$$

but

$$x(z).\, (\overline{z} \mid a) \not\sim x(z).\, (\overline{z}.\, a + a.\, \overline{z})\,. \tag{2.1}$$

Recall that $\overline{z} \mid a$ and $\overline{z}.\, a + a.\, \overline{z}$ were used in Exercise 2.1.21 to show that strong barbed congruence differs from strong barbed equivalence. It is not a coincidence that these processes show also that strong bisimilarity is not preserved by input prefix, for as we will see later, strong bisimilarity coincides with strong barbed equivalence.

The reason why the input-prefixed processes in (2.1) are not strong bisimilar is that one name that can be received via x is a. The respective continuations are then $\overline{a} \mid a$ and $\overline{a}.\, a + a.\, \overline{a}$, and only the first of these has a τ transition. In general, when an input-prefixed process $x(z).\, P$ receives a name free in P, new possibilities for interaction among the components of P may arise. As the example illustrates, however, if P' is a summation strong bisimilar to P, these possibilities may not be represented in $x(z).\, P'$.

The essence of this example is that strong bisimilarity is not preserved by substitution, for

$$(\overline{z} \mid a)\{a/z\} \not\sim (\overline{z}.\, a + a.\, \overline{z})\{a/z\} .$$

In seeking a congruence based on action we are therefore led to:

Definition 2.2.2 (Strong full bisimilarity) P and Q are *strong full bisimilar*, $P \sim^{\mathrm{c}} Q$, if $P\sigma \sim Q\sigma$ for every substitution σ. □

Strong full bisimilarity is strictly finer than strong bisimilarity: $\overline{z} \mid a$ and $\overline{z}.\, a + a.\, \overline{z}$ are strong bisimilar, but not strong full bisimilar because of the substitution $\{a/z\}$ considered above. The match prefix form makes it possible to unfold the behaviour of a composition to a strong-*full*-bisimilar summation, as in, for instance,

$$\overline{z} \mid a \sim^{\mathrm{c}} \overline{z}.\, a + a.\, \overline{z} + [z = a]\tau .$$

This equality holds because if $z\sigma = a\sigma = x$ then

$$\begin{array}{rcl} (\overline{z} \mid a)\sigma & = & \overline{x} \mid x \\ & \sim & \overline{x}.\, x + x.\, \overline{x} + \tau \\ & \sim & \overline{x}.\, x + x.\, \overline{x} + [x = x]\tau \\ & = & (\overline{z}.\, a + a.\, \overline{z} + [z = a]\tau)\sigma , \end{array}$$

while if $z\sigma \neq a\sigma$ then

$$\begin{array}{rcl} (\overline{z} \mid a)\sigma & \sim & \overline{z\sigma}.\, a\sigma + a\sigma.\, \overline{z\sigma} \\ & \sim & \overline{z\sigma}.\, a\sigma + a\sigma.\, \overline{z\sigma} + [z\sigma = a\sigma]\tau \\ & = & (\overline{z}.\, a + a.\, \overline{z} + [z = a]\tau)\sigma . \end{array}$$

We show in Section 2.2.2 that using terms guarded by appropriate match prefixes, for *any* given composition we can find a summation that is strong full bisimilar to it.

In contrast with the previous example, we have that

$$x(z).\, \boldsymbol{\nu} w\, (\overline{z} \mid w) \sim^{\mathrm{c}} x(z).\, \boldsymbol{\nu} w\, (\overline{z}.\, w + w.\, \overline{z}) .$$

The restriction ensures that the name received via x is different from the restricted name, so no liaison can be formed via it.

We saw above that strong bisimilarity is not preserved by arbitrary substitution. It is preserved by injective substitution, however:

Lemma 2.2.3 $P \sim Q$ implies $P\sigma \sim Q\sigma$ for every σ that is injective on $\mathsf{fn}(P, Q)$.

Proof The proof is deferred to Section 2.3, where further proof techniques will be available. □

Moreover, strong full bisimilarity is obviously preserved by substitution:

Lemma 2.2.4 $P \sim^{\mathrm{c}} Q$ implies $P\sigma \sim^{\mathrm{c}} Q\sigma$ for every σ.

Proof The assertion is immediate from the definitions. □

Before examining the relationships among the various relations we note:

Lemma 2.2.5 $\sim$ and $\sim^{\mathrm{c}}$ are equivalence relations.

Proof The assertions follow easily from the definitions, except that transitivity of $\sim$ needs a little work (see the following exercise). □

Exercise 2.2.6

(1) By considering bound-output actions, show that the composition of two strong bisimulations it not necessarily a strong bisimulation.
(2) Using Lemma 2.2.3, show that $\sim$ is transitive. □

We have introduced five relations: strong barbed bisimilarity, equivalence and congruence, and strong bisimilarity and full bisimilarity. The following lemma summarizes the relationships among the barbed relations and the relationships involving the labelled relations that we have already discussed.

Lemma 2.2.7

(1) $P \sim^{\mathrm{c}} Q$ implies $P \sim Q$, and $P \sim Q$ implies $P \stackrel{\cdot}{\sim} Q$.
(2) $P \simeq^{\mathrm{c}} Q$ implies $P \simeq Q$, and $P \simeq Q$ implies $P \stackrel{\cdot}{\sim} Q$.
(3) Each of the implications in (1) and (2) is strict.

Proof The first two assertions follow easily from the definitions, and the last is shown by examples considered earlier. □

To complete the picture, we show exactly how the barbed and labelled equivalences are related (Theorem 2.2.9). For this, we first need to establish the congruence properties of the labelled relations.

Theorem 2.2.8 (Congruence properties of $\sim$ and $\sim^{\mathrm{c}}$)

(1) $\sim$ is a non-input congruence.

(2) If $P\{y/z\} \sim Q\{y/z\}$ for all $y \in \mathsf{fn}(P, Q, z)$, then $x(z).P \sim x(z).Q$.
(3) $\sim^{\mathrm{c}}$ is a congruence.
(4) $\sim^{\mathrm{c}}$ is the largest congruence included in $\sim$.

Proof The proofs of the first two parts are deferred to Section 2.3.

For the third part, suppose $P \sim^{\mathrm{c}} Q$. We show by induction on contexts that for every context C and substitution σ, $C[P\sigma] \sim C[Q\sigma]$. For $C \stackrel{\mathrm{def}}{=} [\cdot]$ this is immediate as $P \sim^{\mathrm{c}} Q$. The other cases follow using the first two parts, the most notable being when $C \stackrel{\mathrm{def}}{=} x(z).C'$. Let $y \in \mathsf{fn}(C'[P]\sigma, C'[Q]\sigma, z)$ and let $\sigma' = \sigma\{y/z\}$. Then by induction hypothesis, $C'\sigma'[P\sigma'] \sim C'\sigma'[Q\sigma']$, that is, $C'[P]\sigma' \sim C'[Q]\sigma'$. (Note that the induction hypothesis is applicable because application of a substitution to a context does not alter the size of the context.) Hence by the second part, $C[P]\sigma \sim C[Q]\sigma$.

For the last part, suppose $\doteq$ is a congruence included in $\sim$, and suppose $P \doteq Q$. Suppose $\sigma = \{\widetilde{y}/\widetilde{z}\}$. Set

$$C \stackrel{\mathrm{def}}{=} \boldsymbol{\nu} x\,(\overline{x}y_1.\ \ldots.\overline{x}y_n \mid x(z_1).\ \ldots.x(z_n).[\cdot])$$

where x is fresh. Then $C[P] \doteq C[Q]$ so $C[P] \sim C[Q]$. But $C[P]\,(\stackrel{\tau}{\longrightarrow})^n \equiv P\sigma$ where $(\stackrel{\tau}{\longrightarrow})^n$ is the n-fold composition of $\stackrel{\tau}{\longrightarrow}$, so $C[Q]\,(\stackrel{\tau}{\longrightarrow})^n \sim P\sigma$. Since $C[Q]\,(\stackrel{\tau}{\longrightarrow})^n \sim Q\sigma$ only, $P\sigma \sim Q\sigma$. Hence $P \sim^{\mathrm{c}} Q$. □

By Theorem 2.2.8(2), to establish $x(z).P \sim x(z).Q$ it suffices to show that $P\{y/z\} \sim Q\{y/z\}$ for the names y free in P or Q and one other name. (Since $\sim$ is preserved by the match operator, Theorem 2.2.8(2) holds if we replace $x(z)$ by $[x_1 = y_1] \ldots [x_n = y_n]x(z)$, for arbitrary $x_1, y_1, \ldots, x_n, y_n$.)

We now have the Strong Characterization Theorem. It asserts that strong barbed equivalence and strong barbed congruence coincide with strong bisimilarity and strong full bisimilarity, respectively. The more important fact is the inclusion of the labelled relations in the barbed, since this licenses the use of the more tractable strong bisimilarities to prove that processes are strong barbed equivalent and congruent. This fact is a simple consequence of earlier results.

Theorem 2.2.9 (Strong Characterization Theorem) For any P, Q,

(1) $P \simeq Q$ iff $P \sim Q$
(2) $P \simeq^{\mathrm{c}} Q$ iff $P \sim^{\mathrm{c}} Q$. □

Before giving the proof we have some notes on the theorem and its proof. First, the proof carries over with little change to show the corresponding result in the *weak case* (Theorem 2.4.29). Secondly, although the construction in the proof employs many observables, a *single observable* is sufficient to establish the theorem. Let us write $P\downarrow$ to mean $P\downarrow_\mu$ for some μ. Consider the relation defined like strong barbed congruence except that in the definition of strong barbed bisimilarity, the clause '$P\downarrow_\mu$ implies $Q\downarrow_\mu$' is replaced by '$P\downarrow$ implies $Q\downarrow$'. The relation so defined coincides with strong full bisimilarity and hence with strong barbed congruence. In the weak case, however, it is not known if the corresponding result holds.

Thirdly, the + *operator* is not needed to prove the theorem. What *is* needed is a form of internal choice (where a process decides autonomously to follow one of several possible paths; see, for instance, the internal choice operator of λ-calculus in Section 17.4), and this can be expressed via other operators. This fact is important when one seeks similar results on subcalculi that lack +.

Fourthly, the result also holds if *matching* is omitted from the calculus. Briefly, the reason is that in the strong case, the role that matching plays in the proof can be achieved by other means. This is a rather technical point, and the following discussion may be best read after the proof. Consider a process

$$x(z).\,([z=a]M+[z=b]N)$$

where $z\notin \mathsf{fn}(M,N)$, which is to proceed as M if it receives a via x, and as N if it receives b. In the proof, such a process can be replaced by

$$x(z).\,((c+\overline{z})\mid(a.\,M+b.\,N))\,,$$

where c is a fresh name. The point is that if a, say, is received via x, then in a single transition, the observable c can be removed and the observables in M exposed. The analogue of the theorem in the weak case does not hold without the match prefix form, however, as we will see at the end of Section 2.4.

2.2.1.1 Proof of Theorem 2.2.9

We first show (1). That $P\sim Q$ implies $P\simeq Q$ follows from the facts that $\sim$ is included in $\dot{\sim}$ by Lemma 2.2.7, that $\simeq$ is the largest non-input congruence included in $\dot{\sim}$ by Lemma 2.1.24, and that $\sim$ is a non-input congruence by Theorem 2.2.8(1).

The proof that $P\simeq Q$ implies $P\sim Q$ is more difficult. We first outline the structure of the argument. We define a family of relations $\sim_n$ for $n<\omega$ by stratifying the definition of strong bisimilarity (Definition 2.2.10), and, using the image-finiteness of the transition relations, show that the intersection $\sim_\omega$ of these relations coincides with strong bisimilarity (Claim 2.2.11). We then show by induction on $n<\omega$ that if $P\not\sim_n Q$ then $C[P]\not\dot{\sim} C[Q]$ for some context C (Claim 2.2.12). The result then follows.

Definition 2.2.10 (Stratification of strong bisimilarity)

(1) $\sim_0$ is the universal relation on processes.

(2) For $1 \leq n < \omega$, the relation $\sim_n$ is defined by: $P \sim_n Q$ if

  (a) $P \xrightarrow{\alpha} P'$ implies $Q \xrightarrow{\alpha}\sim_{n-1} P'$

  (b) $Q \xrightarrow{\alpha} Q'$ implies $P \xrightarrow{\alpha}\sim_{n-1} Q'$.

(3) $P \sim_\omega Q$ if $P \sim_n Q$ for all $n < \omega$. □

Note that $\sim_0, \sim_1, \ldots, \sim_\omega$ is a decreasing sequence of relations.

The following claim is a consequence of the fact that the transition relations are image-finite.

Claim 2.2.11 $P \sim_\omega Q$ iff $P \sim Q$.

Proof First note from the definitions that $P \sim Q$ implies $P \sim_\omega Q$.

We show that $P \sim_\omega Q$ implies $P \sim Q$ by establishing that $\sim_\omega$ is a bisimulation. So suppose $P \sim_\omega Q$ and $P \xrightarrow{\alpha} P'$. Then for each $n < \omega$ there is Q_n such that $Q \xrightarrow{\alpha} Q_n \sim_n P'$. Since $\xrightarrow{\alpha}$ is image-finite, there is Q' such that $Q \xrightarrow{\alpha} Q'$ and $Q' = Q_n$ for infinitely many n. We deduce that $Q' \sim_n P'$ for infinitely many n, and hence $Q' \sim_\omega P'$. □

In what follows, $\Sigma_{i \in I} P_i$ abbreviates $P_{i_1} + \cdots + P_{i_r}$ where $I = \{i_1, \ldots, i_r\}$.

Claim 2.2.12 Suppose that $n \geq 0$ and $P \not\sim_n Q$. Then there is a summation M such that for any $\widetilde{z} \subseteq \mathsf{fn}(P, Q)$ and any fresh name s,

$$(\boldsymbol{\nu}\widetilde{z})\,(P \mid (M + s)) \not\sim (\boldsymbol{\nu}\widetilde{z})\,(Q \mid (M + s))\,.$$

Proof By induction on n. For $n = 0$ there is nothing to prove, so suppose that $n > 0$. Then there are α and P' such that $P \xrightarrow{\alpha} P'$ but $P' \not\sim_{n-1} Q'$ for all Q' such that $Q \xrightarrow{\alpha} Q'$ (or vice versa, when the argument is the same). Since $\xrightarrow{\alpha}$ is image-finite, $\{Q' \mid Q \xrightarrow{\alpha} Q'\} = \{Q_i \mid i \in I\}$ for some finite set I. Appealing to the induction hypothesis, for each $i \in I$ let M_i be a summation such that for any $\widetilde{w} \subseteq \mathsf{fn}(P', Q_i)$ and any fresh name t,

$$(\boldsymbol{\nu}\widetilde{w})\,(P' \mid (M_i + t)) \not\sim (\boldsymbol{\nu}\widetilde{w})\,(Q_i \mid (M_i + t))\,. \qquad (2.2)$$

We consider four cases, one for each form that α can take. We give the details only for the case when α is an input action. The other cases are similar, and for them we just indicate the main point in the construction.

Case 1 Suppose that α is xy. Let s_i $(i \in I)$ be fresh names, and set

$$M \stackrel{\text{def}}{=} \overline{x}y.\,\Sigma_{i \in I}\,\tau.\,(M_i + s_i)\,.$$

We show that M is as required in the claim. So suppose that $\widetilde{z} \subseteq \mathsf{fn}(P,Q)$ and s is fresh. Let $A \stackrel{\mathrm{def}}{=} (\boldsymbol{\nu}\widetilde{z})\,(P \mid (M+s))$ and $B \stackrel{\mathrm{def}}{=} (\boldsymbol{\nu}\widetilde{z})\,(Q \mid (M+s))$, and suppose, for a contradiction, that $A \stackrel{\cdot}{\sim} B$.

We have

$$A \xrightarrow{\tau} A' \stackrel{\mathrm{def}}{=} (\boldsymbol{\nu}\widetilde{z})\,(P' \mid \Sigma_{i\in I}\ \tau.\,(M_i + s_i))\ .$$

Since $A \stackrel{\cdot}{\sim} B$ there is B' such that $B \xrightarrow{\tau} B' \stackrel{\cdot}{\sim} A'$. Since $A' \downarrow_s$ does not hold, $B' \downarrow_s$ does not hold. The only way this is possible is if $I \neq \emptyset$ and

$$B' \stackrel{\mathrm{def}}{=} (\boldsymbol{\nu}\widetilde{z})\,(Q_j \mid \Sigma_{i\in I}\ \tau.\,(M_i + s_i))$$

for some $j \in I$. We now exploit the inductive hypothesis on P', Q_j, and M_j. We have

$$A' \xrightarrow{\tau} A''_j \stackrel{\mathrm{def}}{=} (\boldsymbol{\nu}\widetilde{z})\,(P' \mid (M_j + s_j))\ .$$

Since $A' \stackrel{\cdot}{\sim} B'$ there is B''_j such that $B' \xrightarrow{\tau} B''_j \stackrel{\cdot}{\sim} A''_j$. In particular, since $A''_j \downarrow_{s_j}$ we must have $B''_j \downarrow_{s_j}$. The only possibility is

$$B''_j \stackrel{\mathrm{def}}{=} (\boldsymbol{\nu}\widetilde{z})\,(Q_j \mid (M_j + s_j))\ .$$

But $A''_j \stackrel{\cdot}{\not\sim} B''_j$ by (2.2), a contradiction. Hence $A \stackrel{\cdot}{\not\sim} B$, as required.

Case 2 Suppose that α is $\overline{x}y$. Let s_i $(i \in I)$ and w be fresh names, and set

$$M \stackrel{\mathrm{def}}{=} x(w).\,\Sigma_{i\in I}\ [w = y]\tau.\,(M_i + s_i)\ .$$

The argument is then similar.

Case 3 Suppose that α is $\overline{x}(z)$. Suppose $\mathsf{fn}(P,Q) = \{a_1,\ldots,a_k\}$. Let s_i $(i \in I)$ and t and w be fresh names, and set

$$M \stackrel{\mathrm{def}}{=} x(w).\,(\Sigma_{h=1}^{k}[w = a_h]t + \Sigma_{i\in I}\ \tau.\,(M_i + s_i))\ .$$

The argument is then similar. In this case, using the notation in the first case we have

$$A' \stackrel{\mathrm{def}}{=} \boldsymbol{\nu}\widetilde{z}\,\boldsymbol{\nu}z\,(P' \mid (\Sigma_{h=1}^{k}[z = a_h]t + \Sigma_{i\in I}\ \tau.\,(M_i + s_i)))$$

and not $A' \downarrow_s$ and not $A' \downarrow_t$. It follows that the transition $B \xrightarrow{\tau} B'$ must result from Q performing a bound-output action whose subject is x and whose object we may take to be z by Lemma 1.4.9.

Case 4 Suppose that α is τ. Let s_i $(i \in I)$ be fresh names, and set

$$M \stackrel{\mathrm{def}}{=} \Sigma_{i\in I}\ \tau.\,(M_i + s_i)\ .$$

The argument is then similar.

This completes the proof of the claim. □

To complete the proof of (1) of the theorem, suppose that $P \not\sim Q$. Then by Claim 2.2.11, $P \not\sim_n Q$ for some $n < \omega$. Then let M be as given by Claim 2.2.12, let s be fresh, and set $C \stackrel{\text{def}}{=} [\cdot] \mid (M + s)$. Then $C[P] \not\dot\sim C[Q]$, and so $P \not\simeq Q$.

Finally, (2) of the theorem follows immediately from (1) since $\simeq^{\mathrm{c}}$ is the largest congruence included in $\simeq$ and $\sim^{\mathrm{c}}$ is the largest congruence included in $\sim$. □

2.2.2 Expanding process behaviour

In concurrency theory in general, expanding, or unfolding, a process is a fundamental analytical technique. Expanding a process involves transforming it to an equivalent summation in which all of its capabilities for action are explicit. By iterating the procedure, the behaviour of the process can be calculated to any desired depth. Unfolding is often allied with laws for abstracting from internal action and rules for handling infinite behaviour, with the goal of obtaining simple descriptions of the observable behaviours of processes.

To unfold π-calculus processes it is convenient to introduce an abbreviation for expressing the bound-ouput actions they can perform.

Notation 2.2.13 (Bound-output prefix) $\overline{x}(z).P$ stands for $\boldsymbol{\nu} z\, \overline{x}z.P$. We refer to it as a *bound-output prefix*. We use κ, λ to range over prefixes including bound outputs. We allow bound-output prefixes in summations: $M_1 + \cdots + \overline{x}(z).P + \cdots + M_n$ abbreviates $\boldsymbol{\nu} z\,(M_1 + \cdots + \overline{x}z.P + \cdots + M_n)$ where $z \notin \mathsf{fn}(M_1, \ldots, M_n)$. □

The Expansion Lemma for strong bisimilarity is:

Lemma 2.2.14 (Expansion Lemma for $\sim$) If $M = \kappa_1.P_1 + \cdots + \kappa_n.P_n$ and $N = \lambda_1.Q_1 + \cdots + \lambda_m.Q_m$, then

$$M \mid N \sim \Sigma_i \kappa_i.(P_i \mid N) + \Sigma_j \lambda_j.(M \mid Q_j) + \Sigma_{\kappa_i\, \mathtt{comp}\, \lambda_j} \tau.R_{ij}$$

where $\kappa_i\, \mathtt{comp}\, \lambda_j$ (κ_i *complements* λ_j) if

(1) κ_i is $\overline{x}y$ and λ_j is $x(z)$, when R_{ij} is $P_i \mid Q_j\{y/z\}$, or
(2) κ_i is $\overline{x}(z)$ and λ_j is $x(z)$, when R_{ij} is $\boldsymbol{\nu} z\,(P_i \mid Q_j)$,

or vice versa.

Proof Let K be the summation on the right of the asserted equivalence. It is straightforward to check that the relation obtained by adding the pair $(M \mid N, K)$ to the identity relation is a strong bisimulation. □

To illustrate Lemma 2.2.14, consider

$$M \stackrel{\text{def}}{=} x(z).\,\overline{z}a + y(w).\,\overline{w}b \qquad \text{and} \qquad N \stackrel{\text{def}}{=} \overline{y}(v).\,v(u)\ .$$

We have

$$\begin{aligned} M \mid N \sim\ & x(z).\,(\overline{z}a \mid N) + y(w).\,(\overline{w}b \mid N) + \overline{y}(v).\,(M \mid v(u)) \\ & + \tau.\,\boldsymbol{\nu} v\,(\overline{v}b \mid v(u))\ . \end{aligned}$$

We cannot replace $\sim$ by $\sim^{\mathrm{c}}$ in Lemma 2.2.14: recall the earlier observation that $\overline{z} \mid a \not\sim^{\mathrm{c}} \overline{z}.\,a + a.\,\overline{z}$. Recall also we noted that $\overline{z} \mid a \sim^{\mathrm{c}} \overline{z}.\,a + a.\,\overline{z} + [z = a]\tau$. This is a simple instance of the Expansion Lemma for strong full bisimilarity.

Lemma 2.2.15 (Expansion Lemma for $\sim^{\mathrm{c}}$) Let M and N be as in the previous lemma. Then

$$M \mid N \sim^{\mathrm{c}} \Sigma_i \kappa_i.\,(P_i \mid N) + \Sigma_j \lambda_j.\,(M \mid Q_j) + \Sigma_{\kappa_i\,\mathsf{opp}\,\lambda_j} [x_i = y_j]\tau.\,R_{ij}$$

where $\kappa_i\,\mathsf{opp}\,\lambda_j$ (κ_i *opposes* λ_j) if

(1) κ_i is $\overline{x_i}y$ and λ_j is $y_j(z)$, when R_{ij} is $P_i \mid Q_j\{y/z\}$, or
(2) κ_i is $\overline{x_i}(z)$ and λ_j is $y_j(z)$, when R_{ij} is $\boldsymbol{\nu} z\,(P_i \mid Q_j)$,

or vice versa.

Proof The proof is similar to that of Lemma 2.2.14. □

To illustrate, with M and N as in the example before Lemma 2.2.15,

$$\begin{aligned} M \mid N \sim^{\mathrm{c}}\ & x(z).\,(\overline{z}a \mid N) + y(w).\,(\overline{w}b \mid N) + \overline{y}(v).\,(M \mid v(u)) \\ & + [y = y]\tau.\,\boldsymbol{\nu} v\,(vb \mid v(u)) \\ & + [x = y]\tau.\,\boldsymbol{\nu} v\,(\overline{v}a \mid v(u))\ . \end{aligned}$$

The extra final summand is present as strong full bisimilarity demands strong bisimilarity under arbitrary substitution, and a substitution could identify x and y.

The assertions in the next lemma are useful in manipulating expanded processes. The first allows inert terms to be eliminated, and the second is helpful in iterating the operation of expansion. The *subject*, $\mathsf{subj}(\pi)$, of a prefix π is x if π is $\overline{x}y$ or $x(z)$, τ if π is τ, and $\mathsf{subj}(\pi')$ if π is $[x = y]\pi'$. (Defining the subject of the prefix τ to be τ is just a notational convenience; in Table 1.4 the subject of the action τ is not defined.)

Lemma 2.2.16

(1) If $z = \mathsf{subj}(\pi)$ then $\boldsymbol{\nu} z\,\pi.\,P \sim^{\mathrm{c}} \mathbf{0}$ and $\boldsymbol{\nu} z\,!\pi.\,P \sim^{\mathrm{c}} \mathbf{0}$.
(2) If z does not occur in π then $\boldsymbol{\nu} z\,\pi.\,P \sim^{\mathrm{c}} \pi.\,\boldsymbol{\nu} z\,P$.

Proof For the first assertion in (1), the relation

$$\{((\boldsymbol{\nu} z\, \pi.\, P)\sigma, \mathbf{0}) \mid z = \mathsf{subj}(\pi) \text{ and } \sigma \text{ arbitrary}\}$$

is a strong bisimulation. The argument for the second assertion is entirely similar.

For (2), the union of the identity relation and the relation

$$\{((\boldsymbol{\nu} z\, \pi.\, P)\sigma, (\pi.\, \boldsymbol{\nu} z\, P)\sigma) \mid z \text{ does not occur in } \pi, \text{ and } \sigma \text{ arbitrary}\}$$

is a strong bisimulation. □

So for example,

$$\boldsymbol{\nu} z\; !z(w).\, \overline{w}a \sim^{\mathrm{c}} \mathbf{0}$$

and

$$\boldsymbol{\nu} z\, \overline{x}y.\, \overline{y}z \sim^{\mathrm{c}} \overline{x}y.\, \boldsymbol{\nu} z\, \overline{y}z\ .$$

It is worth recording that the effect of a restriction on a summation is what one would expect given the above. That is, summands whose leading subject is restricted can be deleted, and leading prefixes in which the restricted name does not occur can be moved above the restriction.

Lemma 2.2.17 If $M = \kappa_1.\, P_1 + \cdots + \kappa_n.\, P_n$ where z does not occur in any κ_i, and $N = \lambda_1.\, Q_1 + \cdots + \lambda_m.\, Q_m$ where $z = \mathsf{subj}(\lambda_j)$ for each j, then

$$\boldsymbol{\nu} z\, (M + N) \sim^{\mathrm{c}} \kappa_1.\, \boldsymbol{\nu} z\, P_1 + \cdots + \kappa_n.\, \boldsymbol{\nu} z\, P_n.$$

Proof The union of the identity relation and the relation

$$\{((\boldsymbol{\nu} z\, (M + N))\sigma, (\kappa_1.\, \boldsymbol{\nu} z\, P_1 + \cdots + \kappa_n.\, \boldsymbol{\nu} z\, P_n)\sigma) \mid \sigma \text{ arbitrary}\}$$

is a strong bisimulation. □

In general, match prefixes are essential when reasoning about strong full bisimilarity of processes. Sometimes, however, they can be eliminated. The first observation relating to this is that

$$[x = x]\pi.\, P \sim^{\mathrm{c}} \pi.\, P\ .$$

This holds as the processes have the same transitions and that property is preserved by substitution. The second observation is that

$$[x = y]\pi.\, P \sim \mathbf{0}$$

but that

$$[x = y]\pi.\, P \not\sim^{\mathrm{c}} \mathbf{0}\ .$$

The strong bisimilarity holds as $[x=y]\pi.P$ has no transitions. The strong full bisimilarity fails because that property is not preserved by substitution.

Here is a simple example to illustrate the role of some of these properties in expanding process behaviour. It also uses the property

$$!\pi.P \sim^{c} \pi.(P \mid !\pi.P),$$

whose soundness the reader may care to check. Let

$$\begin{aligned}
P &\stackrel{\text{def}}{=} a(x).\overline{c}x.\overline{n}\\
Q &\stackrel{\text{def}}{=} c(x).\overline{b}x\\
R &\stackrel{\text{def}}{=} (\boldsymbol{\nu}c,n)\,(P \mid !n.P \mid Q)\\
S &\stackrel{\text{def}}{=} d(a).R\,.
\end{aligned}$$

The system R can be thought of as being composed of two cells: P, which receives a name via a, passes it to Q via the restricted name c, and then restores itself; and Q, which sends via b the name it receives via c and then becomes inactive. By repeated expansion and some of the above properties, we show R strong bisimilar to a simple summation. We have:

$$\begin{aligned}
R &\sim (\boldsymbol{\nu}c,n)\,a(x).(\overline{c}x.\overline{n} \mid !n.P \mid Q)\\
&\sim a(x).(\boldsymbol{\nu}c,n)\,(\overline{c}x.\overline{n} \mid !n.P \mid Q)\\
&\sim a(x).\tau.(\boldsymbol{\nu}c,n)\,(\overline{n} \mid !n.P \mid \overline{b}x)\\
&\sim a(x).\tau.(\overline{b}x.(\boldsymbol{\nu}c,n)\,(\overline{n} \mid !n.P) + \tau.(\boldsymbol{\nu}c,n)\,(P \mid !n.P \mid \overline{b}x))\\
&\sim a(x).\tau.(\,\overline{b}x.\tau.(\boldsymbol{\nu}c,n)\,(P \mid !n.P)\\
&\qquad\qquad + \tau.(\,\overline{b}x.(\boldsymbol{\nu}c,n)\,(P \mid !n.P)\\
&\qquad\qquad\qquad + a(y).(\boldsymbol{\nu}c,n)\,(\overline{c}y.\overline{n} \mid !n.P \mid \overline{b}x)))\\
&\sim a(x).\tau.(\,\overline{b}x.\tau.a(y).(\boldsymbol{\nu}c,n)\,(\overline{c}y.\overline{n} \mid !n.P)\\
&\qquad\qquad + \tau.(\,\overline{b}x.a(y).(\boldsymbol{\nu}c,n)\,(\overline{c}y.\overline{n} \mid !n.P)\\
&\qquad\qquad\qquad + a(y).\overline{b}x.(\boldsymbol{\nu}c,n)\,(\overline{c}y.\overline{n} \mid !n.P)))\\
&\sim a(x).\tau.(\,\overline{b}x.\tau.a(y).\mathbf{0} + \tau.(\overline{b}x.a(y).\mathbf{0} + a(y).\overline{b}x.\mathbf{0}))\,.
\end{aligned}$$

It is not the case, however, that

$$S \sim d(a).a(x).\tau.(\overline{b}x.\tau.a(y).\mathbf{0} + \tau.(\overline{b}x.a(y).\mathbf{0} + a(y).\overline{b}x.\mathbf{0}))\,.$$

The reason is that one name S can receive via d is b.

Exercise 2.2.18 Show by similar reasoning, but using the Expansion Lemma for $\sim^{c}$, that

$$S \sim^{c} d(a).a(x).\tau.(\overline{b}x.\tau.a(y).\mathbf{0} + \tau.(\overline{b}x.a(y).\mathbf{0} + a(y).\overline{b}x.\mathbf{0} + [a=b]\tau.\mathbf{0}))\,.$$

□

To simplify terms such as those on the right of the equality in Exercise 2.2.18, we need an equivalence that abstracts from internal action; for this see Exercise 2.4.20.

We will use the following definition and simple observation later in the book.

Definition 2.2.19 We write $P \xrightarrow{\tau}_{\mathrm{d}} Q$ if the transition $P \xrightarrow{\tau} Q$ is *deterministic*, that is, $P \xrightarrow{\tau} Q$ is the only transition of P. We write $P \xrightarrow{\tau}{}^{n}_{\mathrm{d}} Q$ if P evolves to Q by performing n deterministic transitions. □

Lemma 2.2.20 If $P \xrightarrow{\tau}_{\mathrm{d}} P'$ then $P \sim^{\mathrm{c}} \tau.\, P'$. □

Exercise 2.2.21 Show that if the transition rule

$$\frac{P \xrightarrow{\tau} P'}{\pi.\, P \xrightarrow{\tau} \pi.\, P'}$$

were added, then the Expansion Lemma for strong bisimilarity would not hold. □

2.2.3 Replication

Infinite behaviour is expressed by means of the replication operator. This subsection collects a number of results involving replication that are useful for reasoning about processes.

To begin, let us return briefly to structural congruence. The only axiom of structural congruence that involves replication explicitly is: $!P \equiv P \mid !P$. Consequently, although $\boldsymbol{\nu} z\, \mathbf{0} \equiv \mathbf{0}$, $P \mid \mathbf{0} \equiv P$, and $M + \mathbf{0} \equiv M$, it is not the case that $!\mathbf{0} \equiv \mathbf{0}$. Neither $!\mathbf{0}$ nor $\mathbf{0}$ has any transitions, however, and each is impervious to substitution, so $!\mathbf{0} \sim^{\mathrm{c}} \mathbf{0}$.

Recalling the original informal explanation of $!P$ as $P \mid P \mid \cdots$, we would expect $!P \mid !P$ and $!P$ to be equivalent in some sense; and we would expect the same of $!!P$ and $!P$, and of $!(P \mid Q)$ and $!P \mid !Q$. The sense is not that of structural congruence, however.

Exercise* 2.2.22 Show that $!P \mid !P \not\equiv !P$ and $!!P \not\equiv !P$ and $!(P \mid Q) \not\equiv !P \mid !Q$. (Hint: for the second, consider what happens to the maximum depth of nesting of replications in a term when an axiom of structural congruence is applied within it.) □

The processes are, rather, strong full bisimilar.

Lemma 2.2.23

(1) $!P \mid !P \sim^{c} !P$.
(2) $!!P \sim^{c} !P$.
(3) $!(P \mid Q) \sim^{c} !P \mid !Q$.

Proof The proof is deferred to Section 2.3. □

Thus we can freely duplicate, indeed replicate, replicated processes, and we can distribute replication over composition.

To motivate the next result, consider the process

$$R \stackrel{\text{def}}{=} !x(z).\, \boldsymbol{\nu} n\, \overline{z}n.\, n(w).\, !\overline{n}w\ .$$

The subprocess $n(w).\, !\overline{n}w$ represents a simple storage cell. It can repeatedly emit via n the name it initially receives via n. The process R is an inexhaustible supplier of cells, each accessible via a different name. A process P can ask R to supply a cell by sending it a name via x. The supplier uses the name sent by P to return the fresh name of the new cell. In $\boldsymbol{\nu} x\, (P \mid R)$ we can think of R as a private resource of P.

Consider the processes

$$Q \stackrel{\text{def}}{=} \boldsymbol{\nu} x\, (P_1 \mid P_2 \mid R) \qquad \text{and} \qquad Q' \stackrel{\text{def}}{=} \boldsymbol{\nu} x\, (P_1 \mid R) \mid \boldsymbol{\nu} x\, (P_2 \mid R)\ .$$

In Q, the resource is shared by the components P_1 and P_2, while in Q' each component has its own private resource. Processes of these kinds arise very frequently, as representations of client-server systems, for example. Would we expect Q and Q' to be behaviourally equivalent? In some cases yes, but not in general.

A simple counterexample to the general equivalence is: $P_1 \stackrel{\text{def}}{=} \overline{x}a$ and $P_2 \stackrel{\text{def}}{=} x(w)$. In this case Q and Q' are not even barbed bisimilar, because $Q \longrightarrow \boldsymbol{\nu} x\, R \sim^{c} \mathbf{0}$ but $Q' \longrightarrow Q''$ implies $Q'' \downarrow_{\overline{a}}$. In the shared-resource system Q, a request from P_1 for a new cell can be misdirected to P_2. Nothing analogous is possible in Q'.

Allowing P_2 to receive via x is contrary to the spirit of the discussion, however. Suppose we stipulate that x cannot occur as the subject of an input prefix in P_1 or P_2. Does this guarantee the equivalence of Q and Q'? The answer is no, and the reason is that the property that a name does not occur as the subject of an input prefix is not invariant under transition. Suppose, for example, that $P_1 \stackrel{\text{def}}{=} \overline{y}x.\, v(u).\, u(w)$, $P_2 \stackrel{\text{def}}{=} \overline{x}a$, $S \stackrel{\text{def}}{=} y(t).\, \overline{v}t$. Then we have the evolution

$$\begin{aligned} S \mid Q \quad &\longrightarrow \quad \nu x\,(\overline{v}x \mid v(u).\,u(w) \mid P_2 \mid R) \\ &\longrightarrow \quad \nu x\,(x(w) \mid P_2 \mid R) \\ &\longrightarrow \quad \nu x\,R\,, \end{aligned}$$

which has no analogue in $S \mid Q'$.

Counterexamples such as these can be ruled out in more than one way. Here we will be content with a simple condition to achieve the desired outcome. Although it is simple, the condition is often satisfied in practice. (In Part IV we will use a more generous condition, based on types.)

Definition 2.2.24 If the only occurrences of the name x in P are as subjects of output prefixes, then we say that *x occurs in P only in output subject position*. □

If a name x occurs in a process P only in output subject position, then P cannot immediately send x or receive via x. Indeed, if P never receives x then it will never send x or receive via x.

Theorem 2.2.25 (First Replication Theorem) If x occurs in P_1, P_2, and R only in output subject position, then

$$\nu x\,(P_1 \mid P_2 \mid !x(z).\,R) \sim^{c} \nu x\,(P_1 \mid !x(z).\,R) \mid \nu x\,(P_2 \mid !x(z).\,R)\,.$$

Proof The proof is deferred to Section 2.3. □

Clearly this result generalizes to the cases when more than two processes share a resource. Another useful generalization is:

Theorem 2.2.26 (Second Replication Theorem) If x occurs in P and R only in output subject position, then

$$\nu x\,(\,!P \mid !x(z).\,R) \sim^{c} !\nu x\,(P \mid !x(z).\,R)\,.$$

Proof The proof is deferred to Section 2.3. □

One reading of this result is that all instances of a replicated resource P can share some replicated subresource R, or equivalently each instance of P can have its own subresource R. The proviso is that in all the processes concerned, the access-name of the subresource occurs only in output subject position.

Systems of the form we have been considering arise so frequently that it is worth introducing a special notation for them.

Notation 2.2.27 Under the proviso that x occurs in P and R only in output subject position, we write

$$P\{x = (z).R\} \quad \text{for} \quad \boldsymbol{\nu} x\, (P \mid !x(z).\, R)\ .$$

This notation is apposite as it connotes substitution of instances of R for x in P, where by an instance of R we mean $R\{a/z\}$ for some a. We take $\{x = (z).R\}$, like substitution, to bind more tightly than process operators. We refer to $\{x = (z).R\}$ as a *local environment*. □

Using the substitution notation, the assertions in Theorem 2.2.25 and Theorem 2.2.26 become:

$$(P_1 \mid P_2)\{x = (z).R\} \sim^{\mathrm{c}} P_1\{x = (z).R\} \mid P_2\{x = (z).R\}$$

and

$$(!P)\{x = (z).R\} \sim^{\mathrm{c}} !P\{x = (z).R\}\ .$$

Anticipating somewhat Section 2.4 and full bisimilarity, $\approx^{\mathrm{c}}$, we will have

$$\overline{x}a\,\{x = (z).R\} \approx^{\mathrm{c}} R\{a/z\}\,\{x = (z).R\}\ .$$

These equivalences show the 'substitution-like' behaviour of local environments. Staying with the strong equivalences for now, we record a generalization of this property, together with three other simple but useful facts.

Lemma 2.2.28

(1) $(\overline{x}a.\, P)\{x = (z).R\} \sim^{\mathrm{c}} \tau.\, (P \mid R\{a/z\})\{x = (z).R\}$.
(2) If $x \notin \mathsf{fn}(P)$ then $P\{x = (z).R\} \sim^{\mathrm{c}} P$.
(3) $(\boldsymbol{\nu} w\, P)\{x = (z).R\} \sim^{\mathrm{c}} \boldsymbol{\nu} w\, P\{x = (z).R\}$.
(4) If x does not occur in π then $(\pi.\, P)\{x = (z).R\} \sim^{\mathrm{c}} \pi.\, P\{x = (z).R\}$. □

Note that in Lemma 2.2.28(3), by Convention 1.4.10 on bound names, $w \notin \mathsf{fn}(x(z).\, R)$.

Exercise 2.2.29 Prove Lemma 2.2.28. □

The exercise below invites the reader to show that each process is strong full bisimilar to a process in which only prefixed processes are replicated. The exercise is slightly simpler using some of the techniques introduced in Section 2.3.

Exercise* 2.2.30

(1) Show that $!(M + N) \sim^{\mathrm{c}} !M \mid !N$.
(2) Show that $!(\boldsymbol{\nu}\widetilde{z})\,(M + N) \sim^{\mathrm{c}} !(\boldsymbol{\nu}\widetilde{z})\, M \mid !(\boldsymbol{\nu}\widetilde{z})\, N$.

(3) Show that for each P there is a summation M such that $M \sim^{c} P$ and the depth of nesting of replications in M is no greater than it is in P.

(4) Hence show that for each P there is Q such that $Q \sim^{c} P$ and if $!R$ is a subterm of Q then R is of the form $\kappa. R'$. □

2.3 Up-to techniques

Several proofs were deferred in Section 2.2 with promises that they would be given when further proof techniques for bisimilarity were available. This section develops these techniques and uses them to give the missing proofs. The techniques, and their analogues considered in Section 2.4, when we abstract from internal action, will be used frequently later in the book.

Note This section is concerned only with strong equivalences. To avoid repetition, however, the qualifier 'strong' is omitted except in definitions and statements of results.

A simple method for showing that two processes are bisimilar is to find a bisimulation relating them. The correctness of this method follows from the definition of bisimilarity as the union of all bisimulations. To illustrate the method, consider showing that composition preserves bisimilarity of CCS processes, here written $\triangleq$ to avoid confusion with bisimilarity in π-calculus. This can be done by proving that

$$\{(P \mid R, Q \mid R) \mid P, Q, R \text{ are CCS processes with } P \triangleq Q\}$$

is a bisimulation, a task that is easily accomplished via an analysis based on the CCS transition rules for compositions.

To prove the corresponding result in π-calculus is less straightforward, however: the relation

$$\{(P \mid R, Q \mid R) \mid P, Q, R \text{ are } \pi\text{-calculus processes with } P \sim Q\}$$

is not a bisimulation. This becomes apparent on carrying out the corresponding analysis based on the π-calculus transition rules for compositions. The analysis reveals that the relation lacks the essential closure property of a bisimulation: that if two processes are in the relation then each transition of one can be matched by a transition of the other to a *related* process; the point of failure is the accretion of a restriction as a result of inferring an interaction using a CLOSE rule. In seeking a suitable bisimulation, we are therefore led to consider the larger relation

$$\{((\boldsymbol{\nu}\widetilde{z})\,(P \mid R), (\boldsymbol{\nu}\widetilde{z})\,(Q \mid R)) \;\mid\; P, Q, R \text{ are } \pi\text{-calculus processes with } P \sim Q, \text{ and } \widetilde{z} \text{ are arbitrary names}\}\,.$$

By carrying out an analysis of the transitions of compositions and restrictions, it can be checked that this relation is indeed a bisimulation.

The above discussion illustrates that the smallest bisimulation relating two processes may be larger than at first envisaged. Indeed, even in simple cases the smallest bisimulation relating two processes may be infinite: in the case of the processes $x(z).\,\tau.\,\overline{y}z$ and $\boldsymbol{\nu}w\,(x(z).\,\overline{w}z \mid w(v).\,\overline{y}v)$, for instance, it is

$$\begin{aligned}
& \{(x(z).\,\tau.\,\overline{y}z, \boldsymbol{\nu}w\,(x(z).\,\overline{w}z \mid w(v).\,\overline{y}v))\} \\
\cup\; & \{(\tau.\,\overline{y}a, \boldsymbol{\nu}w\,(\overline{w}a \mid w(v).\,\overline{y}v)) \mid a \text{ arbitrary}\} \\
\cup\; & \{(\overline{y}a, \boldsymbol{\nu}w\,(\mathbf{0} \mid \overline{y}a)) \mid a \text{ arbitrary}\} \\
\cup\; & \{(\mathbf{0}, \boldsymbol{\nu}w\,(\mathbf{0} \mid \mathbf{0}))\}\,.
\end{aligned}$$

Moreover, it may not be easy to guess what the smallest bisimulation relating two processes might be: what, for instance, is the smallest bisimulation relating $!!P$ and $!P$ for an arbitrary process P? Finally, even when it is possible correctly to guess the smallest bisimulation relating two processes, it may not be easy to describe it succinctly, and the relation may be awkward to work with.

We therefore seek a technique for showing bisimilarity that is easier to apply than the method of exhibiting and checking a bisimulation. The notion of bisimulation up to bisimilarity ($\simeq$) familiar from CCS is an important pointer. In CCS, a relation $\mathcal{R}$ is a *strong bisimulation up to* $\simeq$ if whenever $(P, Q) \in \mathcal{R}$,

> if $P \xrightarrow{\alpha} P'$ then there is Q' such that $Q \xrightarrow{\alpha} Q'$ and
> for some P'' and Q'' we have $P' \simeq P''$ and $(P'', Q'') \in \mathcal{R}$ and $Q'' \simeq Q'$

and vice versa. A bisimulation up to $\simeq$ is not in general a bisimulation: the definition requires only that to each derivative of one process, there corresponds a derivative of the other such that the two derivatives are *bisimilar to* processes in the relation. It is the case, however, that if $\mathcal{R}$ is a bisimulation up to $\simeq$ then $(P, Q) \in \mathcal{R}$ implies $P \simeq Q$. The reason is that if $\mathcal{R}$ is a bisimulation up to $\simeq$ then $\simeq\mathcal{R}\simeq$ is a bisimulation, and of course $\mathcal{R}$ is included in $\simeq\mathcal{R}\simeq$.

The notion of bisimulation up to bisimilarity carries over straightforwardly to π-calculus. In π-calculus, however, other bisimulation-up-to techniques are useful – for instance, bisimulation up to injective substitution and bisimulation up to context. Moreover, it is often essential to be able to combine different bisimulation-up-to techniques. We therefore present a general account of how to do this.

The broad aim is to find tractable techniques for showing that a relation is included in bisimilarity. The key idea is that this can often be achieved just by examining the effect of applying to the relation a so-called safe function. The class of safe functions enjoys good closure properties, a fact that is important for combining up-to techniques. Moreover, the definition of 'safe function' is crafted to give a class that is closed under the broadest range of operators.

This section comprises three subsections. The first introduces safe functions and establishes their basic properties. The second investigates bisimulation-up-to techniques. The third uses the techniques to give the proofs deferred from Section 2.2.

2.3.1 Strongly safe functions

Before we can isolate the safe functions, we need to introduce the following notion and explore its elementary properties. In what follows, 'relation' means relation on processes.

Definition 2.3.1 (Strong progression) Relation $\mathcal{R}$ *strongly progresses to* relation $\mathcal{S}$, written $\mathcal{R} \rightsquigarrow \mathcal{S}$, if whenever $(P, Q) \in \mathcal{R}$,

(1) $P \xrightarrow{\alpha} P'$ implies $Q \xrightarrow{\alpha} Q'$ with $(P', Q') \in \mathcal{S}$
(2) vice versa. □

Clearly, a relation $\mathcal{R}$ is a bisimulation just if $\mathcal{R} \rightsquigarrow \mathcal{R}$. A simple technique for establishing that a relation is included in bisimilarity is to show that it progresses to some bisimulation.

Lemma 2.3.2 If $\mathcal{R} \rightsquigarrow \mathcal{S}$ where $\mathcal{S}$ is a bisimulation, then $\mathcal{R} \subseteq \sim$.

Proof Observe that $\mathcal{R} \cup \mathcal{S}$ is a bisimulation. □

If one relation progresses to another, then any subset of the first progresses to any superset of the second.

Lemma 2.3.3

(1) If $\mathcal{R} \subseteq \mathcal{S}$ and $\mathcal{S} \rightsquigarrow \mathcal{T}$, then $\mathcal{R} \rightsquigarrow \mathcal{T}$.
(2) If $\mathcal{R} \rightsquigarrow \mathcal{S}$ and $\mathcal{S} \subseteq \mathcal{T}$, then $\mathcal{R} \rightsquigarrow \mathcal{T}$.

Proof The assertions follow immediately from the definitions. □

Next we have two observations about unions of sets of relations some of whose members progress to others. We write I and J for possibly infinite indexing sets.

Lemma 2.3.4 Suppose $\{\mathcal{R}_i \mid i \in I\}$ and $\{\mathcal{S}_j \mid j \in J\}$ are sets of relations, $\mathcal{R} \stackrel{\text{def}}{=} \bigcup_{i \in I} \mathcal{R}_i$, and $\mathcal{S} \stackrel{\text{def}}{=} \bigcup_{j \in J} \mathcal{S}_j$.

(1) If for each i there is j such that $\mathcal{R}_i \rightsquigarrow \mathcal{S}_j$, then $\mathcal{R} \rightsquigarrow \mathcal{S}$.
(2) If for each i there is i' such that $\mathcal{R}_i \rightsquigarrow \mathcal{R}_{i'}$, then $\mathcal{R}$ is a bisimulation. □

Exercise 2.3.5 Prove Lemma 2.3.4. (Hint: (2) follows from (1).) □

We can now isolate the functions on relations that are safe.

Definition 2.3.6 (Strongly safe function) A function $\mathcal{F}$ is *strongly safe* if $\mathcal{R} \subseteq \mathcal{S}$ and $\mathcal{R} \rightsquigarrow \mathcal{S}$ implies $\mathcal{F}(\mathcal{R}) \subseteq \mathcal{F}(\mathcal{S})$ and $\mathcal{F}(\mathcal{R}) \rightsquigarrow \mathcal{F}(\mathcal{S})$. □

Example 2.3.7 Three simple examples of safe functions are the identity function $\mathcal{F}_\iota$, the constant function $\mathcal{F}_\sim$, which maps any relation to $\sim$, and the constant function $\mathcal{F}_\equiv$, which maps any relation to $\equiv$. □

The first key property of safe functions is given in the following lemma.

Lemma 2.3.8 If $\mathcal{F}$ is strongly safe and $\mathcal{R} \rightsquigarrow \mathcal{F}(\mathcal{R})$, then $\mathcal{R}$ and $\mathcal{F}(\mathcal{R})$ are included in $\sim$.

Proof Let $\mathcal{R}_0 = \mathcal{R}$, $\mathcal{R}_{n+1} = \mathcal{R}_n \cup \mathcal{F}(\mathcal{R}_n)$, and $\mathcal{R}_\omega = \bigcup_n \mathcal{R}_n$. Clearly $\mathcal{R}_n \subseteq \mathcal{R}_{n+1}$ for each n. We show by induction that $\mathcal{R}_n \rightsquigarrow \mathcal{R}_{n+1}$ for each n.

For $n = 0$ we have $\mathcal{R}_0 \rightsquigarrow \mathcal{F}(\mathcal{R}_0) \subseteq \mathcal{R}_1$ by hypothesis, so $\mathcal{R}_0 \rightsquigarrow \mathcal{R}_1$ by Lemma 2.3.3(2).

Also, assuming $\mathcal{R}_n \rightsquigarrow \mathcal{R}_{n+1}$, since also $\mathcal{R}_n \subseteq \mathcal{R}_{n+1}$ and $\mathcal{F}$ is safe, $\mathcal{F}(\mathcal{R}_n) \rightsquigarrow \mathcal{F}(\mathcal{R}_{n+1})$. So $\mathcal{R}_n \cup \mathcal{F}(\mathcal{R}_n) \rightsquigarrow \mathcal{R}_{n+1} \cup \mathcal{F}(\mathcal{R}_{n+1})$ by Lemma 2.3.4(1), that is, $\mathcal{R}_{n+1} \rightsquigarrow \mathcal{R}_{n+2}$.

Hence $\mathcal{R}_\omega$ is a bisimulation by Lemma 2.3.4(2). But $\mathcal{R} \rightsquigarrow \mathcal{R}_1 \subseteq \mathcal{R}_\omega$, so $\mathcal{R} \rightsquigarrow \mathcal{R}_\omega$ by Lemma 2.3.3(2). Also, $\mathcal{F}(\mathcal{R}) \subseteq \mathcal{R}_1 \rightsquigarrow \mathcal{R}_\omega$, so $\mathcal{F}(\mathcal{R}) \rightsquigarrow \mathcal{R}_\omega$ by Lemma 2.3.3(1). Hence $\mathcal{R}$ and $\mathcal{F}(\mathcal{R})$ are included in $\sim$ by Lemma 2.3.2. □

So in particular, to show that $P \sim Q$ it suffices to find a relation $\mathcal{R}$ such that $(P, Q) \in \mathcal{R}$ and a safe function $\mathcal{F}$ such that $\mathcal{R} \rightsquigarrow \mathcal{F}(\mathcal{R})$.

Corollary 2.3.9 If $\mathcal{F}$ is strongly safe and $\sim \subseteq \mathcal{F}(\sim)$, then $\mathcal{F}(\sim) = \sim$.

Proof If $\sim \subseteq \mathcal{F}(\sim)$ then $\sim \rightsquigarrow \mathcal{F}(\sim)$ since $\sim$ is a bisimulation, and hence $\mathcal{F}(\sim) \subseteq \sim$ by Lemma 2.3.8. □

We introduced some useful safe functions in Example 2.3.7. We now present some more, and establish some closure properties of the class of safe functions. The following result will be used in particular to prove Lemma 2.2.3 – that bisimilarity is preserved by injective substitution – and Theorem 2.2.8(2) – concerning strong bisimilarity and input prefixes.

Lemma 2.3.10 Suppose $\mathcal{F}_\sigma$ is defined by

$$\mathcal{F}_\sigma(\mathcal{R}) = \{(P\rho, Q\rho) \mid (P, Q) \in \mathcal{R},\ \rho \text{ injective on } \mathsf{fn}(P, Q)\} .$$

Then $\mathcal{F}_\sigma$ is strongly safe.

Proof Suppose $\mathcal{R} \subseteq \mathcal{S}$ and $\mathcal{R} \rightsquigarrow \mathcal{S}$. Clearly $\mathcal{F}_\sigma(\mathcal{R}) \subseteq \mathcal{F}_\sigma(\mathcal{S})$. Suppose ρ is injective on $\mathsf{fn}(P, Q)$, and let θ be a bijective substitution such that θ and ρ agree on $\mathsf{fn}(P, Q)$, so $P\rho = P\theta$ and $Q\rho = Q\theta$. If $P\theta \xrightarrow{\beta} R$ then by Lemma 1.4.12, $P \xrightarrow{\alpha} P'$ with $\alpha\theta = \beta$ and $P'\theta = R$. Since $(P, Q) \in \mathcal{R}$ and $\mathcal{R} \rightsquigarrow \mathcal{S}$, $Q \xrightarrow{\alpha} Q'$ with $(P', Q') \in \mathcal{S}$. Then by Lemma 1.4.8, $Q\theta \xrightarrow{\beta} S \stackrel{\text{def}}{=} Q'\theta$, and $(R, S) \in \mathcal{F}_\sigma(\mathcal{S})$ since θ is injective on $\mathsf{fn}(P', Q')$. Hence $\mathcal{F}_\sigma(\mathcal{R}) \rightsquigarrow \mathcal{F}_\sigma(\mathcal{S})$. □

We call $\mathcal{R}$ a *strong bisimulation up to injective substitution* if $\mathcal{R} \rightsquigarrow \mathcal{F}_\sigma(\mathcal{R})$. By Lemma 2.3.10 and Lemma 2.3.8, if $\mathcal{R}$ is a bisimulation up to injective substitution then $(P, Q) \in \mathcal{R}$ implies $P \sim Q$.

To show that a relation $\mathcal{R}$ is a bisimulation, one must check that for each pair $(P, Q) \in \mathcal{R}$, each action of P can be mimicked by an action of Q to give a pair in $\mathcal{R}$, and vice versa. This holds in particular for every input action and every bound-output action $\overline{x}(z)$ with $z \notin \mathsf{fn}(P, Q)$. The next lemma, which is a consequence of the safety of $\mathcal{F}_\sigma$, establishes that to show that $\mathcal{R}$ is included in bisimilarity, for a given pair (P, Q) it suffices to consider only input of names in $\mathsf{fn}(P, Q)$ and one fresh name, and only output of a single fresh name. This observation is often helpful in reducing the amount of work that is required to show that two processes are bisimilar.

Lemma 2.3.11 Suppose $\mathcal{R}$ is such that if $(P, Q) \in \mathcal{R}$ then there is $z \notin \mathsf{fn}(P, Q)$ such that

(1) if $P \xrightarrow{xy} P'$ where $y \in \mathsf{fn}(P, Q, z)$, then $Q \xrightarrow{xy} Q'$ with $(P', Q') \in \mathcal{R}$
(2) if $P \xrightarrow{\overline{x}(z)} P'$ then $Q \xrightarrow{\overline{x}(z)} Q'$ with $(P', Q') \in \mathcal{R}$
(3) if $P \xrightarrow{\alpha} P'$ where α is a free output or τ, then $Q \xrightarrow{\alpha} Q'$ with $(P', Q') \in \mathcal{R}$

and vice versa. Then $\mathcal{R} \subseteq \sim$. □

Exercise 2.3.12 Prove Lemma 2.3.11 by showing that $\mathcal{R} \rightsquigarrow \mathcal{F}_\sigma(\mathcal{R})$ and appealing to Lemma 2.3.10. □

Starting from safe functions such as $\mathcal{F}_\iota$, $\mathcal{F}_\equiv$, $\mathcal{F}_\sim$, and $\mathcal{F}_\sigma$, more complex safe functions can be constructed by applying safety-preserving operators.

Definition 2.3.13 (Strongly secure operator) An operator on functions on relations is *strongly secure* if when applied to strongly safe arguments, it yields a strongly safe result. □

Clearly, the identity operator is secure, as is any operator that projects a tuple of functions to one of its components. Security of some other operators is asserted in the following lemma.

Lemma 2.3.14 Union ($\bigcup$), composition ($\circ$), and chaining are strongly secure, where

$$\begin{aligned} (\textstyle\bigcup_{i \in I} \mathcal{F}_i)(\mathcal{R}) &\stackrel{\text{def}}{=} \textstyle\bigcup_{i \in I} \mathcal{F}_i(\mathcal{R}) \\ (\mathcal{F} \circ \mathcal{G})(\mathcal{R}) &\stackrel{\text{def}}{=} \mathcal{F}(\mathcal{G}(\mathcal{R})) \\ (\mathcal{F}\mathcal{G})(\mathcal{R}) &\stackrel{\text{def}}{=} \mathcal{F}(\mathcal{R})\mathcal{G}(\mathcal{R}) \end{aligned}$$

where $\mathcal{F}(\mathcal{R})\mathcal{G}(\mathcal{R})$ is the composition of the relations $\mathcal{F}(\mathcal{R})$ and $\mathcal{G}(\mathcal{R})$. □

Exercise 2.3.15 Prove Lemma 2.3.14. □

Given a function $\mathcal{F}$, we define $\mathcal{F}^{(n)}$ for $n < \omega$ by

$$\begin{aligned} \mathcal{F}^{(0)}(\mathcal{R}) &\stackrel{\text{def}}{=} \mathcal{R} \\ \mathcal{F}^{(n)}(\mathcal{R}) &\stackrel{\text{def}}{=} \mathcal{F}(\mathcal{R})\mathcal{F}^{(n-1)}(\mathcal{R}) \qquad \text{for } n > 0 . \end{aligned}$$

We define also

$$\mathcal{F}^*(\mathcal{R}) \stackrel{\text{def}}{=} \bigcup_{n \geq 0} \mathcal{F}^{(n)}(\mathcal{R}) .$$

Then by Lemma 2.3.14, if $\mathcal{F}$ is safe then so are $\mathcal{F}^{(n)}$ for $n \geq 0$ and $\mathcal{F}^*$. In particular, the function $(\mathcal{F}_\iota)^*$, which gives the transitive closure of a relation, is safe.

Since chaining is secure, the functions $\mathcal{F}_\sim\mathcal{F}_\iota\mathcal{F}_\sim$ and $\mathcal{F}_\equiv\mathcal{F}_\iota\mathcal{F}_\equiv$ are safe. Consequently, a *strong bisimulation up to* $\sim$, that is, a relation $\mathcal{R}$ such that $\mathcal{R} \rightsquigarrow {\sim}\mathcal{R}{\sim}$, is included in bisimilarity. (This illustrates how the bisimulation-up-to-bisimilarity technique from CCS mentioned at the beginning of the section arises as an instance of the theory we are presenting.) Also, a *strong bisimulation up to* $\equiv$, that is, a relation $\mathcal{R}$ such that $\mathcal{R} \rightsquigarrow {\equiv}\mathcal{R}{\equiv}$, is included in bisimilarity. Hence if $(P, Q) \in \mathcal{R}$ where $\mathcal{R}$ is a bisimulation up to $\sim$ or a bisimulation up to $\equiv$, then $P \sim Q$.

The following technique for showing that a function is safe will be used in Section 2.3.2.

Lemma 2.3.16 Suppose $\mathcal{F}$ is such that $\mathcal{R} \subseteq \mathcal{S}$ and $\mathcal{R} \rightsquigarrow \mathcal{S}$ implies $\mathcal{F}(\mathcal{R}) \subseteq \mathcal{F}^*(\mathcal{S})$ and $\mathcal{F}(\mathcal{R}) \rightsquigarrow \mathcal{F}^*(\mathcal{S})$. Then $\mathcal{F}^*$ is strongly safe.

Proof Since $\mathcal{F}^*(\mathcal{R}) = \bigcup_{n\geq 0} \mathcal{F}^{(n)}(\mathcal{R})$, by Lemma 2.3.4(1) it suffices to show that if $\mathcal{R} \subseteq \mathcal{S}$ and $\mathcal{R} \rightsquigarrow \mathcal{S}$, then $\mathcal{F}^{(n)}(\mathcal{R}) \subseteq \mathcal{F}^*(\mathcal{S})$ and $\mathcal{F}^{(n)}(\mathcal{R}) \rightsquigarrow \mathcal{F}^*(\mathcal{S})$ for all n. □

Exercise 2.3.17 Complete the proof of Lemma 2.3.16. (Hint: argue by induction on n.) □

2.3.2 Up-to-context techniques

We now introduce safe functions involving classes of contexts. One such function will be used in particular to prove Theorem 2.2.8(1) – that strong bisimilarity is a non-input congruence – and another in particular in proving the Replication Theorems, Theorem 2.2.25 and Theorem 2.2.26. Up-to-context techniques, especially for weak equivalences, will be used frequently later in the book.

Consider first the function $\mathcal{F}_{\text{nil}}$ defined by

$$\mathcal{F}_{\text{nil}}(\mathcal{R}) = \{(C[P], C[Q]) \mid C \text{ is a non-input context and } (P, Q) \in \mathcal{R}\} .$$

This function is not safe. To see this, consider $P \stackrel{\text{def}}{=} \overline{x}y.\,\mathbf{0} \mid x(z).\,\mathbf{0}$ and $Q \stackrel{\text{def}}{=} x(z).\,\mathbf{0} \mid \overline{x}y.\,\mathbf{0}$, and the relation

$$\mathcal{R} = \{(P, Q),\ (\mathbf{0} \mid x(z), x(z) \mid \mathbf{0}),\ (\overline{x}y \mid \mathbf{0}, \mathbf{0} \mid \overline{x}y),\ (\mathbf{0}, \mathbf{0})\} .$$

Clearly, $\mathcal{R} \rightsquigarrow \mathcal{R}$. It is not the case that $\mathcal{F}_{\text{nil}}(\mathcal{R}) \rightsquigarrow \mathcal{F}_{\text{nil}}(\mathcal{R})$, however, because

$$!P \xrightarrow{\tau} P^* \stackrel{\text{def}}{=} \mathbf{0} \mid x(z) \mid (\overline{x}y \mid \mathbf{0}) \mid !P$$

but the only τ transitions of $!Q$ are

$$!Q \xrightarrow{\tau} Q^* \stackrel{\text{def}}{=} x(z) \mid \mathbf{0} \mid (\mathbf{0} \mid \overline{x}y) \mid !Q \quad \text{and} \quad !Q \xrightarrow{\tau} Q^{**} \stackrel{\text{def}}{=} \mathbf{0} \mid \mathbf{0} \mid !Q\,,$$

and there are no context C and $(R, R') \in \mathcal{R}$ such that $P^* = C[R]$ and either $Q^* = C[R']$ or $Q^{**} = C[R']$.

To overcome this, we consider contexts in which there can be any number of holes, each of which can occur any number of times. We have already met multi-hole contexts in Definition 1.2.23, but for convenience we recast some of the definitions in a slightly more general form.

Definition 2.3.18 (Multi-hole context) We assume *holes* $[\cdot]_1, [\cdot]_2, \ldots$, and to be able to consider a context as a multi-hole context, we take $[\cdot]_0$ to be $[\cdot]$. A *multi-hole context* is obtained when zero or more non-degenerate occurrences of $\mathbf{0}$ in a process-term given by the grammar in Definition 1.1.1 are replaced by holes. (The same hole can occur several times.) A multi-hole context is *n-ary* if at most n different holes occur in it. A multi-hole context is *non-input* if no hole occurs under an input prefix. An *instantiation* is a function from hole indices to processes. □

For example,

$$(\,!\boldsymbol{\nu} z\,(\overline{x}z.\,[\cdot]_1 + \overline{x}y.\,[\cdot]_2))\mid !x(w).\,[\cdot]_3$$

is a 3-ary context, composed from a 2-ary non-input context and a 1-ary context. Note that a process is considered to be a 0-ary multi-hole context.

If C is a multi-hole context and η an instantiation, we write $C\eta$ for the process obtained by replacing each occurrence of each $[\cdot]_i$ in C by η_i, where η_i is $\eta(i)$. For example, if $\eta_1 = z(v).\,\mathbf{0}$, $\eta_2 = y(u).\,\mathbf{0}$, and $\eta_3 = w(t).\,\overline{t}a.\,\mathbf{0}$, then writing C for the example context above we have

$$C\eta = (\,!\boldsymbol{\nu} z\,(\overline{x}z.\,z(v).\,\mathbf{0} + \overline{x}y.\,y(u).\,\mathbf{0}))\mid !x(w).\,w(t).\,\overline{t}a.\,\mathbf{0}\;.$$

Clearly, if instantiations η, η' agree on the indices of the holes in a multi-hole context C, then $C\eta = C\eta'$.

We then define the function $\mathcal{F}_{\text{ni}}$ by

$$\mathcal{F}_{\text{ni}}(\mathcal{R}) = \{(C\eta, C\eta') \mid \begin{array}{l} C \text{ is a non-input multi-hole context and} \\ (\eta_i, \eta'_i) \in \mathcal{R} \text{ for all } i\}\;. \end{array}$$

Clearly, $\mathcal{F}_{\text{ni1}}(\mathcal{R}) \subseteq \mathcal{F}_{\text{ni}}(\mathcal{R})$ for any $\mathcal{R}$. Indeed we have:

Lemma 2.3.19 $\mathcal{F}_{\text{ni}} = (\mathcal{F}_{\text{ni1}})^*$. □

Exercise 2.3.20 Prove Lemma 2.3.19. □

This observation is helpful in proving the following result.

Lemma 2.3.21 $\mathcal{F}_{\text{ni}}$ is strongly safe.

Proof Suppose $\mathcal{R} \subseteq \mathcal{S}$ and $\mathcal{R} \rightsquigarrow \mathcal{S}$. To prove the assertion, it suffices, by Lemma 2.3.19 and Lemma 2.3.16, to show that $\mathcal{F}_{\text{ni1}}(\mathcal{R}) \subseteq \mathcal{F}_{\text{ni}}(\mathcal{S})$ and $\mathcal{F}_{\text{ni1}}(\mathcal{R}) \rightsquigarrow \mathcal{F}_{\text{ni}}(\mathcal{S})$.

The inclusion is immediate from the definitions of the functions and the assumption that $\mathcal{R} \subseteq \mathcal{S}$. For the progression, we have to show that if C is a 1-ary non-input context, $(P, Q) \in \mathcal{R}$, and $C[P] \xrightarrow{\alpha} P'$, then $C[Q] \xrightarrow{\alpha} Q'$ with $(P', Q') \in \mathcal{F}_{\text{ni}}(\mathcal{S})$. This is done by induction on C.

(1) Suppose C is $[\cdot]$, so $P \xrightarrow{\alpha} P'$. Then since $(P, Q) \in \mathcal{R}$ and $\mathcal{R} \rightsquigarrow \mathcal{S}$, we have $Q \xrightarrow{\alpha} Q'$ with $(P', Q') \in \mathcal{S}$, as required since $\mathcal{S} \subseteq \mathcal{F}_{\text{ni}}(\mathcal{S})$.

(2) Suppose C is $\pi.C'$. Then $P' = C'[P]$, because C is non-input. Moreover, $C[Q] \xrightarrow{\alpha} C'[Q]$ and $(C'[P], C'[Q]) \in \mathcal{F}_{\text{ni}}(\mathcal{S})$ as required. The assumption $\mathcal{R} \subseteq \mathcal{S}$ licenses this conclusion.

The cases when the main operator of C is $+$ or $|$ or $\boldsymbol{\nu}$ are left as exercises for the interested reader.

(3) Suppose C is $!C'$. There are three cases depending on which replication rule is used to infer the transition $C[P] \xrightarrow{\alpha} P'$.

(a) Suppose $P' = P'' \mid C[P]$ where $C'[P] \xrightarrow{\alpha} P''$. Then $C'[Q] \xrightarrow{\alpha} Q''$ with $(P'', Q'') \in \mathcal{F}_{\text{ni}}(\mathcal{S})$, by induction hypothesis. Thus $P'' = C''\eta$ and $Q'' = C''\eta'$ for some C'', η, and η' with $(\eta_i, \eta'_i) \in \mathcal{S}$ for all i; we may assume that $\eta_0 = P$ and $\eta'_0 = Q$ (we can rename the holes of the context, if necessary). Then $C[Q] \xrightarrow{\alpha} Q' \stackrel{\text{def}}{=} Q'' \mid C[Q]$, and $(P', Q') \in \mathcal{F}_{\text{ni}}(\mathcal{S})$ because $P' = C'''\eta$ and $Q' = C'''\eta'$ where $C''' \stackrel{\text{def}}{=} C'' \mid C$.

(b) Suppose α is τ and $P' = P'' \mid P''' \mid C[P]$ where $C'[P] \xrightarrow{\overline{x}y} P''$ and $C'[P] \xrightarrow{xy} P'''$. Then $C'[Q] \xrightarrow{\overline{x}y} Q''$ and $C'[Q] \xrightarrow{xy} Q'''$ with $(P'', Q'') \in \mathcal{F}_{\text{ni}}(\mathcal{S})$ and $(P''', Q''') \in \mathcal{F}_{\text{ni}}(\mathcal{S})$, by induction hypothesis. Then $P'' = C''\eta$ and $Q'' = C''\eta'$, for some C'', η, and η' with $(\eta_i, \eta'_i) \in \mathcal{S}$ for all i. Similarly, $P''' = C'''\eta''$ and $Q''' = C'''\eta'''$ for some C''', η'', and η''' with $(\eta''_i, \eta'''_i) \in \mathcal{S}$ for all i. We may assume that no hole of C'' occurs in C''', and vice versa. Therefore, since the values of η and η' (respectively η'' and η''') on the indices of holes not in C'' (respectively C''') are not important, we may assume that $\eta = \eta''$ and $\eta' = \eta'''$. We may also assume, as in case (a) above, that $\eta_0 = \eta''_0 = P$ and $\eta'_0 = \eta'''_0 = Q$. Finally, we have $C[Q] \xrightarrow{\tau} Q' \stackrel{\text{def}}{=} Q'' \mid Q''' \mid C[Q]$, and $(P', Q') \in \mathcal{F}_{\text{ni}}(\mathcal{S})$ because $P' = C''''\eta''$ and $Q' = C''''\eta'''$ where $C'''' \stackrel{\text{def}}{=} C'' \mid C''' \mid C$.

(c) The argument when the rule is REP-CLOSE is similar.

This completes the proof. □

Note that in case (2) in the proof of Lemma 2.3.21, we see why the assumption $\mathcal{R} \subseteq \mathcal{S}$ appears in the definition of safe function (Definition 2.3.6): in the case $C' = [\cdot]$, for instance, we need to be able to conclude $(P, Q) \in \mathcal{F}_{\text{ni}}(\mathcal{S})$ from the hypothesis $(P, Q) \in \mathcal{R}$.

We call $\mathcal{R}$ a *bisimulation up to non-input context* if $\mathcal{R} \rightsquigarrow \mathcal{F}_{\text{ni}}(\mathcal{R})$. By definition, if $\mathcal{R}$ is a bisimulation up to non-input context, $(P, Q) \in \mathcal{R}$, and $P \xrightarrow{\alpha} P'$, then there are Q' such that $Q \xrightarrow{\alpha} Q'$, instantiations η and η' such that $(\eta_i, \eta'_i) \in \mathcal{R}$ for all i, and a non-input multi-hole context C such that $P' = C\eta$ and $Q' = C\eta'$. Since a common multi-hole context can be factored out of matching derivatives, a bisimulation up to non-input context need not be a large relation. For instance, as we will see below, given a process P, the singleton relation $\{(!P \mid !P, !P)\}$ is a bisimulation up to non-input context. On the other hand, the smallest bisimulation containing $(!P \mid !P, !P)$ is infinite if P has any transition.

A special case of bisimulation up to non-input context that we will use later is bisimulation up to restriction. We call $\mathcal{R}$ a *bisimulation up to restriction* if $\mathcal{R} \rightsquigarrow \mathcal{F}_\nu(\mathcal{R})$, where the safe function $\mathcal{F}_\nu$ is defined by

$$\mathcal{F}_\nu(\mathcal{R}) = \{((\boldsymbol{\nu}\tilde{z})\, P, (\boldsymbol{\nu}\tilde{z})\, Q) \mid (P, Q) \in \mathcal{R},\ \tilde{z} \text{ arbitrary}\}\ .$$

Thus far we have considered proving bisimilarity. We now consider showing full bisimilarity. Recall that by definition, $P \sim^{\mathrm{c}} Q$ if $P\sigma \sim Q\sigma$ for all σ. Hence by Lemma 2.3.8:

Lemma 2.3.22 If $(P, Q) \in \mathcal{R}$ where $\mathcal{R}$ is closed under substitution, and $\mathcal{R} \rightsquigarrow \mathcal{F}(\mathcal{R})$ where $\mathcal{F}$ is strongly safe, then $P \sim^{\mathrm{c}} Q$. □

In particular by Lemma 2.3.21:

Corollary 2.3.23 If $(P, Q) \in \mathcal{R}$ where $\mathcal{R}$ is closed under substitution and $\mathcal{R} \rightsquigarrow \mathcal{F}_{\mathrm{ni}}(\mathcal{R})$, then $P \sim^{\mathrm{c}} Q$. □

We finish with two results about contexts in which some hole occurs under an input prefix. The first can be proved using a strategy similar to that used to prove Lemma 2.3.21.

Lemma 2.3.24 $\mathcal{F}_C$ is strongly safe, where $\mathcal{F}_C(\mathcal{R})$ is the set of all pairs of the form $(C\eta, C\eta')$ with C a multi-hole context and η, η' such that

(1) $(\eta_j, \eta'_j) \in \mathcal{R}$ for all j, and
(2) if $[\cdot]_i$ occurs under an input prefix in C, then $(\eta_i\sigma, \eta'_i\sigma) \in \mathcal{R}$ for all σ. □

A consequence of this result is the following strengthening of Corollary 2.3.23 for proving processes strong full bisimilar. This result differs from Corollary 2.3.23 in that arbitrary contexts can be used to show the progression.

Corollary 2.3.25 If $(P, Q) \in \mathcal{R}$ where $\mathcal{R}$ is closed under substitution and $\mathcal{R} \rightsquigarrow \mathcal{F}_C(\mathcal{R})$, then $P \sim^{\mathrm{c}} Q$. □

2.3.3 Deferred proofs

We now use some of these techniques to give the proofs deferred from Section 2.2.

Proof (of Lemma 2.2.3)

Suppose $\mathcal{R}$ is a bisimulation with $(P, Q) \in \mathcal{R}$. Then since $\mathcal{R} \subseteq \mathcal{F}_\sigma(\mathcal{R})$ we have $\mathcal{R} \rightsquigarrow \mathcal{F}_\sigma(\mathcal{R})$, and the assertion follows by Lemma 2.3.10 and Lemma 2.3.8. □

Proof (of Theorem 2.2.8(1))

This follows from Corollary 2.3.9 and Lemma 2.3.21. □

Proof (of Theorem 2.2.8(2))

If $\mathcal{R}$ is a bisimulation containing $(P\{y/z\}, Q\{y/z\})$ for each $y \in \mathsf{fn}(P, Q, z)$, then

$$\{(x(z).\,P, x(z).\,Q)\} \cup \mathcal{R}$$

is a bisimulation up to injective substitution. □

Proof (of Lemma 2.2.23)

We prove just the first assertion; the proofs of the other two are similar and are left as exercises for the interested reader.

Let $\mathcal{R}$ be the relation

$$\{(!P \mid !P,\, !P) \mid P \text{ arbitrary}\}\ .$$

Let $\mathcal{G}$ be the safe function $\mathcal{F}_\equiv \mathcal{F}_{\mathrm{ni}} \mathcal{F}_\equiv$. Since $\mathcal{R}$ is closed under substitution, it suffices by Lemma 2.3.22 to show that $\mathcal{R} \rightsquigarrow \mathcal{G}(\mathcal{R})$.

Suppose that $!P \mid !P \xrightarrow{\alpha} Q$. We have to show that there are R such that $!P \xrightarrow{\alpha} R$ and a multi-hole context C and instantiations η and η' such that $Q \equiv C\eta$ and $R \equiv C\eta'$ and $(\eta_i, \eta'_i) \in \mathcal{R}$ for all i. There are four cases.

(1) Suppose $Q = R \mid !P$ where $!P \xrightarrow{\alpha} R$. Then $R = S \mid !P$ where either $P \xrightarrow{\alpha} S$ or $\alpha = \tau$ and $P \mid P \xrightarrow{\alpha} S$. In either case $!P \xrightarrow{\alpha} R$, and $(Q, R) \in \mathcal{G}(\mathcal{R})$ because $Q \equiv S \mid (!P \mid !P)$.

(2) If $Q = !P \mid R$ where $!P \xrightarrow{\alpha} R$, then the argument is similar.

(3) If $Q = R_1 \mid R_2$ where $!P \xrightarrow{\overline{x}y} R_1$ and $!P \xrightarrow{xy} R_2$ and $\alpha = \tau$ (or similarly with the roles of sender and receiver swapped), then $R_1 = S_1 \mid !P$ where $P \xrightarrow{\overline{x}y} S_1$, and $R_2 = S_2 \mid !P$ where $P \xrightarrow{xy} S_2$. Hence by transition rule Rep-comm, $!P \xrightarrow{\alpha} R \stackrel{\mathrm{def}}{=} S_1 \mid S_2 \mid !P$, and $(Q, R) \in \mathcal{G}(\mathcal{R})$ because $Q \equiv S_1 \mid S_2 \mid (!P \mid !P)$.

(4) If $Q = \nu z\,(R_1 \mid R_2)$ where $!P \xrightarrow{\overline{x}(z)} R_1$ and $!P \xrightarrow{xz} R_2$ and $z \notin \mathsf{fn}(P)$ and $\alpha = \tau$ (or similarly with the roles of sender and receiver swapped), then $R_1 = S_1 \mid !P$ where $P \xrightarrow{\overline{x}(z)} S_1$, and $R_2 = S_2 \mid !P$ where $P \xrightarrow{xz} S_2$.

Hence by transition rule REP-CLOSE, $!P \xrightarrow{\alpha} R \stackrel{\text{def}}{=} \nu z\,(S_1 \mid S_2) \mid !P$, and $(Q, R) \in \mathcal{G}(\mathcal{R})$ because $Q \equiv \nu z\,(S_1 \mid S_2) \mid (\,!P \mid !P)$.

Similarly, if $!P \xrightarrow{\alpha} R$ then $!P \mid !P \xrightarrow{\alpha} Q$ with $(Q, R) \in \mathcal{G}(\mathcal{R})$, as the reader may care to check. □

Proof (of Theorem 2.2.25)

Let $\mathcal{R}$ be the relation containing all pairs of processes of the forms

$$\nu x\,(P_1 \mid P_2 \mid !x(z).\,R) \quad \text{and} \quad \nu x\,(P_1 \mid !x(z).\,R) \mid \nu x\,(P_2 \mid !x(z).\,R)$$

such that x occurs in P_1, P_2, and R only in output subject position. Let $\mathcal{G}$ be the safe function $\mathcal{F}_{\sim}\mathcal{F}_{\text{ni}}\mathcal{F}_{\sim}$. Since $\mathcal{R}$ is closed under substitution, it suffices by Lemma 2.3.22 to show that $\mathcal{R} \rightsquigarrow \mathcal{G}(\mathcal{R})$. An important theme in the proof is that the property that x occurs in a process only in output subject position is invariant provided the process does not receive x, and that the processes P_1 and P_2 cannot receive x because x is restricted.

Suppose $\nu x\,(P_1 \mid P_2 \mid !x(z).\,R) \xrightarrow{\alpha} Q$. There are eight cases. They are:

(1) $Q = \nu x\,(P_1' \mid P_2 \mid !x(z).\,R)$ where $P_1 \xrightarrow{\alpha} P_1'$, noting that α cannot be of the form $\overline{a}x$ because x occurs in P_1 only in output subject position
(2) $Q = \nu x\,(P_1' \mid P_2' \mid !x(z).\,R)$ where $P_1 \mid P_2 \xrightarrow{\alpha} P_1' \mid P_2'$ and $\alpha = \tau$
(3) $Q = \nu x\,(\nu y\,(P_1' \mid P_2') \mid !x(z).\,R)$ where $P_1 \mid P_2 \xrightarrow{\alpha} \nu y\,(P_1' \mid P_2')$ and $\alpha = \tau$
(4) $Q = \nu x\,(P_1' \mid P_2 \mid (R\{y/z\} \mid !x(z).\,R))$ where $P_1 \xrightarrow{\overline{x}y} P_1'$
(5) $Q = \nu x\,(\nu y\,(P_1' \mid P_2 \mid (R\{y/z\} \mid !x(z).\,R)))$ where $P_1 \xrightarrow{\overline{x}(y)} P_1'$ and y is fresh

and the three cases similar to (1), (4), and (5) in which P_2 rather than P_1 acts. We give just cases (1), (3), and (5), leaving the rest to the reader.

For (1) we have

$$\begin{array}{ll} & \nu x\,(P_1 \mid !x(z).\,R) \mid \nu x\,(P_2 \mid !x(z).\,R) \\ \xrightarrow{\alpha} & Q' \stackrel{\text{def}}{=} \nu x\,(P_1' \mid !x(z).\,R) \mid \nu x\,(P_2 \mid !x(z).\,R)\,, \end{array}$$

and $(Q, Q') \in \mathcal{G}(\mathcal{R})$ since x occurs in P_1' only in output subject position.

For (3) we have

$$\begin{array}{ll} & \nu x\,(P_1 \mid !x(z).\,R) \mid \nu x\,(P_2 \mid !x(z).\,R) \\ \xrightarrow{\alpha} & Q' \stackrel{\text{def}}{=} \nu y\,(\nu x\,(P_1' \mid !x(z).\,R) \mid \nu x\,(P_2' \mid !x(z).\,R))\,, \end{array}$$

and $(Q, Q') \in \mathcal{G}(\mathcal{R})$ because $Q \sim \nu y\, \nu x\,(P_1' \mid P_2' \mid !x(z).\,R)$ and x occurs in P_1' and P_2' only in output subject position.

For (5) we have

$$\begin{array}{ll} & \boldsymbol{\nu}x\,(P_1 \mid !x(z).\,R) \mid \boldsymbol{\nu}x\,(P_2 \mid !x(z).\,R) \\ \xrightarrow{\alpha} & Q' \stackrel{\text{def}}{=} \boldsymbol{\nu}x\,(\boldsymbol{\nu}y\,(P_1' \mid (R\{y/z\} \mid !x(z).\,R))) \mid \boldsymbol{\nu}x\,(P_2 \mid !x(z).\,R)\,, \end{array}$$

and $(Q, Q') \in \mathcal{G}(\mathcal{R})$ because

$$Q \sim \boldsymbol{\nu}x\,(\boldsymbol{\nu}y\,(P_1' \mid R\{y/z\}) \mid P_2 \mid !x(z).\,R)$$

and

$$Q' \sim \boldsymbol{\nu}x\,(\boldsymbol{\nu}y\,(P_1' \mid R\{y/z\}) \mid !x(z).\,R) \mid \boldsymbol{\nu}x\,(P_2 \mid !x(z).\,R)$$

and x occurs in $P_1' \mid R\{y/z\}$ and P_2' only in output subject position.

Similarly if $\boldsymbol{\nu}x\,(P_1 \mid !x(z).\,R) \mid \boldsymbol{\nu}x\,(P_2 \mid !x(z).\,R) \xrightarrow{\alpha} Q'$, then there is Q such that $\boldsymbol{\nu}x\,(P_1 \mid P_2 \mid !x(z).\,R) \xrightarrow{\alpha} Q$ and $(Q, Q') \in \mathcal{G}(\mathcal{R})$. □

Proof (of Theorem 2.2.26)

The proof involves a similar kind of case analysis to that of Theorem 2.2.25, and uses the same safe function. The proof also appeals to Theorem 2.2.25. It is an instructive exercise. □

2.4 Barbed congruence

The theory of the strong equivalences has now been elaborated in some depth, and many useful techniques and results have been presented. To apply π-calculus, however, it is essential to be able to abstract from internal action. The strong equivalences are deficient in this respect as they treat internal action and visible action equally. The deficiency is overcome by the behavioural equivalences studied in this section. The section is in four subsections. Section 2.4.1 defines barbed congruence and the labelled equivalences (bisimilarity and full bisimilarity), and establishes their basic properties. Section 2.4.2 considers an effect of admitting infinite sums to the calculus. Section 2.4.3 presents sharpened techniques for proving barbed congruence. Section 2.4.4 briefly discusses a variant of barbed congruence.

2.4.1 Barbed congruence and bisimilarity

In many respects, the theory of barbed congruence and bisimilarity differs only in details from the theory of strong barbed congruence and strong bisimilarity, presented in Section 2.1 and Section 2.2. We begin by explaining why this is so, considering bisimilarity first. In the following discussion, α ranges over *Act* as usual, and β ranges over $Act - \{\tau\}$.

The transition relations describe how processes can evolve step by step. The transition $P \xrightarrow{\beta} Q$ expresses that P can evolve to Q by performing the visible action β, sending or receiving a name. The transition $P \xrightarrow{\tau} Q$, on the other hand, expresses that P can evolve to Q as an effect of an internal action, typically an interaction between two of its components. For two processes to be strong bisimilar, they must be able to mimic one another's transitions step by step.

Bisimilarity demands a similar kind of mimicry, but with a different notion of step. The relevant relations are $\Longrightarrow$ and $\stackrel{\beta}{\Longrightarrow}$, defined as follows.

Notation 2.4.1 (Weak transition relations)

(1) $\Longrightarrow$ is the reflexive and transitive closure of $\xrightarrow{\tau}$.
(2) $\stackrel{\alpha}{\Longrightarrow}$ is $\Longrightarrow\xrightarrow{\alpha}\Longrightarrow$, for $\alpha \in Act$. □

Thus, $P \Longrightarrow Q$ expresses that P can evolve to Q by performing some number, possibly zero, of internal actions; and $P \stackrel{\beta}{\Longrightarrow} Q$ expresses that P can evolve to Q as a result of an evolution whose visible content is the action β, but which may involve any number of internal actions before and after β. So, for example, if

$$P \stackrel{\text{def}}{=} (\boldsymbol{\nu} z, w)\,((\overline{z}a + \overline{z}b) \mid z(v).\,(\overline{x}v \mid \overline{w}v) \mid w(u).\,\overline{u}y)$$

then there are five processes Q such that $P \Longrightarrow Q$, among them

$$(\boldsymbol{\nu} z, w)\,(\mathbf{0} \mid \overline{x}a \mid \overline{w}a \mid w(u).\,\overline{u}y) \qquad \text{and} \qquad (\boldsymbol{\nu} z, w)\,(\mathbf{0} \mid \overline{x}b \mid \mathbf{0} \mid \overline{b}y)\,,$$

and there are two processes R such that $P \stackrel{\overline{x}a}{\Longrightarrow} R$, namely

$$(\boldsymbol{\nu} z, w)\,(\mathbf{0} \mid \mathbf{0} \mid \overline{w}a \mid w(u).\,\overline{u}y) \qquad \text{and} \qquad (\boldsymbol{\nu} z, w)\,(\mathbf{0} \mid \mathbf{0} \mid \mathbf{0} \mid \overline{a}y)\,.$$

Bisimilarity is the relation obtained by playing the bisimulation game on the graph whose arrows are given by $\Longrightarrow$ and the $\stackrel{\beta}{\Longrightarrow}$ relations. The only difference between strong bisimilarity and bisimilarity is therefore what counts as a move in the bisimulation game. It is the special treatment accorded to τ transitions in defining the relations $\Longrightarrow$ and $\stackrel{\beta}{\Longrightarrow}$ that makes abstraction from internal action possible using weak equivalences. τ actions cannot be completely disregarded in defining weak equivalences, however. The reason is that they can preempt other actions. For instance, $x + y$ and $\tau.\,x + \tau.\,y$ are not behaviourally equivalent.

In general, it will be more work to determine bisimilarity than strong bisimilarity, if only because there will be more $\Longrightarrow$ and $\stackrel{\beta}{\Longrightarrow}$ arrows than $\xrightarrow{\alpha}$ arrows. More significantly, a proof of strong bisimilarity can often usefully be structured as an induction on the inference of $\xrightarrow{\alpha}$ transitions. An induction on inference of $\Longrightarrow$ and $\stackrel{\beta}{\Longrightarrow}$ steps is invariably much more awkward. All is not lost, however, for by virtue of the recursive nature of bisimulation, the same relation is obtained if in the bisimulation game on the graph whose arrows are given by the $\Longrightarrow$ and $\overset{\beta}{\Longrightarrow}$ relations, the first player's moves are restricted to arrows that involve only single transitions; see Definition 2.4.10 and Lemma 2.4.11.

A more profound difference between the strong and weak cases is that whereas the $\overset{\alpha}{\longrightarrow}$ relations are image-finite, this is not true of $\Longrightarrow$ and hence of the $\overset{\beta}{\Longrightarrow}$ relations. This fact has important consequences, as we will see.

The definition of barbed congruence involves the following predicates.

Notation 2.4.2 (Weak observability predicates) $\Downarrow_\mu$ is $\Longrightarrow\downarrow_\mu$. □

For example, for P above we have $P \Downarrow_{\overline{x}}$, $P \Downarrow_{\overline{a}}$, and $P \Downarrow_{\overline{b}}$. Barbed bisimilarity and congruence are obtained by applying the corresponding definitions from the strong case to the graph whose arrows are given by $\Longrightarrow$ and whose observables are given by the $\Downarrow_\mu$ predicates.

With this preliminary discussion completed, we can now define the equivalences and study their properties. We follow the same order of presentation as in the strong case.

Definition 2.4.3 (Barbed bisimilarity) *Barbed bisimilarity* is the largest symmetric relation, $\dot{\approx}$, such that whenever $P \mathrel{\dot{\approx}} Q$,

(1) $P \downarrow_\mu$ implies $Q \Downarrow_\mu$
(2) $P \overset{\tau}{\longrightarrow} P'$ implies $Q \Longrightarrow\dot{\approx} P'$. □

Note that the clauses of the definition have $P \downarrow_\mu$ and $P \overset{\tau}{\longrightarrow} P'$ as antecedents, rather than $P \Downarrow_\mu$ and $P \Longrightarrow P'$. The reason is to make the definition easier to work with, as discussed above in connection with bisimilarity. The second part of the following lemma justifies the precise form of the definition.

Lemma 2.4.4

(1) $\dot{\approx}$ is an equivalence relation.
(2) $\dot{\approx}$ is the largest symmetric relation, $\doteq$, such that whenever $P \doteq Q$,
   (a) $P \Downarrow_\mu$ implies $Q \Downarrow_\mu$
   (b) $P \Longrightarrow P'$ implies $Q \Longrightarrow\doteq P'$.

Proof The assertions follow easily from the definitions. □

Although barbed bisimilarity, like strong barbed bisimilarity, is lacking in discrimination, it does allow some abstraction from internal activity. For instance,

$$(\boldsymbol{\nu} z, w)\,(\overline{z}a \mid z(v).\,\overline{w}v \mid w(u).\,\overline{u}x) \mathrel{\dot{\approx}} \overline{a}y\ .$$

We are finally ready to define barbed congruence, the relation we adopt as the main behavioural equivalence on π-terms.

Definition 2.4.5 (Barbed congruence) Processes P and Q are *barbed congruent*, $P \cong^{c} Q$, if $C[P] \stackrel{\bullet}{\approx} C[Q]$ for every context C. □

Immediately from the definition we have:

Lemma 2.4.6 $\cong^{c}$ is the largest congruence included in $\stackrel{\bullet}{\approx}$. □

The Context Lemma for barbed congruence is analogous to the result in the strong case (Lemma 2.1.19), and it too holds in all subcalculi considered in the book.

Lemma 2.4.7 (Context Lemma for $\cong^{c}$) $P \cong^{c} Q$ iff $P\sigma \mid R \stackrel{\bullet}{\approx} Q\sigma \mid R$ for any R and σ.

Proof The proof is similar to that of Lemma 2.1.19, using the fact that if $\mathcal{S}$ is a barbed bisimulation up to $\stackrel{\bullet}{\approx}$ and $(P,Q) \in \mathcal{S}$, then $P \stackrel{\bullet}{\approx} Q$, where $\mathcal{S}$ is a *barbed bisimulation up to* $\stackrel{\bullet}{\approx}$ if whenever $(P,Q) \in \mathcal{S}$,

(1) $P \Downarrow_{\mu}$ iff $Q \Downarrow_{\mu}$
(2) if $P \xrightarrow{\tau} P'$ then $Q \Longrightarrow Q'$ for some Q' with $P' \stackrel{\bullet}{\sim} \mathcal{S} \stackrel{\bullet}{\approx} Q'$
(3) if $Q \xrightarrow{\tau} Q'$ then $P \Longrightarrow P'$ for some P' with $P' \stackrel{\bullet}{\approx} \mathcal{S} \stackrel{\bullet}{\sim} Q'$.

□

Definition 2.4.8 (Barbed equivalence) Processes P and Q are *barbed equivalent*, $P \cong Q$, if $P \mid R \stackrel{\bullet}{\approx} Q \mid R$ for any R. □

This relation is important for reasons similar to those explained when its strong analogue was introduced (see the discussion around Definition 2.1.20).

Lemma 2.4.9 $\cong$ is the largest non-input congruence included in $\stackrel{\bullet}{\approx}$.

Proof The proof is similar to that of the analogous result in the strong case (Lemma 2.1.24), but using for replication the kind of argument employed in the proof of the Context Lemma (see Lemma 2.1.19 and Lemma 2.4.7). □

We need tractable techniques for showing barbed congruence. The basis for these is bisimilarity.

Definition 2.4.10 (Bisimilarity) *Bisimilarity* is the largest symmetric relation, $\approx$, such that whenever $P \approx Q$,

(1) $P \xrightarrow{\beta} P'$ implies $Q \stackrel{\beta}{\Longrightarrow}\approx P'$
(2) $P \xrightarrow{\tau} P'$ implies $Q \Longrightarrow\approx P'$. □

The reason why the definition has $\xrightarrow{\alpha}$ transitions in the antecedents has already been discussed. It is justified by:

Lemma 2.4.11 $\dot{\approx}$ is the largest symmetric relation, $\asymp$, such that whenever $P \asymp Q$,

(1) $P \stackrel{\beta}{\Longrightarrow} P'$ implies $Q \stackrel{\beta}{\Longrightarrow}\asymp P'$
(2) $P \Longrightarrow P'$ implies $Q \Longrightarrow\asymp P'$.

Proof The assertion follows easily from the definitions. □

The two clauses in Definition 2.4.10 can be amalgamated with the help of a little notation: $\stackrel{\widehat{\tau}}{\Longrightarrow}$ is $\Longrightarrow$, and $\stackrel{\widehat{\beta}}{\Longrightarrow}$ is $\stackrel{\beta}{\Longrightarrow}$. The definition can then be rewritten:

bisimilarity is the largest symmetric relation, $\approx$, such that whenever $P \approx Q$, if $P \xrightarrow{\alpha} P'$ then $Q \stackrel{\widehat{\alpha}}{\Longrightarrow}\approx P'$.

Like its strong analogue, bisimilarity is preserved by injective substitution.

Lemma 2.4.12 $P \approx Q$ implies $P\sigma \approx Q\sigma$ for every σ that is injective on $\mathsf{fn}(P, Q)$.

Proof The proof is deferred to Section 2.4.3. □

Bisimilarity is not preserved by arbitrary substitution, however: just as in the strong case, if $P \stackrel{\text{def}}{=} \overline{z} \mid a$ and $Q \stackrel{\text{def}}{=} \overline{z}.\,a + a.\,\overline{z}$, then $P \approx Q$ but $P\{a/z\} \not\approx Q\{a/z\}$. Also just as in the strong case, we therefore consider the substitution-closure of bisimilarity.

Definition 2.4.13 (Full bisimilarity) P and Q are *full bisimilar*, $P \approx^{\mathrm{c}} Q$, if $P\sigma \approx Q\sigma$ for every substitution σ. □

Immediately from the definition we have:

Lemma 2.4.14 $P \approx^{\mathrm{c}} Q$ implies $P\sigma \approx^{\mathrm{c}} Q\sigma$ for every σ. □

Using Lemma 2.4.12 we have:

Lemma 2.4.15 $\approx$ and $\approx^{\mathrm{c}}$ are equivalence relations.

Proof The proof is similar to that of Lemma 2.2.5. □

The weak equivalences enjoy the same interrelationships as their strong variants.

Lemma 2.4.16

(1) $P \approx^{c} Q$ implies $P \approx Q$, and $P \approx Q$ implies $P \stackrel{\cdot}{\approx} Q$.
(2) $P \cong^{c} Q$ implies $P \cong Q$, and $P \cong Q$ implies $P \stackrel{\cdot}{\approx} Q$.
(3) Each of the above implications is strict.

Proof Assertions (1) and (2) follow from the definitions and the observation that a bisimulation is a barbed bisimulation. For (3), it suffices to consider the examples that establish the corresponding assertions in the strong case (Lemma 2.2.7). □

Each of the relations strictly includes its strong variant.

Lemma 2.4.17

(1) $P \stackrel{\cdot}{\sim} Q$ implies $P \stackrel{\cdot}{\approx} Q$, $P \simeq Q$ implies $P \cong Q$, and $P \simeq^{c} Q$ implies $P \cong^{c} Q$.
(2) $P \sim Q$ implies $P \approx Q$, and $P \sim^{c} Q$ implies $P \approx^{c} Q$.
(3) Each of the above implications is strict.

Proof Assertions (1) and (2) follow easily from the definitions. For (3), note that if $P = \tau.\mathbf{0}$ and $Q = \mathbf{0}$, then P and Q are equated by each of the weak relations but distinguished by each of the strong relations. □

A useful abstraction property of full bisimilarity is given in the following lemma.

Lemma 2.4.18 $\tau.P \approx^{c} P$.

Proof Clearly, the union of the identity relation and the relation

$$\{(\tau.P, P) \mid P \text{ arbitrary}\}$$

is a bisimulation and is closed under substitution. □

An important observation should be made here. By Lemma 2.4.18 we have, for example, that $\tau.(x \mid y) \approx^{c} (x \mid y)$. As is familiar from CCS, however, the expressions $a + \tau.(x \mid y)$ and $a + (x \mid y)$ are not bisimilar. Nonetheless, as we will see below, $\approx^{c}$ is a congruence, so that $P \approx^{c} Q$ implies $C[P] \approx^{c} C[Q]$ for every context C. The reason why this is coherent is that an expression such as $a + (x \mid y)$ is not a π-process: according to Definition 1.1.1, a summation is a sum of *prefixes* (and $\mathbf{0}$ terms). And according to Definition 1.2.1, a context is an expression obtained by replacing a *non-degenerate* occurrence of $\mathbf{0}$ in a process-term by $[\cdot]$. Thus, in particular, $a + [\cdot]$ is not a context.

It is worth recording explicitly two consequences of Lemma 2.4.18. A special case of the second was anticipated when properties of replication were studied; see Notation 2.2.27 and Lemma 2.2.28.

Corollary 2.4.19

(1) $\boldsymbol{\nu} x\,(\overline{x}y.\,P \mid x(z).\,Q) \approx^{\mathrm{c}} \boldsymbol{\nu} x\,(P \mid Q\{y/z\})$.
(2) $(\overline{x}a.\,P)\,\{x = (z).R\} \approx^{\mathrm{c}} (P \mid R\{a/z\})\,\{x = (z).R\}$. □

Exercise 2.4.20 Returning to Exercise 2.2.18, show that for the process S under consideration there,

$$S \approx^{\mathrm{c}} d(a).\,a(x).\,(\overline{b}x.\,a(y).\,\mathbf{0} + a(y).\,\overline{b}x.\,\mathbf{0} + [a = b]\tau.\,\mathbf{0})\,.$$

(Hint: use Lemma 2.4.18 and another equation.) □

The following exercise gives a kind of cancellation property. A variation of it will be proved and used in Part VI (see Lemma 18.3.10).

Exercise 2.4.21 Suppose $P \mid Q \approx P' \mid Q'$ where $\mathsf{fn}(P) = \mathsf{fn}(P')$ and $\mathsf{fn}(Q) = \mathsf{fn}(Q')$ and $\mathsf{fn}(P) \cap \mathsf{fn}(Q) = \emptyset$. Show that $P \approx P'$ and $Q \approx Q'$. (Hint: make use of Lemma 2.3.11.) □

We now establish basic properties of bisimilarity and full bisimilarity, and then show how they are related to barbed equivalence and barbed congruence.

Theorem 2.4.22 (Congruence properties of $\approx$ and $\approx^{\mathrm{c}}$)

(1) $\approx$ is a non-input congruence.
(2) If $P\{y/z\} \approx Q\{y/z\}$ for all $y \in \mathsf{fn}(P, Q, z)$, then $x(z).\,P \approx x(z).\,Q$.
(3) $\approx^{\mathrm{c}}$ is a congruence.
(4) $\approx^{\mathrm{c}}$ is the largest congruence included in $\approx$.

Proof The proofs of (1) and (2) are deferred to Section 2.4.3. The proofs of (3) and (4) are just like those of their strong variants in Theorem 2.2.8, with the observation for the last that for any R,

$$\boldsymbol{\nu} x\,(\overline{x}y_1.\,\ldots.\,\overline{x}y_n \mid x(z_1).\,\ldots.\,x(z_n).\,R) \approx^{\mathrm{c}} R\{\tilde{y}/\tilde{z}\}$$

where x is fresh. □

From this we have that bisimilarity and full bisimilarity are included in barbed equivalence and barbed congruence, respectively.

Theorem 2.4.23

(1) $P \approx Q$ implies $P \cong Q$.
(2) $P \approx^{c} Q$ implies $P \cong^{c} Q$.

Proof The first assertion follows from Theorem 2.4.22(1), the fact that bisimilarity is included in barbed bisimilarity by Lemma 2.4.16(1), and the fact that barbed equivalence is the largest non-input congruence included in barbed bisimilarity by Lemma 2.4.9. The second follows from Theorem 2.4.22(4) and the fact that barbed congruence is the largest congruence included in barbed bisimilarity by Lemma 2.4.6. □

Thus a way of establishing that two processes are barbed equivalent is to show that they are bisimilar, and a way of establishing that two processes are barbed congruent is to show that they are full bisimilar.

It is not known whether the converses of the implications in Theorem 2.4.23 hold. The reason that the proofs of the analogous implications in the strong case (Theorem 2.2.9) do not carry over is that they exploit the image-finiteness of the transition relations $\xrightarrow{\alpha}$, and as mentioned earlier, the relations $\Longrightarrow$ and $\stackrel{\beta}{\Longrightarrow}$ are *not* image-finite. For instance, we have

$$!\tau.\,x \Longrightarrow \underbrace{x \mid \cdots \mid x}_{k} \mid !\tau.\,x \qquad \text{for each } k \geq 0\,.$$

It is known, however, that the converse of Theorem 2.4.23 holds 'almost always'. We prove this for image-finite processes in Theorem 2.4.29 and for processes that are image-finite up to $\approx$ in Exercise 2.4.32. (The result in Exercise 2.4.32 implies Theorem 2.4.29, but the proof of the theorem is a bit simpler.)

Even though they do not cover all processes, these results are important and satisfactory for two reasons. First, Theorem 2.4.23 shows that bisimilarity and full bisimilarity are sound, in that they can be used to obtain proof techniques for barbed equivalence and barbed congruence. Soundness alone, however, does not tell us whether the techniques are applicable to many processes. (For instance, the identity relation is included in barbed equivalence and barbed congruence and is therefore sound, but it does not give us interesting proof techniques.) Theorem 2.4.29 and Exercise 2.4.32 show that the techniques apply to a very large class of processes. Second, processes that are not image-finite up to $\approx$ tend to arise rarely in practice. For more on the completeness of bisimilarity and full bisimilarity, see Section 2.4.2.

Definition 2.4.24 (Stratification of bisimilarity)

(1) $\approx_0$ is the universal relation on processes.

(2) For $1 \leq n < \omega$, the relation $\approx_n$ is defined by: $P \approx_n Q$ if

(a) $P \stackrel{\alpha}{\longrightarrow} P'$ implies $Q \stackrel{\widehat{\alpha}}{\Longrightarrow} \approx_{n-1} P'$

(b) $Q \stackrel{\alpha}{\longrightarrow} Q'$ implies $P \stackrel{\widehat{\alpha}}{\Longrightarrow} \approx_{n-1} Q'$.

(3) $P \approx_\omega Q$ if $P \approx_n Q$ for all $n < \omega$. □

Note that $\approx_0, \approx_1, \ldots, \approx_\omega$ is a decreasing sequence of relations.

Exercise 2.4.25

(1) Show that $\approx_n$ is not transitive for $1 \leq n < \omega$.

(2) Show that $\approx_\omega$ is transitive. □

Definition 2.4.26 (Image-finite process) A process P is *image-finite* if for each derivative Q of P and each action α, there are $n \geq 0$ and $Q_1, \ldots, Q_n$ such that $Q \stackrel{\widehat{\alpha}}{\Longrightarrow} Q'$ implies $Q' = Q_i$ for some i. □

Theorem 2.4.27 If P, Q are image-finite and $P \cong Q$, then $P \approx Q$.

Proof The proof is very similar to that of the corresponding result in the strong case: see Theorem 2.2.9(1). We indicate the main points of difference. First, the analogue of Claim 2.2.11 for the weak relations does not hold. We therefore have the assumption of image-finiteness in the theorem. Secondly, corresponding to Claim 2.2.12 we have:

Claim 2.4.28 Suppose that $n \geq 0$ and $P \not\approx_n Q$. Then there is a summation M such that for any $\widetilde{z} \subseteq \mathsf{fn}(P, Q)$ and any fresh name s, one of the following holds:

(1) $(\boldsymbol{\nu}\widetilde{z})\,(P' \mid (M + s)) \not\dot{\approx} (\boldsymbol{\nu}\widetilde{z})\,(Q \mid (M + s))$ for all P' such that $P \Longrightarrow P'$

(2) $(\boldsymbol{\nu}\widetilde{z})\,(P \mid (M + s)) \not\dot{\approx} (\boldsymbol{\nu}\widetilde{z})\,(Q' \mid (M + s))$ for all Q' such that $Q \Longrightarrow Q'$.

Proof By induction on n. For $n = 0$ there is nothing to prove, so suppose that $n > 0$. Then there are α and P' such that $P \stackrel{\alpha}{\longrightarrow} P'$ but $P' \not\approx_{n-1} Q''$ for all Q'' such that $Q \stackrel{\widehat{\alpha}}{\Longrightarrow} Q''$ (or vice versa, with the roles of P and Q swapped). By the hypothesis of the theorem, $\{Q'' \mid Q \stackrel{\widehat{\alpha}}{\Longrightarrow} Q''\} = \{Q_i \mid i \in I\}$ for some finite set I. We prove that assertion (2) of the claim holds (in the case when the roles of P and Q are swapped, one would prove assertion (1)). Appealing to the induction hypothesis, for each $i \in I$ let M_i be a summation such that P', Q_i, M_i satisfy the assertion of the claim.

The argument is similar to that in Claim 2.2.12. We give the details only for the case when α is an input action. For the other cases we only show the definition of the process M.

Case 1 Suppose that α is xy. Let s_i $(i \in I)$ and s' be fresh names, and set

$$M \stackrel{\text{def}}{=} \overline{x}y.\,(s' + \Sigma_{i\in I}\ \tau.\,(M_i + s_i))\ .$$

Suppose that $\widetilde{z} \subseteq \mathsf{fn}(P,Q)$ and s is fresh, and let Q' be any process such that $Q \Longrightarrow Q'$. Let $A \stackrel{\text{def}}{=} (\boldsymbol{\nu}\widetilde{z})\,(P \mid (M+s))$ and $B \stackrel{\text{def}}{=} (\boldsymbol{\nu}\widetilde{z})\,(Q' \mid (M+s))$, and suppose, for a contradiction, that $A \stackrel{\bullet}{\approx} B$. We have

$$A \stackrel{\tau}{\longrightarrow} A' \stackrel{\text{def}}{=} (\boldsymbol{\nu}\widetilde{z})\,(P' \mid (s' + \Sigma_{i\in I}\ \tau.\,(M_i + s_i)))$$

and $A' \Downarrow_{s'}$ but not $A' \Downarrow_{s}$. Since $A \stackrel{\bullet}{\approx} B$ there is B' such that $B \Longrightarrow B' \stackrel{\bullet}{\approx} A'$. In particular it must be that $B' \Downarrow_{s'}$ but not $B' \Downarrow_{s}$. The only way this is possible is if $I \neq \emptyset$ and

$$B' \stackrel{\text{def}}{=} (\boldsymbol{\nu}\widetilde{z})\,(Q_j \mid (s' + \Sigma_{i\in I}\ \tau.\,(M_i + s_i)))$$

for some $j \in I$ (a derivative of Q' under $\stackrel{\alpha}{\Longrightarrow}$ is also a derivative of Q).

By induction hypothesis, either (1) or (2) of the claim holds for P', Q_j, and M_j. Suppose that (2) holds. We have

$$A' \stackrel{\tau}{\longrightarrow} A''_j \stackrel{\text{def}}{=} (\boldsymbol{\nu}\widetilde{z})\,(P' \mid (M_j + s_j))$$

and $A''_j \Downarrow_{s_j}$ but not $A''_j \Downarrow_{s'}$. Then $B' \Longrightarrow B''_j$ with $B''_j \stackrel{\bullet}{\approx} A''_j$, and we must have

$$B''_j \stackrel{\text{def}}{=} (\boldsymbol{\nu}\widetilde{z})\,(Q'_j \mid (M_j + s_j))$$

for some Q'_j such that $Q_j \Longrightarrow Q'_j$. But $A''_j \stackrel{\bullet}{\approx} B''_j$ contradicts that (2) of the claim holds for P', Q_j, and M_j.

Dually, if (1) of the claim holds for P', Q_j, and M_j, then we obtain a contradiction by considering how A' can match the transition

$$B' \stackrel{\tau}{\longrightarrow} B''_j \stackrel{\text{def}}{=} (\boldsymbol{\nu}\widetilde{z})\,(Q_j \mid (M_j + s_j))\ .$$

Case 2 Suppose that α is $\overline{x}y$. Let s_i $(i \in I)$ and s' and w be fresh names, and set

$$M \stackrel{\text{def}}{=} x(w).\,(s' + \Sigma_{i\in I}\ [w = y]\tau.\,(M_i + s_i))\ .$$

Case 3 Suppose that α is $\overline{x}(z)$. Suppose that $\mathsf{fn}(P,Q) = \{a_1, \ldots, a_k\}$. Let s_i $(i \in I)$ and t and s' and w be fresh names, and set

$$M \stackrel{\text{def}}{=} x(w).\,(s' + \Sigma_{h=1}^{k}[w = a_h]t + \Sigma_{i\in I}\ \tau.\,(M_i + s_i))\ .$$

Case 4 Suppose that α is τ. Let s_i $(i \in I)$ be fresh names, and set

$$M \stackrel{\text{def}}{=} \Sigma_{i\in I}\ \tau.\,(M_i + s_i)\ .$$

This completes the proof of the claim. □

The remainder of the proof of the theorem is like that of Theorem 2.2.9(1). □

As a consequence of Theorem 2.4.27 and Theorem 2.4.23(1) we have:

Theorem 2.4.29 (Characterization Theorem) On image-finite processes,

(1) $\cong$ and $\approx$ coincide
(2) $\cong^{c}$ and $\approx^{c}$ coincide. □

In contrast with the strong case, on the subcalculus obtained by omitting the match prefixes, the analogue of Theorem 2.4.29 does not hold. The following exercise invites the reader to show this. It can be done using the Context Lemma for the subcalculus without the match prefixes.

Exercise 2.4.30 Show that if $P \stackrel{\text{def}}{=} \overline{a}x \mid E_{xy}$ and $Q \stackrel{\text{def}}{=} \overline{a}y \mid E_{xy}$ where

$$E_{xy} \stackrel{\text{def}}{=} !x(z).\,\overline{y}z \mid !y(z).\,\overline{x}z\,,$$

then $P \not\approx Q$ but for each context C of the subcalculus without the match prefixes, $C[P] \stackrel{\bullet}{\approx} C[Q]$. □

Definition 2.4.31 (Process image-finite up to $\approx$) A process P is *image-finite up to* $\approx$ if for each derivative Q of P and each action α, there are $n \geq 0$ and $Q_1, \ldots, Q_n$ such that $Q \stackrel{\widehat{\alpha}}{\Longrightarrow} Q'$ implies $Q' \approx Q_i$ for some i. □

Exercise 2.4.32 Prove the variant of Theorem 2.4.29 using the hypothesis of image-finiteness up to $\approx$ (Definition 2.4.31) in place of image-finiteness. □

Not all processes are image-finite up to $\approx$. For instance, if

$$P \stackrel{\text{def}}{=} (\boldsymbol{\nu} a, n)\,(\,!a.\,(\overline{n}.\,\overline{a} + \tau) \mid \overline{a}.\,!n.\,x) \tag{2.3}$$

then $P \Longrightarrow\sim^{c} x^k$ for each $k \geq 0$, where $x^0 \stackrel{\text{def}}{=} \mathbf{0}$ and $x^{k+1} \stackrel{\text{def}}{=} x.\,x^k$.

2.4.2 Infinite sums

In this section we show that if we admit sums in which the number of summands is infinite, then Theorem 2.4.29 can be extended to the full calculus with essentially the same proof.

The only caveat for allowing infinite sums is that the possibility of α-converting names into fresh names must be maintained. To ensure this we assume that names are taken from an uncountable set and require sums to have only countably many summands. Accordingly, we replace the form $M + M'$ in Definition 1.1.1 by

$$\Sigma_{i \in I} M_i$$

where I is a countable set. We write $\pi_{\infty+}$ for the resulting calculus. The modifications required to the transition rules are straightforward.

Lemma 2.4.33 For any process P of $\pi_{\infty+}$ and action α, the set

$$\{P' \mid P \stackrel{\alpha}{\Longrightarrow} P'\}$$

is countable.

Proof The proof makes repeated use of the fact that a countable union of countable sets is countable. First one shows, by an argument similar to that used to prove Corollary 1.4.6, that for all P and α, the set $\{P' \mid P \xrightarrow{\alpha} P'\}$ is countable. Then one shows by induction on n that for all P and $n < \omega$, the set $\{P' \mid P \,(\xrightarrow{\tau})^n\, P'\}$ is countable. From this it follows that for all P, the set $\{P' \mid P \Longrightarrow P'\}$ is countable. And from this it follows that for all P and α, the set $\{P' \mid P \stackrel{\alpha}{\Longrightarrow} P'\}$ is countable. The reader may care to check some of the details. □

On $\pi_{\infty+}$, Claim 2.4.28 holds without the assumption that the processes are image-finite. The reader may care to check that, using Lemma 2.4.33, the same proof works (where now I can be countably infinite). We can thus prove that $P \cong Q$ implies $P \approx_\omega Q$. This is not enough to show that $P \cong Q$ implies $P \approx Q$ on $\pi_{\infty+}$, however, because $P \approx_\omega Q$ does not imply $P \approx Q$. For a counterexample we can use the process P in (2.3) and the process

$$Q \stackrel{\text{def}}{=} \tau.\, P + \tau.\, !x\ .$$

We have $P \approx_\omega Q$ but not $P \approx Q$.

To prove that barbed equivalence is included in bisimilarity on $\pi_{\infty+}$, we extend the stratification of $\approx$ to the infinite ordinals and use transfinite induction rather than induction on the natural numbers. Apart from this, very little has to be changed in the proof.

Definition 2.4.34 (Transfinite stratification of bisimilarity)

(1) $\approx_0$ is the universal relation on processes.
(2) For δ an ordinal, the relation $\approx_{\delta+1}$ is defined by: $P \approx_{\delta+1} Q$ if

(a) $P \xrightarrow{\alpha} P'$ implies $Q \stackrel{\widehat{\alpha}}{\Longrightarrow} \approx_\delta P'$

(b) $Q \xrightarrow{\alpha} Q'$ implies $P \stackrel{\widehat{\alpha}}{\Longrightarrow} \approx_\delta Q'$.

(3) For γ a limit ordinal, $P \approx_\gamma Q$ if $P \approx_\delta Q$ for all $\delta < \gamma$. □

Note that if $\delta < \delta'$ then $\approx_{\delta'}$ is included in $\approx_\delta$.

Lemma 2.4.35 On any subcalculus of $\pi_{\infty+}$, $P \approx Q$ iff $P \approx_\delta Q$ for all ordinals δ.

Proof The argument is similar to the proof of Claim 2.2.11, but using the fact that for each R and α, $\{R' \mid R \stackrel{\alpha}{\Longrightarrow} R'\}$ is a set whereas the ordinals are a proper class, and a few simple facts about ordinals. The reader may care to check the details.

The proof can also be done by showing that the non-increasing sequence of relations $\approx_\delta$ reaches a fixed point at some ordinal. □

Theorem 2.4.36 (Characterization Theorem on $\pi_{\infty+}$) On $\pi_{\infty+}$,

(1) $\cong$ and $\approx$ coincide

(2) $\cong^{\mathrm{c}}$ and $\approx^{\mathrm{c}}$ coincide.

Proof The main difference from the proof of Theorem 2.4.29 is that Claim 2.4.28 has to be modified to apply to all processes of $\pi_{\infty+}$ and to be extended from natural numbers to all ordinals. The required result is:

Claim 2.4.37 Suppose that δ is an ordinal and $P \not\approx_\delta Q$. Then there is a summation M such that for any $\widetilde{z} \subseteq \mathsf{fn}(P, Q)$ and any fresh name s, one of the following holds:

(1) $(\boldsymbol{\nu}\widetilde{z})\,(P' \mid (M+s)) \not\dot{\approx} (\boldsymbol{\nu}\widetilde{z})\,(Q \mid (M+s))$ for all P' such that $P \Longrightarrow P'$

(2) $(\boldsymbol{\nu}\widetilde{z})\,(P \mid (M+s)) \not\dot{\approx} (\boldsymbol{\nu}\widetilde{z})\,(Q' \mid (M+s))$ for all Q' such that $Q \Longrightarrow Q'$.

Proof The proof is by induction on δ, and uses Lemma 2.4.33. If δ is a limit ordinal and $P \not\approx_\delta Q$, then $P \not\approx_\gamma Q$ for some $\gamma < \delta$, and the result follows immediately by induction. In the case when δ is a successor ordinal, the argument is essentially the same as in the proof of Claim 2.4.28, but with I possibly being a countably infinite set. □

The remainder of the proof is essentially as for Theorem 2.4.29. □

2.4.3 Proof techniques

This subsection presents some further proof techniques for bisimilarity, and uses them to give the proofs deferred above. First, a unique-solution theorem for systems of equations is presented, together with some small examples of its use. Then bisimulation-up-to techniques are studied.

2.4.3.1 A unique-solution theorem

Theorem 2.4.40 below gives conditions under which a system of equations has a unique solution up to bisimilarity. The unknowns in the equations are abstractions of processes. An abstraction can be thought of as a function from names to processes. More precisely, each abstraction has a fixed arity n and can be applied to n-tuples of names. An abstraction of arity n is formed by abstracting n names $\widetilde{x}$ from a process P, written $(\widetilde{x}).\,P$. In $(\widetilde{x}).\,P$, the occurrences of the names $\widetilde{x}$ are binding with scope P. The abstraction $(\widetilde{x}).\,P$ is applied to the n-tuple $\langle\widetilde{y}\rangle$ by substituting the names $\widetilde{y}$ for the names $\widetilde{x}$ in P. The result, $P\{\widetilde{y}/\widetilde{x}\}$, is referred to as an instance of the abstraction $(\widetilde{x}).\,P$. Two abstractions of arity n are deemed to be bisimilar if for any n-tuple $\langle\widetilde{y}\rangle$, the instances obtained by applying the abstractions to $\langle\widetilde{y}\rangle$ are bisimilar processes. The reason why the unknowns in the equations in Theorem 2.4.40 are abstractions rather than processes is that the unknowns may occur underneath input prefixes, and consequently names free in them are open to instantiation.

Definition 2.4.38 (Abstraction)

(1) An *abstraction* of *arity* $n \geq 0$ is an expression of the form $(x_1, \ldots, x_n).\,P$, where the x_i are distinct.
(2) If $F \stackrel{\text{def}}{=} (\widetilde{x}).\,P$ is of arity n and $\widetilde{y}$ is of length n, then $P\{\widetilde{y}/\widetilde{x}\}$ is an *instance* of F. We abbreviate $P\{\widetilde{y}/\widetilde{x}\}$ to $F\langle\widetilde{y}\rangle$. We refer to this instantiation operation as *pseudo-application*.
(3) Abstractions F and G of arity n are *bisimilar*, $F \approx G$, if $F\langle\widetilde{y}\rangle \approx G\langle\widetilde{y}\rangle$ for every n-tuple $\langle\widetilde{y}\rangle$. □

To write the equations, we introduce variables $\{X_i \mid i \in I\}$ over abstractions; each variable X_i has an arity $n_i \geq 0$. In the equations will appear expressions of the form $X_i\langle\widetilde{y}\rangle$. Indeed, an equation will take the form

$$X \approx (\widetilde{x}).\,(\kappa_1.\,X_{i_1}\langle\widetilde{y}_1\rangle + \cdots + \kappa_m.\,X_{i_m}\langle\widetilde{y}_m\rangle) \tag{2.4}$$

where the κ_j are prefixes, including bound outputs, and the length of $\widetilde{y}_j$ is n_{i_j}, the arity of X_{i_j}. (It is possible to prove a version of Theorem 2.4.40 in which the terms that appear in equations are drawn from a larger class, but the result as stated covers the kind of system arising most often in applications of the theory.) Given a system of equations $\{X_i \approx (\widetilde{x}_i).\, E_i \mid i \in I\}$ each having the form in (2.4), a family of abstractions $\{F_i \mid i \in I\}$ of the appropriate arities is a solution of the system if, for each equation, if X_j is replaced by F_j for each j, then the asserted bisimilarity between the resulting abstractions holds.

Definition 2.4.39 (System of equations) Let $\{X_i \mid i \in I\}$ be a possibly infinite set of variables, and for each i let n_i be the arity of X_i.

(1) An *instance* of X_i is an expression of the form $X_i\langle\widetilde{y}\rangle$, where $\widetilde{y}$ is of length n_i.
(2) An *equational term* is of the form $\kappa_1.\, H_1 + \cdots + \kappa_m.\, H_m$, where each H_j is an instance of some X_i, and the κ_j are prefixes (including bound outputs) as in Notation 2.2.13.
(3) A *system of equations* is a set of equations

$$\{X_i \approx (\widetilde{x}_i).\, E_i \mid i \in I\}\,,$$

where each E_i is an equational term and $\widetilde{x}_i$ consists of n_i distinct names.
(4) A *solution* of the system is a set of abstractions $\{F_i \mid i \in I\}$ such that for each $i \in I$, if $F_i \stackrel{\text{def}}{=} (\widetilde{z}_i).\, P_i$ then
   (a) $\widetilde{z}_i$ is of length n_i, that is, F_i is of arity n_i, and
   (b) for each $\widetilde{y}$ of length n_i, the processes $P_i\{\widetilde{y}/\widetilde{z}_i\}$ and $E_i[\widetilde{F}/\widetilde{X}]\{\widetilde{y}/\widetilde{x}_i\}$ are bisimilar, where $E_i[\widetilde{F}/\widetilde{X}]$ is obtained by replacing each expression $X_j\langle\widetilde{w}\rangle$ in E_i by $P_j\{\widetilde{w}/\widetilde{z}_j\}$. □

A system of equations may have more than one solution. A simple example is the system consisting of the single equation $X \approx \tau.\, X$. By Lemma 2.4.18, any 0-ary abstraction is a solution of this equation. To guarantee uniqueness, we need the condition that the system is guarded. Given a system of equations $\{X_i \approx (\widetilde{x}_i).\, E_i \mid i \in I\}$, we write $i \succ j$ if some summand of E_i is of the form $\tau.\, X_j\langle\widetilde{y}\rangle$. The system is *guarded* if there is no infinite sequence $i_0, i_1, i_2, \ldots$ such that $i_h \succ i_{h+1}$ for each h. We write $\succ^*$ for the reflexive and transitive closure of $\succ$.

Theorem 2.4.40 (Unique-Solution Theorem) If $\{F_i \mid i \in I\}$ and $\{G_i \mid i \in I\}$ are solutions of a guarded system of equations, then $F_i \approx G_i$ for each i.

Proof Suppose $\{F_i \mid i \in I\}$ and $\{G_i \mid i \in I\}$ are solutions of the guarded system of equations $\{X_i \approx (\widetilde{x}_i)E_i \mid i \in I\}$, where $\widetilde{x}_i \cap \mathsf{fn}(F_j, G_j) = \emptyset$ for all i, j. For $i \in I$, let $H_i \stackrel{\text{def}}{=} (\widetilde{x}_i).\, E_i[\widetilde{F}/\widetilde{X}]$ and $J_i \stackrel{\text{def}}{=} (\widetilde{x}_i).\, E_i[\widetilde{G}/\widetilde{X}]$. Set

$$\mathcal{S} \stackrel{\text{def}}{=} \{(P, Q) \mid P \approx F_i\langle\widetilde{y}\rangle \text{ and } Q \approx G_i\langle\widetilde{y}\rangle \text{ for some } i \text{ and } \widetilde{y}\}\,.$$

We show that $\mathcal{S}$ is a bisimulation. The main facts needed in the proof are given in Claims 2.4.43 and 2.4.44. First we have some preparation for those claims.

Claim 2.4.41

(1) If $H_i\langle\widetilde{y}\rangle \xrightarrow{\alpha} R$ then there are j and $\widetilde{z}$ such that $R = F_j\langle\widetilde{z}\rangle$ and $J_i\langle\widetilde{y}\rangle \xrightarrow{\alpha} G_j\langle\widetilde{z}\rangle$. Moreover, if $\alpha = \tau$ then $i \succ j$.

(2) The variant of (1) with the roles of H, F and J, G swapped.

Proof This is immediate from the definitions. □

For any given $i \in I$, let T_i be the directed graph with set of nodes $\{j \mid i \succ^* j\}$ and an edge from j to j' iff $j \succ j'$. Note that if $i \succ i'$ then $T_{i'}$ is a subgraph of T_i. Since the system of equations is guarded, there are no infinite paths in T_i. Moreover, T_i is finite-branching. Hence by König's Lemma, T_i is finite. In detail:

Claim 2.4.42 The set of nodes of T_i, that is $\{j \mid i \succ^* j\}$, is finite.

Proof The proof is by contradiction. Suppose that $\{j \mid i \succ^* j\}$ is infinite. Then since T_i is finite branching there is i_1 such that $i \succ i_1$ and $\{j \mid i_1 \succ^* j\}$ is infinite. And by the same argument there is i_2 such that $i_1 \succ i_2$ and $\{j \mid i_2 \succ^* j\}$ is infinite. By repeating the argument we see that there is an infinite path in T_i, a contradiction. □

Let ℓ_i be the length of a longest path in T_i. Note that if $i \succ i'$ then $\ell_{i'} < \ell_i$.

Claim 2.4.43 If $F_i\langle\widetilde{y}\rangle \Longrightarrow R$ then there are j and $\widetilde{z}$ such that $i \succ^* j$ and $F_j\langle\widetilde{z}\rangle \approx R$ and $G_i\langle\widetilde{y}\rangle \Longrightarrow\approx G_j\langle\widetilde{z}\rangle$.

Proof The proof is by induction on ℓ_i as defined above.

Since $H_i\langle\widetilde{y}\rangle \approx F_i\langle\widetilde{y}\rangle$ we have $H_i\langle\widetilde{y}\rangle \Longrightarrow\approx R$. If $H_i\langle\widetilde{y}\rangle \approx R$, which holds in particular if $\ell_i = 0$ and therefore $R = H_i\langle\widetilde{y}\rangle$, then we can take $j = i$ and $\widetilde{z} = \widetilde{y}$. So suppose $\ell_i > 0$ and $H_i\langle\widetilde{y}\rangle \not\approx R$. Then by Claim 2.4.41(1), for some i' such that $i \succ i'$ and some $\widetilde{w}$ we have $H_i\langle\widetilde{y}\rangle \xrightarrow{\tau} F_{i'}\langle\widetilde{w}\rangle \Longrightarrow\approx R$, and $J_i\langle\widetilde{y}\rangle \xrightarrow{\tau} G_{i'}\langle\widetilde{w}\rangle$ and so $G_i\langle\widetilde{y}\rangle \Longrightarrow\approx G_{i'}\langle\widetilde{w}\rangle$ as $G_i\langle\widetilde{y}\rangle \approx J_i\langle\widetilde{y}\rangle$. Since $i \succ i'$ we have $\ell_{i'} < \ell_i$. Hence by induction hypothesis there are j and $\widetilde{z}$ such that $i' \succ^* j$ and $F_j\langle\widetilde{z}\rangle \approx R$ and $G_{i'}\langle\widetilde{w}\rangle \Longrightarrow\approx G_j\langle\widetilde{z}\rangle$.

In summary, we have that $i \succ^* j$ and $F_j\langle\widetilde{z}\rangle \approx R$ and, using the fact that $\approx$ is an equivalence and commutes with $\Longrightarrow$, also $G_i\langle\widetilde{y}\rangle \Longrightarrow\approx G_j\langle\widetilde{z}\rangle$. □

Clearly, the variant of Claim 2.4.43 with the roles of F and G swapped also holds.

Claim 2.4.44 If $H_i\langle\widetilde{y}\rangle \overset{\beta}{\Longrightarrow} R$ where $\beta \in Act - \{\tau\}$, then there are j and $\widetilde{z}$ such that $F_j\langle\widetilde{z}\rangle \approx R$ and $J_i\langle\widetilde{y}\rangle \overset{\beta}{\Longrightarrow}\approx G_j\langle\widetilde{z}\rangle$.

Proof The proof is again by induction on ℓ_i as defined above.

In the case $\ell_i = 0$ the transition from $H_i\langle\widetilde{y}\rangle$ must be of the form $H_i\langle\widetilde{y}\rangle \xrightarrow{\beta} R' \Longrightarrow R$, because $H_i\langle\widetilde{y}\rangle$ cannot perform a τ action. By Claim 2.4.41(1), for some i' and $\widetilde{w}$ we have $R' = F_{i'}\langle\widetilde{w}\rangle$. By Claim 2.4.43 there are j and $\widetilde{z}$ such that $i' \succ^* j$ and $F_j\langle\widetilde{z}\rangle \approx R$ and $G_{i'}\langle\widetilde{w}\rangle \Longrightarrow\approx G_j\langle\widetilde{z}\rangle$. Since also by Claim 2.4.41(1) $J_i\langle\widetilde{y}\rangle \xrightarrow{\beta} G_{i'}\langle\widetilde{w}\rangle$, we have $J_i\langle\widetilde{y}\rangle \overset{\beta}{\Longrightarrow}\approx G_j\langle\widetilde{z}\rangle$.

Now suppose that $\ell_i > 0$. If the transition from $H_i\langle\widetilde{y}\rangle$ is of the form $H_i\langle\widetilde{y}\rangle \xrightarrow{\beta} R' \Longrightarrow R$, then we can reason as above. So suppose that $H_i\langle\widetilde{y}\rangle \xrightarrow{\tau} R' \overset{\beta}{\Longrightarrow} R$. Then by Claim 2.4.41(1), for some i' and $\widetilde{w}$ we have $R' = F_{i'}\langle\widetilde{w}\rangle$. Moreover, $i \succ i'$ and so $\ell_i > \ell_{i'}$. Since $H_{i'}\langle\widetilde{w}\rangle \approx F_{i'}\langle\widetilde{w}\rangle$, we have $H_{i'}\langle\widetilde{w}\rangle \overset{\beta}{\Longrightarrow}\approx R$, and so by induction hypothesis there are j and $\widetilde{z}$ such that $F_j\langle\widetilde{z}\rangle \approx R$ and $J_{i'}\langle\widetilde{w}\rangle \overset{\beta}{\Longrightarrow}\approx G_j\langle\widetilde{z}\rangle$. Since, again by Claim 2.4.41(1), $J_i\langle\widetilde{y}\rangle \xrightarrow{\tau} G_{i'}\langle\widetilde{w}\rangle$ and $G_{i'}\langle\widetilde{w}\rangle \approx J_{i'}\langle\widetilde{w}\rangle$, we have, using that $\approx$ is an equivalence and commutes with $\overset{\beta}{\Longrightarrow}$, that $J_i\langle\widetilde{y}\rangle \overset{\beta}{\Longrightarrow}\approx G_j\langle\widetilde{z}\rangle$, as required. □

Clearly, the variant of Claim 2.4.44 with the roles of H, F and J, G swapped also holds.

To finish the proof suppose $(P, Q) \in \mathcal{S}$, say $P \approx F_i\langle\widetilde{y}\rangle$ and $Q \approx G_i\langle\widetilde{y}\rangle$. Suppose $P \xrightarrow{\tau} P'$. Then $F_i\langle\widetilde{y}\rangle \Longrightarrow\approx P'$ and so by Claim 2.4.43 there are j and $\widetilde{z}$ such that $F_j\langle\widetilde{z}\rangle \approx P'$ and $G_i\langle\widetilde{y}\rangle \Longrightarrow\approx G_j\langle\widetilde{z}\rangle$. Since $Q \approx G_i\langle\widetilde{y}\rangle$ we have $Q \Longrightarrow Q' \approx G_j\langle\widetilde{z}\rangle$, and so $(P', Q') \in \mathcal{S}$. Now suppose $P \xrightarrow{\beta} P'$ where $\beta \in Act - \{\tau\}$. Then $H_i\langle\widetilde{y}\rangle \overset{\beta}{\Longrightarrow}\approx P'$ and so by Claim 2.4.44 there are j and $\widetilde{z}$ such that $F_j\langle\widetilde{z}\rangle \approx P'$ and $J_i\langle\widetilde{y}\rangle \overset{\beta}{\Longrightarrow}\approx G_j\langle\widetilde{z}\rangle$. Since $Q \approx J_i\langle\widetilde{y}\rangle$ we have $Q \overset{\beta}{\Longrightarrow} Q' \approx G_j\langle\widetilde{z}\rangle$, and so $(P', Q') \in \mathcal{S}$. □

We have not presented a unique-solution theorem for strong bisimilarity because it is seldom useful. It is straightforward, however, to establish such a result by simplifying the proof of Theorem 2.4.40.

The following example illustrates the use of Theorem 2.4.40 in combination with other techniques presented earlier. Let

$$\begin{aligned} P &\overset{\text{def}}{=} a(x).\,\overline{c}x.\,\overline{n} \\ Q &\overset{\text{def}}{=} c(x).\,\overline{b}x.\,\overline{m} \\ R &\overset{\text{def}}{=} (\boldsymbol{\nu} c, n, m)\,(P \mid !n.\,P \mid Q \mid !m.\,Q)\,. \end{aligned}$$

The subsystem $\boldsymbol{\nu} n\,(P \mid !n.\,P)$ is a cell that emits via c the name it receives via a, and then restores itself. The subsystem $\boldsymbol{\nu} m\,(Q \mid !m.\,Q)$ is similar, receiving via c and emitting via b. The system R consists of the two cells chained together via the private name c.

Let also

$$\begin{array}{rcl} A' & \stackrel{\text{def}}{=} & a(x).\,\overline{c}x \\ A & \stackrel{\text{def}}{=} & c(x).\,(\overline{b}x.\,A' + a(y).\,\overline{d}x.\,e.\,\overline{c}y) \\ B & \stackrel{\text{def}}{=} & m.\,d(x).\,\overline{b}x.\,\overline{e}.\,\overline{m} \\ S & \stackrel{\text{def}}{=} & (\boldsymbol{\nu} c, d, e, m)\,(A' \mid !A \mid \overline{m} \mid !B)\ . \end{array}$$

The system S is somewhat similar to R, but the cells behave slightly differently, with an instance of A calling on an instance of B only if a new datum is received via a before the datum received previously via a has been emitted via b.

We claim that the two systems have the same observable behaviour. Indeed, we claim that the systems are indistinguishable for any instantiations of the names a and b, that is, that

$$(a,b).\,R \approx (a,b).\,S\ .$$

This can be established by showing that the two abstractions are solutions for X_0 in the following guarded system of equations:

$$\begin{array}{rcl} X_0 & \approx & (a,b).\,a(x).\,X_1\langle a,b,x\rangle \\ X_1 & \approx & (a,b,x).\,(a(y).\,X_2\langle a,b,x,y\rangle \mid \overline{b}x.\,X_0\langle a,b\rangle) \\ X_2 & \approx & (a,b,x,y).\,\overline{b}x.\,X_1\langle a,b,y\rangle\ . \end{array} \qquad (2.5)$$

We show that $(a,b).\,R$ is a solution for X_0 and invite the reader to show that $(a,b).\,S$ is also. Let

$$\begin{array}{rcl} R_1^x & \stackrel{\text{def}}{=} & (\boldsymbol{\nu} c,n,m)\,(P \mid !n.\,P \mid \overline{b}x.\,\overline{m} \mid !m.\,Q) \\ R_2^{xy} & \stackrel{\text{def}}{=} & (\boldsymbol{\nu} c,n,m)\,(\overline{c}y.\,\overline{n} \mid !n.\,P \mid \overline{b}x.\,\overline{m} \mid !m.\,Q)\ . \end{array}$$

Then by expansion, some of the properties in Section 2.2.2, and Lemma 2.4.18,

$$\begin{array}{rcl} R & \sim^{\mathrm{c}} & a(x).\,\tau.\,(\boldsymbol{\nu} c,n,m)\,(\overline{n} \mid !n.\,P \mid \overline{b}x.\,\overline{m} \mid !m.\,Q) \\ & \approx^{\mathrm{c}} & a(x).\,R_1^x \end{array}$$

and

$$\begin{array}{rcl} R_1^x & \approx^{\mathrm{c}} & a(y).\,R_2^{xy} + \overline{b}x.\,R + [a=b]\tau.\,(\boldsymbol{\nu} c,n,m)\,(\overline{c}x.\overline{n} \mid !n.\,P \mid \overline{m} \mid !m.\,Q) \\ & \approx^{\mathrm{c}} & a(y).\,R_2^{xy} + \overline{b}x.\,R + [a=b]\tau.\,R_1^x \\ & \approx^{\mathrm{c}} & a(y).\,R_2^{xy} + \overline{b}x.\,R \end{array}$$

using the easily-proved fact that if $P' \approx^{\mathrm{c}} M + [a=b]\tau.\,P'$ then $P' \approx^{\mathrm{c}} M$, and

$$\begin{aligned} R_2^{xy} &\sim^{c} \bar{b}x.\,(\nu c, n, m)\,(\bar{c}y.\,\bar{n} \mid !n.\,P \mid \bar{m} \mid !m.\,Q) \\ &\approx^{c} \bar{b}x.\,R_1^{y}\,. \end{aligned}$$

Hence $(a, b).\,R$, $(a, b, x).\,R_1^x$ and $(a, b, x, y).\,R_2^{xy}$ comprise a solution of the system. Given also that $(a, b).\,S$ is the X_0-component of a solution, it follows by Theorem 2.4.40 that $(a, b).\,R \approx (a, b).\,S$.

The fact that the abstraction $(a, b).\,R$ is a solution for X_0 shows that R behaves as a 2-place buffer even if the names that it uses for receiving and for sending are identified. If the definition is changed in the obvious way to describe a system with capacity 3, however, then the system does not behave as a buffer when its access names are identified. The following exercise invites the reader to explore this. An observation useful for tackling it is that in the calculation starting from R_1^x above, a match prefix is absorbed.

Exercise 2.4.45 Suppose the definition of R is changed in the obvious way to describe a system with capacity 3. Find a system of equations analogous to (2.5) that is satisfied by the changed $(a, b).\,R$ and other suitable abstractions. □

2.4.3.2 Further exercises

The following exercise examines an effect of adding input actions as prefixes.

Exercise 2.4.46 Consider the set $\mathcal{U}$ of terms obtained when input *actions* are admitted as prefixes, and the transition rule

$$\frac{}{xy.\,P \xrightarrow{xy} P}$$

is added.

(1) Show that for any given term $\pi.\,P$ of $\mathcal{U}$ and names x and y, there is a context C of $\mathcal{U}$ containing no match prefixes such that $C[P] \approx^{c} [x = y]\pi.\,P$.
(2) Hence show that for each term in $\mathcal{U}$ that contains no $+$ there is a full-bisimilar term in $\mathcal{U}$ that contains no match prefixes.
(3) Does your encoding work for terms involving $+$? □

The next exercise concerns the mismatch prefix form mentioned earlier and another operator on processes.

Exercise* 2.4.47 Consider the set $\mathcal{T}$ of terms obtained when sum is removed from the calculus and two syntactic forms are added: the mismatch prefix form

$[x \neq y]\pi.\, P$, and the form $\{x\}P$, with transition rules:

$$\frac{\pi.\, P \xrightarrow{\alpha} P'}{[x \neq y]\pi.\, P \xrightarrow{\alpha} P'}\quad x \neq y \qquad\qquad \frac{P \xrightarrow{\alpha} P'}{\{x\}P \xrightarrow{\alpha} \{x\}P'}\quad \mathsf{subj}(\alpha) \neq x\,.$$

In $\{x\}P$, the occurrence of x is not binding.

(1) Show that

$$[x = y]\pi.\, P \approx^{c} \boldsymbol{\nu} z\, (z.\, \pi.\, P \mid \{x\}\{y\}(y.\, \overline{z} \mid \overline{x}))$$

where z is fresh.

(2) Hence show that for each term in $\mathcal{T}$ there is a full-bisimilar term in $\mathcal{T}$ that has no subterm of the form $[x = y]\pi.\, P$.

(3) Show that for each term in $\mathcal{T}$ there is a full-bisimilar term in $\mathcal{T}$ that has no subterm of the form $[x \neq y]\pi.\, P$. (Hint: observe that $\{y\}x.\, P$ has a transition iff $x \neq y$.) □

2.4.3.3 Up-to techniques

In Section 2.3 we gave a general account of bisimulation-up-to techniques and how to combine them in the strong case, and used some of the theory developed to prove results about strong equivalences. The notions of progression and safe function carry over straightforwardly to the weak setting.

Definition 2.4.48 (Progression) Relation $\mathcal{R}$ *progresses to* relation $\mathcal{S}$, written $\mathcal{R} \rightsquigarrow \mathcal{S}$, if whenever $(P, Q) \in \mathcal{R}$,

(1) $P \xrightarrow{\alpha} P'$ implies $Q \stackrel{\widehat{\alpha}}{\Longrightarrow} Q'$ for some Q' with $(P', Q') \in \mathcal{S}$

(2) vice versa. □

Definition 2.4.49 (Safe function) A function $\mathcal{F}$ on relations is *safe* if $\mathcal{R} \subseteq \mathcal{S}$ and $\mathcal{R} \rightsquigarrow \mathcal{S}$ implies $\mathcal{F}(\mathcal{R}) \subseteq \mathcal{F}(\mathcal{S})$ and $\mathcal{F}(\mathcal{R}) \rightsquigarrow \mathcal{F}(\mathcal{S})$. □

As we will see shortly, however, chaining is not a secure operator in the weak case. This is so because of the use of $\xrightarrow{\alpha}$ transitions in Definition 2.4.48. If we were to replace these by $\stackrel{\alpha}{\Longrightarrow}$ transitions, then the theory would carry over entirely smoothly from the strong case (see for instance Exercise 2.4.63); but the advantages of using $\xrightarrow{\alpha}$ transitions, discussed before Notation 2.4.2, would be lost; on balance it is better to work with Definition 2.4.48 as stated.

The following key property of safe functions holds.

Lemma 2.4.50 If $\mathcal{F}$ is safe and $\mathcal{R} \rightsquigarrow \mathcal{F}(\mathcal{R})$, then $\mathcal{R}$ and $\mathcal{F}(\mathcal{R})$ are included in $\approx$.

Proof The proof is entirely similar to that of Lemma 2.3.8. □

Thus to show that $P \approx Q$, it suffices to find a relation $\mathcal{R}$ such that $(P, Q) \in \mathcal{R}$ and a safe function $\mathcal{F}$ such that $\mathcal{R} \rightsquigarrow \mathcal{F}(\mathcal{R})$.

The general theory of combining up-to techniques is less settled in the weak case than in the strong, however. The main reason for this is that chaining is not a secure operator, where an operator on functions on relations is *secure* if when applied to safe arguments it yields a safe result. To see this, consider the singleton relation $\mathcal{R} = \{(\tau.x, \mathbf{0})\}$ and the safe functions $\mathcal{F}_\iota$, the identity, and $\mathcal{F}_\approx$, the constant function that maps any relation to $\approx$. Set $\mathcal{G} \stackrel{\text{def}}{=} \mathcal{F}_\approx \mathcal{F}_\iota$. Then $\mathcal{R} \rightsquigarrow \mathcal{G}(\mathcal{R})$, since for the transition $\tau.x \xrightarrow{\tau} x$ we have $x \approx \tau.x$ and so $(x, \mathbf{0}) \in \mathcal{G}(\mathcal{R})$. Hence if chaining were secure then $\mathcal{G}$ would be safe, and it would follow that $\tau.x \approx \mathbf{0}$. Note that as the example shows, this difficulty is not particular to π-calculus.

The fact that chaining is not secure may appear to be a source of possible difficulty. For we wish to establish results for weak equivalences analogous to results that we proved for strong equivalences in Section 2.3.3 using the fact that chaining *is* strongly secure. If we look more closely, however, we see that the strong security of chaining was used in just two ways. First, it gives a convenient way of enlarging a relation, for instance by applying $\mathcal{F}_\sim$ or $\mathcal{F}_\equiv$ to it, while still remaining within strong bisimilarity. And second, chaining allows us to extend the safety of a function to its transitive closure.

In the weak case, we can circumvent the insecurity of chaining as follows. First, we prove *directly* that specific functions of interest are safe. The analogue in the strong case would be proving directly that, for example, the function that maps $\mathcal{R}$ to $\sim\mathcal{R}\sim$ is strongly safe. As we noted above, the corresponding function that maps $\mathcal{R}$ to $\approx\mathcal{R}\approx$ is *not* safe. It turns out to be convenient to have several safe variations of it, involving $\sim$ or $\equiv$ or a relation called *expansion* (Definition 2.4.58) rather than $\approx$. Second, the most important point concerning transitive closure is that, in the strong case, it suffices to work with (single-hole) contexts in the proof of Lemma 2.3.21. In the weak case, we have to work *directly* with multi-hole contexts.

In summary, by overcoming the insecurity of chaining as just outlined, we are able to establish analogues for the weak equivalences of all the techniques for the strong equivalences. We now proceed to do this.

First recall the function $\mathcal{F}_\sigma$ defined by

$$\mathcal{F}_\sigma(\mathcal{R}) = \{(P\rho, Q\rho) \mid (P, Q) \in \mathcal{R},\ \rho \text{ injective on } \mathsf{fn}(P, Q)\}\ .$$

Lemma 2.4.51 $\mathcal{F}_\sigma$ is safe.

Proof The proof is similar to that of Lemma 2.3.10. □

We call $\mathcal{R}$ a *bisimulation up to injective substitution* if $\mathcal{R} \rightsquigarrow \mathcal{F}_\sigma(\mathcal{R})$.

Using this technique we can give the first two proofs deferred above.

Proof (of Lemma 2.4.12)

This follows from Lemma 2.4.51 and Lemma 2.4.50. □

Proof (of Theorem 2.4.22(2))

If $\mathcal{R}$ is a bisimulation containing $(P\{y/z\}, Q\{y/z\})$ for each $y \in \mathsf{fn}(P, Q, z)$, then

$$\{(x(z).\,P, x(z).\,Q)\} \cup \mathcal{R}$$

is a bisimulation up to injective substitution. □

Now recall the function $\mathcal{F}_{\mathrm{ni}}$ defined by

$$\mathcal{F}_{\mathrm{ni}}(\mathcal{R}) = \{(C\eta, C\eta') \mid \begin{array}{l} C \text{ is a non-input multi-hole context and} \\ (\eta_i, \eta'_i) \in \mathcal{R} \text{ for all } i\} \,. \end{array}$$

Lemma 2.4.52 $\mathcal{F}_{\mathrm{ni}}$ is safe.

Proof The proof is similar to that of Lemma 2.3.21, but more complex because we have to use multi-hole contexts. We cannot use the function $\mathcal{F}_{\mathrm{ni1}}$ because of the problem with transitive closure in the weak case discussed above. □

Using this we can then give the final missing proof.

Proof (of Theorem 2.4.22(1))

The proof is similar to that of Theorem 2.2.8(1). It is left as an exercise for the interested reader. □

Analogous to Lemma 2.3.22, Corollary 2.3.23, Lemma 2.3.24, and Corollary 2.3.25, we have the following techniques for proving processes full bisimilar. The proofs of the results are somewhat similar to those of their strong analogues, but with the direct kind of treatment explained above in place of applications of chaining.

Lemma 2.4.53 If $(P, Q) \in \mathcal{R}$ where $\mathcal{R}$ is closed under substitution, and also $\mathcal{R} \rightsquigarrow \mathcal{F}(\mathcal{R})$ where $\mathcal{F}$ is safe, then $P \approx^{\mathrm{c}} Q$. □

Corollary 2.4.54 If $(P, Q) \in \mathcal{R}$ where $\mathcal{R}$ is closed under substitution, and $\mathcal{R} \rightsquigarrow \mathcal{F}_{\mathrm{ni}}(\mathcal{R})$, then $P \approx^{\mathrm{c}} Q$. □

Lemma 2.4.55 The function $\mathcal{F}_C$ (defined in Lemma 2.3.24) is safe.

Proof The proof is similar to that of Lemma 2.3.24, but again more complex because we have to use multi-hole contexts. □

Corollary 2.4.56 If $(P, Q) \in \mathcal{R}$ where $\mathcal{R}$ is closed under substitution, and $\mathcal{R} \rightsquigarrow \mathcal{F}_C(\mathcal{R})$, then $P \approx^c Q$. □

Recall from the discussion about chaining not being a secure operator that $(P, Q) \in \mathcal{R}$ where $\mathcal{R} \rightsquigarrow\ \approx\mathcal{R}\approx$ does *not* imply $P \approx Q$. The following definitions and results give some tools that can sometimes help to get round this difficulty. We use an asymmetric variant of bisimilarity called *expansion*. In practice, it is often possible to show that processes that one expects to be bisimilar are in fact related by expansion. The idea underlying expansion is roughly that if Q expands P, then P and Q are bisimilar, except that in mimicking Q's behaviour, P cannot perform more τ transitions than Q. Expansion is the first preorder on processes we have met that is not an equivalence (it is not symmetric). To define expansion we need the following notation.

Notation 2.4.57

(1) $\xrightarrow{\widehat{\tau}}$ is $\xrightarrow{\tau} \cup \mathcal{I}$, where $\mathcal{I}$ is the identity relation; that is, $P \xrightarrow{\widehat{\tau}} P'$ if $P \xrightarrow{\tau} P'$ or $P' = P$.

(2) If $\alpha \neq \tau$ then $\xrightarrow{\widehat{\alpha}}$ is $\xrightarrow{\alpha}$. □

The expansion relation is then defined as follows.

Definition 2.4.58 (Expansion relation) A relation $\mathcal{S}$ is an *expansion* if whenever $(P, Q) \in \mathcal{S}$,

(1) $P \xrightarrow{\alpha} P'$ implies $Q \stackrel{\alpha}{\Longrightarrow} Q'$ and $(P', Q') \in \mathcal{S}$ for some Q'

(2) $Q \xrightarrow{\alpha} Q'$ implies $P \xrightarrow{\widehat{\alpha}} P'$ and $(P', Q') \in \mathcal{S}$ for some P'.

Q *expands* P, written $Q \succeq P$ or $P \preceq Q$, if $(P, Q) \in \mathcal{S}$ for some expansion $\mathcal{S}$. We call $\succeq$ the *expansion relation*. The *expansion precongruence*, ${}^c\!\!\succeq$, is defined by: $P\ {}^c\!\!\succeq Q$ if $P\sigma \succeq Q\sigma$ for all σ. □

As expected, the expansion relation is preserved by all non-input contexts, and the expansion precongruence by *all* contexts. The expansion relation lies strictly between strong bisimilarity and bisimilarity.

Exercise 2.4.59 Show that:

(1) $P \sim Q$ implies $P \succeq Q$.
(2) $P \succeq Q$ implies $P \approx Q$.
(3) The above implications are strict. □

Definition 2.4.60 (Bisimulation up to expansion)

(1) The function $\mathcal{F}_{\succeq}$ is defined by

$$\mathcal{F}_{\succeq}(\mathcal{R}) \stackrel{\text{def}}{=} \succeq \mathcal{R} \preceq,$$

that is, $(P, Q) \in \mathcal{F}_{\succeq}(\mathcal{R})$ if there is $(P', Q') \in \mathcal{R}$ such that $P \succeq P'$ and $Q \succeq Q'$.

(2) $\mathcal{S}$ is a *bisimulation up to* $\succeq$ if $\mathcal{S} \rightleftarrows \mathcal{F}_{\succeq}(\mathcal{S})$. □

Exercise 2.4.61

(1) Show that $\mathcal{F}_{\succeq}$ is safe.
(2) Hence show that if $(P, Q) \in \mathcal{R}$ where $\mathcal{R}$ is a bisimulation up to $\succeq$, then $P \approx Q$. □

Exercise 2.4.62 Show that the function that maps $\mathcal{R}$ to $\succeq \mathcal{R} \approx$ is *not* safe. □

Exercise 2.4.63 Suppose $\mathcal{R}$ is such that whenever $(P, Q) \in \mathcal{R}$,

(1) if $P \stackrel{\alpha}{\Longrightarrow} P'$ then $Q \stackrel{\widehat{\alpha}}{\Longrightarrow} Q'$ and $P' \approx \mathcal{R} \approx Q'$
(2) vice versa.

Prove that if $(P, Q) \in \mathcal{R}$ then $P \approx Q$. (Note the use of $\stackrel{\alpha}{\Longrightarrow}$ in the premisses.) □

Exercise 2.4.64 Suppose $\mathcal{R}$ is such that whenever $(P, Q) \in \mathcal{R}$,

(1) if $P \stackrel{\alpha}{\longrightarrow} P'$ where $\alpha \neq \tau$, then $Q \stackrel{\alpha}{\Longrightarrow} Q'$ and $P' \approx \mathcal{R} \approx Q'$
(2) if $P \stackrel{\tau}{\longrightarrow} P'$ then $Q \Longrightarrow Q'$ and $P' \sim \mathcal{R} \approx Q'$
(3) the variants of (1) and (2) with the roles of P and Q interchanged.

Prove the following.

(1) If $(P, Q) \in \mathcal{R}$ and $P \Longrightarrow P'$, then $Q \Longrightarrow Q'$ for some Q' with $P' \sim \mathcal{R} \approx Q'$.
(2) If $P \approx \mathcal{R} \approx Q$ and $P \Longrightarrow P'$, then $Q \Longrightarrow Q'$ for some Q' with $P' \approx \mathcal{R} \approx Q'$.
(3) If $P \sim \mathcal{R} \approx Q$ and $P \stackrel{\alpha}{\longrightarrow} P'$ where $\alpha \neq \tau$, then $Q \stackrel{\alpha}{\Longrightarrow} Q'$ for some Q' with $P' \approx \mathcal{R} \approx Q'$.
(4) If $(P, Q) \in \mathcal{R}$ and $P \stackrel{\alpha}{\Longrightarrow} P'$ where $\alpha \neq \tau$, then $Q \stackrel{\alpha}{\Longrightarrow} Q'$ for some Q' with $P' \approx \mathcal{R} \approx Q'$. (Hint: use 1, 3, and 2.)
(5) If $(P, Q) \in \mathcal{R}$ then $P \approx Q$. □

We can usefully combine up to expansion with up to context.

Definition 2.4.65 (Bisimulation up to context and up to expansion) $\mathcal{S}$ is a *bisimulation up to context and up to* $\succeq$ if whenever $(P, Q) \in \mathcal{S}$,

(1) if $P \xrightarrow{\alpha} P'$ then there are Q' such that $Q \stackrel{\widehat{\alpha}}{\Longrightarrow} Q'$, a multi-hole context C, and instantiations η and η' such that $P' \succeq C\eta$ and $Q' \succeq C\eta'$ and
   (a) $(\eta_j, \eta'_j) \in \mathcal{S}$ for all j, and
   (b) if $[\cdot]_i$ occurs under an input prefix in C, then $(\eta_i\sigma, \eta'_i\sigma) \in \mathcal{S}$ for all σ

(2) vice versa with the roles of P and Q interchanged. □

Lemma 2.4.66 Suppose $\mathcal{R}$ is a bisimulation up to context and up to $\succeq$. Then $(P, Q) \in \mathcal{R}$ implies $P \approx Q$.

Exercise 2.4.67 Prove Lemma 2.4.66 as follows.

(1) First show that composition (as defined in Lemma 2.3.14) is a secure operator.
(2) Then apply Lemma 2.4.55 and Exercise 2.4.61(1). □

Lemma 2.4.68 Suppose $\mathcal{R}$ is a bisimulation up to context and up to $\succeq$, and $\mathcal{R}$ is closed under substitution. Then $(P, Q) \in \mathcal{R}$ implies $P \approx^{c} Q$.

Proof This is a consequence of Lemma 2.4.66. □

2.4.4 Reduction-closed barbed congruence

We briefly discuss a variant of barbed congruence in which the quantification over contexts is pushed inside the definition of barbed bisimulation, that is, where the following clause is added to Definition 2.4.3:

$$C[P] \stackrel{\cdot}{\approx} C[Q] \qquad \text{for every context } C\,. \tag{2.6}$$

The resulting relation, *reduction-closed barbed congruence*, is, essentially by definition, both a congruence and a barbed bisimulation; indeed, it is the largest barbed bisimulation that is a congruence. (Although we consider only the weak equivalence, the same arguments apply in the strong case.)

The main advantage of reduction-closed barbed congruence over barbed congruence is that a characterization theorem in terms of labelled bisimilarity can be proved for all processes. This can be done using reasoning similar to that in Theorem 2.4.29 (though without the need to use the relation $\approx_\omega$). Such a proof is possible because (2.6) allows the context surrounding the processes being compared to be changed at any point in the reduction-closed barbed bisimulation game.

On the π-calculus, reduction-closed barbed congruence is stronger and, arguably, less natural, than barbed congruence. On π-calculus processes, reduction-closed barbed congruence coincides with a variant of *open bisimilarity* (studied in Section 4.6) in which names that have been extruded are treated in a special way. Moreover, in calculi where arbitrary processes can be combined with the sum operator, such as CCS, reduction-closed barbed congruence violates the equation

$$\pi.\tau.P = \pi.P\ .$$

The reason why barbed congruence is more robust is that it keeps the intervention of the external observer to a minimum. (Recall that we started from reduction bisimilarity in Section 2.1.) In reduction-closed barbed congruence, on the other hand, the observer has the power to change the context surrounding the processes being tested. Further, as explained before Theorem 2.4.27, the fact that $P \cong^{c} Q$ implies $P \approx^{c} Q$ for a large class of processes (though not all processes) is satisfactory: the important point is that $P \approx^{c} Q$ implies $P \cong^{c} Q$ for all P and Q (Theorem 2.4.23).

Between barbed congruence and reduction-closed barbed congruence is the reduction-closed version of barbed equivalence, where (2.6) is replaced by

$$P \mid R \stackrel{\centerdot}{\approx} Q \mid R \qquad \text{for every } R\ .$$

This equivalence, *reduction-closed barbed equivalence*, is a compromise between barbed congruence and reduction-closed barbed congruence. Thus, for instance, it is less robust than barbed congruence (and barbed equivalence), but it often gives a more natural equivalence than reduction-closed barbed congruence. On the π-calculus, reduction-closed barbed equivalence coincides with bisimilarity, and therefore is not a congruence.

Notes and References for Part I

The first paper on π-calculus, [MPW89, MPW92], was written by Milner, Parrow, and Walker in the spring of 1989, and gave an account of work done intermittently over the preceding two years. The π-calculus developed from the calculus ECCS introduced by Engberg and Nielsen in [EN86]. (See [EN00] for a detailed comparison of the two calculi.) ECCS showed how label-passing could be added to CCS [Mil80], and thus established the possibility of an algebraic calculus of mobility. A summary of other earlier work on formalisms that allow mobility was given in [MPW92]. In particular, Astesiano and Zucca [AZ84] extended CCS with parametric channels, and Clinger [Cli81] gave a semantic treatment of Hewitt's Actors model [Hew77]. A summary of basic theory of the π-calculus was given by Parrow in [Par01].

Structural congruence and reduction were introduced in [Mil92]. The use of rules for manipulating the structure of π-terms was suggested by the Chemical Abstract Machine (CHAM) of Berry and Boudol [BB92]. It is an open question whether structural congruence is decidable. Decidability of relations close to structural congruence was shown by Engelfreit and Gelsema in [EG99] and by Hirschkoff in [Hir99]. The transition rules, with the exception of the rules for replications, are from [MPW92, MPW93], as are many of the basic results about the transition system.

Barbed bisimilarity, congruence, and equivalence were introduced in [MS92a]. They have been applied to a wide variety of languages, including languages with functional, imperative, and object-oriented features, and to concurrent calculi with a range of communication mechanisms. The view of bisimulation as a game has been stressed and developed by Stirling [Sti96]. Testing equivalence was introduced by De Nicola and Hennessy [DH84]. Its adaptation to the π-calculus was studied by Hennessy [Hen91] and by Boreale and De Nicola [BD95].

The Context Lemma for barbed congruence (Lemma 2.4.7) was proved by Pierce and Sangiorgi in [PS96]. The basic theory of bisimilarity and full bisimilarity was presented in [MPW92, MPW93]. The Characterization Theorems (Theorem 2.2.9 and Theorem 2.4.29) were proved in [San92]. The Replication Theorems (Theorem 2.2.25 and Theorem 2.2.26) are from [Mil93]. The results in Exercise 2.2.30 were proved in [San98b].

The theory of safe functions and secure operators was first studied in [San98b]. A unique-solution theorem was shown in [MPW92]; the version that is Theorem 2.4.40 is an elaboration of a result in [Mil99]. Exercise 2.4.47 is based on operators considered by Vivas and Dam in [VD98]. The expansion relation was studied by Arun-Kumar and Hennessy in [AKH92] as a preorder giving information about the 'efficiency' of processes. Its use in up-to techniques was investigated in [SM92]. Lemma 2.4.66 was proved in [San96b].

Montanari and Sassone [MS92b] first used relations that by definition are both bisimulations and congruences, in CCS. These relations are defined like CCS bisimulation, but with an additional requirement similar to (2.6). The largest relation so obtained is different from bisimilarity because bisimilarity is not a congruence. Honda and Yoshida [HY95] applied similar ideas in the setting of reduction-based bisimilarities (where τ transitions, or reductions, are the only relevant transitions of processes). The relation defined is essentially reduction-closed barbed congruence, although the formulation and the calculi are rather different. The results mentioned in Sections 2.4.2 and 2.4.4 are from [San01b].

Part II

Variations of the π-calculus

Introduction to Part II

Part I presented a main line in the theory of the π-calculus, examining processes and behavioural equivalence in some depth. Part II continues the study of the calculus.

Its first segment addresses two of the book's central concerns: how to *use* π-calculus, and the question of its *expressiveness*. These two concerns are intimately connected, since using the calculus involves expressing things in it. Among the things whose expression is explored are computational *data*: simple data such as numbers and strings, and complex data such as records, lists, and graphs. Representing data is an attractive first exercise in using π-calculus, because it is simple and yet allows many common idioms to be demonstrated. The activity has a similar flavour to expressing entities such as numbers and partial recursive functions as terms of λ-calculus. As we will see, however, there are many striking points of contrast. We show by example how values of arbitrary datatypes and operations on them can be expressed as name-passing processes, and how evaluation of data is captured by reduction of those processes.

The calculus of Part I is sometimes referred to as the *monadic* π-calculus, because an interaction involves the communication of a *single* name between processes. The representations of data as processes make use of two additions to the monadic calculus. The first is *polyadicity*: the passing of *tuples* of names in communications. Polyadicity is perhaps the simplest addition to the monadic calculus that retains names as the only atomic data. As we will see, however, polyadicity forces consideration of types, an issue that can be left aside in the monadic calculus. The second addition to the monadic calculus used in representing data is *recursive definition* of processes. Polyadicity and recursion can be convenient when using π-calculus. Anything that can be expressed with their help can also be expressed without it, however. To demonstrate some of the reasoning techniques developed in Part I in alliance with polyadicity and recursion, we give an extended worked example. It establishes the equivalence of two implementations of a priority-queue datatype.

The second segment of Part II continues the study of behavioural equivalence from Chapter 2. We have adopted barbed congruence as the formal expression of behavioural equivalence of processes; and we have seen that bisimilarity is in harmony with it and is an indispensable tool for reasoning about behaviour. We introduce three variants of bisimilarity: *ground bisimilarity*, *late bisimilarity*, and *open bisimilarity*.

The principal reason for studying these equivalences is that they are useful in various ways for reasoning about process behaviour. For instance, ground bisimilarity demands less of processes' ability to mimic one another's input actions than does bisimilarity. Consequently, ground bisimilarity is less discriminating than bisimilarity and often much easier to establish. On the full π-calculus, ground bisimilarity is not a satisfactory equivalence: it is not preserved by composition, for instance. On some important subcalculi, however, it coincides with bisimilarity, and its simpler nature is then extremely valuable.

A second reason for discussing the variants is to give a summary of bisimilarities for the π-calculus. When π-calculus was introduced, it was not clear what the canonical bisimilarity should be. The first paper on π-calculus concentrated on the theory of late bisimilarity, and many others have explored the variants. Subsequent developments, in particular the introduction of barbed congruence and the demonstration of its importance, have clarified the picture and influenced our decision to treat equivalence as we do in the book. An important point is that in practice, the differences among the bisimilarities (possibly excluding ground) are so small as to be unimportant.

A proper treatment of open bisimilarity requires a technical notion called *distinctions*. A distinction is a relation on names whose purpose is to record that certain names cannot be instantiated to the same name. Distinctions crop up in several places in π-calculus, and have various uses.

We also study axiomatizations and proof systems for equivalences on finite processes. This is a popular topic in process calculus generally, and for π-calculus in particular, a fairly complete picture has been built up. We give a survey, only sketching the longer proofs.

The final segment of Part II explores some important subcalculi of the π-calculus. The usefulness of these subcalculi stems from the facts that precise practical intuitions underlie them, they are expressive, and yet there are powerful reasoning techniques for them that are not available on the full π-calculus. To appreciate this point, recall that the definition of barbed congruence is sensitive to the calculus under consideration, since it involves universal quantification over the contexts of the calculus. Although two terms of a subcalculus can be compared as processes of the π-calculus, it is often natural to consider them to be equivalent if they are indistinguishable in all contexts of the subcalculus, that is, if they are barbed congruent *as terms of the subcalculus*. Typically, barbed congruence on a subcalculus is less demanding than barbed congruence on the π-calculus, because terms are compared in fewer contexts. Consequently, sharper algebraic and other tools can often be found for proving equivalence of terms of the subcalculus.

We consider a subcalculus in which communication between processes can be understood as being asynchronous, that is, where the act of sending a datum by one process and the act of receiving it by another are separate. This subcalculus is called the *Asynchronous π-calculus*, Aπ. Its most distinctive syntactic feature – and the basis for the interpretation of communication as asynchronous – is that the only term that can occur under an output prefix is $\mathbf{0}$. Many systems, especially distributed systems, are naturally represented by processes of Aπ. A highlight of the behavioural-equivalence theory of Aπ is that if two Aπ-processes are ground bisimilar, then they are barbed congruent.

We also study a subcalculus, the *Localized π-calculus*, Lπ, in which only the output capabilities of names can be communicated, that is, where the recipient of a name can only use it for sending or send it. This constraint on use of names arises often in practice.

We also examine a subcalculus, the *Private π-calculus*, Pπ, in which only bound names can be communicated. This *internal mobility* is responsible for much of the expressive power of the π-calculus.

Finally, we note some limits to the range of applicability of ground bisimilarity, by showing that it is not preserved by substitution on any subcalculus that has output prefix, input prefix, composition, restriction, and replication.

Structure of the Part Part II consists of three chapters. The first, Chapter 3, has four sections. Section 3.1 introduces polyadicity. Section 3.2 explains recursion, and in particular shows the precise relationship between recursion and replication. Section 3.3 contains the priority-queues example, and Section 3.4 shows how data can be represented as π-calculus processes.

The first of Chapter 4's eight sections, Section 4.1, presents basic results about distinctions. Sections 4.2–4.7 are about ground bisimilarity, late bisimilarity, and open bisimilarity. Section 4.8 presents axiomatizations and proof systems. We begin with summations, and give axiomatizations and proof systems for the various bisimilarities and associated congruences. The mismatching operator, mentioned in Section 1.1, plays an important role in many of these. We then add composition and restriction.

Sections 5.1–5.5 in Chapter 5 are about the Asynchronous π-calculus. The

Localized π-calculus is studied in Section 5.6, internal mobility in Section 5.7, and non-congruence results for bisimilarity in Section 5.8.

3

Polyadicity and Recursion

3.1 Polyadicity

In the monadic π-calculus, an interaction involves the transmission of a single name from one process to another. A natural and convenient extension is to admit processes that pass tuples of names. The enriched language, the polyadic π-calculus, is examined in this section.

Definition 3.1.1 (Polyadic π-calculus) The processes of the *polyadic π-calculus* are defined in the same way as the processes of the monadic calculus, except that the prefixes are given by

$$\pi \ ::= \ \overline{x}\langle\widetilde{y}\rangle \mid x(\widetilde{z}) \mid \tau \mid [x=y]\pi \,,$$

where no name occurs more than once in the tuple $\widetilde{z}$ in an input prefix. □

The intended interpretations of the new polyadic prefixes are that $\overline{x}\langle\widetilde{y}\rangle. P$ can send the tuple $\langle\widetilde{y}\rangle$ via x and continue as P, and that $x(\widetilde{z}). Q$ can receive a tuple $\langle\widetilde{y}\rangle$ via x and continue as $Q\{\widetilde{y}/\widetilde{z}\}$.

The natural way to extend the reduction relation to polyadic terms is to change the first axiom, R-INTER, of reduction to:

$$\text{PR-INTER} \quad \frac{}{(\overline{x}\langle\widetilde{y}\rangle. P_1 + M_1) \mid (x(\widetilde{z}). P_2 + M_2) \longrightarrow P_1 \mid P_2\{\widetilde{y}/\widetilde{z}\}} \quad |\widetilde{y}| = |\widetilde{z}| \,.$$

Thus, in an interaction, sender and receiver must agree on the length of the tuple to be passed. (We write $|\widetilde{x}|$ for the length of the tuple $\widetilde{x}$.) Simply defining reduction using PR-INTER is not the end of the story, however.

To see why, consider a polyadic term in which sender and receiver disagree on the length of tuple to be transmitted via some name, for instance,

$$\overline{x}\langle a,b,c\rangle. \mathbf{0} \mid x(y,z). \mathbf{0} \,. \tag{3.1}$$

A term such as this is somewhat analogous to an ill-typed application term in a typed λ-calculus. It may not be manifest whether a disagreement of the kind illustrated in (3.1) can arise from a given polyadic process. For instance,

$$\overline{s}\langle x, w\rangle. \mathbf{0} \mid w(v). \overline{v}\langle a, b, c\rangle. \mathbf{0} \mid s(t, u). \overline{u}\langle t\rangle. t(y, z). \mathbf{0} \qquad (3.2)$$

can evolve in two reductions to the term in (3.1); and one can easily imagine more complicated examples.

How can such ill-formed polyadic processes be separated out? Taking a cue from λ-calculus and programming languages, we may seek to achieve the separation via a suitable type discipline. Part III and Part IV are devoted to types, and consider in particular typing of polyadic processes. Passing of tuples is so useful, however, that we wish to anticipate a little and develop a suitable treatment here. The treatment will use a *by-name* typing discipline, based on *sorts*. The typing is by name in that different sorts are considered to be different types. From Part III on, we study typing *by structure*, where types are equal if they have the same structure.

In the monadic calculus, no distinctions of type are made among names: any name can be used to communicate any name. In seeking a suitable well-formedness criterion for polyadic processes, one might think of assigning each name an integer arity, and requiring that prefix formation be arity-respecting; that is, if x had arity n then $\overline{x}\langle a_1, \ldots, a_k\rangle. P$ and $x(z_1, \ldots, z_k). Q$ would be well-formed only if $k = n$. As illustrated by the terms in (3.2) and (3.1), however, the set of processes respecting this arity discipline is not closed under reduction. Attention should also be paid to the arities of the names that are passed in communications.

To achieve this, consider a partition S of the set of names into infinite sets called *sorts*. Each sort is infinite to make α-conversion possible (substitution is required to be sort-respecting). We write $x : \gamma$ if x belongs to the sort γ, and $x : y$ if x and y belong to the same sort, and we extend these notations to tuples in the obvious way.

Definition 3.1.2 (Sorting)

(1) A *sorting* is a function $\Sigma : \mathsf{S} \longrightarrow \mathsf{S}^*$, where S^* is the set of all finite tuples of sorts. If $\gamma \in \mathsf{S}$ then we refer to $\Sigma(\gamma)$ as the *object sort* of γ.

(2) A polyadic term P *respects* a sorting Σ if

 (a) for each $\overline{x}\langle\widetilde{y}\rangle$ or $x(\widetilde{y})$ in P, if $x : \gamma$ then $\widetilde{y} : \Sigma(\gamma)$

 (b) for each match $[x = y]$ in P we have $x : y$. □

For example, if there are two sorts γ and δ, and $\Sigma(\gamma) = \langle\gamma, \delta\rangle$ and $\Sigma(\delta) = \langle\delta, \delta, \gamma\rangle$, then

$$a(x, y, z).\,\boldsymbol{\nu} w\, [x = y]\overline{z}\langle w, x\rangle.\,\mathbf{0} \mid \overline{a}\langle b, b, c\rangle.\, c(v, u).\,\mathbf{0}$$

respects Σ, provided $c, v, w, z : \gamma$ and $a, b, u, x, y : \delta$. The terms in (3.1) and (3.2), on the other hand, do not respect any sorting.

Exercise 3.1.3 Show that if P respects Σ and $P \longrightarrow Q$, then Q respects Σ. □

In view of this discussion, we adopt axiom PR-INTER and consider only the polyadic processes that respect a sorting.

To define the transition relations on polyadic processes, we must enrich the set of actions to capture that polyadic processes communicate tuples. Moreover, polyadic processes can perform output actions in whose objects some names are free and others bound. An example is the transition

$$\boldsymbol{\nu} z\, \overline{x}\langle y, z\rangle.\, z(w).\,\mathbf{0} \xrightarrow{(\boldsymbol{\nu} z)\, \overline{x}\langle y, z\rangle} z(w).\,\mathbf{0}\,,$$

where $(\boldsymbol{\nu} z)\, \overline{x}\langle y, z\rangle$ is an output via x in whose object y is free and z is bound. In general, the actions that polyadic processes can perform are given by

$$\alpha \;::=\; (\boldsymbol{\nu}\widetilde{z})\,\overline{x}\langle\widetilde{y}\rangle \;\mid\; x\langle\widetilde{y}\rangle \;\mid\; \tau\,,$$

where in the first, $\widetilde{z} \subseteq \widetilde{y}$, that is, $\widetilde{z}$ is a *subset* of the set of names occurring in the tuple $\widetilde{y}$. So in an action $(\boldsymbol{\nu}\widetilde{z})\,\overline{x}\langle\widetilde{y}\rangle$, the order of the names $\widetilde{z}$ is immaterial.

In Section 6.2, we introduce a language called *Base-π* that serves as a basis for typed calculi and higher-order calculi. Base-π is parametrized on the types of data that processes can communicate. By taking the data to be tuples of names, we obtain the polyadic processes. Since the transition rules for Base-π are presented in full in Table 6.4, we do not give the rules specifically for the polyadic processes here. For now, it suffices to say that if a polyadic process P respects a sorting Σ, then its actions conform to Σ and its derivatives respect Σ, provided that if $P \xrightarrow{x\langle\widetilde{y}\rangle} P'$ where $x : \gamma$, then $\widetilde{y} : \Sigma(\gamma)$. (This is analogous to the Subject Reduction Theorem of Section 6.2.)

Processes P and Q that respect Σ are ***barbed congruent with respect to*** Σ, written $\Sigma \triangleright P \cong^{c} Q$, if $C[P] \overset{\centerdot}{\approx} C[Q]$ for every context C that respects Σ. (Labelled) ***bisimilarity*** on polyadic processes that respect a sorting Σ is given by the standard bisimulation game on the graph determined by the transition relations for those processes, with a similar proviso to that above on tuples received in input actions. Processes P and Q that respect Σ are ***full bisimilar with respect to*** Σ, written $\Sigma \triangleright P \approx^{c} Q$, if $P\sigma \approx Q\sigma$ for every substitution σ that respects Σ, that is, is such that $x : x\sigma$ for every x.

The sorted equivalences on polyadic processes share very many properties with their monadic analogues. In particular, $\Sigma \triangleright P \approx^{c} Q$ implies $\Sigma \triangleright P \cong^{c} Q$. We will not spell out the definitions of the strong variants of the equivalences on sorted processes; they are as expected. Indeed, we will not develop the theory of sorted equivalence here. The theory of equivalence for typed π-calculi will be presented in Part IV. (Although that Part uses mainly by-structure typing, similar results can be obtained for by-name typing.) Now we turn to the question of expressibility.

We have in fact already seen two examples of how passing of tuples can be expressed in the monadic calculus. In Section 2.1, we introduced the abbreviations $x.P$ for $x(w).P$ where $w \notin \mathsf{fn}(P)$, and $\overline{x}.Q$ for $\boldsymbol{\nu} w\,\overline{x}w.Q$ where $w \notin \mathsf{fn}(Q)$. In effect, an interaction between $x.P$ and $\overline{x}.Q$ is simply a synchronization via x: the name sent is fresh and is not free in the continuation of the sender or the continuation of the receiver; the interaction may be viewed as the passing of an empty tuple. Further, in Section 1.2, we saw how the effect of passing a pair of names atomically from one process to another can be achieved in the monadic calculus: if $R \stackrel{\text{def}}{=} x(w).\,w(y).\,w(z).\,P$ and $S \stackrel{\text{def}}{=} \boldsymbol{\nu} w\,\overline{x}w.\,\overline{w}a.\,\overline{w}b.\,Q$ where $w \notin \mathsf{fn}(P, Q, a, b)$, then

$$
\begin{array}{rcl}
R \mid S & \stackrel{\tau}{\longrightarrow} & \boldsymbol{\nu} w\,(w(y).\,w(z).\,P \mid \overline{w}a.\,\overline{w}b.\,Q) \\
& \stackrel{\tau}{\longrightarrow} & \boldsymbol{\nu} w\,(w(z).\,P\{a/y\} \mid \overline{w}b.\,Q) \\
& \stackrel{\tau}{\longrightarrow}\equiv & P\{a,b/y,z\} \mid Q\,.
\end{array}
$$

These are two instances of a general scheme for representing communication of tuples in the monadic calculus.

Definition 3.1.4 The translation $[\![\cdot]\!]$ from polyadic processes to monadic processes is defined by the clauses

$$
\begin{array}{rcl}
[\![x(z_1,\ldots,z_n).\,P]\!] & \stackrel{\text{def}}{=} & x(w).\,w(z_1).\,\cdots.\,w(z_n).\,[\![P]\!] \\
[\![\overline{x}\langle a_1,\ldots,a_n\rangle.\,P]\!] & \stackrel{\text{def}}{=} & \boldsymbol{\nu} w\,\overline{x}w.\,\overline{w}a_1.\,\cdots.\,\overline{w}a_n.\,[\![P]\!]\,,
\end{array}
$$

where in each case, w is a fresh name, together with the stipulation that $[\![\cdot]\!]$ is a homomorphism for the other operators. □

Thus, for example,

$$
\begin{array}{rl}
& [\![x(z_1,\ldots,z_n).\,P \mid \overline{x}\langle a_1,\ldots,a_n\rangle.\,Q]\!] \\
= & x(w).\,w(z_1).\,\cdots.\,w(z_n).\,[\![P]\!] \mid \boldsymbol{\nu} w\,\overline{x}w.\,\overline{w}a_1.\,\cdots.\,\overline{w}a_n.\,[\![Q]\!] \\
\stackrel{\tau}{\longrightarrow} & \boldsymbol{\nu} w\,(w(z_1).\,\cdots.\,w(z_n).\,[\![P]\!] \mid \overline{w}a_1.\,\cdots.\,\overline{w}a_n.\,[\![Q]\!]) \\
\cdots & \\
\stackrel{\tau}{\longrightarrow}\equiv & [\![P]\!]\{a_1,\ldots,a_n/z_1,\ldots,z_n\} \mid [\![Q]\!]\,.
\end{array}
$$

Note that each but the first of the $n+1$ τ transitions is semantically null, in that

$$\nu w\,(w(z_1).\cdots.w(z_n).\,[\![P]\!] \mid \overline{w}a_1.\cdots.\overline{w}a_n.\,[\![Q]\!]) \approx^{\mathrm{c}} [\![P]\!]\{\widetilde{a}/\widetilde{z}\} \mid [\![Q]\!]\,.$$

The first communication, via x, creates a private link w. The remainder transfer the names $a_1, \ldots, a_n$ from sender to receiver via w. The privacy of w ensures that once begun the transfer cannot be interrupted.

Lemma 3.1.5 If P respects a sorting then $[\![P]\!] \stackrel{\bullet}{\approx} P$.

Proof In full detail, the proof is rather long. The reader may care to devise a strategy for it. We will see similar arguments later in the book, for instance in Part V. □

Using Lemma 3.1.5 we can show that the translation is sound.

Exercise 3.1.6 Show that the translation applied to the polyadic processes that respect a fixed sorting Σ is *sound*, that is, that $[\![P]\!] \cong^{\mathrm{c}} [\![Q]\!]$ implies $\Sigma \rhd P \cong^{\mathrm{c}} Q$. □

The translation is not complete, however.

Exercise 3.1.7 Show that the translation is not *complete*, that is, that $\Sigma \rhd P \cong^{\mathrm{c}} Q$ does not imply $[\![P]\!] \cong^{\mathrm{c}} [\![Q]\!]$. (Hint: consider a simple instance of the Expansion Lemma.) □

The translation $[\![\cdot]\!]$ is the first of several we will meet in this Part of the book. These translations are of interest both for the results they give about the expressiveness of various subcalculi, and as illustrations of how to express things in the subcalculi.

We now have a couple of exercises about a translation that exposes disagreements between the parties to a communication. Call a polyadic process P *harmonious* if there is no Q of the form

$$(\nu\widetilde{w})\,((\overline{x}\langle\widetilde{y}\rangle.\,Q_1 + M_1) \mid (x(\widetilde{z}).\,Q_2 + M_2) \mid Q_3)$$

where $|\widetilde{y}| \neq |\widetilde{z}|$ such that $P \Longrightarrow\equiv Q$. Clearly, if P respects a sorting then P is harmonious.

Exercise 3.1.8 Show that the converse is false, that is, that P harmonious does not imply that P respects a sorting. □

Exercise 3.1.9 Fix a name d and a sorting Σ. By modifying $[\![\cdot]\!]$, exhibit a translation $\{\![\cdot]\!\}$ from the polyadic processes in which d does not occur free to monadic processes such that

(1) if P respects Σ then $\{\![P]\!\} \stackrel{\bullet}{\approx} [\![P]\!]$
(2) if P is not harmonious then $\{\![P]\!\} \Downarrow_d$.

The intention is that if $\{\![P]\!\} \Longrightarrow R$ then $R \downarrow_d$ just if a disagreement has arisen between the parties to some communication. □

3.2 Recursion

If a process contains no replications, each of its behaviours is finite. A convenient alternative to replication as a means of expressing infinite behaviour is recursive definition of processes. In fact, recursion is the more familiar of the two primitives: it is present in CCS and in many other calculi and languages, and indeed some papers on π-calculus use recursion rather than replication. Replication is a simple form of recursion, a form that is often just what is needed, for instance in representing data and functions. Moreover, replication permits proof by structural induction. (This will be important in Part V, when we compare the π-calculus with higher-order process calculi.) Further, using replication rather than recursion does not diminish expressive power.

In this section, we first show how to add recursion to π-calculus, and then examine the relationship between replication and recursion. We show that any process involving recursive definitions is representable using replication, and, conversely, that replication is redundant in the presence of recursion.

To be able to give recursive definitions of processes, we introduce process *constants*, ranged over by K, and add two new forms. First, we have *recursive definitions* of the form

$$K \triangleq (\widetilde{x}).\, P$$

where $\mathsf{fn}(P) \subseteq \widetilde{x}$. Secondly, we have a new form of process, the *constant application*,

$$K\lfloor \widetilde{a} \rfloor \,.$$

We sometimes refer to $K\lfloor \widetilde{a} \rfloor$ as an *instance* of the process constant K. The brackets $\lfloor \cdot \rfloor$ indicate that this is a real syntactic construct, not an abbreviation like the pseudo-application for abstractions (Definition 2.4.38).

Formally, processes of the enriched language are interpreted in an environment that records the definitions of the constants. The environment is *finitary*, in the sense that any process depends on only finitely many constant definitions. (Formally, the transitive closure of the relation that relates two different constants

K and K' if an instance of K occurs in the definition of K', is well-founded.) We write const(P) for the finite set of constants on whose definition P depends. Moreover, a fixed sorting Σ is assumed. If $K \triangleq (\widetilde{x}).P$ then a constant application $K\lfloor\widetilde{a}\rfloor$ is well-formed only if $\widetilde{a} : \widetilde{x}$. It is intended that $K\lfloor\widetilde{a}\rfloor$ should behave as $P\{\widetilde{a}/\widetilde{x}\}$.

A simple example is the following description of a kind of 2-place buffer:

$$\begin{array}{lcl} B_0 & \triangleq & (x,y,z).(y(w).B_1\lfloor x,y,z,w\rfloor + x(u).B_0\lfloor x,u,z\rfloor) \\ B_1 & \triangleq & (x,y,z,w).(y(v).B_2\lfloor x,y,z,w,v\rfloor + \overline{z}\langle w\rangle.B_0\lfloor x,y,z\rfloor) \\ B_2 & \triangleq & (x,y,z,w,v).\overline{z}\langle w\rangle.B_1\lfloor x,y,z,v\rfloor\ . \end{array}$$

The instances $B_0\lfloor a,b,c\rfloor$, $B_1\lfloor a,b,c,d\rfloor$, and $B_2\lfloor a,b,c,d,e\rfloor$ represent empty, half-empty, and full states, respectively. In the non-full states, the buffer can accept data via b, and in the non-empty states, it can emit datum d via c. When the buffer is empty, the name to be used for accepting data can be changed by a communication via a. Note that the definitions are mutually recursive. Note also that $x:\gamma$ and $y,z:\gamma'$ and $w,v:\gamma''$, where $\Sigma(\gamma) = \langle\gamma'\rangle$ and $\Sigma(\gamma') = \langle\gamma''\rangle$.

The definition of structural congruence is unchanged. A new reduction rule for constant applications is added to the rules in Table 1.3:

$$\text{R-CONST}\quad \frac{}{K\lfloor\widetilde{a}\rfloor \longrightarrow P\{\widetilde{a}/\widetilde{x}\}}\quad K \triangleq (\widetilde{x}).P\ .$$

And a similar new transition rule is added to the rules in Table 1.5:

$$\text{CONST}\quad \frac{}{K\lfloor\widetilde{a}\rfloor \xrightarrow{\tau} P\{\widetilde{a}/\widetilde{x}\}}\quad K \triangleq (\widetilde{x}).P\ . \qquad (3.3)$$

As an illustration, if the environment is given by the family of three definitions above, then example reductions are

$$\begin{array}{ll} & \boldsymbol{\nu} s\,(\overline{s}\langle d\rangle \mid \overline{a}\langle s\rangle) \mid B_0\lfloor a,b,c\rfloor \\ \longrightarrow & \boldsymbol{\nu} s\,(\overline{s}\langle d\rangle \mid \overline{a}\langle s\rangle) \mid (b(w).B_1\lfloor a,b,c,w\rfloor + a(u).B_0\lfloor a,u,c\rfloor) \\ \longrightarrow & \boldsymbol{\nu} s\,(\overline{s}\langle d\rangle \mid B_0\lfloor a,s,c\rfloor) \\ \longrightarrow & \boldsymbol{\nu} s\,(\overline{s}\langle d\rangle \mid (s(w).B_1\lfloor a,s,c,w\rfloor + a(u).B_0\lfloor a,u,c\rfloor)) \\ \longrightarrow & \boldsymbol{\nu} s\,B_1\lfloor a,s,c,d\rfloor\ , \end{array}$$

and example transitions are

$$\begin{array}{rcl} B_0\lfloor a,b,c\rfloor & \xrightarrow{\tau} & b(w).\,B_1\lfloor a,b,c,w\rfloor + a(u).\,B_0\lfloor a,u,c\rfloor \\ & \xrightarrow{a\langle s\rangle} & B_0\lfloor a,s,c\rfloor \\ & \xrightarrow{\tau} & s(w).\,B_1\lfloor a,s,c,w\rfloor + a(u).\,B_0\lfloor a,u,c\rfloor \\ & \xrightarrow{s\langle d\rangle} & B_1\lfloor a,s,c,d\rfloor \\ & \xrightarrow{\tau} & s(v).\,B_2\lfloor a,s,c,d,v\rfloor + \overline{c}\langle d\rangle.\,B_0\lfloor a,s,c\rfloor \\ & \xrightarrow{\overline{c}\langle d\rangle} & B_0\lfloor a,s,c\rfloor\ . \end{array}$$

Another way to extend reduction to the richer language is to add a new axiom of structural congruence for each constant,

$$K\lfloor\widetilde{a}\rfloor \equiv P\{\widetilde{a}/\widetilde{x}\}\,, \quad \text{if } K \triangleq (\widetilde{x}).\,P\,,$$

instead of the reduction rule R-CONST. And another way to extend the transition relations is to add the rule

$$\frac{P\{\widetilde{a}/\widetilde{x}\} \xrightarrow{\alpha} P'}{K\lfloor\widetilde{a}\rfloor \xrightarrow{\alpha} P'} \quad K \triangleq (\widetilde{x}).\,P \tag{3.4}$$

instead of the rule CONST. We adopt R-CONST and CONST because they conform to the pattern that we will follow in Part III and Part IV to deal with typed processes. (The choice is not significant: it is straightforward to modify the results and proofs below.)

We now turn to showing that any polyadic process involving constants can be represented in the polyadic calculus. Rather than beginning with the general translation scheme, we illustrate the idea by considering the family of three definitions above (the 2-place buffer).

We choose fresh names k_0, k_1, k_2 to stand for the constants B_0, B_1, B_2, and set:

$$\begin{array}{rcl} B_0^* & \stackrel{\text{def}}{=} & !k_0(x,y,z).\,(y(w).\,\overline{k_1}\langle x,y,z,w\rangle.\,\mathbf{0} + x(u).\,\overline{k_0}\langle x,u,z\rangle.\,\mathbf{0}) \\ B_1^* & \stackrel{\text{def}}{=} & !k_1(x,y,z,w).\,(y(v).\,\overline{k_2}\langle x,y,z,w,v\rangle.\,\mathbf{0} + \overline{z}\langle w\rangle.\,\overline{k_0}\langle x,y,z\rangle.\,\mathbf{0}) \\ B_2^* & \stackrel{\text{def}}{=} & !k_2(x,y,z,w,v).\,\overline{z}\langle w\rangle.\,\overline{k_1}\langle x,y,z,v\rangle.\,\mathbf{0}\ . \end{array}$$

A process P interpreted in the environment recording these definitions is represented by

$$(\boldsymbol{\nu} k_0,k_1,k_2)\,(P^* \mid B_0^* \mid B_1^* \mid B_2^*)\,,$$

where P^* is obtained from P by replacing each instance $B_i\lfloor\widetilde{a}\rfloor$ by $\overline{k_i}\langle\widetilde{a}\rangle.\,\mathbf{0}$, for each i.

For instance, here is how the sequence of four reductions above of the term $\boldsymbol{\nu} s\ (\overline{s}\langle d\rangle \mid \overline{a}\langle s\rangle) \mid B_0\lfloor a,b,c\rfloor$ is mimicked, where B^* abbreviates $B_0^* \mid B_1^* \mid B_2^*$, and an output-prefixed process $\overline{x}\langle\widetilde{y}\rangle.\,\mathbf{0}$ is abbreviated to $\overline{x}\langle\widetilde{y}\rangle$:

$$\begin{array}{ll}
& (\boldsymbol{\nu} k_0, k_1, k_2)\,((\boldsymbol{\nu} s\,(\overline{s}\langle d\rangle \mid \overline{a}\langle s\rangle) \mid B_0\lfloor a,b,c\rfloor)^* \mid B^*) \\
= & (\boldsymbol{\nu} k_0, k_1, k_2)\,(\boldsymbol{\nu} s\,(\overline{s}\langle d\rangle \mid \overline{a}\langle s\rangle) \mid \overline{k_0}\langle a,b,c\rangle \mid B^*) \\
\longrightarrow & (\boldsymbol{\nu} k_0, k_1, k_2)\,(\boldsymbol{\nu} s\,(\overline{s}\langle d\rangle \mid \overline{a}\langle s\rangle) \mid (b(w).\,\overline{k_1}\langle a,b,c,w\rangle + a(u).\,\overline{k_0}\langle a,u,c\rangle) \mid B^*) \\
\longrightarrow & (\boldsymbol{\nu} k_0, k_1, k_2, s)\,(\overline{s}\langle d\rangle \mid \overline{k_0}\langle a,s,c\rangle \mid B^*) \\
\longrightarrow & (\boldsymbol{\nu} k_0, k_1, k_2, s)\,(\overline{s}\langle d\rangle \mid (s(w).\,\overline{k_1}\langle a,s,c,w\rangle + a(u).\,\overline{k_0}\langle a,u,c\rangle) \mid B^*) \\
\longrightarrow & (\boldsymbol{\nu} k_0, k_1, k_2, s)\,(\overline{k_1}\langle a,s,c,d\rangle \mid B^*)\,.
\end{array}$$

Note how the first reduction, in which the definition of the constant B_0 is unfolded, is mimicked by the activation of a fresh copy of the appropriate replicated process. The use of replication allows for as many instances of each of the constants as are needed.

The names k_0, k_1, k_2 introduced in the translation are from new sorts γ_0, γ_1, γ_2, respectively, and the sorting is extended in the appropriate way, so that the terms B_0^*, B_1^*, B_2^* respect the extended sorting. Thus, for example, writing Σ also for the extended sorting, $\Sigma(\gamma_1) = \langle \gamma, \gamma', \gamma', \gamma''\rangle$. Note in particular that the names k_0, k_1, k_2 are restricted in the translation of a term, and that they appear only as subjects of prefixes, so there is no possibility of their scopes being extruded.

Turning now to the general case, consider the language π^C of polyadic terms involving instances of an arbitrary set $\{K_i \mid i \in I\}$ of constants. Suppose the environment is given by the definitions: $K_i \triangleq (\widetilde{x}_i).\,P_i$. Fix a sorting Σ. Let $\{\gamma_i \mid i \in I\}$ be new sorts, and extend Σ appropriately, so that $\widetilde{x}_i : \Sigma(\gamma_i)$, where, as before, we write Σ also for the extended sorting. The translation $[\![\cdot]\!]$ from π^C to the language of polyadic processes uses fresh names $\{k_i \mid i \in I\}$ for the constants, where $k_i : \gamma_i$.

First, define an auxiliary translation, $\{\!|\cdot|\!\}$, by setting, for each instance of a constant,

$$\{\!| K_i\lfloor\widetilde{a}\rfloor |\!\} \stackrel{\text{def}}{=} \overline{k_i}\langle\widetilde{a}\rangle.\,\mathbf{0}\,,$$

and stipulating that $\{\!|\cdot|\!\}$ is a homomorphism for the other operators. Then, for each constant K_i set

$$\{\!| K_i |\!\} \stackrel{\text{def}}{=} !k_i(\widetilde{x}_i).\,\{\!| P_i |\!\}\,.$$

Definition 3.2.1 The translation $[\![\cdot]\!]$ from π^C to the polyadic π-calculus is defined by

$$[\![P]\!] \stackrel{\text{def}}{=} (\boldsymbol{\nu} k_1, \ldots, k_n)\,(\{\!|P|\!\} \mid \{\!|K_1|\!\} \mid \ldots \mid \{\!|K_n|\!\})$$

where $\mathsf{const}(P) = \{K_1, \ldots, K_n\}$. □

The translation is not compositional; for instance, $[\![P \mid P']\!] \neq [\![P]\!] \mid [\![P']\!]$.

Using the Replication Theorems, however, we can show that there is a strong correspondence between the actions of P and the actions of $[\![P]\!]$.

Lemma 3.2.2 Suppose $P \in \pi^{\mathcal{C}}$.

(1) If $P \xrightarrow{\alpha} P'$ then $[\![P]\!] \xrightarrow{\alpha}\sim [\![P']\!]$.
(2) If $[\![P]\!] \xrightarrow{\alpha} Q$ then there is P' such that $P \xrightarrow{\alpha} P'$ and $[\![P']\!] \sim Q$.

Proof The first assertion is proved by induction on inference, and the reader may care to check a few cases. □

Exercise 3.2.3 Prove the second part of Lemma 3.2.2. You may find it useful to show:

(1) $[\![K_i\lfloor\tilde{a}\rfloor]\!] \sim^{\mathrm{c}} \tau.\,[\![P_i\{\tilde{a}/\tilde{x}_i\}]\!]$
(2) $[\![\Sigma_j\,\pi_j.\,Q_j]\!] \sim^{\mathrm{c}} \Sigma_j\,\pi_j.\,[\![Q_j]\!]$
(3) $[\![P \mid P']\!] \sim^{\mathrm{c}} [\![P]\!] \mid [\![P']\!]$
(4) $[\![\boldsymbol{\nu} z\,P]\!] \equiv \boldsymbol{\nu} z\,[\![P]\!]$
(5) $[\![!P]\!] \sim^{\mathrm{c}} ![\![P]\!]$. □

Corollary 3.2.4 For $P \in \pi^{\mathcal{C}}$ we have $\Sigma \rhd P \sim^{\mathrm{c}} [\![P]\!]$.

Proof Let $\mathcal{R}$ be the graph of the translation, that is, $\mathcal{R} \stackrel{\mathrm{def}}{=} \{(P, [\![P]\!]) \mid P \in \pi^{\mathcal{C}}\}$. Clearly, $\mathcal{R}$ is closed under substitution. Moreover, by Lemma 3.2.2, $\mathcal{R}$ is a strong bisimulation up to $\sim$. □

Using this, we can obtain the Representation Theorem for Constants. (Note that in the definition of $\simeq^{\mathrm{c}}$ on a π-calculus with constants, the hole does not appear in a constant definition.)

Theorem 3.2.5 (Representation Theorem for Constants) Suppose that $P, Q \in \pi^{\mathcal{C}}$. Then for any Σ we have $\Sigma \rhd P \simeq^{\mathrm{c}} Q$ iff $\Sigma \rhd [\![P]\!] \simeq^{\mathrm{c}} [\![Q]\!]$.

Proof This follows immediately from Corollary 3.2.4 and the inclusion of strong bisimilarity in strong barbed bisimilarity. □

Exercise 3.2.6 Let $[\cdot]$ be the translation from $\pi^{\mathcal{C}}$ to the monadic π-calculus that is the composition of the translation in Definition 3.2.1 followed by the translation in Definition 3.1.4. Show that for any Σ we have $[P] \cong^{\mathrm{c}} [Q]$ implies $\Sigma \rhd P \cong^{\mathrm{c}} Q$. □

In summary, addition of process constants to the π-calculus does not increase expressive power. Note, however, that name-passing and restriction are crucial to the representation of constants in the π-calculus. Replication cannot therefore supplant recursion in CCS in the same way.

We now show, conversely, that if we admit enough constants then replication becomes redundant. To see this, for each polyadic process R of the form $!Q$, choose a listing $\widetilde{x}_R$ of its free names and a constant K_R. Fix a sorting Σ, and define a translation, $\{[\cdot]\}$, from the polyadic processes that respect Σ to terms with instances of the constants K_R instead of replication by setting, for R of the form $!Q$,

$$\{[R]\} \stackrel{\text{def}}{=} K_R\lfloor\widetilde{x}_R\rfloor\,,$$

and stipulating that $\{[\cdot]\}$ is a homomorphism for the other operators. Then, let the (finitary) environment be given by the definitions: for each Q,

$$K_R \triangleq (\widetilde{x}_R)(\{[Q]\} \mid K_R\lfloor\widetilde{x}_R\rfloor) \qquad \text{where } R = !Q\,.$$

We give three examples. First, if $R \stackrel{\text{def}}{=} !Q$ where $Q \stackrel{\text{def}}{=} \overline{x}y.\mathbf{0}$, then

$$K_R \triangleq (x,y).\,(\overline{x}y.\mathbf{0} \mid K_R\lfloor x,y\rfloor)\,,$$

and the transition $R \xrightarrow{\overline{x}y} \mathbf{0} \mid R$ is mimicked by

$$\begin{array}{rcl} K_R\lfloor x,y\rfloor & \xrightarrow{\tau} & \overline{x}y.\mathbf{0} \mid K_R\lfloor x,y\rfloor \\ & \xrightarrow{\overline{x}y} & \mathbf{0} \mid K_R\lfloor x,y\rfloor\,. \end{array}$$

Second, if $R' \stackrel{\text{def}}{=} !Q'$ where $Q' \stackrel{\text{def}}{=} x(z).\mathbf{0}$, and $P \stackrel{\text{def}}{=} R \mid R'$, then the transition $P \xrightarrow{\tau} \mathbf{0} \mid R \mid (\mathbf{0} \mid R')$ is mimicked by

$$\begin{array}{rcl} \{[P]\} & = & K_R\lfloor x,y\rfloor \mid K_{R'}\lfloor x\rfloor \\ & \xrightarrow{\tau} & \overline{x}y.\mathbf{0} \mid K_R\lfloor x,y\rfloor \mid K_{R'}\lfloor x\rfloor \\ & \xrightarrow{\tau} & \overline{x}y.\mathbf{0} \mid K_R\lfloor x,y\rfloor \mid (x(z).\mathbf{0} \mid K_{R'}\lfloor x\rfloor) \\ & \xrightarrow{\tau} & \mathbf{0} \mid K_R\lfloor x,y\rfloor \mid (\mathbf{0} \mid K_{R'}\lfloor x\rfloor)\,. \end{array}$$

Third, if $S \stackrel{\text{def}}{=} !R$ then the transition $S \xrightarrow{\overline{x}y} \mathbf{0} \mid R \mid S$ is mimicked by

$$\begin{array}{rcl} K_S\lfloor x,y\rfloor & \xrightarrow{\tau} & K_R\lfloor x,y\rfloor \mid K_S\lfloor x,y\rfloor \\ & \xrightarrow{\tau} & \overline{x}y.\mathbf{0} \mid K_R\lfloor x,y\rfloor \mid K_S\lfloor x,y\rfloor \\ & \xrightarrow{\overline{x}y} & \mathbf{0} \mid K_R\lfloor x,y\rfloor \mid K_S\lfloor x,y\rfloor\,. \end{array}$$

Lemma 3.2.7

(1) If $P \xrightarrow{\alpha} P'$ then $\{[P]\} \Longrightarrow\xrightarrow{\alpha}\equiv \{[P']\}$.

(2) If $\{\![P]\!\} \xrightarrow{\alpha} Q$ where $\alpha \neq \tau$, then there is P' such that $P \xrightarrow{\alpha} P'$ and $\{\![P']\!\} = Q$.

Proof The proof is by induction on inference. The reader may care to check the cases when P is a replication. □

The result in Lemma 3.2.7(2) does not extend to τ transitions, however. For instance, if $P \stackrel{\text{def}}{=} !\mathbf{0}$ then we have $K_P \triangleq \mathbf{0} \mid K_P$ (omitting empty tuples), and

$$K_P \xrightarrow{\tau} \mathbf{0} \mid K_P \xrightarrow{\tau} \mathbf{0} \mid \mathbf{0} \mid K_P \xrightarrow{\tau} \cdots .$$

Nonetheless, P and $\{\![P]\!\}$ are full bisimilar with respect to the sorting.

Exercise 3.2.8 Show that $\Sigma \rhd P \approx^{\mathrm{c}} \{\![P]\!\}$. (Hint: first show that it suffices to establish $P \approx \{\![P]\!\}$, and then use Lemma 3.2.7 and an additional observation.) □

In view of this result, replication is indeed redundant in the presence of recursion.

Exercise 3.2.9 This exercise illustrates how infinite sums (Section 2.4.2) can be useful for describing succinctly the behaviour of processes. We use a recursive definition to aid readability. Consider the definition

$$K \triangleq (z, x).\,(\tau.\,(z.x \mid K\lfloor z, x \rfloor) + \tau.\,!\overline{z} + \tau.\,\boldsymbol{\nu} y\, K\lfloor y, x \rfloor)\;.$$

Prove that in the π-calculus with infinite sums, $\pi_{\infty +}$,

$$\boldsymbol{\nu} z\, K\lfloor z, x \rfloor \approx \Sigma_{i=0}^{\omega} \tau.\, x^i$$

where $x^0 \stackrel{\text{def}}{=} \mathbf{0}$ and $x^{i+1} \stackrel{\text{def}}{=} x.\,x^i$. (Hint: you may find the technique of bisimulation up to expansion useful.) Is the third summand in the definition of K necessary? □

3.3 Priority-queue data structures

This section is devoted to a worked example. It illustrates the convenience of polyadicity and recursion, and demonstrates how induction and equational reasoning, in particular the Unique-Solution Theorem (Theorem 2.4.40) and the First Replication Theorem (Theorem 2.2.25), can be applied.

The example also illustrates the important fact that name-passing can be combined with communication of other kinds of data. The theory of Part I extends without difficulty to accommodate these other data. We will not go into the details here, as Part III and Part IV discuss many of the points that arise. The non-name data that the processes in the example communicate are integers. The processes also involve obvious operators on integers, and a *conditional* process form:

$$\mathsf{IF}(b_1 \hookrightarrow P_1, \ldots, b_n \hookrightarrow P_n)\ .$$

Informally, this process can behave as P_i if the value of the boolean expression b_i is true; and if the value of every b_i is false, then the process cannot do anything.

Finally, the example illustrates how dynamic data structures can be represented as mobile processes, and introduces several ideas that will be developed further in Section 3.4, which is about data as processes.

The example concerns two implementations of a priority-queue datatype for storing integers. In each case, the queue is implemented as a chain of cells that grows and shrinks as items are inserted and deleted. A dialogue between a process and a queue involves the process requesting an operation, and the queue responding in due course with the appropriate result. In one implementation, at most one operation can be in progress at any time, while in the other, several operations can be in progress simultaneously. Indeed, one can think of the second implementation as being obtained from the first by applying two transformations whose purpose is to increase the scope for concurrent activity. As we will show, however, the two implementations share the observable behaviour prescribed by the following simple recursive definition, which can serve as a specification of the datatype:

$$\begin{aligned} \text{SPEC} \triangleq (i,d,m).\ \ (&i(x,c).\,\overline{c}.\,\text{SPEC}\lfloor i,d,m \oplus x \rfloor \\ \mid\ &d(e,r).\,\mathsf{IF}(\ ?m \hookrightarrow \overline{e}.\,\text{SPEC}\lfloor i,d,m \rfloor, \\ &\qquad\qquad \neg ?m \hookrightarrow \overline{r}\langle m^{\dagger}\rangle.\,\text{SPEC}\lfloor i,d,m\ \ \rfloor))\ . \end{aligned}$$

The constant application $\text{SPEC}\lfloor i,d,\{k_1,\ldots,k_n\}\rfloor$ is a queue storing the multiset $\{k_1,\ldots,k_n\}$ and accessible via the names i and d. A process can request an insertion operation via i, and a deletion via d. To request an insertion, a process sends the integer x to be inserted and a name c to be used by the queue to signal to the process that the operation has been carried out. This signal is akin to the return from a procedure call, or from a method invocation in object-oriented programming. In the definition, $\overline{c}$ represents output of an empty tuple, and $m \oplus x$ the multiset obtained by adding integer x to multiset m. To request a deletion, a process sends two names, e and r. If m is empty, that is, if $?m$ is true, then a signal indicating this is transmitted to the process via e. And if m is not empty then the largest element, $m^{\dagger}$, is removed from m (leaving m^{-}) and returned via r.

A typical inserting process is of the form

$$(\boldsymbol{\nu} c)\,\overline{i}\langle 3,c\rangle.\,c.\,P\ , \tag{3.5}$$

where the c prefixed to P represents input of an empty tuple. The name c is fresh to ensure that the confirmation signal cannot be misdirected to any other process. A typical deleting process is of the form

$$(\boldsymbol{\nu} e, r)\, \overline{d}\langle e, r\rangle. (e. P + r(x). P'),$$

where the names e and r are fresh for the same reason, and the process is prepared for either outcome of the operation.

The notion of sorting introduced in Section 3.1 extends easily to accommodate integers. We write INT for the sort of integers, and introduce sorts INS, DEL, NULL, RES, and GEN. The appropriate sorting has

$$\begin{aligned}
\Sigma(\mathsf{INS}) &\stackrel{\text{def}}{=} \langle \mathsf{INT}, \mathsf{NULL}\rangle \\
\Sigma(\mathsf{DEL}) &\stackrel{\text{def}}{=} \langle \mathsf{NULL}, \mathsf{RES}\rangle \\
\Sigma(\mathsf{NULL}) &\stackrel{\text{def}}{=} \epsilon \\
\Sigma(\mathsf{RES}) &\stackrel{\text{def}}{=} \langle \mathsf{INT}\rangle \\
\Sigma(\mathsf{GEN}) &\stackrel{\text{def}}{=} \langle \mathsf{INS}, \mathsf{DEL}\rangle
\end{aligned}$$

where ϵ is the empty tuple. The sorting is a partial function; it is not defined on INT. In the definition of SPEC, we have $i : \mathsf{INS}$, $d : \mathsf{DEL}$, $x : \mathsf{INT}$, $c, e : \mathsf{NULL}$, and $r : \mathsf{RES}$ (GEN will be explained shortly).

The equivalence we will use to compare the implementations is full bisimilarity with respect to Σ. The processes that feature in the bisimulation game are *closed*, in the sense that no names of sort INT occur free in them. Evolution of processes involves evaluation of truth-valued expressions in conditional processes and of multiset-valued expressions occurring as parameters in instances of constants. In an instance $K\lfloor \widetilde{v} \rfloor$, the arguments $\widetilde{v}$ are evaluated before the transition rule (3.3) is applied. (This corresponds to a call-by-value evaluation strategy; evaluation strategies are discussed further in Remark 6.2.2 and Section 14.3.)

We now describe the implementations. The first is

$$\text{QUEUE} \stackrel{\text{def}}{=} (i, d, m). (\boldsymbol{\nu} g)\, (E\lfloor i, d, g\rfloor \mid G\langle g\rangle)$$

where

$$G \stackrel{\text{def}}{=} (g).\ !g(i, d). E\lfloor i, d, g\rfloor$$

and

$$\begin{aligned}
E \triangleq (i, d, g).\ \ &(i(x, c). (\boldsymbol{\nu} i', d')\, \overline{g}\langle i', d'\rangle. \overline{c}. F\lfloor i, d, x, i', d', g\rfloor \\
&+ d(e, r). \overline{e}. E\lfloor i, d, g\rfloor)
\end{aligned}$$

and

$$\begin{aligned} F \triangleq (i,d,k,i',d',g).\ & \\ (i(x,c).\,\mathsf{IF}(\ & x < k \hookrightarrow (\boldsymbol{\nu} c')\,(\overline{i'}\langle x,c'\rangle \mid c'.\,\overline{c}.\,F\lfloor i,d,k,i',d',g\rfloor), \\ & x \geq k \hookrightarrow (\boldsymbol{\nu} c')\,(\overline{i'}\langle k,c'\rangle \mid c'.\,\overline{c}.\,F\lfloor i,d,x,i',d',g\rfloor)) \\ +\, d(e,r).\,(\boldsymbol{\nu} e',r')\,(\overline{d'}\langle e',r'\rangle & \mid e'.\,\overline{r}\langle k\rangle.\,E\lfloor i,d,g\rfloor \\ & \mid r'(x').\,\overline{r}\langle k\rangle.\,F\lfloor i,d,x',i',d',g\rfloor))\,. \end{aligned}$$

In the definitions, $g : \mathsf{GEN}$.

The process constants E and F represent the two quiescent states of a cell: empty and full, respectively. A quiescent chain will consist of some F-cells, each storing an item, and a terminating E-cell. The instance $\text{QUEUE}\langle i,d,\emptyset\rangle$ represents the empty queue accessible via i and d. It consists of just an E-cell and the replicator G, which allows the queue to grow as necessary. G is an example of how a class in the sense of object-oriented programming can be represented in π-calculus; see Part VII. (We can think of G as representing a class whose objects are cells initially in the empty state.) For instance, when an item x is inserted into an empty queue, the E-cell interacts with G to create a new E-cell with fresh names i' and d', and then becomes an F-cell storing x and the names i' and d'. Thus, after the operation, the queue is

$$(\boldsymbol{\nu} i',d',g)\,(F\lfloor i,d,x,i',d',g\rfloor \mid E\lfloor i',d',g\rfloor \mid G\langle g\rangle)\,.$$

By the First Replication Theorem for the extended language, this process is strong bisimilar with respect to Σ to

$$(\boldsymbol{\nu} i',d')\,((\boldsymbol{\nu} g)\,(F\lfloor i,d,x,i',d',g\rfloor \mid G\langle g\rangle) \mid (\boldsymbol{\nu} g)\,(E\lfloor i',d',g\rfloor \mid G\langle g\rangle))\,,$$

where each cell has its own copy of the generator. We will make use of this fact later.

The items in a non-empty queue are stored in decreasing order. When an item x is inserted into a non-empty queue, the first cell, $F\lfloor i,d,k,i',d',g\rfloor$, requests that the smaller of k and x be inserted into the subqueue accessible via i' and d', and on receiving confirmation that this has been done, confirms via c that the insertion of x has been completed. Thus, in general, when a process requests an insertion into a queue, a wave of activity ripples down the chain until the new item has been inserted at the correct place and a new end cell has been created; a confirmation signal then ripples back up the chain before being transmitted to the inserting process. A deletion proceeds in an analogous sequential fashion. In particular, when a deletion wave reaches the end E-cell in a non-empty queue, the end cell signals to its neighbour that *it* should become an E-cell; the old end cell is then inaccessible, and therefore semantically insignificant, as its names are restricted and no longer free in any other component of the system. Thus, using the general property that if $i, d \notin \mathsf{fn}(P)$ then

$$(\boldsymbol{\nu} i, d)\,(P \mid E\lfloor i, d, g\rfloor) \sim^{\mathrm{c}} P\,, \tag{3.6}$$

up to the equivalence, any quiescent state does indeed consist of some F-cells, a terminating E-cell, and the replicator G.

The second implementation differs from the first mainly in that an F-cell responds to a request from its left neighbour *before* issuing a request to its right neighbour. The new cells, distinguished by the decoration *, are defined by

$$\begin{aligned} E^* \triangleq (i, d, g).\ \ &(i(x, c).\,\overline{c}.\,(\boldsymbol{\nu} i', d')\,\overline{g}\langle i', d'\rangle.\,F^*\lfloor i, d, x, i', d', g\rfloor \\ &+ d(e, r).\,\overline{e}.\,E^*\lfloor i, d, g\rfloor) \end{aligned}$$

and

$$\begin{aligned} F^* \triangleq\ & (i, d, k, i', d', g). \\ & (i(x, c).\,\overline{c}.\,\mathsf{IF}(\ x < k \hookrightarrow (\boldsymbol{\nu} c')\,(\overline{i'}\langle x, c'\rangle \mid c'.\,F^*\lfloor i, d, k, i', d', g\rfloor), \\ & \qquad\qquad\quad x \geq k \hookrightarrow (\boldsymbol{\nu} c')\,(\overline{i'}\langle k, c'\rangle \mid c'.\,F^*\lfloor i, d, x, i', d', g\rfloor)) \\ & + d(e, r).\,\overline{r}\langle k\rangle.\,(\boldsymbol{\nu} e', r')\,(\overline{d'}\langle e', r'\rangle \mid e'.\,E^*\lfloor i, d, g\rfloor \\ & \qquad\qquad\qquad\qquad\qquad\qquad \mid r'(x').\,F^*\lfloor i, d, x', i', d', g\rfloor))\,. \end{aligned}$$

The abstractions G^* and QUEUE* are then defined just like G and QUEUE, but with E^* in place of E.

An F^*-cell differs from an F-cell in that when an insertion is requested, F^* first confirms that it has been done and then requests that its right neighbour carry out the appropriate insertion, and in that when a deletion is requested, F^* first returns its value and then interacts with its right neighbour. There is a similar anticipation in the behaviour of E^* in response to an insertion request. This change in cell behaviour has two related effects. The first is that a process inserting into or deleting from a queue is no longer kept waiting while the operation is carried out: the head cell responds to it immediately; and the second is that several operations can be rippling along a QUEUE*-chain at any one time. The underlying graph structure of the chains is such that there is no possibility of interference between operations, however, and thus the two implementations are behaviourally equivalent, as we now prove.

Lemma 3.3.1 QUEUE $\approx$ QUEUE*.

Proof The strategy is to show that QUEUE and QUEUE* are corresponding components of solutions of a guarded system of equations, and then to appeal to the Unique-Solution Theorem for the extended π-language.

We abbreviate the pair i, d to q, and i', d' to q' etc. For $j \geq 0$ let X_j be a variable over abstractions whose arity is the sequence of sorts $\mathsf{INS}, \mathsf{DEL}, \mathsf{MSET}_j$, where MSET_j is the sort of expressions for multisets of integers of cardinality j. We use m to range over expressions for multisets. The system of equations is

$$\begin{aligned} X_0 \approx (q,m).\ \ &(i(x,c).\,\overline{c}.\,X_1\langle q, m \oplus x\rangle \\ &+ d(e,r).\,\overline{e}.\,X_0\langle q,m\rangle) \end{aligned}$$

and for $j > 0$,

$$\begin{aligned} X_j \approx (q,m).\ \ &(i(x,c).\,\overline{c}.\,X_{j+1}\langle q, m \oplus x\rangle \\ &+ d(e,r).\,\overline{r}\langle m^{\dagger}\rangle.\,X_{j-1}\langle q,m^{-}\rangle)\ . \end{aligned}$$

If m is of sort MSET_j then $k_1^m, \ldots, k_j^m$ stands for its elements in non-increasing order. The putative solutions are Q_j $(j \geq 0)$ and Q_j^* $(j \geq 0)$ where

$$\begin{aligned} Q_j \stackrel{\text{def}}{=}\ \ &(q,m).\,(\boldsymbol{\nu} q_1, \ldots, q_j, g) \\ &(F\lfloor q, k_1^m, q_1, g\rfloor \mid \cdots \mid F\lfloor q_{j-1}, k_j^m, q_j, g\rfloor \mid E\lfloor q_j, g\rfloor \mid G\langle g\rangle) \end{aligned}$$

and

$$\begin{aligned} Q_j^* \stackrel{\text{def}}{=}\ \ &(q,m).\,(\boldsymbol{\nu} q_1, \ldots, q_j, g) \\ &(F^*\lfloor q, k_1^m, q_1, g\rfloor \mid \cdots \mid F^*\lfloor q_{j-1}, k_j^m, q_j, g\rfloor \mid E^*\lfloor q_j, g\rfloor \mid G^*\langle g\rangle)\ . \end{aligned}$$

Note that Q_0 is QUEUE and Q_0^* is QUEUE*. To make terms easier to read, we will elide the fixed parameter g, writing G for $G\langle g\rangle$, $E\lfloor q\rfloor$ for $E\lfloor q, g\rfloor$, and so on.

We prove by induction on j that the equation for X_j is satisfied by Q_j, leaving the proof for Q_j^* to the reader. The proof makes use of some simple equivalences involving conditional process forms.

For the induction base, we have:

$$\begin{aligned} Q_0\langle q,\emptyset\rangle \ &=\ (\boldsymbol{\nu} g)\,(E\lfloor q\rfloor \mid G) \\ &\approx\ i(x,c).\,(\boldsymbol{\nu} g)\,((\boldsymbol{\nu} q')\,\overline{g}\langle q'\rangle.\,\overline{c}.\,F\lfloor q, x, q'\rfloor \mid G) \\ &\quad\ + d(e,r).\,(\boldsymbol{\nu} g)\,(\overline{e}.\,E\lfloor q\rfloor \mid G) \\ &\approx\ i(x,c).\,\tau.\,\overline{c}.\,(\boldsymbol{\nu} q', g)\,(F\lfloor q, x, q'\rfloor \mid E\lfloor q'\rfloor \mid G) \\ &\quad\ + d(e,r).\,\overline{e}.\,(\boldsymbol{\nu} g)\,(E\lfloor q\rfloor \mid G) \\ &\approx\ i(x,c).\,\overline{c}.\,Q_1\langle q, \{x\}\rangle \\ &\quad\ + d(e,r).\,\overline{e}.\,Q_0\langle q,\emptyset\rangle\ . \end{aligned}$$

For the induction step, suppose $j > 0$. As noted earlier, using the First Replication Theorem,

$$\begin{aligned} &(\boldsymbol{\nu} q_1, \ldots, q_j, g)\,(F\lfloor q, k_1^m, q_1\rfloor \mid \cdots \mid F\lfloor q_{j-1}, k_j^m, q_j\rfloor \mid E\lfloor q_j\rfloor \mid G) \\ \approx\ \ &(\boldsymbol{\nu} q_1)\ \ (\ (\boldsymbol{\nu} g)\,(F\lfloor q, k_1^m, q_1\rfloor \mid G) \\ &\qquad\quad \mid (\boldsymbol{\nu} q_2, \ldots, q_j, g)\,(F\lfloor q_1, k_2^m, q_2\rfloor \mid \cdots \mid F\lfloor q_{j-1}, k_j^m, q_j\rfloor \mid E\lfloor q_j\rfloor \mid G))\,, \end{aligned}$$

that is,

$$Q_j\langle q,m\rangle \approx (\boldsymbol{\nu} q_1)\,((\boldsymbol{\nu} g)\,(F\lfloor q,k_1^m,q_1\rfloor \mid G) \mid Q_{j-1}\langle q_1,m^-\rangle)\,.$$

Using this, by the Expansion Lemma and properties of restriction we have

$$\begin{aligned}Q_j\langle q,m\rangle \approx\; & i(x,c).\,(\boldsymbol{\nu} q_1)\,(A \mid Q_{j-1}\langle q_1,m^-\rangle)\\ & + d(e,r).\,(\boldsymbol{\nu} q_1)\,(B \mid Q_{j-1}\langle q_1,m^-\rangle)\end{aligned}$$

where

$$\begin{aligned}A \stackrel{\text{def}}{=} (\boldsymbol{\nu} g)\,(G \mid \mathsf{IF}(\; & x < k_1^m \hookrightarrow (\boldsymbol{\nu} c')\,(\overline{i_1}\langle x,c'\rangle \mid c'.\,\overline{c}.\,F\lfloor q,k_1^m,q_1\rfloor),\\ & x \geq k_1^m \hookrightarrow (\boldsymbol{\nu} c')\,(\overline{i_1}\langle k_1^m,c'\rangle \mid c'.\,\overline{c}.\,F\lfloor q,x,q_1\rfloor)))\end{aligned}$$

and

$$\begin{aligned}B \stackrel{\text{def}}{=} (\boldsymbol{\nu} g)\,(G \mid (\boldsymbol{\nu} e',r')\,(\overline{d_1}\langle e',r'\rangle\; & \mid e'.\,\overline{r}\langle k_1^m\rangle.\,E\lfloor q\rfloor\\ & \mid r'(x').\,\overline{r}\langle k_1^m\rangle.\,F\lfloor q,x',q_1\rfloor))\,.\end{aligned}$$

Hence, using the induction hypothesis, further expansion, and properties of restriction,

$$\begin{aligned}Q_j\langle q,m\rangle \approx\; & i(x,c).\,\mathsf{IF}(x < k_1^m \hookrightarrow \tau.\,\tau.\,\overline{c}.\,D,\; x \geq k_1^m \hookrightarrow \tau.\,\tau.\,\overline{c}.\,D')\\ & + d(e,r).\,\tau.\,\tau.\,\overline{r}\langle k_1^m\rangle.\,D''\end{aligned}$$

where

$$D \stackrel{\text{def}}{=} (\boldsymbol{\nu} q_1)\,((\boldsymbol{\nu} g)\,(F\lfloor q,k_1^m,q_1\rfloor \mid G) \mid Q_j\langle q_1,m^- \oplus x\rangle)$$

and

$$D' \stackrel{\text{def}}{=} (\boldsymbol{\nu} q_1)\,((\boldsymbol{\nu} g)\,(F\lfloor q,x,q_1\rfloor \mid G) \mid Q_j\langle q_1,m\rangle)$$

and, if $j = 1$ then

$$D'' \stackrel{\text{def}}{=} (\boldsymbol{\nu} q_1)\,((\boldsymbol{\nu} g)\,(E\lfloor q\rfloor \mid G) \mid Q_0\langle q_1,\emptyset\rangle)\,,$$

while if $j > 1$ then

$$D'' \stackrel{\text{def}}{=} (\boldsymbol{\nu} q_1)\,((\boldsymbol{\nu} g)\,(F\lfloor q,k_2^m,q_1\rfloor \mid G) \mid Q_{j-1}\langle q_1,m^{--}\rangle)\,.$$

Hence, using Lemma 2.4.18 to eliminate τ prefixes and the First Replication Theorem, and also in the case $j = 1$ property (3.6) above,

$$\begin{aligned}Q_j\langle q,m\rangle \approx\; & i(x,c).\,\overline{c}.\,Q_{j+1}\langle q,m \oplus x\rangle\\ & + d(e,r).\,\overline{r}\langle m^\dagger\rangle.\,Q_{j-1}\langle q,m^-\rangle\,,\end{aligned}$$

as required. □

Moreover, the implementations satisfy the specification SPEC:

Exercise 3.3.2 Show that $\mathrm{QUEUE}\langle i, d, \emptyset\rangle \approx^{\mathrm{c}} \mathrm{SPEC}\lfloor i, d, \emptyset\rfloor$. (Hint: appeal to the Unique-Solution Theorem.) □

We will revisit this example in Section 7.4 and Section 20.4. We will see that in conjunction with a formal semantic definition for an object-oriented programming language by translation to π-calculus, the above reasoning establishes the soundness of program transformations that increase concurrency within systems of objects.

3.4 Data as processes

In general, processes interact by passing one another data. The only data of the π-calculus are names. It may well be convenient, however – as illustrated in the example in Section 3.3, for instance – to admit other atomic data, such as integers, and structured data, such as tuples and multisets. It is in the spirit of process calculus generally to allow the data language to be tailored to the application at hand, admitting sets, lists, trees, and so on as convenient. And one *should* admit the relevant data when using π-calculus to reason about systems.

Remarkably, however, all such data can be expressed in the π-calculus. This section shows how this is possible. The main motivation is to illustrate some techniques for representing systems and reasoning about them that arise frequently when using π-calculus. A further point of interest is the contrast with CCS, where no analogous representation of data is possible.

The section comprises two subsections. The first explains the basic ideas, by showing how to represent truth-values and integers and operations on them. The second illustrates how the values of arbitrary datatypes and operations on them can be expressed, where by a datatype we mean the collection of values built recursively using a finite set of constructors.

Expressing data gives a further illustration of the convenience of recursion and, especially, polyadicity. If desired, the translations studied in Section 3.1 can be applied to obtain representations in the monadic π-calculus. Throughout the section we will use a fixed sorting Σ, which will be revealed as we proceed.

3.4.1 Truth-values and integers

To begin, let us consider the simplest non-degenerate data type: the truth-values, $\{\mathsf{true}, \mathsf{false}\}$. Consider first the abstractions

$$\mathrm{T} \stackrel{\mathrm{def}}{=} (x).\, x(t, f).\, \bar{t}.\mathbf{0} \quad \text{and} \quad \mathrm{F} \stackrel{\mathrm{def}}{=} (x).\, x(t, f).\, \bar{f}.\mathbf{0}\ .$$

An instance of one of these abstractions represents a *located copy* of a truth-value. For example, $\mathrm{T}\langle b\rangle$ is a copy of true located at b. The instance $\mathrm{T}\langle b\rangle$ is the process $b(t,f).\,\bar{t}$ (where as usual we elide $.\,\mathbf{0}$). When this process receives a pair of names via b, it responds by signalling on the first of them. The instance $\mathrm{F}\langle b\rangle$, on the other hand, is the process $b(t,f).\,\bar{f}$, and on receiving a pair of names via b, this process signals on the second of the pair. Note in passing that there is a formal analogy with Church's representation of copies of truth-values in λ-calculus as the λ-terms $\lambda tf.\,t$ and $\lambda tf.\,f$. There is a similar analogy for other types of value, as we will see. The name x has sort BOOL, and the names t and f sort NULL, where

$$\Sigma(\mathsf{BOOL}) \stackrel{\mathrm{def}}{=} \langle \mathsf{NULL}, \mathsf{NULL}\rangle$$

and, as before, $\Sigma(\mathsf{NULL}) \stackrel{\mathrm{def}}{=} \epsilon$, the empty tuple.

A process co-located at $\bar{b}$, such as

$$R \stackrel{\mathrm{def}}{=} (\boldsymbol{\nu} t,f)\,\bar{b}\langle t,f\rangle.\,(t.\,P + f.\,Q)\,,$$

can interact with a copy of a truth-value located at b to determine how to proceed. For instance,

$$R \mid \mathrm{T}\langle b\rangle \Longrightarrow\equiv P$$

and

$$R \mid \mathrm{F}\langle b\rangle \Longrightarrow\equiv Q\,,$$

where it is assumed that $t,f \notin \mathsf{fn}(P,Q)$. The interaction between R and a copy of a truth-value located at b takes the form of a dialogue in which R asks the copy to disclose its value by sending it a pair of names via b, and the copy answers by signalling on the appropriate one. For this to work correctly, it is essential that the names supplied in the question be fresh: if they were not, the answer could be misdirected to some other process, and the questioner could accept an answer from some other process. The restrictions on t and f in R are therefore essential, and an analogous representation is not possible in CCS.

The act of interrogating a process $\mathrm{T}\langle b\rangle$ or $\mathrm{F}\langle b\rangle$ for its value destroys it. Persistence of data is represented using replication. For the truth-values we set

$$\mathrm{TRUE} \stackrel{\mathrm{def}}{=} (x).\,!\mathrm{T}\langle x\rangle \quad \text{and} \quad \mathrm{FALSE} \stackrel{\mathrm{def}}{=} (x).\,!\mathrm{F}\langle x\rangle\,.$$

Instances of these abstractions can conduct arbitrarily-many dialogues, yielding the same value in each. For example, with R as above,

$$R \mid R \mid \mathrm{TRUE}\langle b\rangle \Longrightarrow\equiv P \mid P \mid \mathrm{TRUE}\langle b\rangle$$

and

$$R \mid R \mid \mathrm{FALSE}\langle b \rangle \Longrightarrow= Q \mid Q \mid \mathrm{FALSE}\langle b \rangle \,,$$

again assuming that $t, f \notin \mathsf{fn}(P, Q)$.

We now consider how operations on truth-values can be represented as processes. The simplest example is the abstraction

$$\mathrm{NEG} \stackrel{\mathrm{def}}{=} (x, y).\, !x(t, f).\, (\nu t', f')\, \overline{y}\langle t', f' \rangle.\, (t'.\, \overline{f} + f'.\, \overline{t}) \,.$$

It represents the operation of negation on truth-values: the composition, restricted on b, of the instance $\mathrm{NEG}\langle a, b \rangle$ and a truth-value process located at b behaves as the other truth-value process located at a. For instance:

Lemma 3.4.1 $\nu b\, (\mathrm{NEG}\langle a, b \rangle \mid \mathrm{TRUE}\langle b \rangle) \approx \mathrm{FALSE}\langle a \rangle$.

Proof The proof appeals to the Unique-Solution Theorem.

For $i \geq 0$ let X_i be a variable over abstractions whose arity is the tuple of sorts consisting of BOOL followed by i NULLs. Consider the system

$$X_i \approx (x, \widetilde{f}).\, (x(t, f).\, X_{i+1}\langle x, \widetilde{f}, f \rangle + \Sigma_{f \in \widetilde{f}}\, \overline{f}.\, X_{i-1}\langle x, \widetilde{g} \rangle)$$

where $\widetilde{g}$ is $\widetilde{f}$ with f removed. We will show that the abstractions FALSE and $\mathrm{NT} \stackrel{\mathrm{def}}{=} (x).\, \nu y\, (\mathrm{NEG}\langle x, y \rangle \mid \mathrm{TRUE}\langle y \rangle)$ are corresponding components of solutions of the system. By the Unique-Solution Theorem, it follows that $\mathrm{FALSE}\langle a \rangle \approx \mathrm{NT}\langle a \rangle$ for any $a : \mathsf{BOOL}$.

To this end, set $F_0 \stackrel{\mathrm{def}}{=} \mathrm{FALSE}$ and for $i > 0$

$$F_i \stackrel{\mathrm{def}}{=} (x, \widetilde{f}).\, (F_0\langle x \rangle \mid \Pi_{f \in \widetilde{f}}\, \overline{f}) \,,$$

where Π stands for composition. Set also $G_0 \stackrel{\mathrm{def}}{=} \mathrm{NT}$ and for $i > 0$

$$G_i \stackrel{\mathrm{def}}{=} (x, \widetilde{f}).\, (G_0\langle x \rangle \mid \Pi_{f \in \widetilde{f}}\, \overline{f}) \,.$$

Fix i and $a : \mathsf{BOOL}$ and $\widetilde{f} : \mathsf{NULL}^i$. Then, from the definitions, using the Expansion Lemma,

$$F_i\langle a, \widetilde{f} \rangle \approx a(t, f).\, F_{i+1}\langle a, \widetilde{f}, f \rangle + \Sigma_{f \in \widetilde{f}}\, \overline{f}.\, F_{i-1}\langle a, \widetilde{g} \rangle$$

where $\widetilde{g}$ is $\widetilde{f}$ with f removed, and by a simple calculation using expansion,

$$G_i\langle a, \widetilde{f} \rangle \approx a(t, f).\, \tau.\, \tau.\, G_{i+1}\langle a, \widetilde{f}, f \rangle + \Sigma_{f \in \widetilde{f}}\, \overline{f}.\, G_{i-1}\langle a, \widetilde{g} \rangle \,.$$

The result follows by eliminating the τ prefixes (Lemma 2.4.18). □

A second example is the abstraction

$$\begin{aligned}\text{IMP} \stackrel{\text{def}}{=} \ & (x, y_1, y_2).\\ & !x(t,f).\,(\boldsymbol{\nu} t_1, f_1)\,\overline{y_1}\langle t_1, f_1\rangle.(f_1.\overline{t}\\ & \qquad + t_1.\,(\boldsymbol{\nu} t_2, f_2)\,\overline{y_2}\langle t_2, f_2\rangle.\,(f_2.\overline{f} + t_2.\overline{t}))\ .\end{aligned}$$

It represents the operation of formal implication on truth-values: the composition, restricted on b_1 and b_2, of the instance $\text{IMP}\langle a, b_1, b_2\rangle$ and truth-value processes located at b_1 and b_2, behaves as a truth-value process located at a; if the truth-values located at b_1 and b_2 are v_1 and v_2, then the truth-value located at a is (v_1 implies v_2).

Exercise 3.4.2 Show that if $B_1, B_2 \in \{\text{TRUE}, \text{FALSE}\}$ then

$$(\boldsymbol{\nu} b_1, b_2)\,(\text{IMP}\langle a, b_1, b_2\rangle \mid B_1\langle b_1\rangle \mid B_2\langle b_2\rangle) \approx B\langle a\rangle$$

where if $B_1 = \text{TRUE}$ and $B_2 = \text{FALSE}$, then $B = \text{FALSE}$, and otherwise $B = \text{TRUE}$. □

The kind of question-answer dialogue illustrated above, in which evaluation of data expressions is represented by reduction, is the key to representing all kinds of data as processes, as we will see below.

The idea used in representing truth-values can be extended to any other finite datatype. For the type {*north*,*east*,*south*,*west*}, for example, we can use

$$\begin{aligned}\text{NORTH} &\stackrel{\text{def}}{=} (x)\ !x(n,e,s,w).\,\overline{n}\\ \text{EAST} &\stackrel{\text{def}}{=} (x)\ !x(n,e,s,w).\,\overline{e}\end{aligned}$$

and so on, where $x : \mathsf{DIR}$ and

$$\Sigma(\mathsf{DIR}) \stackrel{\text{def}}{=} \langle \mathsf{NULL}, \mathsf{NULL}, \mathsf{NULL}, \mathsf{NULL}\rangle\ .$$

Before turning to the general case, we examine the simplest infinite datatype: the natural numbers. We will give a representation in base 1; it is straightforward to modify it to obtain representations in other bases (see Exercise 3.4.5).

We write $[\![k]\!]$ for the abstraction representing integer k. It is

$$[\![k]\!] \stackrel{\text{def}}{=} (x).\ !x(z,o).\,(\overline{o}.\,)^k\overline{z}\,,$$

where $(\overline{o}.\,)^k$ abbreviates $\overline{o}.\,\ldots.\overline{o}.$ (k occurrences). The sort of x is $\mathsf{INTEGER}$, and

$$\Sigma(\mathsf{INTEGER}) \stackrel{\text{def}}{=} \langle \mathsf{NULL}, \mathsf{NULL}\rangle\ .$$

Instances of the abstractions $[\![k]\!]$ represent located integers. For example, $[\![3]\!]\langle a\rangle$ is 3 located at a. It is the process $!a(z,o).\overline{o}.\overline{o}.\overline{o}.\overline{z}$. On receiving a pair of names z, o via a, this process signals three times on o and then once on z, the last to indicate that it has finished delivering its value.

Operations on integers can be expressed as processes. The following abstraction, for example, represents successor:

$$succ \stackrel{\text{def}}{=} (x, y).\ !x(z, o).\ \overline{o}.\ \overline{y}\langle z, o\rangle\ .$$

Exercise 3.4.3

(1) Show that

$$\boldsymbol{\nu} b\,(succ\langle a, b\rangle \mid [\![k]\!]\langle b\rangle) \approx [\![k+1]\!]\langle a\rangle\ .$$

(2) Show that $succ^*$ is also a suitable representation of successor, where

$$\begin{array}{rcl} succ^* & \stackrel{\text{def}}{=} & (x, y).\ !x(z, o).\ (\boldsymbol{\nu} z', o')\ \overline{y}\langle z', o'\rangle.\ copy^*\lfloor z, o, z', o'\rfloor \\ copy^* & \triangleq & (z, o, z', o').\ (z'.\ \overline{o}.\ \overline{z} + o'.\ \overline{o}.\ copy^*\lfloor z, o, z', o'\rfloor)\ . \end{array}$$

(3) Give an abstraction that represents the predecessor function on natural numbers. □

On receiving a pair of names z, o, an instance of $[\![k]\!]$ delivers its value by means of k signals on o, and indicates that it has finished with a signal on z. The following exercise shows why the final signal on z is important.

Exercise 3.4.4 Suppose $[k]$ is defined by

$$[k] \stackrel{\text{def}}{=} (x).\ !x(o).\ (\overline{o}.\ )^{k+1}\ .$$

Show that with this representation, it is impossible to express the operation of testing for zero, that is, that there is no process Z such that $\boldsymbol{\nu} x\,(Z \mid [0]\langle x\rangle) \approx \overline{t}$ and $\boldsymbol{\nu} x\,(Z \mid [k]\langle x\rangle) \approx \overline{f}$ if $k > 0$, where t and f are different names. (Hint: suppose Z satisfies the requirements, and observe first that then $\boldsymbol{\nu} x\,(Z \mid [0]\langle x\rangle) \stackrel{\overline{t}}{\Longrightarrow}$.) □

The following exercise explores in more detail how evaluation of data is represented as reduction.

Exercise 3.4.5 This exercise concerns natural-number expressions written in base 2, and truth-valued expressions built from them. Let N be the set of strings over the alphabet $\{0, 1\}$ whose elements are the singleton string 0 and all strings ending with a 1, and think of strings in N as representing natural numbers in base 2 with least significant bit first. Consider the classes of expressions given as follows, where c ranges over N:

$$\begin{array}{rcl} e & ::= & c \mid e + e' \\ b & ::= & \mathsf{true} \mid \mathsf{false} \mid e = e'\ . \end{array}$$

Let *val* map each expression to its value, which is a string in N or one of true and false.

By analogy with the representation in base 1 given above, for each $c \in N$ define $[\![c]\!]$ as follows, where ε is the empty string:

$$\begin{aligned} [\![\varepsilon]\!] &\stackrel{\text{def}}{=} (z,o,e).\,\overline{e}.\,\mathbf{0} \\ [\![0c]\!] &\stackrel{\text{def}}{=} (z,o,e).\,\overline{z}.\,[\![c]\!]\langle z,o,e\rangle \\ [\![1c]\!] &\stackrel{\text{def}}{=} (z,o,e).\,\overline{o}.\,[\![c]\!]\langle z,o,e\rangle\,. \end{aligned}$$

Give abstractions *plus* and *equal* of the appropriate sorts so that

$$\begin{aligned} (\boldsymbol{\nu} a_1,a_2)\,(\mathit{plus}\langle a,a_1,a_2\rangle \mid [\![e_1]\!]\langle a_1\rangle \mid [\![e_2]\!]\langle a_2\rangle) &\approx [\![c]\!]\langle a\rangle \\ (\boldsymbol{\nu} a_1,a_2)\,(\mathit{equal}\langle d,a_1,a_2\rangle \mid [\![e_1]\!]\langle a_1\rangle \mid [\![e_2]\!]\langle a_2\rangle) &\approx [\![b]\!]\langle d\rangle \end{aligned}$$

where $c = \mathit{val}(e_1 + e_2)$ and $b = \mathit{val}(e_1 = e_2)$. □

3.4.2 Arbitrary datatypes

We have seen by example how the values of finite datatypes and operations on them can be represented as processes. We now show the same for arbitrary datatypes.

We begin by looking again at natural numbers. Consider the datatype declaration

$$\texttt{type Nat} \;=\; \texttt{zero} \mid \texttt{succ Nat}\,.$$

Clearly, we could represent the expressions of this datatype as we did the integer constants above. That representation is simple and illustrates some important ideas. But it does not lend itself to generalization. We therefore present another representation scheme that does generalize to arbitrary datatypes.

Corresponding to the constructors `zero` and `succ`, we have abstractions $[\![\texttt{zero}]\!]$ and $[\![\texttt{succ}]\!]$ defined by

$$\begin{aligned} [\![\texttt{zero}]\!] &\stackrel{\text{def}}{=} (x).\,!x(z,s).\,\overline{z} \\ [\![\texttt{succ}]\!] &\stackrel{\text{def}}{=} (x,y).\,!x(z,s).\,\overline{s}\langle y\rangle\,. \end{aligned}$$

Then, for each expression e of type `Nat`, we set

$$[\![\texttt{succ}\ e]\!] \stackrel{\text{def}}{=} (x).\,\boldsymbol{\nu} y\,([\![\texttt{succ}]\!]\langle x,y\rangle \mid [\![e]\!]\langle y\rangle)\,. \qquad (3.7)$$

Note the close affinity between expression structure and process structure. We have $x, y : \mathsf{NAT}$ and $s : \mathsf{SUCC}$ and $z : \mathsf{NULL}$, where the sorting has

$$\begin{aligned} \Sigma(\mathsf{NAT}) &\stackrel{\text{def}}{=} \langle \mathsf{NULL}, \mathsf{SUCC}\rangle \\ \Sigma(\mathsf{SUCC}) &\stackrel{\text{def}}{=} \langle \mathsf{NAT}\rangle\,. \end{aligned}$$

The abstraction $[\![\texttt{zero}]\!]$ is identical to $[\![0]\!]$ in Section 3.4.1. But the instances of $[\![\texttt{succ zero}]\!]$ and $[\![1]\!]$ engage in different dialogues with interrogating processes, and the same is true of $[\![\texttt{succ (succ zero)}]\!]$ and $[\![2]\!]$, and so on. For instance, consider $[\![2]\!]\langle a\rangle$, which is the process $!a(z,o).\,\overline{o}.\,\overline{o}.\,\overline{z}$, and suppose a process is to proceed to P if the value located at a is 2 and to Q if it is not. An appropriate process is

$$(\boldsymbol{\nu} z,o)\,(\overline{a}\langle z,o\rangle \mid (z.\,Q + o.\,(z.\,Q + o.\,(z.\,P + o.\,Q))))\;.$$

Suppose, on the other hand, a process is to evolve similarly, but by examining the a-located process $[\![\texttt{succ (succ zero)}]\!]\langle a\rangle$, which is

$$\boldsymbol{\nu} b\,(\,!a(z,s).\,\overline{s}\langle b\rangle \mid \boldsymbol{\nu} c\,(\,!b(z_1,s_1).\,\overline{s_1}\langle c\rangle \mid !c(z_2,s_2).\,\overline{z_2}))\;.$$

Then an appropriate process is

$$\begin{aligned}&(\boldsymbol{\nu} z,s)\,(\overline{a}\langle z,s\rangle \mid\\ &\qquad (z.\,Q + s(b).\,(\boldsymbol{\nu} z_1,s_1)\,(\overline{b}\langle z_1,s_1\rangle \mid\\ &\qquad\qquad (z_1.\,Q + s_1(c).\,(\boldsymbol{\nu} z_2,s_2)\,(\overline{c}\langle z_2,s_2\rangle \mid\\ &\qquad\qquad\qquad (z_2.\,P + s_2(r).\,Q))))))\;.\end{aligned}$$

The dialogue involving $[\![\texttt{succ (succ zero)}]\!]$ is longer than that involving $[\![2]\!]$. But this is more than compensated for by the fact that the idea illustrated in (3.7) can be applied to arbitrary datatypes. Another advantage is that by using $[\![\texttt{succ (succ zero)}]\!]$ rather than $[\![2]\!]$ and so on, it is sometimes simpler to express operations on natural numbers as processes. (This is more evident in the subcalculus without sum.)

Exercise 3.4.6 Suppose the datatype `Nat` and the abstractions $[\![\texttt{zero}]\!]$ and $[\![\texttt{succ}]\!]$ are as above.

(1) Give an abstraction that represents the test-for-zero operation on `Nat`.
(2) Give an abstraction that represents the predecessor function on `Nat`.
(3) Give an abstraction that represents the addition function on `Nat`. □

When first interrogated, an instance of $[\![\texttt{succ}\ e]\!]$ emits a private name that gives access to an instance of $[\![e]\!]$, and that same name is freely emitted in subsequent interrogations. The instance of $[\![e]\!]$ in question may therefore be shared among interrogating processes. Suppose, on the other hand, that we define $\{[\texttt{zero}]\}$ just as we defined $[\![\texttt{zero}]\!]$, but we define the abstractions $\{[\texttt{succ}\ e]\}$ by

$$\{[\texttt{succ}\ e]\} \stackrel{\text{def}}{=} (x).\ !x(z,s).\,\boldsymbol{\nu} y\,(\overline{s}\langle y\rangle \mid \{[e]\}\langle y\rangle)\;.$$

An instance of $\{\![\texttt{succ}\ e]\!\}$ emits a private name on *each* interrogation, and each such name gives access to a different instance of $\{\![e]\!\}$, so that there is no sharing.

The two representations, $[\![e]\!]$ and $\{\![e]\!\}$, of an expression e of type `Nat` are not bisimilar. As we will see in Example 10.2.3, however, they are equivalent in an appropriate typed calculus.

To see how the construction generalizes, consider now the following declaration of a datatype of binary trees:

$$\texttt{type tree} \;=\; \texttt{leaf Nat} \;\big|\; \texttt{node Nat tree tree}\,.$$

The expression `leaf` e represents a singleton tree storing e, and the expression `node` $e\ t\ t'$ a tree with root storing e, left subtree t, and right subtree t'. The abstractions $[\![\texttt{leaf}]\!]$ and $[\![\texttt{node}]\!]$ that correspond to the constructors `leaf` and `node` are

$$\begin{array}{rcl}[\![\texttt{leaf}]\!] & \stackrel{\text{def}}{=} & (x,v).\,!x(\ell,n).\,\overline{\ell}\langle v\rangle \\ [\![\texttt{node}]\!] & \stackrel{\text{def}}{=} & (x,v,y,z).\,!x(\ell,n).\,\overline{n}\langle v,y,z\rangle\,.\end{array}$$

The instance $[\![\texttt{leaf}]\!]\langle a,b\rangle$ is a leaf-process located at a and storing the location b of a number-process. The instance $[\![\texttt{node}]\!]\langle a,b,c,d\rangle$ is a node-process located at a and storing the location b of a number-process and the locations c and d of the leaf- or node-processes that are its left and right children. A process interrogates $[\![\texttt{leaf}]\!]\langle a,b\rangle$ and $[\![\texttt{node}]\!]\langle a,b,c,d\rangle$ by providing a pair of names, ℓ and n, via a; the leaf-process responds by sending b on ℓ, and the node-process by sending b, c, and d on n. We have $x,y,z:\mathsf{CELL}$ and $\ell:\mathsf{LEAF}$ and $n:\mathsf{NODE}$ and $v:\mathsf{NAT}$, and the sorting has

$$\begin{array}{rcl}\Sigma(\mathsf{CELL}) & \stackrel{\text{def}}{=} & \langle\mathsf{LEAF},\mathsf{NODE}\rangle \\ \Sigma(\mathsf{LEAF}) & \stackrel{\text{def}}{=} & \langle\mathsf{NAT}\rangle \\ \Sigma(\mathsf{NODE}) & \stackrel{\text{def}}{=} & \langle\mathsf{NAT},\mathsf{CELL},\mathsf{CELL}\rangle\,.\end{array}$$

For expressions e of type `Nat` and t, t' of type `tree`, we then define

$$\begin{array}{rcl}[\![\texttt{leaf}\ e]\!] & \stackrel{\text{def}}{=} & (x).\,\boldsymbol{\nu}v\,([\![\texttt{leaf}]\!]\langle x,v\rangle \mid [\![e]\!]\langle v\rangle) \\ [\![\texttt{node}\ e\ t\ t']\!] & \stackrel{\text{def}}{=} & (x).\,(\boldsymbol{\nu}v,y,z)\,([\![\texttt{node}]\!]\langle x,v,y,z\rangle \mid [\![e]\!]\langle v\rangle \mid [\![t]\!]\langle y\rangle \mid [\![t']\!]\langle z\rangle)\,.\end{array}$$

For instance, abbreviating `succ zero` to one and so on,

$$[\![\texttt{node}\ \mathsf{two}\ (\texttt{leaf}\ \mathsf{one})\ (\texttt{node}\ \mathsf{four}\ (\texttt{leaf}\ \mathsf{three})\ (\texttt{leaf}\ \mathsf{five}))]\!]\langle a\rangle$$

is structurally congruent to the tree-process

$$\begin{aligned}(\boldsymbol{\nu} v_1, v_2, v_3, v_4, v_5, \ell_1, \ell_2, \ell_3, b)\,(\; & [\![\mathsf{node}]\!]\langle a, v_2, \ell_1, b\rangle \mid [\![\mathsf{two}]\!]\langle v_2\rangle \\ \mid\; & [\![\mathtt{leaf}]\!]\langle \ell_1, v_1\rangle \mid [\![\mathsf{one}]\!]\langle v_1\rangle \\ \mid\; & [\![\mathsf{node}]\!]\langle b, v_4, \ell_2, \ell_3\rangle \mid [\![\mathsf{four}]\!]\langle v_4\rangle \\ \mid\; & [\![\mathtt{leaf}]\!]\langle \ell_2, v_3\rangle \mid [\![\mathsf{three}]\!]\langle v_3\rangle \\ \mid\; & [\![\mathtt{leaf}]\!]\langle \ell_3, v_5\rangle \mid [\![\mathsf{five}]\!]\langle v_5\rangle) \,.\end{aligned}$$

A process can navigate a tree-process by interrogating its component node- and leaf-processes, and can thereby find and interrogate its component number-processes.

As an example of how operations on trees can be represented, consider the operation mir on expressions of type `tree` defined by: $mir(\mathtt{leaf}\ e) = \mathtt{leaf}\ e$ and $mir(\mathtt{node}\ e\ t_1\ t_2) = \mathtt{node}\ e\ (mir\ t_2)\ (mir\ t_1)$. So $mir(t)$ is the mirror image of t. The operation mir is represented by the abstraction $[\![mir]\!]$ defined by

$$[\![mir]\!] \overset{\text{def}}{=} (x, x').\,(\boldsymbol{\nu} g, h)\,(M\lfloor x, x', g, h\rfloor \mid G\langle g\rangle \mid H\langle h\rangle)$$

where

$$\begin{aligned} M &\triangleq (x, x', g, h).\,(\boldsymbol{\nu}\ell, n)\,\overline{x}\langle \ell, n\rangle. \\ &\quad\;\; (\ell(v).\,\overline{g}\langle x', v\rangle \\ &\quad\;\; + n(v, y, z).\,(\boldsymbol{\nu} y', z')\,\overline{h}\langle x', v, y', z'\rangle.\,(M\lfloor z, y', g, h\rfloor \mid M\lfloor y, z', g, h\rfloor)) \\ G &\overset{\text{def}}{=} (g).\,!g(x, v).\,[\![\mathtt{leaf}]\!]\langle x, v\rangle \\ H &\overset{\text{def}}{=} (h).\,!h(x, v, y, z).\,[\![\mathtt{node}]\!]\langle x, v, y, z\rangle\,. \end{aligned}$$

In the subterm $M\lfloor x, x', g, h\rfloor$ of $[\![mir]\!]$, x is the name by which M can access the root within a tree-process, and x' is the name of the root within the mirror tree-process that M constructs.

Exercise 3.4.7 Show that if t is an expression of type `tree`, then

$$\nu a\,([\![mir]\!]\langle a, b\rangle \mid [\![t]\!]\langle a\rangle) \approx [\![mir(t)]\!]\langle b\rangle\,.$$

□

We close this chapter with an exercise on representing list structures as processes.

Exercise 3.4.8 Consider the following declaration of a datatype of lists of natural numbers:

```
type list  =  nil | cons Nat list .
```

(1) By analogy with the representation of expressions of type `tree`, give an appropriate representation of expressions of type `list`.
(2) Define an abstraction that represents the operation of reversing a list. □

4

Behavioural Equivalence, continued

4.1 Distinctions

The π-calculus makes no syntactic distinction between instantiable names and non-instantiable names, that is, between variables and constants. Sometimes, however, it is desirable to treat certain names as constants, that is, as not subject to instantiation. More generally, it is sometimes useful to work in a setting where certain names cannot be instantiated to the same name. This more general case is no more difficult technically than treating names as constants. This section shows how to treat the more general case, by means of a family of behavioural equivalences indexed by certain binary relations, *distinctions*, on names.

Suppose we wish to model some system as a π-calculus process, and that to achieve this, it is convenient to regard two names, s and r, as constants. For example, suppose s is to signify *send* and r *receive* in a process such as

$$x(u).\,([u=s]\overline{a}y.\,S + [u=r]b(z).\,R)\ .$$

In order that the occurrences of s and r in a process not be open to instantiation when it is placed in a context C, the hole in C must not be underneath an input prefix that binds s or r. Let us call the contexts with this property the (s,r)-*faithful* contexts.

Now suppose that two π-calculus processes describe the system in question, and that we wish to compare them. Then we would like an equivalence, $\doteq$, that treats s and r appropriately, in that it satisfies the preservation property: if $P \doteq P'$ and C is an (s,r)-faithful context, then $C[P] \doteq C[P']$. What is a suitable choice for $\doteq$?

It is easy to see that neither bisimilarity nor full bisimilarity will do. The former is too weak, because in general, $P \approx P'$ does not imply $C[P] \approx C[P']$ if the hole in C occurs under *any* input prefix. And the latter is too strong, because it demands bisimilarity in *all* contexts, not just the (s,r)-faithful contexts.

We therefore need something in between, indeed a new class of equivalences, to handle all varieties of faithfulness. Generalizing slightly from the motivating example, we introduce a family of equivalences each of which demands bisimilarity under all substitutions that maintain the distinction between certain pairs of names. Each member of the family is indexed by a relation that prescribes the relevant pairs.

Definition 4.1.1 (Distinction) A *distinction* is a finite symmetric and irreflexive relation on names. A substitution σ *respects* a distinction D if $(x, y) \in D$ implies $x\sigma \neq y\sigma$. □

The equivalences are then defined as follows.

Definition 4.1.2 (D-full bisimilarity) Suppose D is a distinction.

(1) P and Q are *strong D-full bisimilar*, $P \sim^D Q$, if $P\sigma \sim Q\sigma$ for each σ that respects D.
(2) P and Q are *D-full bisimilar*, $P \approx^D Q$, if $P\sigma \approx Q\sigma$ for each σ that respects D. □

For instance, revisiting the example above,

$$x(u).\,([u=s]\overline{a}y.\,S + [u=r]b(z).\,R) \sim^{\{s,r\}} x(u).\,([u=s]\overline{a}y.\,S \mid [u=r]b(z).\,R)\,,$$

where $\{s, r\}$ abbreviates the distinction $\{(s, r), (r, s)\}$. To see this, suppose σ respects $\{s, r\}$. Then for any name c,

$$[c=s\sigma](\overline{a}y.\,S)\sigma + [c=r\sigma](b(z).\,R)\sigma \sim [c=s\sigma](\overline{a}y.\,S)\sigma \mid [c=r\sigma](b(z).\,R)\sigma\,,$$

because $s\sigma \neq r\sigma$ and so at least one of the match-prefixed processes is strong bisimilar to $\mathbf{0}$. (Note that the equality between the input-prefixed processes does not hold without the distinction index $\{s, r\}$.)

Many distinctions arising in practice are of the form $(M \times M) - \mathcal{I}$ for some finite set M of names, where $\mathcal{I}$ is the identity relation. It is therefore convenient to write M itself as an abbreviation for $(M \times M) - \mathcal{I}$ when used as a superscript to $\sim$ or $\approx$.

The family $\mathcal{D} = \{\sim^D \mid D \text{ a distinction}\}$ has quite a rich structure, and the same is true of $\{\approx^D \mid D \text{ a distinction}\}$. In what follows, we will make observations and state results only for the strong case, but on the understanding that the corresponding observations and results hold for the weak case.

First, inclusion between distinctions implies inclusion between the equivalences they index:

$$\text{if } D \subseteq D' \text{ then } P \sim^D Q \text{ implies } P \sim^{D'} Q.$$

This is so because if a substitution respects a distinction, then it respects any subdistinction. Hence in particular, the relation $\sim^{\emptyset}$ is included in every other $\sim^{D}$. Note that $\sim^{\emptyset}$ coincides with full bisimilarity, since every substitution respects the empty distinction. Further, two members $\sim^{D}$ and $\sim^{D'}$ of $\mathcal{D}$ have a least upper bound $\sim^{D \cup D'}$ in $\mathcal{D}$ and a greatest lower bound $\sim^{D \cap D'}$ in $\mathcal{D}$. Hence, $\mathcal{D}$ is a lattice with a smallest member. It has no largest member, however, because every distinction is finite.

The following notations are useful for expressing further properties of the D-full bisimilarities. We write $\mathcal{R}^{=}$ for the symmetric closure of a relation $\mathcal{R}$. We write also $D\backslash x$ for $D - (\{x\} \times \mathsf{N})^{=}$, where N is the set of all names; so, $D\backslash x$ is the distinction obtained from D by deleting all pairs containing x. Further, for a set M of names, we write $D\lceil M$ for $D \cap (M \times M)$, and we write $\mathsf{n}(D)$ for the set of names that occur in D.

Since substitution affects only the free names of a process,

$$P \sim^{D} Q \text{ implies } P \sim^{D\lceil \mathsf{fn}(P,Q)} Q\,,$$

and of course the converse holds as $D\lceil \mathsf{fn}(P,Q) \subseteq D$.

The other main facts are collected in the following theorem. Its first assertion is that D-full bisimilarity does indeed enjoy the property that motivated its introduction: D-full bisimilarity is preserved by every context in which the hole does not occur underneath an input prefix that binds a name in D. The second and third parts of the theorem highlight the difference in nature between the two binding operators of the π-calculus. The fourth part is a simple observation about matching, the fifth is the Expansion Lemma for D-full bisimilarity, and the last the analogue of a result about input prefixing seen earlier for bisimilarity. We say that a relation, $\triangleq$, is a *D-congruence* if whenever $P \triangleq Q$, then $C[P] \triangleq C[Q]$ for every context C in which the occurrence of the hole is not underneath an input prefix binding a name in D.

Theorem 4.1.3 (Congruence properties of $\sim^{D}$) Let D be a distinction.

(1) $\sim^{D}$ is a D-congruence.
(2) If $P \sim^{D} Q$ then $\boldsymbol{\nu} z\, P \sim^{D\backslash z} \boldsymbol{\nu} z\, Q$.
(3) If $P \sim^{D\backslash z} Q$ then $x(z).\, P \sim^{D} x(z).\, Q$.
(4) $[x = y]\pi.\, P \sim^{\{x,y\}} \mathbf{0}$.
(5) If $M \overset{\text{def}}{=} \kappa_1.\, P_1 + \cdots + \kappa_n.\, P_n$ and $N \overset{\text{def}}{=} \lambda_1.\, Q_1 + \cdots + \lambda_m.\, Q_m$, then

$$M \mid N \sim^{D} \Sigma_i \kappa_i.\, (P_i \mid N) + \Sigma_j \lambda_j.\, (M \mid Q_j) + \Sigma_{\kappa_i\, \mathsf{opp}_D\, \lambda_j} [x_i = y_j]\tau.\, R_{ij}$$

where $\kappa_i\ \mathsf{opp}_D\ \lambda_j$ if

(a) κ_i is $\overline{x_i}y$ and λ_j is $y_j(z)$, where $(x_i, y_j) \notin D$, in which case R_{ij} is $P_i \mid Q_j\{y/z\}$, or
(b) κ_i is $\overline{x_i}(z)$ and λ_j is $y_j(z)$, where $(x_i, y_j) \notin D$, in which case R_{ij} is $\nu z\,(P_i \mid Q_j)$,

or vice versa.

(6) If $P \sim^D Q$ and $P\{y/z\} \sim^D Q\{y/z\}$ for all $y \in \mathsf{fn}(P, Q)$ with $(y, z) \in D$, then $x(z).\,P \sim^D x(z).\,Q$.

Proof The proofs are mostly similar to those of results we have already seen, and they are left as exercises for the interested reader. In particular, (5) follows from (4) using the Expansion Lemma for $\sim$. □

The notion of D-congruence is not as robust as the notion of congruence, as the following exercise shows.

Exercise 4.1.4 Show that in general, $\sim^D$ is *not* the largest D-congruence included in $\sim$. (Hint: consider $D = \{(x, y), (x, z)\}^=$.) □

We will see further uses for distinctions in the following sections, which are about other variants of bisimilarity.

4.2 Variants of bisimilarity

We have seen that bisimilarity is indispensable for reasoning about behavioural equivalence of processes. Later in this chapter, three useful variants of bisimilarity will be introduced: *ground bisimilarity*, *late bisimilarity*, and *open bisimilarity*. This short section explains why these variants are useful, and how they are related to bisimilarity and to one another. It begins with a brief discussion of another family of transition relations, which will be useful for the variant bisimilarities.

The transition relations of Part I are often referred to as the *early* relations, and the new relations as the *late* relations (the terminology will be explained in the next section). The two differ only on input actions, and even there the difference is small. Bisimilarity and each of the three variants can be expressed both using the early relations and using the late relations, though for late bisimilarity the late relations are much more convenient. Section 4.3 introduces the late relations and compares them with the early relations. It also mentions briefly another way of expressing process dynamics, using abstractions and a dual notion: *concretions*.

To determine whether processes P and Q are bisimilar, one factor that must be taken into account is that an input prefix expresses an ability to receive an arbitrary name: one must show that for *each* name y, if $P \xrightarrow{xy} P'$ then $Q \xrightarrow{xy} Q'$ for a suitable Q'. Techniques such as those studied in Section 2.3 can help in achieving this. A main motivation for two of the variants is to ease the task further.

For two processes to be ground bisimilar, rather little is demanded of their abilities to mimic one another's input actions. Indeed, so little is demanded that ground bisimilarity is not a satisfactory equivalence for the full π-calculus. On important subcalculi, however, ground bisimilarity is a congruence, and we can then benefit greatly from its simpler character, as we will later in this Part and also later in the book. Ground bisimilarity is studied in Section 4.4.

Late bisimilarity, which is introduced in Section 4.5, is very close to bisimilarity, but imposes a slightly stronger requirement on mimicry of input actions. Just like bisimilarity, late bisimilarity is not a congruence, and late congruence is its closure under arbitrary substitution. Late bisimilarity and late congruence are of interest principally because they arise naturally in the setting of the late transition relations, in particular when behaviour is explained using abstractions and concretions, and, for reasons related to this, it seems easier to construct denotational models for processes based on them.

Open bisimilarity, studied in Section 4.6, is more demanding even than late bisimilarity, but it is a co-inductively-defined congruence. Its characteristic feature is a kind of closure under substitution at each point in the appropriate bisimulation game. Remarkably, open bisimilarity has a relatively simple characterization using a symbolic account of action, a fact that is useful in building automatic tools to ascertain bisimilarity. This characterization has similar advantages to ground bisimilarity: it involves no explicit or implicit quantification over names received in input actions or over substitutions. To achieve this, the symbolic transitions are necessarily more complicated than the (early or late) transitions used in determining ground bisimilarity. In compensation, however, open bisimilarity can be used on the full calculus, while ground bisimilarity cannot. Further, as we will see in Section 4.8, open bisimilarity has a particularly simple axiomatization on finite terms.

To make their essences clear, the variants are introduced first in their strong forms. Section 4.7 discusses their weak forms, when we abstract from internal action.

4.3 The late transition relations

The transition $P \xrightarrow{xy} Q$ expresses that P can receive the name y via x and evolve to Q. An action of the form xy is sometimes referred to as a *free* input;

it records both the name used for receiving and the name received. In the late relations, the free-input actions are replaced by the input prefixes, referred to in this context as *bound-input actions*. In a late transition $P \overset{x(z)}{\longmapsto} Q$, the label contains a placeholder z for the name to be received, rather than the name itself. If $\alpha = x(z)$ then $\mathsf{fn}(\alpha) = \{x\}$ and $\mathsf{bn}(\alpha) = \{z\}$.

Definition 4.3.1 (Late transition relations) The *late transition relations*, $\{ \overset{\alpha}{\longmapsto} \mid \alpha \in Act' \}$, are defined by the rules in Table 4.1, where Act' is obtained from Act by removing the free-input actions and adding the bound-input actions. Similarly to the definition of the early relations in Section 1.3, four rules are elided from the table: the variant of L-SUM-L with $Q + P$ in place of $P + Q$, and the variants of L-PAR-L, L-COMM-L, and L-CLOSE-L with the roles of the left and right components swapped. □

The arrow $\longmapsto$ is used to distinguish the late relations from the early. Apart from this and the fact that α ranges over Act' rather than Act, the only differences from the rules defining the early relations are in L-INP, L-REP-COMM, L-REP-CLOSE, and L-COMM-L and L-CLOSE-L and their variants. (By the Convention on Bound Names, in L-REP-ACT the bound name of α, if any, is not free in P.)

With the early rules, when an action of a process $x(z).\,P$ is inferred, the actual name received via x is recorded in the free input action and substituted in P: for instance,

$$x(z).\,P \xrightarrow{xy} P\{y/z\} .$$

An internal action of $\overline{x}y.\,Q \mid x(z).\,P$ is then inferred from this transition and $\overline{x}y.\,Q \xrightarrow{\overline{x}y} Q$ using rule COMM-L:

$$\overline{x}y.\,Q \mid x(z).\,P \xrightarrow{\tau} Q \mid P\{y/z\} .$$

Rule COMM-L is applicable as the name sent via x is the same as the name received via x.

With the late rules, the analogous transition

$$\overline{x}y.\,Q \mid x(z).\,P \overset{\tau}{\longmapsto} Q \mid P\{y/z\}$$

is inferred using L-COMM-L from $\overline{x}y.\,Q \overset{\overline{x}y}{\longmapsto} Q$ and

$$x(z).\,P \overset{x(z)}{\longmapsto} P ,$$

the latter being an instance of L-INP. Thus, using the late rules, the placeholder z is instantiated by y when the *communication* is inferred, rather than when the *input* by the receiver is inferred. Thus the early–late terminology is based

$$\text{L-OUT}\quad \frac{}{\overline{x}y.\,P \xmapsto{\overline{x}y} P} \qquad\qquad \text{L-INP}\quad \frac{}{x(z).\,P \xmapsto{x(z)} P}$$

$$\text{L-TAU}\quad \frac{}{\tau.\,P \xmapsto{\tau} P} \qquad\qquad \text{L-MAT}\quad \frac{\pi.\,P \xmapsto{\alpha} P'}{[x=x]\pi.\,P \xmapsto{\alpha} P'}$$

$$\text{L-SUM-L}\quad \frac{P \xmapsto{\alpha} P'}{P+Q \xmapsto{\alpha} P'}$$

$$\text{L-PAR-L}\quad \frac{P \xmapsto{\alpha} P'}{P \mid Q \xmapsto{\alpha} P' \mid Q} \quad \mathsf{bn}(\alpha) \cap \mathsf{fn}(Q) = \emptyset$$

$$\text{L-COMM-L}\quad \frac{P \xmapsto{\overline{x}y} P' \quad Q \xmapsto{x(z)} Q'}{P \mid Q \xmapsto{\tau} P' \mid Q'\{y/z\}}$$

$$\text{L-CLOSE-L}\quad \frac{P \xmapsto{\overline{x}(z)} P' \quad Q \xmapsto{x(z)} Q'}{P \mid Q \xmapsto{\tau} \boldsymbol{\nu} z\,(P' \mid Q')}$$

$$\text{L-RES}\quad \frac{P \xmapsto{\alpha} P'}{\boldsymbol{\nu} z\,P \xmapsto{\alpha} \boldsymbol{\nu} z\,P'} \quad z \notin \mathsf{n}(\alpha) \qquad\qquad \text{L-OPEN}\quad \frac{P \xmapsto{\overline{x}z} P'}{\boldsymbol{\nu} z\,P \xmapsto{\overline{x}(z)} P'} \quad z \neq x$$

$$\text{L-REP-ACT}\quad \frac{P \xmapsto{\alpha} P'}{!P \xmapsto{\alpha} P' \mid !P}$$

$$\text{L-REP-COMM}\quad \frac{P \xmapsto{\overline{x}y} P' \quad P \xmapsto{x(z)} P''}{!P \xmapsto{\tau} (P' \mid P''\{y/z\}) \mid !P}$$

$$\text{L-REP-CLOSE}\quad \frac{P \xmapsto{\overline{x}(z)} P' \quad P \xmapsto{x(z)} P''}{!P \xmapsto{\tau} (\boldsymbol{\nu} z\,(P' \mid P'')) \mid !P}$$

Table 4.1. *The late transition rules*

on when a name is instantiated in inferring an interaction: when the input is inferred (*early*), or when the interaction is inferred (*late*).

Note also that using L-CLOSE-L we can infer

$$(\nu z\,\overline{x}z.\,Q) \mid x(z).\,P \overset{\tau}{\longmapsto} \nu z\,(Q \mid P)$$

from $\nu z\,\overline{x}z.\,Q \overset{\overline{x}(z)}{\longmapsto} Q$ and $x(z).\,P \overset{x(z)}{\longmapsto} P$. The side condition of CLOSE-L is not needed in L-CLOSE-L.

The very close relationship between the early and late relations is given in the following lemma.

Lemma 4.3.2

(1) $P \xrightarrow{\overline{x}y} Q$ iff $P \overset{\overline{x}y}{\longmapsto} Q$.
(2) $P \xrightarrow{xy} Q$ iff there are P' and z such that $P \overset{x(z)}{\longmapsto} P'$ and $Q = P'\{y/z\}$.
(3) $P \xrightarrow{\overline{x}(z)} Q$ iff $P \overset{\overline{x}(z)}{\longmapsto} Q$.
(4) $P \xrightarrow{\tau} Q$ iff $P \overset{\tau}{\longmapsto} Q$.

Proof The proof is a straightforward induction on inference. □

In view of this result, we can freely use the early or late relations as convenient.

4.3.1 Abstractions and concretions

As an intermezzo, we briefly mention another way of presenting the late transition relations.

The transition $P \overset{x(z)}{\longmapsto} Q$ can be written

$$P \overset{x}{\longmapsto} (z).\,Q\,,$$

where the label indicates an input via x and the continuation is the abstraction $(z).\,Q$. To complement this, transitions $R \overset{\overline{x}y}{\longmapsto} S$ and $R \overset{\overline{x}(w)}{\longmapsto} S$ can be written

$$R \overset{\overline{x}}{\longmapsto} \langle y \rangle S$$

and

$$R \overset{\overline{x}}{\longmapsto} \langle \nu w\, \rangle S\,,$$

respectively. The continuations $\langle y \rangle S$ and $\langle \nu w\, \rangle S$ are called *concretions*. Interactions can then be inferred using the rule

$$\frac{P \xrightarrow{x} F \quad R \xrightarrow{\overline{x}} G}{P \mid R \xrightarrow{\tau} F@G}$$

where F stands for an abstraction, G for a concretion, and $F@G$ for their combination. For example,

$$((z).\,Q)@\langle y\rangle S = Q\{y/z\} \mid S$$

and

$$((z).\,Q)@\langle \boldsymbol{\nu} w\,\rangle S = \boldsymbol{\nu} w\,(Q\{w/z\} \mid S)\,.$$

We will not give the definition of the combination operator @, and indeed we will not discuss this approach any further. It allows an elegant and compact presentation of process dynamics. We have chosen not to adopt it, however, because we consider the presentation we have given to be simpler and easier to work with.

4.4 Ground bisimilarity

The first variant of bisimilarity arises when the standard bisimulation game is played on the late transition system. Rather than defining the relation that way, however, we give a definition that is more convenient as it employs the early transition relations, which we use throughout the book. The key point of ground bisimilarity is that it suffices to consider a single fresh name as the object of an input or bound-output action.

Definition 4.4.1 (Strong ground bisimilarity) *Strong ground bisimilarity* is the largest symmetric relation, $\sim_{\mathrm{g}}$, such that whenever $P \sim_{\mathrm{g}} Q$, there is $z \notin \mathsf{fn}(P, Q)$ such that if $P \xrightarrow{\alpha} P'$ where α is $\overline{x}y$ or xz or $\overline{x}(z)$ or τ, then $Q \xrightarrow{\alpha}\sim_{\mathrm{g}} P'$. □

To understand the motivation for considering ground bisimilarity, it is helpful to contrast it with bisimilarity. For two processes to be bisimilar, each transition of one must be matched by a similar transition of the other. This holds in particular of transitions labelled by free-input actions. For instance, to establish that $x(z).\,P \sim x(z).\,Q$, it is necessary to show that $P\{y/z\} \sim Q\{y/z\}$ for every y. This may involve a lot of work. To establish that $x(z).\,P \sim_{\mathrm{g}} x(z).\,Q$, on the other hand, it suffices to show that $P \sim_{\mathrm{g}} Q$. The definition requires that each of the processes in question can mimic those input actions of the other whose object is a *single* fresh name. Moreover, only bound-output actions whose object is that single name need be considered. (We saw this point about bound-output actions for *bisimilarity* in Lemma 2.3.11.)

This reduced level of scrutiny has a cost, however. It is that ground bisimilarity is less discriminating than bisimilarity. For instance,

$$x(z).\,(\overline{z} \mid a) \sim_{\mathrm{g}} x(z).\,(\overline{z}.\,a + a.\,\overline{z})$$

since $\overline{z} \mid a \sim_{\mathrm{g}} \overline{z}.\, a + a.\, \overline{z}$; but the input-prefixed processes are not bisimilar. Moreover, ground bisimilarity is not preserved by composition as, for instance,

$$\overline{x}a \mid x(z).\, (\overline{z} \mid a) \not\sim_{\mathrm{g}} \overline{x}a \mid x(z).\, (\overline{z}.\, a + a.\, \overline{z})\ .$$

Indeed, although the right components of these two processes are ground bisimilar, the processes themselves are not even barbed bisimilar, because the process $\overline{x}a \mid x(z).\, (\overline{z} \mid a)$ can perform two τ transitions and become inactive.

We will see in Section 5.3 and Section 5.7, however, that ground bisimilarity is a congruence on some important subcalculi, and that we are then able to benefit from its relative simplicity. In general, if on some subcalculus, ground bisimilarity (or bisimilarity) is not preserved by substitution, then it is likely that all of the variants will differ from one another and from bisimilarity on that subcalculus. Although many of the examples we will give to illustrate the differences between the equivalences involve + or matching, this is only to give the simplest examples, and not because these operators are needed for the task. (For more on this, see Section 5.8.)

As for bisimilarity (Lemma 2.2.5), a little work is needed to show that ground bisimilarity is an equivalence relation. Indeed, a little more work is needed, because of the existential quantification over names (z) in Definition 4.4.1.

Exercise 4.4.2

(1) Show that $\sim_{\mathrm{g}}$ is preserved by injective substitution.
(2) Hence show that $\sim_{\mathrm{g}}$ is an equivalence relation. □

Returning to the opening sentence of this section:

Exercise 4.4.3 Show that $\sim_{\mathrm{g}}$ is the largest symmetric relation, $\doteq$, such that whenever $P \doteq Q$, if $P \overset{\alpha}{\longmapsto} P'$ then $Q \overset{\alpha}{\longmapsto} \doteq P'$. (Hint: recall from Lemma 4.3.2 that if $z \notin \mathsf{fn}(P, Q)$ then $R \overset{x(z)}{\longmapsto} R'$ iff $R \overset{xz}{\longrightarrow} R'$.) □

Lemma 4.4.4 $P \sim Q$ implies $P \sim_{\mathrm{g}} Q$, but the converse does not hold.

Proof To see that the implication holds, observe that a bisimulation is a ground bisimulation. The pair of processes $x(z).\, (\overline{z} \mid a)$ and $x(z).\, (\overline{z}.\, a + a.\, \overline{z})$ considered above shows that the converse does not hold. □

Exercise 4.4.5 Determine which operators preserve $\sim_{\mathrm{g}}$. □

4.5 Late bisimilarity

Although the definition of bisimilarity was couched in terms of the early relations, it is straightforward to recast it using the late relations instead.

Lemma 4.5.1 $\sim$ is the largest symmetric relation, $\mathrel{\hat{=}}$, such that whenever $P \mathrel{\hat{=}} Q$,

(1) $P \overset{x(z)}{\longmapsto} P'$ implies for each y there is Q' such that $Q \overset{x(z)}{\longmapsto} Q'$ and $P'\{y/z\} \mathrel{\hat{=}} Q'\{y/z\}$
(2) if α is not an input action then $P \overset{\alpha}{\longmapsto} P'$ implies $Q \overset{\alpha}{\longmapsto} \mathrel{\hat{=}} P'$.

Proof The result follows easily from the definitions using Lemma 4.3.2. □

Note that neglect of free-input actions due to use of the late relations is compensated for by universal quantification over names in the first clause. Note also the order of the quantifiers: the matching derivative Q' may be different for different names y. By changing the order of the quantifiers we obtain a slightly stronger relation.

Definition 4.5.2 (Strong late bisimilarity) *Strong late bisimilarity* is the largest symmetric relation, $\sim_\ell$, such that whenever $P \sim_\ell Q$,

(1) $P \overset{x(z)}{\longmapsto} P'$ implies there is Q' such that $Q \overset{x(z)}{\longmapsto} Q'$ and $P'\{y/z\} \sim_\ell Q'\{y/z\}$ for every y
(2) if α is not an input action then $P \overset{\alpha}{\longmapsto} P'$ implies $Q \overset{\alpha}{\longmapsto} \sim_\ell P'$. □

The reason for the appellation 'late' is that to match a transition $P \overset{x(z)}{\longmapsto} P'$, a transition $Q \overset{x(z)}{\longmapsto} Q'$ must be chosen *before* the name y that is to instantiate z is chosen; that is, y is chosen late. In bisimilarity, however, as expressed in Lemma 4.5.1, Q' is chosen *after* y. For this reason, (strong) bisimilarity is sometimes referred to as (strong) *early* bisimilarity, because y is chosen early.

The switch of quantifiers has the expected outcome that late bisimilarity is slightly stronger than bisimilarity.

Lemma 4.5.3 $P \sim_\ell Q$ implies $P \sim Q$, but the converse does not hold.

Proof The implication follows from the definitions and Lemma 4.5.1. To see that the inclusion is strict, consider

$$P \overset{\text{def}}{=} x(z) + x(z).\,\overline{z}$$

and

$$Q \overset{\text{def}}{=} x(z) + x(z).\,\overline{z} + x(z).\,[z = y]\overline{z}\ .$$

To see that $P \not\sim_\ell Q$, consider the transition $Q \overset{x(z)}{\longmapsto} [z=y]\overline{z}$. For $P \sim_\ell Q$ to hold, there would have to be P' such that $P \overset{x(z)}{\longmapsto} P'$ and

$$P'\{a/z\} \sim_\ell ([z=y]\overline{z})\{a/z\} \text{ for every } a.$$

But neither of the two possibilities for P' will do: the first, $\mathbf{0}$, because of the case $a = y$, and the second, $\overline{z}$, because of the case $a = z$.

To see that $P \sim Q$, however, simply note that the union of the identity relation and the relation

$$\{(P, Q), ([y=y]\overline{y}, \overline{y})\} \cup \{([a=y]\overline{y}, \mathbf{0}) \mid a \neq y\}$$

is a bisimulation. The crux is that bisimilarity demands only that, for each a, instantiating z by a in one of the two derivatives of P gives a process bisimilar to $([z=y]\overline{z})\{a/z\}$, and this is indeed the case. □

Exercise 4.5.4 Show that $P \sim Q$ does not imply $P \sim_\ell Q$ on the subcalculus without matching. □

Late bisimilarity, like bisimilarity, is not preserved by substitution, as the same example – $\overline{z} \mid a$ and $\overline{z}.\, a + a.\, \overline{z}$ – shows. Hence, late bisimilarity is not preserved by input prefix. By analogy with full bisimilarity (which is sometimes called *early congruence*), we therefore introduce:

Definition 4.5.5 (Strong late congruence) P and Q are *strong late congruent*, $P \sim_\ell^c Q$, if $P\sigma \sim_\ell Q\sigma$ for every substitution σ. □

Late bisimilarity and congruence share the following properties with bisimilarity and full bisimilarity.

Lemma 4.5.6 (Congruence properties of $\sim_\ell$ and $\sim_\ell^c$)

(1) $\sim_\ell$ is a non-input congruence.
(2) If $P\{y/z\} \sim_\ell Q\{y/z\}$ for all $y \in \mathsf{fn}(P, Q, z)$, then $x(z).\, P \sim_\ell x(z).\, Q$.
(3) $\sim_\ell^c$ is a congruence.
(4) $\sim_\ell^c$ is the largest congruence included in $\sim_\ell$.

Proof The proof is very similar to that of Theorem 2.2.8. □

As an immediate consequence of the fact that late bisimilarity is strictly included in bisimilarity we have:

Lemma 4.5.7 $P \sim_\ell^c Q$ implies $P \sim^c Q$, but the converse does not hold.

Proof The implication follows immediately from the definitions and Lemma 4.5.3. The strictness of the implication follows by considering the pair of processes mentioned in the proof of that lemma. □

This completes the discussion of late bisimilarity; it is not mentioned in the book beyond this Part. It is worth noting that in practice, the difference between bisimilarity and late bisimilarity is so minor as to be unimportant.

4.6 Open bisimilarity

A factor vital to the tractability of bisimilarity is the co-inductive nature of its definition. Bisimilarity is not a congruence, however, because all free names of a process are open to instantiation. Full bisimilarity, the largest congruence included in bisimilarity, is obtained by closing under substitution. It is natural to ask whether it is possible to give a direct co-inductive definition of a useful congruence. This is indeed possible, and the relation obtained is called *open bisimilarity*. It is the final variant of bisimilarity we will consider. In addition to being a co-inductively-defined congruence, open bisimilarity is useful for ascertaining automatically whether processes are bisimilar. We will return to this point at the end of this section. First, however, we need to define open bisimilarity.

To begin, consider the subcalculus without the restriction operator, and let $\doteqdot$ be the largest symmetric relation such that whenever $P \doteqdot Q$ and σ is a substitution, $P\sigma \overset{\alpha}{\longmapsto} P'$ implies $Q\sigma \overset{\alpha}{\longmapsto} \doteqdot P'$.

It turns out that on the restriction-free subcalculus, $\doteqdot$ is a congruence and is strictly included in full bisimilarity. The principal difference between $\doteqdot$ and full bisimilarity is the following. Whenever it is the first player's turn in the bisimulation game defining $\doteqdot$, an arbitrary substitution can be applied to the relevant processes. For P and Q to be full bisimilar, on the other hand, it is required only that, for each substitution σ, the second player has a winning strategy for the ordinary bisimulation game played from $P\sigma$ and $Q\sigma$. Thus, in the case of $\doteqdot$, instantiation of free names is allowed throughout the game, whereas in the case of full bisimilarity, instantiation is allowed only at the beginning. The appellation 'open' emphasizes this susceptibility of names to instantiation.

Exercise 4.6.1 Show that on the subcalculus without restriction,

(1) $\doteqdot$ is the largest ground bisimulation that is closed under substitution
(2) $\doteqdot$ is preserved by input prefix (it is in fact preserved by all the operators of the subcalculus)
(3) $\doteqdot$ is strictly included in strong full bisimilarity. □

Although $\doteq$ is a congruence on the restriction-free subcalculus, it is not a suitable equivalence for the full π-calculus. Its deficiency is that it does not take proper account of the natures of the restriction operator and of bound-output actions. For instance, suppose

$$P \stackrel{\text{def}}{=} (\boldsymbol{\nu} z, w)\, \overline{x}z.\, \overline{x}w.\, (\overline{z} \mid w)$$

and

$$Q \stackrel{\text{def}}{=} (\boldsymbol{\nu} z, w)\, \overline{x}z.\, \overline{x}w.\, (\overline{z}.\, w + w.\, \overline{z})\,.$$

These two processes are distinguished by $\doteq$. The reason is that $\overline{z} \mid w \not\doteq \overline{z}.\, w + w.\, \overline{z}$ as, for instance,

$$(\overline{z} \mid w)\{w/z\} \xrightarrow{\tau} \quad \text{but not} \quad (\overline{z}.\, w + w.\, \overline{z})\{w/z\} \xrightarrow{\tau}\,.$$

We do not wish to distinguish between P and Q, however, because the private names z and w cannot be instantiated to the same name in any π-calculus context.

The key to giving an adequate definition is to use a family of relations indexed by distinctions to record which names cannot be identified with one another.

Definition 4.6.2 (Strong open bisimilarity) $\{\sim_{\text{o}}^{D} \mid D \text{ a distinction}\}$ is the largest family of symmetric relations such that if $P \sim_{\text{o}}^{D} Q$ and σ respects D, then

(1) if $P\sigma \stackrel{\alpha}{\longmapsto} P'$ and α is not a bound output, then $Q\sigma \stackrel{\alpha}{\longmapsto} \sim_{\text{o}}^{D\sigma} P'$

(2) if $P\sigma \stackrel{\overline{x}(z)}{\longmapsto} P'$ then $Q\sigma \stackrel{\overline{x}(z)}{\longmapsto} \sim_{\text{o}}^{D'} P'$ where $D' = D\sigma \cup (\{z\} \times \mathsf{fn}(P\sigma, Q\sigma))^{=}$.

We refer to $\sim_{\text{o}}^{D}$ as *strong open D-bisimilarity*. □

If P and Q are open D-bisimilar, σ respects D, and α is not a bound output, then for each $\stackrel{\alpha}{\longmapsto}$ transition of $P\sigma$ there is a matching transition of $Q\sigma$ to an open $D\sigma$-bisimilar process; the substitutions subsequently of interest are those that respect $D\sigma$. In addition, if α is $\overline{x}(z)$, where $z \notin \mathsf{n}(D) \cup \mathsf{n}(\sigma)$ by the Convention on Bound Names, the distinction D' records also that z cannot be identified with any name free in $P\sigma$ or $Q\sigma$. Note that extending D' to include $(\{z\} \times \mathsf{n}(D\sigma))^{=}$ would make no difference, because only the names free in the processes are important.

For instance, returning to the example $P \stackrel{\text{def}}{=} (\boldsymbol{\nu} z, w)\, \overline{x}z.\, \overline{x}w.\, (\overline{z} \mid w)$ and $Q \stackrel{\text{def}}{=} (\boldsymbol{\nu} z, w)\, \overline{x}z.\, \overline{x}w.\, (\overline{z}.\, w + w.\, \overline{z})$ above, we have $P \sim_{\text{o}}^{\emptyset} Q$, because

$$\overline{z} \mid w \sim_{\text{o}}^{\{z,w\}} \overline{z}.\, w + w.\, \overline{z}$$

where, as in Section 4.1, $\{z, w\}$ abbreviates $\{(z, w), (w, z)\}$.

Note that the same family of relations is obtained if the early transition relations are used in place of the late. Indeed, it would suffice to consider a single fresh input to establish the equivalence: the quantification over substitutions allows for communication of other names.

Theorem 4.6.3 (Congruence properties of $\sim_{\mathrm{o}}^{D}$)

(1) $\sim_{\mathrm{o}}^{D}$ is a D-congruence, so in particular, $\sim_{\mathrm{o}}^{\emptyset}$ is a congruence.
(2) If $P \sim_{\mathrm{o}}^{D} Q$ and σ respects D, then $P\sigma \sim_{\mathrm{o}}^{D\sigma} Q\sigma$.

Proof The proofs are long but do not require new techniques. □

Like the family of D-full bisimilarities defined in Section 4.1, the family $\{\sim_{\mathrm{o}}^{D} \mid D \text{ a distinction}\}$ forms a lattice with a smallest member but no largest member. Strong open $\emptyset$-bisimilarity, which we refer to as *strong open bisimilarity*, is the most discriminating relation we have considered.

Defining *strong late D-congruence*, $\sim_{\ell}^{D}$, analogously to strong D-full bisimilarity we have:

Lemma 4.6.4

(1) $P \sim_{\mathrm{o}}^{D} Q$ implies $P \sim_{\ell}^{D} Q$, but the converse does not hold.
(2) $P \sim_{\ell}^{D} Q$ implies $P \sim^{D} Q$, but the converse does not hold.

Proof For (1), first note that an open bisimulation need not be a late bisimulation: consider, for example, the relation

$$\{(x(z).\,\overline{z}, x(z).\,\overline{z}), (\overline{z}, \overline{z}), (\mathbf{0}, \mathbf{0})\}\ .$$

An open bisimulation is, however, a late bisimulation up to injective substitution. The inclusion in (1) follows from this observation using Theorem 4.6.3(2) and the fact that $\sim_{\mathrm{o}}^{D}$ is preserved by injective substitution.

To show that the inclusion is strict, fix a distinction D, and consider the processes

$$P \stackrel{\mathrm{def}}{=} x.\,x + x$$

and

$$Q \stackrel{\mathrm{def}}{=} x.\,x + x + x.\,[y = z]x$$

where $(y, z) \notin D$. Clearly, $P \sim_{\ell}^{D} Q$; indeed $P\sigma \sim_{\ell} Q\sigma$ for every σ. But $P \not\sim_{\mathrm{o}}^{D} Q$, as $[y = z]x$ is open D-bisimilar neither to $\mathbf{0}$ nor to x, because $([y = z]x)\sigma$ has a transition if $y\sigma = z\sigma$, but does not have a transition if $y\sigma \neq z\sigma$.

The proof of (2) is similar to that of Lemma 4.5.7. □

The proof of Lemma 4.6.4 illustrates the utility of being able to define the various equivalences using the late transition relations.

The fact noted in the proof that an open bisimulation need not be a (late) bisimulation, is a mild hint that it may be less work to show that two processes are open bisimilar than to show directly that they are bisimilar. To explore this possibility, we have to look more closely at open bisimilarity. One immediate difficulty is that the definition of open D-bisimilarity involves quantification over substitutions respecting D. Consequently, some open D-bisimulations are large relations, and it can be a lot of work to check that a relation satisfies the definition. Open bisimilarity has, however, a characterization that does not involve quantification over substitutions. This involves a new kind of 'symbolic' transition, written $P \overset{M,\alpha}{\longmapsto} Q$, where M is a finite sequence $[x_1 = y_1] \cdots [x_n = y_n]$ of matches, and α ranges over Act'. The rules defining these transitions are given in Table 4.2 where: λ ranges over pairs M, α; the empty sequence of matches is written ε; and if λ is M, α then $\mathsf{bn}(\lambda) = \mathsf{bn}(\alpha)$ and $\mathsf{n}(\lambda) = \mathsf{n}(M) \cup \mathsf{n}(\alpha)$ where $\mathsf{n}(M)$ is the set of names in M. (As usual, the symmetric forms of O-SUM-L, O-PAR-L, O-COMM-L, and O-CLOSE-L are omitted.)

The intention is that in $P \overset{M,\alpha}{\longmapsto} Q$, the conjunction of the identities in M is a sufficient condition for P to perform α and thereby evolve to Q. For instance, by O-OUT, O-MAT, O-INP, and O-COMM-L, we have

$$[y = z]\overline{x}y.\, P \mid v(w).\, Q \overset{[y=z][x=v],\tau}{\longmapsto} P \mid Q\{y/w\} \,.$$

The condition is not necessary: consider $\overline{x}x + [y = z]xx$.

To define the form of bisimulation appropriate for the $\overset{M,\alpha}{\longmapsto}$ relations, we need some notation. Given a match sequence M, we write E_M for the equivalence relation on names determined by M (which relates two names if their equality can be inferred from the matches in M), and we choose a name from each E_M-equivalence class and write σ_M for the function that maps each name to the chosen representative of its equivalence class. We write $M \rhd M'$ if $E_M \subseteq E_{M'}$, that is, E_M is a finer relation than $E_{M'}$.

Definition 4.6.5 $\{\simeq_{\mathrm{o}}^{D} \mid D \text{ a distinction}\}$ is the largest family of symmetric relations such that if $P \simeq_{\mathrm{o}}^{D} Q$ and M is such that σ_M respects D, then there is a fresh z such that

(1) if $P \overset{M,\alpha}{\longmapsto} P'$ where α is $\overline{x}y$ or $x(z)$ or τ, then $Q \overset{M',\alpha'}{\longmapsto} Q'$ for some Q', M', α' with $M \rhd M'$ and $\alpha\sigma_M = \alpha'\sigma_M$ and $P'\sigma_M \simeq_{\mathrm{o}}^{D\sigma_M} Q'\sigma_M$

(2) if $P \overset{M,\alpha}{\longmapsto} P'$ where α is $\overline{x}(z)$, then $Q \overset{M',\alpha'}{\longmapsto} Q'$ for some Q', M', α' with

O-OUT $$\frac{}{\overline{x}y.\,P \overset{\varepsilon,\overline{x}y}{\longmapsto} P}$$

O-INP $$\frac{}{x(z).\,P \overset{\varepsilon,x(z)}{\longmapsto} P}$$

O-TAU $$\frac{}{\tau.\,P \overset{\varepsilon,\tau}{\longmapsto} P}$$

O-SUM-L $$\frac{P \overset{\lambda}{\longmapsto} P'}{P+Q \overset{\lambda}{\longmapsto} P'}$$

O-MAT $$\frac{\pi.\,P \overset{M,\alpha}{\longmapsto} P'}{[x=y]\pi.\,P \overset{M',\alpha}{\longmapsto} P'} \qquad M' = \begin{cases} M[x=y] & \text{if } x \neq y \\ M & \text{otherwise} \end{cases}$$

O-PAR-L $$\frac{P \overset{\lambda}{\longmapsto} P'}{P \mid Q \overset{\lambda}{\longmapsto} P' \mid Q} \qquad \mathsf{bn}(\lambda) \cap \mathsf{fn}(Q) = \emptyset$$

O-COMM-L $$\frac{P \overset{M,\overline{x}y}{\longmapsto} P' \quad Q \overset{M',z(w)}{\longmapsto} Q'}{P \mid Q \overset{M'',\tau}{\longmapsto} P' \mid Q'\{y/w\}} \qquad M'' = \begin{cases} MM'[x=z] & \text{if } x \neq z \\ MM' & \text{otherwise} \end{cases}$$

O-CLOSE-L $$\frac{P \overset{M,\overline{x}(z)}{\longmapsto} P' \quad Q \overset{M',y(z)}{\longmapsto} Q'}{P \mid Q \overset{M'',\tau}{\longmapsto} \boldsymbol{\nu} z\,(P' \mid Q')} \qquad M'' = \begin{cases} MM'[x=y] & \text{if } x \neq y \\ MM' & \text{otherwise} \end{cases}$$

O-RES $$\frac{P \overset{\lambda}{\longmapsto} P'}{\boldsymbol{\nu} z\, P \overset{\lambda}{\longmapsto} \boldsymbol{\nu} z\, P'} \qquad z \notin \mathsf{n}(\lambda)$$

O-OPEN $$\frac{P \overset{M,\overline{x}z}{\longmapsto} P'}{\boldsymbol{\nu} z\, P \overset{M,\overline{x}(z)}{\longmapsto} P'} \qquad z \notin \mathsf{n}(M) \cup \{x\}$$

O-REP-ACT $$\frac{P \overset{\lambda}{\longmapsto} P'}{!P \overset{\lambda}{\longmapsto} P' \mid !P}$$

O-REP-COMM $$\frac{P \overset{M,\overline{x}y}{\longmapsto} P' \quad P \overset{M',z(w)}{\longmapsto} P''}{!P \overset{M'',\tau}{\longmapsto} (P' \mid P''\{y/w\}) \mid !P} \qquad M'' = \begin{cases} MM'[x=z] & \text{if } x \neq z \\ MM' & \text{otherwise} \end{cases}$$

O-REP-CLOSE $$\frac{P \overset{M,\overline{x}(z)}{\longmapsto} P' \quad P \overset{M',y(z)}{\longmapsto} P''}{!P \overset{M'',\tau}{\longmapsto} (\boldsymbol{\nu} z\,(P' \mid P'')) \mid !P} \qquad M'' = \begin{cases} MM'[x=y] & \text{if } x \neq y \\ MM' & \text{otherwise} \end{cases}$$

Table 4.2. *The symbolic open transition rules*

$M \rhd M'$ and $\alpha\sigma_M = \alpha'\sigma_M$ and $P'\sigma_M \doteq_o^{D'} Q'\sigma_M$ where $D' = D\sigma_M \cup (\{z\} \times \mathsf{fn}(P\sigma_M, Q\sigma_M))^=$. □

Note that for each pair P, Q, the definition requires that one consider only a single fresh name as the object of input and bound-output actions. This is analogous to the requirement for ground bisimilarity (Definition 4.4.1). Also, in each clause the distinction indexing the relation used to compare the derivatives is analogous to the corresponding distinction in the definition of $\sim_o^D$.

Lemma 4.6.6 (Symbolic Characterization Lemma) $P \doteq_o^D Q$ iff $P \sim_o^D Q$.

Proof The proof is long and quite complicated, though it does not require substantially new techniques.

First, one shows that $\doteq_o^D$ is preserved by all substitutions that respect D, that is, if $P \doteq_o^D Q$ and σ respects D, then $P\sigma \doteq_o^{D\sigma} Q\sigma$. The analogous result for $\sim_o^D$ has already been stated in Theorem 4.6.3.

Then, one establishes the operational correspondence between the $\overset{M,\alpha}{\longmapsto}$ transitions of P and the (early) transitions of $P\sigma_M$. This is in two parts:

(1) if $P\sigma_M \xrightarrow{\alpha} P''$ then $P \overset{N,\beta}{\longmapsto} P'$ with $M \rhd N$ and $\alpha = \beta\sigma_M$ and $P'' = P'\sigma_M$

(2) if $P \overset{M,\alpha}{\longmapsto} P'$ then $P\sigma_M \xrightarrow{\alpha\sigma_M} P'\sigma_M$.

Finally, using these results one shows that $\sim_o^D$ is a $\doteq_o^D$-bisimulation (that is, a bisimulation of the kind defined implicitly in Definition 4.6.5), which proves that $\sim_o^D$ is included in $\doteq_o^D$; and that $\doteq_o^D$ is an open D-bisimulation (as defined implicitly in Definition 4.6.2), which proves the converse. □

The utility of this result lies in the fact that, in general, it is less work to determine whether two processes are related by applying Definition 4.6.5 than Definition 4.6.2: showing $\doteq_o^D$ involves considering only transitions $\overset{M,\alpha}{\longmapsto}$ for α of the form $\overline{x}y$, τ, $x(z)$, and $\overline{x}(z)$ for a single z, rather than arbitrary actions and arbitrary D-respecting substitutions. The characterization is used, for instance, in the Mobility Workbench, a prototype automated tool for reasoning about mobile processes. The characterization also helps to make clearer the nature of open bisimilarity. It shows, for instance, that instantiation of a name can happen only when it is 'needed', in a sense similar to that in call-by-need semantics of λ-calculus. As a final remark, open bisimilarity becomes problematic if mismatching is added to the calculus. In particular, the proof of Lemma 4.6.6 depends on the monotonicity property of action under substitution discussed in Section 1.1.

4.7 The weak equivalences

Thus far, we have considered the ground, late, and open variants of bisimilarity only in their strong forms. By proceeding in this way, we have been able to understand the various equivalences and the relationships between them without the burden of the additional complication that abstraction from internal action brings. As is the case for bisimilarity itself, however, it is the weak versions of the equivalences that are of most interest.

Little new arises in the theories of ground bisimilarity and open bisimilarity. They are defined as expected. For instance:

Definition 4.7.1 (Ground bisimilarity) *Ground bisimilarity* is the largest symmetric relation, $\approx_{\rm g}$, such that whenever $P \approx_{\rm g} Q$, there is $z \notin \mathsf{fn}(P, Q)$ such that if $P \xrightarrow{\alpha} P'$ where α is $\overline{x}y$ or xz or $\overline{x}(z)$ or τ, then $Q \overset{\widehat{\alpha}}{\Longrightarrow}\approx_{\rm g} P'$. □

The appropriate analogues of all of the results presented in the strong case can be shown to hold. We will not, therefore, study ground bisimilarity and open bisimilarity in detail. Further, ground, late, and open variants of the expansion relation (Definition 2.4.58) can be defined, and using them, the up-to techniques for bisimilarity presented in Chapter 2 can be carried over to the ground, late, and open bisimilarities. We will not go into the details, except to record one fact that we will use, namely, writing ${}_{\rm g}\!\succeq$ for the ground expansion relation:

$$\text{if } P \;{}_{\rm g}\!\succeq Q \text{ then } P \approx_{\rm g} Q. \tag{4.1}$$

The definition of late bisimilarity is less straightforward, however. To see this, write $\Longmapsto$ for the reflexive and transitive closure of $\overset{\tau}{\longmapsto}$, and $\overset{\alpha}{\Longmapsto}$ for $\Longmapsto\overset{\alpha}{\longmapsto}\Longmapsto$. Focusing on the significant point, which is the treatment of input actions, by analogy with the definition of bisimilarity, late bisimilarity might be defined as the largest symmetric relation, $\doteqdot$, such that whenever $P \doteqdot Q$,

$P \overset{x(z)}{\longmapsto} P'$ implies there is Q' such that $Q \overset{x(z)}{\Longmapsto} Q'$ and
$P'\{y/z\} \doteqdot Q'\{y/z\}$ for every y.

This relation is not transitive, however. For let $S \overset{\text{def}}{=} \overline{z}.\,a + a.\,\overline{z}$, and $S' \overset{\text{def}}{=} \overline{z}.\,a + a.\,\overline{z} + \tau$, and $S'' \overset{\text{def}}{=} \overline{z} \mid a$, and consider

$$\begin{aligned} P &\overset{\text{def}}{=} x(z).\,(\tau.\,S + \tau.\,S' + y + \tau.\,S'') + x(z).\,S'' \\ Q &\overset{\text{def}}{=} x(z).\,(\tau.\,S + \tau.\,S' + y + \tau.\,S'') \\ R &\overset{\text{def}}{=} x(z).\,(\tau.\,S + \tau.\,S' + y)\;. \end{aligned}$$

Exercise 4.7.2 Show that $P \doteqdot Q$ and $Q \doteqdot R$, but $P \not\doteqdot R$. □

If the definition of $\bumpeq$ is rewritten with $P \overset{x(z)}{\Longmapsto} P'$ in place of $P \overset{x(z)}{\longmapsto} P'$, then this problem is overcome, though the benefits of having a single transition in the antecedent discussed in Section 2.4 are lost. At least with the addition of mismatching, however, the definition with $P \overset{x(z)}{\Longmapsto} P'$ in place of $P \overset{x(z)}{\longmapsto} P'$ is definitely unsatisfactory. For if

$$P \overset{\text{def}}{=} x(z).\,[z \neq y](\tau.\,[z \neq y]y + x)$$

and

$$Q \overset{\text{def}}{=} x(z).\,[z \neq y](\tau.\,y + x)\,,$$

then $P \not\bumpeq Q$; but P and Q *are strong* late bisimilar.

Exercise 4.7.3 Prove that $P \not\bumpeq Q$ but that $P \sim_\ell Q$. □

There are two plausible definitions of late bisimilarity. They treat non-input actions just as bisimilarity does. For input actions, the first requires that

> $P \overset{x(z)}{\longmapsto} P'$ implies there is Q' such that $Q \Longmapsto \overset{x(z)}{\longmapsto} Q'$ and
> for each y there is Q'' such that $Q'\{y/z\} \Longmapsto Q''$ and $P'\{y/z\} \bumpeq Q''$,

while the second requires that

> $P \overset{x(z)}{\longmapsto} P'$ implies there is Q' such that $Q \Longmapsto \overset{x(z)}{\longmapsto} Q'$ and
> $P'\{y/z\} \bumpeq Q'\{y/z\}$ for every y.

The second is a kind of bisimilarity often referred to as 'delayed'. The third τ law,

$$\pi.\,(P + \tau.\,Q) = \pi.\,(P + \tau.\,Q) + \pi.\,Q\,,$$

fails for such bisimilarities. Nonetheless, it can be argued that this second relation is the appropriate notion of late bisimilarity. The reason is that it captures the underlying intuition that an input prefix $x(z).\,P$ is composed of a name x and an abstraction $(z).\,P$: the definition requires that an input be matched by an input that yields a pointwise-equivalent *function* from names to processes. (This point becomes especially clear when processes that pass data built from processes are considered, so the processes and the functions are higher order; see [San96a].)

The relationships among the principal equivalences, on image-finite processes, are summarized in Figure 4.1, where $\approx_{\mathrm{g}}^{\mathrm{c}}$ is ground congruence, $\approx_\ell$ is late bisimilarity, $\approx_\ell^{\mathrm{c}}$ is late congruence, and $\approx_{\mathrm{o}}$ is open bisimilarity. Note that ground congruence coincides with barbed congruence, because ground bisimilarity lies between barbed bisimilarity and bisimilarity, and barbed congruence and full

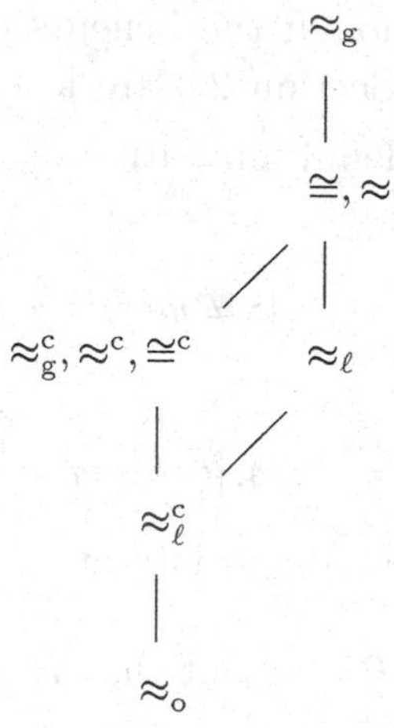

Fig. 4.1. Relationships among equivalences (on image-finite processes)

bisimilarity coincide. It is unknown, however, whether the coincidences hold without the assumption of image-finiteness.

Exercise 4.7.4 Show that $P\sigma \approx_g Q\sigma$ for all σ does not imply $P \approx_g^c Q$. □

The number of equivalences is not a cause of concern. We have adopted barbed congruence as the main behavioural equivalence, and view bisimilarity as an indispensable auxiliary equivalence. We regard ground bisimilarity, late bisimilarity, and open bisimilarity also as useful auxiliary equivalences. All of the relations coincide on some important subcalculi, as will see later. In general, it is important to note that with the possible exception of ground bisimilarity, the differences between the various relations are so fine that it is rare for them to be of practical significance.

4.8 Axiomatizations and proof systems

Equational reasoning is a central technique in process calculus. In carrying out a calculation, appeal can be made to any axiom or rule sound for the equivalence in question.

In general, equivalence of processes is undecidable, indeed it is not even semi-decidable. We will see a very short proof of this in Part VI (Exercise 18.3.19). On finite processes, however, axiomatizations and proof systems are possible. By an *axiomatization* of an equivalence on a set of terms, we mean some equational axioms that, together with the rules of equational reasoning, suffice for proving all (and only) the valid equations. The rules of equational reasoning are reflexivity, symmetry, transitivity, and congruence rules that make it possible to replace any subterm of a process by an equivalent term. A *proof system* achieves the same goal, but may have, in addition to axioms and some of the rules of equational reasoning, other inference rules. Where obtainable, an axiomatization is preferable to a proof system, because for example general techniques from term-rewriting may then be applicable. If the equivalence in question is not a congruence, however, then it has no axiomatization.

Axiomatizations and proof systems are of interest for two main reasons. The first is simply that axioms and rules contributing to completeness are often useful in equational reasoning. Good examples of this are the Expansion Lemma and the τ laws. The second reason is that axiomatizations and proof systems are often good for contrasting equivalences: light can be shed on the differences between equivalences by isolating small collections of axioms and rules that distinguish them.

In process calculus generally, axiomatizations and proof systems are known for very many equivalences on very many languages. For π-calculus and its various subcalculi, a fairly complete picture has been built up, though it is perhaps not as tidy as one might wish. Rather than attempting to present the full picture, we will give an overview, omitting many (long) proofs in favour of exercises that highlight particular points. The equivalences we consider are bisimilarity and full bisimilarity (which on finite π-calculus coincide with barbed equivalence and congruence, respectively), late bisimilarity and congruence, and open bisimilarity.

Since full bisimilarity is defined in terms of bisimilarity, if we had a proof system, say $\mathcal{B}$, for bisimilarity, then we could obtain one for full bisimilarity by adding the rule:

$$\text{if } \mathcal{B} \vdash P\sigma = Q\sigma \text{ for all } \sigma, \text{ then } P = Q.$$

This would not give us an independent characterization of the congruence, however, since it refers to another equivalence and its proof system. We will seek independent characterizations. The same argument applies to late bisimilarity and its congruence.

The proofs that the various axiomatizations and proof systems are complete have a common two-part structure. In the first part, it is shown that using some of the axioms and rules, each term can be proved equal to a term of a special kind, often called a *standard form*. And in the second part, the other axioms and rules are used to show that any two standard forms that are related by the equivalence in question are provably equal. (Sometimes an axiom or rule has a role in both parts.) The proofs give insight into how to prove terms equivalent by algebraic means, and they sometimes bring to light other useful equalities.

The section is in five subsections. The first four are devoted to the strong equivalences, and analyse increasingly rich languages. We start in Section 4.8.1 with terms built using inaction, prefixing without matching, and summation. In this simplest case, all varieties of bisimilarity coincide, and the axiomatization is very straightforward. In Section 4.8.2, we add matching. For convenience, we work with a slightly larger set of summations – and, later in the section, processes – than that given in Definition 1.1.1. (We allow matching to be applied arbitrarily, not just on top of prefixes, and we admit arbitrary sums of processes.) To obtain a simpler proof system for bisimilarity, and any axiomatizations for full bisimilarity and late congruence, we need to make a significant addition to the term language, namely mismatching. We do this in Section 4.8.3. In Section 4.8.4, we see how to handle composition and restriction. We finish, in Section 4.8.5, by looking briefly at how to treat abstraction from internal action.

We do not consider fixed-point rules or induction principles for reasoning about processes that have infinite behaviour. See, however, the approximations of bisimilarity in Definition 2.2.10, which implicitly give an induction principle for strong bisimilarity.

4.8.1 Summations

Let us write $\mathsf{L}(\mathbf{0}, \pi, +)$ for the language of terms given by

$$P \;::=\; \mathbf{0} \;\mid\; \pi.\, P \;\mid\; P + P'$$

where the prefixes are given by

$$\pi \;::=\; \overline{x}y \;\mid\; x(z) \;\mid\; \tau\,.$$

The language $\mathsf{L}(\mathbf{0}, \pi, +)$ differs from the corresponding fragment of CCS only in that the prefixes have a little structure. In $\mathsf{L}(\mathbf{0}, \pi, +)$, however, that structure plays no special role, and all of the bisimilarities coincide and are congruences. We record and name the rules of equational reasoning for this language:

REFL	$P = P$
SYMM	$P = Q$ implies $Q = P$
TRANS	$P = Q$ and $Q = R$ implies $P = R$
PRE	$P = Q$ implies $\pi.\, P = \pi.\, Q$
SUM	$P = Q$ implies $P + R = Q + R\,.$

It is very simple to axiomatize bisimilarity on $\mathsf{L}(\mathbf{0}, \pi, +)$. Since we identify α-convertible terms, we need only add axioms saying that $+$ is associative, commutative, idempotent, and has $\mathbf{0}$ as an identity:

$$\begin{array}{llcl} \text{S1} & (P+Q)+R & = & P+(Q+R) \\ \text{S2} & P+Q & = & Q+P \\ \text{S3} & P+\mathbf{0} & = & P \\ \text{S4} & P+P & = & P\,. \end{array}$$

Let G be the collection of axioms and rules: REFL, SYMM, TRANS, PRE, SUM, S1, S2, S3, S4.

Theorem 4.8.1 G is an axiomatization of strong bisimilarity for the terms in $\mathsf{L}(\mathbf{0}, \pi, +)$. □

Exercise 4.8.2 Prove Theorem 4.8.1. The fact that strong bisimilarity is a congruence on $\mathsf{L}(\mathbf{0}, \pi, +)$ gives a choice about which terms to take as the standard forms. One possibility is to use the *head normal forms*, that is, the terms of the form $\Sigma_{i=1}^{n} \pi_i . P_i$ where $n \geq 0$. The other is to define the standard forms to be the terms of the form $\Sigma_{i=1}^{n} \pi_i . P_i$ where $n \geq 0$ and each P_i is a standard form. This choice is usually available when the equivalence in question is a congruence. When considering an equivalence that is not a congruence, however, we normally have to use the head normal forms. □

4.8.2 Summations with matching

Let us move on to a richer fragment, and write $\mathsf{L}(\mathbf{0}, \pi, +, =)$ for the language of terms given by

$$P \;::=\; \mathbf{0} \mid \pi . P \mid P+P' \mid [x=y]P$$

where the prefixes are given by

$$\pi \;::=\; \overline{x}y \mid x(z) \mid \tau\,.$$

Clearly, $\mathsf{L}(\mathbf{0}, \pi, +, =)$ contains every pure summation of the π-calculus, as well as terms, such as $[x=y]\mathbf{0}+[x=y](\overline{x}y.\mathbf{0}+x(z).\mathbf{0})$, that are not processes according to the grammar in Definition 1.1.1.

On $\mathsf{L}(\mathbf{0}, \pi, +, =)$, the five equivalences we are examining are all different.

4.8.2.1 Open bisimilarity

To axiomatize open bisimilarity, we add to the collection G above the following axioms involving matching:

M1	$[x=x]P$	$=$	P
M2	$[x=y]P$	$=$	$[y=x]P$
M3	$[x=y][x=y]P$	$=$	$[x=y]P$
M4	$[x=y][z=w]P$	$=$	$[z=w][x=y]P$
M5	$[x=y][x=z]P$	$=$	$[x=y][x=z][y=z]P$
M6	$[x=y]P$	$=$	$[x=y]P\{y/x\}$
M7	$[x=y](P+Q)$	$=$	$[x=y]P+[x=y]Q$
M8	$[x=y]P+P$	$=$	P .

Axioms M1–M5 formalize equality on names. They allow a sequence of matches to be replaced by another sequence that is semantically equivalent to it; see Exercise 4.8.4(1). M6 asserts that the two names in a match are interchangeable underneath it, M7 allows distribution of match over +, and M8 is an absorption law, capturing that the only effect of a match may be to block a process.

Let O be obtained by adding to G the axioms M1–M8 and the rule:

$$\text{MAT} \quad P=Q \ \text{ implies } \ [x=y]P=[x=y]Q\ .$$

Theorem 4.8.3 O is an axiomatization of strong open bisimilarity for the terms in $\mathsf{L}(\mathbf{0},\pi,+,=)$. □

The structure of the proof is similar to that of Theorem 4.8.1, but the details are rather more complex. The treatment of matching in the completeness proof is of technical interest. In the proof systems for bisimilarity and late bisimilarity below, conditional constructs are removed by evaluating them. In the system for late bisimilarity in Theorem 4.8.5, for instance, this is done by the axiom

$$\text{M9} \quad [x=y]P=\mathbf{0} \quad \text{if } x \neq y\ .$$

This axiom is not sound, however, for an equivalence – such as open bisimilarity – that is preserved by name-substitution, because the application of a substitution can change the value of a condition. For such equivalences, one needs axioms for manipulating conditions. Remarkably, for open bisimilarity the simple axioms M1–M8 for matching suffice.

Another interesting point about the axiomatization O is that it can be used to transform any process to a canonical representative of its equivalence class under open bisimilarity. Formally, there is a function $\cdot^*$ on processes that picks out an element of each equivalence class, that is, such that $P \sim_o Q$ iff $P^* = Q^*$, and there is an algorithm for proving $P = P^*$ using the axiomatization. (The existence of the algorithm also shows the completeness of O.) Moreover, for any P, the size of P^* is no greater than the size of P, so the canonical representative of a class is no larger than any process in the class. It is an open question whether similar algorithms exist for finding canonical representatives for full bisimilarity or late congruence.

The following exercise highlights some features of the axiomatization O.

Exercise 4.8.4 Recall from before Definition 4.6.5 that if M is the sequence $[x_1 = y_1] \cdots [x_n = y_n]$ of matches, then E_M is the smallest equivalence relation on names such that $(x_i, y_i) \in E_M$ for each i.

(1) Show that if $E_M = E_{M'}$ then $MP = M'P$ can be proved using M1–M5 and equational reasoning.
(2) Show that if $(x, y) \in E_M$ then $MP = M(P\{y/x\})$ can be proved using M1–M6 and equational reasoning.
(3) Suppose σ is a substitution such that $x\sigma = y\sigma$ iff $(x, y) \in E_M$. Show that $MP = M(P\sigma)$ can be proved using M1–M6 and equational reasoning.
(4) Show that S4 is redundant.
(5) Show that $P = P + MP$ can be proved using S1, S2, M8 and equational reasoning. □

4.8.2.2 Late bisimilarity

Now consider late bisimilarity on $\mathsf{L}(\mathbf{0}, \pi, +, =)$. As late bisimilarity is not preserved by input prefix, the rule

$$\text{PRE} \quad P = Q \quad \text{implies} \quad \pi.P = \pi.Q$$

is not sound for $\pi = x(z)$. We therefore separate out the sound part of it,

$$\text{PRE1} \quad P = Q \quad \text{implies} \quad \pi.P = \pi.Q \quad \text{if } \pi \text{ is not of the form } x(z)\,,$$

and introduce the rule:

$$\text{PRE2} \quad P\{y/z\} = Q\{y/z\} \quad \text{for all } y \in \mathsf{fn}(P, Q, z) \quad \text{implies} \quad x(z).P = x(z).Q.$$

We use also the axiom M9, which we presented above. This axiom is sound for late bisimilarity, but not, as we noted, for open bisimilarity.

Let LB be obtained from G by replacing PRE by PRE1 and PRE2, and adding M1 and M9 (M2–M8 are derivable).

Theorem 4.8.5 LB is a proof system for strong late bisimilarity of the terms in $\mathsf{L}(\mathbf{0}, \pi, +, =)$. □

Exercise 4.8.6 Prove Theorem 4.8.5. The standard forms are the head normal forms as defined in Exercise 4.8.2. □

$$\frac{P \xrightarrow{\alpha} P' \quad [\![\varphi]\!] = \mathsf{true}}{\varphi P Q \xrightarrow{\alpha} P'} \qquad \frac{Q \xrightarrow{\alpha} Q' \quad [\![\varphi]\!] = \mathsf{false}}{\varphi P Q \xrightarrow{\alpha} Q'}$$

Table 4.3. *The transition rules for $\varphi P Q$*

4.8.2.3 Other equivalences

It is harder to give a proof system for bisimilarity on $\mathsf{L}(\mathbf{0}, \pi, +, =)$. It can be done by adding to LB the rule:

$$\text{PRE3} \quad \frac{\Sigma_{i=1}^{n} \tau. P_i\{y/z\} = \Sigma_{j=1}^{m} \tau. Q_j\{y/z\} \quad \text{for all } y \in N}{\Sigma_{i=1}^{n} x(z). P_i = \Sigma_{j=1}^{m} x(z). Q_j}$$

where $N = \mathsf{fn}(P_1, \ldots, P_n, Q_1, \ldots, Q_m, z)$. To obtain a simpler proof system for bisimilarity, and to obtain axiomatizations for full bisimilarity and late congruence, we add mismatching to the calculus. It is an open problem how to axiomatize full bisimilarity and late congruence without mismatching.

4.8.3 Summations with conditions

Rather then adding just mismatching, it is more convenient to consider the richer language $\mathsf{L}(\mathbf{0}, \pi, +, \varphi)$ of terms given by

$$P \ ::= \ \mathbf{0} \mid \pi. P \mid P + P' \mid \varphi P P' ,$$

where the prefixes are given by

$$\pi \ ::= \ \overline{x}y \mid x(z) \mid \tau$$

and the *conditions* by

$$\varphi \ ::= \ [x = y] \mid \neg\varphi \mid \varphi \wedge \varphi' .$$

Each condition φ has an obvious truth value, $[\![\varphi]\!]$, obtained by evaluating the atomic conditions $[x = y]$ in φ and applying the boolean operators. The term $\varphi P P'$ is read: if φ then P else P'. The (early) transition rules for the new terms are given in Table 4.3.

Although, for convenience, we allow arbitrary boolean combinations of matches, the only significant addition is mismatching. Of course, having mismatch we will not consider open bisimilarity.

Exercise 4.8.7 Show that each term of $\mathsf{L}(\mathbf{0}, \pi, +, \varphi)$ is strong late congruent to a term of the language given by

$$P \ ::= \ \mathbf{0} \mid \pi.P \mid P+P' \mid [x=y]P \mid [x\neq y]P \ .$$

□

4.8.3.1 Late bisimilarity

First, we give a proof system for late bisimilarity on $\mathsf{L}(\mathbf{0}, \pi, +, \varphi)$. To do this, we generalize axioms M1 and M9 to:

$$\begin{array}{llcll} \text{C1} & \varphi P Q & = & P & \text{if } [\![\varphi]\!] = \mathsf{true} \\ \text{C2} & \varphi P Q & = & Q & \text{if } [\![\varphi]\!] = \mathsf{false}\ . \end{array}$$

Strictly speaking, these are not axioms in the standard sense, because they involve the evaluation function for conditions. Here, however, we are concerned with axiomatizing process equivalences taking for granted that we can prove equivalences between conditions. We therefore refer to C1 and C2 as axioms. If desired, they can be replaced by a number of proper axioms involving matching and mismatching, as hinted at in Exercise 4.8.7. Let LB' be obtained from LB by replacing M1 and M9 by C1 and C2.

Theorem 4.8.8 LB' is a proof system for strong late bisimilarity of the terms in $\mathsf{L}(\mathbf{0}, \pi, +, \varphi)$.

Proof The proof is similar to that of Theorem 4.8.5. □

4.8.3.2 Bisimilarity

It was mentioned early in this section that axiomatizations and proof systems are often good for contrasting equivalences. A nice illustration of this is that to get a proof system for bisimilarity on $\mathsf{L}(\mathbf{0}, \pi, +, \varphi)$, it suffices to add a single axiom to the proof system for late bisimilarity, namely,

$$\text{C3} \quad x(z).P + x(z).Q = x(z).P + x(z).Q + x(z).[z=y]PQ\ .$$

Let B' be obtained from LB' by adding C3.

Theorem 4.8.9 B' is a proof system for strong bisimilarity of the terms in $\mathsf{L}(\mathbf{0}, \pi, +, \varphi)$. □

The following exercise goes some way towards showing the role of C3 in the proof of the completeness of B'.

Exercise* 4.8.10 Suppose that $P \sim Q$ where

$$P \stackrel{\text{def}}{=} \Sigma_{i\in I}\, x(z).\, P_i \qquad \text{and} \qquad Q \stackrel{\text{def}}{=} \Sigma_{j\in J}\, x(z).\, Q_j\,.$$

Then, from the definition, there is a function f such that for $i \in I$ and y a name, $P_i\{y/z\} \sim Q_{f(i,y)}\{y/z\}$. The exercise is to show that if we assume that, for each i and each $y \in \mathsf{fn}(P, Q, z)$,

$$\mathsf{B}' \vdash P_i\{y/z\} = Q_{f(i,y)}\{y/z\}\,,$$

then we can derive $\mathsf{B}' \vdash P = Q$.

Let $\mathsf{fn}(P, Q) = \{y_1, \ldots, y_n\}$. Fix $i \in I$. Set $R_i^0 \stackrel{\text{def}}{=} Q_{f(i,z)}$, and for $1 \le k \le n$,

$$R_i^k \stackrel{\text{def}}{=} [z = y_k]\, Q_{f(i,y_k)}\, R_i^{k-1}\,.$$

Set also $R_i \stackrel{\text{def}}{=} R_i^n$.

(1) Show that $\mathsf{B}' \vdash Q_{f(i,y)}\{y/z\} = R_i^k\{y/z\}$ if $y = y_k$ and $1 \le k \le n$.
(2) Hence show that $\mathsf{B}' \vdash P_i\{y/z\} = R_i\{y/z\}$ for all $y \in \mathsf{fn}(P_i, R_i, z)$.
(3) Deduce that $\mathsf{B}' \vdash x(z).\, P_i = x(z).\, R_i$.
(4) Using C3, prove that $\mathsf{B}' \vdash Q = Q + x(z).\, R_i^k$ for $0 \le k \le n$.
(5) Set $R \stackrel{\text{def}}{=} \Sigma_{i\in I}\, x(z).\, R_i$. Deduce that $\mathsf{B}' \vdash Q = Q + R$.
(6) Hence show that $\mathsf{B}' \vdash P = Q$. □

4.8.3.3 Late congruence and full bisimilarity

We now consider how to axiomatize the congruence relations late congruence and full bisimilarity.

It is instructive to begin by examining where the proof of Theorem 4.8.5 breaks down when applied to late congruence rather than late bisimilarity. Suppose we wish to prove $P \sim_\ell^c Q$, where P and Q are head normal forms. By the definition of late congruence, for each summand $\pi.\, P'$ of P and each substitution σ, there is a summand $\pi'.\, Q'$ of Q such that $\pi\sigma = \pi'\sigma$ and $P'\sigma \sim_\ell Q'\sigma$. The difficulty is that $P'\sigma \sim_\ell Q'\sigma$ does not imply $P' \sim_\ell^c Q'$, in general, and so we cannot appeal to the induction hypothesis.

We overcome this problem by using a new kind of standard form. The standard forms are chosen to conform to Lemma 4.8.12 below, which allows us to lift $\sim_\ell$ up to $\sim_\ell^c$ on certain processes. We need some notation.

First, let us write φP for $\varphi P \mathbf{0}$. We say that φ *implies* φ' if $[\![\varphi\sigma]\!]$ implies $[\![\varphi'\sigma]\!]$ for every σ, where a substitution is applied to a condition by applying it to every name in the condition. Further, we write $\varphi - \varphi'$ if φ implies φ' and φ' implies φ.

Definition 4.8.11 A condition φ is *complete on* a set V of names if for all $x, y \in V$, either φ implies $[x=y]$ or φ implies $\neg[x=y]$. □

If φ is complete on V then E_φ is an equivalence relation on V, where $(x,y) \in E_\varphi$ if φ implies $[x=y]$. Hence, if φ is complete on V then there is a substitution σ such that $[\![\varphi\sigma]\!] = \mathsf{true}$: select a representative of each equivalence class, and let σ map each name in V to the representative of its class. In this case, we say that σ *agrees with* φ. For example, $\varphi \stackrel{\text{def}}{=} [x=y] \wedge [y=z] \wedge \neg[z=w]$ is complete on $V \stackrel{\text{def}}{=} \{x,y,z,w\}$, the equivalence classes are $\{x,y,z\}$ and $\{w\}$, and σ agrees with φ where $x\sigma = y\sigma = z\sigma = x$ and $w\sigma = w$.

The following result shows a key idea in the proofs of completeness of axiomatizations for the congruences. It reveals an interesting relationship between conditionals and substitutions: the outermost condition of processes P and Q can be used to cut down the class of substitutions that has to be considered to prove $P \sim_\ell^{c} Q$. In particular, when the conditions are complete on the free names of the processes, it suffices to consider a single substitution.

Lemma 4.8.12 Suppose that $P = \varphi P'$, $Q = \varphi Q'$, $\mathsf{fn}(P,Q) \subseteq V$, φ is complete on V, and σ agrees with φ. Then

(1) $P\sigma \sim_\ell Q\sigma$ implies $P \sim_\ell^{c} Q$
(2) $P\sigma \sim Q\sigma$ implies $P \sim^{c} Q$. □

To obtain axiomatizations for the congruences, we replace the axioms C1 and C2, which are sound for the bisimilarities but not for the congruences, by axioms for manipulating conditions. This is similar to what we did for axiomatizing open bisimilarity, but here there are more axioms because the conditions are more complex.

First, we have the simple congruence rule:

$$\text{C4} \quad P = Q \quad \text{implies} \quad \varphi P = \varphi Q\,.$$

Then, we have an axiom that allows us to replace a condition by an equivalent one:

$$\text{C5} \quad \varphi P = \varphi' P \quad \text{if } \varphi = \varphi'\,.$$

C5, like C1 and C2, can be replaced by proper axioms, if desired. We then have four axioms for conditional forms, namely

$$\begin{array}{llcl} \text{C6} & \neg[x=x]\,P & = & \neg[x=x]\,Q \\ \text{C7} & \varphi P P & = & P \\ \text{C8} & \varphi P Q & = & \neg\varphi Q P \\ \text{C9} & \varphi(\varphi' P) & = & (\varphi \wedge \varphi')\,P\,. \end{array}$$

These axioms are somewhat analogous to axioms S1–S4 for +. In particular, C7, like S4, expresses a form of idempotence, and C8, like S2, a form of commutativity. Also, S3 and C6 concern, respectively, the special roles of the process **0** and the condition $\neg[x = x]$, and S1 and C9 deal with the nesting of operators.

Then, we have a kind of distribution axiom involving conditions and summations:

$$\text{C10} \quad \varphi\,(P + P')\,(Q + Q') = \varphi\,P\,Q + \varphi\,P'\,Q' \,.$$

And finally, we have two axioms concerning conditions and prefixing, namely

$$\begin{array}{lrcl} \text{C11} & \varphi\,(\pi.\,P) & = & \varphi\,\pi.\,\varphi\,P \\ \text{C12} & [x = y]\,(\pi.\,P) & = & [x = y]\,(\pi\{y/x\}).\,P \,, \end{array}$$

where in C11, if $\pi = x(z)$ then z does not appear in φ. Note that C7, C8, and C10 are the only axioms that involve binary conditionals. Axiom C12 gives that the two names in a match are interchangeable underneath it:

Exercise 4.8.13 Show that $[x = y]\,P \;=\; [x = y]\,(P\{y/x\})$ can be proved using C5, C9, C10, C11, C12, and equational reasoning. □

Let LC' be obtained from LB' by replacing C1 and C2 by C4–C12.

Theorem 4.8.14 LC' is an axiomatization for strong late congruence of the terms in $\mathsf{L}(\mathbf{0}, \pi, +, \varphi)$. □

The key to the completeness proof is a kind of saturation of conditions, in which conditions are made complete on certain sets of names. The standard forms are standard *for* particular sets of names. In the proof, the two processes P and Q under consideration are transformed to standard forms that involve conditions complete on $\mathsf{fn}(P, Q)$.

For V a set of names, a *V-standard form* is a term of the form

$$\textstyle\sum_{i=1}^{n} \varphi_i \pi_i.\, \varphi_i P_i$$

where $n \geq 0$ and for each i,

(1) π_i is a prefix (containing no conditions) with $\mathsf{bn}(\pi_i) \cap V = \emptyset$
(2) φ_i is complete on V.

Note that φ_i occurs on top of π_i and on top of P_i.

The two main steps in the proof are then as follows. First, one shows that for any term P, if $\mathsf{fn}(P) \subseteq V$ then there is a V-standard form P^* such that $\mathsf{LC}' \vdash P = P^*$. Then, one shows that two V-standard forms that are late congruent are provably equal. The induction step appeals to (a generalization of) Lemma 4.8.12(1).

Now let FB' be obtained from LC' by adding the single axiom C3 that distinguishes bisimilarity from late bisimilarity.

Theorem 4.8.15 FB' is an axiomatization for strong full bisimilarity of the terms in $\mathsf{L}(\mathbf{0}, \pi, +, \varphi)$. □

The structure of the proof is similar to that of Theorem 4.8.14. The difference is in the completeness proof on V-standard forms, when the case of input prefixes is handled along the lines of Exercise 4.8.10 (but with some additional complication).

The following exercise gives some insight into these proof systems.

Exercise* 4.8.16 Let $\varphi \vee \varphi'$ abbreviate $\neg(\neg\varphi \wedge \neg\varphi')$.

(1) Show that if $\mathsf{LC}' \vdash P = P'$ and $\mathsf{LC}' \vdash Q = Q'$, then $\mathsf{LC}' \vdash \varphi PQ = \varphi P'Q'$.
(2) Show that $\mathsf{LC}' \vdash \varphi PQ = \varphi P + \neg\varphi Q$.
(3) Show that $\mathsf{LC}' \vdash (\varphi \vee \varphi') P = \varphi P (\varphi' P)$.
(4) Show that $\mathsf{LC}' \vdash (\varphi \vee \varphi') P = \varphi P + \varphi' P$.

(Hint: for (1) and (2), make use of S3, C10, C4, and C8.) □

We noted earlier a proof system for bisimilarity on $\mathsf{L}(\mathbf{0}, \pi, +, =)$ that involves the rule PRE3 instead of the axiom C3, and that therefore does not use mismatching. Similarly, if we replace C3 in FB' by the rule

$$\text{PRE4} \quad \frac{\Sigma_{i=1}^{n}\, \tau.\, P_i = \Sigma_{j=1}^{m}\, \tau.\, Q_j}{\Sigma_{i=1}^{n}\, x(z).\, P_i = \Sigma_{j=1}^{m}\, x(z).\, Q_j}$$

then the result is a proof system for full bisimilarity.

4.8.4 Composition and restriction

We now illustrate how to handle composition and restriction, by considering how to give proof systems for late congruence and full bisimilarity of the terms in the language $\mathsf{L}(\mathbf{0}, \pi, +, \varphi, |, \boldsymbol{\nu})$ given by

$$P \ ::= \ \mathbf{0} \ \mid \ \pi.P \ \mid \ P + P' \ \mid \ \varphi P P' \ \mid \ P \mid P' \ \mid \ \boldsymbol{\nu} z\, P\,,$$

where the prefixes are given by

$$\pi \ ::= \ \overline{x}y \ \mid \ x(z) \ \mid \ \tau \ \mid \ \overline{x}(z)$$

and the conditions by

$$\varphi \ ::= \ [x = y] \ \mid \ \neg\varphi \ \mid \ \varphi \wedge \varphi'\,.$$

Note that $\mathsf{L}(\mathbf{0},\pi,+,\varphi,|,\boldsymbol{\nu}\,)$ has bound-output prefixes. These prefixes are convenient for expanding compositions, as we saw in Section 2.2.2.

We need some axioms for expanding compositions and for manipulating restrictions. Consider expansion first. The expansion axiom schema, E, is the obvious generalization of the Expansion Lemma 2.2.15. It is:

if $P = \Sigma_i \varphi_i\, \pi_i .\, P_i$ and $P' = \Sigma_j \varphi'_j\, \pi'_j .\, P'_j$, then

$$\begin{array}{rcl} P \mid P' & = & \Sigma_i \varphi_i\, \pi_i .\,(P_i \mid P') + \Sigma_j \varphi'_j\, \pi'_j .\,(P \mid P'_j) + \\ & & \Sigma_{\pi_i\, \mathsf{opp}\, \pi'_j} (\varphi_i \wedge \varphi'_j \wedge [x_i = x'_j])\, \tau .\, R_{ij} \end{array}$$

where $\pi_i\, \mathsf{opp}\, \pi'_j$ if

(1) π_i is $\overline{x_i}y$ and π'_j is $x'_j(z)$, when R_{ij} is $P_i \mid P'_j\{y/z\}$, or
(2) π_i is $\overline{x_i}(z)$ and π'_j is $x'_j(z)$, when R_{ij} is $\boldsymbol{\nu} z\,(P_i \mid P'_j)$,

or vice versa.

For manipulating restrictions we have the congruence rule

$$\text{RES} \quad P = Q \quad \text{implies} \quad \boldsymbol{\nu} z\, P = \boldsymbol{\nu} z\, Q$$

and the axioms:

RES1	$\boldsymbol{\nu} z\, \boldsymbol{\nu} w\, P$	$=$	$\boldsymbol{\nu} w\, \boldsymbol{\nu} z\, P$	
RES2	$\boldsymbol{\nu} z\,(P+Q)$	$=$	$\boldsymbol{\nu} z\, P + \boldsymbol{\nu} z\, Q$	
RES3	$\boldsymbol{\nu} z\, \pi .\, P$	$=$	$\pi .\, \boldsymbol{\nu} z\, P$	if $z \notin \mathsf{n}(\pi)$
RES4	$\boldsymbol{\nu} z\, \pi .\, P$	$=$	$\mathbf{0}$	if π is $z(w)$ or $\overline{z}y$ or $\overline{z}(w)$
RES5	$\boldsymbol{\nu} z\, [x = y]P$	$=$	$[x = y]\boldsymbol{\nu} z\, P$	if $x, y \neq z$
RES6	$\boldsymbol{\nu} z\, [z = y]P$	$=$	$\mathbf{0}$	if $y \neq z$.

Note how restriction interacts with matching in axioms RES5 and RES6. These are the axioms that best show the meaning of restriction. By RES5, a restriction can be pushed through a match that does not involve the restricted name. When one of the names in the match is restricted, however, then no substitution can make the match true, and RES6 captures that the process is semantically null. These axioms also show clearly that restriction is a static binder.

As illustrations, we show how the analogues of RES5 and RES6 for mismatch, that is,

$$\boldsymbol{\nu} z\, [x \neq y]P = [x \neq y]\boldsymbol{\nu} z\, P \quad \text{if } x, y \neq z \tag{4.2}$$

and

$$\boldsymbol{\nu} z\, [z \neq y]P = \boldsymbol{\nu} z\, P \quad \text{if } y \neq z, \tag{4.3}$$

can be derived. We only sketch the derivations, leaving the missing details for Exercise 4.8.17. First,

$$P = \varphi P + \neg\varphi P \tag{4.4}$$

is derivable, using C7 and Exercise 4.8.16(2). Then,

$$\boldsymbol{\nu} z\, \mathbf{0} = \mathbf{0} \tag{4.5}$$

is derivable using C7 and RES6. Finally,

$$\varphi(\neg\varphi P) = \mathbf{0} \tag{4.6}$$

is derivable using C9, C5, C6, and C7.

Exercise 4.8.17 Show that (4.4), (4.5), and (4.6) are derivable. □

Then for (4.2) we have

$$\begin{array}{rcll}
\boldsymbol{\nu} z\,[x \neq y]P & = & [x = y]\boldsymbol{\nu} z\,[x \neq y]P + [x \neq y]\boldsymbol{\nu} z\,[x \neq y]P & \text{by (4.4)} \\
& = & \boldsymbol{\nu} z\,[x = y][x \neq y]P + [x \neq y]\boldsymbol{\nu} z\,[x \neq y]P & \text{by RES5} \\
& = & \boldsymbol{\nu} z\,\mathbf{0} + [x \neq y]\boldsymbol{\nu} z\,[x \neq y]P & \text{by (4.6)} \\
& = & \mathbf{0} + [x \neq y]\boldsymbol{\nu} z\,[x \neq y]P & \text{by (4.5)} \\
& = & [x \neq y][x = y]\boldsymbol{\nu} z\,P + [x \neq y]\boldsymbol{\nu} z\,[x \neq y]P & \text{by (4.6)} \\
& = & [x \neq y]\boldsymbol{\nu} z\,[x = y]P + [x \neq y]\boldsymbol{\nu} z\,[x \neq y]P & \text{by RES5} \\
& = & [x \neq y](\boldsymbol{\nu} z\,[x = y]P + \boldsymbol{\nu} z\,[x \neq y]P) & \text{by C10, S3} \\
& = & [x \neq y]\boldsymbol{\nu} z\,([x = y]P + [x \neq y]P) & \text{by RES2} \\
& = & [x \neq y]\boldsymbol{\nu} z\,P & \text{by (4.4)}\,.
\end{array}$$

And for (4.3) we have

$$\begin{array}{rcll}
\boldsymbol{\nu} z\,[z \neq y]P & = & \mathbf{0} + \boldsymbol{\nu} z\,[z \neq y]P & \text{by S2, S3} \\
& = & \boldsymbol{\nu} z\,[z = y]P + \boldsymbol{\nu} z\,[z \neq y]P & \text{by RES6} \\
& = & \boldsymbol{\nu} z\,([z = y]P + [z \neq y]P) & \text{by RES2} \\
& = & \boldsymbol{\nu} z\,P & \text{by (4.4)}\,.
\end{array}$$

We give two sample results: axiomatizations for late congruence and for full bisimilarity on $\mathsf{L}(\mathbf{0}, \pi, +, \varphi, |, \boldsymbol{\nu})$. Late bisimilarity and bisimilarity are handled quite similarly. And open bisimilarity can be axiomatized in an analogous way, starting from the axiomatization in Theorem 4.8.3. We refer to the notes at the end of the Part for more details.

Theorem 4.8.18 LC' plus E, RES, and RES1–RES6 is an axiomatization for strong late congruence of the terms in $\mathsf{L}(\mathbf{0}, \pi, +, \varphi, |, \boldsymbol{\nu})$. □

Theorem 4.8.19 FB' plus E, RES, and RES1–RES6 is an axiomatization for strong full bisimilarity of the terms in $\mathsf{L}(\mathbf{0}, \pi, +, \varphi, |, \boldsymbol{\nu})$. □

Some of the axioms for restriction listed in Theorems 4.8.18 and 4.8.19 can, in fact, be derived from other axioms. The strategy for the completeness proofs is to use the expansion schema and the restriction axioms to convert terms to congruent standard forms of the kinds discussed in connection with the proofs of Theorem 4.8.14 and Theorem 4.8.15. In particular, each restriction either disappears (by RES4 for instance) or gives rise to a bound-output prefix. Note that the only difference between the axiomatizations FB' and LC' is the axiom C3. (This axiom is also the only difference between the proof systems for the bisimilarities.)

4.8.5 Weak equivalences

Finally, to obtain axiomatizations for (weak) late congruence and full bisimilarity on $\mathsf{L}(\mathbf{0}, \pi, +, \varphi)$, it suffices to add to the axioms of LC' and FB' the analogues of the CCS τ laws:

TAU1	$\pi.\tau.P$	$=$	$\pi.P$
TAU2	$\tau.P + P$	$=$	$\tau.P$
TAU3	$\pi.(P + \tau.Q)$	$=$	$\pi.(P + \tau.Q) + \pi.Q$.

Composition and restriction can also be handled, using techniques similar to those in Section 4.8.4. The axiomatization of (weak) open bisimilarity is not completely settled. For this and proof systems for bisimilarity and late bisimilarity, see the notes at the end of the Part.

5

Subcalculi

5.1 The Asynchronous π-calculus

The π-calculus takes over from CCS a kind of synchronized communication, in which an interaction involves the joint participation of two processes. The prefix operator expresses temporal precedence: the sole capability of $\overline{x}y.\,P$ is to send via x, and that of $x(z).\,Q$ to receive via x, and in each case it is only after the relevant capability has been exercised that the behaviour expressed by the term underneath the prefix can unfold. The combination of prefixing and synchronized communication is versatile and tractable.

On the other hand, some concurrent systems, especially distributed systems, use forms of *asynchronous* communication, in which the act of sending a datum and the act of receiving it are separate. Often, such communication involves an explicit *medium* of some kind, and sending and receiving data involve putting them into and taking them out of the medium. Media exhibit a variety of characteristics. For instance, they may have bounded or unbounded capacity, and they may or may not preserve some ordering among the data they contain. There may be an arbitrary delay between a datum being sent and it being received. If the communication medium has unbounded capacity, no process need wait to send a datum.

This section and the following four are about a subcalculus of the π-calculus in which communication can be understood as asynchronous. The key step in achieving this is the decree that, in the subcalculus, the only term that can appear underneath an output prefix is $\mathbf{0}$. Thus, the only output-prefixed terms are of the shape $\overline{x}y.\,\mathbf{0}$, or, in abbreviated form, $\overline{x}y$. In a term of the subcalculus, an unguarded occurrence of a particle $\overline{x}y$ can be thought of as a datum y in an implicit communication medium, tagged with x to indicate that it is available to any unguarded subterm of the form $x(z).\,P$. Thus, in the evolution of a term, the datum y can be considered to be sent when $\overline{x}y$ becomes unguarded, and to be received when $\overline{x}y$ disappears via an intraaction of the form

$$\overline{x}y \mid (x(z).\, P + M) \longrightarrow P\{y/z\}\ .$$

This reduction has two effects: the particle $\overline{x}y$ is consumed and removed from the communication medium; and the unguarded output particles in $P\{y/z\}$ are liberated and put into the medium.

There can be any number of unguarded output particles scattered within a term; the implicit medium therefore has unbounded capacity and preserves no ordering among output particles. In order to carry through this interpretation consistently, it is necessary to disallow output particles as summands (see the discussion below).

The subcalculus is called the *Asynchronous π-calculus*, and it is of interest for a combination of reasons. Many mobile systems are naturally thought of as composed of parts that communicate asynchronously. In particular, communication in many distributed systems involves transmission of data via media, and is therefore asynchronous. Further, many languages for programming concurrent or distributed systems have asynchronous primitives, as they are amenable to efficient implementation. Other language features, in particular for synchronized communication, are usually implemented using asynchronous primitives. The Asynchronous π-calculus and variants of it are helpful in addressing some of the difficulties in reasoning about the behaviour of asynchronous mobile systems and programming languages for expressing them.

The syntax of the Asynchronous π-calculus is introduced and discussed in Section 5.2. Section 5.3 and Section 5.4 present the theory of behavioural equivalence for the subcalculus. This differs in some important respects from the theory for the full π-calculus, briefly because asynchronous observers are less discriminating than synchronous observers. One of the main results is that ground bisimilarity is a congruence on the subcalculus. The expressiveness of the asynchronous subcalculus is examined in Section 5.5.

Note In the following four sections, we will not give details of all proofs. To do so would increase the length substantially, and many of the techniques are by now familiar. We will concentrate on what is particular to asynchrony.

5.2 Syntax of Aπ

We begin by defining the subcalculus formally.

Definition 5.2.1 (Aπ) The *Asynchronous π-calculus* is the subcalculus, Aπ, of the π-calculus whose processes and summations are given by

$$
\begin{array}{rcl}
P & ::= & \overline{x}y.\,\mathbf{0} \mid M \mid P \mid P' \mid \nu z\, P \mid !P \\
M & ::= & \mathbf{0} \mid x(z).\,P \mid \tau.\,P \mid M + M' .
\end{array}
$$

□

As just discussed, the only output-prefixed processes admitted are the degenerate ones of the form $\overline{x}y.\,\mathbf{0}$. Moreover, only input-prefixed and τ-prefixed terms can be summands in sums.

The reason for preventing output particles from being summands is to be consistent with the intention outlined above, that the subcalculus be viewed as capturing asynchronous communication. An unguarded occurrence of a particle $\overline{x}y$ in a term is to be thought of as named datum that *has been* sent and is available to any process that can receive via x. A term such as $\overline{x}y + a(z).\,Q$ is excluded because, although it has an unguarded occurrence of an output particle and is *capable* of sending y via x, it is also capable of receiving via a, and if that second capability is exercised then the first is rendered void. If such terms were admitted, the correspondence between a datum's having been sent but not received, and the appearance of an unguarded particle containing the datum, would be lost.

Terms such as $\overline{x}y + a(z).\,Q$ should be excluded even if we want to model a lossy communication medium. Such a medium might throw away any data that have been sent. But $\overline{x}y + a(z).\,Q$ can itself decide that the offer of $\overline{x}y$ will vanish, by performing an input via a. An asynchronous process that can choose nondeterministically to send y via x or to receive via a should be written $\tau.\,\overline{x}y + a(z).\,Q$. Further, if we want to model a medium that is lossy on x, it suffices to add to the system the term $!x(z).\,\mathbf{0}$.

The match prefix form is also excluded from Aπ. This is not because matching is incompatible with asynchronous communication: the two notions are concordant. The reason is rather that some powerful proof techniques for Aπ terms, which we will use frequently later in the book, are lost if matching is added, and this outweighs any diminution in expressiveness. Indeed, the main reason for including match prefixes in the π-calculus is their importance in the Expansion Lemma and in axiomatizations and proof systems for behavioural equivalences. A significant weakness of the asynchronous subcalculus is that there is no analogous expansion lemma. Consequences of this are that related techniques, such as an analogue of the Unique-Solution Theorem, are missing, and axiomatizations and proof systems are more complicated.

Although output prefixing is degenerate in Aπ, some sequentialization is apparent in the syntax, because in Aπ input prefixes are still *prefixed to* processes. (One could countenance a form of 'delayed input' in which this restriction was relaxed to some extent, and we will consider such a form in Section 10.4.) Although output particles cannot be prefixed to terms other than $\mathbf{0}$, some semantic sequentialization of output actions can nonetheless be achieved using private names, and for this reason the subcalculus retains much of the expressive power of the π-calculus.

As a simple example to illustrate this point, consider the Aπ term

$$(\boldsymbol{\nu} y, z)\,(\overline{x}y \mid \overline{y}z \mid \overline{z}a \mid R)$$

where $y, z \notin \mathsf{fn}(R)$. The subterm R is free to proceed, but the three output particles can be consumed only in left-to-right order.

We now give some examples to illustrate how to express things in Aπ. First, consider the term

$$(\boldsymbol{\nu} x, w)\,(\overline{x}w \mid w(u).\,(\overline{u}a \mid w(v).\,\overline{v}b) \mid x(w).\,\boldsymbol{\nu} u\,(\overline{w}u \mid u(y).\,\boldsymbol{\nu} v\,(\overline{w}v \mid v(z).\,Q)))\ .$$

Although the prefix $w(u)$ is unguarded, the restriction on w ensures that the particle $\overline{x}w$ must be consumed before an input via w can occur. Moreover, the protocol expressed in this term is such that $\overline{u}a$ must be consumed before $\overline{v}b$; the only evolution from the term yields, after five reductions, $Q\{^{a,\,b}\!/\!_{y,\,z}\}$.

This protocol can be used to express synchronized communication in the asynchronous subcalculus. Suppose we augment Aπ by allowing arbitrary output-prefixed terms. The key clauses in a translation, $[\![\cdot]\!]$, from the augmented language to Aπ are

$$[\![\overline{x}y.\,P]\!] = \boldsymbol{\nu} w\,(\overline{x}w \mid w(u).\,(\overline{u}y \mid [\![P]\!]))$$

and

$$[\![x(z).\,Q]\!] = x(w).\,\boldsymbol{\nu} u\,(\overline{w}u \mid u(z).\,[\![Q]\!])\,,$$

where $w, u \notin \mathsf{fn}(P, Q, x, y)$. The transition

$$\overline{x}y.\,P \mid x(z).\,Q \xrightarrow{\tau} P \mid Q\{^{y}\!/\!_{z}\}$$

is mimicked by the sequence

$$\begin{aligned}
[\![\overline{x}y.\,P \mid x(z).\,Q]\!] &\xrightarrow{\tau}\equiv \boldsymbol{\nu} w\,(w(u).\,(\overline{u}y \mid [\![P]\!]) \mid \boldsymbol{\nu} u\,(\overline{w}u \mid u(z).\,[\![Q]\!]))\\
&\xrightarrow{\tau}\equiv \boldsymbol{\nu} u\,(\overline{u}y \mid [\![P]\!] \mid u(z).\,[\![Q]\!])\\
&\xrightarrow{\tau}\equiv [\![P]\!] \mid [\![Q]\!]\{^{y}\!/\!_{z}\}\ .
\end{aligned}$$

We will return to this translation in Section 5.5.

As a final example, we illustrate how to encode input-guarded sums in Aπ without using the $+$ operator. Consider a persistent cell storing a value v, and suppose the value stored can be got (read) via g and set (updated) via s. The cell can be expressed succinctly by the term CELL$\langle v\rangle$ of the polyadic π-calculus, where

$$\mathrm{CELL} \stackrel{\mathrm{def}}{=} (v).\,(\boldsymbol{\nu} c)\,(\overline{c}\langle v\rangle \mid !c(y).\,(g(r).\,\overline{r}\langle y\rangle.\,\overline{c}\langle y\rangle + s(x,d).\,\overline{d}.\,\overline{c}\langle x\rangle))\ .$$

To get the value stored in the cell, a process supplies via g a name on which the value should be returned to it, as in

$$\boldsymbol{\nu} r\,(\overline{g}\langle r\rangle \mid r(y).\,P)\,,$$

and to set the value, a process supplies via s the new value and a name on which the cell can signal that the operation has been carried out, as in

$$\boldsymbol{\nu} d\,(\overline{s}\langle v', d\rangle \mid d.\,Q)\ .$$

Interacting with a CELL is similar to interacting with a priority queue of the kind described in Section 3.3.

We can express such a cell in Aπ without using $+$ (but with polyadicity, for convenience) by

$$\boldsymbol{\nu}\ell\,(\overline{\ell}\langle v\rangle \mid !g(r).\,\ell(w).\,(\overline{\ell}\langle w\rangle \mid \overline{r}\langle w\rangle) \mid !s(x,d).\,\ell(w).\,(\overline{\ell}\langle x\rangle \mid \overline{d}))\ .$$

The value, v, stored in the cell is associated with the restricted name ℓ, which also acts as a lock. A process $\boldsymbol{\nu} d'\,(\overline{s}\langle v', d'\rangle \mid d'.\,Q)$ requests a set operation by interacting with the subterm $!s(x,d).\,\ell(w).\,(\overline{\ell}\langle x\rangle \mid \overline{d})$. The continuation, $\ell(w).\,(\overline{\ell}\langle v'\rangle \mid \overline{d'})$, of an instance of the replicated term first acquires the current value via ℓ, and then makes the new value available, again via ℓ, and signals via d' that the operation has been carried out. The behaviour is similar in the case of a get, except that the relevant instance of the replicated term makes available via ℓ the value it received via ℓ, that is, the value is unchanged. The use of locks, illustrated in this example, is common in asynchronous programming languages.

We will see in Section 5.5 that the subcalculus of Aπ without input-guarded sums is just as expressive as Aπ. A yet more succinct description of a persistent cell storing v is the polyadic π-calculus process CELL$'\langle v\rangle$ where

$$\mathrm{CELL}' \stackrel{\mathrm{def}}{=} (v).\,(\boldsymbol{\nu} c)\,(\overline{c}\langle v\rangle \mid !c(y).\,(\overline{g}\langle y\rangle.\,\overline{c}\langle y\rangle + s(x).\,\overline{c}\langle x\rangle))\ .$$

Although CELL$'$ is slightly more succinct, CELL uses a common idiom, expressing a cell as an object with two methods that can be invoked by sending it appropriate data. Note that CELL$'$ involves a sum of an output-prefixed process and an input-prefixed process. As we will also see in Section 5.5, π-calculus summations involving both output-prefixed summands and input-prefixed summands cannot, in general, be expressed in the subcalculus of the π-calculus that lacks $+$, if certain properties are required of a representation.

5.3 Behavioural equivalence in Aπ

If two Aπ terms P and Q are barbed congruent then they are completely interchangeable, that is, $C[P]$ and $C[Q]$ are barbed congruent for any π-context C. Rather than viewing two Aπ terms as (special) π-calculus processes, however, they can be considered as processes of the Asynchronous π-calculus. It is then natural to compare them in asynchronous contexts, that is, in the contexts of Aπ.

It is therefore useful to consider a variant of barbed congruence in whose definition the quantification is restricted to contexts of Aπ. There is a further consideration, namely, that in an asynchronous setting it is natural to restrict the observables to be the co-names. (This point will be explained in Section 5.4.) It turns out that this variant, *asynchronous barbed congruence*, is coarser than barbed congruence on Aπ.

Before introducing asynchronous barbed congruence, however, we examine the labelled bisimilarities on Aπ. On the π-calculus, bisimilarity and its ground, late, and open variants are all different. On Aπ, however, they all coincide. Moreover, the common relation is a congruence on Aπ; indeed, it is preserved by all contexts of the full π-calculus. An important consequence is that two Aπ terms can be shown to be barbed congruent (and hence also asynchronous barbed congruent) by establishing that they are ground bisimilar.

Our first goal is to show that ground bisimilarity is preserved by substitution on Aπ. To do this, we need three lemmas about transition. The origin of the properties stated in the first two lemmas is the fact that, in Aπ, the occurrence of an output action cannot preclude any other action, because output particles do not appear in sums, and cannot itself enable any action, because the continuation of any particle is $\mathbf{0}$.

Lemma 5.3.1 Suppose P is an Aπ term.

(1) If $P \xrightarrow{\overline{x}y} P'$ then $P \equiv \overline{x}y \mid P'$.

(2) If $P \xrightarrow{\overline{x}(z)} P'$ then $P \equiv \boldsymbol{\nu} z\,(\overline{x}z \mid P')$.

Proof Both parts are proved by straightforward induction on inference, using properties of structural congruence. □

Lemma 5.3.2 Suppose P is an Aπ term.

(1) If $P \xrightarrow{\overline{x}y}\xrightarrow{\alpha} P'$ then $P \xrightarrow{\alpha}\xrightarrow{\overline{x}y}\equiv P'$.

(2) If $P \xrightarrow{\overline{x}(z)}\xrightarrow{\alpha} P'$ where $z \notin \mathsf{n}(\alpha)$, then $P \xrightarrow{\alpha}\xrightarrow{\overline{x}(z)}\equiv P'$.

(3) If $P \xrightarrow{\overline{x}y} \xrightarrow{xw} P'$ where $w \notin \mathsf{fn}(P)$, then $P \xrightarrow{\tau}\equiv P'\{y/w\}$.

(4) If $P \xrightarrow{\overline{x}(z)} \xrightarrow{xw} P'$ where $w \notin \mathsf{fn}(P)$, then $P \xrightarrow{\tau}\equiv \nu z\, P'\{z/w\}$. □

Exercise 5.3.3 Prove Lemma 5.3.2. □

Of course, none of the assertions in Lemma 5.3.1 or Lemma 5.3.2 is correct for the full calculus.

Lemma 5.3.4 Suppose P is an Aπ term.

(1) If $P \stackrel{\overline{x}y}{\Longrightarrow} \stackrel{xw}{\Longrightarrow} P'$ where $w \notin \mathsf{fn}(P)$, then $P \Longrightarrow\equiv P'\{y/w\}$.

(2) If $P \stackrel{\overline{x}(z)}{\Longrightarrow} \stackrel{xw}{\Longrightarrow} P'$ where $w \notin \mathsf{fn}(P)$, then $P \Longrightarrow\equiv \nu z\, P'\{z/w\}$.

Proof We consider (1); (2) is similar.

If $P \stackrel{\overline{x}y}{\Longrightarrow} \stackrel{xw}{\Longrightarrow} P'$ then there are P_1 and P_2 such that $P \Longrightarrow P_1 \xrightarrow{\overline{x}y} P_2 \stackrel{xw}{\Longrightarrow} P'$. By Lemma 5.3.1(1), we have $P_1 \equiv \overline{x}y \mid P_2$. Since $P_2 \stackrel{xw}{\Longrightarrow} P'$ and w is fresh, $\overline{x}y \mid P_2 \Longrightarrow P'\{y/w\}$ using Lemma 1.4.4(2). Hence $P_1 \Longrightarrow\equiv P'\{y/w\}$, and so $P \Longrightarrow\equiv P'\{y/w\}$. (We use here that $\equiv\xrightarrow{\tau}$ is included in $\xrightarrow{\tau}\equiv$.) □

Using these results and Lemma 1.4.13, we can show that ground bisimilarity of Aπ terms is preserved by arbitrary substitution. The proof uses the following definition and result.

Definition 5.3.5 $\mathcal{R}$ is a *ground bisimulation up to restriction and up to* $\sim_{\mathrm{g}}$ if whenever $(P, Q) \in \mathcal{R}$, there is $z \notin \mathsf{fn}(P, Q)$ such that

(1) if $P \xrightarrow{\alpha} P'$ where α is $\overline{x}y$ or xz or $\overline{x}(z)$ or τ, then there are
   (a) Q' such that $Q \stackrel{\widehat{\alpha}}{\Longrightarrow} Q'$ and
   (b) P'', Q'', $\widetilde{w}$ such that $P' \sim_{\mathrm{g}} (\nu\widetilde{w})\, P''$ and $Q' \sim_{\mathrm{g}} (\nu\widetilde{w})\, Q''$ and $(P'', Q'') \in \mathcal{R}$

(2) vice versa. □

Exercise 5.3.6 Show that if $\mathcal{R}$ is a ground bisimulation up to restriction and up to $\sim_{\mathrm{g}}$, then $(P, Q) \in \mathcal{R}$ implies $P \approx_{\mathrm{g}} Q$. □

Lemma 5.3.7 (Preservation of $\approx_{\mathrm{g}}$ by substitution on Aπ) Suppose that P and Q are Aπ terms. If $P \approx_{\mathrm{g}} Q$ then $P\sigma \approx_{\mathrm{g}} Q\sigma$ for any σ.

Proof We show that

$$\mathcal{S} \stackrel{\text{def}}{=} \{(P\sigma, Q\sigma) \mid P, Q \text{ A}\pi \text{ terms with } P \approx_{\mathrm{g}} Q, \text{ and } \sigma \text{ arbitrary}\}$$

is a ground bisimulation up to restriction and up to $\sim_{\mathrm{g}}$.

Suppose $(P\sigma, Q\sigma) \in \mathcal{S}$ with $P \approx_{\mathrm{g}} Q$, and choose $w \notin \mathsf{fn}(P\sigma, Q\sigma)$. Suppose $P\sigma \xrightarrow{\beta} R$, where if β is an input or a bound output, then its object is w. We have to show that there are S such that $Q\sigma \stackrel{\widehat{\beta}}{\Longrightarrow} S$ and P', Q', $\widetilde{u}$ such that $R \sim_{\mathrm{g}} (\boldsymbol{\nu}\widetilde{u})\, P'$ and $S \sim_{\mathrm{g}} (\boldsymbol{\nu}\widetilde{u})\, Q'$ and $(P', Q') \in \mathcal{S}$.

First, suppose $\beta \neq \tau$. Then by Lemma 1.4.13(1), we have $P \xrightarrow{\alpha} P''$ with $\alpha\sigma = \beta$ and $P''\sigma = R$. Since $P \approx_{\mathrm{g}} Q$ we have $Q \stackrel{\alpha}{\Longrightarrow} Q'' \approx_{\mathrm{g}} P''$, and so by Lemma 1.4.8, $Q\sigma \stackrel{\beta}{\Longrightarrow} S \stackrel{\mathrm{def}}{=} Q''\sigma$, as required.

Now suppose $\beta = \tau$. By Lemma 1.4.13(2), there are three cases. We consider just the third possibility, (c): (a) is similar to the above, and (b) is similar to (c).

So suppose $R \sim \boldsymbol{\nu} y\, P''\{y/w\}\sigma$ where $P \xrightarrow{\overline{x}(y)}\xrightarrow{zw} P''$ and $x\sigma = z\sigma$. Since $P \approx_{\mathrm{g}} Q$, we have $Q \stackrel{\overline{x}(y)}{\Longrightarrow}\stackrel{zw}{\Longrightarrow} Q'' \approx_{\mathrm{g}} P''$. Setting $a = x\sigma$ we have $Q\sigma \stackrel{\overline{a}(y)}{\Longrightarrow}\stackrel{aw}{\Longrightarrow} Q''\sigma$, and hence by Lemma 5.3.4(2) – here we use the fact that the terms belong to Aπ – we have $Q\sigma \Longrightarrow S \sim_{\mathrm{g}} \boldsymbol{\nu} y\, Q''\sigma\{y/w\}$ (since $\equiv$ is included in $\sim_{\mathrm{g}}$). Set $P' \stackrel{\mathrm{def}}{=} P''\{y/w\}\sigma$ and $Q' \stackrel{\mathrm{def}}{=} Q''\{y/w\}\sigma = Q''\sigma\{y/w\}$. Then $(P', Q') \in \mathcal{S}$ and $R \sim_{\mathrm{g}} \boldsymbol{\nu} y\, P'$ and $S \sim_{\mathrm{g}} \boldsymbol{\nu} y\, Q'$, as required. $\square$

As a first consequence of this result, we can show that ground bisimilarity is a congruence on the Asynchronous π-calculus. In fact, a stronger result holds: ground bisimilarity of Aπ terms is preserved in every context of the *full* π-calculus.

Theorem 5.3.8 (Congruence property of $\approx_{\mathrm{g}}$ on Aπ) Suppose that P and Q are Aπ terms. If $P \approx_{\mathrm{g}} Q$ then $C[P] \approx_{\mathrm{g}} C[Q]$ for any π-context C.

Proof We show only the most interesting case: that if $P \approx_{\mathrm{g}} Q$ then $P \mid R \approx_{\mathrm{g}} Q \mid R$ for any π-calculus process R. To do this we show that

$$\mathcal{S} \stackrel{\mathrm{def}}{=} \{(P \mid R, Q \mid R) \mid P \approx_{\mathrm{g}} Q,\ R \text{ arbitrary }\}$$

is a ground bisimulation up to restriction.

To see the main point, suppose that $P \mid R \xrightarrow{\tau} P' \mid R'$ is inferred by COMM-R from $P \xrightarrow{xy} P'$ and $R \xrightarrow{\overline{x}y} R'$.

Since $P \approx_{\mathrm{g}} Q$, there is a fresh z such that for any P^*, if $P \xrightarrow{xz} P^*$ then $Q \stackrel{xz}{\Longrightarrow}\approx_{\mathrm{g}} P^*$. Since $P \xrightarrow{xy} P'$, there is P'' such that $P \xrightarrow{xz} P''$ and $P''\{y/z\} = P'$, by Lemma 1.4.4(2). Taking $P^* = P''$ in the above, $Q \stackrel{xz}{\Longrightarrow} Q'' \approx_{\mathrm{g}} P''$ and so $Q \stackrel{xy}{\Longrightarrow} Q' \stackrel{\mathrm{def}}{=} Q''\{y/z\}$ by Lemma 1.4.4(1). Since, by Lemma 5.3.7, $\approx_{\mathrm{g}}$ is preserved by substitution on Aπ processes, $P' \approx_{\mathrm{g}} Q'$.

In summary, $Q \mid R \xrightarrow{\tau} Q' \mid R'$ and $(P' \mid R', Q' \mid R') \in \mathcal{S}$, as required.

Up to restriction is needed for the case when $P \mid R \xrightarrow{\tau} \nu y\,(P' \mid R')$ is inferred by CLOSE-L, for example. □

A very useful consequence of this result is that ground bisimilarity is a sufficient condition for barbed congruence of $A\pi$ terms.

Corollary 5.3.9 If P and Q are $A\pi$ terms and $P \approx_{\mathrm{g}} Q$, then $P \cong^{\mathrm{c}} Q$.

Proof This follows from Theorem 5.3.8 and the fact that ground bisimilarity implies barbed bisimilarity. □

A second consequence is that all variants of bisimilarity coincide on $A\pi$.

Corollary 5.3.10 The relations $\approx_{\mathrm{g}}$, $\approx_{\mathrm{g}}^{\mathrm{c}}$, $\approx$, $\approx^{\mathrm{c}}$, $\approx_{\ell}$, $\approx_{\ell}^{\mathrm{c}}$, and $\approx_{\mathrm{o}}$ coincide on $A\pi$ terms.

Proof It suffices to show that $P \approx_{\mathrm{g}} Q$ implies $P \approx_{\mathrm{o}} Q$ on $A\pi$. To do this, one checks that, on $A\pi$, $\approx_{\mathrm{g}}$ is an open bisimulation, appealing to the fact that $\approx_{\mathrm{g}}$ is closed under substitution. □

We have considered the weak case. The analogous results hold in the strong case. Again, note that ground bisimilarity is preserved by arbitrary π-calculus contexts.

Theorem 5.3.11 Suppose P and Q are $A\pi$ terms.

(1) The relations $\sim_{\mathrm{g}}$, $\sim_{\mathrm{g}}^{\mathrm{c}}$, $\sim$, $\sim^{\mathrm{c}}$, $\sim_{\ell}$, $\sim_{\ell}^{\mathrm{c}}$, and $\sim_{\mathrm{o}}$ coincide on $A\pi$ terms.
(2) If $P \sim_{\mathrm{g}} Q$ then $C[P] \sim_{\mathrm{g}} C[Q]$ for any π-context C.
(3) If $P \sim_{\mathrm{g}} Q$ then $P \simeq^{\mathrm{c}} Q$.

Proof The proof is a simplification of the argument in the weak case. □

The following definition and result, which shows the soundness of a proof technique for $A\pi$ processes, will be used in later work. A special case of this technique is that of Definition 5.3.5. We recall that ${}_{\mathrm{g}}\!\succeq$ is the ground expansion relation.

Definition 5.3.12 $\mathcal{R}$ is a *ground bisimulation up to context and up to* ${}_{\mathrm{g}}\!\succeq$ if whenever $(P, Q) \in \mathcal{R}$, there is $z \notin \mathsf{fn}(P, Q)$ such that

(1) if $P \xrightarrow{\alpha} P'$ where α is $\overline{x}y$ or xz or $\overline{x}(z)$ or τ, then there are

 (a) a process Q' such that $Q \overset{\widehat{\alpha}}{\Longrightarrow} Q'$ and

(b) a multi-hole context C such that $P' \ {}_{\mathrm{g}}\!\succeq C\eta$ and $Q' \ {}_{\mathrm{g}}\!\succeq C\eta'$ for some instantiations η and η' such that
   (i) $(\eta_j, \eta'_j) \in \mathcal{R}$ for all j and
   (ii) if $[\cdot]_i$ occurs under an input prefix in C, then $(\eta_i\sigma, \eta'_i\sigma) \in \mathcal{R}$ for all σ

(2) vice versa. □

Lemma 5.3.13 Suppose that $\mathcal{S}$ is a ground bisimulation up to context and up to ${}_{\mathrm{g}}\!\succeq$ on Aπ. Then for any Aπ processes P and Q, if $(P, Q) \in \mathcal{S}$ then $P \approx_{\mathrm{g}} Q$.

Proof The proof is similar to that of Lemma 2.4.66. □

Notation 5.3.14 (Barbed congruence) For a subcalculus $\mathcal{L}$ of the π-calculus, we write $\mathcal{L} \triangleright P \cong^{\mathrm{c}} Q$ to assert that P and Q are barbed congruent in $\mathcal{L}$, that is, that $C[P] \stackrel{\bullet}{\approx} C[Q]$ for every $\mathcal{L}$-context C. We will later use this notation also for calculi that are not subcalculi of the π-calculus, provided they have a reduction relation and a notion of observability so that barbed congruence can be defined. □

We will often tacitly appeal to the fact that if $\mathcal{L}$ is a subcalculus of the π-calculus and $\mathcal{L}'$ is a subcalculus of $\mathcal{L}$, then $\mathcal{L} \triangleright P \cong^{\mathrm{c}} Q$ implies $\mathcal{L}' \triangleright P \cong^{\mathrm{c}} Q$. For example, by Corollary 5.3.9, if P, Q are Aπ terms then $P \approx_{\mathrm{g}} Q$ implies $\pi \triangleright P \cong^{\mathrm{c}} Q$, and hence A$\pi \triangleright P \cong^{\mathrm{c}} Q$. That is, if two A$\pi$ terms are ground bisimilar then they are indistinguishable in any context of the π-calculus, and hence in any Aπ context.

5.4 Asynchronous equivalences

We now introduce asynchronous barbed congruence, the variant of barbed congruence mentioned at the start of the previous section. It has two significant aspects. The origin of the first is that when considering two asynchronous processes, it is appropriate to consider them to have the same behaviour if they are indistinguishable in any *asynchronous* context.

The second aspect is of a different kind, and is less obvious. It reflects the nature of asynchronous communication. In CCS and the π-calculus, to observe a process *is* to interact with it by performing a complementary action, and both input actions and output actions are observable, because every complementary action has a continuation that is set running when the interaction occurs. In Aπ, there is no difficulty in observing that a process performs an output action, because the complementary input action has a continuation. An input action, on the other hand, is not observable in general, because its complementary action, the output particle, has no continuation. A process may be able to observe an input indirectly, however, for instance by performing some action that would not have been possible had the input not occurred. For example, thinking of the Aπ term $\boldsymbol{\nu} z\,(\overline{x}z \mid z(w).\,P)$ as describing a component of a system, we may say that the component observes that the private name z has been received when it receives a name via z. The upshot of this discussion is that, in defining asynchronous barbed congruence, it is appropriate to restrict the observables to be the co-names.

Definition 5.4.1 (Asynchronous barbed bisimilarity and congruence)

(1) *Asynchronous barbed bisimilarity* is the largest symmetric relation, $\dot{\approx}_{\mathrm{a}}$, such that whenever $P \dot{\approx}_{\mathrm{a}} Q$,

  (a) $P \downarrow_{\overline{x}}$ implies $Q \Downarrow_{\overline{x}}$

  (b) $P \xrightarrow{\tau} P'$ implies $Q \Longrightarrow\dot{\approx}_{\mathrm{a}} P'$.

(2) P and Q are *asynchronous barbed congruent*, $P \cong^{\mathrm{c}}_{\mathrm{a}} Q$, if $C[P] \dot{\approx}_{\mathrm{a}} C[Q]$ for every context C of Aπ. □

It is worth noting in passing that if in the definition of barbed congruence on the π-calculus the observables were taken to be the co-names only (rather than the co-names and the names), then the same relation (that is, barbed congruence) would result.

A first natural question is whether asynchronous barbed congruence differs from barbed congruence on Aπ. It does, and an example that shows this is $P \stackrel{\mathrm{def}}{=} !x(z).\,\overline{x}z$ and $Q \stackrel{\mathrm{def}}{=} \mathbf{0}$. Clearly, P and Q are not barbed congruent. They are, however, asynchronous barbed congruent, as we will see shortly. The equivalence of P and Q expresses that in an asynchronous setting, a buffer process that can repeatedly consume a datum via some name and then emit it via the same name is semantically null.

A second natural question arises, namely, whether we can find tractable techniques for showing that Aπ processes are asynchronous barbed congruent, as we did in Chapter 2 for showing that processes are barbed congruent. The answer is again positive, and the techniques are the analogues of what we saw in the previous section: the appropriate variant of ground bisimilarity is adequate. First, we define the asynchronous variant of bisimilarity.

Definition 5.4.2 (Asynchronous bisimilarity) *Asynchronous bisimilarity* is the largest symmetric relation, $\approx_{\mathrm{a}}$, such that whenever $P \approx_{\mathrm{a}} Q$,

(1) if $P \xrightarrow{\alpha} P'$ and α is $\overline{x}y$ or $\overline{x}(z)$ or τ, then $Q \stackrel{\widehat{\alpha}}{\Longrightarrow}\approx_{\mathrm{a}} P'$

(2) if $P \xrightarrow{xy} P'$ then

(a) $Q \stackrel{xy}{\Longrightarrow} \approx_{\mathrm{a}} P'$ or
(b) $Q \Longrightarrow Q'$ for some Q' with $P' \approx_{\mathrm{a}} (Q' \mid \overline{x}y)$. □

The distinctive clause is the second, concerning input actions. It is based on the earlier observation that in an asynchronous setting, a process cannot directly observe the receipt of data it sends. Thus, an input action of one process can be mimicked not only in the normal way, but also by some internal actions leading to a process that, when composed with the particle consumed in the input action, stands in the appropriate relation.

A little work is needed to show that asynchronous bisimilarity is transitive. The exercise below invites the reader to do this for its strong variant, $\sim_{\mathrm{a}}$, which is defined by replacing $\stackrel{\widehat{\alpha}}{\Longrightarrow}$ by $\stackrel{\alpha}{\longrightarrow}$, and $\stackrel{xy}{\Longrightarrow}$ by $\stackrel{xy}{\longrightarrow}$, and $\Longrightarrow$ by $\stackrel{\tau}{\longrightarrow}$, in Definition 5.4.2. The proof for $\approx_{\mathrm{a}}$ is similar but longer.

Exercise 5.4.3

(1) Show that $P \sim_{\mathrm{a}} Q$ implies $P \mid \overline{x}y \sim_{\mathrm{a}} Q \mid \overline{x}y$.
(2) Hence show that $\sim_{\mathrm{a}}$ is transitive. □

The significant point in Definition 5.4.2 is how one process is allowed to mimic another's performance of an input action. The three exercises below give some insight into the way input actions are treated, by giving equivalent formulations of the second clause in the definition. In fact, the exercises are about *strong* asynchronous bisimilarity, $\sim_{\mathrm{a}}$. The analogous results for the weak case are much harder; indeed some of them are still open. The exercises just state replacements for the second clause in the definition, which is

(2) if $P \stackrel{xy}{\longrightarrow} P'$ then
  (a) $Q \stackrel{xy}{\longrightarrow} \sim_{\mathrm{a}} P'$ or
  (b) $Q \stackrel{\tau}{\longrightarrow} Q'$ for some Q' with $P' \sim_{\mathrm{a}} (Q' \mid \overline{x}y)$.

Exercise 5.4.4 Let $\sim_{\mathrm{a1}}$ be defined like $\sim_{\mathrm{a}}$ except that

(2) if $P \downarrow_x$ then $P \mid \overline{x}y \sim_{\mathrm{a1}} Q \mid \overline{x}y$ for all y.

Show that:

(1) $\sim_{\mathrm{a1}}$ is an equivalence relation.
(2) $\sim_{\mathrm{a1}}$ coincides with $\sim_{\mathrm{a}}$. □

Exercise* 5.4.5 Let $\sim_{\mathrm{a2}}$ be defined like $\sim_{\mathrm{a}}$ except that

(2) if $P \stackrel{xy}{\longrightarrow} P'$ then
  (a) $Q \stackrel{xy}{\longrightarrow} \sim_{\mathrm{a2}} P'$ or

(b) $Q \xrightarrow{\tau} Q'$ for some Q' with $P' \xrightarrow{\overline{x}y} \sim_{a2} Q'$.

Show that:

(1) $\sim_{a2}$ is an equivalence relation.
(2) If $P \sim_{a2} Q$ then $P \mid \overline{x}y \sim_{a2} Q \mid \overline{x}y$.
(3) $\sim_{a2}$ coincides with $\sim_a$. (Hint: use the first two parts of this exercise, and both parts of Exercise 5.4.3. You may also find the last two parts of Lemma 5.3.2 useful.) □

Exercise 5.4.6 Let $\sim_{a3}$ be defined like $\sim_a$ except that

(2) if $P \xrightarrow{xy} P'$ then

(a) $Q \xrightarrow{xy} \sim_{a3} P'$ or
(b) there are P'' and P''' such that $P' \xrightarrow{\overline{x}y} P''$ and $P \xrightarrow{\tau} P'''$ and $P'' \sim_{a3} P'''$.

Show that:

(1) $\sim_{a3}$ is an equivalence relation.
(2) $\sim_{a3}$ coincides with $\sim_{a2}$. □

The ground variant of asynchronous bisimilarity is defined as follows.

Definition 5.4.7 (Asynchronous ground bisimilarity) *Asynchronous ground bisimilarity* is the largest symmetric relation, $\approx_{ag}$, such that whenever $P \approx_{ag} Q$, there is $z \notin \mathsf{fn}(P, Q)$ such that

(1) if $P \xrightarrow{\alpha} P'$ where α is $\overline{x}y$ or $\overline{x}(z)$ or τ, then $Q \stackrel{\widehat{\alpha}}{\Longrightarrow} \approx_{ag} P'$
(2) if $P \xrightarrow{xz} P'$ then

(a) $Q \stackrel{xz}{\Longrightarrow} \approx_{ag} P'$ or
(b) $Q \Longrightarrow Q'$ for some Q' with $P' \approx_{ag} (Q' \mid \overline{x}z)$. □

The following exercise shows that for a name x, in the presence of a persistent 1-place buffer that can repeatedly accept any datum via x and then emit it via x, output prefixing with subject x is redundant.

Exercise 5.4.8 Show that for any π-term P,

$$\overline{x}y.\, P \mid !x(z).\, \overline{x}z \approx \overline{x}y \mid P \mid !x(z).\, \overline{x}z\,.$$

□

We saw earlier that bisimilarity and ground bisimilarity coincide on Aπ, and that the common relation is preserved in all contexts of the full π-calculus. Their asynchronous variants also coincide and are preserved in all Aπ contexts. (Since the asynchronous equivalences are intended for comparing asynchronous processes, only contexts of Aπ are considered.) Hence, asynchronous ground bisimilarity implies asynchronous barbed congruence.

Theorem 5.4.9 Suppose P and Q are Aπ terms.

(1) $P \approx_{\mathrm{ag}} Q$ iff $P \approx_{\mathrm{a}} Q$.
(2) If $P \approx_{\mathrm{ag}} Q$ then $C[P] \approx_{\mathrm{ag}} C[Q]$ for any Aπ context C.
(3) If $P \approx_{\mathrm{ag}} Q$ then $P \cong^{\mathrm{c}}_{\mathrm{a}} Q$.

Proof The proof is similar to arguments seen earlier. □

The strong analogues of the various asynchronous equivalences (notation: $\simeq^{\mathrm{c}}_{\mathrm{a}}$, $\sim_{\mathrm{a}}$, $\sim_{\mathrm{ag}}$) are defined in the expected ways. The following theorem records that strong asynchronous barbed congruence, bisimilarity, and ground bisimilarity all coincide on Aπ.

Theorem 5.4.10 Suppose P and Q are Aπ terms. Then $P \simeq^{\mathrm{c}}_{\mathrm{a}} Q$ iff $P \sim_{\mathrm{a}} Q$ iff $P \sim_{\mathrm{ag}} Q$.

Proof The proof is similar to those of earlier results. □

In the weak case, the various equivalences on Aπ are related just as their analogues on the full π-calculus without matching. (Recall that matching is absent from Aπ.) Thus asynchronous (ground) bisimilarity does *not* coincide with asynchronous barbed congruence on image-finite Aπ processes. The counterexample in Exercise 2.4.30 shows this, that is, the pair of processes $P \stackrel{\mathrm{def}}{=} \overline{a}x \mid E_{xy}$ and $Q \stackrel{\mathrm{def}}{=} \overline{a}y \mid E_{xy}$, where $E_{xy} \stackrel{\mathrm{def}}{=} !x(z).\,\overline{y}z \mid !y(z).\,\overline{x}z$.

Moreover, if matching is added, then the relationship between barbed congruence and labelled bisimilarity is again as for the full calculus. Thus, let AMπ be defined like Aπ but with matching added, and let *asynchronous barbed equivalence*, $\cong_{\mathrm{a}}$, be defined by setting $P \cong_{\mathrm{a}} Q$ if $P \mid R \stackrel{\bullet}{\approx}_{\mathrm{a}} Q \mid R$ for any AMπ term R. Then, asynchronous barbed equivalence and asynchronous barbed congruence do not coincide on AMπ, and asynchronous bisimilarity does not imply asynchronous barbed congruence on AMπ. We record just the main result.

Theorem 5.4.11 Suppose P and Q are image-finite AMπ terms. Then $P \approx_{\mathrm{a}} Q$ iff $P \cong_{\mathrm{a}} Q$.

$$\text{On A}\pi,\ \simeq^{\mathrm{c}} \subset \simeq^{\mathrm{c}}_{\mathrm{a}} = \sim_{\mathrm{a}} = \sim_{\mathrm{ag}}.$$

$$\text{On A}\pi,\ \cong^{\mathrm{c}} \subset \cong^{\mathrm{c}}_{\mathrm{a}} \supset \approx_{\mathrm{a}} = \approx_{\mathrm{ag}}.$$

$$\text{On image-finite AM}\pi,\ \cong^{\mathrm{c}} \subset \cong^{\mathrm{c}}_{\mathrm{a}} \subset \cong_{\mathrm{a}} = \approx_{\mathrm{a}}.$$

Table 5.1. *The asynchronous equivalences on* Aπ

Proof See the reference at the end of the Part. □

Table 5.1 summarizes the relationships among the various equivalences on Aπ. We now turn to other aspects of the subcalculus.

5.5 Expressiveness of asynchronous calculi

This section examines the expressiveness of some asynchronous subcalculi of the π-calculus. The results give insight into the expressiveness of various combinations of operators. They may also be useful in practice, for instance in the implementation of concurrent programming languages.

We begin by looking in detail at how synchronized communication can be expressed in Aπ, a topic that was touched on briefly in Section 5.2. It is useful because programming-language constructs for synchronized communication are usually implemented using asynchronous primitives.

Another construct that is present in many concurrent programming languages is input-guarded choice. It allows expression of processes that can evolve in different ways depending on which of several communications is received first. This construct is also often implemented using asynchronous communication primitives. (This is the case in Pict, for example.) We study a translation of Aπ into the subcalculus of Aπ without sum.

Finally, we discuss whether sum terms involving both input prefixes and output prefixes can be expressed in Aπ.

5.5.1 Expressing polyadic communication

Let us write A$\pi_{-\{+,\tau\}}$ for the subcalculus of Aπ from which the sum and τ-prefix operators are excluded. Thus, the terms of A$\pi_{-\{+,\tau\}}$ are given by

$$P \ ::= \ \mathbf{0} \mid \overline{x}y.\mathbf{0} \mid x(z).P \mid P \mid P' \mid \nu z\, P \mid\ !P\,. \tag{5.1}$$

The translation of the polyadic π-calculus into the monadic π-calculus in Section 3.1 uses output prefixing to ensure that the order within a tuple is preserved when its components are communicated individually. Terms of the polyadic version of $A\pi_{-\{+,\tau\}}$ can be expressed in $A\pi_{-\{+,\tau\}}$ using a different idea. The translation, $\{\cdot\}$, from the polyadic version of $A\pi_{-\{+,\tau\}}$ to $A\pi_{-\{+,\tau\}}$ is a homomorphism, except that

$$\begin{aligned} \{\overline{x}\langle y_1, y_2\rangle\} &\stackrel{\text{def}}{=} \boldsymbol{\nu} w\,(\overline{x}w \mid w(v).\,(\overline{v}y_1 \mid w(v).\,\overline{v}y_2)) \\ \{x(z_1, z_2).\,R\} &\stackrel{\text{def}}{=} x(w).\,\boldsymbol{\nu} v\,(\overline{w}v \mid v(z_1).\,(\overline{w}v \mid v(z_2).\,\{R\}))\,, \end{aligned}$$

where w and v are fresh. (For clarity, we give the definition for pairs. The general case is then as expected.)

Communication of the pair y_1, y_2 via x is achieved as follows. The sender uses x to send a private name w. The receiver accepts w and uses it to send back another private name v. The sender then uses v to send y_1, and the receiver accepts y_1 and acknowledges receipt by sending v via w again (it could just as well send another fresh name). The sender then uses v to send y_2, and the receiver accepts y_2 and proceeds.

Exercise 5.5.1 Check that

$$\{\overline{x}\langle y_1, y_2\rangle \mid x(z_1, z_2).\,R\} \Longrightarrow\equiv \{R\sigma\}$$

where σ is $\{y_1, y_2/z_1, z_2\}$. □

5.5.2 Expressing synchronized communication in $A\pi$

It is well known that a synchronized interaction can in many cases be achieved by means of a pair of asynchronous communications. The sending process emits the data to be sent together with a fresh name, and waits for a signal via the fresh name acknowledging receipt of the data before proceeding. The receiving process accepts the data and the fresh name, and then emits an acknowledgement signal and proceeds.

This can be expressed succinctly in π-calculus terms: the effect of the interaction

$$\overline{x}\langle\tilde{y}\rangle.\,P \mid x(\tilde{z}).\,Q \xrightarrow{\tau} P \mid Q\{\tilde{y}/\tilde{z}\}$$

between polyadic π-terms is achieved by the first two communications within

$$\boldsymbol{\nu} a\,(\overline{x}\langle\tilde{y}, a\rangle \mid a.\,P \mid x(\tilde{z}, a).\,(\overline{a} \mid Q))\,,$$

where a is fresh.

We look more closely at this representation. Consider the extension of $A\pi_{-\{+,\tau\}}$ where arbitrary output-prefixed terms are admitted, that is, the set of terms obtained when $\overline{x}y.\,P$ replaces $\overline{x}y.\,\mathbf{0}$ in the grammar (5.1) above. This is the subcalculus $\pi_{-\{=,+,\tau\}}$ obtained by omitting matching, sum, and τ prefix from the full π-calculus.

The translation, $[\cdot]$, from the polyadic version of $\pi_{-\{=,+,\tau\}}$ to the polyadic version of $\mathrm{A}\pi_{-\{+,\tau\}}$ is a homomorphism, except that

$$\begin{aligned} [\overline{x}\langle\widetilde{y}\rangle.\,P] &\stackrel{\text{def}}{=} \boldsymbol{\nu} a\,(\overline{x}\langle\widetilde{y},a\rangle \mid a.\,[P]) \\ [x(\widetilde{z}).\,Q] &\stackrel{\text{def}}{=} x(\widetilde{z},a).\,(\overline{a} \mid [Q])\,, \end{aligned}$$

where in each case a is fresh.

Suppose Σ is a sorting on the polyadic version of $\pi_{-\{=,+,\tau\}}$. Let Σ^* be the obvious modification of Σ suggested by the translation; that is, if $\Sigma(\gamma) = \langle\widetilde{\delta}\rangle$ then $\Sigma^*(\gamma) = \langle\widetilde{\delta}, \mathsf{NULL}\rangle$, where NULL is a new sort and $\Sigma^*(\mathsf{NULL})$ is the empty tuple. Using techniques similar to those used to obtain analogous results for the translation of the polyadic π-calculus into the monadic π-calculus in Section 3.1, it can be shown that the translation is sound but not complete.

Composing $[\cdot]$ and the translation $\{\cdot\}$ of polyadic $\mathrm{A}\pi_{-\{+,\tau\}}$ to $\mathrm{A}\pi_{-\{+,\tau\}}$ gives the translation $\{[\cdot]\}$, from the polyadic version of $\pi_{-\{=,+,\tau\}}$ to $\mathrm{A}\pi_{-\{+,\tau\}}$, whose effect is illustrated by

$$\begin{aligned} \{[\overline{x}\langle y_1,y_2\rangle.\,P]\} &\stackrel{\text{def}}{=} \boldsymbol{\nu} a\,(\boldsymbol{\nu} w\,(\overline{x}w \mid w(v).\,(\overline{v}y_1 \mid w(v).\,(\overline{v}y_2 \mid w(v).\,\overline{v}a))) \\ &\qquad \mid a(w).\,\boldsymbol{\nu} v\,(\overline{w}v \mid \{[P]\})) \\ \{[x(z_1,z_2).\,Q]\} &\stackrel{\text{def}}{=} x(w).\,\boldsymbol{\nu} v\,(\overline{w}v \mid v(z_1).\,(\overline{w}v \mid \\ &\qquad v(z_2).\,(\overline{w}v \mid v(a).\,\boldsymbol{\nu} w\,(\overline{a}w \mid w(u).\,\{[Q]\})))) \,. \end{aligned}$$

The synchronized communication of an n-tuple is expressed by $2n+5$ asynchronous monadic communications when $n > 0$. This number can be reduced to $2n+1$ by eliminating the last four actions. The last two actions are redundant because they correspond to the obsolete acknowledgement via a; and the preceding two are redundant because they are just preparatory for the last two. (To pass an empty tuple we need two communications.) The result is the optimized translation, $[\![\cdot]\!]$, which is a homomorphism except that

$$\begin{aligned} [\![\overline{x}\langle y_1,y_2\rangle.\,P]\!] &\stackrel{\text{def}}{=} \boldsymbol{\nu} w\,(\overline{x}w \mid w(v).\,(\overline{v}y_1 \mid w(v).\,(\overline{v}y_2 \mid [\![P]\!]))) \\ [\![x(z_1,z_2).\,Q]\!] &\stackrel{\text{def}}{=} x(w).\,\boldsymbol{\nu} v\,(\overline{w}v \mid v(z_1).\,(\overline{w}v \mid v(z_2).\,[\![Q]\!])) \,. \end{aligned}$$

As usual, $[\![\cdot]\!]$ is sound but not complete.

5.5.3 Expressing input-prefixed sums in $\mathrm{A}\pi_{-\{+,\tau\}}$

We now show that sum terms of $\mathrm{A}\pi$ all of whose summands are input prefixes, can be expressed in the subcalculus $\mathrm{A}\pi_{-\{+,\tau\}}$, which lacks the sum operator. For convenience, we use indexed sum rather than binary sum, and therefore consider the terms given by the grammar

$$P \ ::= \ \Sigma_{i \in I}\, x_i(z).\, P_i \ \mid \ \overline{x}y.\, \mathbf{0} \ \mid \ P \mid P' \ \mid \ \boldsymbol{\nu} z\, P \ \mid \ !P\,, \tag{5.2}$$

where I ranges over finite sets. Taking I to be the empty set gives $\mathbf{0}$, and taking it to be a singleton gives an input-prefixed term. So, the grammar essentially describes the terms of $\mathrm{A}\pi$ that contain no τ prefix. (It is actually straightforward to accommodate τ prefixes in what follows.)

The translation, $[\cdot]$, from the terms given by the grammar (5.2) to the polyadic version of $\mathrm{A}\pi_{-\{+,\tau\}}$ is a homomorphism, except that

$$\begin{aligned}[\Sigma_i\, x_i(z).\, P_i] \overset{\text{def}}{=} \boldsymbol{\nu}\ell\ (\ & \text{PROCEED} \\ \mid\ & \Pi_i\, x_i(z).\, (\boldsymbol{\nu} p, f)\ (\overline{\ell}\langle p, f\rangle \mid p.\, (\text{FAIL} \mid [P_i]) \\ & \qquad\qquad\qquad\qquad\quad \mid f.\, (\text{FAIL} \mid \overline{x_i}\langle z\rangle)))\,,\end{aligned}$$

where ℓ, p, and f are fresh and

$$\begin{aligned}\text{PROCEED} &\overset{\text{def}}{=} \ell(p, f).\, \overline{p} \\ \text{FAIL} &\overset{\text{def}}{=} \ell(p, f).\, \overline{f}\,.\end{aligned}$$

To understand the representation, consider first a transition

$$\Sigma_i\, x_i(z).\, P_i \xrightarrow{x_j y} P_j\{y/z\}\,.$$

This is mimicked as follows. The j-indexed component of $[\Sigma_i\, x_i(z).\, P_i]$ accepts y via x_j, and then interacts with PROCEED via the private name ℓ. This interaction is like that used in representing truth-values, and the effect is that $[P_j]\{y/z\}$ can proceed and the process FAIL becomes unguarded: the derivative after three transitions is structurally congruent to

$$\begin{aligned}[P_j]\{y/z\} \mid \boldsymbol{\nu}\ell\ (\ & \text{FAIL} \\ \mid\ & \Pi_{i \neq j}\, x_i(z).\, (\boldsymbol{\nu} p, f)\ (\overline{\ell}\langle p, f\rangle \ \mid p.\, (\text{FAIL} \mid [P_i]) \\ & \qquad\qquad\qquad\qquad\qquad\ \mid f.\, (\text{FAIL} \mid \overline{x_i}\langle z\rangle)))\,.\end{aligned}$$

If subsequently any of the other input-prefixed components, $x_k(z).\, Q$ say, accepts a name, a say, its next interaction via ℓ is with FAIL rather than PROCEED. After that interaction, the name a is emitted again via x_k, and a new instance of FAIL becomes unguarded. Thus, in effect, the name a is absorbed and then emitted by a 1-place buffer named x_k, which, as we have seen, is a semantically null activity in an asynchronous setting.

This illustrates how $[\Sigma_i\, x_i(z).\, P_i]$ can resolve to receive a name via x_j and render the other possibilities void. The resolution occurs when a component interacts with PROCEED via the private name ℓ. Note, however, that several of the input-prefixed components of $[\Sigma_i\, x_i(z).\, P_i]$ can accept names before any of them interacts with PROCEED. All but one, however, will end up interacting with an instance of FAIL and emitting the name they accepted.

The translation $[\cdot]$ differs in an important respect from those we considered earlier: the first action of a term $[P]$ need *not* correspond directly to an action of P, because the component that performs the first action need not be the one that subsequently interacts with PROCEED. This has the effect that the precise statement of the expressibility result and its proof need care. We will not go into the proof here (see the reference at the end of the Part). We do wish to mention the result, however.

The first important point is that, because the tension among the alternatives is not resolved immediately, (asynchronous) bisimilarity is not an appropriate criterion by which to judge the correctness of the encoding. For consider the term

$$P \stackrel{\text{def}}{=} \overline{x}y \mid (x(z).\, \overline{z}.\, \mathbf{0} + w(z).\, \mathbf{0})\ .$$

Let $\{[\cdot]\}$ be the composition of $[\cdot]$ and the translation $\{\cdot\}$ from above that eliminates polyadic prefixes from $\mathrm{A}\pi_{-\{+,\tau\}}$ terms.

Exercise 5.5.2

(1) Prove that $P \not\approx_{\mathrm{a}} \{[P]\}$.
(2) Hence, show that $\{[\cdot]\}$ is not sound with respect to asynchronous bisimilarity, that is, that $\{[Q]\} \approx_{\mathrm{a}} \{[R]\}$ does not imply $Q \approx_{\mathrm{a}} R$. ($\{[\cdot]\}$ is not complete either, that is, $Q \approx_{\mathrm{a}} R$ does not imply $\{[Q]\} \approx_{\mathrm{a}} \{[R]\}$.) □

The translation is sound and complete with respect to the equivalence *asynchronous coupled similarity*, however. This equivalence, $\asymp_{\mathrm{a}}$, (whose definition we do not give) is less demanding than bisimilarity. Informally, it does not distinguish between processes that differ only in how they *gradually* resolve via internal activity how to proceed.

Theorem 5.5.3 For any terms P and Q given by grammar (5.2),

(1) $P \asymp_{\mathrm{a}} \{[P]\}$
(2) $\{[P]\} \asymp_{\mathrm{a}} \{[Q]\}$ iff $P \asymp_{\mathrm{a}} Q$.

Proof See the reference at the end of the Part. □

We leave this topic with an exercise that asks for an encoding that is sound and complete with respect to asynchronous bisimilarity.

Exercise* 5.5.4 Find a variant of the encoding $[\cdot]$ that is sound and complete with respect to asynchronous bisimilarity. (Hint: modify $[\cdot]$ so that no *irrevocable* decision to accept a particular input is taken until a later stage. The modified encoding may introduce the possibility of divergence, that is, an infinite sequence of τ actions representing unending internal computation. Note that $[\cdot]$ does not introduce the possibility of divergence.) □

5.5.4 Expressing other sums in $\mathrm{A}\pi_{-\{+,\tau\}}$

Consider the subcalculus of the π-calculus whose terms are given by

$$\begin{array}{rcl} P & ::= & M \mid N \mid P \mid P' \mid \boldsymbol{\nu} z\, P \mid\, !P \\ M & ::= & \mathbf{0} \mid x(z).\, P \mid M + M' \\ N & ::= & \overline{x}y.\, P \mid N + N'\, . \end{array}$$

In this subcalculus – which is not asynchronous – the summands in a sum term are either all input prefixes or all output prefixes.

The translation $[\cdot]$ just discussed can be modified to yield a translation from this subcalculus to the polyadic version of $\mathrm{A}\pi_{-\{+,\tau\}}$ (and thence, if desired, to $\mathrm{A}\pi_{-\{+,\tau\}}$). The modified translation, $\{\!\!\{\cdot\}\!\!\}$, is a homomorphism, except that

$$\begin{array}{rl} \{\!\!\{\Sigma_i\, \overline{x_i} d_i.\, P_i\}\!\!\} \stackrel{\mathrm{def}}{=} \boldsymbol{\nu} s & (\ \mathrm{PROCEED}\langle s\rangle \\ & \mid \Pi_i\ \boldsymbol{\nu} a\, \overline{x_i}\langle d_i, s, a\rangle.\, (\boldsymbol{\nu} p, f)\, (\overline{a}\langle p, f\rangle \mid p.\, \{\!\!\{P_i\}\!\!\} \mid f.\, \mathbf{0})) \end{array}$$

$$\begin{array}{l} \{\!\!\{\Sigma_i\, y_i(z).\, Q_i\}\!\!\} \stackrel{\mathrm{def}}{=} \\ \boldsymbol{\nu} r\ \ (\ \mathrm{PROCEED}\langle r\rangle \\ \quad\ \mid \Pi_i\ \boldsymbol{\nu} g\ \ (\ \overline{g} \\ \qquad\qquad \mid\, !g.\, y_i(z, s, a).\, (\boldsymbol{\nu} p_1, f_1)\ (\ \overline{r}\langle p_1, f_1\rangle \\ \qquad\qquad\qquad \mid p_1.\, (\boldsymbol{\nu} p_2, f_2)\ (\ \overline{s}\langle p_2, f_2\rangle \\ \qquad\qquad\qquad\qquad \mid p_2.\ (\ \mathrm{FAIL}\langle r\rangle \\ \qquad\qquad\qquad\qquad\qquad \mid \mathrm{FAIL}\langle s\rangle \\ \qquad\qquad\qquad\qquad\qquad \mid \mathrm{PROCEED}\langle a\rangle \\ \qquad\qquad\qquad\qquad\qquad \mid \{\!\!\{Q_i\}\!\!\}) \\ \qquad\qquad\qquad\qquad \mid f_2.\ (\ \mathrm{PROCEED}\langle r\rangle \\ \qquad\qquad\qquad\qquad\qquad \mid \mathrm{FAIL}\langle s\rangle \\ \qquad\qquad\qquad\qquad\qquad \mid \mathrm{FAIL}\langle a\rangle \\ \qquad\qquad\qquad\qquad\qquad \mid \overline{g})) \\ \qquad\qquad\qquad \mid f_1.\, (\mathrm{FAIL}\langle r\rangle \mid \overline{y_i}\langle z, s, a\rangle)))))\, , \end{array}$$

where r, s, a, etc. are fresh, and PROCEED and FAIL are essentially as above:

$$\text{PROCEED} \stackrel{\text{def}}{=} (\ell).\,\ell(p,f).\,\overline{p}$$
$$\text{FAIL} \stackrel{\text{def}}{=} (\ell).\,\ell(p,f).\,\overline{f}\ .$$

The idea underlying this translation is the following.

The subterm PROCEED$\langle s\rangle$ of $\{\!\!\{\Sigma_i\,\overline{x_i}d_i.\,P_i\}\!\!\}$ is to ensure that only one output prefix can proceed, and the subterm PROCEED$\langle r\rangle$ of $\{\!\!\{\Sigma_i\,y_i(z).\,Q_i\}\!\!\}$ that only one input prefix can proceed.

If $x_j = y_k$ ($= x$ say) then the jth component of the first translated term and the kth component of the second can communicate, via x. The datum d_j is sent, together with the private name s and another private name a. The receiver then determines via r whether it can proceed or not.

If it cannot proceed, because a commitment to some other input-prefixed summand has already been made, it emits via x the triple d_j, s, a that it received, so that that triple is available to the translation of any other sum of input prefixes.

If the receiver can proceed, then it determines via s whether also its potential partner in the communication can proceed.

If that is not possible, because a commitment to some other output-prefixed summand has already been made, it continues as the composition of four subterms. The term PROCEED$\langle r\rangle$ is to ensure that an input is possible. The term FAIL$\langle s\rangle$ is to ensure that no further output is possible. The term FAIL$\langle a\rangle$ is to ensure that the continuation of the j-indexed component of the translation of $\{\!\!\{\Sigma_i\,\overline{x_i}d_i.\,P_i\}\!\!\}$ cannot proceed: that continuation tests via a whether it can proceed or not. The particle $\overline{g}$ restores the translation of the j-indexed summand, so that it is available to participate in another attempt at a communication.

Finally, if the continuation of the k-indexed component of $\{\!\!\{\Sigma_i\,y_i(z).\,Q_i\}\!\!\}$ determines that *both* it and the sender can proceed, then the communication takes place. The continuation is the composition of $\{\!\!\{Q_k\}\!\!\}\{^{d_j}\!/z\}$, the term PROCEED$\langle a\rangle$ that allows the sender to proceed, and the terms FAIL$\langle r\rangle$ and FAIL$\langle s\rangle$ that prevent any other component in the translation of either sum term from proceeding.

The translation $\{\!\!\{\cdot\}\!\!\}$ does not introduce the possibility of deadlock, that is, if $\{\!\!\{P\}\!\!\}$ can deadlock then P can deadlock. The translation also does not introduce the possibility of divergence. It is not known, however, whether a result analogous to Theorem 5.5.3 holds for $\{\!\!\{\cdot\}\!\!\}$.

The sum terms of the subcalculus just considered are homogeneous. Let us now consider mixed choice, by examining the subcalculus $\pi_{-\{=,\tau\}}$ of the π-calculus that lacks the τ-prefix and matching operators, that is, the subcalculus whose terms are given by

$$\begin{array}{lcl} P & ::= & M \mid P \,|\, P' \mid \boldsymbol{\nu} z\, P \mid !P \\ M & ::= & \mathbf{0} \mid x(z).\, P \mid \overline{x}y.\, P \mid M + M'\,. \end{array}$$

To implement the choice construct of this language using asynchronous communication primitives, the possibility of deadlock must be considered. A translation of $\pi_{-\{=,\tau\}}$ into (the polyadic version of) $\mathrm{A}\pi_{-\{+,\tau\}}$ that is based directly on $\{\!\{\cdot\}\!\}$ introduces deadlock. For instance, the translations of terms of the form

$$(\overline{x}a.\, P + y(z).\, Q) \mid (x(w).\, R + \overline{y}b.\, S)$$

and

$$\overline{x}a.\, P + x(w).\, R$$

can deadlock even if the terms themselves cannot.

Exercise* 5.5.5 Work out the natural extension of $\{\!\{\cdot\}\!\}$ to $\pi_{-\{=,\tau\}}$, and show how it introduces deadlock when applied to terms of the above forms. □

Two ideas used in implementations to avert deadlock are randomization and ordering among processes. Leaving aside such concerns, we conclude discussion of this topic by mentioning a result of theoretical interest. The result says that there is no translation, $[\![\cdot]\!]$, from $\pi_{-\{=,\tau\}}$ into $\pi_{-\{=,+,\tau\}}$ that enjoys three properties. The first two properties are

$$[\![P\sigma]\!] = [\![P]\!]\sigma \text{ for any injective substitution } \sigma \tag{5.3}$$

and

$$[\![P \mid Q]\!] = [\![P]\!] \mid [\![Q]\!]\,. \tag{5.4}$$

To express the third property, we say that a computation of a process is *maximal* if either it is infinite, or it is finite and the last process in it has no transitions. Then the third property is:

> for any P and any $N \subseteq \mathsf{fn}(P)$, if every maximal computation of P contains exactly one action whose subject is in N, then every maximal computation of $[\![P]\!]$ contains exactly one action whose subject is in N. (5.5)

Theorem 5.5.6 There is no translation from $\pi_{-\{=,\tau\}}$ to $\pi_{-\{=,+,\tau\}}$ that satisfies (5.3), (5.4), and (5.5).

Proof Briefly, the proof is based on showing that a solution to the leadership-election problem for symmetric networks (where, informally, the processes running at the nodes are identical) that can be expressed in $\pi_{-\{=,\tau\}}$ cannot be expressed in $\pi_{-\{=,+,\tau\}}$. See the reference at the end of the Part. □

This elegant theorem is one of the few non-expressiveness results for π-calculus or related languages. The weakness of the Asynchronous π-calculus that is pinpointed by the result is in line with results in the field of distributed systems expressed using other models; see, for instance, [Lyn96]. One may argue, however, that the conditions (5.4) and (5.5) in Theorem 5.5.6 are too strong. First, some encodings introduce extra components for coordinating activities, and (5.4) disallows this. And second, an encoding could have the property that $P \approx [\![P]\!]$ for every P, and yet fail to satisfy (5.5), just because $[\![P]\!]$ can perform an infinite sequence of τ transitions but P cannot, for some P. For this reason, the question of the relative expressiveness of the subcalculi is not settled.

5.6 The Localized π-calculus

In a π-calculus process $x(z).\,P$, the bound name z may occur in the continuation P as subject of an input prefix, as subject or object of an output prefix, or in a match. Consequently, when the process receives a name y via x, there are three capabilities involving y that it may be able to exercise. The first is the *input capability*: the ability to receive via y. The second is the *output capability*, that is, the ability to send via y. And the third is the *match capability*: the ability to compare y with other names.

This section is about the *Localized π-calculus*, Lπ, a subcalculus of the π-calculus in which processes can exercise and communicate output capabilities, but not input capabilities or match capabilities. In Lπ, when a process receives a name, it can only use it for sending or send it to another process, which must itself respect the output-capability constraint. The output capability is separate from the match capability; indeed, many useful properties would be lost if matching were added to Lπ.

The output-capability constraint of Lπ arises frequently in applications. For instance, a process in an operating system that is responsible for managing a printer can communicate to another process the capability to send a job to the printer, but not the capability to receive a job intended for the printer. For another example, think of names as names of objects in the sense of object-oriented programming. The constraint guarantees the basic property that no two objects have the same name. In a system of objects, names of objects can be communicated. The recipient of an object name a can use a to invoke the object's methods, and it can pass a to other objects; but it cannot create an object named a. When objects are represented in π-calculus, this discipline is usually expressed via the output-capability constraint.

A consequence of the output-capability constraint is that in a process $\boldsymbol{\nu} x\, P$ of Lπ, every possible input via x is visible in the syntax of P: no input can be created, either inside or outside P. In other words, every process that receives via a name is local to the process that created that name. This locality property of names gives the Localized π-calculus its name. The locality property may be useful for developing distributed implementations of (extensions of) the language, where processes run at different sites: the constraint may facilitate the task of establishing *to which site* a given message should be delivered. The property may also be useful for typing. For instance, it is needed to develop type inference algorithms in the presence of polymorphism; see the notes at the end of Part III.

Definition 5.6.1 (Lπ) The *Localized π-calculus* is the subcalculus, Lπ, of the π-calculus whose processes and summations are given by

$$\begin{array}{lcl} P & ::= & M \mid P \mid P' \mid \nu z\, P \mid\, !P \\ M & ::= & \mathbf{0} \mid \overline{x}y.\, P \mid x(z).\, P \mid M + M' \end{array}$$

where in $x(z).\, P$, the name z cannot occur free in P as the subject of an input prefix. □

The output-capability constraint can also be formalized via a type system (the i/o types of Section 7.1). It is worth studying on its own, however, because of its importance and the fact that by formalizing the idea by syntactic means, it is easier to see and express its consequences.

The output-capability constraint is often allied with asynchronous communication. Indeed, the first language to impose the constraint and bring out its importance was the Join calculus, which is an asynchronous language. We refer to the intersection of Lπ and Aπ as the *Asynchronous Localized π-calculus*, ALπ. It syntax is as in Definition 5.6.1, except that $\overline{x}y.\, P$ is deleted from the grammar for summations, and $\overline{x}y.\, \mathbf{0}$ is added to the grammar for processes. Several consequences of the output-capability constraint do not depend on asynchrony, however.

5.6.1 Expressiveness

As an illustration of the expressiveness of ALπ without $+$, we show how to encode the sum-free terms of Aπ in it. (Recall that we saw in Section 5.5.3 how to encode arbitrary Aπ processes as sum-free terms of Aπ.) For convenience, we will use the polyadic version of ALπ. The translation will make use of the ALπ processes $x \hookrightarrow y$ defined by

$$x \hookrightarrow y \stackrel{\text{def}}{=}\, !x(z).\, y(s,t).\, \overline{z}\langle s,t\rangle\ .$$

The translation of a term $a(z).\,P$ must allow for the possibility that z may occur as the subject of an input prefix in P. Roughly, the main idea of the translation is to replace each output particle $\overline{a}y$ by the process $\boldsymbol{\nu} x\,(\overline{a}\langle x,y\rangle \mid x \hookrightarrow y)$, and to transform a term of the form $a(z).\,P$ to one that receives a pair such as x, y and, when necessary, interacts with $x \hookrightarrow y$ to effect an input via y without itself performing an input via y. One can think of the x and y in the translation of P as representing the input capability and the output capability of the name y in P, respectively. The process $x \hookrightarrow y$ acts as a coordinator between processes that wish to interact via y. We will explain this further after defining the translation and giving an example.

The translation, $[\![\cdot]\!]$, is indexed by a finite partial function ε on names, which is needed for book-keeping. It is a homomorphism, except that

$$[\![\overline{a}y]\!]_\varepsilon \stackrel{\text{def}}{=} \boldsymbol{\nu} x\,(\overline{a}\langle x,y\rangle \mid x \hookrightarrow y)$$

and

$$[\![a(z).\,P]\!]_\varepsilon \stackrel{\text{def}}{=} \begin{cases} a(x,z).\,[\![P]\!]_{\varepsilon[x/z]} & \text{if } a \notin \mathsf{dom}(\varepsilon) \\ \boldsymbol{\nu} w\,(\overline{x}\langle w\rangle \mid w(x',z).\,[\![P]\!]_{\varepsilon[x'/z]}) & \text{if } \varepsilon(a) = x \end{cases}$$

where x, w, x' are fresh, and $\varepsilon[u/z]$ is the finite partial function that agrees with ε and maps z to u.

To illustrate the translation, consider the Aπ transitions

$$\overline{a}y \mid a(z).\,(\overline{z}b \mid z(u).\,\overline{u}c) \xrightarrow{\tau}\equiv \overline{y}b \mid y(u).\,\overline{u}c \xrightarrow{\tau}\equiv \overline{b}c\,. \tag{5.6}$$

These are mimicked as follows, where the ε is the empty function:

$$\begin{array}{ll}
& [\![\overline{a}y \mid a(z).\,(\overline{z}b \mid z(u).\,\overline{u}c)]\!] \\
= & \boldsymbol{\nu} x_y\,(\overline{a}\langle x_y,y\rangle \mid x_y \hookrightarrow y) \mid a(x,z).\,([\![\overline{z}b]\!] \mid \boldsymbol{\nu} w\,(\overline{x}\langle w\rangle \mid w(x',u).\,[\![\overline{u}c]\!])) \\
\xrightarrow{\tau}\equiv & \boldsymbol{\nu} x_y\,(x_y \hookrightarrow y \mid \boldsymbol{\nu} x_b\,(\overline{y}\langle x_b,b\rangle \mid x_b \hookrightarrow b) \mid \boldsymbol{\nu} w\,(\overline{x_y}\langle w\rangle \mid w(x',u).\,[\![\overline{u}c]\!])) \\
\xrightarrow{\tau}\equiv & (\boldsymbol{\nu} x_y,w)\,(x_y \hookrightarrow y \mid y(s,t).\,\overline{w}\langle s,t\rangle \mid \boldsymbol{\nu} x_b\,(\overline{y}\langle x_b,b\rangle \mid x_b \hookrightarrow b) \mid w(x',u).\,[\![\overline{u}c]\!]) \\
\xrightarrow{\tau}\equiv & (\boldsymbol{\nu} x_y,w,x_b)\,(x_y \hookrightarrow y \mid \overline{w}\langle x_b,b\rangle \mid x_b \hookrightarrow b \mid w(x',u).\,\boldsymbol{\nu} x_c\,(\overline{u}\langle x_c,c\rangle \mid x_c \hookrightarrow c)) \\
\xrightarrow{\tau}\equiv & (\boldsymbol{\nu} x_y,x_b)\,(x_y \hookrightarrow y \mid x_b \hookrightarrow b \mid \boldsymbol{\nu} x_c\,(\overline{b}\langle x_c,c\rangle \mid x_c \hookrightarrow c)) \\
\simeq^{\mathrm{c}} & [\![\overline{b}c]\!]\,.
\end{array}$$

The first transition in (5.6) is mimicked by the first of the four transitions: the process $[\![a(z).\,(\overline{z}b \mid z(u).\,\overline{u}c)]\!]$ receives x_y, y via a. The second transition in (5.6) is mimicked by the remaining three transitions. In the first of these, the process $[\![y(u).\,\overline{u}c]\!]_{[x_y/y]}$ sends a private name w to $x_y \hookrightarrow y$ via x_y. This indicates that the process is willing to receive via w any data that is available at y. The activated coordinator $y(s,t).\,\overline{w}\langle s,t\rangle$ then interacts with $[\![\overline{y}b]\!] \stackrel{\text{def}}{=} \boldsymbol{\nu} x_b\,(\overline{y}\langle x_b,b\rangle \mid x_b \hookrightarrow b)$ to receive the pair x_b, b, and passes it back via w.

The asserted barbed congruence in the final line follows from Lemma 2.2.28(2). We will not go into the properties of the translation here, except to note that it does not easily extend to accommodate + (see the reference at the end of the Part).

5.6.2 Equivalence in Lπ

We now summarize some results about equivalence of Lπ processes. The results will be developed in greater detail and proved using types in Chapter 10, though their formulation will become a little more complex. (We noted above that Lπ can be formulated as a typed calculus, using i/o types.)

Two Lπ processes may be indistinguishable in all Lπ contexts but not equivalent as processes of the π-calculus. For instance, if

$$P \stackrel{\mathrm{def}}{=} \boldsymbol{\nu} z\, \overline{x}z \qquad \text{and} \qquad Q \stackrel{\mathrm{def}}{=} \boldsymbol{\nu} z\, (\overline{x}z \mid \overline{z}y)\,,$$

then P and Q are barbed congruent in Lπ, that is, $\mathrm{L}\pi \rhd P \cong^{\mathrm{c}} Q$, but they are not barbed congruent in the π-calculus (or even in Aπ). The same is true of

$$P \stackrel{\mathrm{def}}{=} \boldsymbol{\nu} z\, \overline{x}z.\, (z(w).\, \overline{w} + \tau.\, \overline{a}) \qquad \text{and} \qquad Q \stackrel{\mathrm{def}}{=} \boldsymbol{\nu} z\, \overline{x}z.\, (z(w).\, \overline{w} \mid \overline{z}a)\,.$$

In each case, a context that distinguishes P and Q is

$$C \stackrel{\mathrm{def}}{=} x(z).\, z(v).\, \overline{c} \mid [\cdot]\,,$$

which is not an Lπ context because of the prefix $z(v)$. A further example is

$$\mathrm{L}\pi \rhd \overline{a}x \mid E_{xy} \cong^{\mathrm{c}} \overline{a}y \mid E_{xy}\,,$$

where E_{xy} is the equator process defined by $E_{xy} \stackrel{\mathrm{def}}{=} !x(z).\, \overline{y}z \mid !y(z).\, \overline{x}z$, which we met in Exercise 2.4.30. Other equivalences that hold in Lπ but not in the π-calculus are given in Examples 10.2.1–10.2.4.

Sharpened forms of the Replication Theorems (Theorems 2.2.25 and 2.2.26) hold in Lπ. In the original theorems, the name x could occur in the processes only in output subject position, so the processes could only send via x. The sharpened results allow also that x may be sent. (See Section 10.5 for further discussion and proofs.)

Theorem 5.6.2 (Sharpened Replication Theorems, in Lπ) If P_1, P_2, and R are Lπ processes and x does not occur as the subject of an input prefix in any of them, then

(1) $\mathrm{L}\pi \rhd \boldsymbol{\nu} x\, (P_1 \mid P_2 \mid !x(z).\, R) \simeq^{\mathrm{c}} \boldsymbol{\nu} x\, (P_1 \mid !x(z).\, R) \mid \boldsymbol{\nu} x\, (P_2 \mid !x(z).\, R)$
(2) $\mathrm{L}\pi \rhd \boldsymbol{\nu} x\, (!P \mid !x(z).\, R) \simeq^{\mathrm{c}} !\boldsymbol{\nu} x\, (P \mid !x(z).\, R)\,.$

Proof See the proof of Theorem 10.5.1. □

The next lemma gives an important equality that is valid in ALπ, the asynchronous variant of Lπ. To state it, we need to use simple buffer processes. Given names x and y, the *wire* from x to y is the process $x(z).\,\overline{y}z$, abbreviated $x \twoheadrightarrow y$. The lemma asserts that in ALπ, a wire can be used to transform a free output into a bound output.

Lemma 5.6.3 $\mathrm{AL}\pi \rhd \overline{x}y \cong^{c} \boldsymbol{\nu} z\,(\overline{x}z \mid !z \twoheadrightarrow y)$.

Proof See the proof of Lemma 10.3.1. □

We will use this lemma in Section 10.8 to obtain a proof technique for ALπ processes. Lemma 5.6.3 is actually a special case of the following result.

Lemma 5.6.4 If z does not occur free in P as the subject of an input prefix, then

$$\mathrm{AL}\pi \rhd P\{^{x}\!/\!_{z}\} \cong^{c} \boldsymbol{\nu} z\,(P \mid !z \twoheadrightarrow x)\ .$$

Proof See Exercise 10.8.2. □

We will see other results that depend on the output-capability constraint, and that therefore have simpler statements in Lπ, in Sections 10.4, 13.2.5, and 15.6.

5.7 Internal mobility

Two kinds of mobility can be distinguished in the π-calculus: *external mobility*, which arises from communication of free names, and *internal mobility*, whose source is communication of private names. In this section, we study the *Private π-calculus*, Pπ, a subcalculus in which there is only internal mobility. Pπ has elegant duality properties, and, in general, its theory is much simpler than that of the π-calculus. Nonetheless, internal mobility is the source of much of the expressive power of the π-calculus, and Pπ succinctly expresses ideas used in implementations of programming languages based on π-calculi.

The section is in four subsections. Section 5.7.1 introduces Pπ and discusses internal and external mobility. The basic theory of Pπ is presented in Section 5.7.2. Section 5.7.3 considers combining internal mobility with asynchrony and with locality, and Section 5.7.4 examines the expressiveness of the subcalculus that combines internal mobility with locality.

5.7.1 The Private π-calculus

There is a fundamental asymmetry between receiving and sending in the π-calculus. It is manifest in the syntax – an input prefix $x(z)$ contains a binder while an output prefix $\overline{x}y$ does not; and it is manifest in the semantics – *any* name can be received in an input but only a *specific* name can be emitted in an output. We have seen that the bound output $\overline{x}(z)$ plays a vital role in π-calculus, for instance in giving the transition rules, in expanding process behaviour, and in axiomatizations.

In the π-calculus, *internal mobility* results when a *bound* output meets an input, as, for instance, in

$$\overline{x}(z).\,P \mid x(z).\,Q \xrightarrow{\tau} \boldsymbol{\nu} z\,(P \mid Q)\,.$$

As an effect of this interaction, two bound names are identified and bound by a restriction. In order for the two parties to the communication to agree on the bound name, α-conversion may be required. The interaction consumes the prefixes but does not change the continuations P and Q: α-conversion is the only kind of substitution required to express internal mobility.

External mobility results when a *free* output meets an input, as in

$$\overline{x}y.\,P \mid x(z).\,Q \xrightarrow{\tau} P \mid Q\{y/z\}\,.$$

This time, a bound name is identified with a free name. Since y may occur free in Q, z cannot, in general, be α-converted to y. Instead, y must be substituted for z in Q.

In Pπ, there is only internal mobility. By studying Pπ, we can investigate internal mobility in isolation, and explore its theory and the impact it has on expressiveness. We obtain Pπ by replacing the free-output prefix by the bound-output prefix.

Definition 5.7.1 (Finite Pπ) The processes and summations of *finite* Pπ are given by

$$\begin{array}{rcl} P & ::= & M \mid P \mid P' \mid \boldsymbol{\nu} z\, P \\ M & ::= & \mathbf{0} \mid \pi.\,P \mid M + M' \\ \pi & ::= & x(z) \mid \overline{x}(z) \mid \tau\,. \end{array}$$

□

Note that there is no matching; we will come back to this later.

The displayed occurrence of z in $\overline{x}(z).\,P$ is binding with scope P. The input and output prefixes of Pπ are dual: the process $\overline{x}(z).\,P$ can only send a fresh name via x, and therefore the process $x(z).\,P$ can only receive a fresh name via

x. More formally, the operation that transforms inputs to outputs and vice versa acts as a homomorphism on transitions (see Lemma 5.7.4).

Note that syntactically, Pπ is not a subcalculus of the π-calculus, because the π-calculus has no bound-output prefix. Thinking of bound output as an abbreviation, however (as we do in the π-calculus), Pπ is semantically a subcalculus.

5.7.1.1 Infinite processes

We saw in Section 3.2 that, in the π-calculus, recursion and replication have the same expressive power. When there is only internal mobility, however, recursion is more powerful. The grammar of Pπ therefore uses recursion.

Definition 5.7.2 (Pπ) The processes of Pπ are obtained by changing the first line of the grammar in Definition 5.7.1 to

$$P \ ::= \ M \mid P \mid P' \mid \nu z\, P \mid K\lfloor \widetilde{x} \rfloor$$

where in $K\lfloor \widetilde{x} \rfloor$, no name may occur more than once in the tuple $\widetilde{x}$. $\square$

The only new point is that in an application $K\lfloor \widetilde{x} \rfloor$, no name may occur more than once in $\widetilde{x}$. This requirement, which is not imposed in the π-calculus, ensures that α-conversion is the only kind of substitution needed in Pπ, because in a constant definition $K \triangleq (\widetilde{x}).\, P$, we have $\mathsf{fn}(P) \subseteq \widetilde{x}$.

Definition 5.7.3 (P$\pi^!$) The processes of P$\pi^!$ are obtained by changing the first line of the grammar in Definition 5.7.1 to

$$P \ ::= \ M \mid P \mid P' \mid \nu z\, P \mid !P\,.$$

$\square$

The encoding of recursion using replication in Section 3.2 is not possible in P$\pi^!$. For instance, consider

$$K \triangleq (x).\, \overline{x}(y).\, K\lfloor y \rfloor\,.$$

Then, $K\lfloor x_0 \rfloor$ has the infinite computation

$$K\lfloor x_0 \rfloor \xrightarrow{\overline{x_0}(x_1)} K\lfloor x_1 \rfloor \xrightarrow{\overline{x_1}(x_2)} K\lfloor x_2 \rfloor \xrightarrow{\overline{x_2}(x_3)} \ldots$$

where the object of one action is the subject of the next. This kind of infinity in depth is not possible in P$\pi^!$. This will be shown in Exercise 6.4.8. (This exercise shows that P$\pi^!$ processes are typable in a simply-typed π-calculus without recursive types, something that guarantees, by Theorem 6.4.7, that infinity in depth is not possible.)

5.7.2 Basic theory of Pπ

Several varieties of bisimilarity can be defined on processes of the π-calculus, and most of them are not congruences. Further, reasoning about behaviour often involves case analysis on names, as shown, for instance, by the appearance of matching in the Expansion Lemma for full bisimilarity (Lemma 2.2.15). In Pπ, however, only ground bisimilarity is sensible: the other variants involve arbitrary substitution, but the transition rules of Pπ involve only α-conversion. Moreover, in Pπ, no case analysis on names is required, as we now explain. In what follows, we consider only strong bisimilarity; the weak case is similar.

5.7.2.1 Case analysis on names

In the π-calculus, the processes $\overline{x} \mid y$ and $\overline{x}.\, y + y.\, \overline{x}$ are bisimilar. They are not full bisimilar, however; for instance

$$a(y).\, (\overline{x} \mid y) \not\sim a(y).\, (\overline{x}.\, y + y.\, \overline{x})\ .$$

To obtain a summation that is full bisimilar to $\overline{x} \mid y$, we have to add a match-prefixed term:

$$\overline{x} \mid y \sim^{\mathrm{c}} \overline{x}.\, y + y.\, \overline{x} + [y = x]\tau\ .$$

This summation can replace the composition in any context; in particular,

$$a(y).\, (\overline{x} \mid y) \sim a(y).\, (\overline{x}.\, y + y.\, \overline{x} + [y = x]\tau)\ .$$

In general, when we manipulate algebraically a subterm P of a π-calculus process, we cannot assume that the different free names in P will remain different. When P becomes active, some of these names may have been identified, a phenomenon known as *aliasing*. Consequently, when reasoning about processes, we have to take into account all possible equalities and inequalities among their free names.

In Pπ, however, no case analysis is needed, because there is no aliasing: only fresh names are communicated, so no two different free names of a process can be identified. For instance, the processes $\overline{x} \mid y$ and $\overline{x}.\, y + y.\, \overline{x}$ are indistinguishable in any Pπ context, and so

$$\mathrm{P}\pi \rhd a(y).\, (\overline{x} \mid y) \simeq^{\mathrm{c}} a(y).\, (\overline{x}.\, y + y.\, \overline{x})\ .$$

No Pπ context can send the name x via a. The lack of a need for case analysis explains why matching is absent from Pπ.

5.7.2.2 Transition system and duality

The transition rules for Pπ are given in Table 5.2. Elided from the table are the variant of P-SUM-L with $Q + P$ in place of $P + Q$, and the variant of P-PAR-L

$$\text{P-PRE} \quad \frac{}{\pi.P \xrightarrow{\pi} P}$$

$$\text{P-SUM-L} \quad \frac{P \xrightarrow{\pi} P'}{P+Q \xrightarrow{\pi} P'} \qquad \text{P-RES} \quad \frac{P \xrightarrow{\pi} P'}{\nu z\, P \xrightarrow{\pi} \nu z\, P'} \quad z \notin \mathsf{n}(\pi)$$

$$\text{P-PAR-L} \quad \frac{P \xrightarrow{\pi} P'}{P \mid Q \xrightarrow{\pi} P' \mid Q} \quad \mathsf{bn}(\pi) \cap \mathsf{fn}(Q) = \emptyset$$

$$\text{P-COMM} \quad \frac{P \xrightarrow{\pi} P' \quad Q \xrightarrow{\overline{\pi}} Q'}{P \mid Q \xrightarrow{\tau} \nu z\,(P' \mid Q')} \quad \mathsf{bn}(\pi) = \{z\}$$

$$\text{P-REC} \quad \frac{}{K\lfloor \widetilde{x} \rfloor \xrightarrow{\tau} P} \quad K \triangleq (\widetilde{x}).\, P$$

Table 5.2. *The transition rules for* $\mathrm{P}\pi$

with the roles of the left and right components swapped. Note that the actions are just the prefixes. We write $\overline{\pi}$ for the *complement* of π, where $\overline{x}(y) = x(y)$, $\overline{x(y)} = \overline{x}(y)$, and $\overline{\tau} = \tau$.

The rules are simpler than the rules for the π-calculus. There are just one prefix rule, one communication rule, and one restriction rule. Note also the simple form of P-REC, which is possible because of the requirement that in $K\lfloor \widetilde{x} \rfloor$, no name may occur more than once in $\widetilde{x}$.

If P is a $\mathrm{P}\pi$ process then $\overline{P}$, the *dual* of P, is obtained from P by replacing each prefix π by its complement $\overline{\pi}$. This transformation is possible because of the *syntactic* symmetry of $\mathrm{P}\pi$. The following result shows that the symmetry is also *semantic*.

Lemma 5.7.4 If $P \xrightarrow{\pi} Q$ then $\overline{P} \xrightarrow{\overline{\pi}} \overline{Q}$.

Proof The proof is a simple induction on inference. □

Note that since $\overline{\overline{P}} = P$, the converse of Lemma 5.7.4 also holds.

5.7.2.3 Bisimilarity

As we have seen, the natural labelled equivalence on $\mathrm{P}\pi$ is ground bisimilarity.

Definition 5.7.5 (Bisimilarity on Pπ) On Pπ, *strong ground bisimilarity* is the largest symmetric relation, $\sim_{\mathrm{g}}$, such that whenever $P \sim_{\mathrm{g}} Q$, there is $z \notin \mathsf{fn}(P, Q)$ such that if $P \xrightarrow{\pi} P'$ where π is $x(z)$ or $\overline{x}(z)$ or τ, then $Q \xrightarrow{\pi}\sim_{\mathrm{g}} P'$. □

It is straightforward to show that ground bisimilarity of Pπ processes is preserved by injective substitution. It is not preserved by arbitrary substitution, however: consider the familiar Pπ processes

$$\overline{x}(y) \mid a(z) \qquad \text{and} \qquad \overline{x}(y).\, a(z) + a(z).\, \overline{x}(y)$$

and substitution $\{a/x\}$. Nonetheless, because α-conversion is the only kind of substitution needed in Pπ, ground bisimilarity is a congruence.

Lemma 5.7.6 If P and Q are Pπ processes and $P \sim_{\mathrm{g}} Q$, then $C[P] \sim_{\mathrm{g}} C[Q]$ for every Pπ context C. □

Exercise 5.7.7 Prove Lemma 5.7.6 for C of the forms $\pi.\, C'$ and $C' \mid R$. □

The notion of observable is more robust in Pπ than in the π-calculus. To explain this, recall that for π-calculus processes P and Q to be bisimilar, each α transition of one must be mimicked by an α transition of the other. This holds in particular for α of the forms $\overline{x}y$ and $\overline{x}(z)$, so the observer is able to discern whether or not the name emitted in an output is private. One may argue that this notion of observation, where the privacy of names is observable, is too strong. Some evidence for this is the fact, noted at the end of Section 2.4.1, that full bisimilarity is strictly finer than barbed congruence on subcalculi without matching. More compelling evidence will be given in Part IV when we study equivalences for typed processes.

This issue does not arise in Pπ, however, because *all* communicated names are fresh. We will make use of this later in the book to develop proof techniques for typed processes using transformations to Pπ, and other transformations that replace external mobility by internal mobility. We will consider a related transformation in Section 5.7.4 below.

5.7.2.4 Axiomatization

Strong ground bisimilarity has a simple axiomatization on finite Pπ. For ease of comparison with the axiomatizations and proof systems in Section 4.8, we consider the terms given by

$$P \ ::= \ \mathbf{0} \mid \pi.\, P \mid P + P' \mid P \mid P' \mid \boldsymbol{\nu} z\, P, \tag{5.7}$$

where π is as in Definition 5.7.1.

$$\begin{array}{llcll}
\text{S1} & (P+Q)+R & = & P+(Q+R) & \\
\text{S2} & P+Q & = & Q+P & \\
\text{S3} & P+\mathbf{0} & = & P & \\
\text{S4} & P+P & = & P & \\
\\
\text{RES2} & \nu z\,(P+Q) & = & \nu z\,P+\nu z\,Q & \\
\text{RES3} & \nu z\,\pi.\,P & = & \pi.\,\nu z\,P & \text{if } z\notin \mathsf{n}(\pi) \\
\text{RES4} & \nu z\,\pi.\,P & = & \mathbf{0} & \text{if } \pi \text{ is } z(w) \text{ or } \overline{z}(w) \\
\text{RES7} & \nu z\,\mathbf{0} & = & \mathbf{0} &
\end{array}$$

If $P = \Sigma_i\, \pi_i.\, P_i$ and $P' = \Sigma_j\, \pi'_j.\, P'_j$ and for some $z \notin \mathsf{fn}(P,Q)$, if $\pi_i \neq \tau$ then $\mathsf{bn}(\pi_i) = \{z\}$ and if $\pi'_j \neq \tau$ then $\mathsf{bn}(\pi'_j) = \{z\}$, then

$$\begin{array}{rcl}
P \mid P' & = & \Sigma_i\, \pi_i.\,(P_i \mid P') + \Sigma_j\, \pi'_j.\,(P \mid P'_j) + \\
& & \Sigma_{\pi_i\, \mathsf{opp}\, \pi'_j}\, \tau.\, \nu z\,(P_i \mid P'_j)
\end{array}$$

where $\pi_i\, \mathsf{opp}\, \pi'_j$ if $\overline{\pi_i} = \pi'_j \neq \tau$.

Table 5.3. *Axioms for strong ground bisimilarity of* Pπ *terms*

Theorem 5.7.8 The axioms in Table 5.3 comprise an axiomatization for strong ground bisimilarity of the terms given by (5.7).

Proof See the reference at the end of the Part. □

The axiomatization comprises familiar axioms for sum and restriction (including RES7, which was derived from axioms for conditionals in Section 4.8), and the appropriate expansion schema. As we have discussed, there is no need for matching or other conditions in Pπ.

5.7.3 Internal mobility, asynchrony, and locality

Internal mobility can usefully be combined with asynchrony and with locality. The terms of *Asynchronous* Pπ, PAπ, are obtained by replacing the form $\overline{x}y.\,\mathbf{0}$ in Definition 5.2.1 by

$$\nu z\,(\overline{x}z.\,\mathbf{0} \mid P) \quad \text{where } z \text{ does not occur free in } P \text{ as the object of a prefix.}$$

The terms of LPπ^- are defined as in Definition 5.6.1, except that the summations are given by

$$M \;::=\; \mathbf{0} \;\mid\; \overline{x}(y).\,P \;\mid\; x(z).\,P \;\mid\; M+M'$$

where:

(1) in $\overline{x}(y).\,P$, the name y can occur in P only as the subject of *input* prefixes
(2) in $x(z).\,P$, the name z can occur in P only as the subject of *output* prefixes.

These syntactic restrictions strengthen the duality between input and output in Pπ. For suppose P is an LPπ^- term. If $P \xrightarrow{\overline{x}(y)} Q$ then Q can only *receive* via y, and if $P \xrightarrow{x(z)} R$ then R can only *send* via z.

The syntactic restrictions of LPπ^- allow some control over interference among processes. To see this, consider the π-calculus, or Pπ, process

$$a(y).\,\overline{y}(z).\,P_1 \mid \overline{a}(x).\,(x(w).\,P_2 \mid \overline{x}(y).\,P_3)\;. \tag{5.8}$$

The derivative after the communication via a is

$$\boldsymbol{\nu}x\,(\overline{x}(z).\,P_1 \mid x(w).\,P_2 \mid \overline{x}(y).\,P_3)\,,$$

and in this process, the two outputs at x are in competition for the lone input. This interference is a result of the communication via a. Moreover, it was not apparent in the syntax of the term in (5.8). Note that the term in (5.8) is not in LPπ^-, because of the subterm $\overline{x}(y).\,P_3$.

In an LPπ^- term $x(y).\,P \mid \overline{x}(y).\,Q$, in contrast, any interference on output at y is localised to P, and any interference on input at y is localised to Q. Remarkably, LPπ^- is a very expressive subcalculus, as we now illustrate.

5.7.4 Expressiveness

Here, we explore a little the expressiveness of internal mobility, by showing how to encode ALπ into LPπ^-. Recall that we have seen earlier how to encode A$\pi_{-\{+\}}$ into ALπ, and how to translate various subcalculi into A$\pi_{-\{+\}}$. The encoding uses *dynamic wires*, the processes defined by

$$x \twoheadrightarrow\!\!\!\!\!\rightarrow y \stackrel{\Delta}{=} x(z).\,\overline{y}(w).\,!w \twoheadrightarrow\!\!\!\!\!\rightarrow z\;.$$

The dynamic wire $x \twoheadrightarrow\!\!\!\!\!\rightarrow y$, to which we will return in Section 10.8, is somewhat similar to the wire $x \twoheadrightarrow y$ introduced in Section 5.6. Instead of emitting at y the name z it receives at x, however, the dynamic wire sends via y a private name w that is 'wired to' z. The following result states two useful properties of dynamic wires.

Lemma 5.7.9

(1) $\boldsymbol{\nu}z\,(!x \twoheadrightarrow\!\!\!\!\!\rightarrow z \mid !z \twoheadrightarrow\!\!\!\!\!\rightarrow y) \cong^{c} !x \twoheadrightarrow\!\!\!\!\!\rightarrow y$.
(2) If $x \notin \mathsf{fn}(P)$ then $\boldsymbol{\nu}x\,(!x \twoheadrightarrow\!\!\!\!\!\rightarrow y \mid P) \simeq^{c} P$. □

Exercise 5.7.10 Prove Lemma 5.7.9. □

The translation, $[\![\cdot]\!]$, from ALπ to LPπ^- is a homomorphism, except that

$$[\![\overline{x}y]\!] \stackrel{\text{def}}{=} \overline{x}(z).\,!z \twoheadrightarrow y\;.$$

We will not go into the correctness of the translation; see the reference at the end of the Part. Rather, we give an example to illustrate how it works.

Example 5.7.11 The transition $\overline{x}y \mid x(w).\,\overline{w}a \stackrel{\tau}{\longrightarrow} \overline{y}a$ is mimicked as follows:

$$\begin{array}{lll}
 & [\![\overline{x}y \mid x(w).\,\overline{w}a]\!] & \\
= & \overline{x}(z).\,!z \twoheadrightarrow y \mid x(w).\,\overline{w}(v).\,!v \twoheadrightarrow a & \\
\stackrel{\tau}{\longrightarrow} & \boldsymbol{\nu} z\,(!z \twoheadrightarrow y \mid \overline{z}(v).\,!v \twoheadrightarrow a) & \\
\Longrightarrow & (\boldsymbol{\nu} z, v)\,(\overline{y}(u).\,!u \twoheadrightarrow v \mid !z \twoheadrightarrow y \mid !v \twoheadrightarrow a) & \\
\simeq^{\mathrm{c}} & \overline{y}(u).\,(\boldsymbol{\nu} z, v)\,(!u \twoheadrightarrow v \mid !z \twoheadrightarrow y \mid !v \twoheadrightarrow a) & \text{(by expansion)} \\
\cong^{\mathrm{c}} & \overline{y}(u).\,\boldsymbol{\nu} z\,(!u \twoheadrightarrow a \mid !z \twoheadrightarrow y) & \text{(by Lemma 5.7.9(1))} \\
\cong^{\mathrm{c}} & \overline{y}(u).\,!u \twoheadrightarrow a & \text{(by Lemma 5.7.9(2))} \\
= & [\![\overline{y}a]\!]\;. &
\end{array}$$

$\square$

There is some similarity between the translation $[\![\cdot]\!]$ and the way communication is implemented in programming languages based on the Asynchronous π-calculus. Typically, a substitution arising from an interaction such as $\overline{x}y \mid x(z).\,Q \longrightarrow Q\{y/z\}$ is not applied directly. Instead, implementations use environments to record the relevant associations between names and values. The dynamic wires used in $[\![\cdot]\!]$ can be thought of as environment entries. Parts (1) and (2) of Lemma 5.7.9 can then be thought of as properties relating to composition and garbage-collection of environment entries.

5.8 Non-congruence results for ground bisimilarity

Of the four varieties of labelled bisimilarity that we have studied, ground bisimilarity – where input of only a single fresh name is considered – is the simplest and the easiest to establish. On the full π-calculus, however, ground bisimilarity is of little use, because it is not preserved by composition. Earlier in this chapter, we studied two interesting subcalculi of the π-calculus, Aπ and Pπ, and we saw that ground bisimilarity is a congruence on both of them. The congruence result is perhaps not surprising for Pπ, where only fresh names can be communicated. It is more surprising in Aπ, where there is no such constraint. More precisely, the surprising result for Aπ is that ground bisimilarity is preserved by substitution. From this it follows that all four varieties of bisimilarity coincide on Aπ, and that the common relation is a congruence.

A natural question is whether any interesting subcalculi containing the output prefix $\overline{x}y.\,P$ enjoy the same property. In this section, we show that the answer is negative: the property fails on any subcalculus that has output prefix, input prefix, composition, restriction, and replication. Consequently, on any such subcalculus all varieties of bisimilarity and the associated congruences are different – with the usual exception of open bisimilarity, which is always a congruence.

On any language with matching, ground bisimilarity, like bisimilarity and late bisimilarity, is not preserved by substitution. For example, if $P \stackrel{\text{def}}{=} [x=y]a(z).\,\mathbf{0}$ then $P \sim_{\text{g}} \mathbf{0}$ but $P\{y/x\}$ can input via a. The same is true on $\pi_{-\{=\}}$, the subcalculus of the π-calculus that lacks the match operator. It is enlightening to think a little more about the counterexamples in Section 2.2.

Counterexample 5.8.1 (Subcalculus $\pi_{-\{=\}}$) Let $P \stackrel{\text{def}}{=} \overline{y} \mid x$ and $Q \stackrel{\text{def}}{=} \overline{y}.\,x + x.\,\overline{y}$. Then $P \sim_{\text{g}} Q$ but $P\{y/x\} \not\sim_{\text{g}} Q\{y/x\}$, because $P\{y/x\}$ has a τ transition that $Q\{y/x\}$ cannot mimic.

The same processes show also that $\approx_{\text{g}}$ is not preserved by substitution. □

The sum operator plays an important role in Counterexample 5.8.1: the counterexample is an instance of the Expansion Lemma, which cannot be formulated without sum. The question whether ground bisimilarity is preserved by substitution is more subtle for the subcalculus $\pi_{-\{=,+\}}$ of the π-calculus that lacks matching and sum. The question is significant because of the tractability of ground bisimilarity, and the fact that sum is often not needed to express systems in π-calculus. As the following two counterexamples show, however, neither $\sim_{\text{g}}$ nor $\approx_{\text{g}}$ is preserved by substitution on $\pi_{-\{=,+\}}$.

Counterexample 5.8.2 (Subcalculus $\pi_{-\{=,+\}}$, strong case) Let

$$P \stackrel{\text{def}}{=} !\overline{x}.\,y.\,\tau.\,a \mid !y.\,\overline{x}.\,\tau.\,a \qquad \text{and} \qquad Q \stackrel{\text{def}}{=} !\boldsymbol{\nu} z\,(\overline{x}.\,\overline{z} \mid y.\,z.\,a)\,.$$

Clearly, $P\{y/x\} \not\sim_{\text{g}} Q\{y/x\}$, because $Q\{y/x\} \xrightarrow{\tau}\xrightarrow{\tau}\xrightarrow{a}$ but $P\{y/x\}$ can perform a only after three τ transitions.

We show, however, that $P \sim_{\text{g}} Q$, indeed that $P \sim Q$. First, using the Expansion Lemma and Lemmas 2.2.16 and 2.2.17 to remove the restriction on z, we have

$$\boldsymbol{\nu} z\,(\overline{x}.\,\overline{z} \mid y.\,z.\,a) \sim \overline{x}.\,y.\,\tau.\,a + y.\,\overline{x}.\,\tau.\,a\,.$$

Hence, since $\sim$ is preserved by replication, using Exercise 2.2.30(1) we have

$$\begin{aligned} Q &\sim !(\overline{x}.\,y.\,\tau.\,a + y.\,\overline{x}.\,\tau.\,a) \\ &\sim !\overline{x}.\,y.\,\tau.\,a \mid !y.\,\overline{x}.\,\tau.\,a \\ &= P\,. \end{aligned}$$

□

To show the analogous result in the weak case, we need a more complicated counterexample.

Counterexample 5.8.3 (Subcalculus $\pi_{-\{=,+\}}$, weak case) Let

$$P \stackrel{\text{def}}{=} !\boldsymbol{\nu} u\,(\overline{x}u.\,y(v).\,\overline{a}(w).\,\overline{w}u.\,\overline{w}v) \mid !\boldsymbol{\nu} u\,(y(v).\,\overline{x}u.\,\overline{a}(w).\,\overline{w}u.\,\overline{w}v)$$

and

$$Q \stackrel{\text{def}}{=} !(\boldsymbol{\nu} u, z)\,(\overline{x}u.\,\overline{z} \mid y(v).\,z.\,\overline{a}(w).\,\overline{w}u.\,\overline{w}v)\;.$$

First, we show that $P \approx_{\mathrm{g}} Q$, indeed that $P \approx Q$. Proceeding as in the previous example, using instead Exercise 2.2.30(2) and in addition the τ law: $\pi.\,\tau.\,R \approx \pi.\,R$, we have:

$$\begin{array}{rcl} Q & \sim & !\boldsymbol{\nu} u\,(\overline{x}u.\,y(v).\,\tau.\,\overline{a}(w).\,\overline{w}u.\,\overline{w}v + y(v).\,\overline{x}u.\,\tau.\,\overline{a}(w).\,\overline{w}u.\,\overline{w}v) \\ & \approx & !\boldsymbol{\nu} u\,(\overline{x}u.\,y(v).\,\overline{a}(w).\,\overline{w}u.\,\overline{w}v + y(v).\,\overline{x}u.\,\overline{a}(w).\,\overline{w}u.\,\overline{w}v) \\ & \sim & !\boldsymbol{\nu} u\,(\overline{x}u.\,y(v).\,\overline{a}(w).\,\overline{w}u.\,\overline{w}v) \mid !\boldsymbol{\nu} u\,(y(v).\,\overline{x}u.\,\overline{a}(w).\,\overline{w}u.\,\overline{w}v) \\ & = & P\,. \end{array}$$

To see that $P\{y/x\} \not\approx_{\mathrm{g}} Q\{y/x\}$, however, consider the computation

$$\begin{array}{rcl} Q\{y/x\} & \xrightarrow{\tau} & (\boldsymbol{\nu} u, z)\,(\overline{z} \mid z.\,\overline{a}(w).\,\overline{w}u.\,\overline{w}u) \mid Q\{y/x\} \\ & \xrightarrow{\tau} & (\boldsymbol{\nu} u, z)\,\overline{a}(w).\,\overline{w}u.\,\overline{w}u \mid Q\{y/x\} \\ & \xrightarrow{\overline{a}(w)} & (\boldsymbol{\nu} u, z)\,\overline{w}u.\,\overline{w}u \mid Q\{y/x\} \\ & \xrightarrow{\overline{w}(u)} & \boldsymbol{\nu} z\,\overline{w}u \mid Q\{y/x\} \\ & \xrightarrow{\overline{w}u} & \boldsymbol{\nu} z\,\mathbf{0} \mid Q\{y/x\}\,. \end{array}$$

The object of the final free output $\overline{w}u$ is the same as the object of the preceding bound output $\overline{w}(u)$. This behaviour cannot be mimicked by $P\{y/x\}$, because in no subterm $\overline{a}(w).\,\overline{w}u.\,\overline{w}v$ can v be instantiated by u. Hence $P\{y/x\} \not\approx_{\mathrm{g}} Q\{y/x\}$. $\square$

Similar counterexamples can be given on the subcalculus of $\pi_{-\{=,+\}}$ in which only input-prefixed processes can be replicated. (This subcalculus, especially its asynchronous variant, is quite often used.) Counterexample 5.8.3 is easily modified, using the fact that

$$!R \approx \boldsymbol{\nu} z\,(!z.\,(R \mid \overline{z}) \mid \overline{z})$$

where $z \notin \mathsf{fn}(R)$. This trick does not work for strong equivalences, however. Indeed modifying Counterexample 5.8.2 to use only input-guarded replication appears hard. Below is a different counterexample.

Counterexample 5.8.4 (Subcalculus of $\pi_{-\{=,+\}}$ with only input-guarded replication, strong case) Let

$$\begin{array}{lcl} P & \stackrel{\text{def}}{=} & \boldsymbol{\nu} z\, (x.\, (\overline{z} \mid A) \mid \overline{y}.\, (z.\, \overline{a} \mid !x.\, R)) \mid !x.\, B \\ Q & \stackrel{\text{def}}{=} & A \mid !x.\, B \\ R & \stackrel{\text{def}}{=} & \tau.\, \overline{a} \mid \overline{y} \\ A & \stackrel{\text{def}}{=} & \overline{y}.\, !x.\, R \\ B & \stackrel{\text{def}}{=} & \overline{y}.\, (\tau.\, \overline{a} \mid !x.\, R)\ . \end{array}$$

Then $P\{y/x\} \not\sim_{\mathrm{g}} Q\{y/x\}$, because $P\{y/x\} \xrightarrow{\tau}\xrightarrow{\tau}\xrightarrow{\overline{a}}$ but $Q\{y/x\}$ can perform $\overline{a}$ only after three τ transitions. The following exercise invites the reader to check, however, that $P \sim Q$ and hence $P \sim_{\mathrm{g}} Q$. □

Exercise* 5.8.5 Show that $P \sim Q$, where P and Q are as in Counterexample 5.8.4. (Hint: use the technique of bisimulation up to $\sim$ and up to non-input context; the contexts that you may find it useful to cut are compositions.) □

It is an open question whether $\sim_{\mathrm{g}}$ or $\approx_{\mathrm{g}}$ is preserved by substitution on the finite subcalculus of $\pi_{-\{=,+\}}$, that is, the subcalculus without replication.

Notes and References for Part II

The polyadic π-calculus and the associated notion of sorting for polyadic processes were introduced by Milner [Mil93]. The translation of polyadic processes into the monadic calculus (Definition 3.1.4) was given, in essence, in [MPW92]. Yoshida [Yos96] and Quaglia and Walker [QW98] used type systems to define a sublanguage of the monadic calculus and show that the translation into that sublanguage is complete. Recursion was used in [MPW92]; replication was introduced in [Mil93]. The priority-queue example in Section 3.3 is based on [Wal94]. The representation of data using π-calculus processes was first explored in [Mil93].

Distinctions were introduced in [MPW92]. The late transition system was studied in [MPW92]. Abstractions and concretions were introduced in [Mil93]. They are the basis for the treatment of process dynamics in [Mil99]. The property of ground bisimilarity that the meaning of processes can be captured without considering more than one instance of input value is important and useful in equivalence and model checking. It is sometimes called *data-independence* [JP93]. See also [Laz99] for an extensive study of data-independence. The theory of late bisimilarity was developed in [MPW92]. For denotational models of π-calculus, see [FT01] and references therein. Open bisimilarity was studied by Sangiorgi [San96d]. The Mobility Workbench was designed by Victor and Moller [VM94, Vic98]. A related tool was developed by Ferrari, Gnesi, Montanari, Pistore, and Ristori [FGM+98]. Other semi-automatic analyses use theorem-provers; see, for instance, [Hir99] by Hirschkoff, and [HMS01] by Honsell, Miculan, and Scagnetto. Symbolic operational semantics were studied for value-passing processes by Hennessy and Lin [HL95], and for the π-calculus in [San96d] and by Lin [Lin94] and Boreale and De Nicola [BD96]. Some of these semantics generalize the idea of a distinction-indexed family of equivalences to a family indexed by conditions, that is, boolean combinations of equalities between names. Ferrari, Montanari, and Quaglia [FMQ96] presented a CCS-like formulation of the π-calculus, again using a symbolic semantics, and gave characterizations of the various equivalences.

The axiomatization of strong open bisimilarity (Theorem 4.8.3) is from [San96d]. The proof system for strong late bisimilarity (Theorem 4.8.5) is from [MPW92]. The proof systems and axiomatizations for strong bisimilarity, late bisimilarity, and their congruences, Theorems 4.8.8, 4.8.9, 4.8.14, and 4.8.15, are due to Parrow and Sangiorgi [PS95]. Lin [Lin94, Lin95] used a symbolic semantics to obtain proof systems for deriving judgments of the form $\varphi \triangleright P = Q$, asserting that the processes P and Q are related by the equivalence indexed by the condition φ. Lin established in particular that addition of analogues of the CCS τ laws to proof systems for strong bisimilarity, late bisimilarity, and their congruences yields proof systems for the corresponding weak equivalences. Parrow [Par99] showed how to transform a proof of $\varphi \triangleright P = Q$ into a proof of $\varphi P = \varphi Q$, and hence obtained proof systems for equations not involving conditions. An axiomatization of weak open bisimilarity was given by Fu [Fu99], using some additional τ laws. It is not clear if these laws are essential. Proof systems were also given in [FMQ96], based on the CCS-like formulation of the π-calculus mentioned above. An axiomatization of a testing preorder was given in [BD95]. Rewriting algorithms based on axiomatizations for finding minimal canonical representatives analogous to those for open bisimilarity are not known for other equivalences. For work on representatives that are canonical with respect to a given set of names, see, for instance, [PS95], and [HLMP98] by Honsell, Lensia, Montanari, and Pistore.

The Asynchronous π-calculus was introduced by Honda and Tokoro [HT91]; later, unaware of this work, Boudol [Bou92] made a similar proposal. (These papers considered what is here called $\text{A}\pi_{-\{+,\tau\}}$.) The theory of behavioural equivalence was developed in [HT91, HT92], based on a variant labelled transition system, and bisimilarity and asynchronous bisimilarity were shown to be congruences. The presentation of the basic theory of the subcalculus in Section 5.4 follows [San00], which showed in particular, together with [HHK96], the importance of ground bisimilarity. The theory of equivalence for $\text{A}\pi$ was developed further in [ACS98]. Most of the results in Section 5.4 were given there, together with an axiomatization of strong asynchronous bisimilarity on finite $\text{A}\pi$-processes. The relationship between the barbed and labelled relations on $\text{A}\pi$, without the assumption of image-finiteness, was studied by Fournet and Gonthier in [FG98]. General definitions of notions of asynchrony were given, using labelled transition systems with input and output, and axiomatized by Selinger in [Sel97]. The translation from $\pi_{-\{=,+,\tau\}}$ to $\text{A}\pi_{-\{+,\tau\}}$ was given in [HT91] and in [Bou92]. It was studied further in [QW00]. The encoding of sums of input-prefixed processes in $A\pi_{-\{+,\tau\}}$ was given by Nestmann and Pierce [NP96], where Theorem 5.5.3 was proved. The encoding of the subcalculus in which there are no mixed summations of input-prefixed processes and output-prefixed processes is from [Nes00]. Theorem 5.5.6 is due to Palamidessi [Pal97]. The programming language Pict was designed and implemented by Pierce and Turner [PT00]. The Join calculus was introduced in [FG96], and studied further in [FGL+96, Fou98]. An important feature of the Join calculus, especially in connection with programming, is its join patterns. These are the basic synchronization construct of the calculus. They permit simple expression of processes that can proceed just when several messages are available.

The Localized π-calculus, in its asynchronous form (under various names), was studied by Merro [Mer00] and Yoshida [Yos98]. The translation of Section 5.6.1 was presented in [Bor98] and shown to be sound for barbed equivalence. Characterizations of barbed congruence on $AL\pi$ were given in [Mer00].

The Private π-calculus was introduced (named πI) by Sangiorgi [San96c]. The subcalculus $LP\pi^-$ was studied in [Mer00] (there named $L\pi I$), but little is known about it beyond the results mentioned in Section 5.7.3. The translation from $AL\pi$ to $LP\pi^-$ was shown to be sound for barbed equivalence in [Bor98] and fully abstract for barbed congruence in [Mer00]. The non-congruence results in Section 5.8 are from [BS98b]; Counterexample 5.8.4 is due to Gonthier and Leifer.

Variations of the π-calculus that have not been discussed, which are similar to one another, are the *Fusion Calculus*, introduced by Parrow and Victor in [PV98], and the χ-*calculus*, introduced by Fu in [Fu97]. These calculi inherit much from the π-calculus but go beyond it in significant ways. For instance, in the Fusion Calculus the input construct does not bind names. Thus one writes $x\, yz.\,P$ rather than $x(y,z).\,P$. The effect of an interaction between $x\, yz.\,P$ and an output prefix $\overline{x}\langle a,b\rangle.\,Q$ is that the corresponding names in the prefixes are identified. This is written

$$x\, yz.\,P \mid \overline{x}\langle a,b\rangle.\,Q \mid R \mid S \xrightarrow{[y=a][z=b]} P \mid Q \mid R \mid S$$

where $[y=a][z=b]$ indicates the smallest equivalence relation on names (*fusion*) that contains (y,a) and (z,b). The processes R and S feel the effect of the fusion too. To limit the effects of fusions, the calculus has a name-binding *scope* operator: in $(w)A$ the name w is bound in the process A. Thus

$$(y)(x\, yz.\,P \mid \overline{x}\langle a,b\rangle.\,Q) \mid R \mid S \xrightarrow{[z=b]} P\{a/y\} \mid Q\{a/y\} \mid R \mid S\,,$$

and

$$(z)((y)(x\, yz.\,P \mid \overline{x}\langle a,b\rangle.\,Q) \mid R) \mid S \xrightarrow{\mathbf{1}} P\{a,b/y,z\} \mid Q\{a,b/y,z\} \mid R\{b/z\} \mid S$$

where **1** is the identity relation. In [VP98], the Fusion Calculus was used to model concurrent constraint programming.

Part III

Typed π-calculi

Introduction to Part III

A type system is, roughly, a mechanism for classifying the expressions of a language. Type systems for programming languages, sequential and concurrent, are useful for several reasons, most notably:

(1) to detect programming errors statically
(2) to extract information that is useful for reasoning about the behaviour of programs
(3) to improve the efficiency of code generated by a compiler
(4) to make programs easier to understand.

Types are an important part of the theory and of the pragmatics of the π-calculus, and they are one of the most important differences between π-calculus and CCS-like languages. Many of the type systems that have been studied for the π-calculus were suggested by well-known type systems for sequential languages, especially λ-calculi. In addition, however, type systems specific to processes have been proposed, for instance for preventing certain forms of interference among processes or certain forms of deadlock.

In the book we will be mainly interested in the purposes (1) and (2) of types; purposes (3) and (4) are more specific to programming languages (as opposed to calculi). In this Part of the book we introduce several important type systems and present their basic properties. In the next Part we study the effect of types on process behaviour and reasoning.

We formalize type systems by means of *typing rules.* The terms that can be typed using these rules are the *well-typed* terms. The most fundamental property of a type system is its agreement with the reduction relation of the calculus, the *subject reduction* property. A consequence of this property is *type soundness*, asserting that well-typed processes do not give rise to run-time errors under reduction. We use a special term `wrong` to represent a process inside which such an error has occurred. Therefore, type soundness will mean that a well-typed process cannot reduce to a process containing `wrong`.

We discussed run-time errors informally in Section 3.1, when we introduced the polyadic π-calculus. There, we used *sorting* as a mechanism for avoiding errors. Sorting is an example of a type system where equality between types is *by name*, as opposed to *by structure*. In the by-name approach, each type has a name (a sort, in the case of a sorting), and two types are equal if they have the same name. In the by-structure approach, two types are equal if they have the same structure. To illustrate the difference, consider two types T_1 and T_2 that may be ascribed to links that carry booleans. In a by-structure typing, T_1 and T_2 would be regarded as equal. In a by-name typing, on the other hand, they may be unequal, simply because the two types might have different names. This happens in a sorting if T_1 and T_2 are different sorts, for example. By-name type equality may be useful for avoiding confusion between types that are structurally equal but are used for different purposes (see Section 9.3 and Remark 9.4.9). By-structure equality, however, is both mathematically more elegant and more flexible. For instance, the by-structure typing rules have a natural interpretation as a logic, more powerful forms of subtyping are available, and two partners can communicate without first agreeing on a name for the type of the data to be exchanged. The last property is important in distributed systems, where the partners may know very little of each other. In this Part, and thereafter in the book, we follow the by-structure approach.

We present several type systems, beginning with a very simple system and then adding type constructs incrementally. For each new type construct, we discuss the associated rules and productions needed for incorporating it in a calculus.

For describing the evolution of processes, we use labelled transition systems, rather than reduction systems. Although some of the proofs of type soundness would be simpler with a reduction system (on this topic, see Remark 6.1.3 and Exercise 6.4.9), the labelled transition systems force us to present more general subject reduction theorems that will in any case be needed in Part IV to obtain proof techniques for reasoning about the behaviour of well-typed processes.

We concentrate on the type systems and omit *type-checking algorithms*, that is, algorithms for deciding the validity of type judgments. Further, we do not consider *type-inference algorithms*, that is, algorithms for finding a type for a term. Type systems are easier to understand if algorithmic concerns are left aside.

Structure of the Part The Part consists of three chapters. Chapter 6 lays the foundations. Section 6.1 collects terminology and notation used for the typed calculi in this and later Parts. In Section 6.2 we present Base-π, essentially the core of CCS with value-passing. Base-π will serve as a basis for the typed π-calculi as well as for the typed higher-order calculi. In Section 6.3 we establish some fundamental properties of the type system for Base-π. In Section 6.4 we present the (core) simply-typed π-calculus – the analogue of the simply-typed λ-calculus – and in Section 6.5 we enrich it with the type constructs for products, tuples, unions, records, and variants. In Section 6.6 we describe some convenient derived process constructs for decomposing composite values. In Section 6.7 we discuss recursive types.

Chapter 7 is about subtyping. In Section 7.1 we explain type systems that separate the input and the output capabilities on names. This gives rise to a natural subtyping relation, whose properties are studied in Section 7.2. In Section 7.3 we extend subtyping to the type constructs of Chapter 6. In Section 7.4 we briefly discuss why types, in particular variants, are handy for the representation of objects in the π-calculus. Section 7.5 is an intermezzo, or an exercise, in which we examine the relative expressiveness of calculi with products, unions, records and variants, with or without subtyping.

In Chapter 8 we look at more refined type systems. First, linearity (Section 8.1), which allows us to control the number of times a name is used; then uniform receptiveness (Section 8.2), which allows us to describe names that are *functional*, in the sense that the service they provide is persistent and unchanging; and finally parametric polymorphism (Section 8.3), which allows us to have names that can carry values of different types.

6

Foundations

6.1 Terminology and notation for typed calculi

We introduce some terminology and notation for describing typed calculi. On a first reading, it may be best to skim over this section. The main reason for collecting the material here is to make it easier for the reader to find where certain terminology and notation is introduced, than it would be if it were scattered throughout the text.

Definition 6.1.1 (Type environment) An *assignment* of a type to a name is of the form $a : T$, where a is a name, called the name of the assignment, and T is a type, called the type of the assignment.

A *type environment* (or *type assumption*, or, briefly, *typing*) is a finite set of assignments of types to names, where the names in the assignments are all different. □

We use Γ, Δ to range over type environments. We ignore the order of the assignments in a type environment. We sometimes regard a type environment Γ as a finite function from names to types. Therefore we write $\Gamma(a)$ for the type assigned to a by Γ, and say that the names of the assignments in Γ are *the names on which* Γ *is defined.* For now, we also call the names of the assignments in Γ the *support* of Γ, written $\mathsf{supp}(\Gamma)$. When we consider polymorphism, however, a type environment Γ will also include a set of type variables, and $\mathsf{supp}(\Gamma)$ will also include these variables.

To facilitate reading, we sometimes omit curly brackets outside a type environment. For instance we write $a : T \,,\, b : S$ for the type environment that assigns T to a, S to b and is undefined on the other names. We write Γ, Δ for the type environment that is the union of Γ and Δ; often Δ consists of a single type assignment, as in $\Gamma, a : T$. Whenever we extend a type environment, we implicitly assume that the environment was not defined on the added names.

Thus, in writing Γ, Δ, we assume that the names on which Γ and Δ are defined are disjoint and, similarly, in $\Gamma, a : T$ we assume that Γ is not defined on a. We write $\Gamma - x$ for the type environment that is undefined on x and is defined as Γ elsewhere.

Type judgments are of the form $\Gamma \vdash E : T$, where E may be a process or a value. If E is a process then T is $\diamond$, the *behaviour type*. A process type judgment $\Gamma \vdash P : \diamond$ asserts that process P respects the type assumptions in Γ, and a value type judgment $\Gamma \vdash v : T$ that value v has type T under the type assumptions Γ. Having $\diamond$ in process judgments gives them the same shape as value judgments, and avoids duplication of notations and results. However, we usually abbreviate a process judgment $\Gamma \vdash P : \diamond$ as $\Gamma \vdash P$. The behaviour type $\diamond$ will have an important role in the higher-order calculi of Chapter 12.

Given a type system, a *valid* type judgment is one that can be proved from the axioms and inference rules of the type system. A proof of the validity of a type judgment is a *typing derivation*. A process or value E is *well typed in* Γ if there is T such that $\Gamma \vdash E : T$ is valid; E is *well typed* if it is well typed in Γ, for some Γ. We write $\widetilde{x} : T$ to mean that each $x \in \widetilde{x}$ has type T, and $\Gamma \vdash E_1, E_2 : T$ as a shorthand for $\Gamma \vdash E_1 : T$ and $\Gamma \vdash E_2 : T$. As we deal with several typed calculi, to avoid ambiguity we sometimes add the name of the calculus to type judgments; thus $\mathcal{L} \triangleright \Gamma \vdash E : T$ indicates the type judgment $\Gamma \vdash E : T$ of the calculus $\mathcal{L}$.

In typed calculi, we annotate restricted names with their types, as in $(\boldsymbol{\nu} a : T)\, P$. Consequently, we add a type also into the notations for bound-output prefixes and local environments, in which a restricted name occurs, and write them as $\overline{b}(a : T).P$ and $P\{a : T = (x).\, Q\}$, respectively. In all these cases, however, the type T will be omitted when not important. By contrast, we do not put a type annotation in the bound name x of an input $a(x).\, P$, as this type can be directly inferred from the type of a (furthermore the type-annotated input prefix is derivable; see Exercise 7.2.13).

A *link* is a name that may be used to engage in communications. The *values* are the objects that can be exchanged along links. The *link types* are the types that can be ascribed to links. The *value types* are the types that can be ascribed to values. In the π-calculus, the link types are usually also value types; in Base-π (Section 6.2) and in the Higher-Order π-calculus (Chapter 12), however, link types are not value types. In every typed calculus the names are included among the values, because names can be used as placeholders for values in input prefixes. (The fact that the grammar of values includes names, but that link types may not be value types, should not confuse. 'Link' is more restrictive than 'name': a name may be used as a link, to exchange values, but also as a placeholder for values; and if link types are not value types, then processes cannot exchange links.)

We write $\pi^{\mathsf{op}_1,\ldots,\mathsf{op}_n}$ for the π-calculus in which the value types are determined by the type constructs $\{\mathsf{op}_1, \ldots, \mathsf{op}_n\}$. If T is a link type, then $\mathcal{O}(T)$ is the type of the values that a name of type T may carry. For instance, $\mathcal{O}(\sharp\, S)$ is S (where $\sharp\, S$ is the connection type, that is, the type of a name that carries values of type S; see Section 6.2). Link-type constructors have syntactic precedence over value-type constructors; see Notation 6.5.1 for an example.

The closed type environments identify the closed processes, which are the processes that are supposed to be run, or to be tested. For now, the only requirement on closed processes is that all their free names have link types. When we discuss linearity, receptiveness, and polymorphism we will add more requirements (for instance, polymorphism uses type variables, and a closed typing will be required to have no free type variables).

Definition 6.1.2 (Closed type environment) A type environment Γ is *closed* if $\Gamma(a)$ is a link type, for all a on which Γ is defined. A process P is *closed* if $\Gamma \vdash P$ for some closed Γ. □

The main subject reduction theorems for typed π-calculi, the analogues of the subject reduction property of typed λ-calculi, say that closed typings are preserved by silent transitions: if Γ is closed and $\Gamma \vdash P$ and $P \xrightarrow{\tau} P'$, then $\Gamma \vdash P'$. This property holds in all type systems that we will consider.

Remark 6.1.3 We present only the *labelled transitions* for the typed calculi. Whenever we introduce a new type construct we give the additional transition rules. These will be rules for inferring τ transitions, and will be of two kinds: *error rules*, for inferring transitions of the form $P \xrightarrow{\tau} \mathtt{wrong}$; and *$\beta$-reduction rules*, for decomposing a composite value into its components. The same rules, without the τ label, are precisely also the additional rules that would be needed for defining the *reduction relation* for the calculus in question. □

We will be very brief about free names, bound names, and related issues. We simply point out, when introducing a new construct, which occurrences of names are binders. As in the previous chapters, round brackets around a name indicate a binding occurrence.

6.2 Base-π

We begin describing a very simple typed calculus, Base-π, essentially the core of CCS with value-passing. The typing and operational rules, however, are set up

			Types
S, T	$::=$	V	value type
	$\mid$	L	link type
	$\mid$	$\diamond$	behaviour type
			Value types
V	$::=$	B	basic type
			Link types
L	$::=$	$\sharp V$	connection type
			Type environments
Γ	$::=$	$\Gamma, x : L$	
	$\mid$	$\Gamma, x : V$	
	$\mid$	$\emptyset$	

Table 6.1. *Base-π: syntax of types*

in such a way as to facilitate later extensions that allow mobility: typed π-calculi and typed higher-order π-calculi. The syntax of Base-π is in Tables 6.1 and 6.2, the typing rules in Table 6.3, and the transition rules in Table 6.4. (As usual, the symmetric forms of PAR-L, COMM-L, and SUM-L are omitted from Table 6.4.) We briefly comment on these rules below. In Base-π and its extensions, the syntactic distinction between value types and link types is made by the use of V to range over value types and L over link types. However, in typing and operational rules, as well as in discussions and proofs, unless important for the sense we will use only the letters S, T, which stand for arbitrary types. Thus, for instance, in rule T-INP of Table 6.3 we write $\Gamma \vdash v : \sharp T$, rather than $\Gamma \vdash v : \sharp V$; the syntax of types guarantees that T is a value type.

In Base-π there is only one link-type constructor, the *connection type* $\sharp T$. A type assignment $a : \sharp T$ means that a can be used as a link to carry values of type T. The only value types are the *basic types*; therefore the values of these types, the *basic values*, are the only values that are exchanged in a closed process. The set of basic types is left unspecified – the definition of Base-π is parametric with

		Values	
v, w	$::=$	x	name
	$\mid$	$basval$	basic value
		Processes	
P, Q, R	$::=$	$(\nu x : L)\, P$	restriction
	$\mid$	$\ldots$	{ the other constructs, as in Definition 1.1.1 }
	$\mid$	`wrong`	error
		Prefixes	
π	$::=$	$v(x)$	input
	$\mid$	$\overline{v}w$	output
	$\mid$	τ	silent prefix
	$\mid$	$[v = w]\pi$	matching

Table 6.2. *Base-π: syntax of processes*

respect to this set. Unless otherwise stated, we will assume that the basic types include at least the unit type `unit`; the only value of type `unit` is the unit value $\star$, whose typing rule is

$$\text{T-UNIT}\ \frac{}{\Gamma \vdash \star : \mathtt{unit}}$$

Other basic types could be, for instance, the integer and boolean types. Were they to be admitted, we would also need operations that manipulate their values, such as addition and negation; see Remark 6.2.2. We have seen in Section 3.4 that integers and booleans are encodable in π-calculus. But they occur so often as values that it would be cumbersome to adopt those encodings as a programming style. In Tables 6.1, 6.2 and 6.3, B is a metavariable over basic types, and $basval$ a metavariable over basic values. Moreover, $basval \in B$ means that $basval$ is a basic value of type B.

One of the purposes of a type system is to avoid run-time errors. To make the meaning of run-time errors precise and to prove theorems about the absence of run-time errors, we add a new process construct, `wrong`, to the syntax of processes. It denotes a process in which a run-time error has occurred.

There is one typing rule for each syntactic form except `wrong`, which is not

Value typing

$$\text{TV-BASE}\ \frac{}{\Gamma \vdash basval : B}\ basval \in B \qquad \text{TV-NAME}\ \frac{}{\Gamma, x : T \vdash x : T}$$

Process typing

$$\text{T-PAR}\ \frac{\Gamma \vdash P : \diamond \qquad \Gamma \vdash Q : \diamond}{\Gamma \vdash P \mid Q : \diamond} \qquad \text{T-SUM}\ \frac{\Gamma \vdash P : \diamond \qquad \Gamma \vdash Q : \diamond}{\Gamma \vdash P + Q : \diamond}$$

$$\text{T-MAT}\ \frac{\Gamma \vdash v : \sharp T \qquad \Gamma \vdash w : \sharp T \qquad \Gamma \vdash P : \diamond}{\Gamma \vdash [v = w]P : \diamond}$$

$$\text{T-NIL}\ \frac{}{\Gamma \vdash \mathbf{0} : \diamond} \qquad \text{T-REP}\ \frac{\Gamma \vdash P : \diamond}{\Gamma \vdash !P : \diamond}$$

$$\text{T-RES}\ \frac{\Gamma, x : L \vdash P : \diamond}{\Gamma \vdash (\nu x : L)\, P : \diamond} \qquad \text{T-TAU}\ \frac{\Gamma \vdash P : \diamond}{\Gamma \vdash \tau . P : \diamond}$$

$$\text{T-INP}\ \frac{\Gamma \vdash v : \sharp T \qquad \Gamma, x : T \vdash P : \diamond}{\Gamma \vdash v(x). P : \diamond}$$

$$\text{T-OUT}\ \frac{\Gamma \vdash v : \sharp T \qquad \Gamma \vdash w : T \qquad \Gamma \vdash P : \diamond}{\Gamma \vdash \overline{v}w. P : \diamond}$$

Table 6.3. *Typing rules for Base-π*

well typed under any assumptions. The inert process $\mathbf{0}$ is well typed in any typing. The parallel composition and the sum of two processes are well typed if each is well typed in isolation. Similarly, a replication $!P$ is well typed if P, the single copy, is. A process whose outermost constructor is a restriction is well typed if its body observes the constraints imposed both by the type environment and by the declared type of the new name. Note that the type of the restricted name is a link type: restrictions introduce new links, not arbitrary new values. The most interesting cases are the rules for input and output. In an input $v(x). P$, the subject v should have a link type (which also implies v should be a name); moreover, from this type, a type for x is determined and then the body P is required to be well typed under the resulting extension of Γ. The case for output is similar: the output $\overline{v}w. P$ is well typed if v has a link type and this type is compatible with that of w; moreover P itself must be well typed. The typing rule for matching stipulates that only names of the same connection type can be tested. We cannot therefore use matching to test equality between arbitrary

$$\text{OUT}\ \frac{}{\overline{a}w.\,P \xrightarrow{\overline{a}w} P} \qquad \text{INP}\ \frac{}{a(x).\,P \xrightarrow{aw} P\{w/x\}}$$

$$\text{TAU}\ \frac{}{\tau.\,P \xrightarrow{\tau} P} \qquad \text{MAT}\ \frac{P \xrightarrow{\alpha} P'}{[x = x]P \xrightarrow{\alpha} P'}$$

$$\text{SUM-L}\ \frac{P \xrightarrow{\alpha} P'}{P + Q \xrightarrow{\alpha} P'}$$

$$\text{PAR-L}\ \frac{P \xrightarrow{\alpha} P'}{P \mid Q \xrightarrow{\alpha} P' \mid Q}\ \mathsf{bn}(\alpha) \cap \mathsf{fn}(Q) = \emptyset$$

$$\text{COMM-L}\ \frac{P \xrightarrow{(\boldsymbol{\nu}\widetilde{z}:\widetilde{T})\,\overline{a}v} P' \qquad Q \xrightarrow{av} Q'}{P \mid Q \xrightarrow{\tau} (\boldsymbol{\nu}\widetilde{z} : \widetilde{T})\,(P' \mid Q')}\ \widetilde{z} \cap \mathsf{fn}(Q) = \emptyset$$

$$\text{RES}\ \frac{P \xrightarrow{\alpha} P'}{(\boldsymbol{\nu}x : T)\,P \xrightarrow{\alpha} (\boldsymbol{\nu}x : T)\,P'}\ x \notin \mathsf{n}(\alpha)$$

$$\text{OPEN}\ \frac{P \xrightarrow{(\boldsymbol{\nu}\widetilde{z}:\widetilde{T})\,\overline{a}v} P'}{(\boldsymbol{\nu}x : T)\,P \xrightarrow{(\boldsymbol{\nu}\widetilde{z}:\widetilde{T},x:T)\,\overline{a}v} P'}\ x \in \mathsf{fn}(v), x \notin \{\widetilde{z}, a\}$$

$$\text{REP-ACT}\ \frac{P \xrightarrow{\alpha} P'}{!P \xrightarrow{\alpha} P' \mid !P}$$

$$\text{REP-COMM}\ \frac{P \xrightarrow{(\boldsymbol{\nu}\widetilde{z}:\widetilde{T})\,\overline{a}v} P' \qquad P \xrightarrow{av} P''}{!P \xrightarrow{\tau} (\boldsymbol{\nu}\widetilde{z} : \widetilde{T})\,(P' \mid P'') \mid !P}\ \widetilde{z} \cap \mathsf{fn}(P) = \emptyset$$

$$\text{OUTERR}\ \frac{\text{(where } v \text{ is not a name)}}{\overline{v}w.\,P \xrightarrow{\tau} \mathtt{wrong}} \qquad \text{INERR}\ \frac{\text{(where } v \text{ is not a name)}}{v(x).\,P \xrightarrow{\tau} \mathtt{wrong}}$$

$$\text{MATERR}\ \frac{\text{(where } v \text{ or } w \text{ is not a name)}}{[v = w]P \xrightarrow{\tau} \mathtt{wrong}}$$

Table 6.4. *The transition rules for Base-π*

values. The reason for this is that the equality test on connection types, and in general on link types, is a semantically subtle construct (see the discussion on rule T-MAT in Section 7.1). We prefer that the equality test on other types (for instance integers), if needed, is introduced as a separate construct. Note also that, in a type environment, the types assigned to names can be link types or value types, but cannot be the behaviour type.

As in the polyadic π-calculus of Section 3.1, transitions can be of three forms:

- τ transitions $P \xrightarrow{\tau} P'$, with the usual meaning
- input transitions $P \xrightarrow{av} P'$, meaning that P can receive a value v at a and continue as P'
- output transitions $P \xrightarrow{(\boldsymbol{\nu}\widetilde{z}:\widetilde{T})\,\overline{a}v} P'$, meaning that P can send the value v along a extruding the set of names $\widetilde{z}$ of types $\widetilde{T}$, and then continue as P'.

In an output transition $P \xrightarrow{(\boldsymbol{\nu}\widetilde{z}:\widetilde{T})\,\overline{a}v} P'$, names $\widetilde{z}$ are free in v. If P is a well-typed process of Base-π, then $\widetilde{z}$ is always empty – because in Base-π links are not values. But when values can include names, as in typed π-calculi, or processes, as in higher-order π-calculi, then $\widetilde{z}$ can be non-empty; see Exercises 6.4.3 and 6.5.2 for examples. We maintain the terminology for actions of the previous chapters; thus in actions av and $(\boldsymbol{\nu}\widetilde{z} : \widetilde{T})\,\overline{a}v$ we call v the *object* and a the *subject*. Having output actions of the form $(\boldsymbol{\nu}\widetilde{z} : \widetilde{T})\,\overline{a}v$, with a special place for the (possibly empty) set $\widetilde{z}$ of extruded names, allows us to accommodate both forms of output actions of the monadic π-calculus (Definition 1.3.1), namely the free output $\overline{x}y$ and the bound outout $\overline{x}(z)$.

The transition rules (Table 6.4) are similar to those of the untyped π-calculus. The differences are: the two communication rules COMM-L and REP-COMM, in place of the four rules COMM-L, CLOSE-L, REP-COMM, and REP-CLOSE; the more general side condition in rule OPEN; and the presence of rules MATERR, INERR, and OUTERR, for signalling run-time errors. In Base-π, an error occurs if a value that is not a name ends up as the subject of a prefix or in a matching; extensions of the type systems in later sections will add more rules for errors.

The operational rules are defined on arbitrary processes – they need not be well typed, let alone closed. Only closed well-typed processes, however, are guaranteed not to produce a run-time error, as will be proved in Section 6.3. As Base-π is very simple, we could have prevented run-time errors by syntactic means. This would however be complicated in later extensions of Base-π. In the grammar of Table 6.2, we cannot use names instead of arbitrary values as subjects of input and output prefixes and as arguments of matches. The operational rules would not be well defined, because the derivative of a process might not be a process, as in

$$\overline{a}\star.\,P \mid a(x).\,\overline{x}c.\,\mathbf{0} \xrightarrow{\tau} P \mid \overline{\star}c\,.\,\mathbf{0}\,.$$

The problem is with substitutions: $P\{v/x\}$ might not be a process. This problem does not exist with the present syntax, as shown by the following lemma:

Lemma 6.2.1 $P\{v/x\}$ is a process, for every process P, name x, and value v. $\square$

As a consequence of this lemma, the expression E in a judgment $P \xrightarrow{\alpha} E$ inferred from the rules of Table 6.4 is a process.

Remark 6.2.2 We might wish to have operations that manipulate values of basic types. For instance, if we have integers, we would probably need addition and multiplication, and, if we have booleans, negation and conjunction. For this, we should add to the syntax of Base-π the syntactic category of *value expressions*, that is, expressions that reduce to values. Value expressions would include, but not coincide with, values. For instance, if succ is the successor function on integers, then $\mathsf{succ}\ 2$ would be a value expression but not a value. We would then need rules for evaluating value expressions, such as

$$\frac{}{\mathsf{succ}\, n \xrightarrow{\tau} n+1}$$

as well as rules for evaluating value expressions in processes, such as, using e for a value expression,

$$\frac{e \xrightarrow{\tau} e'}{\overline{a}e.\, P \xrightarrow{\tau} \overline{a}e'.\, P} \tag{6.1}$$

These rules determine a *reduction strategy*. Different choices of reduction strategies are possible; for instance rule (6.1) is typical of the *call-by-value* strategy.

We do not introduce value expressions, and hence reduction strategies, into the typed calculi that we present. This addition is an orthogonal issue, and can easily be accomplished by analogy with typed λ-calculi. In examples, however, we occasionally use integer and boolean expressions, assuming standard call-by-value reduction rules for them such as rule (6.1). Reduction strategies are discussed in Chapter 14. □

6.3 Properties of typing

We now establish some fundamental properties of the type system for Base-π. *These properties will continue to hold in extensions of Base-π, unless otherwise stated.* To carry out proofs, we have to fix the set of basic types: we take `unit` as the only such type.

Lemmas 6.3.1–6.3.5 are proved by straightforward induction on the depth of the derivation of the judgment in the hypothesis.

Lemma 6.3.1 If $\Gamma \vdash E : T$ and Γ is not defined on x, then x is not free in E. □

Lemma 6.3.2 If $\Gamma \vdash P$ then P does not have `wrong` as a subterm. □

Lemma 6.3.3 For every typing Γ and name x there is at most one type T such that $\Gamma \vdash x : T$. □

Lemma 6.3.4 (Strengthening) If $\Gamma, x : S \vdash E : T$ and x is not free in E, then also $\Gamma \vdash E : T$. □

Lemma 6.3.5 (Weakening) If $\Gamma \vdash E : T$ then $\Gamma, x : S \vdash E : T$ for any type S and any name x on which Γ is not defined. □

Lemma 6.3.6 (Substitution Lemma) Suppose

(1) $\Gamma \vdash E : T$
(2) $\Gamma(x) = S$
(3) $\Gamma \vdash v : S$.

Then $\Gamma \vdash E\{^{v}\!/\!_{x}\} : T$.

Proof Take the derivation of $\Gamma \vdash E : T$. We obtain one for $\Gamma \vdash E\{^{v}\!/\!_{x}\} : T$ as follows. Consider all leaves that look up the type of x. They are of the form

$$\frac{}{\Delta, x : S \vdash x : S}$$

Here the typing $\Delta, x : S$ is an extension of Γ, in the sense that there is Γ' such that $\Delta, x : S = \Gamma, \Gamma'$. Hence, by Weakening, also $\Delta, x : S \vdash v : S$ is valid. Therefore such a leaf may be replaced by a derivation of $\Delta, x : S \vdash v : S$. Replace also all occurrences of x to the right of a turnstile by v. The result is a derivation of $\Gamma \vdash E\{^{v}\!/\!_{x}\} : T$, which can be proved by induction on the depth of the derivation of $\Gamma \vdash E : T$. □

In the present system, the type of a name is unique (Lemma 6.3.3), and hence in Lemma 6.3.6 the condition $\Gamma(x) = S$ could be replaced by $\Gamma \vdash x : S$. However, this will not hold in later extensions of the system; see for instance Exercise 7.2.1.

The *Subject Reduction* Theorem 6.3.7 expresses a consistency between the operational semantics and the typing rules. The theorem shows how the typing of a process evolves under transitions and how the typing can be used to obtain information about the process's possible transitions. For instance, the type of the value sent out by the process in an output must be compatible with the type of the name at which the output takes place. The first clause is the most important one; it shows that a (closed) process maintains its typing as it evolves.

Theorem 6.3.7 (Subject Reduction) Suppose $\Gamma \vdash P$, with Γ closed, and $P \xrightarrow{\alpha} P'$.

(1) If $\alpha = \tau$ then $\Gamma \vdash P'$.
(2) If $\alpha = av$ then there is T such that

  (a) $\Gamma \vdash a : \sharp T$
  (b) if $\Gamma \vdash v : T$ then $\Gamma \vdash P'$.

(3) If $\alpha = (\boldsymbol{\nu}\widetilde{x} : \widetilde{S})\, \overline{a}v$ then there is T such that

  (a) $\Gamma \vdash a : \sharp T$
  (b) $\Gamma,\, \widetilde{x} : \widetilde{S} \vdash v : T$
  (c) $\Gamma,\, \widetilde{x} : \widetilde{S} \vdash P'$
  (d) each component of $\widetilde{S}$ is a link type.

Proof By induction on the depth of the derivation of $P \xrightarrow{\alpha} P'$. All cases are simple. We consider only two of them.

INP **rule** In this case $P = a(x).Q$ and $P' = Q\{v/x\}$ (note that by the usual convention on bound names x does not appear in Γ or, hence, in v). From $\Gamma \vdash P$ we infer that $\Gamma \vdash a : \sharp T$ and $\Gamma, x : T \vdash Q$, for some T. We have to show that if $\Gamma \vdash v : T$ then $\Gamma \vdash Q\{v/x\}$. From $\Gamma \vdash v : T$ and Weakening, $\Gamma, x : T \vdash v : T$. It also holds that $(\Gamma, x : T)(x) = T$ and $\Gamma, x : T \vdash Q$. We can therefore apply the Substitution Lemma 6.3.6 and infer $\Gamma, x : T \vdash Q\{v/x\}$. Since x is not free in $Q\{v/x\}$, by Strengthening, $\Gamma \vdash Q\{v/x\}$.

COMM-L **rule** We have $P = P_1 \mid P_2$, $P_1 \xrightarrow{(\boldsymbol{\nu}\widetilde{x}:\widetilde{S})\,\overline{a}v} P_1'$, $P_2 \xrightarrow{av} P_2'$, and $P' = (\boldsymbol{\nu}\widetilde{x} : \widetilde{S})\,(P_1' \mid P_2')$. By the inductive assumption on P_1, there is T such that $\Gamma \vdash a : \sharp T$,

$$\Gamma,\, \widetilde{x} : \widetilde{S} \vdash v : T\,, \tag{6.2}$$

and $\Gamma,\, \widetilde{x} : \widetilde{S} \vdash P_1'$.

By Weakening, $\Gamma,\, \widetilde{x} : \widetilde{S} \vdash a : \sharp T$. Moreover, by Lemma 6.3.3, T is the unique type with this property. Using this and (6.2), by the inductive assumption on $\Gamma \vdash P_2$ (which by Weakening also holds for $\Gamma,\, \widetilde{x} : \widetilde{S} \vdash P_2$), we also get $\Gamma,\, \widetilde{x} : \widetilde{S} \vdash P_2'$.

Using rule T-PAR we can now infer $\Gamma,\, \widetilde{x} : \widetilde{S} \vdash P_1' \mid P_2'$, and using T-RES and the inductive assumption that $\widetilde{S}$ are link types, $\Gamma \vdash (\boldsymbol{\nu}\widetilde{x} : \widetilde{S})\,(P_1' \mid P_2')$, which concludes the case.

□

In clause (3), because of the subclause (3d), the environment $\Gamma,\, \widetilde{x} : \widetilde{S}$ under which P' is typed is also closed.

Remark 6.3.8 The Subject Reduction Theorem 6.3.7 actually holds for arbitrary type environments – not only the closed ones. This will not be true for some extensions of Base-π; see Exercise 6.5.3. For this reason, here and in later sections, we present subject reduction theorems on typings that are closed (or related to closed, such as link-closed in Section 8.1). □

Subject Reduction is also used to prove the absence of run-time errors.

Corollary 6.3.9 (Type Soundness) If $\Gamma \vdash P$, with Γ closed, and $P \Longrightarrow P'$, then P' does not have `wrong` as a subterm.

Proof This follows from Theorem 6.3.7(1) and Lemma 6.3.2. □

For instance, the processes $\overline{a}\star \mid a(x).\,\overline{x}\star$ and $\overline{a}\star \mid a(x).\,[x = b]\mathbf{0}$ reduce to processes containing `wrong`, and are not typable.

Exercise 6.3.10 Write down a process that is not well typed and yet never reduces to a process containing `wrong`. □

6.4 The simply-typed π-calculus

The first form of typed π-calculus we consider (we regard Base-π as a form of typed CCS) is the *core simply-typed π-calculus*. We write $\pi^{\widetilde{B},\sharp}$ for the core simply-typed π-calculus whose basic types are $\widetilde{B}$. It is obtained from Base-π by adding the following production to the grammar of value types:

$$V \quad ::= \quad L \qquad \text{link type.}$$

The extension allows links to be communicated, and hence allows mobility. The fundamental type construct of $\pi^{\widetilde{B},\sharp}$ is the connection type; but basic types are needed to get the construction of types started.

Exercise 6.4.1 Show that

$$b(y).\,\overline{y}\star \mid \overline{a}b \mid a(x).\,\overline{x}c$$

is well typed in $c : \sharp\,\mathtt{unit}, b : \sharp\sharp\,\mathtt{unit}, a : \sharp\sharp\sharp\,\mathtt{unit}$. □

Exercise 6.4.2 Show that

$$\overline{a}b \mid a(x).\,\overline{x}\star \mid b(y).\,\overline{y}\star$$

is not typable, and that it reduces to a process that contains `wrong`. □

Exercise 6.4.3 To get some familiarity with typed transitions, check that

$$(\boldsymbol{\nu} b : T)\,(\overline{a}b \mid a(x).\,\overline{c}x) \xrightarrow{\tau} \xrightarrow{(\boldsymbol{\nu} b:T)\,\overline{c}b} \mathbf{0} \mid \mathbf{0}\,.$$

□

We will use the phrase *simply-typed π-calculus* for a typed π-calculus defined using the type constructs of the core simply-typed π-calculus, and possibly the type constructs of the following Sections 6.5 and 6.7, such as products and recursive types.

Remark 6.4.4 The properties of typing in Section 6.3 remain true in the simply-typed π-calculus. Something worth pointing out, however, is the following. In clause (2) of Subject Reduction Theorem 6.3.7, the value v received in an input is typed under the original typing Γ. In typed π-calculi a process well typed in Γ may however receive a fresh name x in an input. This case is covered by the combination of Subject Reduction and Weakening: first use Weakening to extend Γ with a type assignment for x, then use Subject Reduction on the process's transition and on the extended typing. □

In the λ-calculus, where functions are the unit of interaction, the key type construct is function type. In the π-calculus, names are the unit of interaction, and therefore the key type construct is the connection type. The programs of the simply-typed λ-calculus – the λ-calculus analogue of the simply-typed π-calculus – have strong properties of termination: every computation of a well-typed term must terminate. This is not true for the simply-typed π-calculus, as shown for instance by the process $!\overline{a}\star$. However, every *logical thread* of a well-typed process has a finite length. We show this for $\pi^{\mathtt{unit},\sharp}$, where $\mathtt{unit}$ is the only basic type.

Definition 6.4.5

(1) A *trace* is a (possibly infinite) sequence of visible actions $\alpha_1, \ldots, \alpha_n, \ldots$ such that, for all $i \neq j$, $\mathsf{bn}(\alpha_i) \cap \mathsf{bn}(\alpha_j) = \emptyset$ and, for all $j < i$, $\mathsf{bn}(\alpha_i) \cap \mathsf{fn}(\alpha_j) = \emptyset$. (These conditions are to ensure that the bound names of the trace are fresh.) The *length* h of the trace is the number of actions in it ($0 \leq h \leq \omega$).

(2) A trace $\ell = \alpha_1, \ldots, \alpha_n, \ldots$ of length h is a *logical thread* if the object of α_i is the same as the subject of α_{i+1}, for all $1 \leq i < h$.

(3) A *subtrace* of a trace $\ell = \alpha_1, \ldots, \alpha_n, \ldots$ is a trace $\ell' = \alpha_{j_1}, \ldots, \alpha_{j_n}, \ldots$ such that if h is the length of ℓ' then for all integers m_1, m_2 with $1 \leq m_1 < m_2 \leq h$ it holds that $j_{m_1} < j_{m_2}$. In this case we also say that *ℓ has a subtrace ℓ' of length h*; if, moreover, ℓ' is a logical thread, then *ℓ has a logical thread ℓ' of length h*.

(4) A trace $\alpha_1, \ldots, \alpha_n, \ldots$ of length h is a *trace of the process P_1* if there are processes $P_2, \ldots, P_{n+1}, \ldots$ such that $P_i \stackrel{\alpha_i}{\Longrightarrow} P_{i+1}$, for all $1 \leq i < h$. □

A subtrace is obtained from a trace ℓ by erasing some of its actions (possibly all of them).

Example 6.4.6 The trace $xa\,,\ (\boldsymbol{\nu} b : T)\,\overline{c}b\,,\ a\star,\ bz\,,\ \overline{z}\star$ has for instance various logical threads of length 2 (among them, $xa\,,\ a\star$) and one of length 3 (namely $(\boldsymbol{\nu} b : T)\,\overline{c}b\,,\ bz\,,\ \overline{z}\star$). □

A logical thread can be thought of as a sequential computation of a process, in which sequentiality is determined by the names that are exchanged, rather than by prefixing constructs. In this sense, the theorem below shows that a process of the simply-typed π-calculus can perform only *finite* sequential computations.

Theorem 6.4.7 Suppose $\pi^{\mathtt{unit},\sharp} \rhd \Gamma \vdash P\ :\diamond$, for some Γ. Then any logical thread of any trace of P is of finite length.

Proof Consider a trace of P, and a logical thread $\ell = \alpha_1, \ldots, \alpha_n, \ldots$ extracted from the trace. By definition of logical thread, the object of action α_i is the same as the subject of α_{i+1}. Therefore, by Theorem 6.3.7, the type of the subject of α_{i+1} must have fewer link type constructs than the type of the subject of α_i. We conclude that ℓ must have a finite length. □

Of course in general the computation of a process will consist of several interleaved logical threads; however, each single thread is finite.

Exercise 6.4.8 Show that all processes of $\mathrm{P}\pi^{!}$ (Definition 5.7.3) are typable in $\pi^{\mathtt{unit},\sharp}$, viewing bound-output prefix as an abbreviation, as by Notation 2.2.13, and adding appropriate type annotations in restrictions. □

Exercise 6.4.9 This exercise invites the reader to prove a subject reduction theorem on reductions using a reduction system, rather than a labelled transition system. Suppose $\pi^{\mathtt{unit},\sharp} \rhd \Gamma \vdash P\ :\diamond$.

(1) Show that if $P \equiv P'$ then $\pi^{\mathtt{unit},\sharp} \rhd \Gamma \vdash P'\ :\diamond$.
(2) Use the previous result to show that if $P \longrightarrow P'$ then $\pi^{\mathtt{unit},\sharp} \rhd \Gamma \vdash P'\ :\diamond$, where $\longrightarrow$ is the relation defined by the reduction system of $\pi^{\mathtt{unit},\sharp}$ (the analogue for $\pi^{\mathtt{unit},\sharp}$ of the reduction system of Definition 1.2.12 for the untyped π-calculus). □

6.5 Products, unions, records, and variants

In this section we introduce four important type constructs: *products* (which will be generalized to *tuples*), *unions*, *records*, and *variants*. These are the π-calculus versions of familiar constructs of sequential languages. The productions and rules for these types are in Tables 6.5–6.8, and are commented on below. A calculus $\pi^{\mathtt{unit},\sharp,\mathsf{op}}$, where op is one of these type constructs, adds to $\pi^{\mathtt{unit},\sharp}$ the productions and rules for op.

Each type construct introduces a new set of composite values, which can be decomposed into their components by means of pattern matching. Each form of pattern matching is a new process construct, with associated operational rules in which the decomposition of a value generates a τ action. Alternatively, the pattern matching could be made part of the input prefix operator. The choice between the two is essentially a matter of taste. We have chosen to separate pattern matching and input because they represent logically-different operations. However, pattern matching in input gives more compact process expressions and behaviours – see Section 6.6 for details. Yet another quite reasonable possibility for decomposing values would be to use special operators on values. In the case of product types, for instance, the operators would be *first* and *second*, with reduction rules $\mathit{first}\langle v, w\rangle \xrightarrow{\tau} v$ and $\mathit{second}\langle v, w\rangle \xrightarrow{\tau} w$, where $\langle v, w\rangle$ is a product value. In a process calculus, decomposition of values by means of process constructs is more elegant, however, and avoids the issue of reduction strategies on value expressions.

6.5.1 Products

The values of a *product type* $T_1 \times T_2$ are pairs $\langle v_1, v_2\rangle$ where each v_i is of type T_i. Product values are broken into their components by the with construct $\mathsf{with}\ (x_1, x_2) = v\ \mathsf{do}\ P$, where the outermost occurrences of x_1 and x_2 are binding with scope P. The productions and rules for products are reported in Table 6.5.

An obvious generalization of product type is the *tuple type* $\times(T_1, \ldots, T_n)$, for $n \geq 0$, whose values are n-tuples $\langle v_1, \ldots, v_n\rangle$ with the ith component v_i of type T_i, for $1 \leq i \leq n$. The value destructor is the n-ary with:

$$\mathsf{with}\ (x_1, \ldots, x_n) = v\ \mathsf{do}\ P\,.$$

When $n \geq 2$, we abbreviate $\times(T_1, \ldots, T_n)$ as $T_1 \times \ldots \times T_n$. Although tuple types can be derived by repeatedly using products, we will take them as primitive, because they are very often used and because having them as primitive gives us more compact process behaviours: for instance, taking tuples as primitive, a process $\mathsf{with}\ (x_1, \ldots, x_n) = \langle v_1, \ldots, v_n\rangle\ \mathsf{do}\ P$ reduces to $P\{v_1, \ldots, v_n/x_1, \ldots, x_n\}$ in a single τ step; taking tuples as derived, the same reduction would take $n-1$ τ steps. We call a π-calculus that has tuple types *polyadic*. In notations for typed π-calculi, $\pi^{\cdots,\times,\cdots}$ will mean that the calculus has tuple types, whereas $\pi^{\cdots,\times_2,\cdots}$ will mean that the calculus has product types.

Grammars

			Values
v	$::=$	$\langle v, w\rangle$	product value
			Processes
P	$::=$	$\mathsf{with}\ (x, y) = v\ \mathsf{do}\ P$	with
			Types for values
V	$::=$	$V_1 \times V_2$	product type

Typing rules

$$\text{T-WITH}\ \frac{\Gamma \vdash v : T_1 \times T_2 \qquad \Gamma, x_1 : T_1, x_2 : T_2 \vdash P : \diamond}{\Gamma \vdash\ \mathsf{with}\ (x_1, x_2) = v\ \mathsf{do}\ P : \diamond}$$

$$\text{TV-PROD}\ \frac{\Gamma \vdash v_1 : T_1 \qquad \Gamma \vdash v_2 : T_2}{\Gamma \vdash \langle v_1, v_2\rangle : T_1 \times T_2}$$

Transition rules

$$\text{PROD}\ \frac{}{\mathsf{with}\ (x_1, x_2) = \langle v_1, v_2\rangle\ \mathsf{do}\ P \xrightarrow{\tau} P\{v_1, v_2/x_1, x_2\}}$$

$$\text{PRODERR}\ \frac{(\text{where } v \text{ does not have the form } \langle v_1, v_2\rangle)}{\mathsf{with}\ (x_1, x_2) = v\ \mathsf{do}\ P \xrightarrow{\tau} \mathsf{wrong}}$$

Table 6.5. *Additional productions and rules for product types*

Notation 6.5.1 Link types have syntactic precedence over value types, therefore $\sharp T \times S$ reads $(\sharp T) \times S$. □

Exercise 6.5.2 Check that $(\boldsymbol{\nu} b : T, c : S)\, a(x).\, \overline{d}\langle b, x, c\rangle \xrightarrow{ae} \xrightarrow{(\boldsymbol{\nu} b:T,c:S)\, \overline{d}\langle b,e,c\rangle} \mathbf{0}$. □

Exercise 6.5.3 Show that the Subject Reduction Theorem 6.3.7 does not hold in a simply-typed π-calculus with products without the hypothesis that Γ is closed. (Hint: use rule PRODERR.) □

6.5.2 Unions

The dual of the product type is the *union type* (Table 6.6). The union type $T_1 \oplus T_2$ is the disjoint union of the types T_1 and T_2. The values of $T_1 \oplus T_2$ are of the form $\mathsf{inl\_}v$ and $\mathsf{inr\_}v$ where inl, inr are tags that tell us which of the types T_1 and T_2 the argument v comes from. The decomposition of a union value is done by the case construct $\mathsf{case}\ v\ \mathsf{of}\ [\,\mathsf{inl\_}(x_1) \rhd P_1\,;\ \mathsf{inr\_}(x_2) \rhd P_2\,]$, which, depending on whether v is of the form $\mathsf{inl\_}w$ or $\mathsf{inr\_}w$, reduces to $P_1\{^w\!/x_1\}$ or $P_2\{^w\!/x_2\}$; if w is not of either form, an error is produced. In the case construct, the name x_i is binding with scope P_i. Also the binary union type can be generalized to an n-ary construct; we will not use this in the book.

6.5.3 Records

Records are labelled forms of tuples. Without subtyping, record and tuple types are interderivable; but subtyping makes them different constructs, see Section 7.3.

A record type has the form $\{\,\ell_1 : T_1, \ldots, \ell_n : T_n\,\}$, where the labels ℓ_i are all different. Its values are of the form $\{\ell_1 = v_1, \ldots, \ell_n = v_n\}$, where each v_i is a value of type T_i. The components of a record are called *fields*; thus v_i is the value of the field ℓ_i. The order of the fields in a record does not matter: the types $\{\,\ell_1 : T_1\,,\ \ell_2 : T_2\,\}$ and $\{\,\ell_2 : T_2\,,\ \ell_1 : T_1\,\}$ are identified, and similarly for the values $\{\ell_1 = v_1\,,\ \ell_2 = v_2\}$ and $\{\ell_2 = v_2\,,\ \ell_1 = v_1\}$. We abbreviate a value $\{\ell_1 = v_1, \ldots, \ell_n = v_n\}$ as $\{_{j\in 1,\ldots,n}\ \ell_j = v_j\}$, and similarly for record types $\{\,\ell_1 : T_1, \ldots, \ell_n : T_n\,\}$.

The destructor for record values is a labelled form of with,

$$\mathsf{with}\ \{\ell_1 = (x_1), \ldots, \ell_n = (x_n)\}\ = v\ \mathsf{do}\ P\,,$$

in which the outermost occurrence of each x_i is a binder with scope P and, again, the order of the components $\ell_i = (x_i)$ does not matter. Note that in the transition rule RECORD of Table 6.7, the value $\{\ell_1 = v_1, \ldots, \ell_{n+m} = v_{n+m}\}$ may have more components than required. This flexibility is useless with the present typing rules – in a well-typed process the formal and actual parameters of a with must have the same components; but it will be important when we add subtyping.

6.5.4 Variants

Variants are to union types what records are to products: labelled disjoint unions of types. As for records, so in a variant (type or value) the order of the components does not matter, and their labels are all different. The destructor for

Grammars

			Values
v	$::=$	$\mathsf{inl\_}v$	union value, left
	$\mid$	$\mathsf{inr\_}v$	union value, right
			Processes
P	$::=$	$\mathsf{case}\ v\ \mathsf{of}\ [\,\mathsf{inl\_}(x_1) \rhd P_1\,;\ \mathsf{inr\_}(x_2) \rhd P_2\,]$	union case
			Types for values
V	$::=$	$V_1 \oplus V_2$	union type

Typing rules

$$\text{T-WITH}\ \frac{\Gamma \vdash v : T_1 \oplus T_2 \qquad \Gamma, x_i : T_i \vdash P_i : \diamond \qquad i = 1,2}{\Gamma \vdash \mathsf{case}\ v\ \mathsf{of}\ [\,\mathsf{inl\_}(x_1) \rhd P_1\,;\ \mathsf{inr\_}(x_2) \rhd P_2\,] : \diamond}$$

$$\text{TV-UNIL}\ \frac{\Gamma \vdash v : T_1}{\Gamma \vdash \mathsf{inl\_}v : T_1 \oplus T_2}$$

$$\text{TV-UNIR}\ \frac{\Gamma \vdash v : T_2}{\Gamma \vdash \mathsf{inr\_}v : T_1 \oplus T_2}$$

Transition rules

$$\text{UNIL}\ \frac{}{\mathsf{case\ inl\_}v\ \mathsf{of}\ [\,\mathsf{inl\_}(x_1) \rhd P_1\,;\ \mathsf{inr\_}(x_2) \rhd P_2\,] \xrightarrow{\tau} P_1\{v/x_1\}}$$

$$\text{UNIR}\ \frac{}{\mathsf{case\ inr\_}v\ \mathsf{of}\ [\,\mathsf{inl\_}(x_1) \rhd P_1\,;\ \mathsf{inr\_}(x_2) \rhd P_2\,] \xrightarrow{\tau} P_2\{v/x_2\}}$$

$$\text{UNIERR}\ \frac{(\text{where } v \text{ does not have the form } \mathsf{inl\_}w \text{ or } \mathsf{inr\_}w)}{\mathsf{case}\ v\ \mathsf{of}\ [\,\mathsf{inl\_}(x_1) \rhd P_1\,;\ \mathsf{inr\_}(x_2) \rhd P_2\,] \xrightarrow{\tau} \mathtt{wrong}}$$

Table 6.6. *Additional productions and rules for union types*

variant values is a labelled form of case. In a case branch $\ell_i\_(x_i) \rhd P_i$, the name x_i is bound in P_i. We sometimes abbreviate an expression

$$[\,\ell_1\_(y_1) \rhd P_1\,;\ \ldots\ ;\ \ell_n\_(y_n) \rhd P_n\,]$$

Grammars

ℓ, h			*Record labels*
			Values
v	$::=$	$\{\ell_1 = v_1, \ldots, \ell_n = v_n\}$	record value
			Processes
P	$::=$	$\mathsf{with}\ \{\ell_1 = (x_1), \ldots, \ell_n = (x_n)\} = v\ \mathsf{do}\ P$	labelled with
			Types for values
V	$::=$	$\{\ell_1 : V_1, \ldots, \ell_n : V_n\}$	record type

Typing rules

$$\text{T-RECORD}\ \frac{\Gamma \vdash v : \{_{j \in 1,\ldots,n}\ \ell_j : T_j\} \qquad \Gamma, x_1 : T_1, \ldots, x_n : T_n \vdash P : \diamond}{\Gamma \vdash \mathsf{with}\ \{_{j \in 1,\ldots,n}\ \ell_j = (x_j)\} = v\ \mathsf{do}\ P : \diamond}$$

$$\text{Tv-RECORD}\ \frac{\text{for each } i \quad \Gamma \vdash v_i : T_i}{\Gamma \vdash \{_{j \in 1,\ldots,n}\ \ell_j = v_j\} : \{_{j \in 1,\ldots,n}\ \ell_j : T_j\}}$$

Transition rules

$$\text{RECORD}\ \frac{}{\mathsf{with}\ \{_{j \in 1,\ldots,n}\ \ell_j = (x_j)\} = \{_{j \in 1,\ldots,n+m}\ \ell_j = v_j\}\ \mathsf{do}\ P \xrightarrow{\tau} P\{v_1, \ldots, v_n/x_1, \ldots, x_n\}}$$

$$\text{RECORDERR}\ \frac{(\text{where } v \text{ does not have the form } \{_{j \in 1,\ldots,n+m}\ \ell_j = v_j\})}{\mathsf{with}\ \{_{j \in 1,\ldots,n}\ \ell_j = (x_j)\} = v\ \mathsf{do}\ P \xrightarrow{\tau} \mathtt{wrong}}$$

Table 6.7. *Additional productions and rules for record types*

as $[_{j \in 1,\ldots,n}\ \ell_j\_(y_j) \rhd P_j]$, and similarly for variant types $[\ell_1\_T_1, \ldots, \ell_n\_T_n]$.

In Table 6.8, the rule Tv-VAR alone is of little use, because it assigns to any variant value a variant type with a single component. In systems with subtyping (Section 7.3), however, from Tv-VAR and subtyping the following rule is derivable:

$$\text{Tv-VAR-LONG}\ \frac{\Gamma \vdash v : T_i \qquad \ell = \ell_i \qquad i \in \{1, \ldots, n\}}{\Gamma \vdash \ell\_v : [\ell_1\_T_1, \ldots, \ell_n\_T_n]}$$

Without subtyping, this rule is taken as primitive. Variants are more interesting than unions only when there is subtyping, just as for records and products.

Grammars

ℓ, h			*Variant labels*
			Values
v	$::=$	ℓ_v	variant value
			Processes
P	$::=$	$\mathsf{case}\ v\ \mathsf{of}\ [\,\ell_1\_(x_1) \rhd P_1\,;\,\ldots\,;\,\ell_n\_(x_n) \rhd P_n\,]$	labelled case
			Types for values
V	$::=$	$[\ell_1\_V_1, \ldots, \ell_n\_V_n]$	variant type

Typing rules

$$\text{T-VAR}\ \frac{\Gamma \vdash v : [\ell_1\_T_1, \ldots, \ell_n\_T_n] \qquad \text{for each } i \in 1, \ldots, n \quad \Gamma, x_i : T_i \vdash P_i : \diamond}{\Gamma \vdash \mathsf{case}\ v\ \mathsf{of}\ [\,\ell_1\_(x_1) \rhd P_1\,;\,\ldots\,;\,\ell_n\_(x_n) \rhd P_n\,] : \diamond}$$

$$\text{TV-VAR}\ \frac{\Gamma \vdash v : T}{\Gamma \vdash \ell\_v : [\ell\_T]}$$

Transition rules

$$\text{CASE}\ \frac{(\text{where } j \in \{1, \ldots, n\})}{\mathsf{case}\ \ell_j\_v\ \mathsf{of}\ [\,\ell_1\_(x_1) \rhd P_1\,;\,\ldots\,;\,\ell_n\_(x_n) \rhd P_n\,] \xrightarrow{\tau} P_j\{v/x_j\}}$$

$$\text{CASEERR}\ \frac{(\text{where } v \text{ does not have the form } \ell_j\_w \text{ for } j \in \{1, \ldots, n\})}{\mathsf{case}\ v\ \mathsf{of}\ [\,\ell_1\_(x_1) \rhd P_1\,;\,\ldots\,;\,\ell_n\_(x_n) \rhd P_n\,] \xrightarrow{\tau} \mathtt{wrong}}$$

Table 6.8. *Additional productions and rules for variant types*

6.6 Pattern matching in input

Since tuple and variant types are frequently used in the book, we introduce some convenient notations for them. We often wish to decompose a tuple or a variant value immediately after receiving it in an input. A less verbose syntax, combining input and pattern matching into a single construct, is then useful. For tuples, this is the polyadic input prefix

$$a(x_1, \ldots, x_n).\, P\,.$$

We can take it as an abbreviation,

$$a(x_1,\ldots,x_n).\,P \stackrel{\text{def}}{=} a(x).\ \mathsf{with}\ (x_1,\ldots,x_n) = x\ \mathsf{do}\ P\,,$$

for x not free in P, with the following derived operational rules:

$$\begin{array}{lll} a(x_1,\ldots,x_n).\,P \xrightarrow{a\langle v_1,\ldots,v_n\rangle}\xrightarrow{\tau} P\{v_1,\ldots,v_n/x_1,\ldots,x_n\} & \\ a(x_1,\ldots,x_n).\,P \xrightarrow{av}\xrightarrow{\tau} \mathtt{wrong} & \text{if } v \text{ is not an } n\text{-tuple.} \end{array} \qquad (6.3)$$

Or, as discussed in the introduction to Section 6.5 (and as done in Section 3.1), the polyadic input could be taken as primitive, in place of the with construct. In this case the operational rules for the polyadic input are

$$\begin{array}{lll} a(x_1,\ldots,x_n).\,P \xrightarrow{a\langle v_1,\ldots,v_n\rangle} P\{v_1,\ldots,v_n/x_1,\ldots,x_n\} & \\ a(x_1,\ldots,x_n).\,P \xrightarrow{av} \mathtt{wrong} & \text{if } v \text{ is not an } n\text{-tuple} \end{array} \qquad (6.4)$$

and the typing rules for input are modified in the obvious way. Semantically, rules (6.3) and (6.4) are the same: the process behaviours that they produce are indistinguishable (the extra τ in (6.3) is deterministic, in the sense of Definition 2.2.19, and hence the typed analogue of Lemma 2.2.20 holds). A small advantage of rules (6.4) is that the resulting process behaviours are more compact, because they avoid one τ step. In the remainder of the book we sometimes use the polyadic input, assuming rules (6.4) for it (we will point out when this is being done): one can think that the polyadic input is primitive, or that we abstract away from the extra τ in (6.3).

The polyadic input notation $a(x_1,\ldots,x_n).\,P$ could cause some ambiguity when $n = 1$ (are the values exchanged along a tuples or not?). To avoid this, we will use the notation only when $n > 1$. In any case, the surrounding text will clarify any doubt.

Similarly, in the case of variants, we sometimes use the variant input prefix

$$z[\,\ell_1\_(y_1) \rhd P_1,\ldots,\ell_n\_(y_n) \rhd P_n\,]$$

in place of

$$z(x).\,\mathsf{case}\ x\ \mathsf{of}\ [\,\ell_1\_(y_1) \rhd P_1\,;\ \ldots\ ;\ \ell_n\_(y_n) \rhd P_n\,]$$

with x not free in $P_1,\ldots,P_n$, assuming the operational rules

$$\frac{j \in \{1,\ldots,n\}}{z[\,\ell_1\_(y_1) \rhd P_1,\ldots,\ell_n\_(y_n) \rhd P_n\,] \xrightarrow{z\,\ell_j\_v} P_j\{v/y_j\}}$$

$$\frac{(\text{where } v \text{ does not have the form } \ell_j\_w \text{ for } j \in \{1,\ldots,n\})}{z[\,\ell_1\_(y_1) \rhd P_1,\ldots,\ell_n\_(y_n) \rhd P_n\,] \xrightarrow{zv} \mathtt{wrong}}$$

6.7 Recursive types

In programming languages, one normally has the possibility of defining *recursive type* expressions. Typical applications are defining the type of lists and the type of trees. Recursive types are also important in object-oriented programming. To include recursive types in a π-calculus, we add type variables $X, Y, \ldots$ and a new type construct $\mu X.T$, for both value and link types, to the grammar:

$$\begin{array}{lcl} V & ::= & X \mid \mu X.V \\ L & ::= & \mu X.L\,. \end{array}$$

Recursive expressions are finite representations of infinite objects. Similarly, a recursive type $\mu X.T$ can be thought of as the (possibly infinite) type expression that is the solution of the equation $X = T$. This solution is obtained by replacing the free occurrences of X in T with T, and continuing with the same replacement on the resulting terms *ad infinitum*. It is convenient to view this solution as a tree (an abstract syntax tree). For instance, the expression $\mu X.\sharp X$ gives rise to the infinite tree

$$\begin{array}{c} \sharp \\ | \\ \sharp \\ | \\ \vdots \end{array}$$

To avoid vacuous expressions like $\mu X.X$, we impose the constraint that in $\mu X.T$ the variable X of the recursion should be *guarded* in T, that is, X may occur free in T only underneath at least one of the other type constructs. For instance, in $\pi^{\mathtt{unit},\sharp,\mu}$, which has unit, connection, and recursive types, X should be underneath a connection type. This constraint avoids multiple solutions for the equation $X = T$. In $\mu X.T$, the outermost occurrence of X is binding for the free occurrences of X in T. In processes and type judgments, we will assume that the types assigned to names have no free variables (types with free type variables will be allowed only with polymorphism, Section 8.3). Note that we need not add type variables to the grammar of link types because, as all recursive types are guarded, the variables always occur within a value type.

With recursive types, an issue that deserves care is the meaning of type equality. If recursive types are abbreviations for possibly infinite trees, then it is natural to declare two types equal if their underlying trees are the same. This is the approach we follow; we write $T_1 \sim_{\text{type}} T_2$ to mean that types T_1 and T_2 are equal in this sense, and say that T_1 and T_2 are *type equivalent*. We will not attempt to give rules or algorithms that capture the relation $\sim_{\text{type}}$. For this, see the literature on type systems, as indicated in the notes at the end of the Part. For our purposes, it suffices to say that $\sim_{\text{type}}$ is a congruence relation and that the following rule is sound:

$$\text{EQ-UNFOLD} \quad \frac{}{\mu X.T \sim_{\text{type}} T\{\mu X.T/X\}}$$

Exercise 6.7.1 It holds that

$$\mu X.\sharp X \sim_{\text{type}} \mu X.\sharp\sharp X.$$

Why cannot one prove this fact using just rule EQ-UNFOLD and the fact that $\sim_{\text{type}}$ is a congruence? □

The equivalence $\sim_{\text{type}}$ on types is introduced into the typing rules by means of the rule

$$\text{T-EQ} \quad \frac{\Gamma \vdash v : S \qquad S \sim_{\text{type}} T}{\Gamma \vdash v : T}$$

One problem with viewing recursive types as trees is that implementing the equivalence relation $\sim_{\text{type}}$ may be expensive. Another is that under this approach various aspects of the theory of recursive types remain unsettled, in λ-calculi and hence also in π-calculi. (The theory is however well understood for well-established type systems like those presented so far.) The alternative treatment is to have explicit coercion functions (like unfold and fold), from a recursive type $\mu X.T$ to its unfolding $T\{\mu X.T/X\}$ and vice versa, as part of the syntax of terms. Type equivalence then coincides with syntactic identity. We will stick to the former treatment; the results in this Part and later in the book can be adapted to the alternative.

An example of a process expression that can be typed using recursive types, but not with the types in previous sections, is $\overline{a}a.\mathbf{0}$.

Exercise 6.7.2 Prove that $a : \mu X.\sharp X \vdash \overline{a}a.\mathbf{0}$. □

When recursive types are added to the simply-typed π-calculus, Lemma 6.3.3 has to be weakened. The type T of a type judgment $\Gamma \vdash x : T$ is unique only up to type equivalence. The modifications needed to the proofs of the results in Section 6.3 that use the lemma (such as Subject Reduction) are straightforward.

Having recursive types – hence type variables – we do not need basic types to get the construction of types started. Thus, we can give a typed presentation of the pure untyped π-calculus of Part I. Let $\pi^{\sharp,\mu}$ be the simply-typed π-calculus with recursive types and no basic types. All types of the calculus are equivalent to the type $\mu X.\sharp X$. The calculus is 'isomorphic' to the pure untyped π-calculus: a process of $\pi^{\sharp,\mu}$ has exactly the same behaviour as the process of the pure untyped π-calculus in which type annotations on restrictions are omitted.

Another interesting calculus is $\pi^{\sharp,\times,\mu}$, which extends $\pi^{\sharp,\mu}$ with tuple types. Adopting a polyadic input prefix as described in Section 6.6, $\pi^{\sharp,\times,\mu}$ is essentially the polyadic π-calculus studied in Section 3.1. The only differences are: the sorting system is replaced by more conventional types; and the components of a tuple of $\pi^{\sharp,\times,\mu}$ need not be names, but may themselves be tuples. Therefore, we will sometimes call $\pi^{\sharp,\times,\mu}$ itself *the polyadic π-calculus*.

7

Subtyping

Subtyping is a preorder on types that can be thought of as inclusion between the sets of the values of the types. If S is a subtype of T then a value of type S is a also a value of type T. For instance if `Nat`, `Int`, and `Real` are the types of natural numbers, integers and reals, respectively, then we could naturally stipulate that `Nat` is a subtype of `Int` and that `Int` is a subtype of `Real`.

If S is a subtype of T then an expression of type S can always replace an expression of type T; if the program before the replacement is well typed, then also the program after the replacement will be so. This is so because the operations available on values of type T – both the pre-defined and the user-defined operations – are also available on values of type S. For instance, operations such as multiplication and division that are available on `Real` are also available on `Int`. The converse, by contrast, may be false; for instance on `Int` there are operations like successor and predecessor that do not make sense on `Real`. The possibility of having operations that work on all subtypes of a given type is a major advantage of subtyping in a programming language. (In the implementation of programming languages, the subtyping from integers to reals requires a conversion that modifies the representation of a number; therefore operations defined on both types will have different implementations for the two types. Due to this non-uniformity, the subtyping between integers and reals is called 'ad hoc' subtyping. In general, all subtyping between basic types is ad hoc. The subtyping on structured types – the non-basic types – that will be presented in this section is, by contrast, uniform.)

Programming language constructs that are usually associated with subtyping are records, variants, and objects. Subtyping is a key feature of object-oriented languages (perhaps *the* key feature). Indeed, the study of subtyping and of the associated programming constructs has been motivated mainly by the interest in object-oriented languages. Understanding how subtyping is achieved in the

π-calculus is important both for designing programming languages based on it, and for being able to use it to give the semantics of object-oriented languages.

We begin by showing how to add subtyping to the core simply-typed π-calculus. The analogy between π-calculus names and reference cells in imperative languages will guide us. Thereafter, we show the subtype rules for the other type constructs previously examined.

For simplicity, and because they are less fundamental, in the book we do not study other forms of subtyping. For instance we do not consider subtyping for the type constructs of Chapter 8: linearity, receptiveness, and polymorphism. (Furthermore, for some of these type systems, certain aspects of the theory of subtyping are, at present, still a research topic.)

We first fix some terminology for subtyping. A *subtype judgment* has the form $S \leq T$; it asserts that S is a *subtype* of T, and T is a *supertype* of S. A type construct is *covariant* in its ith argument if the construct preserves the direction of subtyping in that argument; for instance a binary construct *op* is covariant in the second argument if $S_2 \leq S_2'$ implies $op(S_1, S_2) \leq op(S_1, S_2')$. Dually, a construct is *contravariant* in its ith argument if the construct inverts the direction of subtyping in that argument; and it is *invariant* in its ith argument if it is both covariant and contravariant in that argument. Invariance forbids subtyping; it allows only type equivalence.

7.1 i/o types

To have non-trivial forms of subtyping on names, we refine the set of link types. The refinement is necessary because the connection type $\sharp T$ – the only link type in a simply-typed π-calculus $\pi^{\widetilde{B},\sharp}$ – is invariant in its argument. To see why, suppose we stipulate that the connection type is covariant, and therefore allow the rule

$$\frac{S \leq T}{\sharp S \leq \sharp T} \qquad (7.1)$$

We show that this rule can make a type system unsound. Take names a and b of type $\sharp$ `Int`, and let succ be the successor function on integers. Under these hypotheses, the process (for readability in this example we add angle brackets around the object of output prefixes)

$$a(x).\,\overline{b}\langle \mathsf{succ}\ x\rangle.\,\mathbf{0}$$

makes perfect sense and, using also standard typing rules for integer expressions, is indeed well typed. However, with (7.1) we can also type the process

$$\overline{a}\langle 3{\cdot}5\rangle.\,\mathbf{0}$$

where 3·5 is a `Real` number (Exercise 7.1.1). But the composition of the two processes, which by rule T-PAR should be well typed, may lead to a run-time error:

$$a(x).\,\overline{b}\langle \mathsf{succ}\; x\rangle.\,\mathbf{0} \mid \overline{a}\langle 3{\cdot}5\rangle.\,\mathbf{0} \xrightarrow{\tau} \overline{b}\langle \mathsf{succ}\; 3{\cdot}5\rangle.\,\mathbf{0} \mid \mathbf{0}$$
$$\xrightarrow{\tau} \mathtt{wrong} \mid \mathbf{0}.$$

The error occurs because `succ` is not defined on `Real`. Similarly, there can be run-time errors if we allow the connection type to be contravariant (the reader may try this as an exercise).

Exercise 7.1.1 Show that using (7.1) with the ad hoc subtyping $\mathtt{Int} \leq \mathtt{Real}$, and the SUBSUMPTION rule of Table 7.1, we can derive

$$a : \sharp\,\mathtt{Int} \vdash a : \sharp\,\mathtt{Real}\,. \qquad \square$$

We refine link types by distinguishing between the capabilities of using a name in output or in input. For this we introduce the types $\mathsf{o}\,T$ and $\mathsf{i}\,T$, with the following informal meanings:

- $\mathsf{o}\,T$ is the type of a name that can be used only in output and that carries values of type T
- $\mathsf{i}\,T$ is the type of a name that can be used only in input and that carries values of type T.

For instance, $p : \mathsf{o}\,\mathsf{i}\,S$ says that the name p can be used *only to emit* and that any message at p carries a name that can be used by the recipient *only to receive* values of type S.

The types $\mathsf{o}\,T$ and $\mathsf{i}\,T$ are not only essential for introducing subtyping into the π-calculus; they are also semantically very important, as they allow us to prevent certain kinds of interference among processes. We discuss the typing aspects in this section, and the semantic aspects in Chapter 10. We call $\sharp\,T$, $\mathsf{i}\,T$ and $\mathsf{o}\,T$ the i/o *types*, and $\sharp$, i, o the i/o *tags*. For readability, we sometimes use brackets with i/o types, as in $\mathsf{o}\,(T)$. We call the extension of $\pi^{\widetilde{B},\sharp}$ with i/o types the *simply-typed π-calculus with subtyping*, written $\pi^{\widetilde{B},\mathsf{i}/\mathsf{o}}$. The additional productions and rules are reported in Table 7.1. There can also be (ad hoc) subtyping rules for basic types, such as $\mathtt{Int} \leq \mathtt{Real}$.

We comment on the subtyping rules. The rules SUB-REFL and SUB-TRANS show that $\leq$ is a preorder. The axioms SUB-$\sharp$I and SUB-$\sharp$O show that tag $\sharp$ gives more freedom than i and o in the use of names: we can use a name of which we possess all capabilities in places where only the input or only the output capability is required. The converse of neither rule is sound, because the input or the output capability gives us only *partial* access to a name.

Grammars

Link types

$$L ::= \mathsf{i}\,V \quad \text{input capability}$$
$$\mid \ \mathsf{o}\,V \quad \text{output capability}$$

Subtyping rules

$$\textsc{Sub-refl}\ \frac{}{T \leq T} \qquad \textsc{Sub-trans}\ \frac{S \leq S' \quad S' \leq T}{S \leq T}$$

$$\textsc{Sub-}\sharp\textsc{I}\ \frac{}{\sharp T \leq \mathsf{i}\,T} \qquad \textsc{Sub-}\sharp\textsc{O}\ \frac{}{\sharp T \leq \mathsf{o}\,T}$$

$$\textsc{Sub-II}\ \frac{S \leq T}{\mathsf{i}\,S \leq \mathsf{i}\,T} \qquad \textsc{Sub-OO}\ \frac{T \leq S}{\mathsf{o}\,S \leq \mathsf{o}\,T}$$

$$\textsc{Sub-BB}\ \frac{T \leq S \quad S \leq T}{\sharp S \leq \sharp T}$$

Typing rules

$$\textsc{T-InpS}\ \frac{\Gamma \vdash a : \mathsf{i}\,S \qquad \Gamma, x : S \vdash P : \diamond}{\Gamma \vdash a(x).\,P : \diamond}$$

$$\textsc{T-OutS}\ \frac{\Gamma \vdash a : \mathsf{o}\,T \qquad \Gamma \vdash w : T \qquad \Gamma \vdash P : \diamond}{\Gamma \vdash \overline{a}w.\,P : \diamond}$$

$$\textsc{Subsumption}\ \frac{\Gamma \vdash v : S \qquad S \leq T}{\Gamma \vdash v : T}$$

(rules T-InpS and T-OutS replace T-Inp and T-Out)

Table 7.1. *Additional productions and rules for* i/o *types*

The rules Sub-♯I and Sub-♯O give us subtyping on the surface – the right to change the outermost construct of a type. The rules Sub-II and Sub-OO, by contrast, give us subtyping in depth. Precisely, rule Sub-II says that i is a covariant construct, and Sub-OO that o is a contravariant construct. By contrast, ♯ is an invariant construct, as shown by rule Sub-BB.

The reason why i is covariant and o is contravariant should be clear if we think of subtyping as type inclusion. If a has type o S then surely it is safe to send along a values of a subtype of S; dually if a has type i S then we can safely assume that a value received at a belongs to a supertype of S – the values of a supertype include those of S.

The subtyping on names of $\pi^{\widetilde{B},\mathsf{i/o}}$ can also be understood by analogy with the subtyping rules for references of imperative languages. A reference is a variable that can be written to and read from. If T is the type of the values stored in the variable, then this variable has the *reference type* `ref` (T). The reference type, like the connection type, is an invariant construct. If we wish to have non-trivial subtyping on references, then we have to separate the capability of reading from and the capability of writing to the variable. This amounts to viewing a reference both as a *value* that can be *read from* and as a *location* where a value can be *written to* (these are sometimes called the R-value and the L-value of the variable). The reading capability of a reference, like the input capability of the π-calculus, yields covariance; the writing capability, like the output capability, yields contravariance; the reference type, like the connection type, is invariant.

When we discussed type equivalence (Section 6.7), we introduced a typing rule that allows us to change the type of a value to an equivalent type (rule T-EQ). Similarly, in the presence of subtyping, the rule SUBSUMPTION allows us to replace a type with a supertype. SUBSUMPTION is the only typing rule that uses subtyping. In the presence of subtyping, we take type equivalence $S \sim_{\mathrm{type}} T$ as an abbreviation to mean that both $S \leq T$ and $T \leq S$ hold. The rule T-EQ (and the associated congruence rules) therefore becomes obsolete.

The typing rules T-INPS and T-OUTS are similar to the rules T-INP and T-OUT, except that now the subject of a prefix is checked to have the appropriate input or output capability. The old rules are derivable from new ones; for instance, T-INPS implies T-INP because $\Gamma \vdash a : \sharp T$ implies $\Gamma \vdash a : \mathsf{i}\, T$ (using rule SUB-$\sharp$I of subtyping). Therefore the rules T-INP and T-OUT can be eliminated.

Note that we do not modify the typing rule T-MAT for matching. Therefore a process is allowed to test equality between names of which the process possesses both the input and the output capabilities (i.e., names of a connection type), but not names of which the process possesses only the input or only the output capability. One reason is that allowing matching on arbitrary $\mathsf{i/o}$ types would destroy important semantic properties – see Chapter 10. Another reason for keeping rule T-MAT as the only rule for matching is the following similarity between matching and communication: a process $[a = a]P$ can continue as P, and, similarly, $a(x).\, P \mid \overline{a}v$ (where x is fresh) can evolve to P; but if $a(x).\, P \mid \overline{a}v$ does so, then it must possess both capabilities on the name; by analogy we therefore require that also $[a = a]P$ possesses both capabilities.

Exercise 7.1.2 Show that:

(1) $a : \sharp\, \mathtt{Int}, b : \sharp\, \mathtt{Real} \vdash \overline{a}5 \mid a(x).\, \overline{b}x$, assuming $\mathtt{Int} \leq \mathtt{Real}$
(2) $x : \mathsf{o}\,\mathsf{o}\, T \vdash (\boldsymbol{\nu} y : \sharp\, T)(\overline{x}y.\, !y(z).\, \mathbf{0})$
(3) $x : \mathsf{o}\,\mathsf{o}\, T, z : \mathsf{o}\,\mathsf{i}\, T \vdash (\boldsymbol{\nu} y : \sharp\, T\,)(\overline{x}y \mid \overline{z}y)$
(4) $b : \sharp\, S, x : \sharp\,\mathsf{i}\, S, a : \sharp\,\mathsf{o}\,\mathsf{i}\, S \vdash \overline{a}x \mid x(y).\, y(z) \mid a(x).\, \overline{x}b$. □

7.2 Properties of the type systems with i/o

We revisit those statements of Section 6.3 that need modification in the presence of subtyping, and we present some new ones. The calculus under consideration is $\pi^{\mathtt{unit},\mathsf{i}/\mathsf{o}}$.

Exercise 7.2.1 Suppose that in the Substitution Lemma 6.3.6, clause (2) is replaced by $\Gamma \vdash x : S$. Show that the lemma is then false for $\pi^{\mathtt{unit},\mathsf{i}/\mathsf{o}}$. □

Lemma 7.2.2

(1) If $S \leq \sharp\, T$ then $S = \sharp\, S'$ for some S' with $T \sim_{\text{type}} S'$.
(2) If $S \leq \mathsf{i}\, T$ then $S = I\, S'$ with $I \in \{\sharp, \mathsf{i}\}$ and $S' \leq T$.
(3) If $S \leq \mathsf{o}\, T$ then $S = I\, S'$ with $I \in \{\sharp, \mathsf{o}\}$ and $T \leq S'$. □

Exercise 7.2.3 Prove Lemma 7.2.2. □

Lemma 7.2.4 If $S \leq \mathsf{o}\, T_1$ and $S \leq \mathsf{i}\, T_2$, then $T_1 \leq T_2$.

Proof Type S is of the form $I\, S'$. Using Lemma 7.2.2(3) we infer that $I \in \{\sharp, \mathsf{o}\}$ and $T_1 \leq S'$. Similarly, from Lemma 7.2.2(2), we infer $I \in \{\sharp, \mathsf{i}\}$ and $S' \leq T_2$. Hence $I = \sharp$ and, by transitivity of subtyping, $T_1 \leq T_2$. □

Lemma 7.2.5 (Narrowing) If $\Gamma, a : S \vdash E : T$ and $S' \leq S$, then also $\Gamma, a : S' \vdash E : T$. □

Exercise 7.2.6 Prove Lemma 7.2.5. (Hint: proceed by induction on the derivation of $\Gamma, a : S \vdash E : T$.) □

Exercise 7.2.7 If $\Gamma \vdash \overline{p}x.\, P$ and $\Gamma(p) = \mathsf{o}\, T$, then $\Gamma(x) \leq T$. □

Exercise 7.2.8 If $\Gamma \vdash p(x).\, P, \overline{p}v.\, Q$, then for some T it holds that $\Gamma(p) = \sharp\, T$ and $\Gamma \vdash v : T$ and $\Gamma \vdash P\{v/x\} \mid Q$. □

With i/o types, as well as with the type constructs of the following sections, two processes may have different 'points of view' on the type of the same name. For instance, one process may possess only the output capability on that name, whereas the other process may possess both capabilities. Therefore in a typing judgment $\Gamma \vdash P$, the type environment Γ can be thought as P's 'point of view' on the types of its free names. The Subject Reduction Theorem below, a refinement of Theorem 6.3.7, shows how this point of view evolves under transitions and how it can be used to obtain information about P's possible transitions. The theorem shows that process P can perform input actions only at names for which the type environment Γ grants the input capability, and dually for outputs. The modifications required to the statement of Theorem 6.3.7 are simple: in the input clause (2a), the type $\sharp T$ has to be replaced by $\mathsf{i}\, T$; and in the output clause (3a) the type $\sharp T$ has to be replaced by $\mathsf{o}\, T$.

Theorem 7.2.9 (Subject Reduction for i/o types) Suppose $\Gamma \vdash P$, with Γ closed, and $P \xrightarrow{\alpha} P'$.

(1) If $\alpha = \tau$ then $\Gamma \vdash P'$.
(2) If $\alpha = av$ then there is T such that
   (a) $\Gamma \vdash a : \mathsf{i}\, T$
   (b) if $\Gamma \vdash v : T$ then $\Gamma \vdash P'$.
(3) If $\alpha = (\boldsymbol{\nu}\widetilde{x} : \widetilde{S})\, \overline{a}v$ then there is T such that
   (a) $\Gamma \vdash a : \mathsf{o}\, T$
   (b) $\Gamma, \widetilde{x} : \widetilde{S} \vdash v : T$
   (c) $\Gamma, \widetilde{x} : \widetilde{S} \vdash P'$
   (d) each component of $\widetilde{S}$ is a link type.

Proof By transition induction on $P \xrightarrow{\alpha} P'$. The proof is quite similar to that of Theorem 6.3.7, except for rule COMM-L, which we consider below.

Suppose $P = P_1 \mid P_2$, $P_1 \xrightarrow{(\boldsymbol{\nu}\widetilde{x}:\widetilde{S})\, \overline{a}v} P_1'$, $P_2 \xrightarrow{av} P_2'$, and $P' = (\boldsymbol{\nu}\widetilde{x} : \widetilde{S})(P_1' \mid P_2')$. Let Γ^+ be $\Gamma, \widetilde{x} : \widetilde{S}$. Since $\Gamma \vdash P_1$, by the inductive assumption on P_1 there is T such that

$$\Gamma \vdash a : \mathsf{o}\, T\,, \tag{7.2}$$

$$\Gamma^+ \vdash v : T\,, \tag{7.3}$$

and $\Gamma^+ \vdash P_1'$. Since $\Gamma \vdash P_2$, also $\Gamma^+ \vdash P_2$. By the inductive assumption on P_2 and Γ^+, there is S such that

$$\Gamma^+ \vdash a : \mathsf{i}\, S \tag{7.4}$$

and

$$\text{if } \Gamma^+ \vdash v : S \text{ , then also } \Gamma^+ \vdash P_2' \text{ .} \tag{7.5}$$

Because of (7.2), it holds that $\Gamma(a) \leq \mathsf{o}\,T$; similarly, (7.4) means that $\Gamma(a) \leq \mathsf{i}\,S$. By Lemma 7.2.4, $T \leq S$. Therefore we can apply SUBSUMPTION to (7.3) and infer $\Gamma^+ \vdash v : S$. Now, by (7.5), we get $\Gamma^+ \vdash P_2'$. Finally using rules T-PAR and T-RES, we infer $\Gamma \vdash (\boldsymbol{\nu}\widetilde{x} : \widetilde{S})\,(P_1' \mid P_2')$. □

Since with subtyping the type of a value is not unique, in clauses (2) and (3) there may be several types that can be ascribed to a. The next exercise invites the reader to play with these types.

Exercise 7.2.10

(1) Show that clause (2b) of Theorem 7.2.9 cannot be replaced by the following: for all S such that $\Gamma \vdash a : \mathsf{i}\,S$ and $\Gamma \vdash v : S$, we have $\Gamma \vdash P'$. (Hint: you may find it easier to exhibit first an example in a π-calculus that includes `Int` and `Real` as basic types with the subtyping `Int` $\leq$ `Real`.)

(2) Show that clause (2b) of Theorem 7.2.9 can be replaced by this: if $\Gamma \vdash v : \mathcal{O}(\Gamma(a))$ then $\Gamma \vdash P'$. (Recall that $\mathcal{O}(T)$ is the type of the values that a name of type T may carry.) Similarly, show that clause (3b) can be replaced by $\Gamma, \widetilde{x} : \widetilde{S} \vdash v : \mathcal{O}(\Gamma(a))$. □

Remark 7.2.11 As in the simply-typed π-calculus, the case where a well-typed process receives a fresh name is covered by the combination of Subject Reduction and Weakening; see Remark 6.4.4.

By contrast, the case in which the process receives a known name but with a different – yet legal – type is covered by the combination of Subject Reduction and Narrowing. For instance, suppose $x : \mathsf{i}\,T, a : \sharp\,\mathsf{o}\,T \vdash P$ and P receives x along a. This means that P receives the output capability on x, something that P did not possess beforehand. This situation is not described in the Subject Reduction Theorem 7.2.9. We therefore have to understand two things: why this situation is possible, and how we can derive a typing judgment for the derivative of P. First, this situation can happen if the process that sent x along a is well typed in $x : \mathsf{o}\,T, a : \sharp\,\mathsf{o}\,T$. Different processes in a system may have different visibility of a name; see the discussion preceding the Subject Reduction Theorem 7.2.9. The different types must however be compatible: they should be supertypes of the same type. In this case the name is x, the different types are $\mathsf{i}\,T$ and $\mathsf{o}\,T$, and the common subtype is $\sharp\,T$.

Secondly, we expect that the derivative of P is well typed in the typing $x : \sharp\,T, a : \sharp\,\mathsf{o}\,T$. Here is how we prove this. By Narrowing, we have $x : \sharp\,T, a :$

$\sharp \mathsf{o} T \vdash P$. From this and Subject Reduction, we can then infer that if $P \xrightarrow{ax} P'$ then $x : \sharp T, a : \sharp \mathsf{o} T \vdash P'$.

A subtle point here is the following. The final type judgment $x : \sharp T, a : \sharp \mathsf{o} T \vdash P'$ does not tell the whole truth about the possible usage of names by P'. Acquiring the input and the output capabilities on x separately, as in the case of P', gives less freedom than acquiring the capability $\sharp$: the process P' can use, separately, the input and the output capabilities on x, but cannot use the capability $\sharp$. For instance, if the type environment of P' contained a name y of type $\mathsf{o} \sharp T$, then P' could *not* send x along y. This information is not revealed by the present subject reduction theorem. A more precise subject reduction theorem is possible, and this could in principle be useful for the proof techniques of Part IV. The price is a more complicated definition of type environment. In practice this lack of precision is rarely a hindrance. □

Exercise 7.2.12 Suppose rule T-INPS is weakened thus:

$$\frac{\Gamma(a) = I\,S \quad (\text{for } I \in \{\sharp, \mathsf{i}\}) \qquad \Gamma, x : S \vdash P : \diamond}{\Gamma \vdash a(x).\,P : \diamond}$$

Show that if this rule is adopted in place of the original rule, then the Narrowing Lemma 7.2.5 and the Subject Reduction Theorem 7.2.9 are still valid. (Hint: show that adopting the new rule does not affect the set of valid type judgments.) □

The rule of Exercise 7.2.12, unlike rule T-INPS, does not require us to guess the type S for x. A similar modification is also possible to the output rule, weakening T-OUTS thus:

$$\frac{\Gamma(a) = I\,T \quad (\text{for } I \in \{\sharp, \mathsf{o}\}) \qquad \Gamma \vdash v : T \qquad \Gamma \vdash P : \diamond}{\Gamma \vdash \overline{a}v.\,P : \diamond}$$

Exercise 7.2.13 In this exercise we consider a typed form $a(x : T).\,P$ of input prefix, where the bound name is annotated with a type. The typing rule for this input prefix is

$$\frac{\Gamma \vdash a : \mathsf{i}\,S \qquad \Gamma, x : S \vdash P : \diamond}{\Gamma \vdash a(x : S).\,P : \diamond}$$

Show that the calculus $\pi_{\star}^{\mathtt{unit},\mathsf{i/o}}$, resulting from $\pi^{\mathtt{unit},\mathsf{i/o}}$ by such modification, can be encoded into $\pi^{\mathtt{unit},\mathsf{i/o}}$, by proving that

$$\pi_{\star}^{\mathtt{unit},\mathsf{i/o}} \triangleright \Gamma \vdash a(x : T).\,P \;:\diamond \quad \text{iff} \quad \pi^{\mathtt{unit},\mathsf{i/o}} \triangleright \Gamma \vdash a(y).\,(\boldsymbol{\nu} b : \sharp T)(\overline{b}y \mid b(x).\,P) \;:\diamond$$

where y, b are fresh. □

With previous type systems, operational correctness was witnessed by the Type Soundness property, a corollary of the Subject Reduction Theorem. With i/o types, Type Soundness still holds but is more subtle, in the sense that a misuse of the i/o discipline need not give rise to a run-time error. Suppose for instance that a process is given only the input capability on a name a but nevertheless the process uses a to perform an output. This process is 'wrong' but its output action on a will not give an error, provided that the value sent along a has the right type.

The Subject Reduction Theorem, however, can still be used to give us evidence that the rules for i/o types are correct. For instance, clause (3) of Theorem 7.2.9 shows that a well-typed process can perform outputs only along names for which it possesses the output capability. The following corollary expresses a similar notion of correctness in a more direct way. The corollary shows that if a process P is typable in an environment that gives P only the input capability on a name a, then no matter how P evolves, the only things P can do with a are to use it in input and to communicate it; and dually if P has only the output capability on a.

Corollary 7.2.14 Suppose $\Gamma \vdash P$ and $P \Longrightarrow P'$.

(1) If $\Gamma(a) = \mathsf{i}\,T$ then each free occurrence of a in P' is either the subject of an input prefix or the object of an output prefix.
(2) If $\Gamma(a) = \mathsf{o}\,T$ then each free occurrence of a in P' is in an output prefix. □

Exercise 7.2.15 Prove Corollary 7.2.14. □

Exercise 7.2.16 Suppose that the output type $\mathsf{o}\,T$ is stipulated to be a co-variant – rather than a contravariant – construct. Show that this breaks Corollary 7.2.14. Show the same if $\mathsf{i}\,T$ is stipulated to be a contravariant construct. (Hint: bear in mind the discussion at the beginning of Section 7.1.) □

For stronger results about the correctness of i/o types, see the references at the end of the Part.

We have seen in Section 1.4 that process transitions are invariant under name substitutions only if these are injective. The i/o types allow us to extend the invariance to some non-injective substitutions.

Lemma 7.2.17 Suppose that $\Gamma, a : I\,T, a' : I\,T \vdash P$, for $I \in \{\mathsf{i}, \mathsf{o}\}$.

(1) If $P \xrightarrow{\alpha} Q$ then $P\{a'/a\} \xrightarrow{\alpha\{a'/a\}} Q\{a'/a\}$.

$$\text{SUB-PROD}\ \frac{S_1 \le T_1 \qquad S_2 \le T_2}{S_1 \times S_2 \le T_1 \times T_2}$$

$$\text{SUB-UNI}\ \frac{S_1 \le T_1 \qquad S_2 \le T_2}{S_1 \oplus S_2 \le T_1 \oplus T_2}$$

$$\text{SUB-RECORD}\ \frac{\text{for each } i \in 1, \ldots, n \qquad S_i \le T_i}{\{\, \ell_1 : S_1, \ldots, \ell_{n+m} : S_{n+m} \,\} \le \{\, \ell_1 : T_1, \ldots, \ell_n : T_n \,\}}$$

$$\text{SUB-VAR}\ \frac{\text{for each } i \in 1, \ldots, n \qquad S_i \le T_i}{[\, \ell_1\_S_1, \ldots, \ell_n\_S_n \,] \le [\, \ell_1\_T_1, \ldots, \ell_{n+m}\_T_{n+m} \,]}$$

Table 7.2. *Subtyping rules for product, union, record, and variant types*

(2) Conversely, suppose $P\{^{a'}\!/a\} \xrightarrow{\alpha'} Q'$, and if α' is an input then a does not appear in the object part of α'. Then there are Q, α such that $P \xrightarrow{\alpha} Q$ with $\alpha\{^{a'}\!/a\} = \alpha'$ and $Q\{^{a'}\!/a\} = Q'$.

Proof Item (1) is Lemma 1.4.8. Item (2) is proved by a straightforward transition induction. Since P may use only one of the input capability and the output capability on a and a', by Corollary 7.2.14 these names cannot appear both in input and in output position and consequently no interaction along a' is possible in $P\{^{a'}\!/a\}$. Hence, the substitution of a' for a does not add new transitions. □

7.3 Other subtyping

7.3.1 Products, unions, records, and variants

The subtpying rules for products, unions, records, and variants are well known from typed λ-calculi, and are shown in Table 7.2 (again, the rule for tuple types is an obvious generalization to n components of the rule for products). Subtyping modifies product and union types componentwise, and record and variant types both componentwise and lengthwise. For records the modification of the length is sound because all operations that are admitted on a record value $\{\ell_1 = v_1, \ldots, \ell_n = v_n\}$ are also admitted on a longer value $\{\ell_1 = v_1, \ldots, \ell_{n+m} = v_{n+m}\}$. In the case of variants the modification of the length is the opposite, and can be justified by similar reasoning.

7.3.2 Subtyping on recursive types

In Section 6.7 we said that type equivalence between recursive types means equality between the underlying trees. Subtyping, by contrast, captures the idea of *similarity* between trees, as induced by the covariances and contravariances of the type constructs.

As an example, we (informally) consider $\pi^{\mathtt{unit},\times,\mu,\mathsf{i/o}}$, the simply-typed π-calculus with unit, $\mathsf{i/o}$, tuple, and recursive types. The trees underlying the types of $\pi^{\mathtt{unit},\times,\mu,\mathsf{i/o}}$ are finite-branching trees whose nodes are labelled with symbols from $\{\mathsf{i},\mathsf{o},\sharp,\times\}$ and whose leaves are labelled $\mathtt{unit}$; moreover, a node labelled from $\{\mathsf{i},\mathsf{o},\sharp\}$ has only one child.

To each type S with no free type variables we associate a tree, called $\mathsf{Tree}(S)$; it is the unique tree satisfying the following equations:

(1) if $S = I\,T$ for $I \in \{\mathsf{i},\mathsf{o},\sharp\}$, then $\mathsf{Tree}(S) = I\,[\mathsf{Tree}(T)]$
(2) if $S = \times(T_1,\ldots,T_n)$ then $\mathsf{Tree}(S) = \times\,[\mathsf{Tree}(T_1),\ldots,\mathsf{Tree}(T_n)]$
(3) if $S = \mathtt{unit}$ then $\mathsf{Tree}(S) = \mathtt{unit}$
(4) if $S = \mu X.T$ then $\mathsf{Tree}(S) = \mathsf{Tree}(T\{^{\mu X.T}/_X\})$.

(For the uniqueness of this tree, it is important that the variables of the recursions are guarded.)

We can then define *tree similarity* as the largest relation $\leq_{tr}$ on trees such that whenever $Tr \leq_{tr} Tr'$ at least one of the following clauses holds, for some $Tr_1,\ldots,Tr_n$, and $Tr'_1,\ldots,Tr'_n$:

(1) $Tr = \sharp\,[Tr_1]$ and $Tr' = \mathsf{i}\,[Tr'_1]$ and $Tr_1 \leq_{tr} Tr'_1$
(2) $Tr = \sharp\,[Tr_1]$ and $Tr' = \mathsf{o}\,[Tr'_1]$ and $Tr'_1 \leq_{tr} Tr_1$
(3) $Tr = \mathsf{i}\,[Tr_1]$ and $Tr' = \mathsf{i}\,[Tr'_1]$ and $Tr_1 \leq_{tr} Tr'_1$
(4) $Tr = \mathsf{o}\,[Tr_1]$ and $Tr' = \mathsf{o}\,[Tr'_1]$ and $Tr'_1 \leq_{tr} Tr_1$
(5) $Tr = \times\,[Tr_1,\ldots,Tr_n]$ and $Tr' = \times\,[Tr'_1,\ldots,Tr'_n]$ and $Tr_i \leq_{tr} Tr'_i$, for all $1 \leq i \leq n$
(6) $Tr = Tr'$.

For types S and T of $\pi^{\mathtt{unit},\times,\mu,\mathsf{i/o}}$ we then set $S \leq T$ if $\mathsf{Tree}(S) \leq_{tr} \mathsf{Tree}(T)$.

In general, a subtyping rule

$$\frac{S_i \leq T_i \quad i \in I \subseteq \{1,\ldots,n\} \qquad T_j \leq S_j \quad j \in J \subseteq \{1,\ldots,n\}}{op(S_1,\ldots,S_n) \leq op(T_1,\ldots,T_n)}$$

becomes, in terms of trees, the clause

$Tr = op\,[Tr_1,\ldots,Tr_n]$, and $Tr' = op\,[Tr'_1,\ldots,Tr'_n]$, and $Tr_i \leq_{tr} Tr'_i$ for all $i \in I$, and $Tr'_j \leq_{tr} Tr_j$ and for all $j \in J$.

An example is clause (5) above, which is the obvious translation of the subtyping clause for tuple types. Some care is sometimes needed, to make sure that the tree simulation remains transitive, as in clauses (1)–(4) above for i/o types.

We discuss, but briefly, inference rules for subtyping on recursive types. In the presence of recursive types, subtype judgments have *subtyping assumptions*. Thus subtyping judgments take the form $\Sigma \vdash S \leq T$, where Σ represents the subtyping assumptions

$$\Sigma \ ::= \ \Sigma, S \leq T \mid \emptyset \,.$$

In the previous rules for subtyping, a judgment $S \leq T$ is then taken as an abbreviation for $\emptyset \vdash S \leq T$. Here are the main rules for handling subtyping in recursive types:

$$\textsc{Sub-Rec} \ \frac{\Sigma,\, X \leq Y \vdash S \leq T}{\Sigma \vdash \mu X.\, S \leq \mu Y.\, T}$$

$$\textsc{Sub-Assum} \ \frac{}{\Sigma, S \leq T \vdash S \leq T}$$

(Note that rule Sub-Rec introduces a subtyping between type variables.) The rule Eq-Unfold of type equivalence (Section 6.7), and the associated rules that make type equivalence a congruence relation, are replaced by

$$\textsc{Sub-unfold} \ \frac{}{\Sigma \vdash \mu X.\, S \leq S\{^{\mu X.\, S}/_X\}}$$

$$\textsc{Sub-fold} \ \frac{}{\Sigma \vdash S\{^{\mu X.\, S}/_X\} \leq \mu X.\, S}$$

The rules above are sound for the tree simulation. They are not complete, however, essentially because rule Eq-Unfold, from which we have extracted rules Sub-unfold and Sub-fold, is not complete for type equivalence. (See [PS96] for a sound and complete system of inference rules.)

Exercise 7.3.1 Show that if $\pi^{\times,\mu,\mathsf{i/o}} \triangleright \Gamma \vdash \langle v_1, v_2 \rangle \ : T_1 \times T_2$ then $\pi^{\times,\mu,\mathsf{i/o}} \triangleright \Gamma \vdash v_i \ : T_i$, for $i = 1, 2$. Beware that the last rule used in the derivation of $\pi^{\times,\mu,\mathsf{i/o}} \triangleright \Gamma \vdash \langle v_1, v_2 \rangle \ : T_1 \times T_2$ may be Subsumption. (Similar results hold for unions, records, and variants.) □

7.4 The priority queues, revisited

Variants are handy for representing *typed objects* in the π-calculus: variants allow syntactically compact descriptions of objects and their operations, and subtyping on variant types can be used to model subtyping on objects. As an example, we revisit the specification and the implementation of the priority queues of

Section 3.3. In that section, however, we used recursive definitions of processes. We therefore first briefly discuss the typing rules for them.

7.4.1 Typed abstractions and constants

The notation of typed π-calculi is adapted to *abstractions* in the expected way. Thus a typed abstraction has the form $(x).\, P$; and if F indicates an abstraction $(x).\, P$ then the *pseudo-application* Fv is an abbreviation for $P\{^v\!/\!_x\}$. As in input prefixes, we often combine abstraction and pattern matching on tuples into a single construct, $(\widetilde{x}).\, P$, the *polyadic* abstraction.

For typing constants, i.e., recursive definitions of processes, we have to say how to type constant definitions and applications. The typing rules can either be derived from the encoding of constants in terms of replication in Section 3.2, or given as primitives. The two approaches are only notationally different. We will follow the latter; the interested reader may check that the encoding in Section 3.2 respects the typing rules we give.

A constant K has a definition of the form $K \triangleq (x).\, P$, and a type of the form $V \to \diamond$. This type, called a *function type*, indicates that the argument x of the constant is of type V. The function type is contravariant in its first argument: if $W \le V$, then $V \to \diamond \le W \to \diamond$. The types of constants are recorded in type environments, which thus now contain assignments of function types to constants; this type information is accessed via the following rule (analogous to the rule TV-NAME for looking up names):

$$\text{TV-CONS}\ \frac{\Gamma(K) = T}{\Gamma \vdash K : T}$$

The following well-formedness condition on type environments is however added. For each constant assignment $K : V \to \diamond$ in Γ, if $K \triangleq (x).\, P$ is the definition of K then $\Gamma, x : V \vdash P : \diamond$ holds. All type environments we consider are assumed to be well formed in this sense. The typing rule for constant application checks that the argument has the appropriate type:

$$\text{T-CONSAPP}\ \frac{\Gamma \vdash K : V \to \diamond \qquad \Gamma \vdash v : V}{\Gamma \vdash K\lfloor v \rfloor : \diamond}$$

Function types, and typing rules for the constructs of abstraction and application, are discussed in depth in Chapter 12, dedicated to higher-order calculi, where these constructs play a fundamental role. In Chapter 12, however: (i) constants are not used, and hence typing environments do not include assignments to constants; (ii) applications are annotated with the type of the argument (in a constant application, by contrast, this type can be inferred from the type of the constant).

Notation 7.4.1 The notations for typed abstractions and typed constants are in accordance with those in use in Parts I and II. There, the argument of an abstraction was always a *tuple* of *names*. Hence pseudo-applications were always of the form $F\langle\widetilde{a}\rangle$. Similarly, the argument of a constant was always a tuple of names; the notation $K\lfloor\widetilde{a}\rfloor$ that we used was in fact an abbreviation for the more cumbersome $K\lfloor\langle\widetilde{a}\rangle\rfloor$. □

7.4.2 The queues

Having variants, the specification SPEC of the queues in Section 3.3 is rewritten as follows, using the notation of Section 3.3 for manipulating multisets, and the input pattern-matching notation of Section 6.6 for decomposing variant values:

$$\begin{array}{lll} \text{SPEC} \triangleq (a,m).\,a[& \mathsf{ins\_}(x,c) \rhd \overline{c}.\,\text{SPEC}\lfloor\langle a, m\oplus x\rangle\rfloor\,; & \\ & \mathsf{del\_}(e,r) \rhd (\mathsf{IF} \;\; ?m \;\hookrightarrow\; \overline{e}.\,\text{SPEC}\lfloor\langle a,m\rangle\rfloor, & \\ & \qquad\qquad\quad \neg?m \;\hookrightarrow\; \overline{r}\,m^{\dagger}\,.\,\text{SPEC}\lfloor\langle a,m^{-}\rangle\rfloor\,) &]\,. \end{array}$$

A queue $\text{SPEC}\lfloor\langle a,m\rangle\rfloor$ has a single name, a, for communications with other processes. A value communicated at a is a variant value whose tag specifies which operation (insert or delete) should be performed. For instance, the code for a client that wishes to insert 3 – the analogue of (3.5) in Section 3.3 – is

$$\boldsymbol{\nu} c\,\overline{a}\,\mathsf{ins\_}\langle 3,c\rangle.\,c.\,P$$

and similarly for a client that wishes to perform a delete operation. Setting

$$T_a \stackrel{\text{def}}{=} [\,\mathsf{ins\_}(\mathtt{Int}\times \mathsf{o}\,\mathtt{unit}), \mathsf{del\_}(\mathsf{o}\,\mathtt{unit}\times\mathsf{o}\,\mathtt{Int})\,]$$

a valid type judgment for $\text{SPEC}\lfloor\langle a,\emptyset\rangle\rfloor$ is

$$\text{SPEC} : (\mathsf{i}\,T_a \times \mathtt{MSet}) \to \diamond, a : \mathsf{i}\,T_a \vdash \text{SPEC}\lfloor\langle a,\emptyset\rangle\rfloor \tag{7.6}$$

where MSet is the type of multisets. Intuitively, $\text{SPEC}\lfloor\langle a,\emptyset\rangle\rfloor$ is the description of an object with name a and methods ins and del.

The cells for the sequential and parallel implementations of the queue are modified similarly. Below are the definitions QUEUE, G, E, F of the sequential queue, the analogues to the homonymous definitions of Section 3.3; we omit type annotations in restrictions.

$$
\begin{array}{rcl}
\mathrm{QUEUE} & \stackrel{\mathrm{def}}{=} & (a).\,\boldsymbol{\nu} g\,(E\lfloor\langle a,g\rangle\rfloor \mid G\,g)\\
G & \stackrel{\mathrm{def}}{=} & (g).\,!g(a).\,E\lfloor\langle a,g\rangle\rfloor\\
E & \triangleq & (a,g).\,a[\;\mathsf{ins\_}(x,c) \rhd (\boldsymbol{\nu} a')\,\overline{g}a'.\,\overline{c}.\,F\lfloor\langle a,x,a',g\rangle\rfloor\;;\\
 & & \qquad\quad \mathsf{del\_}(e,r) \rhd \overline{e}.\,E\lfloor\langle a,g\rangle\rfloor \qquad\qquad\qquad\qquad]\\
F & \triangleq &
\end{array}
$$

$$
\begin{array}{l}
(a,k,a',g).\,a[\;\mathsf{ins\_}(x,c) \rhd (\mathsf{IF}\ x<k \hookrightarrow \boldsymbol{\nu} c'\,(\,\overline{a'}\,\mathsf{ins\_}\langle x,c'\rangle \mid\\
\qquad\qquad\qquad\qquad\qquad\qquad\qquad\qquad c'.\,\overline{c}.\,F\lfloor\langle a,k,a',g\rangle\rfloor),\\
\qquad\qquad\qquad\qquad\qquad\quad x\geq k \hookrightarrow \boldsymbol{\nu} c'\,(\,\overline{a'}\,\mathsf{ins\_}\langle k,c'\rangle \mid\\
\qquad\qquad\qquad\qquad\qquad\qquad\qquad\qquad c'.\,\overline{c}.\,F\lfloor\langle a,x,a',g\rangle\rfloor))\;;\\
\qquad\qquad\mathsf{del\_}(e,r) \rhd (\boldsymbol{\nu} e',r')\,(\,\overline{a'}\,\mathsf{del\_}\langle e',r'\rangle \mid\\
\qquad\qquad\qquad\qquad\qquad\qquad e'.\,\overline{r}k.\,E\lfloor\langle a,g\rangle\rfloor \mid\\
\qquad\qquad\qquad\qquad\qquad\qquad r'(x').\,\overline{r}k.\,F\lfloor\langle a,x',a',g\rangle\rfloor) \qquad]\,.
\end{array}
$$

The following type environment collects the types of the above constants:

$$
\begin{array}{rcl}
\Gamma \stackrel{\mathrm{def}}{=} E & : & (\mathsf{i}\,T_a \times \mathsf{o}\,\mathsf{i}\,T_a) \rightarrow \diamond,\\
F & : & (\mathsf{i}\,T_a \times \mathtt{Int} \times \mathsf{o}\,T_a \times \mathsf{o}\,\mathsf{i}\,T_a) \rightarrow \diamond\,.
\end{array}
$$

Adding the type information for a, we obtain a valid typing for the queues resulting from this implementation. For instance, for the empty queue we have

$$\Gamma, a : \mathsf{i}\,T_a \vdash \mathrm{QUEUE}\;a\;.$$

Putting together all assignments for constants, we obtain a typing under which the queues derived from both the specification and the implementation are well typed; for instance, for the empty queues we have

$$\Gamma, \mathrm{SPEC} : (\mathsf{i}\,T_a \times \mathtt{MSet}) \rightarrow \diamond, a : \mathsf{i}\,T_a \vdash \mathrm{SPEC}\lfloor\langle a,\emptyset\rangle\rfloor, \mathrm{QUEUE}\;a\;.$$

We now present a simple example of the use of subtyping, of the kind one finds in object-oriented programming. For this we play with the specification SPEC; we could have acted on the implementations in the same way. Suppose we want to add another method to the queue, a method search that clients can use to check whether a given integer is in the queue. Let us call the specification for the new queue SPEC$^+$. In SPEC$^+$ the definitions of the ins and del methods remain the same (with SPEC replaced by SPEC$^+$, of course). The new method search has two parameters: the integer that is queried about, and a name along which the boolean result is returned:

$$\begin{array}{lll} \mathrm{SPEC}^+ \triangleq (a,m).\,a[& \mathsf{ins\_}(x,c) \rhd \{ \text{ as before } \}; & \\ & \mathsf{del\_}(e,r) \rhd \{ \text{ as before } \}; & \\ & \mathsf{search\_}(y,s) \rhd \ \mathtt{if}\ y \in m & \mathtt{then}\ \overline{s}\,\mathsf{true}.\,\mathrm{SPEC}^+\lfloor\langle a,m\rangle\rfloor \\ & & \mathtt{else}\ \overline{s}\,\mathsf{false}.\,\mathrm{SPEC}^+\lfloor\langle a,m\rangle\rfloor\,]\,. \end{array}$$

Setting

$$T_a^+ \stackrel{\mathrm{def}}{=} [\,\mathsf{ins\_}(\mathtt{Int} \times \mathsf{o}\,\mathtt{unit}), \mathsf{del\_}(\mathsf{o}\,\mathtt{unit} \times \mathsf{o}\,\mathtt{Int}), \mathsf{search\_}(\mathtt{Int} \times \mathsf{o}\,\mathtt{Bool})\,],$$

a valid type judgment for $\mathrm{SPEC}^+\lfloor\langle a,\emptyset\rangle\rfloor$ is

$$\mathrm{SPEC}^+ : (\mathsf{i}\,T_a^+ \times \mathtt{MSet}) \to \diamond, a : \mathsf{i}\,T_a^+ \vdash \mathrm{SPEC}^+\lfloor\langle a,\emptyset\rangle\rfloor\ . \tag{7.7}$$

The searchable queue offers more services than a plain queue. But if the added method is not used, the searchable queue behaves as a plain queue. In other words, a searchable queue can be used in places where a plain queue is expected. This is reflected in the typing: T_a is a subtype of T_a^+, hence also $\mathsf{i}\,T_a$ is a subtype of $\mathsf{i}\,T_a^+$. We can therefore apply Narrowing (Lemma 7.2.5) to (7.7), and infer

$$\mathrm{SPEC}^+ : (\mathsf{i}\,T_a^+ \times \mathtt{MSet}) \to \diamond, a : \mathsf{i}\,T_a \vdash \mathrm{SPEC}^+\lfloor\langle a,\emptyset\rangle\rfloor\ .$$

Thinking of $\mathrm{SPEC}\lfloor\langle a,\emptyset\rangle\rfloor$ and $\mathrm{SPEC}^+\lfloor\langle a,\emptyset\rangle\rfloor$ as objects named a, the assertion above and (7.6) show that the two objects have the same type $\mathsf{i}\,T_a$.

Exercise 7.4.2 Add the type annotations in restrictions to the definitions of the constants QUEUE, E, F, and then prove (7.6) and (7.7). □

7.5 Encodings between union and product types

We show that product types can be encoded using union types and vice versa, both with and without subtyping. Similar encodings can be given between record and variant types. The main objective of the section is, however, to let the reader play with product, union, record, and variant types, and become familiar with them.

The encodings are annotated with a type environment that shows the types of the free names of the processes that are being translated. To have simple encodings: we use the pattern matching prefixes of Section 6.6 for decomposing values; and we assume that union and product types are not consecutively nested (i.e., in $T_1 \oplus T_2$, the outermost type in T_1 and T_2 is not a union, and similarly for $T_1 \times T_2$). Table 7.3 shows the encoding of $\pi^{\mathtt{unit},\sharp,\oplus}$ (simply-typed π-calculus with unit and union types) into $\pi^{\mathtt{unit},\sharp,\times_2}$ (simply-typed π-calculus with unit and product types). The communication of a union value w is rendered by the communication of a tuple of fresh names b, c. Thus, if w has the form $\mathsf{inl\_}v$ then value v is communicated at b, otherwise w has the form $\mathsf{inr\_}v$ and v is communicated at c.

Exercise 7.5.1 Suppose $\Gamma \vdash P$ with Γ closed. Show that $[\![\Gamma]\!] \vdash [\![P]\!]^{\Gamma}$. $\square$

Exercise 7.5.2 Suppose $\Gamma \vdash P$ and $P \longrightarrow P'$. Then there is P_1 such that $[\![P]\!]^{\Gamma} \Longrightarrow P_1$ and $P_1 \equiv [\![P']\!]^{\Gamma}$. (Hint: it is simpler to prove this using the reduction system, rather than the labelled transition system.) $\square$

The encoding of Table 7.3 can be extended to $\mathsf{i/o}$ types. For this, it suffices to replace the translation of types with

$$
\begin{aligned}
[\![I\,T]\!] &\stackrel{\text{def}}{=} I\,[\![T]\!] && \text{for } I \in \{\mathsf{i}, \mathsf{o}, \sharp\} \\
[\![\mathtt{unit}]\!] &\stackrel{\text{def}}{=} \mathtt{unit} \\
[\![T_1 \oplus T_2]\!] &\stackrel{\text{def}}{=} \mathsf{i}\,[\![T_1]\!] \times \mathsf{i}\,[\![T_2]\!] \,.
\end{aligned}
$$

Exercise 7.5.3 Show that the above extension of the encoding to $\mathsf{i/o}$ types preserves subtyping, i.e., $T \leq S$ iff $[\![T]\!] \leq [\![S]\!]$. $\square$

The opposite encoding, from $\pi^{\mathtt{unit},\sharp,\times_2}$ into $\pi^{\mathtt{unit},\sharp,\oplus}$, is presented in Table 7.4. The translation is very similar to that of the polyadic π-calculus into monadic π-calculus in Section 3.1 (the translation into the monadic π-calculus does not preserve typing, for the monadic π-calculus is untyped; but the idea of the translation is the same). As before, the encoding can be extended to handle subtyping, refining the translation of types thus:

$$
\begin{aligned}
[\![I\,T]\!] &\stackrel{\text{def}}{=} I\,[\![T]\!] && \text{for } I \in \{\mathsf{i}, \mathsf{o}, \sharp\} \\
[\![\mathtt{unit}]\!] &\stackrel{\text{def}}{=} \mathtt{unit} \\
[\![T_1 \times T_2]\!] &\stackrel{\text{def}}{=} \mathsf{i}\,([\![T_1]\!] \oplus [\![T_2]\!]) \,.
\end{aligned}
$$

Exercise 7.5.4 State and prove the analogues of Exercises 7.5.1, 7.5.2 and 7.5.3 for this encoding. $\square$

Reasoning as for encodings in earlier chapters, such as those in Part II, one can prove that the encodings in this section are sound for barbed congruence (precisely *typed* barbed congruence). Full abstraction, by contrast, fails for reasons similar to those that cause failure in the encoding of polyadic communications in Section 3.1.

Translation of types

$$\llbracket \sharp T \rrbracket \stackrel{\text{def}}{=} \sharp \llbracket T \rrbracket$$
$$\llbracket \texttt{unit} \rrbracket \stackrel{\text{def}}{=} \texttt{unit}$$
$$\llbracket T_1 \oplus T_2 \rrbracket \stackrel{\text{def}}{=} \sharp \llbracket T_1 \rrbracket \times \sharp \llbracket T_2 \rrbracket$$

Translation of type environments

$$\llbracket \emptyset \rrbracket \stackrel{\text{def}}{=} \emptyset$$
$$\llbracket \Gamma, x : S \rrbracket \stackrel{\text{def}}{=} \llbracket \Gamma \rrbracket, x : \llbracket S \rrbracket$$

Translation of input and output constructs (We assume that b, c, z_1, z_2 are fresh)

$$\llbracket \overline{x}\, \mathsf{inl\_}v\,.\, P \rrbracket^{\Gamma} \stackrel{\text{def}}{=} (\boldsymbol{\nu} b : \sharp \llbracket T_1 \rrbracket, c : \sharp \llbracket T_2 \rrbracket\,)\overline{x}\langle b, c\rangle .\, \overline{b}v.\, \llbracket P \rrbracket^{\Gamma} \quad \text{if } \mathcal{O}(\Gamma(x)) = T_1 \oplus T_2$$

$$\llbracket \overline{x}\, \mathsf{inr\_}v\,.\, P \rrbracket^{\Gamma} \stackrel{\text{def}}{=} (\boldsymbol{\nu} b : \sharp \llbracket T_1 \rrbracket, c : \sharp \llbracket T_2 \rrbracket\,)\overline{x}\langle b, c\rangle .\, \overline{c}v.\, \llbracket P \rrbracket^{\Gamma} \quad \text{if } \mathcal{O}(\Gamma(x)) = T_1 \oplus T_2$$

$$\llbracket x[\mathsf{inl\_}(x_1) \rhd P_1\,;\, \mathsf{inr\_}(x_2) \rhd P_2] \rrbracket^{\Gamma} \stackrel{\text{def}}{=} x(z_1, z_2).\, \Big(z_1(x_1).\, \llbracket P_1 \rrbracket^{\Gamma, x_1 : T_1} + z_2(x_2).\, \llbracket P_2 \rrbracket^{\Gamma, x_2 : T_2}\Big) \quad \text{if } \mathcal{O}(\Gamma(x)) = T_1 \oplus T_2$$

$$\llbracket \overline{x}v.\, P \rrbracket^{\Gamma} \stackrel{\text{def}}{=} \overline{x}v.\, \llbracket P \rrbracket^{\Gamma} \quad \text{if } v \text{ is a name or the unit value}$$

$$\llbracket y(x).\, P \rrbracket^{\Gamma} \stackrel{\text{def}}{=} y(x).\, \llbracket P \rrbracket^{\Gamma, x:T} \quad \text{if } \mathcal{O}(\Gamma(y)) = T$$

The encoding is the obvious homomorphism on the other process constructs. For instance

$$\llbracket (\boldsymbol{\nu} x : T)\, P \rrbracket^{\Gamma} \stackrel{\text{def}}{=} (\boldsymbol{\nu} x : \llbracket T \rrbracket)\, \llbracket P \rrbracket^{\Gamma, x:T} \qquad \llbracket !P \rrbracket^{\Gamma} \stackrel{\text{def}}{=} !\llbracket P \rrbracket^{\Gamma}$$

Table 7.3. *Encoding of* $\pi^{\texttt{unit},\sharp,\oplus}$ *into* $\pi^{\texttt{unit},\sharp,\times_2}$

The exercise below invites the reader to modify the encodings in this section so that the results, although a little more complex, will also work for records and variants.

Translation of types

$$[\![\sharp\, T]\!] \stackrel{\text{def}}{=} \sharp\, [\![T]\!]$$
$$[\![\mathtt{unit}]\!] \stackrel{\text{def}}{=} \mathtt{unit}$$
$$[\![T_1 \times T_2]\!] \stackrel{\text{def}}{=} \sharp\,(T_1 \oplus T_2)$$

Translation of type environments

$$[\![\emptyset]\!] \stackrel{\text{def}}{=} \emptyset$$
$$[\![\Gamma, x : S]\!] \stackrel{\text{def}}{=} [\![\Gamma]\!], x : [\![S]\!]$$

Translation of input and output constructs (We assume that b, c, z are fresh; the encoding is the obvious homomorphism on the other process constructs)

$$[\![\overline{x}\langle v, w\rangle .\, P]\!]^{\Gamma} \stackrel{\text{def}}{=} (\boldsymbol{\nu} b : \sharp\,([\![T_1]\!] \oplus [\![T_2]\!]))\, \overline{x}b.\, \overline{b}\,\mathsf{inl\_}v\,.\,\overline{b}\,\mathsf{inr\_}w\,.\,[\![P]\!]^{\Gamma} \quad \text{if } \mathcal{O}(\Gamma(x)) = T_1 \times T_2$$

$$[\![x(z_1, z_2).\, P]\!]^{\Gamma} \stackrel{\text{def}}{=} x(z).\, z\Big[\ \mathsf{inl\_}(z_1) \rhd z[\ \mathsf{inl\_}(y) \rhd \mathbf{0}\,;\ \mathsf{inr\_}(z_2) \rhd [\![P]\!]^{\Gamma, z_1:T_1, z_2:T_2}\ ]\,;\ \mathsf{inr\_}(y) \rhd \mathbf{0}\Big] \quad \text{if } \mathcal{O}(\Gamma(x)) = T_1 \times T_2$$

$$[\![\overline{y}v.\, P]\!]^{\Gamma} \stackrel{\text{def}}{=} \overline{y}v.\, [\![P]\!]^{\Gamma} \qquad \text{if } v \text{ is a name or the unit value}$$

$$[\![y(x).\, P]\!]^{\Gamma} \stackrel{\text{def}}{=} y(x).\, [\![P]\!]^{\Gamma, x:T} \qquad \text{if } \mathcal{O}(\Gamma(y)) = T$$

Table 7.4. *Encoding of* $\pi^{\mathtt{unit},\sharp,\times_2}$ *into* $\pi^{\mathtt{unit},\sharp,\oplus}$

Exercise* 7.5.5

(1) Extend the encodings in Tables 7.3 and 7.4 to calculi with records and variants in place of products and unions, without considering subtyping (as there is no subtyping, assume that there is also the typing rule TV-VAR-LONG, for variant types).
(2) Explain why the resulting encodings do not work in the presence of subtyping.
(3) Modify the translations in Tables 7.3 and 7.4 so that their extensions to records and variants will also work in presence of subtyping. (Hint: in the

clause for the translation of union types, use only o as i/o tag; and do the same for the translation of product types.) □

8

Advanced Type Systems

8.1 Linearity

The purpose of the type systems for linearity is to control the number of times a resource is used. In the specific case of the π-calculus the resources are the names.

The linear types for the π-calculus are a refinement of the i/o types that allow us to impose not only *polarity*, but also *multiplicity* constraints: we can say that a name should be used in input or in output *only once*. A *linear type* can take three forms: $\ell_{\mathsf{o}}\,T$, $\ell_{\mathsf{i}}\,T$, and $\ell_{\sharp}\,T$. They are, respectively, the linear versions of the types $\mathsf{o}\,T$, $\mathsf{i}\,T$, and $\sharp\,T$. A type $\ell_{\mathsf{o}}\,T$ for a name gives the capability of transmitting a value of type T along that name once. Dually, $\ell_{\mathsf{i}}\,T$ gives the capability of receiving a value of type T once. Finally $\ell_{\sharp}\,T$ is the type of a name that can be used once for transmitting and once for receiving a value of type T, type $\ell_{\sharp}\,T$ is the union of the capabilities offered by $\ell_{\mathsf{i}}\,T$ and $\ell_{\mathsf{o}}\,T$. (By contrast with $\sharp\,T$, the linear type $\ell_{\sharp}\,T$ does not give the right to test the identity of a name; a name that is used both for a communication *and* for a test is not linear, because it is used twice.) For instance, the processes

$$\overline{a}b, \qquad \overline{c}a, \qquad \overline{c}a \mid c(x).\,\overline{x}b$$

are well typed in $\{a : \ell_{\mathsf{o}}\,T\,,\, b : T\,,\, c : \sharp\,\ell_{\mathsf{o}}\,T\}$. Note that the process $\overline{c}a$ does not itself exercise the output capability on a, but passes it to another process. By contrast, the same typing is not respected by the processes

$$\overline{a}b \mid \overline{a}b, \qquad \overline{a}b \mid \overline{c}a.$$

We add linear types to a simply-typed π-calculus with i/o types; $\pi^{\mathtt{unit},\mathsf{i}/\mathsf{o},\ell}$ is the resulting calculus. Types, and related operations, are presented in Table 8.1. Moving from $\pi^{\mathtt{unit},\mathsf{i}/\mathsf{o}}$ to $\pi^{\mathtt{unit},\mathsf{i}/\mathsf{o},\ell}$, all typing rules for processes and values, except that for restriction, that for matching, and that for subsumption, have to be modified. Table 8.2 reports the complete set of typing rules for $\pi^{\mathtt{unit},\mathsf{i/o},\ell}$. The most important rule to understand is that for parallel composition. When we type $P_1 \mid P_2$ under a typing Γ, we have to make sure that each linear capability in Γ is exercised exactly once, either in P_1 or in P_2. For this we split the linear capabilities in Γ, and derive two type environments under which we type P_1 and P_2. For instance, a judgment

$$a : \ell_\sharp\, \mathtt{unit}\, ,\, b : \ell_\mathsf{o}\, \mathtt{unit} \vdash a(x).\, \overline{b}x \mid \overline{a}\star$$

is split into

$$a : \ell_\mathsf{i}\, \mathtt{unit}\, ,\, b : \ell_\mathsf{o}\, \mathtt{unit} \vdash a(x).\, \overline{b}x \qquad \text{and} \qquad a : \ell_\mathsf{o}\, \mathtt{unit} \vdash \overline{a}\star\ .$$

The split of the type environment is indicated, in the typing rules, by the operator $\uplus$ of *combination* of types, defined in Table 8.1. $\Gamma_1 \uplus \Gamma_2$ may be undefined (i.e., fail to be a type environment) if, for instance, $\Gamma_1(x)$ and $\Gamma_2(x)$ are the same linear type. Only linear types of opposite polarities combine into a type. If $\Gamma_1(x)$ and $\Gamma_2(x)$ are the same non-linear type, then this type is also $(\Gamma_1 \uplus \Gamma_2)(x)$: a non-linear type has unlimited multiplicity and can therefore be copied in the split of a type environment. The operator $\uplus$ is associative, so we omit brackets in $\Gamma_1 \uplus \Gamma_2 \uplus \Gamma_3$.

The type environment is also split in the typing rules for prefixes, to make sure that the linear capabilities are split among the constituents of the prefixes (names and derivative process). This explains, for instance, the condition $m \in \{\mathsf{i}, \ell_\mathsf{i}\}$ of rule LIN-INP: the output capability, if present, is pushed onto Γ_2. In the typing rule for sum, by contrast, there is no split of the type environment, because the capabilities exercised by the two summands are exclusive. The only new ingredient in the rules for **0** and replication is the side condition. This checks that the type environment has no pending linear capability, which could not be exercised by **0** and could be violated by $!P$, as many instances of P could become active. A similar check is made in the typing rule LIN-NAME for names and LIN-UNIT. The rule LIN-RES is the same as rule T-RES of the simply-typed π-calculus. Another rule for restriction, LIN-RES2, is however added. This rule allows us to type a restriction $(\boldsymbol{\nu} x : T)\, P$ where x does not appear in P. Such a rule is needed for the Subject Reduction Theorem 8.1.5 (see the second item in its proof).

Linear types can be used together with the type constructs of Section 6.5. For instance, the typing rule for values of product type is

$$\text{LIN-PROD}\ \frac{\Gamma_1 \vdash v_1 : T_1 \qquad \Gamma_2 \vdash v_2 : T_2}{\Gamma_1 \uplus \Gamma_2 \vdash \langle v_1, v_2 \rangle : T_1 \times T_2}$$

(which is in fact the common typing rule for products in linear typed λ-calculi).

Grammars

			Link types
L	$::=$	$\ell_\sharp V$	linear connection
	$\mid$	$\ell_\mathsf{i} V$	linear input
	$\mid$	$\ell_\mathsf{o} V$	linear output

Combination of types

$$
\begin{array}{rcll}
\ell_\mathsf{i} T \uplus \ell_\mathsf{o} T & \stackrel{\text{def}}{=} & \ell_\sharp T & \\
T \uplus T & \stackrel{\text{def}}{=} & T & \text{if } T \text{ is not a linear type} \\
T \uplus S & \stackrel{\text{def}}{=} & \texttt{error} & \text{otherwise}
\end{array}
$$

Combination of type environments

If, for some x, both $\Gamma_1(x)$ and $\Gamma_2(x)$ are defined and $\Gamma_1(x) \uplus \Gamma_2(x) = \texttt{error}$ then $\Gamma_1 \uplus \Gamma_2$ is undefined. Otherwise $\Gamma_1 \uplus \Gamma_2$ is the type environment defined by

$$
(\Gamma_1 \uplus \Gamma_2)(x) \stackrel{\text{def}}{=} \begin{cases}
\Gamma_1(x) \uplus \Gamma_2(x) & \text{if both } \Gamma_1(x) \text{ and } \Gamma_2(x) \text{ are defined} \\
\Gamma_1(x) & \text{if } \Gamma_1(x)\text{, but not } \Gamma_2(x)\text{, is defined} \\
\Gamma_2(x) & \text{if } \Gamma_2(x)\text{, but not } \Gamma_1(x)\text{, is defined} \\
\text{undefined} & \text{if both } \Gamma_1(x) \text{ and } \Gamma_2(x) \text{ are undefined}
\end{cases}
$$

Extraction of linear names

$$
\begin{array}{rcl}
Lin(\Gamma) & \stackrel{\text{def}}{=} & \{x \mid \Gamma(x) \text{ is a linear type}\} \\
Lin_\mathsf{i}(\Gamma) & \stackrel{\text{def}}{=} & \{x \mid \Gamma(x) = \ell_\mathsf{i}\, S \text{ or } \Gamma(x) = \ell_\sharp\, S, \text{ for some } S\}
\end{array}
$$

Table 8.1. *Additional productions for linear types, and operations for them*

We rectify the definition of closed typing to take account of linearity. Remember that the closed typings identify the processes that can be tested by an external observer. Now, suppose $\Gamma, a : \ell_\sharp T \vdash P$; so the name a is linear and P uses both the input and the output capability on it. This means that all capabilities on a are owned by P: a (well-typed) external observer cannot use a. In other words, input or output actions of P along a should not be observable. This masking is easy to obtain: it suffices to add a restriction on a outside P.

Value typing

$$\text{LIN-NAME}\ \frac{}{\Gamma\,,\,x:T\vdash x:T}\ Lin(\Gamma)=\emptyset$$

$$\text{LIN-UNIT}\ \frac{}{\Gamma\vdash\star:\mathtt{unit}}\ Lin(\Gamma)=\emptyset$$

plus rule SUBSUMPTION and the rules for subtyping in Table 7.1

Process typing

$$\text{LIN-INP}\ \frac{\Gamma_1\vdash v:m\,S\quad\text{for } m\in\{\mathsf{i},\ell_{\mathsf{i}}\}\qquad \Gamma_2\,,\,x:S\vdash P:\diamond}{\Gamma_1\uplus\Gamma_2\vdash v(x).\,P:\diamond}$$

$$\text{LIN-OUT}\ \frac{\Gamma_1\vdash v:m\,S\quad\text{for } m\in\{\mathsf{o},\ell_{\mathsf{o}}\}\qquad \Gamma_2\vdash w:S\qquad\Gamma_3\vdash P:\diamond}{\Gamma_1\uplus\Gamma_2\uplus\Gamma_3\vdash\overline{v}w.\,P:\diamond}$$

$$\text{LIN-PAR}\ \frac{\Gamma_1\vdash P_1:\diamond\qquad\Gamma_2\vdash P_2:\diamond}{\Gamma_1\uplus\Gamma_2\vdash P_1\mid P_2:\diamond}$$

$$\text{LIN-SUM}\ \frac{\Gamma\vdash P_1:\diamond\qquad\Gamma\vdash P_2:\diamond}{\Gamma\vdash P_1+P_2:\diamond}$$

$$\text{LIN-TAU}\ \frac{\Gamma\vdash P:\diamond}{\Gamma\vdash\tau.\,P:\diamond}$$

$$\text{LIN-REP}\ \frac{\Gamma\vdash P:\diamond}{\Gamma\vdash !P:\diamond}\ Lin(\Gamma)=\emptyset$$

$$\text{LIN-NIL}\ \frac{}{\Gamma\vdash\mathbf{0}:\diamond}\ Lin(\Gamma)=\emptyset$$

$$\text{LIN-MAT}\ \frac{\Gamma_1\vdash v:\sharp T\qquad\Gamma_1\vdash w:\sharp T\qquad\Gamma_2\vdash P:\diamond}{\Gamma_1\uplus\Gamma_2\vdash[v=w]P:\diamond}$$

$$\text{LIN-RES}\ \frac{\Gamma\,,\,x:L\vdash P:\diamond}{\Gamma\vdash(\boldsymbol{\nu}x:L)\,P:\diamond}$$

$$\text{LIN-RES2}\ \frac{\Gamma\vdash P:\diamond}{\Gamma\vdash(\boldsymbol{\nu}x:L)\,P:\diamond}$$

Table 8.2. *The typing rules for* $\pi^{\mathtt{unit},\mathsf{i}/\mathsf{o},\ell}$

Doing so makes sense: a may be regarded as a name private to P because the observer has no visibility at all on a. We accordingly add the requirement below to Definition 6.1.2 of closed typing.

Definition 8.1.1 (Closed type environments, additional requirement for linear types) In a closed type environment Γ there is no name a such that $\Gamma(a) = \ell_\sharp\, T$ (if there are recursive types, replace $=$ with $\sim_{\text{type}}$). □

The 'old' definition of closed typing will still be useful, and therefore we rename it *link-closed*:

Definition 8.1.2 (Link-closed type environment) A type environment Γ is *link-closed* if $\Gamma(a)$ is a link type, for all a on which Γ is defined. □

The assertion of the following exercise implies that weakening and strengthening do not hold on linear types; however, they continue to hold on non-linear types.

Exercise 8.1.3 Prove that if $\Gamma \vdash E : T$ and $\Gamma(a)$ is a linear type, then a is free in E. □

Since weakening and strengthening on linear types do not hold, the analogue of Substitution Lemma 6.3.6 is false if the substituted name has a linear type. Hence we refine the assertion of the lemma. Without linear types, the new lemma and the old are equivalent.

Lemma 8.1.4 (Substitution Lemma, linear types) Suppose $\Gamma, x : S \vdash E : T$, and $\Gamma \uplus \Gamma'$ is defined, and $\Gamma' \vdash v : S$. Then $\Gamma \uplus \Gamma' \vdash E\{v/x\} : T$.

Proof If $S = \ell_\sharp\, S'$ then v must be a fresh name, otherwise $\Gamma \uplus \Gamma'$ would not be defined; then the conclusion is easy. Otherwise, the proof is similar to that of Lemma 6.3.6. □

For technical reasons, to prove subject reduction for closed typings we have to prove a slightly more general result, on link-closed typings. Since the notions of link-closed and closed coincide on previous type systems, this theorem is the analogue of previous subject reduction theorems such as Theorems 6.3.7 and 7.2.9. The theorem asserts that a process well typed in a type environment Γ can only perform input or output actions for which Γ offers the appropriate capabilities, and moreover, the used linear capabilities are lost after the action. In the input clause, the original typing Γ may be extended using the environment Γ_3. In previous type systems, this extension was unnecessary, because weakening and strengthening were possible (see for instance Remark 6.4.4). We recall that $\Gamma - a$ is the type environment that is undefined on a and coincides with Γ on the other names.

Theorem 8.1.5 (Subject Reduction, linear types) Suppose $\Gamma \vdash P$, with Γ link-closed, and $P \xrightarrow{\alpha} P'$.

(1) If $\alpha = \tau$ then either $\Gamma \vdash P'$, or there is a with $\Gamma(a) = \ell_\sharp T$, for some T, such that $\Gamma - a \vdash P'$.
(2) If $\alpha = av$ then there are Γ_1, Γ_2, T such that
  (a) $\Gamma = \Gamma_1 \uplus \Gamma_2$
  (b) $\Gamma_1 \vdash a : m\,T$ for $m \in \{\mathsf{i}, \ell_\mathsf{i}\}$
  (c) if $\Gamma_3 \vdash v : T$ and $\Gamma_2 \uplus \Gamma_3$ is defined, then $\Gamma_2 \uplus \Gamma_3 \vdash P'$.
(3) If $\alpha = (\boldsymbol{\nu}\widetilde{x} : \widetilde{S})\,\overline{a}v$ then there are $\Gamma_1, \Gamma_2, \Gamma_3$, and T such that
  (a) $\Gamma, \widetilde{x} : \widetilde{S} = \Gamma_1 \uplus \Gamma_2 \uplus \Gamma_3$
  (b) $\Gamma_1 \vdash a : m\,T$, with $m \in \{\mathsf{o}, \ell_\mathsf{o}\}$
  (c) $\Gamma_2 \vdash v : T$
  (d) $\Gamma_3 \vdash P'$
  (e) each component of $\widetilde{S}$ is a link type.

Proof By transition induction on $P \xrightarrow{\alpha} P'$. The main differences from the proof of Theorem 7.2.9 are in rules COMM-L and RES when α is τ and originates from a communication along a linear name. We consider only these two cases.

- Suppose $P = P_1 \mid P_2$, $P_1 \xrightarrow{(\boldsymbol{\nu}\widetilde{z}:\widetilde{T})\,\overline{a}v} P_1'$, $P_2 \xrightarrow{av} P_2'$, and $P' = (\boldsymbol{\nu}\widetilde{z} : \widetilde{T})(P_1' \mid P_2')$; moreover, $\Gamma(a)$ is a linear type.

  From $\Gamma \vdash P$ we infer that $\Gamma = \Gamma_1 \uplus \Gamma_2$, for some Γ_i with $\Gamma_i \vdash P_i$.

  By the inductive assumption on P_1, there are $\Delta_{a1}, \Delta_{v1}, \Delta_{p1}$ such that $\Gamma_1, \widetilde{z} : \widetilde{T} = \Delta_{a1} \uplus \Delta_{v1} \uplus \Delta_{p1}$, and

$$\Delta_{a1} \vdash a : \ell_\mathsf{o}\,T\,, \tag{8.1}$$

$$\Delta_{v1} \vdash v : T\,, \tag{8.2}$$

$$\Delta_{p1} \vdash P_1'\,. \tag{8.3}$$

  By the inductive assumption on P_2, there are $\Delta_{a2}, \Delta_{vp2}$ such that $\Gamma_2 = \Delta_{a2} \uplus \Delta_{vp2}$,

$$\Delta_{a2} \vdash a : \ell_\mathsf{i}\,T \tag{8.4}$$

  and, for all Δ' such that $\Delta_{vp2} \uplus \Delta'$ is defined and $\Delta' \vdash v : T$,

$$\Delta_{vp2} \uplus \Delta' \vdash P_2'\,. \tag{8.5}$$

(The type T in (8.1) and (8.4) is the same because there is no subtyping on linear types.) Take $\Delta' \stackrel{\text{def}}{=} \Delta_{v1}$. Then $\Delta_{vp2} \uplus \Delta_{v1}$ is defined because the two environments are obtained by decomposing a single environment, namely $\Gamma, \widetilde{z} : \widetilde{T}$ (formally, this is a consequence of the commutativity and associativity of $\uplus$). Also (8.5) holds, because of (8.2).

From (8.1) and rule LIN-NAME, we get

$$\Delta_{a1} = a : \ell_{\mathsf{o}}\, T, \Delta'_{a1}$$

where $Lin(\Delta'_{a1}) = \emptyset$. Similarly, using (8.4),

$$\Delta_{a2} = a : \ell_{\mathsf{i}}\, T, \Delta'_{a2}$$

and $Lin(\Delta'_{a2}) = \emptyset$. Therefore we have

$$\begin{aligned} \Gamma, \widetilde{z} : \widetilde{T} &= \Gamma_1, \widetilde{z} : \widetilde{T} \uplus \Gamma_2 \\ &= \Delta_{a1} \uplus \Delta_{v1} \uplus \Delta_{p1} \uplus \Delta_{a2} \uplus \Delta_{vp2} \\ &= a : \ell_{\mathsf{o}}\, T \uplus \Delta'_{a1} \uplus \Delta_{v1} \uplus \Delta_{p1} \uplus a : \ell_{\mathsf{i}}\, T \uplus \Delta'_{a2} \uplus \Delta_{vp2} \\ &= a : \ell_{\sharp}\, T \uplus \Delta'_{a1} \uplus \Delta_{v1} \uplus \Delta_{p1} \uplus \Delta'_{a2} \uplus \Delta_{vp2}\, . \end{aligned}$$

This shows that

$$\Delta'_{a1} \uplus \Delta_{v1} \uplus \Delta_{p1} \uplus \Delta'_{a2} \uplus \Delta_{vp2} = (\Gamma, \widetilde{z} : \widetilde{T}) - a\, . \tag{8.6}$$

From (8.3), (8.5) and weakening on non-linear types,

$$\begin{aligned} \Delta'_{a1} \uplus \Delta_{p1} &\vdash P'_1 \\ \Delta'_{a2} \uplus \Delta_{vp2} \uplus \Delta_{v1} &\vdash P'_2\, . \end{aligned}$$

Hence using rule LIN-PAR and (8.6),

$$(\Gamma, \widetilde{z} : \widetilde{T}) - a \vdash P'_1 \mid P'_2\, .$$

Using rule LIN-RES,

$$\Gamma - a \vdash (\boldsymbol{\nu} \widetilde{z} : \widetilde{T})\, (P'_1 \mid P'_2) = P'\, .$$

This conclude the case.

- Suppose $P = (\boldsymbol{\nu} x : \ell_\sharp\, T)\, Q$ and $P \xrightarrow{\tau} (\boldsymbol{\nu} x : \ell_\sharp\, T)\, Q'$. We have $\Gamma, x : \ell_\sharp\, T \vdash Q$ and, by induction, either $\Gamma, x : \ell_\sharp\, T \vdash Q'$, or there is a name a such that $(\Gamma, x : \ell_\sharp\, T) - a \vdash Q'$. In the first case, or in the second one if $a \neq x$, we can conclude using rule LIN-RES; while, in the second case, if $a = x$, we infer $\Gamma \vdash (\boldsymbol{\nu} x : \ell_\sharp\, T)\, Q'$ using LIN-RES2.

□

Exercise 8.1.6 Work out the cases of rules INP, OUT, and PAR in the proof of Theorem 8.1.5. □

Corollary 8.1.7 Suppose $\Delta \vdash P$, with Δ closed, and $P \xrightarrow{\tau} P'$. Then also $\Delta \vdash P'$. □

Exercise 8.1.8 Prove Corollary 8.1.7. □

Exercise 8.1.9 Write down and prove the analogue of Corollary 7.2.14 for linear types. □

A linear capability expresses the obligation of using a name once. The fact that a process is well typed in an environment that assigns a linear type to a particular name does not guarantee, however, that the process will ever perform an action along that name. For instance,

$$a : \ell_{\text{¡}}\, \texttt{unit} \vdash (\boldsymbol{\nu} b : \sharp\, \texttt{unit})\, \overline{b}\star.\, a(x).\, \mathbf{0}$$

but $(\boldsymbol{\nu} b : \sharp\, \texttt{unit})\, \overline{b}\star.\, a(x).\, \mathbf{0}$ is deadlocked. The property of exercising the *input* capability of a linear name will be guaranteed by the type system for linear receptiveness in the next section.

Exercise* 8.1.10 (Affine types) Modify the type system for linearity so that a linear type expresses a capability that can be used *at most* once, instead of *exactly* once. (This variation of linear types is usually called *affine types.*) In the new type system the result of Exercise 8.1.3 would not hold.

Show that in the new type system a limited form of weakening and strengthening holds on affine types. What simplifications can be made to the Reduction Subject Theorem? □

Linear types constrain processes to using names only once. It is possible to generalize the idea and constrain processes to using names n times, for arbitrary $n \geq 0$. In practice this generalization does not seem very useful, so we do not consider it.

8.2 Receptiveness

In this section we study type systems for *uniform receptiveness.* Intuitively, a name x is *receptive* in a process P if at any time P is ready to accept an input at x – at least as long as there are processes that could send messages at x. The receptiveness of x is *uniform* if all inputs at x are syntactically the same. Receptiveness ensures that any message sent at x can be processed immediately;

uniformity ensures that all messages are processed in the same way. For brevity, we often omit the adjective 'uniform'.

The above are *semantic* conditions, and are undecidable. To obtain decidable conditions we impose some restrictions; these reflect the typical way in which receptive names are actually used. We demand that a receptive name a appears only in subterms of the form (omitting type annotations)

$$\nu a\,(!a(b).\,P \mid Q) \tag{8.7}$$

where P and Q possess only the output capability on a, or of the form

$$\nu a\,(a(b).\,P \mid Q) \tag{8.8}$$

where, in addition, a can be used only once in output (that is, a is linear). We call the first form *ω-receptiveness*, the second *linear receptiveness*.

Receptive names have advantages. First, they can be implemented more efficiently than arbitrary names; see the notes at the end of the Part. Another advantage of receptive names is their algebraic properties, among which are copying, distributivity, τ-insensitivity, and parallelization laws. We will examine these in Section 11.2.

Uniform receptiveness occurs often in the π-calculus. An important example is the encoding of functions, a topic that will be developed in depth in Part VI. Anticipating a little, a process Q with a local function $\lambda r.\,M$ accessible via a name z is usually written

$$\nu z\,(!z(r, y).\,P \mid Q) \tag{8.9}$$

where P is the encoding of M and y is (a placeholder for) the name where the result of a function call will be delivered. Within Q, a call of the function with argument n is written

$$\nu x\,(\overline{z}\langle n, x\rangle \mid x(p).\,R) \tag{8.10}$$

where p is (a placeholder for) the result of the call. In the function declaration (8.9), z is ω-receptive; in the function call (8.10), x is linear receptive (the order of the parallel components does not matter, so (8.10) does match (8.8)). Similar combinations of linear and ω-receptiveness occur in the encoding of higher-order communications, as we will see in Chapter 13, and of object-oriented languages, as we will see in Part VII. Typically, ω-receptiveness occurs in the modelling of resources that are private to one or more client processes (above, the resource is a function). An important example of linear receptiveness – indeed, perhaps the most important – is found in process interactions based on the *Remote Procedure Call* (RPC) paradigm. An RPC interaction involves two synchronizations between a caller and a callee where, after the first synchronization, the caller waits for the callee to elaborate a response. When we model an RPC in the π-calculus, the return name at which the callee delivers its response is linear receptive. RPC communications can be found in operating systems and object-oriented languages. The function call (8.10) is itself an example of an RPC interaction.

8.2.1 Linear Receptiveness

We study $\pi^{\mathtt{unit},\mathsf{i/o},\ell\mathrm{rec}}$, a simply-typed π-calculus with $\mathsf{i/o}$ and linear-receptive types. It is the same calculus as that in Section 8.1, but with linear receptiveness in place of linearity.

A linear-receptive name differs from a linear name in that the input end must be immediately available after the creation of the name, and only the output capability of the name can be communicated. In practice, it is rare to find names that are linear but not also linear receptive. Types and typing rules for linear receptiveness are easy variations of those for linearity. Types are presented in Table 8.3 and typing rules in Table 8.4. They are the linear-receptive analogues of Tables 8.1 and 8.2 for linear types. We call $\ell\mathrm{rec}_{\mathsf{i}}\, T, \ell\mathrm{rec}_{\mathsf{o}}\, T, \ell\mathrm{rec}_{\sharp}\, T$ the *linear-receptive types.* The type $\ell\mathrm{rec}_{\mathsf{o}}\, T$ represents the output capability on a linear-receptive name, $\ell\mathrm{rec}_{\mathsf{i}}\, T$ the input capability, and $\ell\mathrm{rec}_{\sharp}\, T$ the union of the two capabilities. Combinations of types ($S \uplus T$), type environments ($\Gamma_1 \uplus \Gamma_2$), and extractions of linear-receptive names ($LRec(\Gamma)$ and $LRec_{\mathsf{i}}(\Gamma)$) are defined as for linear types: just replace ℓ with $\ell\mathrm{rec}$, and Lin with $LRec$ in Table 8.1.

As only the output capability of a receptive name can be communicated, $\ell\mathrm{rec}_{\mathsf{i}}\, T$ and $\ell\mathrm{rec}_{\sharp}\, T$ cannot be used as value types. Further, it does not make sense to create a name x with type $\ell\mathrm{rec}_{\mathsf{i}}\, T$ or $\ell\mathrm{rec}_{\mathsf{o}}\, T$, because the input or the output end of x will give a deadlocked process. Therefore type $\ell\mathrm{rec}_{\mathsf{i}}\, T$ is essentially a notational device for writing type judgment proofs.

The only differences between the typing rules for linear receptiveness and those for linearity are the side conditions of the rules LREC-INP, LREC-OUT, LREC-TAU, LREC-MAT, and LREC-SUM. In LREC-INP, LREC-OUT, LREC-TAU, and LREC-MAT the additional side condition makes sure that the input end of a linear-receptive name does not appear underneath a prefix or a match. In rule LREC-SUM, the side condition forbids choices on inputs at receptive names; this constraint can be relaxed but it simplifies some of the theory of receptiveness.

We write $\equiv_M$ for the relation defined as $\equiv$ (structural congruence, Definition 1.2.3), but without rule SC-MAT for match.

Exercise 8.2.1

(1) Show that if $\Gamma \vdash P$ and $P \equiv_M Q$, then also $\Gamma \vdash Q$.

Grammars

			Link types
L	$::=$	$\ell\text{rec}_\sharp\, V$	linear-receptive connection
	$\mid$	$\ell\text{rec}_\text{i}\, V$	linear-receptive input
	$\mid$	$\ell\text{rec}_\text{o}\, V$	linear-receptive output

(With the constraint that $\ell\text{rec}_\sharp\, V$ and $\ell\text{rec}_\text{i}\, V$ *cannot be used as value types*, because only the output end of receptive names can be transmitted.)

Table 8.3. *Additional productions for linear-receptive types*

(2) Show that $\Gamma \vdash P$ and $P \equiv Q$ does not imply $\Gamma \vdash Q$. □

The next lemma shows that if a type environment Γ grants the input capability on a linear-receptive name x, then a process well typed in Γ makes the input end of x immediately available. This is a key property of linear receptiveness.

Lemma 8.2.2 If $\Gamma \uplus x : \ell\text{rec}_\text{i}\, S \vdash P$ then there are $\widetilde{a}, q, \widetilde{T}, P_1, P_2$ such that $P \equiv_M (\boldsymbol{\nu}\widetilde{a} : \widetilde{T})\, (x(q).\, P_1 \mid P_2)$ with $x \notin \widetilde{a}$; moreover, if $x \notin \mathsf{supp}(\Gamma)$ then also $x \notin \mathsf{fn}(P_2) \cup \mathsf{fn}(P_1)$. □

Exercise 8.2.3

(1) Prove Lemma 8.2.2.
(2) Show that Lemma 8.2.2 is not true for linear types. □

In the presence of linear-receptive types, we have to modify the definition of closed type environments. Similarly to what we did for linear types, we require that in a closed type environment no name has type $\ell\text{rec}_\sharp\, T$; in addition, however, we also require that no name has type $\ell\text{rec}_\text{o}\, T$. The second condition is imposed so that in a closed process outputs at receptive names can be immediately consumed – this is the essence of receptiveness. The two conditions, on $\ell\text{rec}_\sharp\, T$ and $\ell\text{rec}_\text{o}\, T$, amount to saying that processes well typed in a closed type environment should have no free occurrences of receptive names in output position.

Definition 8.2.4 (Closed type environments, additional requirement for receptive types) In a closed type environment Γ there is no name x such

Value typing

$$\text{LREC-NAME} \quad \frac{}{\Gamma, x : T \vdash x : T} \quad LRec(\Gamma) = \emptyset$$

$$\text{LREC-UNIT} \quad \frac{}{\Gamma \vdash \star : \mathtt{unit}} \quad LRec(\Gamma) = \emptyset$$

plus rule SUBSUMPTION and the rules for subtyping in Table 7.1

Process typing

$$\text{LREC-INP} \quad \frac{\begin{array}{c}\Gamma_1 \vdash v : m\, S \quad \text{for } m \in \{\mathsf{i}, \ell\mathrm{rec}_{\mathsf{i}}\} \\ \Gamma_2 , x : S \vdash P : \diamond\end{array}}{\Gamma_1 \uplus \Gamma_2 \vdash v(x).\, P : \diamond} \quad LRec_{\mathsf{i}}(\Gamma_2) = \emptyset$$

$$\text{LREC-OUT} \quad \frac{\begin{array}{c}\Gamma_1 \vdash v : m\, S \quad \text{for } m \in \{\mathsf{o}, \ell\mathrm{rec}_{\mathsf{o}}\} \\ \Gamma_2 \vdash w : S \qquad \Gamma_3 \vdash P : \diamond\end{array}}{\Gamma_1 \uplus \Gamma_2 \uplus \Gamma_3 \vdash \overline{v}w.\, P : \diamond} \quad LRec_{\mathsf{i}}(\Gamma_1 \uplus \Gamma_2 \uplus \Gamma_3) = \emptyset$$

$$\text{LREC-PAR} \quad \frac{\Gamma_1 \vdash P_1 : \diamond \qquad \Gamma_2 \vdash P_2 : \diamond}{\Gamma_1 \uplus \Gamma_2 \vdash P_1 \mid P_2 : \diamond}$$

$$\text{LREC-SUM} \quad \frac{\Gamma \vdash P_1 : \diamond \qquad \Gamma \vdash P_2 : \diamond}{\Gamma \vdash P_1 + P_2 : \diamond} \quad LRec_{\mathsf{i}}(\Gamma) = \emptyset$$

$$\text{LREC-TAU} \quad \frac{\Gamma \vdash P : \diamond}{\Gamma \vdash \tau.\, P : \diamond} \quad LRec_{\mathsf{i}}(\Gamma) = \emptyset$$

$$\text{LREC-REP} \quad \frac{\Gamma \vdash P : \diamond}{\Gamma \vdash !P : \diamond} \quad LRec(\Gamma) = \emptyset$$

$$\text{LREC-NIL} \quad \frac{}{\Gamma \vdash \mathbf{0} : \diamond} \quad LRec(\Gamma) = \emptyset$$

$$\text{LREC-MAT} \quad \frac{\Gamma_1 \vdash v : \sharp T \qquad \Gamma_1 \vdash w : \sharp T \qquad \Gamma_2 \vdash P : \diamond}{\Gamma_1 \uplus \Gamma_2 \vdash [v = w]P : \diamond} \quad LRec_{\mathsf{i}}(\Gamma_2) = \emptyset$$

$$\text{LREC-RES} \quad \frac{\Gamma , x : L \vdash P : \diamond}{\Gamma \vdash (\boldsymbol{\nu} x : L)\, P : \diamond}$$

$$\text{LREC-RES2} \quad \frac{\Gamma \vdash P : \diamond}{\Gamma \vdash (\boldsymbol{\nu} x : L)\, P : \diamond}$$

Table 8.4. *The typing rules for* $\pi^{\mathtt{unit},\mathsf{i}/\mathsf{o},\ell\mathrm{rec}}$

that $\Gamma(x) = \ell\mathsf{rec}_\sharp\, T$ or $\Gamma(x) = \ell\mathsf{rec}_\mathsf{o}\, T$ (if there are recursive types, replace $=$ with $\sim_{\mathsf{type}}$). □

The Subject Reduction Theorem 8.1.5 holds also for linear receptiveness: just replace ℓ with $\ell\mathsf{rec}$.

Exercise 8.2.5 Continuing Exercise 8.1.10: give typing rules for *affine-receptive types*; these are to the affine types of Exercise 8.1.10 what linear-receptive types are to the linear types. □

8.2.2 ω-receptiveness

The other interesting example of uniform receptiveness is *ω-receptiveness*, where: the input of a name is always available, and always with the same continuation; and there are no limitations on the utilization of the name in output. A simple way of ensuring the uniformity condition on inputs is to require that the only input occurrence is replicated, i.e., of the form $!x(a).\,P$. For this reason, the type system for ω-receptiveness will have a special rule for input-replicated processes.

In this section we sketch the modifications that need to be made to the theory of Section 8.2.1 when ω-receptive types replace linear-receptive types. The calculus we study is $\pi^{\mathsf{unit,i/o,\omega rec}}$. All the modifications are simple. We briefly explain them, omitting definitions and properties that are straightforward adaptations of those for linear and linear-receptive types. Types and typing rules for ω-receptiveness are presented in Tables 8.5 and 8.6. We call $\omega\mathsf{rec}_\mathsf{i}\, T, \omega\mathsf{rec}_\mathsf{o}\, T, \omega\mathsf{rec}_\sharp\, T$ the *ω-receptive types*.

In the typing system, the interpretation of a judgment

$$\Gamma \uplus \{a : \omega\mathsf{rec}_\mathsf{i}\, S\,,\, b : \omega\mathsf{rec}_\mathsf{o}\, S\} \vdash P : \diamond$$

is that P must make the input end of a immediately available, in input-replicated form, whereas it may use b arbitrarily many times in output. In contrast to the rules for linear receptiveness, in a few rules, such as OREC-INP and OREC-OUT (for prefixes), and the rules for replication and $\mathbf{0}$, the output capabilities on receptive names are the same in the premises and in the conclusions. This is so because there is no requirement that the output of a receptive name is used in only one place. For the same reason, the operation for combining types allows copying of an ω-receptive output ($\omega\mathsf{rec}_\mathsf{o}\, S \uplus \omega\mathsf{rec}_\mathsf{o}\, S = \omega\mathsf{rec}_\mathsf{o}\, S$). The analogues for ω-receptiveness of rules LIN-RES2 and LREC-RES2 of linear and linear-receptive types are not needed. In the rules OREC-INP and OREC-OUT, the premises $\Gamma \vdash v : \mathsf{i}\, S$ and $\Gamma \vdash v : m\, S$ for $m \in \{\mathsf{o}, \omega\mathsf{rec}_\mathsf{o}\}$ imply $ORec_\mathsf{i}(\Gamma) = \emptyset$, because of the side condition in OREC-NAME; similarly in OREC-MAT. (The same side

Grammars

$$
\begin{array}{lcll}
 & & \textit{Link types} & \\
L & ::= & \omega\mathrm{rec}_{\sharp}\ V & \omega\text{-receptive connection} \\
 & | & \omega\mathrm{rec}_{\mathrm{i}}\ V & \omega\text{-receptive input} \\
 & | & \omega\mathrm{rec}_{\mathrm{o}}\ V & \omega\text{-receptive output}
\end{array}
$$

(With the constraint that $\omega\mathrm{rec}_{\sharp}\ V$ and $\omega\mathrm{rec}_{\mathrm{i}}\ V$ *cannot be used as value types,* because only the output end of receptive names can be transmitted.)

Combination of types

$$
\begin{array}{rcll}
\omega\mathrm{rec}_{\mathrm{i}}\ T \uplus \omega\mathrm{rec}_{\mathrm{o}}\ T & \stackrel{\mathrm{def}}{=} & \omega\mathrm{rec}_{\sharp}\ T & \\
\omega\mathrm{rec}_{\mathrm{o}}\ T \uplus \omega\mathrm{rec}_{\mathrm{o}}\ T & \stackrel{\mathrm{def}}{=} & \omega\mathrm{rec}_{\mathrm{o}}\ T & \\
\omega\mathrm{rec}_{\mathrm{o}}\ T \uplus \omega\mathrm{rec}_{\sharp}\ T & \stackrel{\mathrm{def}}{=} & \omega\mathrm{rec}_{\sharp}\ T & \\
T \uplus T & \stackrel{\mathrm{def}}{=} & T & \text{if } T \text{ is not an } \omega\text{-receptive type} \\
T \uplus S & \stackrel{\mathrm{def}}{=} & \mathtt{error} & \text{otherwise}
\end{array}
$$

Extraction of ω-receptive names

$$
ORec_{\mathrm{i}}(\Gamma) \stackrel{\mathrm{def}}{=} \{x \mid \Gamma(x) = \omega\mathrm{rec}_{\mathrm{i}}\ S \text{ or } \Gamma(x) = \omega\mathrm{rec}_{\sharp}\ S, \text{ for some } S\}
$$

Table 8.5. *Additional productions and operations for ω-receptive types*

condition could be removed from OREC-UNIT, in the calculus $\pi^{\mathtt{unit},\mathsf{i/o},\omega\mathtt{rec}}$; but it may be needed in extensions of $\pi^{\mathtt{unit},\mathsf{i/o},\omega\mathtt{rec}}$.) The main difference, however, from previous type systems is the rule OREC-REP$\star$, for introducing ω-receptive names.

Lemma 8.2.6 If $ORec_{\mathrm{i}}(\Gamma) = \emptyset$ then $\Gamma = \Gamma \uplus \Gamma$. □

Exercise 8.2.7 Write down and prove the analogue of Lemma 8.2.2 for ω-receptiveness. □

In the case of ω-receptiveness, weakening and strengthening on output capa-

Value typing

$$\text{OREC-NAME}\ \frac{}{\Gamma, x : T \vdash x : T}\ ORec_{\mathsf{i}}(\Gamma) = \emptyset$$

$$\text{OREC-UNIT}\ \frac{}{\Gamma \vdash \star : \mathtt{unit}}\ ORec_{\mathsf{i}}(\Gamma) = \emptyset$$

plus rule SUBSUMPTION and the rules for subtyping in Table 7.1

Process typing

$$\text{OREC-INP}\ \frac{\Gamma \vdash v : \mathsf{i}\, S \qquad \Gamma, x : S \vdash P : \diamond}{\Gamma \vdash v(x).\, P : \diamond}$$

$$\text{OREC-OUT}\ \frac{\begin{array}{c}\Gamma \vdash v : m\, S \quad \text{for } m \in \{\mathsf{o}, \omega\mathsf{rec}_{\mathsf{o}}\} \\ \Gamma \vdash w : S \qquad \Gamma \vdash P : \diamond\end{array}}{\Gamma \vdash \overline{v}w.\, P : \diamond}$$

$$\text{OREC-PAR}\ \frac{\Gamma_1 \vdash P_1 : \diamond \qquad \Gamma_2 \vdash P_2 : \diamond}{\Gamma_1 \uplus \Gamma_2 \vdash P_1 \mid P_2 : \diamond}$$

$$\text{OREC-SUM}\ \frac{\Gamma \vdash P_1 : \diamond \qquad \Gamma \vdash P_2 : \diamond}{\Gamma \vdash P_1 + P_2 : \diamond}\ ORec_{\mathsf{i}}(\Gamma) = \emptyset$$

$$\text{OREC-TAU}\ \frac{\Gamma \vdash P : \diamond}{\Gamma \vdash \tau.\, P : \diamond}\ ORec_{\mathsf{i}}(\Gamma) = \emptyset$$

$$\text{OREC-REP}\star\ \frac{\Gamma_1 \vdash v : \omega\mathsf{rec}_{\mathsf{i}}\, S \qquad \Gamma_2, x : S \vdash P : \diamond}{\Gamma_1 \uplus \Gamma_2 \vdash !v(x).\, P : \diamond}\ ORec_{\mathsf{i}}(\Gamma_2) = \emptyset$$

$$\text{OREC-REP}\ \frac{\Gamma \vdash P : \diamond}{\Gamma \vdash !P : \diamond}\ ORec_{\mathsf{i}}(\Gamma) = \emptyset$$

$$\text{OREC-NIL}\ \frac{}{\Gamma \vdash \mathbf{0} : \diamond}\ ORec_{\mathsf{i}}(\Gamma) = \emptyset$$

$$\text{OREC-MAT}\ \frac{\Gamma \vdash v : \sharp T \qquad \Gamma \vdash w : \sharp T \qquad \Gamma \vdash P : \diamond}{\Gamma \vdash [v = w]P : \diamond}$$

$$\text{OREC-RES}\ \frac{\Gamma, x : L \vdash P : \diamond}{\Gamma \vdash (\boldsymbol{\nu} x : L)\, P : \diamond}$$

Table 8.6. *The typing rules for* $\pi^{\mathtt{unit},\mathsf{i/o},\omega\mathsf{rec}}$

bilities hold, which was not the case for linearity and linear receptiveness. Here is the weakening property:

Lemma 8.2.8 Suppose $\Gamma \vdash P$ and $ORec_{\mathsf{i}}(\Gamma') = \emptyset$ and $\Gamma \uplus \Gamma'$ is defined. Then $\Gamma \uplus \Gamma' \vdash P$. □

It is a common feature of type systems that some semantically meaningful terms are ruled out:

Exercise 8.2.9 Explain why with ω-receptive types the structural law of replication $!R \equiv R \mid !R$ may not preserve typing. □

The definition of closed typing under ω-receptiveness is like that for linear receptiveness.

Exercise 8.2.10

(1) Do the typing rules for constants need modification in presence of receptive types?
(2) Check that in the definitions of the constants QUEUE, G, E, F in Section 7.4, the name g can be given an ω-receptive type, and the names c, c' can be given linear-receptive types. Why cannot the names r, r', e, e' be given a receptive type? Can these names be given affine receptive types, in the sense of Exercise 8.2.5? □

Exercise* 8.2.11 Work out Substitution and Subject Reduction results for $\pi^{\mathtt{unit},\mathsf{i/o},\omega\mathtt{rec}}$ on link-closed typings. (Hint: in Subject Reduction, the clause for τ transitions can be simpler than that of Theorem 8.1.5, just saying: if $\Gamma \vdash P$ and $P \xrightarrow{\tau} P'$, then $\Gamma \vdash P'$.) □

8.3 Polymorphism

In this section, we discuss *type abstraction*. We study $\pi^{\mathtt{unit},\sharp,\exists}$, a simply-typed π-calculus extended with type abstraction. This calculus can be regarded as being to the π-calculus what Girard's and Reynolds's polymorphic λ-calculus (or system F) is to the λ-calculus. Following the analogy, we call the calculus the *polymorphic π-calculus*, and call its type system a *polymorphic* type system. Type abstraction can however be added to any of the typed π-calculi presented in the previous sections. Although the typing rules for polymorphism in the π-calculus and in the λ-calculus have similar syntactic forms, the semantic effects of polymorphism are quite different in the two calculi, as we will see in Section 11.3. In examples, we also use product types.

Type abstraction is common in modern programming languages. For instance, it allows us to define operations that are generic, that is, they work on many different types of argument. Examples of such operations are list reversal and concatenation, whose definitions are independent of the type of the elements of the lists. In polymorphic languages, such operations are made parametric on the type of the elements; the missing type is supplied later, when the operation is actually used. Another important application of type abstraction is in hiding details about the representation of data, which is the basis for the definition of Abstract Data Types (ADTs). A client of an ADT must be able to work independently of the hidden representation type of the ADT. Polymorphism gives us a useful flexibility in programming, but it also has important consequences for reasoning techniques.

Remark 8.3.1 In a broad sense, in programming languages, polymorphism indicates the possibility of using an expression with several types. Therefore also subtyping can be considered a form of polymorphism, often called *subtyping* (or *inclusion*) *polymorphism*. With subtyping, the different types that an expression may take are related to each other: they differ in how much they reveal about the behaviour of that expression. For instance, the expression 2 may be given type `Int` or type `Real`, the former being more precise. The polymorphism that is studied in this section is, by contrast, referred to as *parametric polymorphism*. The adjective 'parametric' indicates the possibility of defining expressions that behave uniformly on many types.

Parametric and subtyping polymorphism are often presented in opposition to *ad hoc polymorphism*, which refers to expressions that work on a family of types but may behave in unrelated ways for different members of the family. An example is a print function that executes different code depending on whether the type of the argument it receives is a PostScript or ASCII application.

In the book, the word 'polymorphism' is used for parametric polymorphism only. □

We illustrate the use of polymorphism in the π-calculus with an example. Consider the process

$$!a(z, y).\,\overline{z}y.$$

It implements a simple service: it receives values z and y from name a and then sends y along z. A client of this server is of the form $\overline{a}\langle b, v\rangle.\,P$. It does not matter what the type of v is: as long as b can carry v, and P is well typed, the parallel composition of this client and the server does not give a run-time error. Indeed, we can even compose the server with two clients that send values of completely different types, and obtain a perfectly reasonable system, such as

$$\overline{a}\langle c, 5\rangle \mid \overline{a}\langle d, \mathsf{true}\rangle \mid !a(z, y).\,\overline{z}y\ . \tag{8.11}$$

This system does not give rise to run-time errors, but is not well typed under any of the type systems previously examined. For instance, the server could be typed in a type environment that assigns a the type $\sharp\,(\sharp\,T \times T)$; but we need two different T's, namely `Int` and `Bool`, for typing the two clients. This rigidity is annoying, because the type judgment

$$a : \sharp\,(\sharp\,T \times T) \vdash !a(z, y).\,\overline{z}y$$

is valid for *arbitrary* T. Polymorphism allows us to capture this uniformity, by abstracting on type T and turning it into a type parameter. To achieve this, we redefine a to be a polymorphic name, and make the server polymorphic:

$$a : \sharp\,\langle X; \sharp\,X \times X\rangle \vdash !a(x).\,\mathsf{open}\ x\ \mathsf{as}\ (X; z, y)\ \mathsf{in}\ \overline{z}y\ . \tag{8.12}$$

In the type of a and in the server process, X is a type variable that represents the type that is being abstracted. Each time the server is used, a concrete type for X will have to be supplied. For instance, $\overline{a}\,\langle \mathtt{Int}; c, 5\rangle$ is a client that uses integers for X. It interacts with the server as follows:

$$\begin{array}{rl} & \overline{a}\,\langle \mathtt{Int}; c, 5\rangle \mid !a(x).\,\mathsf{open}\ x\ \mathsf{as}\ (X; z, y)\ \mathsf{in}\ \overline{z}y \\ \xrightarrow{\tau} & \mathbf{0} \mid \mathsf{open}\ \langle \mathtt{Int}; c, 5\rangle\ \mathsf{as}\ (X; z, y)\ \mathsf{in}\ \overline{z}y \mid !a(x).\,\mathsf{open}\ x\ \mathsf{as}\ (X; z, y)\ \mathsf{in}\ \overline{z}y \\ \xrightarrow{\tau} & \mathbf{0} \mid \overline{c}5 \mid !a(x).\,\mathsf{open}\ x\ \mathsf{as}\ (X; z, y)\ \mathsf{in}\ \overline{z}y\ . \end{array}$$

The construct $\mathsf{open}\ v\ \mathsf{as}\ (X; x)\ \mathsf{in}\ P$ opens a polymorphic package v into its type and value components, which are respectively bound to X and x, with scope P. We can now rewrite (8.11) thus:

$$\overline{a}\,\langle \mathtt{Int}; c, 5\rangle \mid \overline{a}\,\langle \mathtt{Bool}; d, \mathsf{true}\rangle \mid !a(x).\,\mathsf{open}\ x\ \mathsf{as}\ (X; z, y)\ \mathsf{in}\ \overline{z}y\ .$$

This process is well typed under the type assignment

$$a : \sharp\,\langle X; \sharp\,X \times X\rangle\ ,\ c : \sharp\,\mathtt{Int}\ ,\ d : \sharp\,\mathtt{Bool}\ .$$

Notation 8.3.2 In (8.12), and elsewhere in the section, we use some convenient *pattern-matching* notation for decomposing tuple values, of the kind discussed in Section 6.6. Without abbreviations, the process in (8.12) is written

$$!a(x).\,\mathsf{open}\ x\ \mathsf{as}\ (X; b)\ \mathsf{in}\ (\ \mathsf{with}\ (z, y) = b\ \mathsf{do}\ \overline{z}y)\ .$$

Similarly, in outputs such as $\overline{a}\,\langle \mathtt{Int}; c, 5\rangle$ we omit angle brackets around product values; the full process is $\overline{a}\,\langle \mathtt{Int}; \langle c, 5\rangle\rangle$. □

In the polymorphic server (8.12), the type parameter X does not appear in the body (the process $\overline{z}y$). In general, however, a type parameter may appear in the types of private names. An example is the process

$$a(x).\,\mathsf{open}\ x\ \mathsf{as}\ (X;c)\ \mathsf{in}\ (\nu b : \sharp\, X)\,\overline{c}b\,,$$

which is well typed in $a : \sharp\,\langle X; \sharp\,\sharp\,X\rangle$. This process receives a name c with a partially hidden type, and sends a private name b back; b can then be used to exchange values of the hidden type.

Values such as $\langle \mathtt{Bool}; d, \mathsf{true}\rangle$ that are exchanged along a polymorphic name can be thought of as packages in which typing information, namely Bool, is chosen by the client and is hidden from the server. In λ-calculi, similar packages are defined using existential types. There is indeed a precise correspondence between the typing rules for creating and decomposing polymorphic values in the π-calculus and existential values in the λ-calculus. It is interesting to note that the natural primitive form of polymorphism in the π-calculus is existential quantification, as opposed to universal quantification which is the natural primitive in the λ-calculus. (Both in the λ-calculus and in the π-calculus existential and universal quantification are interdefinable; this can be shown via encodings of the kind discussed in Section 7.5.)

Like existential types in the λ-calculus, polymorphic types in the π-calculus can be used to create information-hiding barriers. The recipient of a value sent along a polymorphic name has only partial visibility of the type of that value. For instance, if the polymorphic name has type $\sharp\,\langle X; T\rangle$ then the recipient's view of the type of the value is T; it is partial because X may appear in T. A (well-typed) recipient can make no assumptions about the hidden part of the type. As we will see, this may severely constrain the behaviour of the recipient.

We anticipate from Part VI that the server $!a(z, y).\,\overline{z}y$ above is (the body of) the π-calculus encoding of the identity function (under the call-by-name strategy). Similarly, $!a(X; z, y).\,\overline{z}y$ is the encoding of the polymorphic identity function.

Rules and productions for polymorphic types are presented in Table 8.7. The calculus $\pi^{\mathtt{unit},\sharp,\exists}$ is defined by adding the productions and rules in this table to those for $\pi^{\mathtt{unit},\sharp}$. A polymorphic value is a pair, consisting of a type component and a value component. Polymorphic values are therefore written, like product values, using angle brackets. In $\langle X; V\rangle$, the type variable X is a binding occurrence with scope V. The same conventions about α-conversion on names apply to type variables; we therefore identify types that differ syntactically only in their bound type variables, and we implicitly α-convert types to satisfy side conditions about distinctness of bound and free variables. We write $\mathsf{tvar}(T)$,

Grammars

			Values
v	$::=$	$\langle V; v\rangle$	polymorphic value
			Processes
P	$::=$	$\mathsf{open}\ v\ \mathsf{as}\ (X; x)\ \mathsf{in}\ P$	unpacking
			Types for values
V	$::=$	$\langle X; V\rangle$	polymorphic type
	$\mid$	X	type variable
			Type environments
Γ	$::=$	Γ, X	type variable

Typing rules

$$\text{T-Open}\ \frac{\Gamma \vdash v : \langle X; T\rangle \qquad \Gamma, x : T, X \vdash P : \diamond}{\Gamma \vdash \mathsf{open}\ v\ \mathsf{as}\ (X; x)\ \mathsf{in}\ P : \diamond}$$

$$\text{Tv-Poly}\ \frac{\Gamma \vdash v : T\{S/X\}}{\Gamma \vdash \langle S; v\rangle : \langle X; T\rangle}$$

Transition rules

$$\text{Poly}\ \frac{}{\mathsf{open}\ \langle T; v\rangle\ \mathsf{as}\ (X; x)\ \mathsf{in}\ P \xrightarrow{\tau} P\{T/X\}\{v/x\}}$$

$$\text{PolyErr}\ \frac{(\text{where } v \text{ does not have the form } \langle T; v\rangle)}{\mathsf{open}\ v\ \mathsf{as}\ (X; x)\ \mathsf{in}\ P \xrightarrow{\tau} \mathtt{wrong}}$$

Table 8.7. *Additional productions and rules for polymorphic types*

$\mathsf{tvar}(P)$, $\mathsf{tvar}(v)$ for the free type variables of type T, process P, and value v, respectively.

We add a production for variables to the grammar for type environments. Thus a type environment Γ now has two parts: an assignment of types to names, and a set of type variables. We write $\mathsf{varpart}(\Gamma)$ for this set of variables; they represent the missing type information. In a type judgment, the variable part of the type environment tells us which variables may occur free in the objects of the judgment (processes, values, types). In other words, the variables in the type environment can be thought of as the binders for the free occurrences of the variables in the objects of the judgment. (If we were to introduce more sophisticated forms of polymorphism such as bounded polymorphism, the variables in the type environment would have subtyping information attached.) Accordingly we place the following well-formedness condition on type environments and type judgments:

- if a type environment Γ is defined on a name a, then we must have $\mathsf{tvar}(\Gamma(a)) \subseteq \mathsf{varpart}(\Gamma)$
- in $\Gamma \vdash E : T$, we must have $(\mathsf{tvar}(E) \cup \mathsf{tvar}(T)) \subseteq \mathsf{varpart}(\Gamma)$.

In every type environment and type judgment we write, we will implicitly assume that these conditions hold.

Having added type variables, the support of a typing Γ, that is $\mathsf{supp}(\Gamma)$, is the union of the set of names on which Γ is defined and the set of type variables $\mathsf{varpart}(\Gamma)$. A *type substitution* $\{\widetilde{T}/\widetilde{X}\}$, where $\widetilde{X}$ are not free in $\widetilde{T}$, maps the type variables $\widetilde{X}$ onto the types $\widetilde{T}$ componentwise. (As the variables are value types, the types $\widetilde{T}$ should be value types too.) The application of this substitution to a process P, written $P\{\widetilde{T}/\widetilde{X}\}$, replaces the free occurrences of the variables $\widetilde{X}$ in P with the types $\widetilde{T}$; similarly for application of the substitution to values or types. When applied to a type environment, the substitution $\{\widetilde{T}/\widetilde{X}\}$ removes the variables $\widetilde{X}$ and adds those in $\mathsf{tvar}(\widetilde{T})$:

$$(\widetilde{a} : \widetilde{S}, \widetilde{Y})\{\widetilde{T}/\widetilde{X}\} = \widetilde{a} : \widetilde{S}\{\widetilde{T}/\widetilde{X}\}, (\widetilde{Y} - \widetilde{X}) \cup \mathsf{tvar}(\widetilde{T})$$

where $(\widetilde{Y} - \widetilde{X}) \cup \mathsf{tvar}(\widetilde{T})$ are the variables in $\widetilde{Y}$ but not in $\widetilde{X}$, plus the variables free in $\mathsf{tvar}(\widetilde{T})$.

In a type judgment $\Gamma \vdash \langle S; v\rangle : \langle X; T\rangle$, the type T represents the visible part of the type of v, and S the hidden part. Therefore the concrete type of v is $T\{S/X\}$. This explains the form of the typing rule TV-POLY in Table 8.7. The other rule, T-OPEN, shows how to type a process that uses a polymorphic value. The body P of the process $\mathsf{open}\ v\ \mathsf{as}\ (X; x)\ \mathsf{in}\ P$ should type without any assumption about the hidden part X of v. Following our conventions on α-conversion, in rule T-OPEN it is implicitly intended that x and X are not in the support of Γ.

Note that since the type of a restriction must be a link type, we cannot introduce a restriction with a completely abstract type, as in

$$P \stackrel{\text{def}}{=} a(y).\,\mathsf{open}\ y\ \mathsf{as}\ (X;x)\ \mathsf{in}\ (\boldsymbol{\nu} b : X)\,\overline{x}b.$$

A type variable can be instantiated with an arbitrary type, including types such as **unit** and **Bool** that cannot be ascribed to links. It is therefore reasonable to reject processes such as P, as they may end up creating new values of arbitrary types (for instance, a new boolean value!).

We say that a process or a type or a type environment is *ground* if it has no free type variables; it is *non-ground* otherwise. We revise the definition of closed type environment, so that type variables are taken into account.

Definition 8.3.3 (Closed type environments, additional requirement for polymorphic types) A closed type environment should be ground (that is, if Γ is closed then $\mathsf{tvar}(\Gamma) = \emptyset$). □

To understand the constraints on process behaviours imposed by polymorphism we will find useful also the notion of semi-closed type environment:

Definition 8.3.4 (Semi-closed type environments) A type environment is *semi-closed* if for all x on which Γ is defined, $\Gamma(x)$ is either a link type or a type variable. □

Since a semi-closed type environment Γ may contain types with free variables, the well-formedness condition on type environments implies that in general $\mathsf{varpart}(\Gamma)$ is non-empty. Note also that if Γ is semi-closed, then a type substitution can make Γ closed: it suffices to instantiate each free type variable of Γ with a ground link type.

Exercise 8.3.5 We have met a few times in the book π-calculus representations of references, or cells, for instance

$$!cell(x, get, put).\,(\overline{get}\,x.\,\overline{cell}\langle x, get, put\rangle + \ put(y).\,\overline{cell}\langle y, get, put\rangle)\,.$$

An output at *cell* has three arguments: the value x to be stored, and names *get* and *put* for reading and overwriting the value stored. Without polymorphism we have to write separate cell processes for each type of value that we want to store in a cell.

Write in $\pi^{\sharp,\times,\exists}$ a polymorphic cell that accepts values of arbitrary types, and then show that it is well typed by proving the appropriate type judgment. □

8.3.1 Properties of polymorphic types

In the assertions below we omit the calculus name $\pi^{\texttt{unit},\sharp,\exists}$. Lemmas 8.3.6 and 8.3.7 show that a type substitution does not affect the transitions of processes (this is not true for substitutions of names for names; see Section 1.4.3). We use χ to range over type substitutions.

Lemma 8.3.6 $P \xrightarrow{\alpha} P'$ implies $P\chi \xrightarrow{\alpha\chi} P'\chi$ for any type substitution χ. □

Lemma 8.3.7 Suppose that $P\chi \xrightarrow{\alpha} Q$.

(1) If α is an output or is τ, then there are α' and P' such that $P \xrightarrow{\alpha'} P'$, with $\alpha'\chi = \alpha$ and $P'\chi = Q$.
(2) If α is an input then for all α' such that $\alpha'\chi = \alpha$ we have $P \xrightarrow{\alpha'} P'$ for some P' with $P'\chi = Q$. □

Exercise 8.3.8 Prove Lemmas 8.3.6 and 8.3.7. □

A type substitution does not affect typing either:

Lemma 8.3.9 Suppose $\Gamma \vdash E : T$. Then also $\Gamma\chi \vdash E\chi : T\chi$, for any type substitution χ. □

Exercise 8.3.10 Prove Lemma 8.3.9. □

With polymorphism, the statements of all results in Section 6.3, including the Subject Reduction Theorem 6.3.7, do not change. (The well-formedness condition for type judgments concerning type variables is maintained, which is straightforward to check.) Moreover, the results are already true on semi-closed type environments (without polymorphic types, the notions of closed and semi-closed type environments coincide). For the reasoning techniques of Part IV, it is indeed important to have those results on semi-closed type environments: Subject Reduction thus allows us to infer important constraints on the behaviour of well-typed processes. For instance, if $\Gamma(a) = X$ then Subject Reduction tells us that a process well typed in Γ cannot perform input or output actions along a. The more non-ground the types of Γ are, the more constraints on the process can be inferred.

Example 8.3.11 Suppose $a : X, b : \sharp X, \Gamma, X \vdash P$. From the Subject Reduction Theorem for semi-closed environments, we deduce that P cannot perform visible actions along a; and if X is not free in Γ, we can also deduce that if P performs an output at b, the value emitted will be a. We will see more such examples in Section 11.3. □

Indeed, looking at the Subject Reduction Theorem 6.3.7 on semi-closed typings, and Lemmas 8.3.6 and 8.3.7, we can make the following observation. Suppose $\Gamma \vdash R$ with Γ closed; and suppose we succeed in removing some type information from Γ and R while preserving well-typedness, that is, we obtain a judgment $\Gamma' \vdash R'$, where R' and Γ' may have free type variables, with $\Gamma'\chi = \Gamma$ and $R'\chi = R$ for some type substitution χ. We can now use Subject Reduction to deduce that R' cannot perform certain actions, for instance input or output actions along a name a for which $\Gamma'(a) = X$; by Lemmas 8.3.6 and 8.3.7 we can lift up these constraints to R. We will develop this point further in Section 11.3, to obtain a proof technique for behavioural equivalence with polymorphic types.

To complete the proof of the Subject Reduction Theorem 6.3.7 for $\pi^{\mathtt{unit},\sharp,\exists}$ it suffices to add the case for the new transition rules POLY and POLYERR. We consider these separately, in the following lemma.

Lemma 8.3.12 Suppose $\Gamma \vdash \mathsf{open}\ v\ \mathsf{as}\ (X; x)\ \mathsf{in}\ P$, with Γ semi-closed, and $\mathsf{open}\ v\ \mathsf{as}\ (X; x)\ \mathsf{in}\ P \xrightarrow{\tau} P'$. Then also $\Gamma \vdash P'$.

Proof The transition rule that has been applied must be POLY; if it were POLYERR then v would not be a polymorphic value and so $\mathsf{open}\ v\ \mathsf{as}\ (X; x)\ \mathsf{in}\ P$ would not be well typed.

Thus, suppose $v = \langle W; w\rangle$. Then $P' = P\{W/X\}\{w/x\}$. We know that $\Gamma \vdash \mathsf{open}\ \langle W; w\rangle\ \mathsf{as}\ (X; x)\ \mathsf{in}\ P$. This means, by rule T-OPEN,

$$\Gamma \vdash \langle W; w\rangle : \langle X; V\rangle \quad \text{and} \quad \Gamma, x : V, X \vdash P$$

and then, by rule TV-POLY,

$$\Gamma \vdash w : V\{W/X\} .$$

By Lemma 8.3.9 (note that X is not free in Γ),

$$\Gamma, x : V\{W/X\} \vdash P\{W/X\} .$$

Finally, from the Substitution Lemma 6.3.6 and Strengthening,

$$\Gamma \vdash P\{W/X\}\{w/x\} .$$

$\square$

Notes and References for Part III

Most of the type constructs examined in this Part were inspired by well-known type constructs of sequential languages, in particular λ-calculi. A reader who wishes to know more about these type systems should therefore first consult textbooks, or tutorials, on type systems or typed languages, such as [Car96, AC96, Mit96, Gun92]. The standard reference paper for type equivalence and subtyping for recursive types is [AC93].

Milner's sorting system [Mil93], discussed in Section 3.1 and in the introduction to this Part of the book, should be regarded as the first form of type system for the π-calculus. i/o types were introduced in [PS96]. The subtyping that they give rise to is similar to that used for reference types in imperative languages such as Reynolds's Forsythe [Rey88]. In [PS96] a form of correctness for i/o types stronger than that seen in Section 7.2 was presented. This was accomplished by defining a refined reduction semantics in which each occurrence of a name in a process is *tagged* to indicate whether that occurrence may validly be used for input and/or output. Attempts to misuse names during communication are caught by checking the consistency of the tags. On well-typed processes, this semantics is isomorphic to the one given, in the sense that every process development in the tagged semantics can be mirrored in the original semantics, and vice versa. Thus, the soundness theorem for the tagged semantics yields the soundness of the original semantics as a corollary.

A type system with i/o and variant types and subtyping was presented in [San98a]. Sewell [Sew98], Hennessy and Riely [HR98c, HR98b], and Yoshida and Hennessy [YH99] extended the i/o type system with richer sets of capabilities for distributed versions of the π-calculus; also [DNFP98] extended i/o types, on a Linda-based distributed language. In these works, the control of capabilities was used for obtaining *security* guarantees on access to resources.

The type system for linearity in Section 8.1 follows [KPT99]. It borrows ideas from *linear logic* [Gir87]. More precisely, the typing rules for parallel composition and prefixes remind us of the multiplicative operators of linear logic, whereas the rule for summation reminds us of the additive operators. Similar ideas have been studied in type systems for λ-calculi; see for instance [Abr93, Bak92, Mac94, TWM95].

The type system for uniform receptiveness in Section 8.2 follows [San99b]. The typing rules in [San99b] are a little more liberal than those we have presented, mainly because in [San99b] bound output is a primitive operator. Uniformly receptive names are sometimes called *functional* names, precisely because they offer a service that is immediately available and does not change over time. We mentioned that uniform receptive names can be implemented more efficiently than arbitrary names: for instance, in Pict [PT00] the compiler can recognize receptive names, and then perform optimizations in the code that implements communications. Languages and calculi based on the π-calculus, such as Pict, Join [FG96], TyCO [VB98], and Blue Calculus [Bou97a], have syntactic constructs of the form (the syntax itself may be different) $\mathsf{def}\ z(a) = P\ \mathsf{in}\ Q$ for introducing a resource, or a function, P named z and with argument a; translated into π-calculus, this is written $\boldsymbol{\nu} z\ (!z(a).\, P \mid Q)$; the new name z is ω-receptive.

Type systems similar to those for linearity and uniform receptiveness were proposed by Niehren [Nie00]. Amadio, Boudol, and Lhoussaine [ABL99] developed a type system for names that are receptive but not necessarily uniform receptive. König [Kön00] and Igarashi and Kobayashi [IK01] explored a general framework for the above-mentioned types, as well as other type systems, using respectively hypergraphs and notions from abstract interpretation. Honda, Vasconcelos, and Kubo [HVK98] proposed a syntactic modification of the π-calculus and a type system for it that are able to describe sessions (i.e., sequences) of interactions between two processes. The resulting calculus has similarities with the π-calculus with *linearized types* discussed in [KPT99].

The basic metatheory of the polymorphic π-calculus was studied by Turner [Tur96] and further developed in [PS00]. Process calculi with weaker ML-style polymorphism were developed by Gay [Gay93], Vasconcelos and Honda [VH93, Vas94], Fournet, Laneve, Maranget, and Rémy [FLMR97], and Dal-Zilio [DZ97]. These works show, among other things, that ML-style polymorphism is possible on those names of which only the output capability can be communicated. A rather different style of polymorphism was considered by Liu and Walker [LW95]; here, polymorphism arises not from type quantification, but by explicitly declaring the possible set of types of values that a given name may carry. Typing itself does not guarantee absence of run-time errors; for this a notion of consistent type is separately introduced.

Pict adopts a form of polymorphism more powerful than that examined in Section 8.3, based on Girard's System F^ω [Gir72]. Join and TyCO use ML-like polymorphism. Other typed concurrent programming languages strongly related to these, and again based on an ML-like polymorphism, are Concurrent ML [Rep99] and Facile [GMP89, TLK96].

The *Ambient Calculus*, AC, [CG98] addresses process mobility and incorporates primitives of location and distribution. AC uses ideas from the π-calculus, but at the heart of its computational model is the notion of movement, rather than interaction as in the π-calculus. The type systems for AC, although formally different, are related to those for the π-calculus discussed here. For instance, in the simply-typed π-calculus types guarantee that all messages exchanged along a given name belong to the same type; similarly in 'simply-typed' AC [CG99] types guarantee that all messages exchanged within a given ambient belong to the same type.

Other type systems, whose emphasis is more on the induced behavioural properties, are discussed in the notes to Part IV.

We conclude by mentioning a few more proposals for types for concurrent languages. In Nierstrasz's regular types [Nie95], types are constructed using the combinators of regular expressions. These systems are intuitively quite appealing, though their formal properties have so far proved difficult to establish.

Another direction of work is that on *effect systems* [LG88, Wri92, NN94, TJ94, Tho94, ANN99]. Effect systems have been developed mainly on higher-order sequential languages, such as ML, but a number of proposals target extensions of these languages with concurrency primitives, such as Concurrent ML and Facile. The effect of an expression may record information about creation of channels and references, and communications and accesses to references performed by that expression; it may also contain information about the partial ordering of these events, such as sequentializations and branching points. Effect systems have been used primarily as a means of enhancing polymorphism, but also as a basis for various forms of static analysis of process behaviours. The separation between some of the most advanced type systems mentioned above and effect-based type systems may not be sharp. For instance Kobayashi, Nakade, and Yonezawa [KNY95] presented an effect system for finding an upper bound on the maximum number of receivers that a given channel can have at the same time, a piece of information that is similar to that given by the type systems for linearity.

Abramsky, Gay and Nagarajan [AGN95] proposed *Interaction Categories* as a semantic foundation for typed concurrent languages, based on category theory and linear logic. In Interaction Categories, objects are types, morphisms are processes respecting types, and composition is process interaction. Interaction Categories have been used to give the semantics to data-flow languages such as Lustre and Signal, and to define classes of processes that are deadlock-free in a compositional way. [GN95] presented a typed process calculus whose design follows the structure of Interaction Categories. It is not clear at present how Interaction Categories can handle process mobility and distribution.

Part IV

Reasoning about Processes using Types

Introduction to Part IV

In this Part we study the use of types for reasoning about behavioural properties of mobile processes.

Although well-developed, the theory of the pure untyped π-calculus is often insufficient to prove 'expected' properties of processes. The reason is that when one uses π-calculus to describe a system, one normally follows a discipline that governs how names may be used; but this discipline is not explicit in π-terms, and therefore it cannot play a part in proofs. (The same happens for the λ-calculus, which is hardly ever used untyped, since each variable usually has an 'intended' functionality.) *Types* can be used to make such disciplines explicit. In Section 9.1, we illustrate this point with two examples that have to do with *encapsulation*.

The use of types affects contextually-defined behavioural equivalences such as barbed congruence, for in a typed calculus the processes being compared must obey the same typing, and the contexts in which they are tested must be compatible with this typing. Typically, in a typed calculus the class of legal contexts in which two processes may be tested is smaller than in the untyped calculus. As a consequence, more behavioural equivalences among processes hold. The behavioural effects of types are important for types such as i/o, linear, receptive, and polymorphic types, because such types express *behavioural guarantees* on the use of names. Types are important not only for behavioural equivalences, but more generally for behavioural properties; see for instance the security property discussed in Section 9.3.

Basic definitions, such as those of typed barbed congruence and typed labelled equivalences, will be parametric on the type system. However, most results will be presented on concrete π-calculi, usually extensions of $\pi^{\sharp,\times,\mu}$, the polyadic π-calculus. $\pi^{\sharp,\times,\mu}$ is simple (for instance it has no basic types), it is an adequate testbed for the results, and it is a common core calculus in applications. The equivalences we present are also valid in other type systems, as long as the key conditions on the usage of names (such as i/o capabilities and receptiveness) are respected. We will point out when this is not the case. In examples we will often use also integer and boolean values.

The notations and terminology for types and typed calculi introduced in Part III (see in particular Sections 6.1 and 6.6) will also be important for this Part. We recall that the phrase 'simply-typed π-calculus' refers to any typed π-calculus that does not use the advanced type constructs for subtyping, linearity, receptiveness and polymorphism; that is, only the types presented in Chapter 6 are used. The main reason for separating these π-calculi from π-calculi with richer types is that the behavioural theory of the former is a straightforward extension of that of the untyped π-calculus, but this is not the case when the more advanced types are admitted. In examples, we often omit type annotations from restrictions. Also, if a name a carries values of `unit` type, we sometimes omit the object part of output and input prefixes at a, writing for instance $\overline{a}.\, P$ and $a.\, P$.

Structure of the Part The structure of this Part mirrors that of the previous one. Thus there are three chapters. Chapter 9 serves both as an introduction to the Part, and as a presentation of essential technical concepts. In Sections 9.1 and 9.2 we discuss informally the usefulness of types for reasoning. In Section 9.3 we exploit the sort system to derive a security property; this is an example of the behavioural consequences of a type system, such as the sorting, in which type equality is by name. Elsewhere we follow the by-structure approach, as in Part III. In Section 9.4 we present the typed version of the most important behavioural equivalences and preorders studied in the book, in particular barbed congruence, bisimilarity, and full bisimilarity. In Section 9.5 we examine these relations in simply-typed π-calculi.

In Chapter 10 we discuss the effect of the i/o types on behavioural equivalences, and we present proof techniques for proving typed equivalences. In Chapter 11 we do the same for the more advanced type systems: linearity, receptiveness, and polymorphism.

9

Groundwork

9.1 Using types to obtain encapsulation

It is desirable that a language, whether sequential or parallel, should have facilities for encapsulation, that is, features that make it possible to constrain access to components such as data and resources. The need for encapsulation led to the development of abstract data types. Encapsulation is also a key feature of objects in object-oriented languages.

In CCS, encapsulation is achieved by the *restriction* operator. Restricting a name x on a process P, written (using π-calculus notation) $\boldsymbol{\nu} x\, P$, guarantees that interactions along x between subcomponents of P occur without interference from outside. For instance, suppose we have two 1-place buffers, *Buf1* and *Buf2*. Suppose *Buf1* receives values along a name x and resends them along y, whereas *Buf2* receives at y and resends at z. They can be composed into a 2-place buffer that receives at x and resends at z thus: $\boldsymbol{\nu} y\,(\mathit{Buf1} \mid \mathit{Buf2})$. Here, the restriction ensures that actions at y from *Buf1* and *Buf2* are not consumed by the external environment. With the formal definitions of *Buf1* and *Buf2* at hand, one can indeed prove that the system $\boldsymbol{\nu} y\,(\mathit{Buf1} \mid \mathit{Buf2})$ is behaviourally equivalent to a 2-place buffer.

The restriction operator provides a quite satisfactory level of protection in CCS, where the visibility of names in processes is fixed. By contrast, restriction alone is very often not satisfactory in the π-calculus, where the visibility of names can change dynamically. Here are two examples.

Example 9.1.1 (A printer with mobile ownership) Consider a situation in which several client processes cooperate in the use of a shared resource such as a printer. Data are sent for printing by the client processes along a name p. Clients can also communicate name p so that new clients can get access to the printer. Suppose that initially there are two clients

$$\begin{aligned} \mathit{C1} &\stackrel{\text{def}}{=} \overline{p}j_1.\overline{p}j_2 \\ \mathit{C2} &\stackrel{\text{def}}{=} \overline{b}p \end{aligned}$$

and therefore, writing P for the printer process, the initial system is

$$\nu p\ (P \mid \mathit{C1} \mid \mathit{C2}).$$

One might wish to prove that when *C1*'s print jobs, represented by j_1 and j_2, are delivered, they are received and processed in that order by the printer. Unfortunately this is false: a misbehaving new client *C3* that has obtained p from *C2* can disrupt the protocol expected by P and *C1* just by reading print requests from p and throwing them away:

$$\mathit{C3} \stackrel{\text{def}}{=} b(p).\ !p(j)\ .$$

□

Example 9.1.2 (A boolean package implementation) A *package* is a structure that provides implementations of a set of values and a set of operators for manipulating, or obtaining information about, those values (for example, finding out whether two values are equal). It is intended that the clients of the package will use the values *only* via the operators provided in the package.

For an even more dramatic example of the unsatisfactory protection given by the restriction operator in the π-calculus, consider a π-calculus representation of a small boolean package:

$$\mathit{BoolPack1} \stackrel{\text{def}}{=} (\boldsymbol{\nu} t, f, \mathit{test}\,)\Big(\ \begin{array}{l} \overline{\mathit{getBool}}\langle t, f, \mathit{test}\rangle \\ \mid t(x,y).\,\overline{x} \\ \mid f(x,y).\,\overline{y} \\ \mid \mathit{test}(b,x,y).\,\overline{b}\langle x,y\rangle \end{array}\ \Big).$$

The package provides an implementation of the values true and false, and of a test function that can be interrogated to learn whether a boolean value is true or false. As seen in Section 3.4, in the π-calculus a boolean value is implemented as a process located at a certain name; above the name is t for the value true and f for the value false. (To make things simpler, the values are ephemeral, i.e., not replicated.) The process implementing true receives two names and signals on the first, while the process implementing false receives two names and signals on the second. The test function is located at *test*, where it receives three arguments: the location b of a boolean value, and two return names x and y; it interacts with the boolean located at b and, depending on whether this is true or false, an answer is produced at x or y. Other functionalities, such as and, or and not functions, can be added to the package in a similar way.

A client can use the package by reading at *getBool* the names t, f and *test*. After this, what remains of the package is

$$\begin{aligned} & t(x,y).\overline{x} \\ & \mid f(x,y).\overline{y} \\ & \mid test(b,x,y).\overline{b}\langle x,y\rangle . \end{aligned}$$

But now the implementation of the package is completely uncovered! A misbehaving client has free access to the internal representation of the components. It may interfere with these components, by attempting to read from t, f or *test*. It may also send at *test* a tuple of names the first of which is not the location of a boolean value. For these reasons, an observer can distinguish the package *BoolPack1* from the package

$$BoolPack2 \stackrel{\text{def}}{=} (\boldsymbol{\nu} t, f, test)\Big(\begin{aligned} & \overline{getBool}\langle t, f, test\rangle \\ & \mid t(x,y).\overline{y} \\ & \mid f(x,y).\overline{x} \\ & \mid test(b,x,y).\overline{b}\langle y,x\rangle \end{aligned} \Big).$$

BoolPack2 has a different internal representation of the boolean values – the true process responds on the second of the two return names, rather than on the first, and dually for the false process – and of the test function. □

In each of the examples, the protection of the resource fails if access to it is transmitted, because no assumptions can be made about *how* a recipient may access it. Simple and powerful encapsulation barriers against the mobility of names can be created using the type systems examined in the previous sections, however. We discuss the two examples.

The misbehaving printer client *C3* of Example 9.1.1 can be excluded by separating the input and output capabilities of a name, that is, by adopting the i/o *types* of Section 7.1. It suffices that the printer has only the input capability on name p, and the initial clients *C1* and *C2* only the output capability. In this way, new clients that receive p from existing clients will receive only the output capability on p. The misbehaving *C3* is thus ruled out as ill-typed, as it uses p in input.

On the other hand, the *polymorphic types* of Section 8.3 can be used in the boolean package *BoolPack1* to hide the implementation details of the components. We can make the name *getBool* polymorphic by abstracting away the type of the boolean names t and f. This forces a well-typed observer to use t and f *only* as arguments of the *test* function. The observer cannot, for instance, communicate along t or f; the observer can access the boolean package only through the operations that have been explicitly provided, such as *test*. Indeed, using polymorphism the package *BoolPack1* is indistinguishable from the package *BoolPack2*. By 'indistinguishable', we mean that no well-typed observer can tell the difference between the two packages by interacting with them. This equivalence will be proved in Section 11.3.1.

In an untyped π-calculus, or in a simply-typed π-calculus, the packages *BoolPack1* and *BoolPack2* are not behaviourally equivalent, for good reasons: they have several quite different traces of actions. For instance,

$$\overline{getBool}\langle t, f, test\rangle, t\langle x, y\rangle, \overline{x}$$

is a trace of *BoolPack1* but not of *BoolPack2*.

Exercise 9.1.3 Define a context C of a simply-typed π-calculus that distinguishes *BoolPack1* from *BoolPack2* (that is, is such that $C[BoolPack1]$ and $C[BoolPack2]$ are not barbed bisimilar). □

Similarly, with polymorphism we can make *BoolPack1* equivalent to the package *BoolPack3* obtained from *BoolPack1* by replacing the line implementing the conditional test with

$$test(b, x, y).\,([b = t]\overline{b}\langle x, y\rangle + [b = f]\overline{b}\langle x, y\rangle)\,. \tag{9.1}$$

Now the test function acts when interrogated only if the first argument is t or f. This new package is equivalent to *BoolPack1* because the value received at *test* for b is always either t or f. This example shows that a client of the package is not authorized to make up new values of the abstracted type (the type of t and f), since the client knows nothing about this type. Again, this equivalence goes well beyond those that are valid in an untyped or simply-typed π-calculus. The example can be made even more striking using mismatching (whose typing rules are the same as for matching). *BoolPack1* remains equivalent to *BoolPack3* if (9.1) is

$$test(b, x, y).\,([b = t]\overline{b}\langle x, y\rangle + [b = f]\overline{b}\langle x, y\rangle + [b \neq t][b \neq f]BAD)$$

where BAD can be any process.

9.2 Why types for reasoning?

Type systems can be used to guarantee safety properties. The most basic safety property is of course type soundness, i.e., absence of run-time errors, studied in Part III. Examples 9.1.1 and 9.1.2, however, show more refined properties: types can prevent undesirable interactions among processes – even if these interactions would not produce run-time errors – thus guaranteeing that certain *security* constraints are not violated. In Example 9.1.1 the security constraint is that the jobs of clients to the printer are not stolen by other processes; in Example 9.1.2 the security constraint is that the implementation details of the package are not made visible to clients. Another example is given in Section 9.3.

Such security constraints are achieved because types give us (some) control over interference among processes. This is important: interference is, notoriously, a major problem in concurrency; in mobile systems, where the process topology may change dynamically, the problem is particularly delicate. This control has several benefits for reasoning. First, types reduce the number of legal contexts in which a given process can be tested. The consequence is that desirable behavioural equalities hold that would otherwise fail. Examples of this have been given in Section 9.1; other examples are in the remainder of this Part. The equalities considered in these examples fail without the appropriate types because there are contexts that are able to detect the difference between the processes concerned. With types, these contexts are ruled out as ill-typed, and the processes are indistinguishable in the remaining well-typed contexts.

Secondly, types facilitate reasoning, by allowing the use of certain proof techniques or simplifying their application. For instance, we will see that linear and receptive types guarantee that certain communications are not preemptive. This is a partial confluence property, in the presence of which only parts of process behaviours need be explored.

Another way types are useful for reasoning is in limiting the explosion in the number of derivatives of a process. To see why this can be a serious problem, consider a process $a(x).\,P$. In the untyped π-calculus, its behaviour is determined by the set of all derivatives $P\{b/x\}$, where b ranges over the free names of P plus a fresh one. In the case of a cascade of inputs, as in $a_1(x_1).\,\ldots\,.\,a_n(x_n).\,P$, this gives rise to state explosion, which can make the analysis of the behaviour of a process very tedious. The number of legal derivatives of processes can be reduced using types. For instance, in Example 9.1.2 of the boolean package *BoolPack1*, having polymorphic types we know that the *only* names that can be received as first argument of the test function are t and f.

9.3 A security property

In this section we apply the sort system (Section 3.1) to derive a *security* property of processes. The calculus we work with here is therefore the sorted polyadic π-calculus of Section 3.1. The sort system, in which type equality is by name, allows us to make fine-grained separations among names. This feature allows us to obtain a more powerful result than we would obtain with a by-structure type equality (Exercise 9.3.3). See Remark 9.4.9 for another example.

The property that we derive says that a certain name will always remain private to a given process. This name can be thought of as a secret, which the process is not supposed to reveal to the outside.

We consider processes of the form $\boldsymbol{\nu}a\, P$, in which the outermost restricted name a is the secret. (We consider only processes of this form for simplicity; the results can be generalized to arbitrary processes.) We say that the well-sorted process $\boldsymbol{\nu}a\, P$ *does not leak* if no derivative of this process performs an output action in which a is exported. Formally, $\boldsymbol{\nu}a P$ does not leak if there is no sequence of transitions

$$\boldsymbol{\nu}a\, P \xrightarrow{\alpha_1} P_1 \cdots P_{n-1} \xrightarrow{\alpha_n} P_n \qquad (n \geq 1),$$

in which the last rule in the transition derivation of $P_{n-1} \xrightarrow{\alpha_n} P_n$ (taking $P_0 \stackrel{\text{def}}{=} P$) is OPEN. Were OPEN used as the last rule, the name in the outermost restriction would be exported. We assume that, as the initial process is well sorted, all input transitions are well sorted too, that is, the names received in the inputs are of sorts compatible with those of the subjects of the inputs (analogous to the condition of clause (2b) in the Subject Reduction Theorem 6.3.7). This ensures that well-sortedness is preserved under transition. (This assumption on input transitions could be removed, however.)

Theorem 9.3.1 specifies a condition under which $\boldsymbol{\nu}a\, P$ does not leak. This property is trivially true if a occurs only in subject position in P. The strength of the theorem is that it can also be applied to processes that communicate a; of course, in this case the names along which a is sent will themselves be private names of $\boldsymbol{\nu}a\, P$.

Let Σ be the sorting that $\boldsymbol{\nu}a\, P$ respects. We write $\gamma \in \Sigma(\delta)$ if the sort γ is in the object sort of δ; that is, if names in γ can be communicated along names in δ, possibly as part of a tuple of names. Now, if T is a set of sorts, then $\mathcal{OS}(\mathsf{T})$ are the object sorts of T, that is

$$\mathcal{OS}(\mathsf{T}) \stackrel{\text{def}}{=} \{\gamma \mid \gamma \in \Sigma(\delta), \text{ for some } \delta \in \mathsf{T}\}.$$

The operation *ObComp* adds the object sorts to a given set of sorts:

$$\mathit{ObComp}(\mathsf{T}) \stackrel{\text{def}}{=} \mathsf{T} \cup \mathcal{OS}(\mathsf{T}).$$

Let $\{a_1, \ldots, a_r\}$ be the free names of $\boldsymbol{\nu}a\, P$, with a_i of sort γ_i, $1 \leq i \leq r$, and let S be their object sorts:

$$\mathsf{S} \stackrel{\text{def}}{=} \mathcal{OS}(\{\gamma_1, \ldots, \gamma_r\}).$$

Finally, the *sort completion* of $\nu a\, P$ is the smallest set T of sorts that includes S and is closed under *ObComp*, that is, $ObComp(\mathsf{T}) \subseteq \mathsf{T}$.

Theorem 9.3.1 Suppose $\nu a\, P$ respects Σ and $a : \gamma$, and let T be the sort completion of $\nu a\, P$. If $\gamma \notin \mathsf{T}$ then $\nu a\, P$ does not leak. □

Exercise 9.3.2 Prove Theorem 9.3.1. (Hint: recall that well-sortedness is preserved under transition.) □

A similar theorem can be formulated using a type system where type equality is by structure, such as the type systems of Part III (Exercise 9.3.3). However, the by-name equality of the sorting gives us, in general, a more powerful theorem. For instance, the by-structure version of the theorem does not apply to processes $\nu a P$ in which the type of a happens – accidentally – to be a subterm of the type of one of the free names of $\nu a P$. These accidental coincidences are avoided with a by-name equality.

Exercise 9.3.3 Here is the analogue of Theorem 9.3.1 for $\pi^{\mathtt{unit},\sharp,\times}$ (where type equality is by structure). Suppose $\Gamma \vdash (\nu a : T)\, P$. Prove that if there is no b on which Γ is defined such that T is a subterm of $\Gamma(b)$, then $(\nu a : T)\, P$ does not leak. □

The property that a process does not leak is undecidable (see Exercise 18.3.20), and hence the conditions in Theorem 9.3.1 and Exercise 9.3.3 are sufficient but not necessary.

9.4 Typed behavioural equivalences

In this section we present the typed versions of barbed congruence and labelled equivalences and preorders. As in the untyped case, so in typed π-calculi barbed congruence will be our principal behavioural equivalence, and the labelled relations, in particular bisimilarity and full bisimilarity, will serve as proof techniques for it. We define only the weak equivalences, and (as elsewhere in the book) we usually omit the adjective 'weak'. The differences between weak and strong relations, in definitions and notations, are as in the untyped π-calculus. The definitions are given for a generic process calculus $\mathcal{L}$. We assume that typing and the transitions for the terms of $\mathcal{L}$ are of the same form as in the π-calculus. For instance, typing judgments for processes and values are of the forms $\mathcal{L} \triangleright \Gamma \vdash P : \diamond$ and $\mathcal{L} \triangleright \Gamma \vdash v : T$.

9.4.1 Typed barbed congruence

We concentrate on typed barbed congruence and ignore typed barbed equivalence, because the congruence is more interesting as a behavioural equivalence and is technically more difficult.

Definition 9.4.1 Let Γ and Δ be type environments of $\mathcal{L}$. We say that Γ *extends* Δ if $\mathsf{supp}(\Delta) \subseteq \mathsf{supp}(\Gamma)$ and $\mathcal{L} \triangleright \Gamma \vdash x : \Delta(x)$ for all $x \in \mathsf{supp}(\Delta)$. □

Intuitively, if a type environment Γ extends Δ, then Γ agrees with the type assignments and variables in Δ; the support of Γ may however be larger. Note that:

- the condition $\mathsf{supp}(\Delta) \subseteq \mathsf{supp}(\Gamma)$ is a requirement both on names and on type variables, the latter requirement being $\mathsf{varpart}(\Delta) \subseteq \mathsf{varpart}(\Gamma)$ (type environments have a variable part if there is polymorphism, Section 8.3)
- if there is subtyping, $\mathcal{L} \triangleright \Gamma \vdash x : \Delta(x)$ holds iff $\Gamma(x) \leq \Delta(x)$
- without subtyping and polymorphism, the above definition says that $\Gamma(x)$ and $\Delta(x)$ are equal (or type equivalent, if types can be recursive) for all x on which Δ is defined.

Exercise 9.4.2 If $\Delta \vdash P$ and Γ extends Δ, then also $\Gamma \vdash P$. Show this for $\pi^{\times,\mu,\mathsf{i/o}}$ and $\pi^{\mathtt{unit},\sharp,\exists}$. □

To express well-typed quantification over contexts we introduce the notion of (Γ/Δ)-context. A (Γ/Δ)-context, when filled with a process well typed in Δ, becomes a process well typed in Γ. The typing Γ may contain names not in Δ; for instance, Γ may have free names that do not appear in the process. The converse might be true too, because of binders in the context that embrace the hole. For instance, if $\Gamma \stackrel{\text{def}}{=} \{a : \sharp T\}$ and $\Delta \stackrel{\text{def}}{=} \{c : T\,,\, b : S\}$ then $C \stackrel{\text{def}}{=} a(c).\,(\boldsymbol{\nu} b : S)\,[\cdot]$ is a (Γ/Δ)-context. Any process P that goes in the hole of C must respect the types T and S for the names b and c, in addition to $\sharp T$ for a. If C is a (Γ/Δ)-context then the type environment Γ' obtained from Γ by scanning the context from the outside towards the hole and keeping track of the binders met along the way is an extension of Δ.

Definition 9.4.3 ((Γ/Δ)-context) Let Γ and Δ be type environments of $\mathcal{L}$. We say that C is a (Γ/Δ)-*context* if $\mathcal{L} \triangleright \Gamma \vdash C : \diamond$ is a valid type judgment in $\mathcal{L}$ when the hole $[\cdot]$ of C is considered as a process and the following typing rule for $[\cdot]$ is added to the rules of $\mathcal{L}$:

$$\text{T-}\Delta\text{-HOLE}\quad \frac{\Theta \text{ extends } \Delta}{\Theta \vdash [\cdot] : \diamond}$$

(In the rule, Δ is a fixed type environment and Θ is a metavariable over type environments.) □

Exercise 9.4.4 If C is a (Γ/Δ)-context and $\Delta \vdash P$, then $\Gamma \vdash C[P]$. Show this for $\pi^{\times,\mu,\mathsf{i/o}}$. □

We need not redefine barbed bisimilarity, because types do not affect the transition relations or the observation predicates:

Lemma 9.4.5 Suppose that $\mathcal{L} \triangleright \Gamma_i \vdash P_i$, where each Γ_i is closed, and the processes P_i and Q_i differ only in their typing annotations, for $i = 1, 2$. Then $P_1 \dot{\approx} P_2$ iff $Q_1 \dot{\approx} Q_2$.

Proof Types do not play a role in reductions. □

It makes sense, however, to consider barbed bisimilarity only on processes that are closed and that are well typed in the same type environment. This explains the definition of barbed congruence in terms of (Γ/Δ)-contexts with Γ closed:

Definition 9.4.6 (Typed barbed congruence) Let Δ be a typing, with $\mathcal{L} \triangleright \Delta \vdash P, Q$. We say that processes P, Q are *barbed congruent at Δ (in $\mathcal{L}$)*, written $\mathcal{L}(\Delta) \triangleright P \cong^{\mathrm{c}} Q$, if, for each closed type environment Γ and (Γ/Δ)-context C, we have $C[P] \dot{\approx} C[Q]$. □

The subject reduction theorems for closed typings in Part III ensure that a closed typing is preserved by τ transitions. Therefore $C[P] \dot{\approx} C[Q]$ can be established using a barbed bisimulation in which all processes in the pairs are well typed in the same type environment. When there is no ambiguity about what the calculus $\mathcal{L}$ is, we may drop $\mathcal{L}$, and abbreviate $\mathcal{L}(\Delta) \triangleright P \cong^{\mathrm{c}} Q$ as $\Delta \triangleright P \cong^{\mathrm{c}} Q$. We write $\mathcal{L}(\Delta) \triangleright P \cong^{\mathrm{c}} Q$ and $\Delta \triangleright P \cong^{\mathrm{c}} Q$ without recalling the assumption that P and Q are well typed in Δ.

Lemma 9.4.7 (Weakening, Strengthening, and Narrowing for typed barbed congruence) Suppose $\mathcal{L}(\Delta) \triangleright P \cong^{\mathrm{c}} Q$.

(1) If $a \notin \mathsf{supp}(\Delta)$ then also $\mathcal{L}(\Delta, a : S) \triangleright P \cong^{\mathrm{c}} Q$, for all S.
(2) If $a \notin \mathsf{fn}(P, Q)$ then also $\mathcal{L}(\Delta - a) \triangleright P \cong^{\mathrm{c}} Q$.
(3) Suppose in $\mathcal{L}$ there is subtyping, $\Delta = \Delta', a : S$, and $T \leq S$. Then also $\mathcal{L}(\Delta', a : T) \triangleright P \cong^{\mathrm{c}} Q$.

Proof Assertions (1) and (3) hold because if Δ_1 extends Δ_2 then a (Γ/Δ_1)-context is also a (Γ/Δ_2)-context. □

The converse of Lemma 9.4.7(3) does not hold; see Exercise 10.2.7.

We study the effect of types on behavioural equivalences in Section 9.5 and in Chapters 10 and 11. We can already make some simple observations, however, in preparation for that. The following example shows that types have semantic consequences, as soon as the type system is non-trivial and names can be communicated.

Example 9.4.8 Let

$$\begin{aligned} P &\stackrel{\text{def}}{=} a(b).\,(\bar{b}v.\,\mathbf{0} \mid c(z).\,\mathbf{0}) \\ Q &\stackrel{\text{def}}{=} a(b).\,(\bar{b}v.\,c(z).\,\mathbf{0} + c(z).\,\bar{b}v.\,\mathbf{0})\,. \end{aligned}$$

In the untyped calculus P and Q are not behaviourally equivalent, because if the name received at a is c then P, but not Q, can silently terminate. This difference of behaviour is no longer possible if b and c have different types, because b cannot then be instantiated to c; as a consequence, the two processes become behaviourally equivalent. For instance, if S is `Bool` and T is `Int` and v is a truth-value, then in any typed π-calculus we have:

$$a : \sharp\sharp S\,,\; c : \sharp T \triangleright P \cong^{\mathrm{c}} Q\,.$$

□

Types prevent names of different types being identified, something that reminds us of the behavioural effects of *distinctions* (Section 4.1).

Remark 9.4.9 (By-name versus by-structure) In Example 9.4.8, if the types S and T are the same, then P and Q are not equivalent, for the same reason that they are not equivalent in the untyped π-calculus. We can separate P and Q even if b and c carry values of the same type if we use a *by-name* approach to type equivalence, as in the sort system of Section 3.1. To distinguish P and Q it suffices to assign different sorts, γ_b and γ_c say, to b and c, and to take γ_b as the object sort of the sort of a. □

On the other hand, behavioural equivalences that are true in the untyped π-calculus remain true when types are added, because in the untyped case names are used in a completely unconstrained way. Consequently, in typed π-calculi we will freely refer to the basic laws of the untyped calculus, for instance the Expansion Lemma, on the understanding that we are using their typed versions.

For similar reasons, behavioural equivalences are preserved by refinements of types, provided that the refinement preserves typing judgments. By 'refinement' we mean a replacement of types with more precise types. For instance the i/o types are a refinement of the connection type, and the linear types are a refinement of the i/o types. We will prove one result of this kind in Section 10.1, refining the connection type with the i/o types, and another one in Section 11.1 for the linear types.

9.4.2 Typed labelled equivalences and preorders

In the untyped π-calculus we have introduced labelled bisimilarities and their congruences as proof techniques for barbed congruence. In this section we extend the idea of labelled bisimilarity – every action of a process should be matched by a bisimilar process with syntactically the same action and the derivatives should be again bisimilar – to the typed case. The extension is easy; the main points to notice are:

- in the input clause of bisimulation, the value that a process receives should be of a type compatible with that of the name at which the input is made
- some types (linear and receptive types) have to be coerced before applying the definition
- in general, typed full bisimilarity is not a complete proof technique for typed barbed congruence; the latter may be strictly coarser.

We show only the extensions of the definitions of bisimilarity and full bisimilarity. The same extensions can be made for other labelled relations. In the book, we will sometimes use *typed expansion* and *typed expansion precongruence*; we omit the definitions.

9.4.2.1 Typed bisimilarity

A *typed $\mathcal{L}$-relation* is a set of triples $(\Delta \,;\, P \,;\, Q)$ where Δ is a closed typing and $\mathcal{L} \triangleright \Delta \vdash P, Q$. We say that Γ is a *closed extension* of Δ if Γ is closed and extends Δ. In clause (1b) below, '$\mathcal{L} \triangleright \Gamma \vdash a : S$ and $\mathcal{O}(S) = T$' means that a can carry values of type T. (As usual, if there are recursive types, replace $\mathcal{O}(S) = T$ with $\mathcal{O}(S) \sim_{\text{type}} T$.)

Definition 9.4.10 (Typed bisimilarity) *Typed $\mathcal{L}$-bisimilarity* is the largest symmetric typed $\mathcal{L}$-relation $\mathcal{R}$ such that $(\Delta \,;\, P \,;\, Q) \in \mathcal{R}$ implies:

(1) whenever

(a) Γ is a closed extension of Δ

(b) $\mathcal{L} \triangleright \Gamma \vdash a : S$ and $\mathcal{O}(S) = T$ and $\mathcal{L} \triangleright \Gamma \vdash v : T$

(c) $P \xrightarrow{av} P'$

there is Q' such that $Q \stackrel{av}{\Longrightarrow} Q'$ and $(\Gamma \,;\, P' \,;\, Q') \in \mathcal{R}$

(2) whenever $P \xrightarrow{(\nu \widetilde{b}:\widetilde{T})\,\overline{a}v} P'$ there is Q' such that $Q \xRightarrow{(\nu \widetilde{b}:\widetilde{T})\,\overline{a}v} Q'$ and $(\Delta\, , \widetilde{b} : \widetilde{T}\ ; P'\ ; Q') \in \mathcal{R}$

(3) whenever $P \xrightarrow{\tau} P'$ there is Q' such that $Q \Longrightarrow Q'$ and $(\Delta\ ; P'\ ; Q') \in \mathcal{R}$.

Let Δ be a closed typing with $\mathcal{L} \rhd \Delta \vdash P, Q$. We say that P and Q are *typed bisimilar at* Δ *(in* $\mathcal{L}$*)*, written $\mathcal{L}(\Delta) \rhd P \approx Q$, if $(\Delta\ ;\ P\ ;\ Q)$ is in some typed $\mathcal{L}$-bisimulation. □

We adopt for typed bisimilarity the same conventions as for typed barbed congruence; for instance we abbreviate $\mathcal{L}(\Delta) \rhd P \approx Q$ to $\Delta \rhd P \approx Q$ if $\mathcal{L}$ is clear, and then we simply talk of 'typed bisimilarity'.

Remark 9.4.11 (Typed bisimilarity with linearity and receptiveness) For Definition 9.4.10 to make sense, in clause (1) the hypotheses should imply $\Gamma \vdash P', Q'$, and similarly in clause (2). This is true in all type systems we have seen, except those with linearity or receptiveness. For instance, if a is a linear name, then an action on a removes a capability from the type environment. (There are other reasons why the above definition does not make much sense with linearity and receptiveness; for instance there is no split of type environment in clause (1b).) The definition may however still be useful for type systems with linearity and receptiveness: it suffices to coerce all linear and receptive types to connection types before applying the definition. For instance, types $\ell_{\natural}\, T$ and $\omega\mathrm{rec}_{\sharp}\, T$, where T does not contain linear or receptive types, are coerced to $\sharp\, T$. The reason why this may be useful is that bisimilarity is a proof technique for barbed congruence, and two processes are barbed congruent if their type-coerced versions are barbed congruent (see Exercise 11.1.1(2)). □

9.4.2.2 Typed full bisimilarity

In typed bisimilarity we compare closed process. To be able to compare arbitrary well-typed processes, and to have a behavioural relation that is a full congruence, we introduce *typed full bisimilarity*. This equates processes whose bisimilarity is preserved by all well-typed substitutions, that is, substitutions that map names onto values of the same type.

Definition 9.4.12 Let Γ and Δ be type environments of $\mathcal{L}$, and σ a substitution from names to values of $\mathcal{L}$. We say that σ is a Δ*-to-*Γ *substitution (in* $\mathcal{L}$*)* if

(1) for all x on which Δ is defined, $\mathcal{L} \rhd \Gamma \vdash \sigma(x) : \Delta(x)$

(2) $\mathsf{varpart}(\Delta) \subseteq \mathsf{varpart}(\Gamma)$. □

In Definition 9.4.12, the value $\sigma(x)$ is constructed using the names in Γ. The type of this value in Γ is the same as that of the original name x in Δ. More generally, the definition of Δ-to-Γ substitution is such that any expression that has a type T in Δ will maintain this type in Γ after the application of the substitution σ:

Lemma 9.4.13 If σ is a Δ-to-Γ substitution in $\mathcal{L}$ and $\mathcal{L} \triangleright \Delta \vdash E : T$, then $\mathcal{L} \triangleright \Gamma \vdash E\sigma : T$. □

Leaving aside linearity and receptiveness, the property of Lemma 9.4.13 holds in all typed π-calculi in the book. (The problem with linearity and receptiveness is that the typing rules for names are not the only ones to look up the content of the type environment; we have pointed out in Remark 9.4.11 that typed bisimilarity does not work with linearity and receptiveness.)

Exercise 9.4.14 Prove Lemma 9.4.13, in $\pi^{\mathtt{unit},\sharp,\times}$. □

We give the definition of full bisimilarity only on ground type environments (that is, without free type variables): the definition is simpler and is sufficient for all our uses of full bisimilarity in the book.

Definition 9.4.15 (Typed full bisimilarity for ground typing) Suppose $\mathcal{L} \triangleright \Delta \vdash P, Q$ and Δ is ground. We say that P and Q are *typed full bisimilar at* Δ *(in* $\mathcal{L}$*)*, written $\mathcal{L}(\Delta) \triangleright P \approx^{\mathrm{c}} Q$, if for each closed Γ, and for each Δ-to-Γ substitution σ, it holds that $\mathcal{L}(\Gamma) \triangleright P\sigma \approx Q\sigma$. □

In Definition 9.4.15, Lemma 9.4.13 guarantees that $\mathcal{L} \triangleright \Gamma \vdash P\sigma, Q\sigma$. As usual, when possible we abbreviate $\mathcal{L}(\Delta) \triangleright P \approx^{\mathrm{c}} Q$ as $\Delta \triangleright P \approx^{\mathrm{c}} Q$.

Remark 9.4.16 In the case Δ itself is closed, the above definition involves a substitution of names for names as in the untyped case. Thus in a typed presentation of the untyped π-calculus, as outlined in Section 6.7, typed full bisimilarity is the same as the untyped relation. □

9.4.2.3 Properties of the typed labelled relations

Typed bisimilarity and full bisimilarity have congruence properties similar to the untyped relations. As a consequence, typed full bisimilarity is sound for typed barbed congruence. Soundness is very useful; it can be used to establish many important properties for barbed congruence. For instance, all proofs of laws of the untyped π-calculus that use the labelled relations, e.g., the law $!P \simeq^{\mathrm{c}} !P \mid !P$, carry over to the typed case.

Strengthening and weakening properties analogous to those for barbed congruence (Lemma 9.4.7) hold for bisimilarity and full bisimilarity too. (Narrowing also holds; but with respect to Lemma 9.4.7 the order of subtyping between S and T is reversed; narrowing on bisimilarity is however less often useful.)

Remark 9.4.17 Also the theory of *progressions* and *safe functions* of Section 2.3 can be lifted up to typed calculi. In addition to the typed versions of the safe functions presented in Section 2.3, other useful safe functions can be defined that allow manipulation of the type environments in the triples of a typed bisimulation. We mention one of them, the *strengthening function*, *Strength*:

$$Strength(\mathcal{R}) \stackrel{\text{def}}{=} \{(\Delta - a\ ;\ P\ ;\ Q) \mid (\Delta\ ;\ P\ ;\ Q) \in \mathcal{R} \text{ and } a \text{ is not free in } P, Q\}\,.$$

This function gives us a very useful up-to technique: due to clause (1) of Definition 9.4.10, which allows an arbitrary extension of the initial type environment, all non-trivial bisimulations would otherwise be infinite. □

The most important property of the untyped full bisimilarity that may fail in the typed case is the completeness for barbed congruence (on image-finite processes). Completeness holds for the type systems of Sections 6.2–6.7: products, unions, recursive types, etc. But it fails on more sophisticated type systems, such as those with subtyping, linearity, receptiveness, and polymorphism, where typed full bisimilarity is strictly finer than typed barbed congruence. For these type systems we will therefore discuss other proof methods: context lemmas and transformations to the Private π-calculus.

Lemma 9.4.18 gives an example of the congruence properties of the typed labelled relations. The assertions in the lemma are proved in the same ways as the corresponding assertions for the untyped π-calculus.

Lemma 9.4.18 Suppose $\mathcal{L}(\Delta) \triangleright P \approx Q$, and the grammar of $\mathcal{L}$ has the process operators of composition, replication, restriction, matching, and output prefix. We have:

(1) if $\mathcal{L} \triangleright \Delta \vdash R$ then also $\mathcal{L}(\Delta) \triangleright P \mid R \approx Q \mid R$
(2) $\mathcal{L}(\Delta) \triangleright !P \approx !Q$
(3) if $\Delta(a) = T$ then $\mathcal{L}(\Delta - a) \triangleright (\boldsymbol{\nu} a : T)\, P \approx (\boldsymbol{\nu} a : T)\, Q$
(4) if $\mathcal{L} \triangleright \Delta \vdash [a = b]P, [a = b]Q$ then $\mathcal{L}(\Delta) \triangleright [a = b]P \approx [a = b]Q$
(5) if $\mathcal{L} \triangleright \Delta \vdash \overline{a}v.\, P, \overline{a}v.\, Q$ then $\mathcal{L}(\Delta) \triangleright \overline{a}v.\, P \approx \overline{a}v.\, Q$. □

We consider the soundness of full bisimilarity with respect to barbed congruence for $\pi^{\sharp,\times,\mu}$ (Corollary 9.4.20).

Lemma 9.4.19 Suppose $\pi^{\sharp,\times,\mu}(\Delta) \triangleright P \approx^{\mathrm{c}} Q$ and C is a (Γ/Δ)-context. Then also $\pi^{\sharp,\times,\mu}(\Gamma) \triangleright C[P] \approx^{\mathrm{c}} C[Q]$.

Proof By induction on the structure of the context. The most interesting case is when the outermost construct in the context C is a with. Thus suppose $\Delta \triangleright P \approx^{\mathrm{c}} Q$, and $\mathsf{with}\ (x_1, x_2) = v\ \mathsf{do}\ D$ is a (Γ/Δ)-context (for ease of readability we show the proof for a binary, rather than n-ary, with). We want to prove that

$$\Gamma \triangleright \text{with } (x_1, x_2) = v \text{ do } D[P] \approx^{\mathrm{c}} \text{ with } (x_1, x_2) = v \text{ do } D[Q].$$

Let T_i be the type assigned to x_i ($i = 1, 2$) in the derivation of $\Gamma \vdash C$. Let $\Gamma_\star \stackrel{\text{def}}{=} \Gamma, x_1 : T_1, x_2 : T_2$. Then D is a $(\Gamma_\star/\Delta)$-context and, by the induction hypothesis,

$$\Gamma_\star \triangleright D[P] \approx^{\mathrm{c}} D[Q] . \tag{9.2}$$

We have to show that for any closed Γ' and Γ-to-Γ' substitution σ,

$$\Gamma' \triangleright \text{with } (x_1, x_2) = v\sigma \text{ do } (D[P])\sigma \approx \text{ with } (x_1, x_2) = v\sigma \text{ do } (D[Q])\sigma.$$

The first transition of both processes uses the β-reduction rule of the with; moreover, as $v\sigma$ is closed, $v\sigma = \langle v_1, v_2 \rangle$ for some v_1 and v_2. It is therefore sufficient to check that

$$\Gamma' \triangleright (D[P])\sigma\{^{v_1, v_2}/_{x_1, x_2}\} \approx (D[Q])\sigma\{^{v_1, v_2}/_{x_1, x_2}\} .$$

This follows from (9.2), for $\sigma\{^{v_1, v_2}/_{x_1, x_2}\}$ is a $\Gamma_\star$-to-Γ' substitution. The reason why $\sigma\{^{v_1, v_2}/_{x_1, x_2}\}$ is a $\Gamma_\star$-to-Γ' substitution is that σ is a Γ-to-Γ' substitution, and $\Gamma' \vdash v_i : T_i$. The latter holds because since $\Gamma \vdash v : T_1 \times T_2$ and σ is a Γ-to-Γ' substitution, by Exercise 9.4.14, also $\Gamma' \vdash v\sigma : T_1 \times T_2$; hence, by Exercise 7.3.1, $\Gamma' \vdash v_i : T_i$. □

Corollary 9.4.20 $\pi^{\sharp, \times, \mu}(\Delta) \triangleright P \approx^{\mathrm{c}} Q$ implies $\pi^{\sharp, \times, \mu}(\Delta) \triangleright P \cong^{\mathrm{c}} Q$. □

9.4.3 Ground bisimilarity and asynchronous calculi

As in the untyped case, so in typed *asynchronous* π-calculi bisimilarity and full bisimilarity coincide at closed type environments (bisimilarity is defined only on closed type environments). They also coincide with the *ground* version of bisimilarity, in which, as in the untyped case (Definition 4.7.1), no substitutions are required on names of link type in the input clause of bisimilarity. Precisely, in clause (1) of Definition 9.4.10 all names in v should be fresh, i.e., they should not appear free in P or Q. We write $\mathcal{L}(\Delta) \triangleright P \approx_{\mathrm{g}} Q$ if P and Q are typed ground bisimilar at Δ, where P and Q are processes of the calculus $\mathcal{L}$ well typed under Δ, again when possible omitting $\mathcal{L}$ from the notation.

Remark 9.4.21 On typed π-calculi without basic types (i.e., where all atomic values are names), such as $\pi^{\sharp, \times, \mu}$, the definitions of *ground bisimilarity* and *ground expansion* are the same as those on untyped π-calculus. In particular we do not need to look at the type environment in which the processes compared are well typed. The reason is the following. On other typed labelled relations, such as typed bisimilarity, types are needed to make sure that the names received in an input are of types compatible with that of the subject name of the input (clause (1) of Definition 9.4.10). In ground relations, however, the names received in an input are all fresh, so we can implicitly assume that they are of the right types. $\square$

9.5 Equivalences and preorders in simply-typed π-calculi

There are no surprises with behavioural equivalences and preorders in simply-typed π-calculi: all the theory of the untyped π-calculus can be transplanted to these calculi in the expected way. The only points to remember are: the difference between closed and non-closed type environments; substitutions are well typed, in the sense of Definition 9.4.12; and types forbid identification of names of different types, as shown in Example 9.4.8.

It is nevertheless worthwhile to write down the typed version of the Context Lemmas 2.1.19 and 2.4.7. In extensions of simply-typed π-calculi where full bisimilarity is strictly finer than barbed congruence, such as with i/o or polymorphic types, the Context Lemma together with the appropriate subject reduction theorem will yield a valuable proof method for barbed congruence. We present the Context Lemma both for strong and for weak barbed congruence as we will use them both several times.

Definition 9.5.1 Suppose $\Delta \vdash P_1, P_2$. We write $\Delta \triangleright P_1 \cong^{\mathrm{s}} P_2$ if for each closed type environment Γ that extends Δ, each Δ-to-Γ substitution σ, and each process Q such that $\Gamma \vdash Q$, it holds that $Q \mid P_1\sigma \stackrel{\bullet}{\approx} Q \mid P_2\sigma$. $\square$

Again, the strong version of the equivalence, written $\Delta \triangleright P \simeq^{\mathrm{s}} Q$, is defined using $\stackrel{\bullet}{\sim}$ (strong barbed bisimilarity) in place of $\stackrel{\bullet}{\approx}$.

Lemma 9.5.2 (Context Lemma, typed π-calculus) Suppose $\Delta \vdash P, Q$.

(1) $\Delta \triangleright P \simeq^{\mathrm{s}} Q$ if and only if $\Delta \triangleright P \simeq^{\mathrm{c}} Q$
(2) $\Delta \triangleright P \cong^{\mathrm{s}} Q$ if and only if $\Delta \triangleright P \cong^{\mathrm{c}} Q$. $\square$

The proof is similar to that of the Context Lemma for untyped π-calculus. The proof becomes more subtle, however, if subtyping is added; this will be analysed in Section 10.7.

10

Behavioural Effects of i/o Types

In the first half of this chapter, comprising Sections 10.1–10.5, we discuss the consequences of i/o types for behavioural properties of processes. For this, we compare the polyadic π-calculus ($\pi^{\sharp,\times,\mu}$) with the polyadic π-calculus with i/o types ($\pi^{\times,\mu,\mathsf{i/o}}$). In the former calculus the only constraint that types impose is that arities of names must be respected; in the latter, i/o information is also taken into account. In the second half of the chapter, comprising Sections 10.6 to 10.8, we study techniques for proving behavioural equivalences that crucially rely on the i/o constraints.

10.1 Type coercion

We first show that if processes of $\pi^{\times,\mu,\mathsf{i/o}}$ are equivalent when i/o information is forgotten, then they are also equivalent in $\pi^{\times,\mu,\mathsf{i/o}}$, where by 'forgotten' we mean that all i/o types are coerced to connection types. The result is useful because proving equivalences in the π-calculus with only the connection type is easier (for instance, the definition of typed bisimilarity is simpler).

Theorem 10.1.1 Suppose that $\pi^{\times,\mu,\mathsf{i/o}} \rhd \Delta \vdash P, Q$ and that the typing $\Delta_\sharp$ and the processes $P_\sharp$ and $Q_\sharp$ are obtained from the typing Δ and the processes P and Q by coercing all i/o tags in Δ, P, and Q to the tag $\sharp$. Then

(1) $\pi^{\sharp,\times,\mu} \rhd \Delta_\sharp \vdash P_\sharp, Q_\sharp$
(2) $\pi^{\sharp,\times,\mu}(\Delta_\sharp) \rhd P_\sharp \simeq^{c} Q_\sharp$ implies $\pi^{\times,\mu,\mathsf{i/o}}(\Delta) \rhd P \simeq^{c} Q$, and $\pi^{\sharp,\times,\mu}(\Delta_\sharp) \rhd P_\sharp \cong^{c} Q_\sharp$ implies $\pi^{\times,\mu,\mathsf{i/o}}(\Delta) \rhd P \cong^{c} Q$.

Proof Assertion (1) is straightforward. For (2), we consider only $\cong^{c}$; the case of $\simeq^{c}$ is analogous. By definition, $\Delta \rhd P \cong^{c} Q$ holds if, for any closed Γ and (Γ/Δ)-context C, we have $C[P] \mathrel{\dot{\approx}} C[Q]$. Let $C_\sharp$ and $\Gamma_\sharp$ be the context and typing obtained from C and Γ by replacing all i/o tags with $\sharp$. By assertion

(1), $\Gamma_\sharp \vdash C_\sharp[P_\sharp], C_\sharp[Q_\sharp]$. Since $\Delta_\sharp \triangleright P_\sharp \cong^c Q_\sharp$ and $\Gamma_\sharp$ is closed and $C_\sharp$ is a $(\Gamma_\sharp/\Delta_\sharp)$-context, we have $C_\sharp[P_\sharp] \stackrel{\bullet}{\approx} C_\sharp[Q_\sharp]$. Hence $C[P] \stackrel{\bullet}{\approx} C[Q]$ follows from Lemma 9.4.5. □

The reason why Theorem 10.1.1 holds is that in $\pi^{\times,\mu,\mathsf{i/o}}$ the coercion of i/o to connection types preserves type judgments. This may however be false in calculi with a richer subtyping relation:

Exercise* 10.1.2 Show that Theorem 10.1.1(1) fails in $\pi^{\mathtt{unit},\mathrm{records},\mathsf{i/o}}$, where tuple types are replaced by records. □

Most important is the behavioural effect of the refinement of connection types to i/o types. Processes that are distinguishable in $\pi^{\sharp,\times,\mu}$ may become equivalent when types are so refined. The equivalences so gained are often highly desirable. In Section 10.2 we present five concrete examples of such equivalences. Then, in Sections 10.3 and 10.5, we present two very useful results: a law about wire processes in the Asynchronous π-calculus, and the Sharpened Replication Theorems. The equivalences in the examples and the results will be proved in the second half of the chapter. In Section 10.4 we exploit the wire processes and their laws to model the *delayed input* construct, in the Asynchronous π-calculus. More examples of the use of i/o types for reasoning can be found in Parts V and VI; see Theorem 13.2.22 and discussion afterwards, and Remark 15.3.17.

10.2 Examples

Example 10.2.1 (A deadlock) Consider the processes

$$P_1 \stackrel{\text{def}}{=} \boldsymbol{\nu} x\,(\overline{a}x \mid \overline{x}b)$$
$$P_2 \stackrel{\text{def}}{=} \boldsymbol{\nu} x\,\overline{a}x\,.$$

In untyped or simply-typed π-calculi these processes are behaviourally different, for P_1 can exhibit two visible actions but P_2 only one. A context that distinguishes them is

$$C \stackrel{\text{def}}{=} \boldsymbol{\nu} a\,(a(x).\,x(z).\,\overline{c} \mid [\cdot])\,.$$

The two processes are equivalent, however, if only the output capability of names can be transmitted at a. Under this condition the recipient of x can use it only in output. Thus no process can create an input at x and, therefore, the particle $\overline{x}b$ cannot be consumed – it is a deadlocked process. Such a constraint can be imposed using i/o types. Thus in a typed π-calculus with i/o we have

$$a : \sharp\, \mathsf{o}\, S\,,\, b : S \triangleright P_1 \simeq^c P_2\,.$$

(The type annotation for the restricted name x of P_1 and P_2 is $\sharp\, S$.) Under the type $\sharp\,\mathsf{o}\, S$ for a, context C is ill-typed because it uses the name received at a in input. □

Example 10.2.2 (Non-observability of name identities) The processes

$$\begin{aligned} P_1 &\stackrel{\text{def}}{=} (\boldsymbol{\nu} x, y)\,(\overline{a}x \mid \overline{a}y \mid !y.\,Q \mid !x.\,Q) \\ P_2 &\stackrel{\text{def}}{=} (\boldsymbol{\nu} x)\,(\overline{a}x \mid \overline{a}x \mid !x.\,Q) \end{aligned} \tag{10.1}$$

are not equivalent in untyped or simply-typed π-calculi, because P_1 can send two different private names, whereas P_2 can only send the same name twice. For instance, both these contexts distinguish P_1 from P_2:

$$\begin{aligned} C &\stackrel{\text{def}}{=} [\cdot] \mid a(z_1).\,a(z_2).\,[z_1 = z_2]\overline{c} \\ D &\stackrel{\text{def}}{=} [\cdot] \mid a(z_1).\,a(z_2).\,(z_1.\,\overline{c} \mid \overline{z_2})\,. \end{aligned}$$

However, P_1 and P_2 become indistinguishable if only the output capability on names can be communicated at a. For instance C and D are then ill-typed because they use more than the output capabilities on the names received at a. Indeed, in a typed π-calculus with i/o, if $\Gamma \vdash P_1, P_2$ and $\Gamma \vdash a : \mathsf{o}\,\mathsf{o}\,\mathtt{unit}$, then

$$\Gamma \rhd P_1 \simeq^{c} P_2\,.$$

□

Example 10.2.3 (Sharing data) In Section 3.4 we presented two encodings of the natural numbers that differ in the way sharing is accomplished. The two encodings, $[\![.]\!]$ and $\{\![.]\!\}$, and rewritten using the notation of typed calculi, are the same on $\mathtt{zero}$, but differ on succ:

$$\begin{aligned} [\![\mathtt{zero}]\!] = \{\![\mathtt{zero}]\!\} &\stackrel{\text{def}}{=} (x).\,!x(z,s).\,\overline{z} \\ [\![\mathsf{succ}\; n]\!] &\stackrel{\text{def}}{=} (x).\,\boldsymbol{\nu} y\,(!x(z,s).\,\overline{s}y \mid [\![n]\!]y) \\ \{\![\mathsf{succ}\; n]\!\} &\stackrel{\text{def}}{=} (x).\,!x(z,s).\,\boldsymbol{\nu} y\,(\overline{s}y \mid \{\![n]\!\}y)\,. \end{aligned}$$

The first encoding of $\mathsf{succ}\, n$ uses a single copy of n and a single access name for it. The second encoding, by contrast, creates a new copy of n and a new access name each time it is used (because $\{\![n]\!\}y$ and the restriction on y are underneath the replication at x). We observed in Section 3.4 that the two encodings are not equivalent in the untyped or polyadic π-calculus. They become indistinguishable, however, if only the output capability of the access names is transmitted. First, we have to understand how to type the encodings using i/o types. Let

$$T \stackrel{\text{def}}{=} \mu X.\,\mathsf{o}\,(\mathsf{o}\,\mathtt{unit} \times \mathsf{o}\,X)$$

and

$$T^{\leftarrow\sharp} \stackrel{\mathrm{def}}{=} \sharp\,(\mathtt{o}\,\mathtt{unit} \times \mathtt{o}\,T)$$

(the type obtained by unfolding T once and then changing its outermost i/o tag into $\sharp$). Annotating the restricted name y in $[\![\mathsf{succ}\,n]\!]$ and $\{\![\mathsf{succ}\,n]\!\}$ with $T^{\leftarrow\sharp}$, we obtain, for all n, the type judgments

$$x : T^{\leftarrow\sharp} \vdash [\![n]\!]x, \{\![n]\!\}x$$

and the behavioural equivalence

$$\pi^{\mathtt{unit},\times,\mu,\mathsf{i/o}}(x : T^{\leftarrow\sharp}) \rhd [\![n]\!]x \simeq^{\mathrm{c}} \{\![n]\!\}x\,.$$

□

Example 10.2.4 (Functional programming) This example uses i/o types to prove a behavioural property of functional programs written as mobile processes. The example also gives us some intuition about how functions can be modelled in π-calculus, a topic developed in Part VI. The example uses integers, with standard operations on them, and an `if-then-else` construct. Also, for readability, we sometimes add angle brackets around the objects of output prefixes.

We consider π-calculus representations of the factorial function. The function can be interrogated using the name f. Each interrogation involves two arguments: an integer x and a return name r; the function returns the factorial of x at r. The following can be regarded as a specification of the service:

$$\mathit{SPEC} \stackrel{\mathrm{def}}{=} !f(x,r).\,\overline{r}\langle \mathit{fact}\,(x)\rangle$$

where $\mathit{fact}\,(x)$ is the factorial of x. The process *IMP* below implements the function in the standard recursive way, relying on the operations of integer subtraction and multiplication. If the integer is 0 then the result 1 is returned at r; otherwise the factorial of $x-1$ is calculated and returned at some fresh name r'; this value is multiplied by x to produce the final result:

$$\begin{array}{rcl} \mathit{IMP} & \stackrel{\mathrm{def}}{=} & !f(x,r). \\ & & \quad \mathtt{if}\ x = 0\ \mathtt{then}\ \overline{r}1 \\ & & \quad \mathtt{else}\ \boldsymbol{\nu} r'\,(\overline{f}\langle x-1, r'\rangle \mid r'(m).\,\overline{r}\langle x * m\rangle)\,. \end{array}$$

We would expect the implementation *IMP* to satisfy the specification *SPEC*. Without i/o types, however, it does not. In a polyadic π-calculus with integers and booleans, it holds that, for $T \stackrel{\mathrm{def}}{=} \mathtt{Int} \times \sharp\,\mathtt{Int}$,

$$f : \sharp\,T \rhd \mathit{SPEC} \not\simeq^{\mathrm{c}} \mathit{IMP}\,.$$

To see why, consider the computation that is made for the integer 1 and return name r. The process *SPEC* immediately returns 1 at r. By contrast, *IMP* makes a recursive call of factorial, as an output at f. This output is visible to the external observer, since f is a free name. Therefore a malicious process in the environment could interfere with the recursive call of the factorial, using f in input, and disrupt the protocol for the calculation of the factorial.

With i/o types we can rule out such malicious environments by making only the output end of f available to the outside. One way to achieve this is to restrict f, and to transmit only its output end to clients. We thus have, in a polyadic π-calculus with i/o types and integers,

$$a : \sharp \mathsf{o} T \triangleright (\boldsymbol{\nu} f : \sharp T)\, (\overline{a} f \mid \mathit{SPEC}) \cong^{\mathrm{c}} (\boldsymbol{\nu} f : \sharp T)\, (\overline{a} f \mid \mathit{IMP})\,.$$

(Type T can also be refined to be $\mathtt{Int} \times \mathtt{o}\,\mathtt{Int}$.) Note that, both in the specification and in the implementation, each computation of a factorial is sequential, but several factorials may be computed concurrently. □

Exercise 10.2.5 Consider the following implementation of factorial, obtained by unfolding the definition of *IMP* a few times:

$$\begin{array}{lll} \mathit{IMP2} & \stackrel{\mathrm{def}}{=} & !f(x,r).\\ & & \mathtt{if}\ x = 0\ \mathtt{then}\ \overline{r}1\\ & & \mathtt{else}\quad \mathtt{if}\ x = 1\ \mathtt{then}\ \overline{r}1\\ & & \qquad\quad \mathtt{else}\quad \mathtt{if}\ x = 2\ \mathtt{then}\ \overline{r}2\\ & & \qquad\qquad\qquad \mathtt{else}\ \boldsymbol{\nu} r'\,(\overline{f}\langle x-1, r'\rangle \mid r'(m).\,\overline{r}\langle x * m\rangle)\,. \end{array}$$

Are *IMP* and *IMP2* behaviourally equivalent as processes of a simply-typed π-calculus? □

Example 10.2.6 (Imperative programming) We use i/o types to reason about π-calculus representations of imperative programs. We can model a reference cell, briefly a cell, as follows:

$$\begin{array}{ll} \mathit{Cell} \triangleq (x, \mathit{get}, \mathit{put}).\ (& \overline{\mathit{get}}\, x.\ \mathit{Cell}\lfloor\langle x, \mathit{get}, \mathit{put}\rangle\rfloor\\ & +\ \mathit{put}(y).\ \mathit{Cell}\lfloor\langle y, \mathit{get}, \mathit{put}\rangle\rfloor\ ) \end{array}$$

where *get* is used for reading the content of the cell, and *put* for overwriting it. Using replication in place of recursion, the cell is written

$$\begin{array}{l} \mathit{Cell} \stackrel{\mathrm{def}}{=} (z, \mathit{get}, \mathit{put}).\, \boldsymbol{\nu}\, \mathit{cell}\ (\ \overline{\mathit{cell}}\langle z, \mathit{get}, \mathit{put}\rangle\\ \qquad\qquad \mid\ !\mathit{cell}(x, \mathit{get}, \mathit{put}).\ (\ \overline{\mathit{get}}\, x.\, \overline{\mathit{cell}}\langle x, \mathit{get}, \mathit{put}\rangle\\ \qquad\qquad\qquad +\ \mathit{put}(y).\, \overline{\mathit{cell}}\langle y, \mathit{get}, \mathit{put}\rangle\ ))\,. \end{array}$$

(Note that if we added type annotations in restrictions, as required by the syntax of typed processes, we would need different cell definitions for different types of the content of the cell. The misuse of notation is harmless in this simple example. The separation of definitions of cells can be avoided using polymorphism; see Exercise 8.3.5.)

The example uses three cells, with access names a_{get}, a_{put}, etc. We write $A\langle v\rangle$ as an abbreviation for $Cell\langle v, a_{get}, a_{put}\rangle$, and similarly for $D\langle v\rangle$ and $H\langle v\rangle$. Cells A and D each store an integer; H stores a pointer to a cell that, like A and D, stores an integer. In some imperative languages, the type of A and D would be written ref(Int), to be read 'reference Int', and the type of H as ref(ref(Int)). Storing the pointer to a cell becomes, in the π-calculus, storing the pair of names that give access to the cell. Consider now the process

$$H\langle v\rangle \mid P_1$$

where v is some initial value of H and

$$P_1 \stackrel{\text{def}}{=} (\boldsymbol{\nu} a_{put}, a_{get}, d_{put}, d_{get})\Big(A\langle 0\rangle \mid D\langle 1\rangle \mid \overline{h_{put}}\langle d_{get}, d_{put}\rangle.\, d_{get}(z).\, \overline{a_{put}}z \Big).$$

P_1 first stores a pointer to D into H, then the content of D into A. In an imperative language these operations might be written as

$$H := D; A := \mathsf{deref}(D).$$

We would expect that $d_{get}(z).\,\overline{a_{put}}z$ can be deleted from the last parallel component of P_1 without affecting the observable behaviour, because cell A is local to P_1 and is not used anywhere else. The resulting process is

$$P_2 \stackrel{\text{def}}{=} (\boldsymbol{\nu} a_{put}, a_{get}, d_{put}, d_{get})\Big(A\langle 0\rangle \mid D\langle 1\rangle \mid \overline{h_{put}}\langle d_{get}, d_{put}\rangle \Big).$$

The processes P_1 and P_2 can be thought of as π-calculus representations of the following imperative programs:

$$\begin{array}{lll} \mathsf{new} & \Big(& A : \mathsf{ref}(\mathtt{Int}) := 0 \\ & & D : \mathsf{ref}(\mathtt{Int}) := 1 \;\Big) \\ \mathsf{in} & & H := D; A := \mathsf{deref}(D) \end{array} \qquad \begin{array}{lll} \mathsf{new} & \Big(& A : \mathsf{ref}(\mathtt{Int}) := 0 \\ & & D : \mathsf{ref}(\mathtt{Int}) := 1 \;\Big) \\ \mathsf{in} & & H := D \end{array}$$

In a Pascal-like imperative language these two programs would indeed be equivalent: A is not accessible from the outside and therefore a modification of its content is not visible.

However, without i/o types P_1 and P_2 are distinguishable. The same holds for $H\langle v\rangle \mid P_1$ and $H\langle v\rangle \mid P_2$, and even for $\boldsymbol{\nu} h_{put}\, (H\langle v\rangle \mid P_1)$ and $\boldsymbol{\nu} h_{put}\, (H\langle v\rangle \mid P_2)$, in which the restriction on h_{put} guarantees that P_1 and P_2 are the only processes that can modify the content of the cell H. We explain the last inequality, which implies all the others. In $\nu h_{put}\,(H\langle v\rangle \mid P_1)$, after D is stored into H, a malicious external process can obtain the name d_{get} (by reading on h_{get}) and then use it in output to consume the input $d_{get}(z)$ of P_1. Such a behaviour would be impossible with P_2, which does not contain any input at d_{get}. Precisely, in a polyadic π-calculus with integers we have:

$$h_{get} : \sharp\,(\sharp\,\mathtt{Int} \times \sharp\,\mathtt{Int}) \rhd\ (\nu h_{put} : \sharp\,(\sharp\,\mathtt{Int} \times \sharp\,\mathtt{Int}))\,(H\langle v\rangle \mid P_1) \ \not\cong^{c} \\ (\nu h_{put} : \sharp\,(\sharp\,\mathtt{Int} \times \sharp\,\mathtt{Int}))\,(H\langle v\rangle \mid P_2)\,.$$

Again, the malicious process can be ruled out by means of i/o types. We assign h_{put} and h_{get} the type $T \stackrel{\text{def}}{=} \sharp\,(\mathsf{i}\,\mathtt{Int} \times \mathsf{o}\,\mathtt{Int})$. This ensures that, when d_{get} and d_{put} are stored into H, an external observer obtains only the input capability on d_{get} and the output capability on d_{put}. Thus the operations of reading and writing on D are not visible to external observers. In a polyadic π-calculus with integers and i/o, we therefore have

$$h_{get} : T \rhd (\nu h_{put} : T)\,(H\langle v\rangle \mid P_1) \cong^{c} (\nu h_{put} : T)\,(H\langle v\rangle \mid P_2)\,. \tag{10.2}$$

□

The next exercise shows that the converse of Lemma 9.4.7(3) is false.

Exercise 10.2.7 Show that in $\pi^{\mathtt{unit},\mathsf{i/o}}$: $\Delta \rhd P \cong^{c} Q$, and $\Delta = \Delta'\,,\, a : S$ with $S \leq T$, and $\Delta'\,,\, a : T \vdash P, Q$, do not imply $\Delta'\,,\, a : T \rhd P \cong^{c} Q$. (Hint: use the equivalence in Example 10.2.2 assuming that $\Gamma(a) = \mathsf{o}\,\mathsf{o}\,\mathtt{unit}$; you may also find the matching operator useful.) □

10.3 Wires in the Asynchronous π-calculus

The semantic consequences of i/o types are even more important in the Asynchronous π-calculus.

A useful law of the Asynchronous π-calculus, for whose validity i/o types are necessary, is Lemma 10.3.1 below. In this lemma, we use special processes called *wires*. A wire between a name x and a name y, written $x \multimap y$, behaves like an ephemeral 1-place buffer from x to y: it receives names at x and emits them at y. The names x and y must be of the same type. The definition, which we saw briefly in Section 5.6.2, is

$$x \multimap y \stackrel{\text{def}}{=} x(u).\,\overline{y}u.$$

Lemma 10.3.1 says that if only the output capability of names can be communicated along a name a (this is the hypothesis $a : \mathsf{o}\,\mathsf{o}\,S$; because of subtyping it also covers the case $a : \sharp\, \mathsf{o}\, S$), then sending a *known* name b along a is the same as sending a *fresh* name c that is wired to b. The first action of the process on the left is a free output, whereas that of the process on the right is a bound output; using the terminology of Section 5.7, this law transforms external mobility into internal mobility. We can call the law an *η-law*, for it makes explicit the functionality of name b, that is, the fact that b may only be used in output.

Lemma 10.3.1 Let $A\pi^{\times,\mu,\mathsf{i/o}}$ be the polyadic Asynchronous π-calculus with $\mathsf{i/o}$, and suppose $A\pi^{\times,\mu,\mathsf{i/o}} \triangleright \Gamma \vdash \overline{a}b$ and $A\pi^{\times,\mu,\mathsf{i/o}} \triangleright \Gamma \vdash a : \mathsf{o}\,\mathsf{o}\, S$, for some S. Then

$$A\pi^{\times,\mu,\mathsf{i/o}}(\Gamma) \triangleright \overline{a}b \cong^{c} (\boldsymbol{\nu} c : \sharp\, S)\,(\overline{a}c \mid\, !c \multimap b). \tag{10.3}$$

Proof Deferred to Exercise 10.7.6. □

For instance, suppose Γ satisfies the hypotheses of the lemma, and $\Gamma \vdash P \stackrel{\text{def}}{=} a(x).\,\overline{x}v$. Then $P \mid \overline{a}b \xrightarrow{\tau}\xrightarrow{\overline{b}v}$. On the other hand,

$$P \mid (\boldsymbol{\nu} c : \sharp\, S)\,(\overline{a}c \mid\, !c \multimap b) \mid P \xrightarrow{\tau}\xrightarrow{\tau}\xrightarrow{\overline{b}v}.$$

Exercise 10.3.2 Explain why Lemma 10.3.1 is not valid in the full π-calculus. □

We will see that when $\mathsf{i/o}$ types are refined to receptive types, Lemma 10.3.1 holds for the full π-calculus. A consequence, and (to some extent) a generalization, of Lemma 10.3.1 is the following result. It shows that, under certain hypotheses, wires behave like explicit substitutions. Suppose $\Gamma \vdash P$ and $\Gamma(y) = \Gamma(x) = \mathsf{o}\, T$. Then in $A\pi^{\times,\mu,\mathsf{i/o}}$ it holds that

$$\Gamma - x \triangleright P\{y/x\} \cong^{c} (\boldsymbol{\nu} x : \sharp\, T)\,(P \mid\, !x \multimap y)\,.$$

The proof is deferred to Exercise 10.8.2.

10.4 Delayed input

In the Asynchronous π-calculus, input prefix is the only syntactic construct for sequentializing process actions. Consider the Asynchronous π-calculus process

$$a(x).\,(\overline{b}v \mid \overline{x}w)\,.$$

The subject of the particle $\overline{x}w$ is bound by the prefix $a(x)$, and it is therefore natural that the particle should be liberated only after a name is received via a. The particle $\overline{b}v$, on the other hand, has no syntactic dependency on the input $a(x)$, and yet the prefixing operator introduces a temporal dependency between particle and prefix. One may argue that the temporal dependency of

DINP $\dfrac{}{a(x):P \xrightarrow{ab} P\{b/x\}}$	DACT $\dfrac{P \xrightarrow{\alpha} P'}{a(x):P \xrightarrow{\alpha} a(x):P'}$ $x \notin \mathsf{n}(\alpha)$
DCLOSE $\dfrac{P \xrightarrow{\overline{a}(b)} P'}{a(x):P \xrightarrow{\tau} \nu b\,(P'\{b/x\})}$	DCOMM $\dfrac{P \xrightarrow{\overline{a}b} P'}{a(x):P \xrightarrow{\tau} P'\{b/x\}}$ $b \neq x$

Table 10.1. *Rules for delayed input (incomplete)*

$\overline{b}v$ on input $a(x)$ is not justified. Accordingly, one might wish to replace the input prefix $a(x).\,P$ of the π-calculus with a *delayed input prefix* $a(x):P$ whose transition rules include those in Table 10.1. The rule DINP is analogous to the rule for the ordinary input prefix. DACT allows the continuation of the delayed input to interact with the environment. Rules DCLOSE and DCOMM allow the continuation to interact with the prefix itself. For instance, we have

$$a(x):(\overline{b}v \mid \overline{x}w) \xrightarrow{\overline{b}v}\equiv a(x):\overline{x}w \xrightarrow{ac} \overline{c}w$$

and

$$a(x):\nu b\,(\overline{a}b \mid P) \xrightarrow{\tau}\equiv \nu b\,(P\{b/x\}).$$

The delayed prefix is attractive because it allows more parallelism in processes. However, the sequentialization forced by the ordinary prefix is useful both for expressing many interesting behaviours, and for having simple algebraic laws in axiomatizations. Moreover, in some cases a delayed prefix can be derived, as we are going to show. To achieve this, we make use of the wire processes, from Section 10.3. We show how to code a delayed prefix $a(x):P$ of the Asynchronous π-calculus, under the assumption that P possesses only the output capability on x.

Consider the equality

$$a(x):P = \nu x\,((a(y).\,!x \twoheadrightarrow y) \mid P)\,. \qquad (10.4)$$

Under the hypothesis that P is asynchronous and possesses only the output capability on x, the two processes have the same behaviour. Exercise 10.4.1 asks for a proof of this claim, under the hypothesis that P cannot communicate x (hence x occurs only in output subject position in P). With this additional hypothesis the rules in Table 10.1 completely define the behaviour of the delayed input construct; without it, other rules are needed, and the proof of the correctness of (10.4) is more complex (see the notes at the end of the Part). Moreover, with the additional hypothesis the output capability constraint can be formulated as a syntactic constraint. Therefore, for simplicity, we present the results on untyped calculi.

Exercise 10.4.1 Let P be a process of the Asynchronous π-calculus, and suppose that x occurs only in output subject position in P. Assume that the behaviour of the delayed input construct is defined by the rules in Table 10.1. Show that

$$a(x) : P \approx_{\mathrm{g}} \boldsymbol{\nu} x\, ((a(y).\, !x \multimap y) \mid P)$$

where y is fresh for P and x. (Hint: use the fact that, under the given hypothesis for P, it holds that $\boldsymbol{\nu} x\, (P \mid !x \multimap y) \;{}_{\mathrm{g}}\!\succeq P\{y/x\}$.) □

Note that the equivalence in the exercise is expressed in terms of ground bisimilarity. This is stronger than using barbed congruence on some form of asynchronous π-calculus: it implies that the processes in the equality are indistinguishable in *any* context built from the π-calculus operators plus the delayed input prefix. (To prove this, reason as in Theorem 5.3.8.) That is, although the process P is asynchronous, the surrounding context need not be asynchronous. Writing π_{DI} for the π-calculus extended with the delayed input, under the hypothesis of Exercise 10.4.1 we indeed have

$$\pi_{\mathrm{DI}} \rhd a(x) : P \cong^{\mathrm{c}} \boldsymbol{\nu} x\, ((a(y).\, !x \multimap y) \mid P)\,. \tag{10.5}$$

A similar encoding of a delayed prefix $a(x) : P$ can be given under the hypothesis that P possesses only the input capability on x: we just invert the direction of the wire, to obtain

$$\boldsymbol{\nu} y\, ((a(y).\, !y \multimap x) \mid P)\,. \tag{10.6}$$

However, the correctness of this transformation is more delicate. It requires additional assumptions about the contexts in which the processes can be used. The context must be composed of processes that are asynchronous, and the context must keep only the output capability on names that are sent at a. These conditions can easily be formalized using a behavioural equivalence for asynchronous calculi (a topic touched on in Section 5.4) and type systems; we omit the details. Both in (10.4) and in (10.6), the replication in front of the wire can be eliminated if x is used linearly in P.

10.5 Sharpened Replication Theorems

The Replication Theorems, shown in Section 2.2.3, express distributivity laws for local environments. These talk about systems of the form

$$(\boldsymbol{\nu} a : T)\, (P \mid !a(x).\, R)\,.$$

We recall that one should think of R as a private resource of P, for P is the only process that can access R; moreover P can activate as many copies of R as needed. The resource R, however, like a recursively-defined function, when activated, can invoke itself. In a typed calculus, we abbreviate such a system as $P\{a : T = (x).\, R\}$.

The most interesting algebraic laws for local environments are distributivity over parallel composition and replication. That for parallel composition is

$$(P_1 \mid P_2)\{a : T = (x).\, R\} \simeq^{c} P_1\{a : T = (x).\, R\} \mid P_2\{a : T = (x).\, R\}\,.$$

The assertion can be read thus: a resource that is shared among several clients can be made private to each of them.

As discussed in Section 2.2.3, in an untyped (and a simply-typed) π-calculus the validity of such a law requires a side condition on the use of names in P_1, P_2, and R, namely that a occurs only in output subject position. This is an onerous condition. It implies that the name a cannot be transmitted. Therefore, the set of clients of the resource $\{a : T = (x).\, R\}$ is fixed. (P_1 and P_2 may be replicated and several copies of R may be activated, so that the number of clients can actually increase; but the syntax of P_1, P_2, and R fixes the possible clients.) In a mobile system, this constraint can be unacceptably strong.

The following two processes, similar to those in Section 2.2.3 where we first discussed the theorems, show the need for the side condition:

$$\begin{array}{lcl} P_1 & \stackrel{\mathrm{def}}{=} & (\overline{b}a \mid \overline{a}v)\,\{a = (x).\, R\} \\ P_2 & \stackrel{\mathrm{def}}{=} & \overline{b}a\,\{a = (x).\, R\} \mid \overline{a}v\,\{a = (x).\, R\}\,. \end{array} \qquad (10.7)$$

The context

$$C \stackrel{\mathrm{def}}{=} b(y).\, y(z).\, \overline{c} \mid [\cdot]\,,$$

where $c \notin \mathsf{fn}(R)$, can tell P_1 and P_2 apart: when used with P_1, context C receives a along b and then uses it in input position to interfere with an attempt by $\overline{a}v$ to trigger R; this is not possible with P_2, where $\overline{a}v$ has its own private access to R. That is, we have $C[P_1] \Downarrow_c$ but not $C[P_2] \Downarrow_c$. The context C ignores the intended role of a as a trigger for R. We would therefore like to consider C as inadmissible. With i/o types, this can be achieved by imposing that only the output end of a is transmissible. Thus the condition 'a occurs in P_1, P_2 and R only in output subject position' of the original theorem can be relaxed by requiring, roughly, that the typing of processes P_1, P_2, and R requires only the output capability on a. This means that these processes, like those of the original theorem, may not use a in input. But, by contrast with those of the original theorem, these processes can communicate a, in which case the constraint on the output capability on a is passed on to the recipients. We met a special case of the theorem when discussing the Localized π-calculus; see Theorem 5.6.2.

Theorem 10.5.1 (Sharpened Replication Theorems) In $\pi^{\times,\mu,\mathsf{i/o}}$, suppose that

(i) $\Gamma, a : \mathsf{o}\,T \vdash P_1, P_2$
(ii) $\Gamma, a : \mathsf{o}\,T, x : T \vdash R$.

Then:

(1) $\Gamma \triangleright (P_1 \mid P_2)\{a : \sharp T = (x).\,R\} \simeq^{\mathrm{c}} P_1\{a : \sharp T = (x).\,R\} \mid P_2\{a : \sharp T = (x).\,R\}$
(2) $\Gamma \triangleright (!P_1)\{a : \sharp T = (x).\,R\} \simeq^{\mathrm{c}} !P_1\{a : \sharp T = (x).\,R\}$.

Proof Deferred to Section 10.7. □

The equivalence in the next exercise reminds us of *inline expansion*, an optimization technique for functional languages that replaces a function call with a copy of the function body. In the exercise, think of $\overline{a}v$ as a call of a function with argument v.

Exercise 10.5.2 Suppose that $\Gamma, a : \mathsf{o}\,T \vdash C[\overline{a}v.\,P]$, and $\Gamma, a : \mathsf{o}\,T, x : T \vdash R$, where C is a context that does not contain binding occurrences of a. Use the Sharpened Replication Theorems to prove

$$\begin{aligned}\pi^{\times,\mu,\mathsf{i/o}}(\Gamma)\triangleright\quad & (C[\overline{a}v.\,P])\{a : \sharp T = (x).\,R\} \simeq^{\mathrm{c}} \\ & (C[\tau.\,(P \mid R\{^{v}\!/\!_{x}\})])\{a : \sharp T = (x).\,R\}\,.\end{aligned}$$

□

Exercise 10.5.3 In $\pi^{\times,\mu,\mathsf{i/o}}$, suppose that $\Gamma, a : \mathsf{o}\,T \vdash \overline{a}a.\,P$, and $\Gamma, x : T \vdash R$. Prove that, if a' is a fresh name,

$$\begin{aligned}\pi^{\times,\mu,\mathsf{i/o}}(\Gamma) \triangleright\ & \Big((\overline{a}a'.\,P)\{a : \sharp T = (x).\,R\}\Big)\{a' : \sharp T = (x).\,R\} \ \simeq^{\mathrm{c}} \\ & (\overline{a}a.\,P)\{a : \sharp T = (x).\,R\}\,.\end{aligned}$$

(Hint: use Exercise 10.5.2, for $C = [\cdot]$, and the Sharpened Replication Theorems.) □

10.6 Proof techniques

In the examples and laws in the first half of the chapter we have asserted several behavioural equivalences between processes of π-calculi with i/o types. But we did not say *how to prove* the equivalences. In untyped or simply-typed π-calculi behavioural equivalences are usually proved using (labelled) bisimilarity.

Bisimilarity is not satisfactory with i/o types, however: none of the equivalences stated in the first half of the chapter relate processes that are bisimilar.

Examples 10.2.1 and 10.2.2 show that the observations allowed by bisimilarity are in general too fine with i/o types, for two reasons.

(a) Only a (possibly proper) subset of the actions of processes is observable. Processes can be tested by an external observer only on those actions for which the observer has the necessary capabilities. For instance, in Example 10.2.1, the observer receives only the output capability on x and cannot therefore use it in input to observe the output of P_1 at x.
(b) The labels of matching transitions of equivalent processes may be syntactically different. For instance, in Example 10.2.2, P_1 has a sequence of transitions $P_1 \xrightarrow{\bar{a}(x)}\xrightarrow{\bar{a}(y)}\xrightarrow{yv}$ that is matched by the sequence $P_2 \xrightarrow{\bar{a}(x)}\xrightarrow{\bar{a}x}\xrightarrow{xv}$ from P_2.

In Definition 9.4.10 of typed bisimilarity, only the types Δ of the tested process are looked at. Modifying the definition to take points (a) and (b) into account requires making the distinction between the processes' and the observer's points of view on the types of the names: the processes and the observer should be allowed to have different capabilities on names. We will not pursue this direction here; see however the notes at the end of the Part.

Point (b) is particularly subtle. The cause of the problem is the combination of type constraints with *name aliasing*, that is, the instantiation of two names in a process with the same name. Aliasing occurs in an observer $O \stackrel{\text{def}}{=} a(y).\,a(z).\,R$ that interacts with process P_2 of Example 10.2.2: the two names y and z in R are instantiated to the same name x. However, because of the type constraints with which x is received (output capability only), the observer cannot see the aliasing. The two names received at a could be different, as happens when O interacts with P_1, without O noticing the fact.

We present two proof methods for barbed congruence with i/o types that can be used where typed bisimilarity fails. The first method is based on the Subject Reduction Theorem 7.2.9 and the Context Lemma. The second method consists in

(1) applying some algebraic transformations that rewrite processes into processes of the Private π-calculus (Pπ) or processes that are at least closer to Pπ processes, and
(2) applying bisimilarity to the results of the transformations.

The reason for aiming at Pπ is that its notion of observable is more robust than that of the ordinary π-calculus, because the names transmitted are private. The method works only in the Asynchronous π-calculus, for the algebraic transformations on which it is based are valid only in this subcalculus. (To apply the method to the full π-calculus we need receptive types; see Section 11.2.) We discuss the first method in Section 10.7, and the second in Section 10.8.

10.7 Context Lemma

The assertion of the Context Lemma 9.5.2 for barbed congruence in simply-typed π-calculi remains true when i/o types are added. Its proof however becomes more subtle and we therefore analyse it below. In applications, such as the proofs of the Sharpened Replication Theorems and of the examples of Section 10.2, we use the Context Lemma together with the Subject Reduction Theorem 7.2.9. The latter allows us to infer constraints on the possible actions of a tester. It is this combination of Context Lemma and Subject Reduction that gives the strength of the proof method. Unless otherwise stated, all results are proved on the polyadic π-calculus with i/o types, $\pi^{\times,\mu,\mathsf{i/o}}$.

The proofs of the Context Lemma for strong and weak barbed congruence are similar. We show only the latter. The judgment $\Delta \triangleright P \cong^{\mathrm{s}} Q$ is defined as in Definition 9.5.1.

Lemma 10.7.1 If $\Delta \triangleright P \cong^{\mathrm{s}} Q$ and Γ extends Δ, then $\Gamma \triangleright P \cong^{\mathrm{s}} Q$. □

Lemma 10.7.2 If $\Delta \triangleright P \cong^{\mathrm{s}} Q$ and $\Delta(a) = S$, then $\Delta - a \triangleright (\boldsymbol{\nu} a : S)\, P \cong^{\mathrm{s}} (\boldsymbol{\nu} a : S)\, Q$. □

We recall the assertion of the Context Lemma. Suppose $\Delta \vdash P, Q$. Then $\Delta \triangleright P \cong^{\mathrm{s}} Q$ if and only if $\Delta \triangleright P \cong^{\mathrm{c}} Q$.

Proof (of the Context Lemma 9.5.2(2) for i/o types) The proof that $\cong^{\mathrm{c}}$ implies $\cong^{\mathrm{s}}$ is easy, proceeding as in the Context Lemma of the untyped π-calculus. For the opposite implication, we prove that for each closed Γ and (Γ/Δ)-context C

$$\Delta \triangleright P \cong^{\mathrm{s}} Q \quad \text{implies} \quad \Gamma \triangleright C[P] \cong^{\mathrm{s}} C[Q]$$

proceeding by induction on the structure of C.

The induction base, when $C = [\cdot]$, follows by Lemma 10.7.1. The case when $C = R \mid C'$ is immediate using the inductive assumption. The case $C = (\boldsymbol{\nu} a : T)C'$ is a consequence of Lemma 10.7.2. The cases when $C = !C'$, or $C = M + C'$, or $C = \overline{a}v.\, C'$, or $C = \tau.\, C'$, or $C = [a = b]C'$, or $C = \mathbf{0}$ are similar to those of the proof of the Context Lemma 2.4.7 for the untyped π-calculus. The case

$C =$ with $(x_1, \ldots, x_n) = v$ do C' is similar to, but simpler than, the case of input prefix dealt with below.

The most interesting case is $C = a(x).\, C'$. The remainder of the proof is devoted to this. If C is a (Γ/Δ)-context, then for some T,

$$\Gamma \vdash a : \mathsf{i}\, T \tag{10.8}$$

and C' is a $(\Gamma, x : T/\Delta)$-context. We have to prove that for any closed Γ' that extends Γ, any Γ-to-Γ' substitution σ, and any R such that $\Gamma' \vdash R$, it holds that

$$R \mid (a(x).\, C'[P])\sigma \stackrel{\approx}{\cdot} R \mid (a(x).\, C'[Q])\sigma\,.$$

For this we take the set $\mathcal{R}$ of all pairs

$$\Big(R \mid (a(x).\, C'[P])\sigma, R \mid (a(x).\, C'[Q])\sigma\Big)$$

for σ and R as above, and prove that $\mathcal{R} \cup \stackrel{\approx}{\cdot}$ is a barbed bisimulation.

Consider a pair of processes in $\mathcal{R}$. We show that any reduction of one process, say $R \mid (a(x).\, C'[P])\sigma$, can be matched by the other one, $R \mid (a(x).\, C'[Q])\sigma$. The interesting case is when the reduction comes from a communication between R and $(a(x).\, C'[P])\sigma$. Therefore the reduction is

$$R \mid (a(x).\, C'[P])\sigma \xrightarrow{\tau} (\boldsymbol{\nu}\widetilde{c} : \widetilde{T})\,(R' \mid C'[P]\sigma\{v/x\}) \tag{10.9}$$

for some $\widetilde{c}, \widetilde{T}$ and v. We show that this reduction is matched by

$$R \mid (a(x).\, C'[Q])\sigma \xrightarrow{\tau} (\boldsymbol{\nu}\widetilde{c} : \widetilde{T})\,(R' \mid C'[Q]\sigma\{v/x\})\,.$$

For this, we exploit the inductive assumption and prove that the derivatives are barbed bisimilar, that is

$$(\boldsymbol{\nu}\widetilde{c} : \widetilde{T})\,(R' \mid C'[P]\sigma\{v/x\}) \stackrel{\approx}{\cdot} (\boldsymbol{\nu}\widetilde{c} : \widetilde{T})\,(R' \mid C'[Q]\sigma\{v/x\})\,.$$

Since $\stackrel{\approx}{\cdot}$ is preserved by restriction, it suffices to prove that

$$R' \mid C'[P]\sigma\{v/x\} \stackrel{\approx}{\cdot} R' \mid C'[Q]\sigma\{v/x\}\,.$$

Since C' is a $(\Gamma, x : T/\Delta)$-context, we can infer the equivalence above from the inductive assumption if we can find a closed Γ'' such that

$$\sigma\{v/x\} \text{ is a } (\Gamma, x : T)\text{-to-}\Gamma'' \text{ substitution} \tag{10.10}$$

$$\Gamma'' \vdash R'\,. \tag{10.11}$$

We show that this holds for $\Gamma'' \stackrel{\text{def}}{=} \Gamma', \widetilde{c} : \widetilde{T}$.

In the reduction (10.9), process R performs the output

$$R \xrightarrow{(\boldsymbol{\nu}\widetilde{c}:\widetilde{T})\,\overline{a}v} R'\,.$$

Since $\Gamma' \vdash R$, by the Subject Reduction Theorem 7.2.9 there is S such that

$$\Gamma' \vdash a : \mathsf{o}\, S \tag{10.12}$$
$$\Gamma', \widetilde{c} : \widetilde{T} \vdash v : S \tag{10.13}$$
$$\Gamma', \widetilde{c} : \widetilde{T} \vdash R' . \tag{10.14}$$

Thus (10.11) holds. Also, Γ'' is closed because Γ' is closed and $\widetilde{T}$ are link types (Theorem 7.2.9(3d)). It remains to show (10.10). This holds if

$$\text{for all } y \text{ on which } \Gamma \text{ is defined,} \quad \Gamma', \widetilde{c} : \widetilde{T} \vdash \sigma(y) : \Gamma(y)$$

and

$$\Gamma', \widetilde{c} : \widetilde{T} \vdash v : T .$$

The former is true because σ is a Γ-to-Γ' substitution. We prove the latter. From (10.8) and Narrowing, $\Gamma' \vdash a : \mathsf{i}\, T$; from (10.12), $\Gamma' \vdash a : \mathsf{o}\, S$. This means that $\Gamma'(a) \leq \mathsf{i}\, T$ and $\Gamma'(a) \leq \mathsf{o}\, S$. By Lemma 7.2.4, $S \leq T$. Hence, by (10.13) and SUBSUMPTION, $\Gamma', \widetilde{c} : \widetilde{T} \vdash v : T$. This concludes the proof. □

10.7.1 Proofs of the Sharpened Replication Theorems

We use the Context Lemma 9.5.2(1) and Subject Reduction to prove the Sharpened Replication Theorems. The crux of the proofs is Lemma 10.7.3.

Lemma 10.7.3 Suppose that

(1) $\Gamma, a : \mathsf{o}\, T, a' : \mathsf{o}\, T \vdash P$
(2) $\Gamma, a : \mathsf{o}\, T, x : T \vdash R$.

Then $\Gamma \triangleright (\boldsymbol{\nu} a : \sharp T)\, (P\{a/a'\} \mid !a(x).\, R) \simeq^{\mathrm{c}} (\boldsymbol{\nu} a : \sharp T)\, (\boldsymbol{\nu} a' : \sharp T)\, (P \mid !a(x).\, R \mid !a'(x).\, R\{a'/a\})$.

Proof We omit type annotations on the restrictions of names a, a'. Let $\mathcal{R}$ be the set of all pairs of processes

$$\Big(\boldsymbol{\nu} a\, (P\{a/a'\} \mid !a(x).\, R), (\boldsymbol{\nu} a, a')\, (P \mid !a(x).\, R \mid !a'(x).\, R\{a'/a\})\Big)$$

that satisfy the hypotheses of the lemma, for some T and closed Γ. We show that $\mathcal{R}$ is a barbed bisimulation up to $\dot{\sim}$. By the Context Lemma 9.5.2(1) this proves the theorem, because $\mathcal{R}$ is closed under name substitution and, up to the structural law SC-RES of restriction, it is also closed under parallel composition.

Let (Q_1, Q_2) be a pair in $\mathcal{R}$. Suppose $Q_1 \xrightarrow{\tau} Q_1'$ (the case where Q_2 moves is analogous). There are two cases to examine, according to whether the move comes from the subterm $P\{a/a'\}$ alone or from a communication between $P\{a/a'\}$ and $a(x).\,R$. For the former case, a matching transition from Q_2 is found using Lemma 7.2.17(2). The Subject Reduction Theorem 7.2.9 then guarantees that condition (1) of the lemma holds also on the derivatives. Let us consider now the latter case. Process $P\{a/a'\}$ makes an output transition,

$$P\{a/a'\} \xrightarrow{(\boldsymbol{\nu}\widetilde{b}:\widetilde{T})\,\overline{a}v} P', \tag{10.15}$$

process $!a(x).\,R$ makes the input transition

$$!a(x).\,R \xrightarrow{av} R\{v/x\} \mid !a(x).\,R\,,$$

and the derivative Q_1' is $(\boldsymbol{\nu}a)\,(\boldsymbol{\nu}\widetilde{b}:\widetilde{T})\,(P' \mid R\{v/x\} \mid !a(x).\,R)$.

We now find a matching transition from Q_2. From (10.15) and Lemma 7.2.17,

$$P \xrightarrow{(\boldsymbol{\nu}\widetilde{b}:\widetilde{T})\,\overline{a_\star}\,v_\star} P_\star \tag{10.16}$$

for some $v_\star, a_\star$, and $P_\star$ with $v = v_\star\{a/a'\}$ and $a = a_\star\{a/a'\}$ and $P' = P_\star\{a/a'\}$. Suppose $a_\star = a$; the case $a_\star = a'$ is analogous. The output transition (10.16) combines with the input

$$!a(x).\,R \xrightarrow{a\,v_\star} R\{v_\star/x\} \mid !a(x).\,R$$

to give a reduction, namely

$$Q_2 \xrightarrow{\tau} Q_2' \stackrel{\text{def}}{=} (\boldsymbol{\nu}a,a')\,(\boldsymbol{\nu}\widetilde{b}:\widetilde{T})\,(P_\star \mid R\{v_\star/x\} \mid !a(x).\,R \mid !a'(x).\,R\{a'/a\})\,.$$

Let $Q_\star \stackrel{\text{def}}{=} (\boldsymbol{\nu}\widetilde{b}:\widetilde{T})\,(P_\star \mid R\{v_\star/x\})$. We have

$$\begin{array}{lcl} Q_1' & \equiv & \boldsymbol{\nu}a\,(Q_\star\{a/a'\} \mid !a(x).\,R) \\ Q_2' & \equiv & (\boldsymbol{\nu}a,a')\,(Q_\star \mid !a(x).\,R \mid !a'(x).\,R\{a'/a\})\,. \end{array}$$

We now show that $Q_\star$ satisfies hypothesis (1) of the lemma, that is

$$\Gamma, a : \mathsf{o}\,T, a' : \mathsf{o}\,T \vdash (\boldsymbol{\nu}\widetilde{b}:\widetilde{T})\,(P_\star \mid R\{v_\star/x\})\,. \tag{10.17}$$

From hypothesis (1) of the lemma, and (10.16), using the Subject Reduction Theorem 7.2.9,

$$\Gamma, a : \mathsf{o}\,T, a' : \mathsf{o}\,T, \widetilde{b} : \widetilde{T} \vdash P_\star \tag{10.18}$$

and

$$\Gamma, a : \mathsf{o}\,T, a' : \mathsf{o}\,T, \widetilde{b} : \widetilde{T} \vdash v_\star : T\,.$$

From the latter and hypothesis (2) of the lemma, by the Substitution Lemma 6.3.6, Weakening, and Strengthening we deduce

$$\Gamma, a : \mathsf{o}\,T, a' : \mathsf{o}\,T, \widetilde{b} : \widetilde{T} \vdash R\{v_\star/x\}\,. \tag{10.19}$$

From (10.18) and (10.19), using typing rules T-PAR and T-RES, we derive (10.17).

Thus, up to $\equiv$, Q_1' and Q_2' are in $\mathcal{R}$. This concludes the proof, because $\equiv$ is included in $\dot{\sim}$. □

Using Lemma 10.7.3, we can now prove the first Sharpened Replication Theorem 10.5.1(1). We recall its assertion. Suppose that

(1) $\Gamma, a : \mathsf{o}T \vdash P_1 \mid P_2$,
(2) $\Gamma, a : \mathsf{o}T, x : T \vdash R$.

Then $\Gamma \triangleright (P_1 \mid P_2)\{a : \sharp T = (x).\, R\} \simeq^{\mathrm{c}} P_1\{a : \sharp T = (x).\, R\} \mid P_2\{a : \sharp T = (x).\, R\}$.

Proof (of Theorem 10.5.1(1)) Let a' be a fresh name. We have, omitting the type of a,

$$\begin{array}{ll} & (P_1 \mid P_2)\,\{a = (x).\, R\} \\ = & \boldsymbol{\nu} a\,(P_1 \mid P_2 \mid !a(x).\, R) \\ \simeq^{\mathrm{c}} & (\boldsymbol{\nu} a, a')\,(P_1 \mid P_2\{^{a'}\!/\!_a\} \mid !a(x).\, R \mid !a'(x).\, R\{^{a'}\!/\!_a\}) \qquad \text{(by Lemma 10.7.3)} \\ \equiv & \boldsymbol{\nu} a\,(P_1 \mid !a(x).\, R) \mid \boldsymbol{\nu} a'\,(P_2\{^{a'}\!/\!_a\} \mid !a'(x).\, R\{^{a'}\!/\!_a\}) \\ = & \boldsymbol{\nu} a\,(P_1 \mid !a(x).\, R) \mid \boldsymbol{\nu} a\,(P_2 \mid !a(x).\, R) \\ = & P_1\,\{a = (x).\, R\} \mid P_2\,\{a = (x).\, R\}\,. \end{array}$$

The appearance of $\equiv$ above is justified by the structural laws for parallel composition and restriction, together with the facts that a is not free in $P_2\{^{a'}\!/\!_a\}$ and $a'(x).\, R\{^{a'}\!/\!_a\}$, and that a' is not free in P_1 and $a(x).\, R$. □

Now, exploiting the first Sharpened Replication Theorem, we can prove the second. We recall its assertion. Suppose that

(1) $\Gamma, a : \mathsf{o}T \vdash P$,
(2) $\Gamma, a : \mathsf{o}T, x : T \vdash R$.

Then $\Gamma \triangleright !(P\{a : \sharp T = (x).\, R\}) \simeq^{\mathrm{c}} (!P)\{a : \sharp T = (x).\, R\}$.

Proof (of Theorem 10.5.1(2)) Omitting types, we consider the set $\mathcal{R}$ of all pairs of the form

$$(Q \mid !(P\,\{a = (x).\, R\}), Q \mid (!P)\,\{a = (x).\, R\})$$

where P, a, x, R satisfy the hypothesis of the lemma, for some T and closed Γ, and $\Gamma \vdash Q$. We show that $\mathcal{R}$ is a barbed bisimulation up to $\dot{\sim}$. By the Context Lemma 9.5.2(1) this proves the theorem, because $\mathcal{R}$ is closed under name substitution and under parallel composition (up to $\equiv$).

Let $(P_1, P_2) \in \mathcal{R}$ and consider a possible reduction in P_1. The terms that might participate in the interaction are Q and $P\{a = (x).\,R\}$. Therefore, if

$$H \stackrel{\text{def}}{=} Q \mid P\{a = (x).\,R\},$$

then any interaction in P_1 can be written in the form

$$P_1 \xrightarrow{\tau} P_1' \stackrel{\text{def}}{=} H' \mid !(P\{a = (x).\,R\}), \tag{10.20}$$

where H' is a derivative of H, i.e.,

$$H \xrightarrow{\tau} H'. \tag{10.21}$$

Let us see how P_2 can match the move (10.20), up to $\dot{\sim}$. We have

$$P_2 \equiv Q \mid (P \mid !P)\{a = (x).\,R\},$$

which, using the first Sharpened Replication Theorem 10.5.1(1), is barbed congruent, hence also barbed bisimilar, to

$$P_2^\star \stackrel{\text{def}}{=} Q \mid P\{a = (x).\,R\} \mid (!P)\{a = (x).\,R\}\,.$$

Now, by (10.21), we have

$$P_2^\star \xrightarrow{\tau} P_2' \stackrel{\text{def}}{=} H' \mid (!P)\{a = (x).\,R\},$$

and $(P_1', P_2') \in \mathcal{R}$. Summarizing, we have $P_2 \dot{\sim} P_2^\star \xrightarrow{\tau} P_2'$ and $(P_1', P_2') \in \mathcal{R}$. From the former, by definition of $\dot{\sim}$, for some P_2'' we also have

$$P_2 \xrightarrow{\tau} P_2'' \dot{\sim} P_2'.$$

This proves that $P_1' \,\mathcal{R}\dot{\sim}\, P_2''$, which is enough to show that $\mathcal{R}$ is a bisimulation up to $\dot{\sim}$. □

Exercise 10.7.4 Use the Subject Reduction Theorem and the Context Lemma 9.5.2 to prove the equality (10.2) of Example 10.2.6. □

Exercise 10.7.5 Use the Sharpened Replication Theorems to prove the equivalences in

(1) Example 10.2.2
(2) Example 10.2.3. □

The same Context Lemma 9.5.2 holds in the Asynchronous π-calculus. Using this, it is easy to prove law (10.3) of Lemma 10.3.1:

Exercise 10.7.6 Use the Subject Reduction Theorem 7.2.9 and the Context Lemma 9.5.2 in the Asynchronous π-calculus to prove Lemma 10.3.1. □

10.8 Adding internal mobility

The second proof method is for the Asynchronous π-calculus, and goes as follows. Suppose we wish to prove $\Gamma \triangleright P \cong^{c} Q$. First we apply law (10.3) of Lemma 10.3.1 to those output particles of P and Q that give troublesome aliasing; we thus transform some external mobility into internal mobility. Let $P^\star$ and $Q^\star$ be the resulting processes. Then we prove $\Gamma \triangleright P^\star \approx_{\mathrm{g}} Q^\star$ where $\approx_{\mathrm{g}}$ is (typed) ground bisimilarity. The proof method is sound for barbed congruence in the Asynchronous π-calculus: law (10.3) is valid for barbed congruence, and ground bisimilarity implies barbed congruence.

For instance, suppose we wish to prove $\Gamma \triangleright P_1 \cong^{c} P_2$, for Γ, P_1, and P_2 as in Example 10.2.2. We apply law (10.3) to the second particle $\overline{a}x$ of P_2, obtaining the process

$$P_2^\star \stackrel{\text{def}}{=} (\boldsymbol{\nu} x, y)\,(\overline{a}x \mid \overline{a}y \mid !y \multimap x \mid !x.\,Q)\,.$$

We do not modify P_1, therefore $P_1^\star \stackrel{\text{def}}{=} P_1$. We can now prove $\Gamma \triangleright P_1^\star \approx_{\mathrm{g}} P_2^\star$; we leave this as an exercise for the reader (Exercise 10.8.1(2)).

The proof method is based on law (10.3), which is valid for *weak* barbed congruence in the *Asynchronous* π-calculus. The method cannot be used for proving results about *strong* barbed congruence, or for reasoning on the *full* π-calculus. The proof method can also be used for the asynchronous version of weak barbed congruence (Definition 5.4.1), coupling it with the asynchronous version of ground bisimilarity. For simplicity here and elsewhere in the book we will prefer the more standard (synchronous) behavioural equivalences.

Exercise 10.8.1 Prove in $\mathrm{A}\pi^{\times,\mu,\mathsf{i/o}}$, proceeding as above:

(1) the equivalence in Example 10.2.1
(2) the equivalence in Example 10.2.2
(3) the equivalence at the end of Example 10.2.4. □

Exercise 10.8.2 Prove in $\mathrm{A}\pi^{\times,\mu,\mathsf{i/o}}$: if $\Gamma \vdash P$ and $\Gamma(y) = \Gamma(x) = \mathsf{o}\,T$, then

$$\Gamma - x \triangleright P\{y/x\} \cong^{c} (\boldsymbol{\nu} x : \sharp\, T)\,(P \mid !x \multimap y)\,.$$

□

We introduced ALπ, the Asynchronous Localized π-calculus, in Section 5.6; it is an asynchronous π-calculus where only the output capability of names may be transmitted, i.e., $\mathsf{o}\,V$ is the only link type that is also a value type. In ALπ, the above method is also complete: if two ALπ processes P and Q are barbed congruent, then they can be proved so using the method. As usual with barbed congruence, completeness is established for image-finite processes only. Since on ALπ the constraint on the output capability of names is in the definition of the calculus, we can directly present the result, namely Theorem 10.8.6, on untyped ALπ. The method in the theorem is actually based on a form of wire more sophisticated than $a \rightarrow b$, which we now introduce.

The law (10.3) transforms a process $\overline{a}b$, whose first (and only) action is a free output, into the process $\nu c\,(\overline{a}c \mid !c \rightarrow b)$, whose first action is a bound output. However, the resulting process can still perform free outputs, this time at b. We can eliminate these by applying the law again, to obtain

$$\nu c\,(\overline{a}c \mid !c(e).\, \nu d\,(\overline{b}d \mid !d \rightarrow e))\,;$$

and again we can eliminate the free outputs at e, giving

$$\nu c\,(\overline{a}c \mid !c(e).\, \nu d\,(\overline{b}d \mid !d(z).\, \nu f\,(\overline{e}f \mid !f \rightarrow z)))\,;$$

and so on. If we could apply the law an infinite number of times, we would obtain the following process, that never performs free outputs:

$$\nu c\,(\overline{a}c \mid !c \twoheadrightarrow b)$$

where $a \twoheadrightarrow b$, called a *dynamic wire process* and briefly mentioned in Section 5.7.4, is defined using recursion thus:

$$a \twoheadrightarrow b \triangleq a(x).\, \nu c\,(\overline{b}c \mid !c \twoheadrightarrow x). \tag{10.22}$$

For ease of reading, in the above we have not respected the syntax for the use of parameters in recursive definitions, as specified in Sections 3.2 and 7.4.1; respecting this syntax, the definition would be

$$\twoheadrightarrow\ \triangleq (a, b).\, a(x).\, \nu c\,(\overline{b}c \mid !\twoheadrightarrow \lfloor\langle c, x\rangle\rfloor).$$

The dynamic wire does not perform free outputs: the name sent at b is not the name x received at a, but a wire to x. The definition of dynamic wire can be rewritten using replication but with recursion it is easier to read. Rewriting the dynamic wires using only replication is not straightforward, however: the encoding of recursion using replication in Section 3.2 does not work because it would destroy the locality condition on names of ALπ in input prefixes; see the exercise below.

Exercise* 10.8.3 Consider the following process (for simplicity, we make use of polyadicity):

$$DW_{a,b} \stackrel{\text{def}}{=} a(x).\, \nu p\,(\overline{p}\langle b, x\rangle \mid !p(z, r).\, \nu c\,(\overline{z}c \mid !c(y).\, \overline{p}\langle r, y\rangle))\,.$$

Prove that $DW_{a,b} \approx_{\mathrm{g}} a \twoheadrightarrow b$. The process on the right-hand side uses recursion, but this does not affect the definition of ground bisimilarity and the related 'up-to' proof techniques. (Hint: show that the singleton relation

$$\{(DW_{a,b}, a \twoheadrightarrow b)\}$$

is a ground bisimulation up to context, up to expansion, and up to injective substitution (see Definition 5.3.12; it does not use injective substitutions, but this is a straightforward addition, see Section 2.4.3.3).) □

In the light of Exercise 10.8.3, in ALπ we can think of $a \twoheadrightarrow b$ as an ALπ process whose behaviour is the same as that of the process defined in (10.22). We are thus led to the following stronger version of law (10.3):

$$\mathrm{AL}\pi \triangleright \overline{a}b \cong^{c} \nu c\,(\overline{a}c \mid !c \twoheadrightarrow b)\,.$$

Exercise 10.8.4 Prove the correctness of the above law, proceeding as in Exercise 10.7.6. Use (10.22) as the definition of $c \twoheadrightarrow b$. □

Using dynamic wires we can define a transformation $\mathcal{C}$ that takes a process of ALπ and returns a process of ALPπ, a subset of ALπ where all names communicated are private (ALPπ is the intersection of ALπ and Pπ). This transformation is a homomorphism on all constructs except output, for which we have

$$\mathcal{C}[\![\overline{a}b]\!] \stackrel{\text{def}}{=} \nu c\,(\overline{a}c \mid !c \twoheadrightarrow b)\,.$$

Lemma 10.8.5 Let $P \in \mathrm{AL}\pi$. Then $\mathrm{AL}\pi \triangleright P \cong^{c} \mathcal{C}[\![P]\!]$.

Proof Induction on the structure of P. The base case, $P = \overline{a}b$, is Exercise 10.8.4. □

Theorem 10.8.6 Let $P, Q \in \mathrm{AL}\pi$ be image-finite. Then $\mathrm{AL}\pi \triangleright P \cong^{c} Q$ iff $\mathcal{C}[\![P]\!] \approx_{g} \mathcal{C}[\![Q]\!]$.

Proof The implication from right to left follows by Lemma 10.8.5 (this holds for arbitrary processes P and Q). The converse is more complex, details can be found in [Mer00]. □

11

Techniques for Advanced Type Systems

11.1 Some properties of linearity

We present some behavioural properties of linear types, on the polyadic π-calculus with i/o and linear types, $\pi^{\times,\mu,\mathsf{i/o},\ell}$. First, as linear types refine i/o types, behavioural equivalences that are true with i/o types are also true with linearity.

Exercise 11.1.1

(1) Prove the analogue of Theorem 10.1.1, with $\pi^{\times,\mu,\mathsf{i/o},\ell}$ in place of $\pi^{\times,\mu,\mathsf{i/o}}$, and $\pi^{\times,\mu,\mathsf{i/o}}$ in place of $\pi^{\sharp,\times,\mu}$. (In this case, typing $\Delta_\sharp$ and processes $P_\sharp$ and $Q_\sharp$ are obtained by coercion of the linear tag ℓ_I to the i/o tag I, for $I \in \{\mathsf{i}, \mathsf{o}, \sharp\}$.)

(2) Conclude that also the analogue of Theorem 10.1.1 with $\pi^{\times,\mu,\mathsf{l/o},\ell}$ in place of $\pi^{\times,\mu,\mathsf{i/o}}$ is valid. (In this case, each linear tag ℓ_I is coerced to the connection tag $\sharp$, for $I \in \{\mathsf{i}, \mathsf{o}, \sharp\}$.) $\square$

Lemma 11.1.2 shows that communications along linear names are τ-insensitive, that is, they do not affect behaviour, under the condition that such communications do not involve sum. τ-insensitivity is a useful property: when comparing the behaviour of two processes there are fewer configurations to take into account.

We say that $P \xrightarrow{\tau} P'$ is a *sum-free communication at a linear name* if $P \xrightarrow{\tau} P'$ originates from a communication along a linear name between subterms of P that are not within a sum (more formally, if the transition derivation of $P \xrightarrow{\tau} P'$ uses a rule COMM-L or COMM-R or REP-COMM whose premises are input and output actions along a linear name, and rules SUM-L and SUM-R are not used).

Lemma 11.1.2 Suppose $\Gamma \vdash P$, with Γ closed, and $P \xrightarrow{\tau} P'$ is a sum-free communication at an linear name. Then $\Gamma \triangleright P \cong^{\mathrm{c}} P'$.

Proof (Sketch) Under the hypothesis of the lemma, it must be, for some $\widetilde{z}$, $\widetilde{T}$, x, S, v, y, P_1, P_2, and P_3, that

$$\begin{aligned} P &\equiv (\boldsymbol{\nu}\widetilde{z} : \widetilde{T}) \left((\boldsymbol{\nu}x : \ell_\sharp\, S)\, (\overline{x}v.\, P_1 \mid x(y).\, P_2) \mid P_3 \right) \\ P' &\equiv (\boldsymbol{\nu}\widetilde{z} : \widetilde{T})\, (P_1 \mid P_2\{^v\!/\!_y\} \mid P_3)\,, \end{aligned}$$

and then the assertion of the lemma is an application of the π-calculus law

$$\boldsymbol{\nu}a\, (\overline{a}v.\, Q \mid a(c).\, R) \cong^{\mathrm{c}} Q \mid R\{^v\!/\!_c\} \qquad \text{if } a \notin \mathsf{fn}(Q, R)\,.$$

This law is valid in untyped or simply-typed π-calculus (it is an immediate consequence of Corollary 2.4.19(1)), hence also with linear types, by Exercise 11.1.1(2). □

Using linearity, in the Asynchronous π-calculus the following law – the linear version of law (10.3) – is valid for barbed congruence:

Lemma 11.1.3 Let $\mathrm{A}\pi^{\times,\mu,\mathsf{i/o},\ell}$ be the asynchronous version of $\pi^{\times,\mu,\mathsf{i/o},\ell}$, and suppose $\mathrm{A}\pi^{\times,\mu,\mathsf{i/o},\ell} \triangleright \Gamma \vdash \overline{a}b$ and $\mathrm{A}\pi^{\times,\mu,\mathsf{i/o},\ell} \triangleright \Gamma \vdash a : \mathsf{o}\, \ell_{\mathsf{o}}\, S$. Then

$$\mathrm{A}\pi^{\times,\mu,\mathsf{i/o},\ell}(\Gamma) \triangleright \overline{a}b \cong^{\mathrm{c}} (\boldsymbol{\nu}c : \ell_\sharp\, S)\, (\overline{a}c \mid c \twoheadrightarrow b)\,.$$

□

11.2 Behavioural properties of receptiveness

We will not dwell on the details of the behavioural theory and proof techniques for receptive types. We present only a few key laws, some of which (law (2) of Lemma 11.2.1 and law (2) of Lemma 11.2.4) transform external mobility into internal mobility. The combination of these laws with standard proof techniques of the π-calculus, such as bisimilarity, gives us a powerful proof method for establishing behavioural properties involving receptiveness, essentially the analogue for receptiveness of the proof method for i/o types examined in Section 10.8. We will see this method at work later in this section, and in Sections 13.2.5 and 20.3.

The results in this section are proved for the polyadic π-calculus with i/o and (linear- or ω-) receptive types, $\pi^{\times,\mu,\mathsf{i/o},\ell\mathrm{rec}}$ and $\pi^{\times,\mu,\mathsf{i/o},\omega\mathrm{rec}}$.

11.2.1 Properties of linear receptiveness

In Lemma 11.2.1 we show two laws and two structural properties for linear-receptive names. Law (1) of the lemma transforms a 'synchronous' output into an 'asynchronous' one: an output prefix at a receptive name is not blocking and therefore can be replaced by a parallel composition. This is useful for performing process transformations that enhance parallelism; see Section 20.4. Law (2) generalizes law (10.3) to the full π-calculus: it transforms a free-output prefix into a bound-output prefix. Law (3) transforms a global (i.e., observable) input into a local (i.e., unobservable) input; (4) does the same for outputs. Laws (3) and (4) allow us to reduce the set of free receptive names in a process.

The validity of these equalities depends crucially on the receptiveness hypothesis on names x and y; none of the equalities is true in the untyped π-calculus or in typed π-calculi without receptiveness.

Lemma 11.2.1

(1) $\Gamma \uplus \{x : \ell\mathrm{rec}_{\mathsf{o}}\, S\} \triangleright \overline{x}a.\, P \cong^{\mathrm{c}} \overline{x}a \mid P$.

(2) $\Gamma \uplus \{x : \ell\mathrm{rec}_{\mathsf{o}}\, S\} \triangleright \overline{a}x.\, P \cong^{\mathrm{c}} (\boldsymbol{\nu} y : \ell\mathrm{rec}_{\sharp}\, S)\, (\overline{a}y.\, P \mid y \rightarrow x)$.

(3) Suppose that $\Gamma(x) = \ell\mathrm{rec}_{\mathsf{i}}\, T$ and a is fresh. Then

$$\Gamma \triangleright P \cong^{\mathrm{c}} Q \text{ iff}$$
$$\Gamma - x\,,\, a : \sharp T \triangleright (\boldsymbol{\nu} x : \ell\mathrm{rec}_{\sharp}\, T)\, (a \rightarrow x \mid P) \cong^{\mathrm{c}} (\boldsymbol{\nu} x : \ell\mathrm{rec}_{\sharp}\, T)\, (a \rightarrow x \mid Q).$$

(4) Suppose that $\Gamma(x) = \ell\mathrm{rec}_{\mathsf{o}}\, T$ and a is fresh. Then

$$\Gamma \triangleright P \cong^{\mathrm{c}} Q \text{ iff}$$
$$\Gamma - x\,,\, a : \sharp T \triangleright (\boldsymbol{\nu} x : \ell\mathrm{rec}_{\sharp}\, T)\, (x \rightarrow a \mid P) \cong^{\mathrm{c}} (\boldsymbol{\nu} x : \ell\mathrm{rec}_{\sharp}\, T)\, (x \rightarrow a \mid Q).$$

Proof We prove law (2). Let $\Gamma' \stackrel{\mathrm{def}}{=} \Gamma \uplus \{x : \ell\mathrm{rec}_{\mathsf{o}}\, S\}$. We show that for any closed Δ and (Δ/Γ') context C, it holds that

$$\Delta \triangleright C[\overline{a}x.\, P] \cong^{\mathrm{c}} C[(\boldsymbol{\nu} y : \ell\mathrm{rec}_{\sharp}\, S)\, (\overline{a}y.\, P \mid y \rightarrow x)]\,.$$

It suffices to prove this equality when all receptive types are coerced to a connection type (appealing to the analogue of Exercise 11.1.1(2) for linear receptiveness). The remainder of the proof is devoted to showing this; we omit types and typings. The facts that $C[\overline{a}x.\, P]$ and $C[(\boldsymbol{\nu} y : \ell\mathrm{rec}_{\sharp}\, S)\, (\overline{a}y.\, P \mid y \rightarrow x)]$ are well typed in Δ, and that x is linear receptive, will however allow us to infer useful information about the possible occurrences of x in the processes.

Since x is receptive and Δ is closed, by Definition 8.2.4 of closed typing, the context C must create x and make it immediately available in input. Thus C has a subcontext C' with

$$C' \equiv (\boldsymbol{\nu} x\ )(x(q).\, R \mid D)$$

where D is another context. We prove $C'[\overline{a}x.\, P] \cong^{\mathrm{c}} C'[\boldsymbol{\nu} y\ (\overline{a}y.\, P \mid y \rightarrow x)]$ proceeding by induction on the structure of D. Note that the typing rules of linear receptiveness guarantee that $a \neq x$ and that the hole of D is not underneath a replication.

$D = [\cdot]$ Using the laws of structural congruence, the Expansion Lemma, and Corollary 2.4.19(1), we have

$$\begin{array}{rl} & C'[\boldsymbol{\nu} y\,(\overline{a}y.\,P \mid y \twoheadrightarrow x)] \\ \equiv & \boldsymbol{\nu} x\,(x(q).\,R \mid \boldsymbol{\nu} y\,(\overline{a}y.\,P \mid y \twoheadrightarrow x)) \\ \equiv & (\boldsymbol{\nu} y\,)(\boldsymbol{\nu} x\,(y \twoheadrightarrow x \mid x(q).\,R) \mid \overline{a}y.\,P) \\ \cong^{\mathrm{c}} & (\boldsymbol{\nu} y\,)(y(q).\,R \mid \overline{a}y.\,P) \\ = & (\boldsymbol{\nu} x\,)(x(q).\,R \mid \overline{a}x.\,P) \\ \equiv & C'[\overline{a}x.\,P]\,. \end{array}$$

$D = M + D'$ The most interesting case is when M has a summand $\pi_1.\,Q$ where π_1 is an output at x, say $\overline{x}v$. To ease readability, we assume that M has no other summands and, similarly, that D' consists of a single summand $\pi_2.\,D''$. Thus $D = \overline{x}v.\,Q + \pi_2.\,D''$. We assume that the name x does not appear in π_2 (this would mean that the summand with π_2 is deadlocked, because π_2 would be an input at x whose partner is in the process underneath π_2). Using the Expansion Lemma we have

$$C'[\overline{a}x.\,P] \simeq^{\mathrm{c}} \tau.\,(Q \mid R\{v/q\}) + \pi_2.\,\boldsymbol{\nu} x\,(x(q).\,R \mid D''[\overline{a}x.\,P])$$

which, using the inductive assumption,

$$\cong^{\mathrm{c}} \tau.\,(Q \mid R\{v/q\}) + \pi_2.\,\boldsymbol{\nu} x\,(x(q).\,R \mid D''[\boldsymbol{\nu} y\,(\overline{a}y.\,P \mid y \twoheadrightarrow x)])$$

which, again by expansion

$$\simeq^{\mathrm{c}} C'[\boldsymbol{\nu} y\,(\overline{a}y.\,P \mid y \twoheadrightarrow x)]\,.$$

$D = \pi.\,D'$ Similar to the above.

$D = Q \mid D'$ Since x is linear receptive, it cannot occur free in Q (both the input and the output capability of x are used by other processes). Therefore, for any process $Q_\star$,

$$C'[Q_\star] \simeq^{\mathrm{c}} Q \mid \boldsymbol{\nu} x\,(x(q).\,R \mid D'[Q_\star])\,.$$

Using this fact, the thesis follows by the inductive assumption.

$D = \boldsymbol{\nu} b\,D'$ Easy, using the inductive assumption.

$D = \mathsf{with}\ (x_1, \ldots, x_n) = v\ \mathsf{do}\ D'$ Follows from induction and

$$\boldsymbol{\nu} x\,(x(q).\,R \mid D) \simeq^{\mathrm{c}} \mathsf{with}\ (x_1, \ldots, x_n) = v\ \mathsf{do}\ \boldsymbol{\nu} x\,(x(q).\,R \mid D')\,.$$

□

Exercise 11.2.2 Prove law (1) of Lemma 11.2.1. □

Exercise 11.2.3 Prove laws (3) and (4) of Lemma 11.2.1. (Hint for (3): the behaviour obtained by plugging P and Q into a closed context C is the same as that obtained by plugging $(\boldsymbol{\nu}x : \ell\mathrm{rec}_\sharp\, T)(a \multimap x \mid P)$ and $(\boldsymbol{\nu}x : \ell\mathrm{rec}_\sharp\, T)(a \multimap x \mid Q)$ into the context obtained from C by replacing x with a; to prove this, you may find law (1) useful. To prove (4) proceed in a similar way.) □

The variant of law (2) of Lemma 11.2.1 with the dynamic wire process $x \twoheadrightarrow y$ of Section 10.8 in place of $x \multimap y$ is also valid.

11.2.2 Properties of ω-receptiveness

Here are the ω-versions of the laws of Lemma 11.2.1. Their proof is along the lines of those of their linear counterparts, though the fact that the hole of a closed context can also be underneath a replication makes things a bit more complicated.

Lemma 11.2.4

(1) $\Gamma \uplus \{x : \omega\mathrm{rec}_\mathsf{o}\, S\} \rhd \overline{x}a.\, P \cong^{\mathrm{c}} \overline{x}a \mid P$.
(2) $\Gamma \uplus \{x : \omega\mathrm{rec}_\mathsf{o}\, S\} \rhd \overline{a}x.\, P \cong^{\mathrm{c}} (\boldsymbol{\nu}y : \omega\mathrm{rec}_\sharp\, S)\,(\overline{a}y.\, P \mid !y \multimap x)$.
(3) Suppose that $\Gamma(x) = \omega\mathrm{rec}_\sharp\, T$ and a is fresh. Then

$$\Gamma \rhd P \cong^{\mathrm{c}} Q \text{ iff}$$
$$\Gamma - x\,,\, a : \sharp T \rhd (\boldsymbol{\nu}x : \omega\mathrm{rec}_\sharp\, T)\,(!a \multimap x \mid P) \cong^{\mathrm{c}} (\boldsymbol{\nu}x : \omega\mathrm{rec}_\sharp\, T)\,(!a \multimap x \mid Q).$$

(4) Suppose that $\Gamma(x) = \omega\mathrm{rec}_\mathsf{o}\, T$ and a is fresh. Then

$$\Gamma \rhd P \cong^{\mathrm{c}} Q \text{ iff}$$
$$\Gamma - x\,,\, a : \sharp T \rhd (\boldsymbol{\nu}x : \omega\mathrm{rec}_\sharp\, T)\,(!x \multimap a \mid P) \cong^{\mathrm{c}} (\boldsymbol{\nu}x : \omega\mathrm{rec}_\sharp\, T)\,(!x \multimap a \mid Q).$$

Proof We show the proof of law (2). The schema of the proof is the same as that of law (2) of Lemma 11.2.1, but there are differences in the details. Let $\Gamma' \stackrel{\mathrm{def}}{=} \Gamma \uplus \{x : \omega\mathrm{rec}_\mathsf{o}\, S\}$. We show that for any closed Δ and (Δ/Γ')-context C, it holds that

$$\Delta \rhd C[\overline{a}x.\, P] \cong^{\mathrm{c}} C[(\boldsymbol{\nu}y : \omega\mathrm{rec}_\sharp\, S)\,(\overline{a}y.\, P \mid !y \multimap x)]\,.$$

It suffices to prove the equality above when all receptive types are coerced to i/o types (appealing to the analogue of Exercise 11.1.1(1) for ω receptiveness.) The remainder of the proof is devoted to showing this; we omit types and typings.

Since x is receptive and Δ is closed, by Definition 8.2.4 of closed typing the context C must create x and make it immediately available in input. Thus C has a subcontext C' with

$$C' \equiv (\boldsymbol{\nu}x\,)(!x(q).\, R \mid D)$$

where D is another context. We prove $C'[\overline{a}x.\, P] \cong^{c} C'[\boldsymbol{\nu} y\, (\overline{a}y.\, P \mid !y \multimap x)]$ proceeding by induction on the structure of D. We show the details only for the base case. The other cases are easier; for the cases of parallel composition and replication, use the Sharpened Replication Theorems 10.5.1 and induction. Thus suppose $D = [\cdot]$. We have

$$C'[\boldsymbol{\nu} y\, (\overline{a}y.\, P \mid !y \multimap x)] \equiv \boldsymbol{\nu} x\, (!x(q).\, R \mid \boldsymbol{\nu} y\, (\overline{a}y.\, P \mid !y \multimap x))\,.$$

Using the laws of structural congruence on the right-hand side,

$$\equiv (\boldsymbol{\nu} x, y)\, (!x(q).\, R \mid !y \multimap x \mid \overline{a}y.\, P)\,.$$

Applying the Sharpened Replication Theorem 10.5.1(1),

$$\simeq^{c} \boldsymbol{\nu} x\, (!x(q).\, R \mid !y \multimap x) \mid \boldsymbol{\nu} x\, (!x(q).\, R \mid \overline{a}y.\, P)$$

and now, from the Sharpened Replication Theorem 10.5.1(2), the Expansion Lemma, and Corollary 2.4.19(2),

$$\cong^{c} !y(q).\, \boldsymbol{\nu} x\, (R \mid !x(q).\, R) \mid \boldsymbol{\nu} x\, (!x(q).\, R \mid \overline{a}y.\, P)\,.$$

Reversing the steps,

$$\simeq^{c} (\boldsymbol{\nu} x, y)\, (!x(q).\, R \mid !y(q).\, R \mid \overline{a}y.\, P)\,.$$

Finally, applying Lemma 10.7.3 (with $a = x$ and $a' = y$),

$$\simeq^{c} \boldsymbol{\nu} x\, (!x(q).\, R \mid \overline{a}x.\, P) \equiv C'[\overline{a}x.\, P]\,.$$

□

Below we consider some copying and distributivity properties. Their effect is to localize computation. In this way, analysing a process's behaviour becomes easier. We then consider some τ-insensitivity properties.

11.2.2.1 Sharpened Replication Theorems, with receptiveness

In Section 10.5 we used i/o types to get sharpened versions of the Replication Theorems. These sharpened versions allow communications of the restricted name (the access name for the replicated resource), under the constraint that the recipients use only the output capability of the name. Adding this requirement is the same as declaring the name ω-receptive. It is worth pointing out that there is a straightforward proof of the Sharpened Replication Theorems, shown below, exploiting the law of Lemma 11.2.4(2) for receptiveness. The careful reader will rightly complain now, because we used the Sharpened Replication Theorems in the proof of Lemma 11.2.4(2). The reasons for showing the proofs below are that: Lemma 11.2.4(2) may also be proved in other ways; and the proofs are a good illustration of a proof method for π-calculi with receptive names, based on the laws for receptiveness plus the standard proof techniques of the π-calculus. A small disadvantage of proving the theorems from Lemma 11.2.4(2) is that we obtain the results for *weak*, rather than strong, barbed congruence (the theorems are also valid in the strong case; see for instance the statement of them in Section 10.5).

Theorem 11.2.5 (Sharpened Replication Theorems, using receptiveness)

(1) $\Gamma \triangleright (\boldsymbol{\nu} x : \omega\mathrm{rec}_\sharp)\, (!x(a).\, R \mid P \mid Q) \cong^{\mathrm{c}} (\boldsymbol{\nu} x : \omega\mathrm{rec}_\sharp)\, (!x(a).\, R \mid P) \mid (\boldsymbol{\nu} x : \omega\mathrm{rec}_\sharp)\, (!x(a).\, R \mid Q)$

(2) $\Gamma \triangleright (\boldsymbol{\nu} x : \omega\mathrm{rec}_\sharp)\, (!x(a).\, R \mid !P) \cong^{\mathrm{c}} !(\boldsymbol{\nu} x : \omega\mathrm{rec}_\sharp)\, (!x(a).\, R \mid P)$.

Proof We prove (1); (2) is similar. By repeatedly applying the algebraic law of Lemma 11.2.4(2) in the processes P, Q and R we get new processes in which the name x occurs only in output subject position. We then infer the thesis from the ordinary Replication Theorems of Section 2.2.3 (an equality valid in untyped or simply-typed π-calculus is also valid with receptiveness). □

11.2.2.2 Open Replication Theorems

To apply the replication theorems (in their sharpened or ordinary forms) one is obliged to consider a system that is 'closed' on the access name x for the replicated resource, that is, a system that contains all processes (resource and clients) that have acquaintance of x. Exploiting receptiveness, we can derive the Sharpened Replication Theorems 11.2.5 from more primitive laws on 'open' systems:

Theorem 11.2.6 (Open Replication Theorems)

(1) $\Gamma \uplus \{x : \omega\mathrm{rec}_\sharp\, T\} \triangleright !x(a).\, R \mid P \cong^{\mathrm{c}} !x(a).\, R \mid (\boldsymbol{\nu} x : \omega\mathrm{rec}_\sharp\, T)\, (!x(a).\, R \mid P)$

(2) $\Gamma \uplus \{x : \omega\mathrm{rec}_\sharp\, T\} \triangleright !x(a).\, R \mid !P \cong^{\mathrm{c}} !x(a).\, R \mid !(\boldsymbol{\nu} x : \omega\mathrm{rec}_\sharp\, T)\, (!x(a).\, R \mid P)$.

Proof We show the proof of (1); that of (2) is similar. By Lemma 11.2.4(3), it is sufficient to prove

$$\begin{aligned} \Gamma - x \;\triangleright\; & (\boldsymbol{\nu} x : \omega\mathrm{rec}_\sharp\, T)\, (!a \twoheadrightarrow x \mid !x(a).\, R \mid P) \cong^{\mathrm{c}} \\ & (\boldsymbol{\nu} x : \omega\mathrm{rec}_\sharp\, T)\, (!a \twoheadrightarrow x \mid !x(a).\, R \mid (\boldsymbol{\nu} x : \omega\mathrm{rec}_\sharp\, T)\, (!x(a).\, R \mid P)) \end{aligned}$$

where a is fresh. Moreover, by Lemma 11.2.4(2), we can assume that x occurs free in P and R only as subject of prefixes. We can then conclude the proof using the ordinary Replication Theorems (after coercing the receptive types to the connection type). □

Exercise 11.2.7 Show that the Sharpened Replication Theorems 11.2.5 can be derived from Theorem 11.2.6. □

Theorem 11.2.8 (Self Open Replication Theorem)

$$\Gamma \uplus \{x : \omega\mathrm{rec}_\sharp\, T\} \triangleright\, !x(a).\, R \cong^{\mathrm{c}}\, !x(a).\, (\boldsymbol{\nu} x : \omega\mathrm{rec}_\sharp\, T)\, (!x(a).\, R \mid R)\,.$$

□

Exercise 11.2.9 Prove Theorem 11.2.8. (Hint: use Lemma 11.2.4(3).) □

The Self Open Replication Theorem can be used to show that the specification and the implementation of the factorial function in Example 10.2.4 are behaviourally equivalent without protecting the location of the function under a restriction, as we did for the proof in Exercise 10.8.1:

Exercise 11.2.10 Prove that

$$f : \omega\mathrm{rec}_\sharp\, (\mathtt{Int} \times \sharp\, \mathtt{Int}) \triangleright \mathit{SPEC} \cong^{\mathrm{c}} \mathit{IMP}\,.$$

(Hint: use the Self Open Replication Theorem.) □

Note that in the definitions of *SPEC* and *IMP*, the return names r, r' can be given the linear-receptive type $\ell\mathrm{rec}_\sharp\, \mathtt{Int}$ and, accordingly, *SPEC* and *IMP* can be typed in $f : \omega\mathrm{rec}_\sharp\, (\mathtt{Int} \times \ell\mathrm{rec}_{\mathsf{o}}\, \mathtt{Int})$.

The following exercise extends the equality of Exercise 10.8.2, relating wires to substitutions, to the full π-calculus. We say that P is *receptive-sum-free* if P does not contain a subterm $\pi.\, M + Q$ or $Q + \pi.\, M$ where π is an output at an ω-receptive name (that is, the first action of any sum in P is not an output at an ω-receptive name).

Exercise 11.2.11 Suppose $\Gamma \vdash P$ with P receptive-sum-free, and $\Gamma(y) = \Gamma(x) = \omega\mathrm{rec}_{\mathsf{o}}\, T$. Then

$$\Gamma - x \triangleright P\{^{y}\!/\!_{x}\} \cong^{\mathrm{c}} (\boldsymbol{\nu} x : \omega\mathrm{rec}_\sharp\, T)\, (P \mid\, !x \multimap y)\,.$$

□

Exercise 11.2.12 Explain why Exercise 11.2.11 is not true without the hypothesis that P is receptive-sum-free. □

11.2.2.3 τ-insensitivity

A consequence of the Open Replication Theorems is:

Lemma 11.2.13 $\Gamma \uplus \{x : \omega\mathrm{rec}_{\sharp}\, T\} \triangleright\, !x(a).\, R \mid \overline{x}b.\, P \cong^{\mathrm{c}}\, !x(a).\, R \mid R\{b/a\} \mid P$. □

Exercise 11.2.14 Prove Lemma 11.2.13. □

In Lemma 11.2.13, the process on the right is a derivative of the process on the left. The result therefore expresses a τ-insensitivity (or partial-confluence) property for certain interactions at receptive names. We can make this into a general property:

Corollary 11.2.15 Suppose that $\Gamma \vdash P$ with P receptive-sum-free, and $P \xrightarrow{\tau} P'$ is a communication at an ω-receptive name (that is, the transition derivation of $P \xrightarrow{\tau} P'$ uses a rule COMM-L or COMM-R or REP-COMM whose premises are input and output actions along an ω-receptive name). Then $\Gamma \triangleright P \cong^{\mathrm{c}} P'$. □

The analogue of Corollary 11.2.15 for linear receptiveness (which is also the analogue of Lemma 11.1.2 for linear types) is valid too.

11.3 A proof technique for polymorphic types

We use the terminology introduced in Section 8.3 (ground processes and typings, type variables, etc.)

The proof method for polymorphic types presented in this section relies, like the method in Section 10.7 for i/o types, on the Context Lemma and the Subject Reduction Theorem. The method also relies on Lemmas 8.3.6 and 8.3.7, which show that a type substitution does not affect the actions that a process can perform. The use of the substitution lemmas is essential, because the Subject Reduction Theorem allows us to infer non-trivial constraints on the actions of non-ground processes.

To exploit the proof method on a ground process Q and ground environment Δ we proceed roughly thus: (1) we take a non-ground process P and a type environment Γ in which P is well typed and of which Q and Δ are ground instances; (2) we use the Subject Reduction Theorem to infer constraints on the behaviour of P; and (3) we use the substitution lemmas to lift these constraints to Q. The non-ground P and Γ can be constructed 'on the fly', while examining sequences of transitions beginning from the initial ground process and type environment. The proofs in Section 11.3.1 follow this schema, exploiting Corollary 11.3.1, which directly combines the Subject Reduction and substitution results.

The Context Lemma 9.5.2 also holds in π-calculi with polymorphic types, provided that both in Definition 9.5.1 and in the assertion of the Context Lemma the typing Δ is ground. Such a Context Lemma for ground typings is simpler than that for arbitrary typings, and it is sufficient for proving many interesting examples, as we will see in Section 11.3.1. The enterprising reader might try to extend the Context Lemma to arbitrary typings.

Informally, the corollary below says that if P is well typed and $P\chi$ can perform an action, then P itself can perform 'the same' action and become a well-typed process, whose typing environment is determined by the Subject Reduction Theorem. There are three clauses, corresponding to the different forms of action that $P\chi$ might perform. Each clause has several conclusions, where the first two use substitution properties to obtain a transition from P corresponding to that of $P\chi$, and the remainder use Subject Reduction to calculate the relationship between P's transition and the original typing Γ.

Corollary 11.3.1 In the calculus $\pi^{\mathtt{unit},\sharp,\exists}$, suppose $\Gamma \vdash P$, with Γ semi-closed, and $P\chi \xrightarrow{\alpha} R$.

(1) If $\alpha = \tau$ then there is P' such that

  (a) $P \xrightarrow{\tau} P'$
  (b) $P'\chi = R$
  (c) $\Gamma \vdash P'$.

(2) If $\alpha = a\,v\chi$ then there are P' and T such that

  (a) $P \xrightarrow{av} P'$
  (b) $P'\chi = R$
  (c) $\Gamma \vdash a : \sharp T$
  (d) if $\Gamma \vdash v : T$ then $\Gamma \vdash P'$.

(3) If $\alpha = (\boldsymbol{\nu}\widetilde{x} : \widetilde{S}\chi)\,\overline{a}\,v\chi$ then there are P' and T such that

  (a) $P \xrightarrow{(\boldsymbol{\nu}\widetilde{x}:\widetilde{S})\,\overline{a}v} P'$
  (b) $P'\chi = R$
  (c) $\Gamma \vdash a : \sharp T$
  (d) $\Gamma, \widetilde{x} : \widetilde{S} \vdash v : T$
  (e) $\Gamma, \widetilde{x} : \widetilde{S} \vdash P'$
  (f) each component of $\widetilde{S}$ is a link type.

Proof By Theorem 6.3.7 and Lemma 8.3.7. For instance, in (3), parts (a) and (b) follow from Lemma 8.3.7 and parts (c)–(f) follow from Theorem 6.3.7. □

11.3.1 An example: boolean ADTs

We show that the two implementations *BoolPack1* and *BoolPack2* of the boolean package discussed in Section 9.1 are behaviourally indistinguishable when the constraints imposed by the polymorphic types are taken into account. Let

$$\begin{array}{rcl} TRUE_1 & \stackrel{\mathrm{def}}{=} & t(x,y).\,\overline{x} \\ TRUE_2 & \stackrel{\mathrm{def}}{=} & t(x,y).\,\overline{y} \\ FALSE_1 & \stackrel{\mathrm{def}}{=} & f(x,y).\,\overline{y} \\ FALSE_2 & \stackrel{\mathrm{def}}{=} & f(x,y).\,\overline{x} \\ TEST_1 & \stackrel{\mathrm{def}}{=} & test(b,x,y).\,\overline{b}\langle x,y\rangle \\ TEST_2 & \stackrel{\mathrm{def}}{=} & test(b,x,y).\,\overline{b}\langle y,x\rangle . \end{array}$$

Using these abbreviations, and writing $\mathtt{Bool}$ for $\sharp\,(\sharp\,\mathtt{unit}\times\sharp\,\mathtt{unit})$, the definitions of *BoolPack1* and *BoolPack2* are, including type annotations

$$\begin{array}{rcl} \mathit{BoolPack1} & \stackrel{\mathrm{def}}{=} & (\boldsymbol{\nu} t:\mathtt{Bool}\,,\ f:\mathtt{Bool}\,,\ \mathit{test}:\sharp\,(\mathtt{Bool}\times\sharp\,\mathtt{unit}\times\sharp\,\mathtt{unit}))\\ & & (\overline{\mathit{getBool}}\,\langle\mathtt{Bool};t,f,\mathit{test}\rangle \mid TRUE_1 \mid FALSE_1 \mid TEST_1) \end{array}$$

$$\begin{array}{rcl} \mathit{BoolPack2} & \stackrel{\mathrm{def}}{=} & (\boldsymbol{\nu} t:\mathtt{Bool}\,,\ f:\mathtt{Bool}\,,\ \mathit{test}:\sharp\,(\mathtt{Bool}\times\sharp\,\mathtt{unit}\times\sharp\,\mathtt{unit}))\\ & & (\overline{\mathit{getBool}}\,\langle\mathtt{Bool};t,f,\mathit{test}\rangle \mid TRUE_2 \mid FALSE_2 \mid TEST_2)\,. \end{array}$$

To have fewer process transitions, we take the polyadic input, with transition rules as in (6.4), as primitive. We use the Context Lemma 9.5.2, which, as mentioned in the introduction to this section, also holds with polymorphic types, provided that the typing of the processes being compared is ground.

Let $\Delta \stackrel{\mathrm{def}}{=} \mathit{getBool} : \sharp\,\langle X; X\times X\times\sharp\,(X\times\sharp\,\mathtt{unit}\times\sharp\,\mathtt{unit})\rangle$. By the Context Lemma, to show that $\Delta \triangleright \mathit{BoolPack1} \simeq^{\mathrm{c}} \mathit{BoolPack2}$, we have to prove $\mathit{BoolPack1} \mid R \stackrel{\centerdot}{\sim} \mathit{BoolPack2} \mid R$ for every R and closed Γ that extends Δ and is such that $\Gamma \vdash R$. We need not apply name substitutions, as in the assertion of the Context Lemma, because *BoolPack1* and *BoolPack2* have only one free name (the fact that there is only one free name implies that all name substitutions would act as injective substitutions, and these preserve bisimilarity).

We now verify that the union $\mathcal{R}$ of the following sets $\mathcal{R}_i$ of pairs of processes is a barbed bisimulation up to $\stackrel{\centerdot}{\sim}$. For $(P,Q)\in\mathcal{R}$, we check that if $P \xrightarrow{\tau} P'$ then $Q \xrightarrow{\tau} Q'$ with $P'\ \mathcal{R}\ Q'$; the converse is similar, and the assertion concerning observability is straightforward. We omit type annotations in restrictions.

- $\mathcal{R}_1$ has all pairs of the form $(\mathit{BoolPack1} \mid R, \mathit{BoolPack2} \mid R)$ such that $\Gamma \vdash R$.

- $\mathcal{R}_2$ has all pairs of the form

$$\Big(\begin{array}{l} (\boldsymbol{\nu} t, f, \mathit{test})\,(\mathit{TRUE}_1 \mid \mathit{FALSE}_1 \mid \mathit{TEST}_1 \mid R\{^{\mathtt{Bool}}\!/\!_X\}), \\ (\boldsymbol{\nu} t, f, \mathit{test})\,(\mathit{TRUE}_2 \mid \mathit{FALSE}_2 \mid \mathit{TEST}_2 \mid R\{^{\mathtt{Bool}}\!/\!_X\}) \end{array} \Big)$$

  for R such that

$$\Gamma, t : X, f : X, \mathit{test} : \sharp\,(X \times \sharp\,\mathtt{unit} \times \sharp\,\mathtt{unit}) \vdash R.$$

- $\mathcal{R}_3$ has all pairs of the form

$$\Big(\begin{array}{l} (\boldsymbol{\nu} t, f, \mathit{test})\,(\boldsymbol{\nu} \widetilde{p} : \sharp\,\mathtt{unit})\,(\mathit{TRUE}_1 \mid \mathit{FALSE}_1 \mid \overline{h}\langle c, d\rangle \mid R\{^{\mathtt{Bool}}\!/\!_X\}), \\ (\boldsymbol{\nu} t, f, \mathit{test})\,(\boldsymbol{\nu} \widetilde{p} : \sharp\,\mathtt{unit})\,(\mathit{TRUE}_2 \mid \mathit{FALSE}_2 \mid \overline{h}\langle d, c\rangle \mid R\{^{\mathtt{Bool}}\!/\!_X\}) \end{array} \Big)$$

  for c, d, R such that

$$\begin{array}{l} \Gamma, t : X, f : X, \mathit{test} : \sharp\,(X \times \sharp\,\mathtt{unit} \times \sharp\,\mathtt{unit}), \widetilde{p} : \sharp\,\mathtt{unit} \vdash R \\ \widetilde{p} \subseteq \{c, d\} \\ h \in \{t, f\}. \end{array}$$

- $\mathcal{R}_4$ has all pairs of the form

$$\Big(\begin{array}{l} (\boldsymbol{\nu} t, f, \mathit{test})\,(\boldsymbol{\nu} \widetilde{p} : \sharp\,\mathtt{unit})\,(N_1 \mid \overline{c} \mid R\{^{\mathtt{Bool}}\!/\!_X\}), \\ (\boldsymbol{\nu} t, f, \mathit{test})\,(\boldsymbol{\nu} \widetilde{p} : \sharp\,\mathtt{unit})\,(N_2 \mid \overline{c} \mid R\{^{\mathtt{Bool}}\!/\!_X\}) \end{array} \Big)$$

  for c, R, N_1, N_2 such that

$$\begin{array}{l} \Gamma, t : X, f : X, \mathit{test} : \sharp\,(X \times \sharp\,\mathtt{unit} \times \sharp\,\mathtt{unit}), \widetilde{p} : \sharp\,\mathtt{unit} \vdash R \\ \widetilde{p} \subseteq \{c\} \\ \{N_1, N_2\} \subseteq \{\mathit{TRUE}_1, \mathit{FALSE}_1, \mathit{TRUE}_2, \mathit{FALSE}_2\}\,. \end{array}$$

- $\mathcal{R}_5$ has all pairs of the form

$$\Big(\begin{array}{l} (\boldsymbol{\nu} t, f, \mathit{test})\,(N_1 \mid R\{^{\mathtt{Bool}}\!/\!_X\}), \\ (\boldsymbol{\nu} t, f, \mathit{test})\,(N_2 \mid R\{^{\mathtt{Bool}}\!/\!_X\}) \end{array} \Big)$$

  for R, N_1, N_2 such that

$$\begin{array}{l} \Gamma, t : X, f : X, \mathit{test} : \sharp\,(X \times \sharp\,\mathtt{unit} \times \sharp\,\mathtt{unit}) \vdash R \\ \{N_1, N_2\} \subseteq \{\mathit{TRUE}_1, \mathit{FALSE}_1, \mathit{TRUE}_2, \mathit{FALSE}_2\}. \end{array}$$

These sets are constructed so that each pair of processes in $\mathcal{R}_i$ can match each other's reductions with the derivatives forming pairs of processes that are in $\mathcal{R}_i$ or in $\mathcal{R}_{i+1}$. Note that the pairs in $\mathcal{R}_4$ can actually be removed, since using $\equiv$ they can be transformed into pairs in $\mathcal{R}_5$.

In the case of $\mathcal{R}_1$, the interesting case is the interaction between *BoolPack1* and R, where *BoolPack1* makes the output at *getBool* and R the input. Using Corollary 11.3.1(2), one can infer that the input by R is of the form

$$R \xrightarrow{getBool\langle X\chi;t,f,test\rangle} R'\chi$$

where $\chi = \{\mathtt{Bool}/X\}$ and R' satisfies the side conditions in the definition of $\mathcal{R}_2$. The process $BoolPack2 \mid R$ matches this interaction in the similar way.

We now show in detail the argument for $\mathcal{R}_2$ (the argument for the other $\mathcal{R}_i$ is similar or easier). Suppose the process

$$(\nu t, f, test)\,(TRUE_1 \mid FALSE_1 \mid TEST_1 \mid R\{\mathtt{Bool}/X\})$$

has a reduction, say

$$(\nu t, f, test)\,(TRUE_1 \mid FALSE_1 \mid TEST_1 \mid R\{\mathtt{Bool}/X\}) \xrightarrow{\tau} A_1.$$

We reason by case analysis on the subprocess that originated the action.

(1) If only the subprocess $R\{\mathtt{Bool}/X\}$ contributes to the action, then

$$A_1 = (\nu t, f, test)\,(TRUE_1 \mid FALSE_1 \mid TEST_1 \mid R_\star)$$

for some $R_\star$ such that $R\{\mathtt{Bool}/X\} \xrightarrow{\tau} R_\star$. By Corollary 11.3.1, $R_\star = R'\{\mathtt{Bool}/X\}$ for some R' that is well typed under the same typing as R.

The process $(\nu t, f, test)\,(TRUE_2 \mid FALSE_2 \mid TEST_2 \mid R\{\mathtt{Bool}/X\})$ can make a matching step thus:

$$(\nu t, f, test)\,(TRUE_1 \mid FALSE_1 \mid TEST_1 \mid R\{\mathtt{Bool}/X\}) \xrightarrow{\tau} (\nu t, f, test)\,(TRUE_1 \mid FALSE_1 \mid TEST_1 \mid R_\star),$$

and the two derivatives are again in $\mathcal{R}_2$.

(2) By definition, no reduction is possible within the system

$$TRUE_1 \mid FALSE_1 \mid TEST_1.$$

(3) The remaining case to consider is that of an interaction between $TRUE_1 \mid FALSE_1 \mid TEST_1$ and $R\{\mathtt{Bool}/X\}$. Process R is well typed under the assumptions $t : X, f : X, test : \sharp\,(X \times \sharp\,\mathtt{unit} \times \sharp\,\mathtt{unit})$. Since the type of t and f is not a connection type, by Corollary 11.3.1 $R\{\mathtt{Bool}/X\}$ cannot perform visible actions with t or f as subject. Therefore the only possible reductions between $TRUE_1 \mid FALSE_1 \mid TEST_1$ and $R\{\mathtt{Bool}/X\}$ are along the name *test*. In this case, $R\{\mathtt{Bool}/X\}$ contributes an output. Moreover, since for R the first argument in the type of *test* is X, by Corollary 11.3.1 (clauses (3d) and (3f)) any output at *test* by $R\{\mathtt{Bool}/X\}$ will have either t or f as first argument (the appeal to 11.3.1(3f) is needed to exclude the case in which

this argument is a fresh name). Suppose it is t (the other case is symmetric). Then the output from $R\{\texttt{Bool}/X\}$ is

$$R\{\texttt{Bool}/X\} \xrightarrow{(\boldsymbol{\nu}\widetilde{p}:\sharp\,\texttt{unit})\,\overline{test}\langle t,c,d\rangle} R'\{\texttt{Bool}/X\},$$

where c and d have type $\sharp\,\texttt{unit}$ and $\widetilde{p} \subseteq \{c,d\}$, and the input from $TEST_1$ is

$$TEST_1 \xrightarrow{test\langle t,c,d\rangle} \overline{t}\langle c,d\rangle.$$

Therefore we have, using the laws of structural congruence,

$$A_1 \stackrel{\cdot}{\sim} (\boldsymbol{\nu}t,f,test)\,(\boldsymbol{\nu}\widetilde{p}:\sharp\,\texttt{unit})\,(\;TRUE_1 \mid FALSE_1 \mid \overline{t}\langle c,d\rangle \mid R'\{\texttt{Bool}/X\}\;). \tag{11.1}$$

Similarly, we infer

$$\begin{array}{ll} & (\boldsymbol{\nu}t,f,test)\,(\;TRUE_2 \mid FALSE_2 \mid TEST_2 \mid R\{\texttt{Bool}/X\}\;) \\ \xrightarrow{\tau}\stackrel{\cdot}{\sim} & (\boldsymbol{\nu}t,f,test)\,(\boldsymbol{\nu}\widetilde{p}:\sharp\,\texttt{unit})\,(\;TRUE_2 \mid FALSE_2 \mid \overline{t}\langle d,c\rangle \mid R'\{\texttt{Bool}/X\})\;. \end{array} \tag{11.2}$$

The final processes in (11.1) and (11.2) form a pair of $\mathcal{R}_3$ since, by Corollary 11.3.1(3e), we have

$$\Gamma, t:X, f:X, test:\sharp\,(X \times \sharp\,\texttt{unit} \times \sharp\,\texttt{unit}), \widetilde{p}:\sharp\,\texttt{unit} \vdash R'$$

and therefore the side condition in the definition of $\mathcal{R}_3$ is satisfied.

This completes the argument.

Exercise* 11.3.2 Prove $\Delta \triangleright$ *BoolPack1* $\simeq^{c}$ *BoolPack3*, proceeding as above, for *BoolPack3* as defined in (9.1), in Section 9.1. □

Notes and References for Part IV

Reasoning techniques for typed behavioural equivalences in name-passing process calculi were presented in [PS96, BS98a, HR98c] for i/o or related types, in [KPT99] for linear types, in [San99b] for receptive types, and in [PS00] for polymorphic types. Most of the examples and techniques presented are based on the work in these papers. Sections 10.3 and 10.8 are from [Mer00]. In the literature, wires are sometimes called *forwarders* (a terminology borrowed from Actors), or *links* (a term that in the book we leave for names). Semantic properties of wires were first studied by Honda and Yoshida [HY95]. The use of polymorphic types to hide the implementation details of the boolean package of Example 9.1.2 is reminiscent of Mitchell and Plotkin's representation of abstract data types in the λ-calculus [MP88]. Example 10.2.4 is due to Pierce, Example 10.2.6 to Röckl [Röc01]. Theorem 9.3.1 is similar to results formulated in [BDNN98] and in [CGG00] that use, respectively, *control-flow* analysis [NNH99] and a π-calculus extended with a construct for creating new sorts. The complete set of transition rules for the delayed input and results stronger than Exercise 10.4.1 can be found in [Mer00].

We have seen that typed bisimilarity and full bisimilarity are in general finer than barbed congruence on typed calculi that go beyond simply-typed π-calculi. We have therefore presented alternative proof methods, based on algebraic laws and context lemmas. Another technique [BS98a, San99b, PS00] is to relax the definition of bisimilarity to allow, for instance, the matching actions of bisimilar processes to be different. Bisimilarities of this kind usually separate the typing of an observer from the typing of the tested processes (observer and processes may have different points of views on types, see Section 7.1 and Remark 7.2.11). We have not pursued this direction in the book, on the one hand because it is, at present, a research topic, and on the other because the definitions tend to be fairly complex, mainly due to the possibility of *name aliasing* (cf. Section 10.6).

We discuss other uses of types for process reasoning that we have not covered.

Yoshida [Yos96] used a type system where types have a graph structure to prove full abstraction of an encoding of the polyadic π-calculus into the monadic calculus. Graphs allow sophisticated communication protocols among processes to be expressed, but introduce some complications in the typing rules and in the type checking. Boudol [Bou97b], Kobayashi and Sumii [Kob98, SK98], and Ravara and Vasconcelos [RV97] developed type systems for asynchronous π-calculus-like languages that guarantee that messages sent along some special channels are always consumed. (Receptiveness may be seen as a very special case of these systems; these type systems go beyond receptiveness, because the input end of channels need not be replicated.) In [Bou97b] types are trace languages over, roughly, a fragment of Hennessy-Milner Logic. Steffen and Nestmann [SN97] and Niehren [Nie00] showed type systems that guarantee confluent behaviours of processes. Abadi [Aba99] used types for guaranteeing secrecy properties in security protocols. The typing rules guarantee that a well-typed protocol does not leak its secret information. Typing rules and protocols are presented in the Spi calculus, an extension of the π-calculus with shared-key cryptographic primitives.

Here are some other works that apply types to security, on calculi or languages that are not based on the π-calculus. Smith and Volpano [SV98] used type systems to control information flow and to guarantee that private information is not improperly disclosed. Program variables are separated into high-security and low-security variables; the type system prevents information flowing from high variables to low variables, so that the final values of the low variables are independent of the initial values of the high variables. On the use of type systems for controlling the flow of secure information, see also Heintze and Riecke [HR98a]. Leroy and Rouaix [LR98] showed how types can guarantee certain security properties of applets.

Part V

The Higher-Order Paradigm

Introduction to Part V

We have seen in the General Introduction that the incarnations of mobility can be quite different. To a first approximation, however, we can distinguish two categories: models involving movement of computational entities, such as processes and parametrized processes, and models involving movement of communication links. Correspondingly, there are two main approaches to representing mobility in process calculi: the *higher-order* (or *process-passing*) paradigm, and the *first-order* (or *name-passing*) paradigm. The higher-order paradigm inherits from the λ-calculus the idea that a computation step involves instantiation of variables by terms.

The first-order paradigm is the mathematically simpler of the two. A fundamental point – without which the significance of the π-calculus would be strongly diminished – is that communication of names is enough to model communications involving processes. The formalization and validation of this claim is a central topic of this Part. The study has two main motivations. The first is expressiveness – two different paradigms are being compared. The second is semantics of higher-order languages: we wish to understand whether the π-calculus can be used as a metalanguage for describing and reasoning about such languages. Especially interesting is the possibility of using the theory of the π-calculus to derive proof techniques for higher-order languages. Obtaining proof techniques directly on these languages may be hard; see the discussion in the notes at the end of the Part. The basis for the study is laid down in this Part; the study is continued in Part VI, where we look at reduction strategies.

We begin Part V by introducing the *Higher-Order π-calculus*, HOπ, a higher-order extension of the core calculus Base-π of Section 6.2. In HOπ, parametrized processes, that is, *abstractions*, may be transmitted. An abstraction has a *functional* type. Applying an abstraction of type $T \to \diamond$ to an argument of type T yields a process. The argument can itself be an abstraction; therefore the order of an abstraction, that is, the level of arrow nesting in its type, can be arbitrarily high. The order can also be ω, if there are recursive types. We then show that HOπ is *representable* in π-calculus. We also study the opposite direction, from first order to higher order, although more briefly.

But what does it mean for a given source language to be representable within a given target language? Typically there are three phases:

(1) formal definition of the semantics of the two languages
(2) definition of the encoding from the source to the target language
(3) proof of the correctness of the encoding with respect to the semantics.

Regarding (2), the encoding must be *compositional*, that is, its definition on a term should depend only upon the definition on the term's immediate constituents.

Some further comment on (1) and (3) is worthwhile. There are two dominant approaches to the formal semantics of programming languages. In a *denotational* semantics, a valuation function maps a program directly to its mathematical meaning or *denotation*. Here the correctness of an encoding can be investigated by considering the relationship between the meaning of a source-language term and the meaning of its translation. Denotational semantics has been very successful in modelling many sequential languages; programs are typically viewed as functions from a domain of input values to a domain of output values. However, to date there has not been an equally satisfactory denotational treatment of concurrency. The tools employed for sequential programs are inadequate for the task, because an account of the behaviour of a concurrent system must take into account the *intermediate* states it can reach.

The predominant approach to the semantics of concurrent systems is *operational*. As we have seen for the π-calculus, the semantics is usually given in two steps: first, a transition (or reduction) system, to describe the possible evolutions of a process; then a behavioural equivalence, to abstract from unwanted details. The operational method necessitates a different approach to translation-correctness, where *behaviours* rather than *meanings* are compared. The behavioural equivalence should be the same on the two calculi. Further, the behavioural equivalence should be interesting, in the sense that it should be a congruence and the equalities and inequalities that it gives should be justifiable with respect to an abstract notion of observation. Moreover, the encoding, besides being compositional, should be *fully abstract*, i.e., two source-language terms should be equivalent if and only if their translations are equivalent. Finally, to reveal how the encoding modifies transitions, the full-abstraction result should be completed by an *operational correspondence* showing the connection between the transitions of a term and the transitions of its translation.

With the full-abstraction demand, we take a strong point of view on representability. Full abstraction has two parts: *soundness*, which says that the equivalence between the translations of two source terms implies that of the source terms themselves, and *completeness*, which says the converse. While soundness is a necessary property, one might well consider milder forms of completeness. Assuming that the behavioural equivalence is a congruence, completeness means that the translations of equivalent terms are indistinguishable in every context of the target language. A milder form of completeness would require indistinguishability only in contexts that are translations of source contexts. We ask for full abstraction because we wish to use the target terms in *arbitrary* contexts; and when two source terms are indistinguishable, their encodings should *always* be interchangeable. In other words, we want to be able to switch freely between the two calculi. In our case, where the source language is HOπ and the target language is π-calculus, this allows us to do two things. First, we can make use of the abstraction power of HOπ, which comes from its higher-order nature, when describing systems. Second, we can rely on the more elementary and better-developed theory of the π-calculus when reasoning about processes; in virtue of the full-abstraction result this theory can be lifted up to HOπ.

Structure of the Part The Part is composed of two chapters: Chapter 12 presents higher-order calculi, and Chapter 13 compares them with first-order calculi.

Section 12.1 introduces HOπ. Roughly, HOπ adds to Base-π the λ-calculus constructs of abstraction and application. However, in HOπ the only expressions of functional type are abstractions: no expression *evaluates to* an abstraction. Therefore the λ-calculus is not a subcalculus of HOπ. Admitting expressions that evaluate to abstractions would force us to consider *reduction strategies*, which we regard as an orthogonal matter and study in the next Part. The first HOπ language we study is HO$\pi^{\mathtt{unit},\rightarrow\diamond}$, whose value types are the function and unit types. We present the typing and operational rules of HO$\pi^{\mathtt{unit},\rightarrow\diamond}$, and discuss some properties: derivability of replication, strong normalization of β-contractions, and η-saturated normal forms. Since HOπ values may contain processes, we also extend behavioural equivalence to values. In Section 12.2 we touch on some extensions and variants of the language, namely recursive types and asynchronous calculi.

In Section 13.1 we show that the higher-order constructs of HO$\pi^{\mathtt{unit},\rightarrow\diamond}$ can be compiled into the π-calculus. Intuitively, this compilation, $\mathcal{D}$, replaces communication of an abstraction by communication of *access* to that abstraction. The target calculus is $\pi^{\mathtt{unit},\mathsf{i/o}}$ – a π-calculus with $\mathsf{i/o}$ and unit types. The compilation acts on both processes and types. We show the operational correspondence between source and target terms of the compilation, and from this we derive adequacy and soundness for (weak) barbed congruence.

Both in $\pi^{\mathtt{unit},\mathsf{i/o}}$ and in $\mathrm{HO}\pi^{\mathtt{unit},\to\diamond}$, we can discriminate between processes according to the order of the types needed to type them. In $\pi^{\mathtt{unit},\mathsf{i/o}}$, the order of a type is the level of nesting of $\mathsf{i/o}$ types; in $\mathrm{HO}\pi^{\mathtt{unit},\to\diamond}$, it is the level of nesting of function types. We thus obtain a hierarchy of first-order calculi $\{\pi^n\}_{n<\omega}$ and a hierarchy of higher-order calculi $\{\mathrm{HO}\pi^n\}_{n<\omega}$. A calculus π^n (resp. $\mathrm{HO}\pi^n$) contains those $\pi^{\mathtt{unit},\mathsf{i/o}}$ (resp. $\mathrm{HO}\pi^{\mathtt{unit},\to\diamond}$) processes that can be typed using types of order at most n. Moving up the hierarchies, the calculi allow an increasing 'degree' of mobility. Neither π^1 nor $\mathrm{HO}\pi^1$ allows any mobility; each is, essentially, the core of CCS. We show that the compilation $\mathcal{D}$ preserves the order of types: $\mathrm{HO}\pi^n$ is compiled into π^n.

The compilation $\mathcal{D}$ is not defined in the presence of recursive types. In Section 13.2 we study some optimizations of the compilation that enable us to handle recursive types, and prove soundness for both weak and strong barbed congruence. The resulting compilation $\mathcal{C}$ will be used in Part VI to derive encodings of the λ-calculus into π-calculus. In the section, we also use the compilations to validate some laws of $\mathrm{HO}\pi$, and discuss simpler proofs of the optimizations that exploit receptive types and asynchrony.

In Section 13.3 we investigate the opposite direction, namely encodings of first-order calculi into higher-order calculi. In order to have simpler encodings, the source calculus is $\mathrm{AL}\pi$ (the Asynchronous Localized π-calculus, where name-passing is asynchronous and constrained so that only the output capability of names may be passed). The encoding of $\mathrm{AL}\pi$ can be extended to less constrained calculi, for instance synchronous calculi or calculi where also the input capability of names can be transmitted, but at the price of increased complexity and weaker correctness results. Finally, in Section 13.4 we study the full abstraction of the encodings in the previous sections. We consider asynchronous calculi, for which the proofs are very simple. We touch on synchronous calculi in Remark 13.4.7.

12

Higher-Order π-calculus

12.1 Simply-typed HOπ

We extend Base-π and move to higher order by allowing values built out of processes. We use *Higher-Order π-calculus*, briefly HOπ, as a general name for a higher-order extension of Base-π.

Passing a process is like passing a parameterless procedure. The recipient of a process can do nothing with it but execute it, possibly several times. Procedures gain great utility if they can be *parametrized* so that, when invoked, some arguments may be supplied. In the same way a higher-order process calculus gains power if the processes that are communicated may be parametrized (see also the discussion at the end of Section 13.1.1). A parametrized process, an *abstraction*, is an expression of the form $(x). P$. We have already met abstractions in previous Parts of the book – Definition 2.4.38, Section 7.4.1; in this Part and the next, they play a central role. We may also regard abstractions as components of input-prefixed processes, viewing $a(x). P$ as an abstraction *located* at a. Indeed, the part $(x). P$ of $a(x). P$ behaves exactly like an abstraction. In $(x). P$ as in $a(x). P$, the displayed occurrence of x is binding with scope P.

When an abstraction $(x). P$ is applied to an argument w it yields the process $P\{^w\!/\!_x\}$. *Application* is the destructor for abstractions. The application of an abstraction v to a value v' is written $v\lfloor v' : T\rfloor$, where T is the type of v'. (The type annotation is to ensure that the typing derivation of a process is unique, which will facilitate the encoding of HOπ into π-calculus. An alternative is to annotate the binding occurrences of names in abstractions, as is common in λ-calculi. Our choice keeps the syntax of abstraction closer to that of input.) At the level of types, adding parametrization means adding *function types*; thus in $v\lfloor v' : T\rfloor$ the value v has type $T \to \diamond$, where $\diamond$ is the behaviour type (the type of processes, Section 6.1).

We begin by studying the HOπ language HO$\pi^{\mathtt{unit},\to\diamond}$, the *simply-typed*

Productions and rules to be added to those for Base-π (Tables 6.1–6.4)

Grammars

			Values
v	$::=$	$(x).\,P$	abstraction
			Processes
P	$::=$	$v\lfloor w : T \rfloor$	application
			Value types
V	$::=$	$V \to \diamond$	function type

Transition rules

$$\textsc{App}\ \frac{}{((x).\,P)\lfloor v : T \rfloor \xrightarrow{\tau} P\{^v\!/\!_x\}}$$

Typing rules for processes

$$\text{T-}\textsc{App}\ \frac{\Gamma \vdash v : T \to \diamond \qquad \Gamma \vdash w : T}{\Gamma \vdash v\lfloor w : T \rfloor : \diamond}$$

Typing rules for values

$$\text{Tv-}\textsc{Abs}\ \frac{\Gamma, x : T \vdash P : \diamond}{\Gamma \vdash (x).\,P : T \to \diamond}$$

Table 12.1. *The calculus* $\mathrm{HO}\pi^{\mathtt{unit},\to\diamond}$

Higher-Order π-calculus, in which the type constructs for values are the function type $T \to \diamond$ and the unit type `unit`.

Definition 12.1.1 ($\mathrm{HO}\pi^{\mathtt{unit},\to\diamond}$) The syntax and the operational semantics of $\mathrm{HO}\pi^{\mathtt{unit},\to\diamond}$ are defined by adding the productions and rules in Table 12.1 to those of Base-π, taking `unit` as the only basic type. □

In $\mathrm{HO}\pi$, abstractions can be communicated, but not processes themselves. To send a process we must add a dummy parameter to it. We forbid direct communication of processes for economy in the calculus (passing processes would require additional productions in the grammars of values and processes) and because it does not add expressiveness. Note that, due to the separation of values from processes, in HOπ a process can execute iff it is not inside an abstraction or underneath a prefix.

Notation 12.1.2 We call an abstraction $(x).P$ of type $\mathtt{unit} \to \diamond$ a *process value*, and often abbreviate it as $@P$, assuming x not free in P (which is reasonable, given that x has unit type). We omit the type T in $v\lfloor w : T\rfloor$ when it is clear from the context or it is not important. Thus we usually abbreviate an expression $v\lfloor \star : \mathtt{unit}\rfloor$ to $v\lfloor\star\rfloor$ (recall that $\star$ denotes the unique value of type $\mathtt{unit}$), and an expression $v\lfloor (x).P : \mathtt{unit} \to \diamond\rfloor$, with x not free in P, to $v\lfloor @P\rfloor$. The abstraction construct has the same syntactic precedence as process prefixing; application has higher precedence. Thus $(x).\,x\lfloor v : T\rfloor$ reads $(x).\,(x\lfloor v : T\rfloor)$. As pointed out above, an input $a(x).P$ may be seen as constructed by juxtaposition of the name a and the abstraction $(x).P$ (rather than a prefix and a process as in the grammar in Definition 1.1.1). Accordingly, if F is the abstraction $(x).P$, we sometimes write $a\,F$ for the process $a(x).P$.

We sometimes add angle brackets around the objects of output prefixes, as in $\overline{a}\langle @P\rangle.\,Q$, to enhance readability; similarly with input actions $a\langle @P\rangle$. We recall that we often abbreviate a type judgment $\Gamma \vdash P : \diamond$ to $\Gamma \vdash P$. □

Example 12.1.3 Here are a process Q that is willing to send a process P along a channel a, and a process R that is willing to receive and execute what Q sends on a:

$$\begin{aligned} Q &\stackrel{\text{def}}{=} \overline{a}\langle @P\rangle.\,Q' \\ R &\stackrel{\text{def}}{=} a(y).\,y\lfloor\star\rfloor\,. \end{aligned}$$

These processes interact as follows:

$$\begin{aligned} Q \mid R &\xrightarrow{\tau} Q' \mid (@P)\lfloor\star\rfloor \\ &\xrightarrow{\tau} Q' \mid P\,. \end{aligned}$$

□

Example 12.1.4 $v \stackrel{\text{def}}{=} (z).\,(P \mid z\lfloor\star\rfloor)$ is an abstraction of type $(\mathtt{unit} \to \diamond) \to \diamond$, and represents a function from process values to processes that runs the process-argument in parallel with P. We have

$$v\lfloor @R\rfloor \xrightarrow{\tau} P \mid (@R)\lfloor\star\rfloor \xrightarrow{\tau} P \mid R\,.$$

$w \stackrel{\text{def}}{=} (y).\,(P \mid y\lfloor @R\rfloor)$ has type $((\mathtt{unit} \to \diamond) \to \diamond) \to \diamond$, and takes an abstraction of the same type as v as argument. We have

$$w\lfloor v \rfloor \xrightarrow{\tau} P \mid v\lfloor @R \rfloor \ (\xrightarrow{\tau})^2 \ P \mid P \mid R. \qquad \square$$

It is worth stressing that in the higher-order calculi of the book, restriction remains a static binder. Therefore the mechanism of scope extrusion exists also in HOπ. For instance, suppose z is a name that occurs free in P and Q, and consider the process

$$\boldsymbol{\nu} z\, (\overline{x}\langle @P \rangle .\, Q).$$

This process interacts with a process $x(y).\, (y\lfloor\star\rfloor \mid R)$ as follows:

$$\begin{array}{ll} & x(y).\, (y\lfloor\star\rfloor \mid R) \mid \boldsymbol{\nu} z\, (\overline{x}\langle @P\rangle .\, Q) \\ \xrightarrow{\tau} & \boldsymbol{\nu} z\, ((@P)\lfloor\star\rfloor \mid R \mid Q) \\ \xrightarrow{\tau} & \boldsymbol{\nu} z\, (P \mid R \mid Q)\,. \end{array}$$

The name z is initially local to the sender. At the end, the scope of z embraces both sender and receiver: a scope extrusion has therefore been accomplished. Static binding says that binders cannot be broken or changed: if a name is bound by a restriction, then that name, and all copies of it that may be made (for instance, by communicating it), will be bound by that restriction for ever; similarly, if a name is not bound by a restriction, then that name, and its copies, will never be so.

Had we decided that restriction were a *dynamic*, rather than static, operator, then the interaction above would become

$$\begin{array}{ll} & x(y).\, (y\lfloor\star\rfloor \mid R) \mid \boldsymbol{\nu} z\, (\overline{x}\langle @P\rangle .\, Q) \\ \xrightarrow{\tau} & (@P)\lfloor\star\rfloor \mid R \mid \boldsymbol{\nu} z\, Q \\ \xrightarrow{\tau} & P \mid R \mid \boldsymbol{\nu} z\, Q\,. \end{array}$$

Note that the communication has destroyed the privacy of the z-link between P and Q: the free occurrences of z in P have evaded the restriction that embraced them. In this case, since a restricted name can later be visible outside the restriction, α-conversion cannot be applied. (Hence one may argue that restriction is not even a binder any more.) The main advantage of restriction as a dynamic operator is an easier semantics, operationally and denotationally. On the other hand, the static operator facilitates the analysis of a process from its text and is pragmatically more useful. For this reason, in this book we consider only the static operator.

Remark 12.1.5 (Values) The values of HOπ cannot reduce autonomously: no reduction of the form $v \xrightarrow{\tau} v'$ is possible. We could say that values are in normal form. This property would not hold if, for instance, the grammar for values allowed applications and nesting of abstractions. In that case, $v \stackrel{\text{def}}{=} ((x).\, (y).\, P)\lfloor w \rfloor$ would be a value, and $\overline{a}v$ would be a process. However, v is not a normal form, for it has a reduction $v \xrightarrow{\tau} (y).\, P\{w/x\}$. Admitting values that are not normal forms would force us to specify a reduction strategy, in order to say, for instance, whether in an expression such as $\overline{a}v \mid a(x).\, P$ the value v should be reduced to a normal form before the communication at a takes place (a positive answer would mean adopting a call-by-value strategy). We require that values in HOπ are normal forms in order to avoid having to specify a reduction strategy for value expressions. We are thus able to concentrate on basic issues of higher-order process calculi, including their expressivity. We regard reduction strategies as an important but orthogonal issue. Reduction strategies are best understood separately. We will study them in Part VI. □

Remark 12.1.6 (Matching) A matching operator for testing equality between names is not very useful in HOπ, because names cannot be communicated and therefore any match in a process could be statically resolved. On the other hand, a matching operator for syntactic equality between higher-order values would be far too powerful: it would allow inspection of the syntax of processes, thus violating elementary algebraic laws such as commutativity and associativity of parallel composition. Hence in HOπ there is no matching. □

Remark 12.1.7 ('Higher order') We call a value whose type involves function types – and which may therefore contain processes – a *higher-order value*; and by a *higher-order calculus* we mean a calculus that may have higher-order values.

'Higher-order' is therefore a *syntactic* qualification. As such, the π-calculus is not higher order. However, the encodings of higher-order calculi into π calculus in Chapter 13 show that the π-calculus is *semantically* higher order. □

Exercise 12.1.8 (Subject Reduction in HO$\pi^{\mathtt{unit},\to\diamond}$) Prove the analogue of Theorem 6.3.7 (Subject Reduction) for HO$\pi^{\mathtt{unit},\to\diamond}$. □

Definition 12.1.9 We say that a type is *functional* if its outermost construct is a function type; formally T is a functional type if $T = S \to \diamond$ for some S (if there are recursive types, replace $=$ with $\sim_{\mathrm{type}}$). □

12.1.1 Derivability of replication

The replication-free fragment of HO$\pi^{\mathtt{unit},\to\diamond}$ – indeed, of any similar language in which processes may be communicated – has already the power of replication. To see this, define

$$R \stackrel{\mathrm{def}}{=} a(x).\, (z\lfloor\star\rfloor \mid x\lfloor\star\rfloor \mid \overline{a}x)$$

and consider the abstraction

$$\texttt{Bang} \stackrel{\text{def}}{=} (z).\, \nu a\, (R \mid \overline{a}\langle @R \rangle)\,.$$

For any process P we have, for $R' \stackrel{\text{def}}{=} R\{^{@P}\!/\!_z\}$ and $R^* \stackrel{\text{def}}{=} \nu a\, (R' \mid \overline{a}\langle @R' \rangle)$,

$$\texttt{Bang}\lfloor @P \rfloor \xrightarrow{\tau} R^* (\xrightarrow{\tau})^3 \equiv P \mid R^* (\xrightarrow{\tau})^3 \equiv P \mid P \mid R^* \ldots\,.$$

That is, $\texttt{Bang}\lfloor @P \rfloor$ behaves as $!P$. The definition of $\texttt{Bang}$ closely resembles that of the fixed point combinator Y of the λ-calculus [Bar84, page 131]. The correctness of this encoding of replication is proved in Exercise 13.2.18.

Despite its derivability, replication is incorporated in the syntax because it facilitates the comparison with the π-calculus, whose operators include replication, in Section 13.1.

12.1.2 Normalization

We show that every well-typed $\text{HO}\pi^{\texttt{unit},\rightarrow\diamond}$ expression is *strongly normalizing* with respect to β-contraction, and has an *η-saturated normal form.* These normal forms are useful when reasoning with the calculus.

Following λ-calculus terminology, we call an expression $((x).\, P)\lfloor v : T \rfloor$ a *β-redex*, and the replacement of a subterm $((x).\, P)\lfloor v : T \rfloor$ of an expression with $P\{^v\!/\!_x\}$ a *β-contraction step.* We then say:

Definition 12.1.10

(1) An expression E *β-contracts to* E', written $E \succ_\beta E'$, if E' can be obtained from E by a finite sequence of β-contraction steps; formally, $\succ_\beta$ is the least precongruence on processes and values that satisfies the rule

$$((x).\, P)\lfloor v : T \rfloor \;\; \succ_\beta \;\; P\{^v\!/\!_x\}\,. \tag{12.1}$$

(2) An expression E is in *β-normal form* if E does not contain any β-redexes.

(3) *β-conversion*, written $=_\beta$, is the least congruence on processes and values that satisfies the rule

$$((x).\, P)\lfloor v : T \rfloor \;\; =_\beta \;\; P\{^v\!/\!_x\}\,.$$

(4) We write $P \longrightarrow_\beta P'$, and say that P *β-reduces* to P', if $P \xrightarrow{\tau} P'$ and the transition derivation of $P \xrightarrow{\tau} P'$ uses rule APP. □

Note that $P \succ_\beta P'$ does not imply $P \Longrightarrow P'$, for the β-redexes contracted in $P \succ_\beta P'$ may be in arbitrary subterms, in particular in subterms underneath prefixes and replications.

In a process in β-normal form, every application has the form $x\lfloor v : T \rfloor$, where the operator of the application is a name. It is not obvious a priori whether every well-typed process has a β-normal form: since v may contain processes, performing the β-step (12.1) does not necessarily simplify the original process, in the sense of reducing the number of process constructs in its syntax. We show below that the β-normal form property holds for $\mathrm{HO}\pi^{\mathtt{unit},\to\diamond}$; indeed we show something stronger; see Corollary 12.1.14. We will see in Section 12.2.1 that the property is lost with the addition of recursive types. These are the analogues of well-known results for typed λ-calculi (see, for instance [Kri93, GLT88]); the proofs are also analogous, and are therefore omitted.

Example 12.1.11 Let v and w be as defined in Example 12.1.4. For any process value $@R$, the β-normal form of $v\lfloor @R \rfloor$ is $P \mid R$; the β-normal form of $w\lfloor v \rfloor$ is $P \mid P \mid R$. For any prefix π, the β-normal form of $!\pi.\, w\lfloor v \rfloor$ is $!\pi.\,(P \mid P \mid R)$. $\square$

Lemma 12.1.12 (Confluence for $\succ_\beta$) Suppose that P is a well-typed process of $\mathrm{HO}\pi^{\mathtt{unit},\to\diamond}$. If $P \succ_\beta P_1$ and $P \succ_\beta P_2$, then there is P_3 such that $P_1 \succ_\beta P_3$ and $P_2 \succ_\beta P_3$. $\square$

Lemma 12.1.13 (Strong normalization) Suppose that P is a well-typed process of $\mathrm{HO}\pi^{\mathtt{unit},\to\diamond}$. Then there is no infinite sequence of β-contraction steps starting from P. $\square$

Corollary 12.1.14 For every well-typed $\mathrm{HO}\pi^{\mathtt{unit},\to\diamond}$ process P there is a unique β-normal form P' such that $P \succ_\beta P'$, and there is no infinite sequence of β-contraction steps beginning at P. (Hence all sequences of β-contractions beginning at P will eventually lead to P'.) $\square$

The following lemma, which asserts that relation $\succ_\beta$ is an expansion relation (Definition 2.4.58), will also be useful:

Lemma 12.1.15 Suppose $\Gamma \vdash P, Q$ with Γ closed, and $P \succ_\beta Q$.

(1) If $P \xrightarrow{\tau} P'$ then there is Q' such that $Q \xrightarrow{\hat{\tau}} Q'$ and $P' \succ_\beta Q'$.
(2) Conversely, if $Q \xrightarrow{\tau} Q'$ then there is P' such that $P \xrightarrow{\tau} P'$ and $P' \succ_\beta Q'$. $\square$

Having considered β-redexes, we now briefly look at *η-redexes.* But we consider the addition of redexes, rather than their elimination. We will use the resulting *η-saturated normal forms* in some proofs in later sections.

We recall that the notation $\mathcal{O}(\Delta(a))$ indicates the type of the values that may be carried along a under the type assignment Δ. We say that a well-typed process is in η-saturated normal form if no name with a functional type appears as an argument of an output or of an application. Formally:

Definition 12.1.16 A process P well typed in Δ is an *η-saturated normal form* if all nodes in the transition derivation of $\Delta \vdash P$ have the following property: if the node is of the form $\Gamma \vdash \overline{a}w.\, Q$ and $\mathcal{O}(\Gamma(a))$ is a functional type, or of the form $\Gamma \vdash v\lfloor w : T \rfloor$ and T is a functional type, then the argument w is an abstraction. $\square$

Exercise 12.1.17 Show that every well-typed $\mathrm{HO}\pi^{\mathtt{unit},\to\diamond}$ process has a unique η-saturated normal form obtained by applying the following rules from left to right:

$$\begin{array}{rcll} v\lfloor y : S \rfloor & = & v\lfloor (z).\, y\lfloor z : T \rfloor : S \rfloor & \text{if } S = T \to \diamond \\ \overline{x}y.\, P & = & \overline{x}\langle (z).\, y\lfloor z : T \rfloor \rangle.\, P & \text{if } \mathcal{O}(\Gamma(x)) = T \to \diamond \end{array}$$

where, in the second line, Γ is the type environment for $\overline{x}y.\, P$. Moreover, if $\Gamma \vdash P$ and P_η is the η-saturated normal form obtained from P, then also $\Gamma \vdash P_\eta$. $\square$

12.1.3 Barbed congruence on values

In Section 9.4 we defined the notion of (Γ/Δ)-context; these are typed contexts whose hole is to be filled in with a process well typed in Δ. We used (Γ/Δ)-contexts to define typed barbed congruence. In $\mathrm{HO}\pi$, since values may contain processes, it is useful to define barbed congruence also on values. We call a $(\Gamma/\Delta /\!\!/ T)$-context a context that, when filled in with a value v such that $\mathrm{HO}\pi \triangleright \Delta \vdash v : T$, becomes a process well typed in Γ.

Definition 12.1.18 (Value context) A *value context* is a process expression in which an occurrence of a value has been replaced by a hole of the form $[_T]$. A $(\Gamma/\Delta /\!\!/ T)$*-context* is a value context C with hole $[_T]$ such that $\Gamma \vdash C : \diamond$ assuming the typing rule

$$\text{TV-}\Delta\text{T-HOLE} \quad \frac{\Theta \text{ extends } \Delta}{\Theta \vdash [_T] : T}$$

for the hole. $\square$

As we are not considering subtyping in $\mathrm{HO}\pi$, Θ extends Δ simply means that $\Theta = \Delta', \Delta$, for some Δ'.

Definition 12.1.19 (Barbed congruence on values) Suppose $\mathrm{HO}\pi^{\mathtt{unit},\to\diamond} \triangleright \Delta \vdash v_i : T \ (i = 1, 2)$. We say that v_1 and v_2 are *barbed congruent at* $(\Delta; T)$, written $\mathrm{HO}\pi^{\texttt{unit},\to\diamond} \triangleright \Delta \vdash v_1 \cong^{c} v_2 : T$ if, for each closed type environment Γ and $(\Gamma/\Delta/\!\!/T)$-context C, we have $C[v_1] \dot{\approx} C[v_2]$. □

The following lemma is useful for manipulating values; it relates barbed congruence between two values to barbed congruence between two processes.

Lemma 12.1.20 Suppose $\mathrm{HO}\pi^{\texttt{unit},\to\diamond} \triangleright \Delta \vdash v_i : T$ $(i = 1, 2)$, and a is fresh for Δ. Then $\mathrm{HO}\pi^{\texttt{unit},\to\diamond} \triangleright \Delta \vdash v_1 \cong^{c} v_2 : T$ iff $\mathrm{HO}\pi^{\texttt{unit},\to\diamond}(\Delta, a : \sharp T) \triangleright \overline{a}v_1 \cong^{c} \overline{a}v_2$.

Proof The implication from left to right follows from the definitions of barbed congruence on processes and on values: both definitions use quantification on contexts, and a context for the $\overline{a}v_i$'s determines a context for the v_i's. For the opposite implication we have to show that for each type environment Γ and $(\Gamma/\Delta/\!\!/T)$-context C, we have $C[v_1] \dot{\approx} C[v_2]$. We prove, by induction on C, that we can find a $(\Gamma/\Delta, a : \sharp T)$-context D such that $\Gamma \triangleright C[v_i] \cong^{c} D[\overline{a}v_i]$, for some a fresh for v_i $(i = 1, 2)$. This will conclude the proof because from the hypothesis $\mathrm{HO}\pi^{\texttt{unit},\to\diamond}(\Delta, a : \sharp T) \triangleright \overline{a}v_1 \cong^{c} \overline{a}v_2$ we have

$$D[\overline{a}v_1] \dot{\approx} D[\overline{a}v_2],$$

hence also $C[v_1] \dot{\approx} C[v_2]$, by transitivity.

We consider only the base case when $C \stackrel{\text{def}}{=} w\lfloor[\cdot]\rfloor$ (we omit types). Define $D \stackrel{\text{def}}{=} \boldsymbol{\nu} a\,([\cdot] \mid a(x).\, w\lfloor x \rfloor)$, for some fresh a. We have

$$\begin{array}{rcl} D[\overline{a}v_i] & = & \boldsymbol{\nu} a\,(\overline{a}v_i \mid a(x).\, w\lfloor x \rfloor) \\ & \cong^{c} & w\lfloor v_i \rfloor \\ & = & C[v_i] \end{array}$$

where the occurrence of $\cong^{c}$ is due to the application of the HOπ version of the π-calculus law of Corollary 2.4.19(1), whose proof is considered in Section 13.2.4. □

12.2 Other HOπ languages

12.2.1 Recursive types

In a higher-order calculus such as the λ-calculus, recursive types allow us to type self applications. The same happens in HOπ: if $S \stackrel{\text{def}}{=} \mu X.\,(X \to \diamond)$, then (omitting type annotations) the abstraction $(x).\, x\lfloor x \rfloor$ has type S, and therefore the process $((x).\, x\lfloor x \rfloor)\lfloor (x).\, x\lfloor x \rfloor \rfloor$ is well typed. Typability of self application implies loss of strong normalization, for we have

$$((x).\, x\lfloor x \rfloor)\lfloor (x).\, x\lfloor x \rfloor \rfloor \succ_{\beta} ((x).\, x\lfloor x \rfloor)\lfloor (x).\, x\lfloor x \rfloor \rfloor \succ_{\beta} \dots\,.$$

Similarly, with recursive types the transformation of processes into η-saturated normal form may not be possible. As a consequence, certain aspects of the theory of process-passing calculi become more complex. Examples are the definition of behavioural equivalences (we will not look into this here; most of the results discussed in the notes at the end of the Part rely on strong normalization), and the proofs of correctness of the encodings into first-order calculi. The extension of $\mathrm{HO}\pi^{\mathtt{unit},\rightarrow\diamond}$ with recursive types is $\mathrm{HO}\pi^{\mathtt{unit},\mu,\rightarrow\diamond}$; the extension involves the standard additions to the grammar of types and to the typing rules, as described in Section 6.7.

12.2.2 Asynchronous HOπ

The asynchronous version of HOπ, called AHOπ, is obtained in the usual way, dropping continuations underneath output prefixes and disallowing output particles in summations (matching is already absent from HOπ). In AHOπ, the output and application constructs are strikingly similar. An output $\overline{a}w$ gives rise to interactions such as $a(x).\,P \mid \overline{a}w \xrightarrow{\tau} P\{w/x\}$; an application $v\lfloor w \rfloor$ to interactions such as $((x).\,P)\lfloor w \rfloor \xrightarrow{\tau} P\{w/x\}$. We may think of the former as a *located interaction*, and the latter as a *non-located interaction*. In the former case, the name a is needed to identify the abstraction $(x).\,P$ and the argument w, since they may not be in contiguous positions. Following this analogy, output and application may be coalesced into a single construct; see the references at the end of the Part.

13

Comparing First-Order and Higher-Order Calculi

13.1 Compiling higher order into first order

Passing processes looks like a drastic departure from passing names. We show in this section and the next, however, that process-passing can be faithfully compiled down to name-passing. We present two main compilations. The second is an optimization of the first. Moreover, the second, unlike the first, is also defined on calculi with recursive types. However, the first compilation is mathematically easier to work with.

We begin with the first compilation, which we call $\mathcal{D}$. The communication of a higher-order value v is translated as the communication of a private name that acts as a pointer to (the translation of) v and that the recipient can use to trigger a copy of (the translation of) v, with appropriate arguments. For instance a process $\overline{a}\langle (x).\, R\rangle.\, \mathbf{0}$ is translated to the process $(\boldsymbol{\nu} y)\overline{a}y.\, !y(x).\, \mathcal{D}[\![R]\!]$; a recipient of the pointer y can use it to activate as many copies of $\mathcal{D}[\![R]\!]$ as needed, with appropriate arguments. The compilation separates the acts of *copying* and of *activating* the value $(x).\, R$; copying is rendered by the replication, and activation by communications along the pointer y. Here are some simple examples of how the compilation works. We omit, for now, all type annotations.

Example 13.1.1 Let $P \stackrel{\text{def}}{=} a(x).\, x\lfloor\star\rfloor \mid \overline{a}\langle (z).\, R\rangle$. It holds that

$$P \xrightarrow{\tau} ((z).\, R)\lfloor\star\rfloor \xrightarrow{\tau} R\{\star/z\}.$$

The translation of P is, with y fresh,

$$\mathcal{D}[\![P]\!] = a(x).\, \overline{x}\star \mid (\boldsymbol{\nu} y)\, \overline{a}y.\, !y(z).\, \mathcal{D}[\![R]\!]$$

and we have

$$\begin{array}{rcl} \mathcal{D}[\![P]\!] & \xrightarrow{\tau} & \boldsymbol{\nu} y\, (\overline{y}\star \mid !y(z).\, \mathcal{D}[\![R]\!]) \\ & \xrightarrow{\tau} & \boldsymbol{\nu} y\, (\mathcal{D}[\![R]\!]\{\star/z\} \mid !y(z).\, \mathcal{D}[\![R]\!]) \end{array}$$

$$\sim^{\mathrm{c}} \quad \mathcal{D}[\![R]\!]\{\star/z\} \tag{13.1}$$

where (13.1) is derived from the law $\boldsymbol{\nu} x\,(P \mid !x(z).\, Q) \sim^{\mathrm{c}} P$ if $x \notin \mathsf{fn}(P)$. □

In the example above, it is important that the trigger name y is private: if it were not, a process in the surrounding environment could interfere with the second communication step.

Example 13.1.2 Let $v \stackrel{\text{def}}{=} (z).\,(z\lfloor\star\rfloor \mid z\lfloor\star\rfloor)$, and $P \stackrel{\text{def}}{=} \overline{a}v \mid a(y).\, y\lfloor(x).\, R\rfloor$. We have $P \Longrightarrow R\{\star/x\} \mid R\{\star/x\}$. The translation of P is

$$\mathcal{D}[\![P]\!] = (\boldsymbol{\nu} b)\, \overline{a}b.\, !b(z).\,(\overline{z}\star \mid \overline{z}\star) \mid a(y).\,(\boldsymbol{\nu} c)\, \overline{y}c.\, !c(x).\, \mathcal{D}[\![R]\!]$$

and we have, proceeding as in the previous example,

$$\begin{array}{rcl}
\mathcal{D}[\![P]\!] & \stackrel{\tau}{\longrightarrow} & \boldsymbol{\nu} b\,(!b(z).\,(\overline{z}\star \mid \overline{z}\star) \mid (\boldsymbol{\nu} c)\, \overline{b}c.\, !c(x).\, \mathcal{D}[\![R]\!]) \\
& \stackrel{\tau}{\longrightarrow} & (\boldsymbol{\nu} b, c)\,(\overline{c}\star \mid \overline{c}\star \mid !b(z).\,(\overline{z}\star \mid \overline{z}\star) \mid !c(x).\, \mathcal{D}[\![R]\!]) \\
& \stackrel{\tau}{\longrightarrow}\stackrel{\tau}{\longrightarrow}\equiv & (\boldsymbol{\nu} b, c)\,(\mathcal{D}[\![R]\!]\{\star/x\} \mid \mathcal{D}[\![R]\!]\{\star/x\} \mid !b(z).\,(\overline{z}\star \mid \overline{z}\star) \mid !c(x).\, \mathcal{D}[\![R]\!]) \\
& \sim^{\mathrm{c}} & \mathcal{D}[\![R\{\star/x\}]\!] \mid \mathcal{D}[\![R\{\star/x\}]\!] \\
& = & \mathcal{D}[\![R\{\star/x\} \mid R\{\star/x\}]\!].
\end{array}$$

□

The examples above show translations of applications $v\lfloor w\rfloor$ in which v is a name; in this case the application is translated in the same way as an output $\overline{v}w$. Here is an example in which v is an abstraction (it is similar to Example 13.1.1, except that $(z).\, R$ is the argument of an application, rather than the value being output):

Example 13.1.3 Let $P \stackrel{\text{def}}{=} ((x).\, x\lfloor\star\rfloor)\lfloor(z).\, R\rfloor$. It holds that

$$P \stackrel{\tau}{\longrightarrow} ((z).\, R)\lfloor\star\rfloor \stackrel{\tau}{\longrightarrow} R\{\star/z\}.$$

The translation of P is, with q, y fresh,

$$\mathcal{D}[\![P]\!] = (\boldsymbol{\nu} q, y)\,\Big(q(x).\, \overline{x}\star \mid \overline{q}y.\, !y(z).\, \mathcal{D}[\![R]\!]\Big)$$

and, proceeding as in Example 13.1.1, we have $\mathcal{D}[\![P]\!] \stackrel{\tau}{\longrightarrow}\stackrel{\tau}{\longrightarrow}\sim^{\mathrm{c}} \mathcal{D}[\![R\{\star/z\}]\!]$. □

The compilation modifies types: a name used in HOπ to exchange processes becomes, in π-calculus, a name used for exchanging other names. The definition of the compilation on types, type environments, values, and terms is given in Table 13.1. The source calculus is HO$\pi^{\mathtt{unit},\rightarrow\diamond}$; the target calculus is $\pi^{\mathtt{unit},\mathsf{i/o}}$. We translate only well-typed expressions. The translation of an expression is annotated with a type environment and (for higher-order values) a type ascribed to the expression. Thus $\mathcal{D}[\![P]\!]^{\Gamma}$ is defined if $\mathrm{HO}\pi^{\mathtt{unit},\to\diamond} \triangleright \Gamma \vdash P$, and $\mathcal{D}[\![v]\!]^{\Gamma;T}$ if $\mathrm{HO}\pi^{\mathtt{unit},\to\diamond} \triangleright \Gamma \vdash v : T$. These annotations are used for assigning the appropriate types to the names introduced by the compilation. The notation $S^{\leftarrow\sharp}$ indicates the replacement of the outermost $\mathsf{i/o}$ tag in S with $\sharp$. We recall that if $\mathcal{D}[\![v]\!]^{\Gamma;T}$ is an abstraction, say $(x).\,P$, then $a\,\mathcal{D}[\![v]\!]^{\Gamma;T}$ is the input-prefixed process $a(x).\,P$.

In the translation of an application $v\lfloor w : S\rfloor$, we distinguish four cases, depending on whether v is a name or an abstraction, and whether S is `unit` or a functional type. If v is a name, the application is translated as an output, namely the output of w, or a trigger for w, at v; otherwise v is an abstraction and it receives its argument via a communication. If S is `unit` then w is a transmissible value in the π-calculus; otherwise w is a higher-order value and has to be translated.

The translation of a name x (second clause in the translation of higher-order values in Table 13.1) uses the translation of $x\lfloor y : S\rfloor$, which, if y has a functional type, recursively requires the translation of name y. This recursion is well-founded (that is, the translation terminates) because the order of the type of y is smaller than that of the type of x. The translation would loop if the types were recursive, which explains why the source calculus has no recursive types.

As in Notation 2.2.13, we take an expression such as

$$M + \boldsymbol{\nu} x\, \overline{a}x.\, P$$

as an abbreviation for

$$\boldsymbol{\nu} x\, (M + \overline{a}x.\, P)$$

assuming x not free in M.

Exercise 13.1.4 Add the type annotations to the source and target processes in Examples 13.1.1–13.1.3. □

Exercise 13.1.5 Prove that

$$\mathcal{D}[\![(\boldsymbol{\nu} a : \sharp T)\,(a(x).\,P \mid \overline{a}w)]\!]^{\Gamma} = \mathcal{D}[\![((x).\,P)\lfloor w : T\rfloor]\!]^{\Gamma}.$$

□

The equality in Exercise 13.1.5 is acceptable because the source processes, $(\boldsymbol{\nu} a : \sharp T)\,(a(x).\,P \mid \overline{a}w)$ and $((x).\,P)\lfloor w : T\rfloor$, have the same observable behaviour.

Exercise 13.1.6 Let $T \stackrel{\mathrm{def}}{=} \mathtt{unit} \to \diamond$, and $\Gamma \stackrel{\mathrm{def}}{=} b : \sharp T,\, x : \sharp T$. Show that $\mathcal{D}[\![b(y).\,\overline{x}y]\!]^{\Gamma} = \mathcal{D}[\![b(y).\,\overline{x}\langle (z).\, y\lfloor z : \mathtt{unit}\rfloor\rangle]\!]^{\Gamma}$. □

In this table we abbreviate $\mathcal{D}[\![E]\!]$ as $[\![E]\!]$, for any expression E.

Translation of types

$$[\![\sharp\, T]\!] \stackrel{\text{def}}{=} \sharp\, [\![T]\!] \qquad [\![\mathtt{unit}]\!] \stackrel{\text{def}}{=} \mathtt{unit}$$

$$[\![T \to \diamond]\!] \stackrel{\text{def}}{=} \mathsf{o}\, [\![T]\!]$$

Translation of type environments

$$[\![\emptyset]\!] \stackrel{\text{def}}{=} \emptyset$$

$$[\![\Gamma, x : S]\!] \stackrel{\text{def}}{=} [\![\Gamma]\!], x : [\![S]\!]$$

Translation of higher-order values

$$[\![(x).\, P]\!]^{\Gamma;T} \stackrel{\text{def}}{=} (x).\, [\![P]\!]^{\Gamma, x:S} \qquad \text{if } T = S \to \diamond$$

$$[\![x]\!]^{\Gamma;T} \stackrel{\text{def}}{=} (y).\, [\![x\lfloor y : S\rfloor]\!]^{\Gamma, y:S} \qquad \text{if } T = S \to \diamond$$

Translation of processes (We assume that names a, b are fresh)

$$[\![\overline{x}v.\, P]\!]^{\Gamma} \stackrel{\text{def}}{=} \begin{cases} \overline{x}v.\, [\![P]\!]^{\Gamma} & \text{if } \Gamma \vdash x : \sharp\, \mathtt{unit} \\ (\boldsymbol{\nu} b : [\![S]\!]^{\leftarrow\sharp})\, \overline{x}b.\, ([\![P]\!]^{\Gamma} \mid !b\, [\![v]\!]^{\Gamma;S}) & \\ \qquad \text{if } \Gamma \vdash x : \sharp\, S \text{ and } S \text{ is a functional type} & \end{cases}$$

$$[\![v\lfloor w : S\rfloor]\!]^{\Gamma} \stackrel{\text{def}}{=} \begin{cases} \overline{v}w & \text{if } v \text{ is a name and } S = \mathtt{unit} \\ (\boldsymbol{\nu} a : \sharp\, \mathtt{unit})\, (a\, [\![v]\!]^{\Gamma;\mathtt{unit}\to\diamond} \mid \overline{a}w) & \\ \qquad \text{if } v \text{ is not a name and } S = \mathtt{unit} & \\ (\boldsymbol{\nu} b : [\![S]\!]^{\leftarrow\sharp})\, \overline{v}b.\, !b\, [\![w]\!]^{\Gamma;S} & \\ \qquad \text{if } v \text{ is a name and } S \text{ is a functional type} & \\ (\boldsymbol{\nu} a : \sharp\, [\![S]\!], b : [\![S]\!]^{\leftarrow\sharp})(a\, [\![v]\!]^{\Gamma;S\to\diamond} \mid \overline{a}b.\, !b\, [\![w]\!]^{\Gamma;S}) & \\ \qquad \text{if } v \text{ is not a name and } S \text{ is a functional type} & \end{cases}$$

$$[\![y(x).\, P]\!]^{\Gamma} \stackrel{\text{def}}{=} y(x).\, [\![P]\!]^{\Gamma, x:T} \qquad \text{if } \Gamma \vdash y : \sharp\, T$$

$$[\![\tau.\, P]\!]^{\Gamma} \stackrel{\text{def}}{=} \tau.\, [\![P]\!]^{\Gamma} \qquad [\![M + N]\!]^{\Gamma} \stackrel{\text{def}}{=} [\![M]\!]^{\Gamma} + [\![N]\!]^{\Gamma}$$

$$[\![P \mid Q]\!]^{\Gamma} \stackrel{\text{def}}{=} [\![P]\!]^{\Gamma} \mid [\![Q]\!]^{\Gamma} \qquad [\![!P]\!]^{\Gamma} \stackrel{\text{def}}{=} ![\![P]\!]^{\Gamma}$$

$$[\![(\boldsymbol{\nu} x : T)\, P]\!]^{\Gamma} \stackrel{\text{def}}{=} (\boldsymbol{\nu} x : [\![T]\!])\, [\![P]\!]^{\Gamma, x:T} \qquad [\![\mathbf{0}]\!]^{\Gamma} \stackrel{\text{def}}{=} \mathbf{0}$$

Table 13.1. *The compilation* $\mathcal{D}$ *of* $\mathrm{HO}\pi^{\mathtt{unit},\to\diamond}$ *into the* π*-calculus.*

Exercise 13.1.6 shows that the process $b(y).\,\overline{x}y$, which, syntactically, is both an HOπ process and a π-calculus process, is not translated onto itself. In Section 13.2 we will study optimizations of the compilation, under which such processes are left unchanged by the translation. The syntactic equality in Exercise 13.1.6 will then be replaced by behavioural equivalence. The next exercise generalizes Exercise 13.1.6.

Exercise 13.1.7 (η-expansion) Suppose $S \stackrel{\text{def}}{=} T \to \diamond$. Show that

(1) $\mathcal{D}[\![v\lfloor y : S\rfloor]\!]^{\Gamma} = \mathcal{D}[\![v\lfloor((z).\,y\lfloor z : T\rfloor) : S\rfloor]\!]^{\Gamma}$
(2) $\mathcal{D}[\![\overline{x}y.\,P]\!]^{\Gamma} = \mathcal{D}[\![\overline{x}\langle(z).\,y\lfloor z : T\rfloor\rangle.\,P]\!]^{\Gamma}$, if $\mathcal{O}(\Gamma(x)) = S$. □

Exercises 12.1.17 and 13.1.7 show that a well-typed process P can be rewritten into an η-saturated normal form P' that is well typed under the same type environment as P, and that the translations of P and P' are the same. We will exploit this property in the proof of Lemma 13.1.11.

Lemma 13.1.8 Suppose $z \notin \mathsf{fn}(P)$. Then $\mathcal{D}[\![P]\!]^{\Gamma} = \mathcal{D}[\![P]\!]^{\Gamma, z:T}$, for all T. □

Lemma 13.1.9 For any name x and type T,

$$\mathrm{HO}\pi^{\mathtt{unit},\to\diamond} \triangleright \Gamma \vdash x : T \quad \text{implies} \quad \pi^{\mathtt{unit},\mathsf{i/o}} \triangleright \mathcal{D}[\![\Gamma]\!] \vdash x : \mathcal{D}[\![T]\!] \ .$$

Proof $\mathrm{HO}\pi^{\mathtt{unit},\to\diamond} \triangleright \Gamma \vdash x : T$ implies that $\Gamma(x) = T$, hence also $(\mathcal{D}[\![\Gamma]\!])(x) = \mathcal{D}[\![T]\!]$ and therefore $\pi^{\mathtt{unit},\mathsf{i/o}} \triangleright \mathcal{D}[\![\Gamma]\!] \vdash x : \mathcal{D}[\![T]\!]$. □

Exercise 13.1.10 Find a T and a Γ such that $\pi^{\mathtt{unit},\mathsf{i/o}} \triangleright \mathcal{D}[\![\Gamma]\!] \vdash x : \mathcal{D}[\![T]\!]$ holds but $\mathrm{HO}\pi^{\mathtt{unit},\to\diamond} \triangleright \Gamma \vdash x : T$ does not. (Hint: exploit the subtyping in $\pi^{\mathtt{unit},\mathsf{i/o}}$.) □

Lemma 13.1.11 If $\mathrm{HO}\pi^{\mathtt{unit},\to\diamond} \triangleright \Gamma \vdash P$ then $\pi^{\mathtt{unit},\mathsf{i/o}} \triangleright \mathcal{D}[\![\Gamma]\!] \vdash \mathcal{D}[\![P]\!]^{\Gamma}$.

Proof We can assume that P is in η-saturated normal form (see discussion after Exercise 13.1.7). We prove the assertion by induction on the structure of P.

- Suppose $P = x(y).\,Q$. By rule T-INP, $\Gamma \vdash P$ holds only if, for some T,

$$\Gamma \vdash x : \sharp T \text{ and } \Gamma, y : T \vdash Q \ .$$

From the latter, by induction, we derive

$$\mathcal{D}[\![\Gamma]\!], y : \mathcal{D}[\![T]\!] \vdash \mathcal{D}[\![Q]\!]^{\Gamma, y:T}$$

and, from the former, by Lemma 13.1.9,

$$\mathcal{D}[\![\Gamma]\!] \vdash x : \sharp\,\mathcal{D}[\![T]\!]\,.$$

Hence by rule T-INP we can conclude $\mathcal{D}[\![\Gamma]\!] \vdash \mathcal{D}[\![x(y).\,Q]\!]^{\Gamma}$.

- Suppose $P = v\lfloor w : T\rfloor$, where v is not a name and T is a functional type. Since v is not a name, it must be an abstraction, say $(x).\,Q$, and since P is an η-saturated normal form, w must be an abstraction too, say $(z).\,R$. Then $\Gamma \vdash P$ implies that

$$\Gamma \vdash (x).\,Q : T \to \diamond \qquad \text{and} \qquad \Gamma \vdash (z).\,R : T\ . \tag{13.2}$$

Since T is a functional type, $T = S \to \diamond$, for some S; therefore, from (13.2), by rule TV-ABS we infer

$$\Gamma, x : T \vdash Q \qquad \text{and} \qquad \Gamma, z : S \vdash R\ .$$

Both Q and R are subterms of P; we can therefore apply the induction hypothesis to derive

$$\mathcal{D}[\![\Gamma]\!], x : \mathcal{D}[\![T]\!] \vdash \mathcal{D}[\![Q]\!]^{\Gamma,x:T} \qquad \text{and} \qquad \mathcal{D}[\![\Gamma]\!], z : \mathcal{D}[\![S]\!] \vdash \mathcal{D}[\![R]\!]^{\Gamma,z:S}\ . \tag{13.3}$$

From (13.3), for any fresh a, b we derive

$$\mathcal{D}[\![\Gamma]\!], a : \sharp\,\mathcal{D}[\![T]\!] \vdash a(x).\,\mathcal{D}[\![Q]\!]^{\Gamma,x:T} \qquad \mathcal{D}[\![\Gamma]\!], b : \sharp\,\mathcal{D}[\![S]\!] \vdash b(z).\,\mathcal{D}[\![R]\!]^{\Gamma,z:S}\ .$$

Hence, using also Lemma 13.1.8 and the fact that $\sharp\,\mathcal{D}[\![S]\!]$ is a subtype of $\mathcal{D}[\![T]\!]$,

$$\mathcal{D}[\![\Gamma]\!] \vdash (\nu a : \sharp\,\mathcal{D}[\![T]\!], b : \sharp\,\mathcal{D}[\![S]\!]\,)(a(x).\,\mathcal{D}[\![Q]\!]^{\Gamma,x:T} \mid \overline{a}b.\,!b(z).\,\mathcal{D}[\![R]\!]^{\Gamma,z:S})$$

which concludes the case, for the process on the right of the turnstile is precisely $\mathcal{D}[\![v\lfloor w : T\rfloor]\!]^{\Gamma}$.

The other cases of the induction are similar. □

Lemma 13.1.11 shows that the compilation preserves type judgments. The converse of the lemma is false. For instance,

$$\mathcal{D}[\![x : \sharp\,\mathtt{unit}]\!] \vdash \mathcal{D}[\![x\lfloor\star\rfloor]\!]^{x:\sharp\,\mathtt{unit}}$$

but $x : \sharp\,\mathtt{unit} \vdash x\lfloor\star\rfloor$ does not hold.

In the remainder of the section we prove the operational correspondence, adequacy, and soundness of the compilation. The easiest parts of the proofs are omitted, while others are deferred to exercises at the end of the section.

Lemmas 13.1.12–13.1.14, which show the operational correspondence between a process P and its translation $\mathcal{D}[\![P]\!]^{\Gamma}$, are proved using induction on the depth of the proof of the transition from P (item 1) and of the transition from $\mathcal{D}[\![P]\!]^{\Gamma}$

(item 2). For item (2), note that the outermost operator of $\mathcal{D}[\![P]\!]^\Gamma$ is restriction in three cases: if P itself has restriction as the outermost operator, if P is an application, and if P is an output prefix.

Lemma 13.1.12 (Operational correspondence for $\mathcal{D}$ on inputs and outputs of unit value) Suppose $\mathrm{HO}\pi^{\mathtt{unit},\to\diamond} \triangleright \Gamma \vdash P$ with Γ closed, $\mathcal{O}(\Gamma(a)) = \mathtt{unit}$, and α is an input $a\star$ or an output $\overline{a}\star$.

(1) If $P \xrightarrow{\alpha} P'$ then $\mathcal{D}[\![P]\!]^\Gamma \xrightarrow{\alpha} \mathcal{D}[\![P']\!]^\Gamma$.
(2) Conversely, if $\mathcal{D}[\![P]\!]^\Gamma \xrightarrow{\alpha} P''$ then there is P' such that $P \xrightarrow{\alpha} P'$ and $P'' = \mathcal{D}[\![P']\!]^\Gamma$. □

Lemma 13.1.13 (Operational correspondence for $\mathcal{D}$ on higher-order input actions) Suppose $\mathrm{HO}\pi^{\mathtt{unit},\to\diamond} \triangleright \Gamma \vdash P$ with Γ closed, $\mathcal{O}(\Gamma(a)) = T \to \diamond$, $\mathrm{HO}\pi^{\mathtt{unit},\to\diamond} \triangleright \Gamma \vdash v : T \to \diamond$, and x is fresh for Γ.

(1) If $P \xrightarrow{av} P'$ then there is P'' such that $\mathcal{D}[\![P]\!]^\Gamma \xrightarrow{ax} \mathcal{D}[\![P'']\!]^{\Gamma,x:T\to\diamond}$ and $P' = P''\{v/x\}$.
(2) Conversely, if $\mathcal{D}[\![P]\!]^\Gamma \xrightarrow{ax} P'''$ then there are P', P'' such that $P \xrightarrow{av} P'$ with $P' = P''\{v/x\}$ and $P''' = \mathcal{D}[\![P'']\!]^{\Gamma,x:T\to\diamond}$. □

Lemma 13.1.14 (Operational correspondence for $\mathcal{D}$ on higher-order output actions) Suppose $\mathrm{HO}\pi^{\mathtt{unit},\to\diamond} \triangleright \Gamma \vdash P$ with Γ closed, and $\mathcal{O}(\Gamma(a)) = T \to \diamond$.

(1) If $P \xrightarrow{(\boldsymbol{\nu}\widetilde{z}:\widetilde{T})\,\overline{a}v} P'$ then there is y fresh for Γ and $\widetilde{z}$ such that

$$\mathcal{D}[\![P]\!]^\Gamma \xrightarrow{(\boldsymbol{\nu}y:\sharp\,\mathcal{D}[\![T]\!])\,\overline{a}y} \equiv (\boldsymbol{\nu}\widetilde{z} : \widetilde{\mathcal{D}[\![T]\!]})\,(\mathcal{D}[\![P']\!]^{\Gamma,\widetilde{z}:\widetilde{T}} \mid !y\,\mathcal{D}[\![v]\!]^{\Gamma,\widetilde{z}:\widetilde{T};T\to\diamond}).$$

(2) Conversely, if $\mathcal{D}[\![P]\!]^\Gamma \xrightarrow{(\boldsymbol{\nu}y:S)\,\overline{a}y} P''$ then $S = \sharp\,\mathcal{D}[\![T]\!]$ and there are $\widetilde{z}$, $\widetilde{T}$, v and P' such that $P \xrightarrow{(\boldsymbol{\nu}\widetilde{z}:\widetilde{T})\,\overline{a}v} P'$ and

$$P'' \equiv (\boldsymbol{\nu}\widetilde{z} : \widetilde{\mathcal{D}[\![T]\!]})\,(\mathcal{D}[\![P']\!]^{\Gamma,\widetilde{z}:\widetilde{T}} \mid !y\,\mathcal{D}[\![v]\!]^{\Gamma,\widetilde{z}:\widetilde{T};T\to\diamond}).$$

□

Lemma 13.1.15 If $\mathrm{HO}\pi^{\mathtt{unit},\to\diamond} \triangleright \Gamma, y : T \vdash P$ where T is not $\mathtt{unit}$, then y may occur free in $\mathcal{D}[\![P]\!]^\Gamma$ only as subject of prefixes. Moreover, if T is a functional type, then y occurs only in output subject position (Definition 2.2.24). □

Lemma 13.1.15 shows that the target language of the compilation is actually Pπ – all names emitted by the translation of a closed process are private.

Lemma 13.1.16 Suppose $\mathrm{HO}\pi^{\mathtt{unit},\to\diamond} \rhd \Gamma, y : T \vdash P$, and $\mathrm{HO}\pi^{\mathtt{unit},\to\diamond} \rhd \Gamma \vdash v : T$, where T is a functional type. Then

$$(\boldsymbol{\nu} y : (\mathcal{D}[\![T]\!])^{\leftarrow\sharp})\,(\mathcal{D}[\![P]\!]^{\Gamma,y:T} \mid {!y}\,\mathcal{D}[\![v]\!]^{\Gamma;T}) \;{}^{\mathrm{c}}\!\succeq \mathcal{D}[\![P\{v/y\}]\!]^{\Gamma}\,.$$

Proof By induction on the order n of T, that is, the depth of arrow-nesting in T (the order of types is studied in Section 13.1.1; see Definition 13.1.29). For $n = 0$ there is nothing to prove: since T is a functional type, its order must be at least 1. For the case $n > 0$ we proceed by induction on the structure of P. We will use the Replication Theorems 2.2.25 and 2.2.26 on $(\boldsymbol{\nu} y : (\mathcal{D}[\![T]\!])^{\leftarrow\sharp})\,(\mathcal{D}[\![P]\!]^{\Gamma,y:T} \mid {!y}\,\mathcal{D}[\![v]\!]^{\Gamma})$; this is possible for, by Lemma 13.1.15, y occurs only in output subject position in $\mathcal{D}[\![P]\!]^{\Gamma}$. Below, for the sake of readability we omit all type annotations in processes. We show the details for only some of the cases; those for the remainder are similar.

- Suppose $P = P_1 \mid P_2$. We have

  $$\boldsymbol{\nu} y\,(\mathcal{D}[\![P]\!] \mid {!y}\,\mathcal{D}[\![v]\!]) = \boldsymbol{\nu} y\,(\mathcal{D}[\![P_1]\!] \mid \mathcal{D}[\![P_2]\!] \mid {!y}\,\mathcal{D}[\![v]\!])$$

  and hence, by the Replication Theorems,

  $$\sim^{\mathrm{c}} \boldsymbol{\nu} y\,(\mathcal{D}[\![P_1]\!] \mid {!y}\,\mathcal{D}[\![v]\!]) \mid \boldsymbol{\nu} y\,(\mathcal{D}[\![P_2]\!] \mid {!y}\,\mathcal{D}[\![v]\!])\,.$$

  By the structural induction,

  $${}^{\mathrm{c}}\!\succeq \mathcal{D}[\![P_1\{v/y\}]\!] \mid \mathcal{D}[\![P_2\{v/y\}]\!] = \mathcal{D}[\![P\{v/y\}]\!]\,.$$

- Suppose $P = x\lfloor y \rfloor$. Then

  $$\begin{aligned}\boldsymbol{\nu} y\,(\mathcal{D}[\![P]\!] \mid {!y}\,\mathcal{D}[\![v]\!]) &\equiv (\boldsymbol{\nu} a, y\,)(\overline{x}a.\,{!a}\,\mathcal{D}[\![y]\!] \mid {!y}\,\mathcal{D}[\![v]\!]) \\ &= (\boldsymbol{\nu} a, y\,)(\overline{x}a.\,{!a}(z).\,\mathcal{D}[\![y\lfloor z \rfloor]\!] \mid {!y}\,\mathcal{D}[\![v]\!])\,.\end{aligned}$$

  Call the last process Q. The type of z can be `unit` or a functional type. We consider only the latter case, which is the more difficult. We have $\mathcal{D}[\![y\lfloor z \rfloor]\!] = \boldsymbol{\nu} b\,(\overline{y}b.\,{!b}\,\mathcal{D}[\![z]\!])$, so, using the Replication Theorems and the other simple laws for garbage-collecting a restricted replication, or pushing it underneath a prefix or a restriction (Lemma 2.2.28(4)),

  $$Q \;\sim^{\mathrm{c}}\; Q' \stackrel{\mathrm{def}}{=} \boldsymbol{\nu} a\,(\overline{x}a.\,{!a}(z).\,(\boldsymbol{\nu} b, y)\,(\overline{y}b.\,{!b}\,\mathcal{D}[\![z]\!] \mid {!y}\,\mathcal{D}[\![v]\!]))\,.$$

  Since $\mathcal{D}[\![v]\!] = (c).\,R$, for some c, R, we have, using a simple law of expansion (Corollary 2.4.19(2), with expansion congruence in place of full bisimilarity) and garbage-collection of useless restricted replications,

  $$Q' \;{}^{\mathrm{c}}\!\succeq\; \boldsymbol{\nu} a\,(\overline{x}a.\,{!a}(z).\,\boldsymbol{\nu} b\,({!b}\,\mathcal{D}[\![z]\!] \mid \mathcal{D}[\![R\{b/c\}]\!]))\,. \tag{13.4}$$

  Since z was the argument of y, the order of the type of z is smaller than that of

y. We can therefore apply the inductive hypothesis on the order of the types to the subterm $\boldsymbol{\nu} b\,(!b\,\mathcal{D}[\![z]\!] \mid \mathcal{D}[\![R\{^{b}\!/\!_{c}\}]\!])$ and infer that

$$\boldsymbol{\nu} b\,(!b\,\mathcal{D}[\![z]\!] \mid \mathcal{D}[\![R\{^{b}\!/\!_{c}\}]\!]) \;{}^{c}\!\succeq \mathcal{D}[\![R\{^{b}\!/\!_{c}\}\{^{z}\!/\!_{b}\}]\!] = \mathcal{D}[\![R\{^{z}\!/\!_{c}\}]\!]\,. \tag{13.5}$$

Using this fact, we can rewrite the right-hand side of (13.4) as

$$\boldsymbol{\nu} a\,(\overline{x}a.\,!a(z).\,\mathcal{D}[\![R\{^{z}\!/\!_{c}\}]\!])$$

and then conclude thus:

$$\begin{aligned} &= \boldsymbol{\nu} a\,(\overline{x}a.\,!a(c).\,\mathcal{D}[\![R]\!]) \\ &= \mathcal{D}[\![x\lfloor v\rfloor]\!] \\ &= \mathcal{D}[\![P\{^{v}\!/\!_{y}\}]\!]\,. \end{aligned}$$

- Suppose $P = y\lfloor w\rfloor$ with $w \stackrel{\text{def}}{=} (x).\,Q$. We have

$$\begin{aligned} \boldsymbol{\nu} y\,(\mathcal{D}[\![P]\!] \mid !y\,\mathcal{D}[\![v]\!]) &\equiv (\boldsymbol{\nu} y, b\,)(\overline{y}b.\,!b(x).\,\mathcal{D}[\![Q]\!] \mid !y\,\mathcal{D}[\![v]\!]) \\ &\simeq^{c} (\boldsymbol{\nu} y, b\,)(\overline{y}b \mid !b(x).\,\mathcal{D}[\![Q]\!] \mid !y\,\mathcal{D}[\![v]\!])\,. \end{aligned}$$

Applying the Replication Theorems and the induction hypothesis we infer

$$\begin{aligned} &\sim^{c} (\boldsymbol{\nu} b\,)(\boldsymbol{\nu} y\,(\overline{y}b \mid !y\,\mathcal{D}[\![v]\!]) \mid \boldsymbol{\nu} y\,(!b(x).\,\mathcal{D}[\![Q]\!] \mid !y\,\mathcal{D}[\![v]\!])) \\ &\sim^{c} (\boldsymbol{\nu} b\,)(\boldsymbol{\nu} y\,(\overline{y}b \mid !y\,\mathcal{D}[\![v]\!]) \mid !b(x).\,\boldsymbol{\nu} y\,(\mathcal{D}[\![Q]\!] \mid !y\,\mathcal{D}[\![v]\!])) \\ &{}^{c}\!\succeq (\boldsymbol{\nu} b\,)(\boldsymbol{\nu} y\,(\overline{y}b \mid !y\,\mathcal{D}[\![v]\!]) \mid !b\,\mathcal{D}[\![w\{^{v}\!/\!_{y}\}]\!])\,. \end{aligned}$$

Since y is used only once, and only to send, we can remove the replication in front of $y\,\mathcal{D}[\![v]\!]$. Rearranging terms, we get

$$\begin{aligned} &\sim^{c} (\boldsymbol{\nu} b, y\,)(y\,\mathcal{D}[\![v]\!] \mid \overline{y}b \mid !b\,\mathcal{D}[\![w\{^{v}\!/\!_{y}\}]\!]) \\ &\sim^{c} (\boldsymbol{\nu} b, y\,)(y\,\mathcal{D}[\![v]\!] \mid \overline{y}b.\,!b\,\mathcal{D}[\![w\{^{v}\!/\!_{y}\}]\!])\,. \end{aligned}$$

Now, if v is an abstraction then we conclude thus:

$$\begin{aligned} &= \mathcal{D}[\![(y\lfloor w\rfloor)\{^{v}\!/\!_{y}\}]\!] \\ &= \mathcal{D}[\![P\{^{v}\!/\!_{y}\}]\!]\,. \end{aligned}$$

Otherwise, v is a name and we have

$$\mathcal{D}[\![v]\!] = (h).\,\boldsymbol{\nu} k\,(\overline{v}k.\,!k\,\mathcal{D}[\![h]\!])$$

hence

$$\begin{array}{rl} & (\boldsymbol{\nu} b, y\,)(y\,\mathcal{D}[\![v]\!] \mid \overline{y}b.\,!b\,\mathcal{D}[\![w\{{}^{v}\!/\!_{y}\}]\!]) \\ \equiv & (\boldsymbol{\nu} b, y, k\,)(y(h).\,\overline{v}k.\,!k\,\mathcal{D}[\![h]\!] \mid \overline{y}b.\,!b\,\mathcal{D}[\![w\{{}^{v}\!/\!_{y}\}]\!]) \\ {}^{c}\!\succeq & (\boldsymbol{\nu} b, k\,)(\overline{v}k.\,!k\,\mathcal{D}[\![b]\!] \mid !b\,\mathcal{D}[\![w\{{}^{v}\!/\!_{y}\}]\!]) \\ \sim^{c} & (\boldsymbol{\nu} k\,)\overline{v}k.\,(\boldsymbol{\nu} b\,)(!k\,\mathcal{D}[\![b]\!] \mid !b\,\mathcal{D}[\![w\{{}^{v}\!/\!_{y}\}]\!])\,. \end{array}$$

We need to expand the translation once more. Assuming that also the argument of v has a functional type (the case of unit type is simpler), we have

$$\mathcal{D}[\![b]\!] = (p).\,\boldsymbol{\nu} q\,(\overline{b}q.\,!q\,\mathcal{D}[\![p]\!])\,.$$

Hence, since $\mathcal{D}[\![w]\!] = (x).\,Q$, for some x, Q, we have, reasoning as previously in the proof,

$$\begin{array}{rl} & (\boldsymbol{\nu} k\,)\overline{v}k.\,(\boldsymbol{\nu} b\,)(!k\,\mathcal{D}[\![b]\!] \mid !b\,\mathcal{D}[\![w\{{}^{v}\!/\!_{y}\}]\!]) \\ = & (\boldsymbol{\nu} k\,)\overline{v}k.\,(\boldsymbol{\nu} b\,)(!k(p).\,\boldsymbol{\nu} q\,\overline{b}q.\,!q\,\mathcal{D}[\![p]\!] \mid !b(x).\,\mathcal{D}[\![Q\{{}^{v}\!/\!_{y}\}]\!]) \\ \sim^{c} & (\boldsymbol{\nu} k\,)\overline{v}k.\,!k(p).\,(\boldsymbol{\nu} b, q\,)(\overline{b}q.\,!q\,\mathcal{D}[\![p]\!] \mid b(x).\,\mathcal{D}[\![Q\{{}^{v}\!/\!_{y}\}]\!]) \\ {}^{c}\!\succeq & (\boldsymbol{\nu} k\,)\overline{v}k.\,!k(p).\,(\boldsymbol{\nu} q\,)(q\,\mathcal{D}[\![p]\!] \mid \mathcal{D}[\![Q\{{}^{v}\!/\!_{y}\}\{{}^{q}\!/\!_{x}\}]\!])\,. \end{array}$$

Now, reasoning as in (13.5), we get

$$\begin{array}{rl} {}^{c}\!\succeq & (\boldsymbol{\nu} k\,)\overline{v}k.\,!k(p).\,\mathcal{D}[\![Q\{{}^{v}\!/\!_{y}\}\{{}^{p}\!/\!_{x}\}]\!] \\ = & (\boldsymbol{\nu} b\,)\overline{v}b.\,!b\,\mathcal{D}[\![w\{{}^{v}\!/\!_{y}\}]\!] \\ = & \mathcal{D}[\![P\{{}^{v}\!/\!_{y}\}]\!]\,. \end{array}$$

□

Remark 13.1.17 The proof above would be much simpler if P were an η-saturated normal form. However, the result for η-saturated normal forms does not imply the result for arbitrary terms; for this, we would also need to prove that, if P_η is the η-saturated normal form of P, then $\mathcal{D}[\![P_\eta\{{}^{v}\!/\!_{y}\}]\!] \;{}^{c}\!\succeq \mathcal{D}[\![P\{{}^{v}\!/\!_{y}\}]\!]$, which is true but requires some work to prove (it is not a consequence of Exercise 13.1.7). □

We can now present the operational correctness of $\mathcal{D}$ on reductions.

Theorem 13.1.18 (Operational correspondence for $\mathcal{D}$ on τ transitions) Suppose $\mathrm{HO}\pi^{\mathtt{unit},\to\diamond} \triangleright \Gamma \vdash P$ and Γ is closed.

(1) If $P \xrightarrow{\tau} P'$ then $\mathcal{D}[\![P]\!]^{\Gamma} \xrightarrow{\tau}\,{}^{c}\!\succeq \mathcal{D}[\![P']\!]^{\Gamma}$.
(2) Conversely, if $\mathcal{D}[\![P]\!]^{\Gamma} \xrightarrow{\tau} P''$ then there is P' such that $P \xrightarrow{\tau} P'$ and $P'' \;{}^{c}\!\succeq \mathcal{D}[\![P']\!]^{\Gamma}$.

Proof Another transition induction, where Lemmas 13.1.12–13.1.16 are used. We consider only the proof of (1), in the case when the last step of the transition derivation of $P \xrightarrow{\tau} P'$ is due to rule COMM-L, and the value transmitted has a functional type T. Thus, $P = P_1 \mid P_2$, and we have

$$P_1 \xrightarrow{(\boldsymbol{\nu}\widetilde{z}:\widetilde{T})\,\overline{a}v} P_1' \quad \text{and} \quad P_2 \xrightarrow{av} P_2'$$

and $P' = (\boldsymbol{\nu}\widetilde{z} : \widetilde{T})\,(P_1' \mid P_2')$. By Lemma 13.1.14

$$\mathcal{D}[\![P_1]\!]^{\Gamma} \xrightarrow{(\boldsymbol{\nu}y:(\mathcal{D}[\![T]\!])^{\leftarrow\sharp})\,\overline{a}y}\equiv (\boldsymbol{\nu}\widetilde{z} : \widetilde{\mathcal{D}[\![T]\!]})\,(\mathcal{D}[\![P_1']\!]^{\Gamma,\widetilde{z}:\widetilde{T}} \mid !y\,\mathcal{D}[\![v]\!]^{\Gamma,\widetilde{z}:\widetilde{T};T\to\diamond}) . \quad (13.6)$$

We also have, using Subject Reduction, that is, Exercise 12.1.8, and Weakening, $\Gamma, \widetilde{z} : \widetilde{T} \vdash P_2$ and $\Gamma, \widetilde{z} : \widetilde{T} \vdash v : T$. We can apply Lemma 13.1.13 and infer that there is P_2'' such that

$$\mathcal{D}[\![P_2]\!]^{\Gamma,\widetilde{z}:\widetilde{T}} \xrightarrow{ay} \mathcal{D}[\![P_2'']\!]^{\Gamma,\widetilde{z}:\widetilde{T},y:T} \quad (13.7)$$

and $P_2' = P_2''\{^{v}\!/\!_{y}\}$. Since the names $\widetilde{z}$ are not free in P_2, by Lemma 13.1.8

$$\mathcal{D}[\![P_2]\!]^{\Gamma,\widetilde{z}:\widetilde{T}} = \mathcal{D}[\![P_2]\!]^{\Gamma} \quad \text{and} \quad \mathcal{D}[\![P_2'']\!]^{\Gamma,\widetilde{z}:\widetilde{T},y:T} = \mathcal{D}[\![P_2'']\!]^{\Gamma,y:T} . \quad (13.8)$$

From (13.6)–(13.8) we can infer

$$\mathcal{D}[\![P_1 \mid P_2]\!]^{\Gamma} \xrightarrow{\tau}\equiv$$
$$(\boldsymbol{\nu}\widetilde{z} : \widetilde{\mathcal{D}[\![T]\!]})\,(\mathcal{D}[\![P_1']\!]^{\Gamma,\widetilde{z}:\widetilde{T}} \mid (\boldsymbol{\nu}y : (\mathcal{D}[\![T]\!])^{\leftarrow\sharp})\,(\mathcal{D}[\![P_2'']\!]^{\Gamma,\widetilde{z}:\widetilde{T},y:T} \mid !y\,\mathcal{D}[\![v]\!]^{\Gamma,\widetilde{z}:\widetilde{T};T\to\diamond}))$$

and now, applying Lemma 13.1.16,

$$\begin{aligned}
&\,^{c}\!\succeq\; (\boldsymbol{\nu}\widetilde{z} : \widetilde{\mathcal{D}[\![T]\!]})\,(\mathcal{D}[\![P_1']\!]^{\Gamma,\widetilde{z}:\widetilde{T}} \mid \mathcal{D}[\![P_2''\{^{v}\!/\!_{y}\}]\!]^{\Gamma,\widetilde{z}:\widetilde{T}}) \\
&= (\boldsymbol{\nu}\widetilde{z} : \widetilde{\mathcal{D}[\![T]\!]})\,(\mathcal{D}[\![P_1']\!]^{\Gamma,\widetilde{z}:\widetilde{T}} \mid \mathcal{D}[\![P_2']\!]^{\Gamma,\widetilde{z}:\widetilde{T}}) \\
&= \mathcal{D}[\![P']\!]^{\Gamma} .
\end{aligned}$$

□

Lemmas 13.1.12–13.1.14 and Theorem 13.1.18 can be composed to give the operational correspondence on weak transitions. We report only the result for weak internal transitions.

Theorem 13.1.19 (Operational correspondence for $\mathcal{D}$ on weak silent transitions) Suppose $\mathrm{HO}\pi^{\mathtt{unit},\to\diamond} \triangleright \Gamma \vdash P$ and Γ is closed.

(1) If $P \overset{\tau}{\Longrightarrow} P'$ then $\mathcal{D}[\![P]\!]^{\Gamma} \overset{\tau}{\Longrightarrow}\succeq \mathcal{D}[\![P']\!]^{\Gamma}$.
(2) Conversely, if $\mathcal{D}[\![P]\!]^{\Gamma} \overset{\tau}{\Longrightarrow} P''$ then there is P' such that $P \overset{\tau}{\Longrightarrow} P'$ and $P'' \succeq \mathcal{D}[\![P']\!]^{\Gamma}$.

Proof By induction on the number of τ steps in $P \stackrel{\tau}{\Longrightarrow} P'$ or $\mathcal{D}[\![P]\!]^{\Gamma} \stackrel{\tau}{\Longrightarrow} P''$, using Theorem 13.1.18. □

In Theorem 13.1.19 it is important to use the expansion relation ($\succeq$) rather than the expansion precongruence (${}^{c}\!\succeq$). The latter is not a bisimulation, and hence does not allow a proof by composition of diagrams.

From the operational correspondence results we derive adequacy.

Corollary 13.1.20 (Adequacy of $\mathcal{D}$) Suppose $\mathrm{HO}\pi^{\mathtt{unit},\to\diamond} \rhd \Gamma \vdash P$ and Γ is closed. Then, for all a, $P \Downarrow_a$ iff $\mathcal{D}[\![P]\!]^{\Gamma} \Downarrow_a$. □

Lemma 13.1.21 Suppose $\mathrm{HO}\pi^{\mathtt{unit},\to\diamond} \rhd \Gamma \vdash P, Q$ and Γ is closed. It holds that $P \stackrel{\centerdot}{\approx} Q$ iff $\mathcal{D}[\![P]\!]^{\Gamma} \stackrel{\centerdot}{\approx} \mathcal{D}[\![Q]\!]^{\Gamma}$.

Proof From Theorem 13.1.19 and Corollary 13.1.20. □

From Lemma 13.1.21 and the compositionality of the encoding we now derive soundness for barbed congruence:

Theorem 13.1.22 (Soundness for $\mathcal{D}$) Suppose $\mathrm{HO}\pi^{\mathtt{unit},\to\diamond} \rhd \Gamma \vdash P, Q$. Then $\pi^{\mathtt{unit},\mathrm{i/o}}(\mathcal{D}[\![\Gamma]\!]) \rhd \mathcal{D}[\![P]\!]^{\Gamma} \cong^{c} \mathcal{D}[\![Q]\!]^{\Gamma}$ implies $\mathrm{HO}\pi^{\mathtt{unit},\to\diamond}(\Gamma) \rhd P \cong^{c} Q$.

Proof We can extend the compilation to contexts by mapping the hole of a context onto itself. Since the encoding is compositional and respects types, for any R with $\Gamma \vdash R$ and any (Δ/Γ)-context C, we have $\mathcal{D}[\![C[R]]\!]^{\Delta} = \mathcal{D}[\![C]\!]^{\Delta}[\mathcal{D}[\![R]\!]^{\Gamma}]$. From this, the assertion follows by Lemma 13.1.21. □

Completeness, the converse of soundness, is generally a harder result for a translation. The proof technique for soundness does not work because there may be contexts of the target language that are not translations of contexts of the source language. We will study completeness in Section 13.4, for the case of asynchronous calculi.

The exercise below shows concretely that a computation of a process $\mathcal{D}[\![P]\!]$ may require more steps (i.e., more reductions) than the corresponding computation by P. But if we do not weight internal work, then P and $\mathcal{D}[\![P]\!]$ have the 'same' behaviour.

Exercise 13.1.23 Let $P \stackrel{\mathrm{def}}{=} a(y).\,\overline{b}y \mid \overline{a}v.\,b(z).\,z\lfloor \star : \mathtt{unit} \rfloor$, and $v \stackrel{\mathrm{def}}{=} (u).\,\overline{c}u$. Then $\Gamma \vdash P$, for $\Gamma \stackrel{\mathrm{def}}{=} a : \sharp\,(\mathtt{unit} \to \diamond), b : \sharp\,(\mathtt{unit} \to \diamond), c : \sharp\,\mathtt{unit}$. How many τ steps does P need to produce $\overline{c}\star$? How many τ steps does $\mathcal{D}[\![P]\!]^{\Gamma}$ need to do the same? □

Exercise 13.1.24 Prove Lemma 13.1.13. □

Exercise 13.1.25 Show the inductive case of the proof of Lemma 13.1.14(1), for rules OUT, PAR-L, RES, and OPEN. □

Exercise 13.1.26 Complete the inductive proof of Lemma 13.1.16, for the cases when P is of the forms $\overline{x}\langle(z).\, P_1\rangle.\, P_2$, $((z).\, P')\lfloor y\rfloor$, and $\boldsymbol{\nu} x\, P'$. □

Exercise 13.1.27 Show the inductive cases of the proof of Theorem 13.1.18(1), for rules APP and PAR-L. □

Exercise 13.1.28 Prove Lemma 13.1.21. (Hint: you may find the technique of 'barbed bisimulation up to $\dot{\approx}$' useful; this technique is defined similarly to the 'bisimilarity up to $\approx$' in Exercise 2.4.63.) □

13.1.1 Hierarchies

We can distinguish types according to their *orders*. The order of a type says how 'high-order' is a value or a name of that type.

Definition 13.1.29 We define the *order* of a type of $\mathrm{HO}\pi^{\mathtt{unit},\to\diamond}$ thus:

$$\begin{aligned} \mathsf{ord}(\mathtt{unit}) &\stackrel{\text{def}}{=} 0 \\ \mathsf{ord}(T \to \diamond) = \mathsf{ord}(\sharp\, T) &\stackrel{\text{def}}{=} \mathsf{ord}(T) + 1\,. \end{aligned}$$

□

The order of a value type of $\mathrm{HO}\pi^{\mathtt{unit},\to\diamond}$ is precisely the level of arrow-nesting in the type. For instance, $(\mathtt{unit} \to \diamond) \to \diamond$ has order 2. We can discriminate processes on the basis of the order of the types needed in their typing; we thus obtain a hierarchy of calculi.

Definition 13.1.30 (Calculi $\{\mathrm{HO}\pi^n\}_\omega$) We write $\mathrm{HO}\pi^n \triangleright \Gamma \vdash P$ if there is a typing derivation for $\mathrm{HO}\pi^{\mathtt{unit},\to\diamond} \triangleright \Gamma \vdash P$ in which all types used (including the types in Γ) have order at most n. □

In $\mathrm{HO}\pi^1$ no non-trivial value (that is, different from the unit value) may be exchanged in communications; $\mathrm{HO}\pi^1$ is, essentially, pure CCS. In $\mathrm{HO}\pi^2$ process values can be communicated. In $\mathrm{HO}\pi^3$, also abstractions whose parameter is a process value – such as the abstraction v in Example 12.1.4 – can be communicated.

Lemma 13.1.31 If $\mathrm{HO}\pi^n \triangleright \Gamma \vdash P$ then also $\mathrm{HO}\pi^m \triangleright \Gamma \vdash P$ for all $m \geq n$. □

We can also define a hierarchy of calculi within $\pi^{\mathtt{unit},\mathsf{i/o}}$, using the orders of the types. The order of a type of π-calculus shows the depth of nested communications that are possible starting from names of that type.

Definition 13.1.32 We define the *order* of a type of $\pi^{\mathtt{unit},\mathsf{i/o}}$ thus:

$$\begin{aligned} \mathsf{ord}(\mathtt{unit}) &\stackrel{\text{def}}{=} 0 \\ \mathsf{ord}(\sharp\, T) = \mathsf{ord}(\mathsf{i}\, T) = \mathsf{ord}(\mathsf{o}\, T) &\stackrel{\text{def}}{=} \mathsf{ord}(T) + 1\,. \end{aligned}$$

□

Definition 13.1.33 (Calculi $\{\pi^n\}_\omega$) If there is a typing derivation of $\pi^{\mathtt{unit},\mathsf{i/o}} \triangleright \Gamma \vdash P$ in which all types used (including the types in Γ) have order at most n, then we write $\pi^n \triangleright \Gamma \vdash P$. □

Lemma 13.1.34 If $\pi^n \triangleright \Gamma \vdash P$ then also $\pi^m \triangleright \Gamma \vdash P$ for all $m \geq n$. □

Thus π^1 is essentially the same as $\mathrm{HO}\pi^1$ and pure CCS, for in π^1 names can be used only for pure synchronization. ($\mathrm{HO}\pi^1$ is not exactly the same as π^1, because $\mathrm{HO}\pi^1$ still has some applications, namely applications of the form $((x).\, P)\lfloor v : \mathtt{unit}\rfloor$; by β-conversion, all these applications can be eliminated; the resulting calculus is indeed the same as π^1.) π^2 contains processes like

$$x(y).\, \overline{y}\star \quad \text{and} \quad \overline{x}y.\, \overline{y}\star$$

where if a name carries another name, then the latter can only be used for pure synchronizations.

Thus the two hierarchies give us a scale of 'degrees of mobility' and an incremental view of the transition from CCS to $\pi^{\mathtt{unit},\mathsf{i/o}}$ and $\mathrm{HO}\pi^{\mathtt{unit},\rightarrow\diamond}$. (It is intuitively clear that the two hierarchies define calculi of increasing expressiveness, but it is not clear how best to make this into a formal statement.)

The compilation $\mathcal{D}$ respects the order of types, in the sense that it maps the calculus $\mathrm{HO}\pi^n$ into the calculus π^n. It is easy to check that if T is an $\mathrm{HO}\pi$ type of order n, then $\mathcal{D}[\![T]\!]$ is a π-calculus type of order n. From this and Lemma 13.1.11, we get:

Corollary 13.1.35 If $\mathrm{HO}\pi^n \triangleright \Gamma \vdash P$ then $\pi^n \triangleright \mathcal{D}[\![\Gamma]\!] \vdash \mathcal{D}[\![P]\!]^\Gamma$. □

The reader might want to check that process P of Example 13.1.2 is in $\mathrm{HO}\pi^3$, and that $\mathcal{D}[\![P]\!]$ is in π^3.

It is worth pausing a little at $\mathrm{HO}\pi^2$. In this calculus, the only non-trivial values that can be transmitted are process values. Intuitively, in $\mathrm{HO}\pi^2$ we can pass processes, but no 'real' abstractions (that is, abstractions whose argument is not the unit value). Transmitting processes seems a powerful mechanism but, in fact, it gives us little more expressiveness than CCS. This is clear by the translation into π-calculus, in particular the translation of types. The language of the value types of π^2, sufficient for translating $\mathrm{HO}\pi^2$, is

$$T ::= \mathtt{o\,unit} \mid \mathtt{unit}.$$

That is, we can translate $\mathrm{HO}\pi^2$ into a π-calculus where names either are 'CCS names' – in the sense that they serve only for pure synchronizations – or carry CCS names.

What is missing with communication of process values is *dynamic linking*. A process that is received in a communication cannot be 'linked' to resources local to the recipient process. Thus, for instance, sending a process Q to a process P that has no names in common with Q is of little use, because P and Q will not be able to interact. This deficiency can be overcome by allowing communication of *parametrized* processes (the abstractions) in which the parameter is other than the unit value.

However, the replication-free fragment of $\mathrm{HO}\pi^2$ is more powerful than the corresponding fragment of π^2. The latter can express only finite processes, that is, processes that terminate after a finite number of transitions. In contrast, in the replication-free fragment of $\mathrm{HO}\pi^2$ we can write processes with infinite behaviours: this fragment has already the power of replication (Section 12.1.1). In general, the replication-free fragment of $\mathrm{HO}\pi^n$ is more powerful than the replication-free fragment of π^n.

13.2 Optimizations

In this section we introduce two simple but useful optimizations of the compilation. We will use the compilation obtained by applying them both in Part VI, to derive encodings of the λ-calculus into the π-calculus. The two optimizations are of different natures, and it is therefore useful to analyse them separately. (There is also a technical reason for analysing them separately; see Remark 13.2.13.)

13.2.1 First optimization

Consider the translation of an output whose argument is a name of functional type (we omit types):

$$\mathcal{D}[\![\overline{x}y.\,P]\!] \stackrel{\text{def}}{=} (\boldsymbol{\nu} z)\,\overline{x}z.\,(\mathcal{D}[\![P]\!] \mid\, !z(u).\,\mathcal{D}[\![\overline{y}u]\!])\,.$$

In the source process, y is a name that during computation will be instantiated to some value, say v (because y has a functional type and therefore cannot occur free in a closed process). In the target π-calculus process, y is used as a trigger for v. The translation introduces a new name z that, in turn, is used as a trigger for y. Therefore a recipient of z has to go through two levels of indirection via triggers before activating v. The optimization we now introduce eliminates one level of indirection, by simply communicating at x the trigger y itself. Writing $\mathcal{C}^+$ for the optimized translation, we have

$$\mathcal{C}^+[\![\overline{x}y.\,P]\!]^\Gamma \stackrel{\text{def}}{=} \overline{x}y.\,\mathcal{C}^+[\![P]\!]^\Gamma\ .$$

In a similar way, we optimize the encoding of higher-order names (i.e., names of functional type), and the encoding of application. For instance, the translation of higher-order names becomes

$$\mathcal{C}^+[\![q]\!]^{\Gamma;T} \stackrel{\text{def}}{=} (y).\,\overline{q}y\ .$$

The optimization has two noteworthy consequences: the new encoding is sound with respect to both weak and *strong* behavioural equivalences; and it is also defined on calculi with recursive types. The latter holds because the translation of names is not recursive.

Table 13.2 reports the new clauses for $\mathcal{C}^+$; on the others, $\mathcal{C}^+$ is the same as $\mathcal{D}$. Since $\mathcal{C}^+$ can also handle recursive types, we can take the source calculus to be $\mathrm{HO}\pi^{\mathtt{unit},\mu,\rightarrow\diamond}$; the target calculus is then $\pi^{\mathtt{unit},\mu,\mathsf{i/o}}$.

Convention (Type equality in encodings) In the clause for output prefix in Table 13.2, the compilation looks up the type of the subject of the output. This type is unique only up to type equality. Since we want to treat $\mathcal{C}^+$ as a function, we assume that the compilation selects a (canonical) representative of the equivalence class. This is a harmless decision: the processes obtained for different choices of the representative are the same modulo type equality. The same convention is assumed for forthcoming encodings. □

We call the optimization via which $\mathcal{C}^+$ is obtained *η-contraction on variables* because we have, for instance,

$$\begin{aligned} \mathcal{C}^+[\![(u).\,y\lfloor u : \mathtt{unit}\rfloor]\!]^{\Gamma;\mathtt{unit}\rightarrow\diamond} &= (u).\,\overline{y}u \\ &= \mathcal{D}[\![y]\!]^{\Gamma;\mathtt{unit}\rightarrow\diamond}\ . \end{aligned} \tag{13.9}$$

That is, on the subcalculus without recursive types, the result of applying the original compilation $\mathcal{D}$ to a process P is the same as that of applying the optimized $\mathcal{C}^+$ to the η-saturated normal form of P (Definition 12.1.16):

In this table we abbreviate $\mathcal{C}^+[\![E]\!]$ as $[\![E]\!]$, for any expression E.

Translation of types

$$[\![\mu X.\, T]\!] \stackrel{\text{def}}{=} \mu X.\, [\![T]\!] \qquad\qquad [\![X]\!] \stackrel{\text{def}}{=} X$$

Translation of higher-order values

$$[\![x]\!]^{\Gamma;T} \stackrel{\text{def}}{=} (y).\, \overline{x}y \qquad \text{where } T \text{ is a functional type}$$

Translation of processes

(We say that a value v is π-transmissible if v is a name or $v = \star$; we assume a, b are fresh names)

$$[\![\overline{x}v.\, P]\!]^{\Gamma} \stackrel{\text{def}}{=} \begin{cases} \overline{x}v.\, [\![P]\!]^{\Gamma} & \text{if } v \text{ is } \pi\text{-transmissible} \\ (\boldsymbol{\nu} a : [\![S]\!]^{\leftarrow\sharp})\, \overline{x}a.\, ([\![P]\!]^{\Gamma} \mid !a\, [\![v]\!]^{\Gamma;S}) & \\ \qquad \text{if } v \text{ is not } \pi\text{-transmissible and } \Gamma \vdash x : \sharp\, S & \end{cases}$$

$$[\![v\lfloor w : S\rfloor]\!]^{\Gamma} \stackrel{\text{def}}{=} \begin{cases} \overline{v}w \quad \text{if } v \text{ is a name and } w \text{ is } \pi\text{-transmissible} \\ (\boldsymbol{\nu} a : \sharp\, [\![S]\!])\, (a\, [\![v]\!]^{\Gamma;S\rightarrow\diamondsuit} \mid \overline{a}w) \\ \qquad \text{if } v \text{ is not a name and } w \text{ is } \pi\text{-transmissible} \\ (\boldsymbol{\nu} a : [\![S]\!]^{\leftarrow\sharp})\, \overline{v}a.\, !a\, [\![w]\!]^{\Gamma;S} \\ \qquad \text{if } v \text{ is a name and } w \text{ is not } \pi\text{-transmissible} \\ (\boldsymbol{\nu} a : \sharp\, [\![S]\!], b : [\![S]\!]^{\leftarrow\sharp})(a\, [\![v]\!]^{\Gamma;S\rightarrow\diamondsuit} \mid \overline{a}b.\, !b\, [\![w]\!]^{\Gamma;S}) \\ \qquad \text{if } v \text{ is not a name and } w \text{ is not } \pi\text{-trasmissible} \end{cases}$$

Table 13.2. *The new clauses for $\mathcal{C}^+$.*

Exercise 13.2.1 Suppose $\mathrm{HO}\pi^{\mathtt{unit},\rightarrow\diamondsuit} \triangleright \Gamma \vdash P$, and let P_η be the η-saturated normal form of P, as defined in Exercise 12.1.17. Show that

$$\mathcal{D}[\![P]\!]^{\Gamma} = \mathcal{C}^+[\![P_\eta]\!]^{\Gamma} \ .$$

□

We did not introduce the η-contraction optimization at the very beginning because it makes the proofs of correctness harder. With the previous compilation $\mathcal{D}$ we can use the ordinary expansion preorder to prove some of the key results for deriving soundness, most notably Lemma 13.1.16. By contrast, Lemma 13.1.16

is false for the optimized compilation $\mathcal{C}^+$, even if expansion is replaced with bisimilarity. To see this, take $P = x\lfloor y \rfloor$ and $v = z$ and $T = \mathtt{unit} \to \diamond$. We have

$$\begin{aligned} \boldsymbol{\nu} y\, (\mathcal{C}^+[\![x\lfloor y\rfloor]\!] \mid !y\; \mathcal{C}^+[\![z]\!]) &= \boldsymbol{\nu} y\, (\overline{x}y \mid !y(u).\, \overline{z}u) \\ &\not\approx \overline{x}z \\ &= \mathcal{C}^+[\![x\lfloor z\rfloor]\!] \\ &= \mathcal{C}^+[\![(x\lfloor y\rfloor)\{z/y\}]\!]\,. \end{aligned}$$

This problem with bisimilarity is due to the fact that it does not take into account the capability types that are used in the translation. We can obtain the analogue of Lemma 13.1.16 by replacing bisimilarity with barbed congruence. This is an instance of a general fact: properties about $\mathcal{D}$ can be proved using labelled equivalences, such as bisimilarity, whereas properties about $\mathcal{C}^+$ often have to proved directly in terms of barbed congruence. This may complicate the proofs (even if we can use *strong* barbed congruence), for barbed congruence is harder to manipulate than the labelled equivalences.

Summarizing: the new compilation $\mathcal{C}^+$ is more efficient and can also accommodate recursive types; but the original compilation is easier to manipulate mathematically. Below we report the main results concerning the correctness of $\mathcal{C}^+$, pointing out only those parts of the proofs that differ conceptually from those in the previous section.

Lemma 13.2.2 For all x and T,

$$\mathrm{HO}\pi^{\mathtt{unit},\mu,\to\diamond} \triangleright \Gamma \vdash x : T \quad \text{implies} \quad \pi^{\mathtt{unit},\mu,\mathsf{i/o}} \triangleright \mathcal{C}^+[\![\Gamma]\!] \vdash x : \mathcal{C}^+[\![T]\!]\;.$$

□

Lemma 13.2.3 If $\mathrm{HO}\pi^{\mathtt{unit},\mu,\to\diamond} \triangleright \Gamma \vdash P$ then $\pi^{\mathtt{unit},\mu,\mathsf{i/o}} \triangleright \mathcal{C}^+[\![\Gamma]\!] \vdash \mathcal{C}^+[\![P]\!]^{\Gamma}$.

Proof Similar to the proof of Lemma 13.1.11. The main difference is that we now need not assume that P is in η-saturated normal form because $\mathcal{C}^+$ never expands terms (in contrast with $\mathcal{D}$, which may expand higher-order values), and therefore we can use a straightforward induction on the structure of P. □

We briefly discuss the operational correspondence results for $\mathcal{C}^+$ on strong transitions. The assertions for visible actions are as for $\mathcal{D}$ (Lemmas 13.1.12–13.1.14; just replace $\mathrm{HO}\pi^{\mathtt{unit},\to\diamond}$ with $\mathrm{HO}\pi^{\mathtt{unit},\mu,\to\diamond}$, and $\mathcal{D}$ with $\mathcal{C}^+$). In the case of internal transitions, in contrast with the original compilation $\mathcal{D}$, we can now prove a 1-to-1 correspondence up to *strong* barbed congruence. This is possible because we can use the strong equivalence in the new version of

Lemma 13.1.16. The proof of this lemma depends crucially on the *Sharpened* Replication Theorems 10.5.1 (rather than the ordinary Replication Theorems, which suffice for proving Lemma 13.1.16).

Lemma 13.2.4 Suppose $\mathrm{HO}\pi^{\mathtt{unit},\mu,\to\diamond} \rhd \Gamma, y : T \vdash P$, and $\mathrm{HO}\pi^{\mathtt{unit},\mu,\to\diamond} \rhd \Gamma \vdash v : T$, where T is a functional type and v an abstraction. Then

$$\mathcal{C}^{+}[\![\Gamma]\!] \rhd (\nu y : (\mathcal{C}^{+}[\![T]\!])^{\leftarrow\sharp})\, (\mathcal{C}^{+}[\![P]\!]^{\Gamma,y:T} \mid !y\, \mathcal{C}^{+}[\![v]\!]^{\Gamma}) \simeq^{\mathrm{c}} \mathcal{C}^{+}[\![P\{v/y\}]\!]^{\Gamma} .$$

Proof The proof goes by induction on the structure of P; the cases of the induction are similar to, but simpler than, those of Lemma 13.1.16. The simplifications are due to the fact that we need not argue by induction on the order of T, as in Lemma 13.1.16, for here we have the extra hypothesis that v is an abstraction. One of the main differences is the case of application for $P = y\lfloor y \rfloor$. Using the law of Exercise 10.5.3, we have

$$\nu y\, (\overline{y}y \mid !y\, \mathcal{C}^{+}[\![v]\!]^{\Gamma;T}) \;\; \simeq^{\mathrm{c}} \;\; (\nu y, y'\,)(\overline{y}y' \mid !y\, \mathcal{C}^{+}[\![v]\!]^{\Gamma;T} \mid !y'\, \mathcal{C}^{+}[\![v]\!]^{\Gamma;T}) .$$

Since the name y is used only once, and only to send, we can remove the replication in front of $y\, \mathcal{C}^{+}[\![v]\!]^{\Gamma;T}$. Rearranging terms, we get

$$\begin{aligned} &\simeq^{\mathrm{c}} \;\; (\nu y, y'\,)(y\, \mathcal{C}^{+}[\![v]\!]^{\Gamma;T} \mid \overline{y}y' \mid !y'\, \mathcal{C}^{+}[\![v]\!]^{\Gamma;T}) \\ &\simeq^{\mathrm{c}} \;\; \mathcal{C}^{+}[\![v\lfloor v \rfloor]\!]^{\Gamma} . \end{aligned}$$

□

Theorem 13.2.5 (Operational correspondence for $\mathcal{C}^{+}$ on τ transitions) Suppose $\mathrm{HO}\pi^{\mathtt{unit},\mu,\to\diamond} \rhd \Gamma \vdash P$ and Γ is closed.

(1) If $P \xrightarrow{\tau} P'$ then there is P'' such that $\mathcal{C}^{+}[\![P]\!]^{\Gamma} \xrightarrow{\tau} P''$ and $\mathcal{C}^{+}[\![\Gamma]\!] \rhd P'' \simeq^{\mathrm{c}} \mathcal{C}^{+}[\![P']\!]^{\Gamma}$.
(2) Conversely, if $\mathcal{C}^{+}[\![P]\!]^{\Gamma} \xrightarrow{\tau} P''$ then there is P' such that $P \xrightarrow{\tau} P'$ and $\mathcal{C}^{+}[\![\Gamma]\!] \rhd P'' \simeq^{\mathrm{c}} \mathcal{C}^{+}[\![P']\!]^{\Gamma}$. □

We can thus derive soundness of $\mathcal{C}^{+}$ both for *strong* and for *weak* barbed congruence. We report only the assertion for the strong case.

Theorem 13.2.6 (Soundness of $\mathcal{C}^{+}$ for strong barbed congruence) Suppose $\mathrm{HO}\pi^{\mathtt{unit},\mu,\to\diamond} \rhd \Gamma \vdash P, Q$. Then $\pi^{\mathtt{unit},\mu,\mathsf{i/o}}(\mathcal{C}^{+}[\![\Gamma]\!]) \rhd \mathcal{C}^{+}[\![P]\!]^{\Gamma} \simeq^{\mathrm{c}} \mathcal{C}^{+}[\![Q]\!]^{\Gamma}$ implies $\mathrm{HO}\pi^{\mathtt{unit},\mu,\to\diamond}(\Gamma) \rhd P \simeq^{\mathrm{c}} Q$. □

The converse, completeness, is, again, much harder to achieve. Indeed, it fails when the target language is $\pi^{\mathtt{unit},\mu,\mathsf{i/o}}$:

Exercise 13.2.7 Suppose that the processes $\overline{x}y.\, P$ and $\overline{x}\langle(z).\, y\lfloor z : T\rfloor\rangle.\, P$ of $\mathrm{HO}\pi^{\mathtt{unit},\mu,\to\diamond}$ are well typed in Γ. These processes are barbed congruent at Γ; prove that that their images under $\mathcal{C}^+$ are not barbed congruent at $\mathcal{C}^+[\![\Gamma]\!]$. (Hint: Exercise 10.3.2 should help.) □

To obtain completeness, and hence full abstraction, we can either

- add receptive types to π-calculus, or
- restrict ourselves to asynchronous calculi.

(On this issue, see also Section 13.2.5.) In Section 13.4 we will follow the latter course; see the notes at the end of the Part for references to the former.

13.2.2 Second optimization

Consider an application $((y).\, P)\lfloor w : T\rfloor$; we have, omitting type annotations and assuming w not π-transmissible

$$\begin{array}{rcl}\mathcal{C}^+[\![((y).\, P)\lfloor w\rfloor]\!] & \stackrel{\mathrm{def}}{=} & (\boldsymbol{\nu} a, b\,)(a(y).\, \mathcal{C}^+[\![P]\!] \mid \overline{a}b.\, !b\,\mathcal{C}^+[\![w]\!]) \\ & \sim & \tau.\, \boldsymbol{\nu} y\,(\mathcal{C}^+[\![P]\!]\{b/y\} \mid !b\,\mathcal{C}^+[\![w]\!])\,.\end{array}$$

The optimization consists in eliminating this initial τ step; similarly, we eliminate the initial τ step in the translation of an application where w is π-transmissible. Let $\mathcal{C}$ be the resulting optimized translation. Its definition is the same as for $\mathcal{C}^+$, except for applications. Since we will use this compilation in Part VI, for ease of reference we report its complete definition (Table 13.3), and the results that we will need (below).

We use the pseudo-application notation for abstraction, from Section 7.4.1. Thus, if F is an abstraction, say $(x).\, P$, then Fy stands for $P\{y/x\}$ – the actual parameter y replaces the formal parameter x in the body P of F. For instance, $\mathcal{C}[\![(x).\, P]\!]^{\Gamma;S\to\diamond}$ is $(x).\, \mathcal{C}[\![P]\!]^{\Gamma,x:S}$, therefore $\mathcal{C}[\![(x).\, P]\!]^{\Gamma;S\to\diamond}y$ is the process $\mathcal{C}[\![P]\!]^{\Gamma,x:S}\{y/x\}$.

Lemma 13.2.8 For all P, v, Γ, T, and p fresh for Γ, we have:

(1) $\mathrm{HO}\pi^{\mathtt{unit},\mu,\to\diamond} \triangleright \Gamma \vdash P$ implies $\pi^{\mathtt{unit},\mu,\mathsf{i/o}} \triangleright \mathcal{C}[\![\Gamma]\!] \vdash \mathcal{C}[\![P]\!]^{\Gamma}$
(2) $\mathrm{HO}\pi^{\mathtt{unit},\mu,\to\diamond} \triangleright \Gamma \vdash v : T \to \diamond$ implies

$$\pi^{\mathtt{unit},\mu,\mathsf{i/o}} \triangleright \mathcal{C}[\![\Gamma]\!], p : \mathcal{C}[\![T]\!] \vdash \mathcal{C}[\![v]\!]^{\Gamma;T\to\diamond}p\,.$$

□

Exercise 13.2.9 Prove that $\mathcal{C}^+[\![P]\!]^{\Gamma} \cong^{\mathrm{c}} \mathcal{C}[\![P]\!]^{\Gamma}$. (Hint: prove the result for $\approx^{\mathrm{c}}$, and use the law $\tau.\, P \approx^{\mathrm{c}} P$.) □

In this table we abbreviate $\mathcal{C}[\![E]\!]$ as $[\![E]\!]$, for any expression E.

Translation of types

$$[\![\sharp T]\!] \stackrel{\mathrm{def}}{=} \sharp [\![T]\!] \qquad [\![\mathtt{unit}]\!] \stackrel{\mathrm{def}}{=} \mathtt{unit}$$

$$[\![T \to \diamond]\!] \stackrel{\mathrm{def}}{=} \mathrm{o}\, [\![T]\!] \qquad [\![\mu X.\, T]\!] \stackrel{\mathrm{def}}{=} \mu X.\, [\![T]\!] \qquad [\![X]\!] \stackrel{\mathrm{def}}{=} X$$

Translation of type environments

$$[\![\emptyset]\!] \stackrel{\mathrm{def}}{=} \emptyset$$

$$[\![\Gamma, x : T]\!] \stackrel{\mathrm{def}}{=} [\![\Gamma]\!], x : [\![T]\!]$$

Translation of higher-order values

$$[\![(x).\, P]\!]^{\Gamma;T} \stackrel{\mathrm{def}}{=} (x).\, [\![P]\!]^{\Gamma,x:S} \quad \text{if } T \sim_{\mathrm{type}} S \to \diamond$$

$$[\![x]\!]^{\Gamma;T} \stackrel{\mathrm{def}}{=} (y).\, \overline{x}y$$

Translation of processes
(We say that a value v is π-transmissible if v is a name or $v = \star$; we assume a is a fresh name)

$$[\![\overline{x}v.\, P]\!]^{\Gamma} \stackrel{\mathrm{def}}{=} \begin{cases} \overline{x}v.\, [\![P]\!]^{\Gamma} & \text{if } v \text{ is } \pi\text{-transmissible} \\ (\boldsymbol{\nu} a : [\![S]\!]^{\leftarrow\sharp})\, \overline{x}a.\, ([\![P]\!]^{\Gamma} \mid !a\, [\![v]\!]^{\Gamma;S}) & \\ & \text{if } v \text{ is not } \pi\text{-transmissible and } \Gamma \vdash x : \sharp S \end{cases}$$

$$[\![v\lfloor w : S\rfloor]\!]^{\Gamma} \stackrel{\mathrm{def}}{=} \begin{cases} [\![v]\!]^{\Gamma;S\to\diamond} w & \text{if } w \text{ is } \pi\text{-transmissible} \\ (\boldsymbol{\nu} a : [\![S]\!]^{\leftarrow\sharp})\, ([\![v]\!]^{\Gamma;S\to\diamond} a \mid !a\, [\![w]\!]^{\Gamma;S}) & \\ & \text{if } w \text{ is not } \pi\text{-transmissible} \end{cases}$$

$$[\![z(x).\, P]\!]^{\Gamma} \stackrel{\mathrm{def}}{=} z(x).\, [\![P]\!]^{\Gamma,x:T} \quad \text{if } \Gamma \vdash z : \sharp T$$

$$[\![\tau.\, P]\!]^{\Gamma} \stackrel{\mathrm{def}}{=} \tau.\, [\![P]\!]^{\Gamma} \qquad [\![M + N]\!]^{\Gamma} \stackrel{\mathrm{def}}{=} [\![M]\!]^{\Gamma} + [\![N]\!]^{\Gamma}$$

$$[\![P \mid Q]\!]^{\Gamma} \stackrel{\mathrm{def}}{=} [\![P]\!]^{\Gamma} \mid [\![Q]\!]^{\Gamma} \qquad [\![!P]\!]^{\Gamma} \stackrel{\mathrm{def}}{=} ![\![P]\!]^{\Gamma}$$

$$[\![(\boldsymbol{\nu} x : T)\, P]\!]^{\Gamma} \stackrel{\mathrm{def}}{=} (\boldsymbol{\nu} x : [\![T]\!])\, [\![P]\!]^{\Gamma,x:T} \qquad [\![\mathbf{0}]\!]^{\Gamma} \stackrel{\mathrm{def}}{=} \mathbf{0}$$

Table 13.3. *The optimized compilation* $\mathcal{C}$ *of* $\mathrm{HO}\pi^{\mathtt{unit},\mu,\to\diamond}$ *into the* π*-calculus.*

Using Exercise 13.2.9, and the adequacy and soundness of $\mathcal{C}^+$, we derive those for $\mathcal{C}$.

Theorem 13.2.10 (Adequacy of $\mathcal{C}$) Suppose $\mathrm{HO}\pi^{\mathtt{unit},\mu,\to\diamond} \triangleright \Gamma \vdash P$ and Γ is closed. Then $P \Downarrow_a$ iff $\mathcal{C}[\![P]\!]^\Gamma \Downarrow_a$, for any a. □

Adequacy can be extended to an arbitrary typing, not necessarily closed. Although by itself this extension is not interesting, we show it below because we will use it in Part VI of the book. If P is an $\mathrm{HO}\pi$ process, then we write $P \Downarrow^\star$ if

- $P \Downarrow_a$ holds, for some a, or
- there is P' such that $P \Longrightarrow P'$ and (omitting types) $P' \equiv \boldsymbol{\nu}\widetilde{z}\,(x\lfloor v \rfloor \mid P'')$, for some $\widetilde{z}, x, v, P''$ (that is, P' has an unguarded application whose head is a variable).

Theorem 13.2.11 (Adequacy of $\mathcal{C}$, arbitrary typing) Suppose that $\mathrm{HO}\pi^{\mathtt{unit},\mu,\to\diamond} \triangleright \Gamma \vdash P$. Then $P \Downarrow^\star$ iff, for some a, $\mathcal{C}[\![P]\!]^\Gamma \Downarrow_a$. □

Theorem 13.2.12 (Soundness of $\mathcal{C}$) Suppose $\mathrm{HO}\pi^{\mathtt{unit},\mu,\to\diamond} \triangleright \Gamma \vdash P, Q$. We have

$$\pi^{\mathtt{unit},\mu,\mathsf{i/o}}(\mathcal{C}[\![\Gamma]\!]) \triangleright \mathcal{C}[\![P]\!]^\Gamma \cong^{\mathrm{c}} \mathcal{C}[\![Q]\!]^\Gamma \text{ implies } \mathrm{HO}\pi^{\mathtt{unit},\mu,\to\diamond}(\Gamma) \triangleright P \cong^{\mathrm{c}} Q.$$

□

Remark 13.2.13 We have proved the adequacy and soundness of $\mathcal{C}$ by going through $\mathcal{C}^+$. Proving the results directly for $\mathcal{C}$ is more difficult. For this, we would need to establish an operational correspondence for $\mathcal{C}$, as we did for $\mathcal{D}$ and $\mathcal{C}^+$: but a β-reduction in P might not correspond to a reduction in $\mathcal{C}[\![P]\!]$, which introduces complications. □

For the reverse implication, completeness, what we said for $\mathcal{C}^+$ in Section 13.2.1 is true also for $\mathcal{C}$. Here is a result much simpler than completeness, which, together with soundness, will be sufficient for our uses of the compilation in Part VI:

Lemma 13.2.14 Suppose $\mathrm{HO}\pi^{\mathtt{unit},\mu,\to\diamond} \triangleright \Gamma \vdash P, Q$. If $P =_\beta Q$ then

$$\pi^{\mathtt{unit},\mu,\mathsf{i/o}}(\mathcal{C}[\![\Gamma]\!]) \triangleright \mathcal{C}[\![P]\!]^\Gamma \cong^{\mathrm{c}} \mathcal{C}[\![Q]\!]^\Gamma .$$

Proof This is essentially a consequence of the first law of Section 13.2.4. □

13.2.3 Extensions

Other type constructs It is simple to extend the compilation $\mathcal{C}$ and its correctness results to HOπ languages with other type constructs, for instance with tuples and linearity. For tuples, see Exercise 13.2.15. If we have linear types, so that we know that the argument w in the expressions $\overline{x}w.\, P$ and $v\lfloor w : T\rfloor$ is used at most once, then in the clauses of Table 13.3 no replication is needed before $a\,\mathcal{C}[\![w]\!]^{\Gamma;T}$. The same holds for the previous encodings $\mathcal{D}$ and $\mathcal{C}^+$.

Exercise 13.2.15 (Tuple types) This exercise is about extending the compilation $\mathcal{C}$ to tuple types. You may assume that the source language is HO$\pi^{\mathtt{unit},\times,\mu,\to\diamond}$, and the target language $\pi^{\mathtt{unit},\times,\mu,\mathtt{i/o}}$ (that is, HO$\pi^{\mathtt{unit},\mu,\to\diamond}$ and $\pi^{\mathtt{unit},\mu,\mathtt{i/o}}$ with the addition of tuple types).

As discussed in Section 6.6, it is often handy to decompose tuple values by pattern matching in inputs, that is, to adopt polyadic inputs $a(x_1,\ldots,x_n).\, P$ as primitive. For this case, show the clauses for translating binary outputs, inputs, applications, and types: $\overline{a}\langle v_1, v_2\rangle.\, P$, $a(x_1, x_2).\, P$, $v\lfloor\langle v_1, v_2\rangle\rfloor$, and $T_1 \times T_2$. $\square$

Dynamic operators The second optimization via which $\mathcal{C}$ was derived may not be sound in languages that include unguarded dynamic operators such as unguarded sum. As an example, take $P \stackrel{\text{def}}{=} a + b$ and $Q \stackrel{\text{def}}{=} ((x).\, a)\lfloor v\rfloor + b$. We have

$$\begin{aligned} \mathcal{C}[\![Q]\!] &\stackrel{\text{def}}{=} \boldsymbol{\nu} y\,(a \mid !y\,\mathcal{C}[\![v]\!]) + b \\ &\simeq^{\mathrm{c}} a + b \\ &= \mathcal{C}[\![P]\!]\,. \end{aligned}$$

However, the source processes P and Q are not even barbed bisimilar, as $Q \xrightarrow{\tau} a$, but P cannot match this. Roughly, soundness fails because in a language with unguarded sum $\tau.\, P = P$ is not a congruence law. On the other hand, $\mathcal{D}$ and $\mathcal{C}^+$ can handle unguarded sum.

13.2.4 Some laws for HOπ

We can exploit the soundness of the encodings examined so far to prove some algebraic properties of HOπ languages, such as

$$\begin{aligned} \Gamma \triangleright ((x).\, P)\lfloor w : T\rfloor &\cong^{\mathrm{c}} P\{w/x\} \\ \Gamma \triangleright P \mid Q &\cong^{\mathrm{c}} Q \mid P \\ \Gamma \triangleright \overline{a}\langle(y).\, P\rangle.\, Q &\cong^{\mathrm{c}} (\boldsymbol{\nu} z : \sharp T)\,(\overline{a}\langle(u).\, \overline{z}u\rangle \mid !z(y).\, P \mid Q) \\ \Gamma \triangleright (\boldsymbol{\nu} a : T)\,(\overline{a}v.\, P \mid a(x).\, Q) &\cong^{\mathrm{c}} (\boldsymbol{\nu} a : T)\,(P \mid Q\{v/x\}) \end{aligned}$$

where, in the third law, z is fresh and $\Gamma \vdash a : \sharp\,(T \to \diamond)$.

Exercise 13.2.16 Use $\mathcal{C}$ to prove the laws above, assuming the source language is $\mathrm{HO}\pi^{\mathtt{unit},\mu,\to\diamond}$. (Hint: use $\approx^{\mathrm{c}}$; for the first law, use Lemma 13.2.4; for the third law, use the (standard) Replication Theorems.) □

In Section 12.1.1 we stated that replication is derivable in HOπ: we defined the abstraction $\mathtt{Bang}$ and claimed that for any process P, the processes $\mathtt{Bang}\lfloor @P \rfloor$ and $!P$ behave alike. The two exercises below invite the reader to prove this claim.

Exercise* 13.2.17 Suppose $\mathrm{HO}\pi^{\mathtt{unit},\mu,\to\diamond} \triangleright \Gamma \vdash P$. Show that $\mathcal{C}[\![\mathtt{Bang}\lfloor @P \rfloor]\!]^{\Gamma} \approx \mathcal{C}[\![!P]\!]^{\Gamma}$. (Hint: first show that $\mathcal{C}[\![\mathtt{Bang}\lfloor @P \rfloor]\!]^{\Gamma} \succeq \tau.\,(\mathcal{C}[\![P]\!]^{\Gamma} \mid \mathcal{C}[\![\mathtt{Bang}\lfloor @P \rfloor]\!]^{\Gamma})$; then use this fact to prove that the pair $(\mathcal{C}[\![\mathtt{Bang}\lfloor @P \rfloor]\!]^{\Gamma}, \mathcal{C}[\![!P]\!]^{\Gamma})$ is a bisimulation up to context and up to expansion.) □

Exercise 13.2.18 Suppose $\mathrm{HO}\pi^{\mathtt{unit},\mu,\to\diamond} \triangleright \Gamma \vdash P$. Use Exercise 13.2.17 to infer that

$$\mathrm{HO}\pi^{\mathtt{unit},\mu,\to\diamond}(\Gamma) \triangleright \mathtt{Bang}\lfloor @P \rfloor \cong^{\mathrm{c}} !P.$$

Conclude that for any $\mathrm{HO}\pi^{\mathtt{unit},\mu,\to\diamond}$ process Q and type environment Γ with $\mathrm{HO}\pi^{\mathtt{unit},\mu,\to\diamond} \triangleright \Gamma \vdash Q$, there is a process Q_{rep} that does not contain replications and is such that $\mathrm{HO}\pi^{\mathtt{unit},\mu,\to\diamond} \triangleright \Gamma \vdash Q_{\mathrm{rep}}$ and $\mathrm{HO}\pi^{\mathtt{unit},\mu,\to\diamond}(\Gamma) \triangleright Q_{\mathrm{rep}} \cong^{\mathrm{c}} Q$. □

With recursive types, we can derive replication in an even simpler way, exploiting self-application as follows. As seen in Section 12.2.1, the type $S \stackrel{\mathrm{def}}{=} \mu X.\,(X \to \diamond)$ can be used to type self-applications. Let $v_P \stackrel{\mathrm{def}}{=} (x).\,(P \mid x\lfloor x : S \rfloor)$, for x not free in P. If $\Gamma \vdash P$ then $\Gamma \vdash v_P : S$. We have $v_P\lfloor v_P : S \rfloor \Longrightarrow P^n \mid v_P\lfloor v_P : S \rfloor$, for all n; indeed it holds that $\mathrm{HO}\pi^{\mathtt{unit},\mu,\to\diamond}(\Gamma) \triangleright v_P\lfloor v_P : S \rfloor \cong^{\mathrm{c}} !P$.

Exercise 13.2.19 Use the compilation $\mathcal{C}$ to prove the equivalence above. □

13.2.5 Receptiveness and asynchrony

We can give a straightforward proof of the optimization in Section 13.2.1 (the η-contraction optimization) using *receptive* types, at least on calculi without recursive types ($\mathcal{D}$ is defined only on such calculi). The trigger names introduced by the compilation (the names b of Table 13.1) are receptive because there is only one, replicated, input occurrence of them, and only their output capability can be transmitted.

The η-contraction optimization is essentially a consequence of the law of

Lemma 11.2.4(2) for receptive types. Indeed, for any P, the process $\mathcal{D}[\![P]\!]^{\Gamma}$ can be transformed into $\mathcal{C}^{+}[\![P]\!]^{\Gamma}$ by repeatedly applying that law. Precisely, let $\mathcal{D}_{\text{rec}}$ and $\mathcal{C}^{+}_{\text{rec}}$ be the compilations defined as are $\mathcal{D}$ and $\mathcal{C}^{+}$ but with receptive types in place of i/o types in the translation of value types; therefore, for instance

$$\mathcal{D}_{\text{rec}}[\![T \to \diamond]\!] \stackrel{\text{def}}{=} \omega\text{rec}_{\text{o}}\mathcal{D}_{\text{rec}}[\![T]\!]$$

(the type annotation for the restricted names b in Table 13.1 is then changed accordingly). Connection types are translated as before; therefore

$$\mathcal{D}_{\text{rec}}[\![\sharp\, T]\!] \stackrel{\text{def}}{=} \sharp\, \mathcal{D}_{\text{rec}}[\![T]\!] .$$

The target calculus is $\pi^{\texttt{unit},\text{i/o},\omega\text{rec}}$. We have:

Theorem 13.2.20 Suppose $\text{HO}\pi^{\texttt{unit},\to\diamond} \triangleright \Gamma \vdash P$. Then $\pi^{\texttt{unit},\text{i/o},\omega\text{rec}}(\mathcal{D}_{\text{rec}}[\![\Gamma]\!]) \triangleright \mathcal{D}_{\text{rec}}[\![P]\!]^{\Gamma} \cong^{\text{c}} \mathcal{C}^{+}_{\text{rec}}[\![P]\!]^{\Gamma}$ (note that $\mathcal{D}_{\text{rec}}[\![\Gamma]\!] = \mathcal{C}^{+}_{\text{rec}}[\![\Gamma]\!]$). □

Exercise* 13.2.21 Prove Theorem 13.2.20. □

In Theorem 13.2.20, receptive types are necessary. The equality is false if only i/o types are taken into account, for the same reason that the equality of the law of Lemma 11.2.4(2) fails. However, i/o types allow us to prove the law in the *Asynchronous* π-calculus; therefore, we have:

Theorem 13.2.22 Suppose $\text{AHO}\pi^{\texttt{unit},\to\diamond} \triangleright \Gamma \vdash P$. Then $\text{A}\pi^{\texttt{unit},\text{i/o}}(\mathcal{D}[\![\Gamma]\!]) \triangleright \mathcal{D}[\![P]\!]^{\Gamma} \cong^{\text{c}} \mathcal{C}^{+}[\![P]\!]^{\Gamma}$ (note that $\mathcal{D}[\![\Gamma]\!] = \mathcal{C}^{+}[\![\Gamma]\!]$). □

Theorem 13.2.20 and (13.9) imply that with receptive types we can prove, assuming that $\Gamma \vdash x : \sharp\,(T \to \diamond)$,

$$\mathcal{D}_{\text{rec}}[\![\Gamma]\!] \triangleright \mathcal{D}_{\text{rec}}[\![\overline{x}y.\, P]\!]^{\Gamma} \cong^{\text{c}} \mathcal{D}_{\text{rec}}[\![\overline{x}\langle (z).\, y\lfloor z : T\rfloor\rangle.\, P]\!]^{\Gamma} . \qquad (13.10)$$

Similarly, Theorem 13.2.22 and (13.9) imply that on asynchronous calculi

$$\mathcal{C}^{+}[\![\Gamma]\!] \triangleright \mathcal{C}^{+}[\![\overline{x}y]\!]^{\Gamma} \cong^{\text{c}} \mathcal{C}^{+}[\![\overline{x}\langle (z).\, y\lfloor z : T\rfloor\rangle]\!]^{\Gamma} .$$

These laws are actually at the heart of the proof of Theorems 13.2.20 and 13.2.22. The laws are also necessary for proving full abstraction of the optimized compilation $\mathcal{C}$, since the source terms are indistinguishable in $\text{HO}\pi$. When we study full abstraction of the compilation in Section 13.4, we will use asynchronous calculi, where i/o types are sufficient for deriving the laws. Were we to study full abstraction on synchronous calculi (i.e., with the full output prefix), receptive types would be necessary. For instance, ignoring receptiveness, (13.10) would not be true (Exercise 13.2.7).

By contrast, neither receptiveness nor asynchrony is necessary for the full abstraction of the non-optimized compilation $\mathcal{D}$.

13.3 Reversing the compilation

In Sections 13.1 and 13.2 we saw that process-passing calculi can be encoded into name-passing calculi. In this section we show that the converse also holds. To have simpler encoding and simpler proofs, the source name-passing calculus is the *Asynchronous Localized π-calculus*, ALπ, the Asynchronous π-calculus in which only the output capability of names can be communicated. The typed version of the calculus with recursive types and unit type is $\mathrm{AL}\pi^{\mathtt{unit},\mu,\mathrm{o}}$. We translate it to the Asynchronous HOπ with recursive types and unit type, $\mathrm{AHO}\pi^{\mathtt{unit},\mu,\to\diamond}$ (whose only difference from $\mathrm{HO}\pi^{\mathtt{unit},\mu,\to\diamond}$ is asynchrony). We call the encoding $\mathcal{R}$; intuitively it works as follows. Suppose a process of $\mathrm{AL}\pi^{\mathtt{unit},\mu,\mathrm{o}}$ communicates a name b; a recipient of b can use it to send a value v. In the encoding into $\mathrm{AHO}\pi^{\mathtt{unit},\mu,\to\diamond}$, this is simulated by the communication of an abstraction that, when applied to a value v, sends v along b.

Example 13.3.1 Omitting types, consider the reduction

$$P \stackrel{\mathrm{def}}{=} \overline{a}b \mid a(x).\,\overline{x}c \xrightarrow{\tau}\equiv \overline{b}c\,.$$

Encoding P, we get

$$\begin{array}{rcl}\mathcal{R}[\![P]\!] & = & \overline{a}\langle(y).\,\overline{b}y\rangle \mid a(x).\,x\lfloor(z).\,\overline{c}z\rfloor \\ & \xrightarrow{\tau}\equiv & ((y).\,\overline{b}y)\lfloor(z).\,\overline{c}z\rfloor \\ & \xrightarrow{\tau} & \overline{b}\langle(z).\,\overline{c}z\rangle \\ & = & \mathcal{R}[\![\overline{b}c]\!]\,.\end{array}$$

□

The encoding, defined only on well-typed terms, is presented in Table 13.4. Note that in the clause for restriction the type of the restricted name is a connection type (i.e., it is of the form $\sharp T$). This is to exclude the other link type, $\mathrm{o}\,T$: it would not be useful to introduce names with this type, because they cannot be used to interact; and it would make the definition of the encoding ill-formed. (In the informal Example 13.3.1 types were omitted; the encoding $\mathcal{R}[\![P]\!]$ was obtained assuming that all free names of P are of connection type, otherwise $\mathcal{R}[\![P]\!]$ would not be a closed process.)

We first show in Lemmas 13.3.3 and 13.3.4 that the encoding is syntactically meaningful. The proofs of these lemmas, which are along the lines of the proofs in the previous sections, use Lemma 13.3.2.

Lemma 13.3.2 If $\mathrm{AL}\pi^{\mathtt{unit},\mu,\mathrm{o}} \triangleright \Gamma \vdash x : T$ then either $\Gamma(x) \sim_{\mathrm{type}} T$ or $\Gamma(x) \sim_{\mathrm{type}} T^{\leftarrow\sharp}$.

In this table we abbreviate $\mathcal{R}[\![E]\!]$ as $[\![E]\!]$, for any expression E.

Translation of types

$$[\![\sharp\, S]\!] \stackrel{\mathrm{def}}{=} \sharp\,[\![S]\!] \qquad [\![\mathrm{o}\, S]\!] \stackrel{\mathrm{def}}{=} [\![S]\!] \to \diamond$$
$$[\![\mathtt{unit}]\!] \stackrel{\mathrm{def}}{=} \mathtt{unit} \qquad [\![\mu X.\, T]\!] \stackrel{\mathrm{def}}{=} \mu X.\, [\![T]\!] \qquad [\![X]\!] \stackrel{\mathrm{def}}{=} X$$

Translation of type environments

$$[\![\emptyset]\!] \stackrel{\mathrm{def}}{=} \emptyset$$
$$[\![\Gamma, x : T]\!] \stackrel{\mathrm{def}}{=} [\![\Gamma]\!], x : [\![T]\!]$$

Translation of values

$$[\![v]\!]^{\Gamma} \stackrel{\mathrm{def}}{=} \begin{cases} v & \text{if } \Gamma(v) \sim_{\mathrm{type}} \mathtt{unit} \\ (z).\, \overline{v}z & \text{if } \Gamma(v) \sim_{\mathrm{type}} \sharp\, T, \text{ for some } T \\ (z).\, v\lfloor z : [\![T]\!]\rfloor & \text{if } \Gamma(v) \sim_{\mathrm{type}} \mathrm{o}\, T \end{cases}$$

Translation of terms

$$[\![\overline{x}v]\!]^{\Gamma} \stackrel{\mathrm{def}}{=} \begin{cases} \overline{x}\,[\![v]\!]^{\Gamma} & \text{if } \Gamma(x) \sim_{\mathrm{type}} \sharp\, T, \text{ for some } T \\ x\lfloor [\![v]\!]^{\Gamma} : [\![T]\!]\rfloor & \text{if } \Gamma(x) \sim_{\mathrm{type}} \mathrm{o}\, T \end{cases}$$

$$[\![x(y).\, P]\!]^{\Gamma} \stackrel{\mathrm{def}}{=} x(y).\, [\![P]\!]^{\Gamma, y:T} \qquad \text{if } \Gamma(x) \sim_{\mathrm{type}} \sharp\, T$$

$$[\![\tau.\, P]\!]^{\Gamma} \stackrel{\mathrm{def}}{=} \tau.\, [\![P]\!]^{\Gamma} \qquad [\![M + N]\!]^{\Gamma} \stackrel{\mathrm{def}}{=} [\![M]\!]^{\Gamma} + [\![N]\!]^{\Gamma}$$

$$[\![P \mid Q]\!]^{\Gamma} \stackrel{\mathrm{def}}{=} [\![P]\!]^{\Gamma} \mid [\![Q]\!]^{\Gamma} \qquad [\![!P]\!]^{\Gamma} \stackrel{\mathrm{def}}{=} ![\![P]\!]^{\Gamma}$$

$$[\![(\nu x : \sharp\, T)\, P]\!]^{\Gamma} \stackrel{\mathrm{def}}{=} (\nu x : [\![\sharp\, T]\!])\, [\![P]\!]^{\Gamma, x:\sharp\, T} \qquad [\![\mathbf{0}]\!]^{\Gamma} \stackrel{\mathrm{def}}{=} \mathbf{0}$$

Table 13.4. *The encoding* $\mathcal{R}$ *of* AL$\pi^{\mathtt{unit},\mu,\mathrm{o}}$ *into* AHO$\pi^{\mathtt{unit},\mu,\to\diamond}$.

Proof The assertion follows from the fact that, in ALπ, $\sharp\, S$ is not a value type, for all S. □

Lemma 13.3.3 For all x, T and Γ, if $\Gamma(x) \sim_{\mathrm{type}} T$ then

$$\mathrm{AHO}\pi^{\mathtt{unit},\mu,\to\diamond} \triangleright \mathcal{R}[\![\Gamma]\!] \vdash x : \mathcal{R}[\![T]\!]\,.$$

□

Lemma 13.3.4 If $\mathrm{AL}\pi^{\mathtt{unit},\mu,\mathtt{o}} \triangleright \Gamma \vdash P$ then $\mathrm{AHO}\pi^{\mathtt{unit},\mu,\to\diamond} \triangleright \mathcal{R}[\![\Gamma]\!] \vdash \mathcal{R}[\![P]\!]^{\Gamma}$.

Proof By induction on the structure of P. The cases of the induction are similar to those of the proof of Lemma 13.2.3, using Lemmas 13.3.2 and 13.3.3. □

We say that a type environment Γ is *connection-closed* if the type of each name on which Γ is defined is a connection type (connection-closed is stronger than closed, for in the latter case the type of a name may be any link type, including $\mathtt{o}\,T$). In the definition of typed barbed congruence for $\mathrm{AL}\pi^{\mathtt{unit},\mu,\mathtt{o}}$ processes well typed in Δ, we can use (Γ/Δ)-contexts in which Γ is connection-closed, rather than closed. This does not affect the class of contexts: since $\sharp\, T$ is a subtype of $\mathtt{o}\,T$ a context that is well typed in, for instance, $\Gamma', a : \mathtt{o}\,T$ is also well typed in $\Gamma', a : \sharp\, T$. The advantage in using connection-closed type environments is that if Γ is connection-closed then its translation is a closed $\mathrm{HO}\pi$ type environment; this might not be true if Γ is simply closed.

Lemma 13.3.5 Suppose $\mathrm{AL}\pi^{\mathtt{unit},\mu,\mathtt{o}} \triangleright \Gamma, y : \mathtt{o}\,T \vdash P$ and $\mathrm{AL}\pi^{\mathtt{unit},\mu,\mathtt{o}} \triangleright \Gamma \vdash z : \sharp\, T$. Then $\mathcal{R}[\![P]\!]^{\Gamma, y:\mathtt{o}\,T}\{(u).\,\overline{z}u/y\} \succ_{\beta} \mathcal{R}[\![P\{z/y\}]\!]^{\Gamma}$.

Proof By induction on the structure of P. We consider only the case when $P = \overline{y}y$. We have

$$\begin{array}{rcl} \mathcal{R}[\![P]\!]^{\Gamma, y:\mathtt{o}\,T}\{(u).\,\overline{z}u/y\} & = & ((u).\,\overline{z}u)\lfloor (x).\,(((u).\,\overline{z}u)\lfloor x : \mathcal{R}[\![T]\!]\rfloor)\rfloor \\ & \succ_{\beta} & \overline{z}\langle (x).\,\overline{z}x\rangle \\ & = & \mathcal{R}[\![P\{z/y\}]\!]^{\Gamma}. \end{array}$$

□

Lemma 13.3.6 Suppose $\mathrm{AL}\pi^{\mathtt{unit},\mu,\mathtt{o}} \triangleright \Gamma \vdash P$ and Γ is connection-closed.

(1) If $P \xrightarrow{\tau} P'$ then $\mathcal{R}[\![P]\!]^{\Gamma} \xrightarrow{\tau}\succ_{\beta} \mathcal{R}[\![P']\!]^{\Gamma}$.
(2) Conversely, if $\mathcal{R}[\![P]\!]^{\Gamma} \xrightarrow{\tau} P''$ then there is P' such that $P \xrightarrow{\tau} P'$ and $P'' \succ_{\beta} \mathcal{R}[\![P']\!]^{\Gamma}$.

Proof Using transition induction and Lemma 13.3.5. □

Exercise 13.3.7 Complete the proofs of Lemmas 13.3.5 and 13.3.6. □

Exercise 13.3.8 Suppose $\mathrm{AL}\pi^{\mathtt{unit},\mu,\mathtt{o}} \triangleright \Gamma \vdash P$ and Γ is connection-closed. Establish the operational correspondence between P and $\mathcal{R}[\![P]\!]^{\Gamma}$ on weak reductions. (Hint: use Lemmas 12.1.15 and 13.3.6.) □

Theorem 13.3.9 (Adequacy of $\mathcal{R}$) Suppose that $\mathrm{AL}\pi^{\mathtt{unit},\mu,\mathsf{o}} \triangleright \Gamma \vdash P$ and Γ is connection-closed. Then $P \Downarrow_a$ iff $\mathcal{R}[\![P]\!]^\Gamma \Downarrow_a$, for all a. □

Theorem 13.3.10 (Soundness of $\mathcal{R}$ for barbed congruence) Suppose that $\mathrm{AL}\pi^{\mathtt{unit},\mu,\mathsf{o}} \triangleright \Gamma \vdash P, Q$. We have

$$\mathrm{AHO}\pi^{\mathtt{unit},\mu,\to\diamond}(\mathcal{R}[\![\Gamma]\!]) \triangleright \mathcal{R}[\![P]\!]^\Gamma \cong^{\mathrm{c}} \mathcal{R}[\![Q]\!]^\Gamma \text{ implies } \mathrm{AL}\pi^{\mathtt{unit},\mu,\mathsf{o}}(\Gamma) \triangleright P \cong^{\mathrm{c}} Q.$$

□

Exercise* 13.3.11 Prove Theorem 13.3.10. (Hint: the proof is similar to that of Theorem 13.1.22.) □

The encoding $\mathcal{R}$, like those in the previous section, preserves the order of the types (cf. Section 13.1.1).

The encoding presented in this section can be extended to synchronous calculi, but with an increase in complexity. The reason is that while an asynchronous output can be translated as an application, in synchronous calculi outputs have continuations, and it not obvious how to accommodate those since applications do not have continuations.

Exercise* 13.3.12 Let $\mathrm{A}\pi^{\mathtt{unit},\mu,\mathsf{i}}$ be the calculus defined like $\mathrm{AL}\pi^{\mathtt{unit},\mu,\mathsf{o}}$ except that only the input capability of names can be communicated. Define an encoding $\mathcal{R}_\mathsf{i}$ of $\mathrm{A}\pi^{\mathtt{unit},\mu,\mathsf{i}}$ into $\mathrm{AHO}\pi^{\mathtt{unit},\mu,\to\diamond}$. Consider then the $\mathrm{A}\pi^{\mathtt{unit},\mu,\mathsf{i}}$ process

$$P \stackrel{\mathrm{def}}{=} \overline{a}b \mid \overline{b}c \mid a(x).\, x(y).\, y$$

which is well typed at $\Gamma \stackrel{\mathrm{def}}{=} a : \sharp\sharp\sharp\,\mathtt{unit}\,,\, b : \sharp\sharp\,\mathtt{unit}\,,\, c : \sharp\,\mathtt{unit}$, and has a reduction

$$P \Longrightarrow\equiv c\,.$$

Apply the encoding to P and show that

$$\mathcal{R}_\mathsf{i}[\![P]\!]^\Gamma \Longrightarrow\bowtie c$$

where $\bowtie$ is an appropriate behavioural equivalence; specify the behavioural equivalence used. □

Exercise* 13.3.13 The same exercise as above, but now the source calculus is $L\pi^{\mathtt{unit},\mu,\mathsf{o}}$, which is defined like $\mathrm{AL}\pi^{\mathtt{unit},\mu,\mathsf{o}}$ but without the constraint on asynchrony (i.e., there are output prefixes $\overline{a}v.\,P$; you may however assume that there is no sum). Take $\mathrm{HO}\pi^{\mathtt{unit},\times,\mu,\to\diamond}$ as the target calculus; product types are useful to handle the derivatives underneath output prefixes. After defining the encoding, call it $\mathcal{R}_s$, consider the $L\pi^{\mathtt{unit},\mu,\mathtt{o}}$ process

$$P \stackrel{\text{def}}{=} \overline{a}b.\, b(x).\, \overline{x} \mid a(y).\, \overline{y}c.\, \overline{c}$$

which is well typed in $\Gamma \stackrel{\text{def}}{=} a : \sharp\sharp\sharp\,\mathtt{unit}\,,\, b : \sharp\sharp\,\mathtt{unit}\,,\, c : \sharp\,\mathtt{unit}$, and has a reduction

$$P \Longrightarrow\equiv \overline{c} \mid \overline{c}\,.$$

Apply the encoding to P and show that

$$\mathcal{R}_s[\![P]\!]^{\Gamma} \Longrightarrow\bowtie \overline{c} \mid \overline{c}$$

where $\bowtie$ is an appropriate behavioural equivalence; specify the behavioural equivalence used. □

13.4 Full abstraction

In this section we prove the full abstraction of encoding $\mathcal{C}$, from process-passing to name-passing, and of encoding $\mathcal{R}$, from name-passing to process-passing. We actually prove that the two encodings are the inverses of each other, up to some simple algebraic laws. We carry out our study on asynchronous calculi, because the proofs are much simpler (see Section 13.2.5 and the end of this section).

The encoding $\mathcal{R}$ is presented in Table 13.4, $\mathcal{C}$ in Table 13.3. ($\mathcal{C}$ is presented on synchronous calculi. When the source calculus is AHOπ, the target calculus is ALπ, provided that bound output prefixes $(\boldsymbol{\nu}x : T)\, \overline{a}x.\, !x(y).\, P$ are rewritten as $(\boldsymbol{\nu}x : T)\, (\overline{a}x \mid !x(y).\, P)$; this modification is semantically harmless, because the subject of the input is restricted.)

On types, $\mathcal{C}$ and $\mathcal{R}$ are syntactically the inverses of each other. On processes, the difference between the composition of the two encodings and the identity encoding is captured by two simple laws. We show the laws, and then we prove the full-abstraction theorems. The first law is the η-law of ALπ:

$$\overline{a}b = \boldsymbol{\nu}c\, (\overline{a}c \mid !c(x).\, \overline{b}x). \qquad (\eta)$$

We showed in Lemma 10.3.1 that this law is valid for barbed congruence in ALπ (the constraint on output capability in the lemma is guaranteed by the locality hypothesis of ALπ). The second law we need is on AHOπ:

$$\overline{a}\langle (y).\, P\rangle = (\boldsymbol{\nu}z : \sharp T)\, (\overline{a}\langle (u).\, \overline{z}u\rangle \mid !z(y).\, P)\ ,\ z \text{ fresh.}$$

We call this law **L**. We examined it in Section 13.2.4 where, exploiting the encoding $\mathcal{C}$, we proved that the law is valid for barbed congruence (we proved this on the synchronous calculus, which is a stronger result).

We write $\mathrm{AL}\pi^{\mathtt{unit},\mu,\mathtt{o}} \triangleright \eta \vdash P = Q$ if the equality between $\mathrm{AL}\pi^{\mathtt{unit},\mu,\mathtt{o}}$ processes P and Q can be proved using law η; and we write $\mathrm{AHO}\pi^{\mathtt{unit},\mu,\to\diamond} \triangleright \mathbf{L} \vdash P = Q$ if P and Q are $\mathrm{AHO}\pi^{\mathtt{unit},\mu,\to\diamond}$ processes that can be equated using law $\mathbf{L}$. The two lemmas below show that $\mathcal{C}$ and $\mathcal{R}$ are the inverses of each other up to the laws η and $\mathbf{L}$. Both lemmas are proved by structural induction on P.

Lemma 13.4.1 Suppose $\mathrm{AL}\pi^{\mathtt{unit},\mu,\mathtt{o}} \triangleright \Gamma \vdash P$. Then

$$\mathrm{AL}\pi^{\mathtt{unit},\mu,\mathtt{o}} \triangleright \eta \vdash P = \mathcal{C}[\![\mathcal{R}[\![P]\!]^{\Gamma}]\!]^{\mathcal{R}[\![\Gamma]\!]}.$$

□

Lemma 13.4.2 Suppose $\mathrm{AHO}\pi^{\mathtt{unit},\mu,\to\diamond} \triangleright \Gamma \vdash P$. Then

$$\mathrm{AHO}\pi^{\mathtt{unit},\mu,\to\diamond} \triangleright \mathbf{L} \vdash P = \mathcal{R}[\![\mathcal{C}[\![P]\!]^{\Gamma}]\!]^{\mathcal{C}[\![\Gamma]\!]}.$$

□

Exercise 13.4.3 Prove Lemmas 13.4.1 and 13.4.2. □

From the soundness of $\mathcal{C}$ and $\mathcal{R}$, and the two lemmas above, we can prove completeness.

Theorem 13.4.4 (Full abstraction of $\mathcal{C}$) Suppose $\mathrm{AHO}\pi^{\mathtt{unit},\mu,\to\diamond} \triangleright \Gamma \vdash P, Q$. We have $\Gamma \triangleright P \cong^{\mathrm{c}} Q$ iff $\mathcal{C}[\![\Gamma]\!] \triangleright \mathcal{C}[\![P]\!]^{\Gamma} \cong^{\mathrm{c}} \mathcal{C}[\![Q]\!]^{\Gamma}$.

Proof The soundness of $\mathcal{C}$ is Theorem 13.2.12. (Theorem 13.2.12 is about synchronous calculi; the same proof works on asynchronous calculi.) For completeness, omitting types, suppose $P \cong^{\mathrm{c}} Q$. By Lemma 13.4.2, $P \cong^{\mathrm{c}} \mathcal{R}[\![\mathcal{C}[\![P]\!]]\!]$ and $Q \cong^{\mathrm{c}} \mathcal{R}[\![\mathcal{C}[\![Q]\!]]\!]$, hence also $\mathcal{R}[\![\mathcal{C}[\![P]\!]]\!] \cong^{\mathrm{c}} \mathcal{R}[\![\mathcal{C}[\![Q]\!]]\!]$. By the soundness of $\mathcal{R}$ we conclude that $\mathcal{C}[\![P]\!] \cong^{\mathrm{c}} \mathcal{C}[\![Q]\!]$. □

Theorem 13.4.5 (Full abstraction of $\mathcal{R}$) Suppose $\mathrm{AL}\pi^{\mathtt{unit},\mu,\mathtt{o}} \triangleright \Gamma \vdash P, Q$. We have $\Gamma \triangleright P \cong^{\mathrm{c}} Q$ iff $\mathcal{R}[\![\Gamma]\!] \triangleright \mathcal{R}[\![P]\!]^{\Gamma} \cong^{\mathrm{c}} \mathcal{R}[\![Q]\!]^{\Gamma}$.

Proof Similar to the proof of Theorem 13.4.4. □

Remark 13.4.6 In the case of asynchronous calculi, the optimizations that brought us from $\mathcal{D}$ to $\mathcal{C}$ preserve barbed congruence (Theorem 13.2.22 and Exercise 13.2.9), and hence Theorem 13.4.4 remains true when $\mathcal{C}$ is replaced by $\mathcal{D}$ or $\mathcal{C}^{+}$. We believe that $\mathcal{C}^{+}$ is fully abstract also for strong barbed congruence. □

Remark 13.4.7 (Synchronous calculi) These full-abstraction results are on asynchronous calculi. In the case of synchronous calculi, full-abstraction results for encodings of higher-order calculi into first-order calculi similar to that in Section 13.1 exist [San92]. However, the proofs are quite different (and more complex), as they are based on labelled characterizations of barbed congruence on the first-order and higher-order calculi. The proof above does not obviously carry through because on synchronous calculi we do not know encodings like $\mathcal{R}$ that are semantically the inverse of $\mathcal{C}$. On the issue of full abstraction for synchronous calculi, see also the discussions at the ends of Sections 13.2.1 and 13.2.5. □

Exercise 13.4.8 Let $\mathcal{R}_\mathsf{s}$ be the encoding of Exercise 13.3.13, and P, Γ the process and type environment in the same exercise. What is $\mathcal{C}[\![\mathcal{R}_\mathsf{s}[\![P]\!]^\Gamma]\!]^{\mathcal{R}_\mathsf{s}[\![\Gamma]\!]}$? Explain why the behaviours of P and $\mathcal{C}[\![\mathcal{R}_\mathsf{s}[\![P]\!]^\Gamma]\!]^{\mathcal{R}_\mathsf{s}[\![\Gamma]\!]}$ are not comparable. □

Notes and References for Part V

The first attempt to encode a higher-order process calculus into π-calculus was made by Thomsen [Tho90]. He studied Plain CHOCS, which is similar to the calculus $\text{HO}\pi^2$ of Section 13.1.1. $\text{HO}\pi$ was introduced in [San92]. A compilation from $\text{HO}\pi$ to π-calculus (extending Thomsen's) was also presented, and its full abstraction for barbed congruence proved. The definitions of $\text{HO}\pi$ and its encodings into π-calculus that we have presented follow [San92]; the full-abstraction proofs follow [San01a]. The full-abstraction proof in [San92] is more complex than the proof we have shown, mainly because the language translated in [San92] is synchronous. The main difference between this Part of the book and [San01a] is that in the latter all calculi are asynchronous and therefore the output and application constructs (and, correspondingly, the connection- and function-type constructs) are combined into a single construct, as hinted at in Section 12.2.2. A similar coalescing construct is found in Pict [PT00] and in the Blue Calculus [Bou97a].

Compilations of higher-order calculi into first-order calculi can be used to derive reasoning principles for higher-order processes. We derived some laws for $\text{HO}\pi$ in this way in Section 13.2.4. The compilations may also guide us towards definitions of suitable labelled bisimilarities for higher-order calculi, and help us prove results about them. Proving results directly on higher-order calculi may be hard. For instance, it may be hard to prove that a bisimilarity is a congruence. In sequential higher-order calculi bisimilarities are often proved to be congruences using Howe's method [How96]; but in concurrent languages this method seems to work only in a limited number of cases. Technically, the bisimulation should be in a 'delayed late' style, hinted at in Section 4.7, and even in this case private names and scope extrusion may cause problems; see [FHJ95] for discussion. A different technique, related to the compilations into first-order calculi presented in this Part, was followed in [San96a, JR00].

The full abstraction of the compilations of $\text{HO}\pi$ into π-calculus also makes it possible to use the higher-order constructs of HOπ as abbreviations, or 'macros', for the π-calculus, allowing more succinct and more readable descriptions of systems. We will see examples of this in Part VI for the interpretation of the λ-calculus. More generally, encodings of useful constructs into the π-calculus may be relevant for the definition of programming languages based on the π-calculus.

The compilations, in which communication of a higher-order value is replaced by communication of a name giving access to the value, remind us of techniques for implementing communications or substitutions involving terms in higher-order languages. Indeed, the compilation $\mathcal{C}$ is at the heart of the compiler for Pict [PT00]. Pict permits communications of terms; it is therefore a higher-order language. Its compiler transforms Pict programs into an intermediate π-calculus-like language. (The extension of π-calculus with higher-order constructs similar to those of HOπ, and an encoding of the extended language into the core π-calculus were the first steps in the design of Pict and of its compiler.) Other calculi or languages that belong to the higher-order paradigm are CHOCS [Tho90], CML [Rep99], and Facile [GMP89, TLK96]. An important difference between fully-fledged programming languages such as Pict, Facile and CML, and calculi such as CHOCS and HOπ is that the former have reduction strategies (in the languages mentioned, call-by-value); reduction strategies are studied in the next Part.

In this Part the encodings were proved correct with respect to barbed congruence. It is very likely that similar correctness results hold for other forms of weak behavioural equivalences that admit a uniform definition over higher-order and first-order calculi, such as *testing equivalence* [DH84], and *refusal semantics* [Phi87]. Moreover, the results can be adapted to *asynchronous* behavioural equivalences (cf. Section 5.4), where only the output actions are directly observable.

An issue not yet fully understood is the extent to which the results presented in this Part are specific to the operators of HOπ and π-calculus. The encodings may no longer be correct when other operators are added to the calculi. For instance, we have already mentioned that the second of the optimizations in Section 13.2 is not correct if unguarded sum is added to HOπ; similarly, one can imagine different forms of sum (for instance in which summands are not discharged after a reduction that originates from a β-reduction) that would be hard to handle. Other dangerous operators are interrupts like LOTOS disabling [BB89], dynamic forms of restriction [VD98], and operators that assign explicit locations to processes. If processes have locations, then communicating a process may make it move from one location to another; in this case encodings like $\mathcal{D}$ or $\mathcal{C}$, in which a pointer is communicated but the process itself does not move, may not be satisfactory. It is possible, however, that appropriate modifications of these encodings will work; evidence for this is that calculi with explicit locations have been modelled in the π-calculus [San96b, AP94, FGL$^+$96].

Astesiano, Giovini, and Reggio studied higher-order process calculi within the framework of *generalized algebraic specifications* [AGR92]; they introduced algebraic structures called *observational structures* – roughly first-order signatures equipped with a notion of observation – where processes can be treated as data. In that work, restriction was treated as a dynamic operator. Studies of operational semantics for higher-order calculi include [AGR88, Tho90, San92, San96a, FHJ95, HK94, AD95, Bal98, JR00]. Studies of the denotational approach include those by Brookes [Bro96], Hartonas and Hennessy [Hen93, HH98], and Cattani and Winskel [Cat99]. Brookes considered a concurrent extension of Idealized Algol, a language that has local mutable variables and higher-order procedures. (Röckl [Röc01] studied a semantics of this language by translation into the π-calculus.) Hennessy and Hartonas considered CHOCS and a subset of Facile and proved full-abstraction results for forms of testing equivalence; in their languages, restriction, when present, was treated as a dynamic operator. Cattani and Winskel considered *presheaf models* for CCS-like languages without restriction and with a form of linear process-passing. The presheaf approach guarantees that bisimilarity, expressed in terms of open maps [JNW96], is a congruence, though how to provide a concrete, i.e., operational, understanding of open-map bisimulation for higher-order processes is an open question. The semantics of higher-order process calculi with private names is an active topic of research, and it remains a very challenging issue for denotational semantics.

Part VI

Functions as Processes

Introduction to Part VI

This Part is concerned with the relationship between λ-calculus and π-calculus. The λ-calculus is the prototypical functional language. The λ-calculus talks about *functions* and their *applicative* behaviour. This contrasts with the π-calculus, which talks about *processes* and their *interactive* behaviour. Application is a special form of interaction, and therefore functions can be seen as a special kind of processes. In this Part we study how the functions of the λ-calculus (the *computable* functions) can be represented as π-calculus processes. The π-calculus semantics of a language induces a notion of equality on the terms of that language. We therefore also analyse the equality among functions that is induced by their representation as π-calculus processes.

A deep study of representations of functions as π-calculus processes is of interest for several reasons. From the π-calculus point of view, the representation is a significant test of expressiveness, and is helpful in getting deeper insight into the theory. From the λ-calculus point of view, the representation makes it possible to apply process-calculus techniques to λ-calculus, and also to analyse λ-terms in contexts that are not purely sequential. This study may be useful for providing a semantic foundation for languages having constructs for functions and for concurrency, and techniques for reasoning about them. (Behavioural equalities between functions preserved in sequential contexts may not be preserved in non-sequential contexts; we will see examples of this in Chapter 17.) The study may also be helpful in developing parallel implementations of functional languages and in the design of programming languages based on process calculi.

Structure of the Part The Part is composed of five chapters. The first, Chapter 14, is about the λ-calculus. The second, Chapter 15, is about the encoding of the untyped λ-calculus into π-calculus. Chapter 16 does the same for the typed λ-calculus. Chapters 17 and 18 are about the full-abstraction problem for the simplest of the π-calculus encodings, namely that of the untyped call-by-name λ-calculus. A more detailed summary follows.

In Section 14.1 we review the syntax and reduction rules of the untyped λ-calculus. In Section 14.2, we look at some properties of the λ-calculus that make it strikingly different from the π-calculus: sequentiality and confluence. We also touch on the differences and the similarities between the basic computational rules of the two calculi.

A λ-term may have several reducible subterms. A *reduction strategy* specifies a reduction order. The most important reduction strategies are call-by-name and call-by-value, and variants of these such as parallel call-by-value and call-by-need (the last is actually an implementation technique, rather than a reduction strategy). We review these strategies and their properties in Section 14.3.

Section 15.1 begins the main topic of this Part of the book, which is interpretation of λ-calculus strategies into π-calculus. The general schema that will be followed for deriving the encodings is presented and, in Section 15.2, some notations are recalled. We derive (most of) the encodings from well-known *Continuation Passing Style* transforms, which transform functions by adding continuations to them, and the compilation $\mathcal{C}$ of the Higher-Order π-calculus into π-calculus of Chapter 13. We analyse the encoding of call-by-value in Section 15.3, and that of call-by-name in Section 15.4. Variants of these strategies and encodings are examined in Sections 15.5 and 15.6. The strategies considered up to this point do not allow reduction inside the body of a function. Technically speaking, they do not allow the ξ rule of the λ-calculus. In Section 15.7 we discuss when and how the ξ rule may be encoded.

In Chapter 16 we address what happens to the type structure of functions when they are represented as processes. In λ-calculi, types are assigned to terms, and provide an abstract view of their behaviour. In contrast, in the type systems for the π-calculus, types are assigned to names and hence reveal very little about behavioural properties of processes. The semantic relationship between the two forms of types is therefore not obvious. Understanding how λ-calculus types are transformed by the π-calculus encodings is important if we wish to use the π-calculus as a semantic basis for typed programming languages. We look at the simply-typed λ-calculus in detail, and briefly discuss extensions.

Both for typed and for untyped λ-calculi, we derive π-calculus encodings of call-by-name and call-by-value in three steps: a CPS transform, the inclusion of CPS terms into HOπ, and the compilation from HOπ to π-calculus. This is useful for understanding the encodings and for proving their properties. Conversely, a reader familiar with π-calculus might find the encodings helpful for understanding the CPS transforms; indeed, one can also go the other way round, and use the π-calculus encodings to derive results about the correctness of the CPS transforms – see Remark 15.3.25, for instance.

The encoding of untyped call-by-name λ-calculus (λN) is the simplest and perhaps the most natural encoding of λ-calculus into π-calculus. In Chapters 17 and 18 we study the equality on λ-terms induced by this encoding. This equality, $=_\pi$, relates two λ-terms if their encodings are behaviourally-equivalent π-calculus processes. The behavioural equivalence for the π-calculus is barbed congruence – the principal behavioural equivalence in the book. The results obtained are, however, largely independent of this choice, due to the special form of the processes encoding λ-terms. The same results hold, for instance, for testing equivalence or trace equivalence.

We begin by comparing $=_\pi$ with the equality given by the operational semantics of λN. The latter can be formulated as a form of bisimilarity, ***applicative bisimilarity***. We will see in Section 17.3 that the π-calculus interpretation of λN is sound, but not complete.

When an interpretation of a calculus is sound but not fully abstract, one may hope to achieve full abstraction by enriching the calculus. (This is exemplified by the solution to the full-abstraction problem for PCF – a typed λ-calculus extended with fixed points, boolean and arithmetic features – proposed by Plotkin [Plo77], in which PCF is augmented with a 'parallel or' operator.) We follow this approach for λN in Section 17.4. We augment λN with operators, that is, symbols equipped with reduction rules defining their behaviour. We prove that the addition of certain operators that yield non-confluent reductions is necessary and sufficient to make the π-calculus interpretation fully abstract (on pure λ-terms). The operators needed are rather simple. One example is a unary operator that when applied to an argument either behaves like the argument itself or diverges. These results imply that the operational equivalence of simple non-confluent extensions of λN is robust: its equalities remain valid in rich extensions of λN, possibly including operators for expressing concurrency.

In Chapter 18 we investigate the meaning of $=_\pi$: which λ-terms does it equate? To determine this, we prove a few characterizations of $=_\pi$ on the pure λ-terms. The most important one is a characterization in terms of a tree structure of the λ-calculus, the *Lévy–Longo Trees.* We also discuss how to obtain a characterization in terms of the other main tree structure of the λ-calculus, the *Böhm Trees.* Tree structures are an important part of the theory of the λ-calculus; they are especially useful in studying its (denotational) models. A corollary of the characterizations in terms of trees is that the equality induced by the π-calculus encoding is the same as that induced by well-known models of the λ-calculus. This is a remarkable agreement between the classical theory of functions and their interpretation as processes.

14

The λ-calculus

14.1 The formal system

The beauty of the λ-calculus is that it achieves Turing completeness – all computable functions are definable in it – with a very simple syntax. The basic operators of the λ-calculus, in its pure form, are λ-abstraction, for forming functions, and application, for applying a function to an argument. A λ-abstraction has the form $\lambda x.\, M$; in the body M of the function, the variable x is a placeholder for the argument. (We stick to the standard λ-calculus terminology, and call x a *variable*, rather than a *name*.) Letting x and y range over the set of λ-calculus variables, the set Λ of λ-*terms* is defined by the grammar

$$M ::= x \;\mid\; \lambda x.\, M \;\mid\; M_1 M_2\,.$$

In $\lambda x.\, M$, the initial x is a static binder, binding all free occurrences of x in M. As we have already met static binders in previous chapters, we omit the definitions of α-conversion, free variable, substitution, etc. We identify α-convertible terms, and therefore write $M = N$ if M and N are α-convertible. A λ-term is *closed* if it contains no free variables. The set of free variables of a term M is written $\mathsf{fv}(M)$. The subset of Λ containing only the closed terms is Λ^0.

To avoid too many brackets, we assume that application associates to the left, so that MNL should be read $(MN)L$, and that the scope of a λ extends as far as possible to the right, so that $\lambda x.\, MN$ should be read $\lambda x.\,(MN)$. We also abbreviate $\lambda x_1.\cdots.\lambda x_n.\, M$ to $\lambda x_1 \cdots x_n.\, M$, or $\lambda \widetilde{x}.\, M$ if the length of $\widetilde{x}$ is not important. We follow Barendregt [Bar84] and Hindley and Seldin [HS86] in notations and terminology for the λ-calculus.

The basic computational step of the λ-calculus is β-reduction:

$$\beta \; \frac{}{(\lambda x.\, M)N \longrightarrow M\{N/x\}}$$

$$\mu\ \frac{M = M'}{MN = M'N} \qquad \nu\ \frac{N = N'}{MN = MN'} \qquad \xi\ \frac{M = M'}{\lambda x.\, M = \lambda x.\, M'}$$

$$\textsc{Refl}\ \frac{}{M = M} \qquad \textsc{Symm}\ \frac{M = N}{N = M} \qquad \textsc{Trans}\ \frac{M = N \quad N = L}{M = L}$$

Table 14.1. *The rules for a λ-calculus congruence*

in which the placeholder x is replaced by the argument N in the body M of the function. An expression of the form $(\lambda x.\, M)N$ is called a *β-redex*, and the derivative $M\{^N\!/x\}$ is its *contractum*.

The following rules of inference allow us to replace a β-redex by its contractum in any context:

$$\mu\ \frac{M \longrightarrow M'}{MN \longrightarrow M'N} \qquad \nu\ \frac{N \longrightarrow N'}{MN \longrightarrow MN'} \qquad \xi\ \frac{M \longrightarrow M'}{\lambda x.\, M \longrightarrow \lambda x.\, M'} \tag{14.1}$$

We write $M \longrightarrow_\beta N$ if $M \longrightarrow N$ is derivable from the rules β, μ, ν, ξ. Relation $\longrightarrow_\beta$ is the *reduction relation of the λ-calculus,* also called *full β-reduction.*

Relation $\longrightarrow_\beta$ defines a directed form of rewriting. A λ-term M without β-redexes (i.e., for which no N exists such that $M \longrightarrow_\beta N$) is a *normal form* (briefly *nf*). A *reduction path* is a sequence of reduction steps

$$M_1 \longrightarrow_\beta M_2 \longrightarrow_\beta \cdots$$

that may have finite or infinite length.

The axiom β and the rules of inference (14.1) define a single-step reduction relation on λ-terms. Adding rules for reflexivity and transitivity we obtain the multistep reduction relation, $\Longrightarrow_\beta$. The resulting formulas $M \Longrightarrow_\beta N$ define the *formal theory of β-reduction* of the λ-calculus. The predicate $\downarrow$ distinguishes the abstractions; that is, $M \downarrow$ holds just if M is of the form $\lambda x.\, N$. Further, $M \Downarrow_\beta N$ means that $M \Longrightarrow_\beta N$ and $N \downarrow$, and $M \Downarrow_\beta$ means that $M \Downarrow_\beta N$ for some N. Turning the oriented rules defining $\Longrightarrow_\beta$ into equations gives rise to the *λβ-theory,* also called the *formal theory of β equality.* It is defined by the axiom

$$\beta\ \frac{}{(\lambda x.\, M)N = M\{^N\!/x\}}$$

plus the axiom and inference rules for congruence in Table 14.1. We write $\lambda\beta \vdash M = N$ if $M = N$ can be proved in the λβ-theory.

We give names to some special λ-terms:

$$\begin{aligned} I &\stackrel{\text{def}}{=} \lambda x.\, x \\ \Omega &\stackrel{\text{def}}{=} (\lambda x.\, xx)(\lambda x.\, xx) \\ \Xi &\stackrel{\text{def}}{=} (\lambda x.\, \lambda y.\, xx)(\lambda x.\, \lambda y.\, xx). \end{aligned}$$

I is the identity function, because for all N, we have $IN \longrightarrow_\beta N$; we may call Ω a 'purely divergent term', because $\Omega \longrightarrow_\beta \Omega \longrightarrow_\beta \cdots$; and we may call Ξ a 'purely convergent term', because $\Xi \longrightarrow_\beta \lambda y.\, \Xi \longrightarrow_\beta \lambda y.\, \lambda y.\, \Xi \longrightarrow_\beta \cdots$; indeed, for all n, we have $\Xi \Longrightarrow_\beta (\lambda y.\,)^n \Xi$.

14.2 Contrasting λ and π

Without doubt the λ-calculus had an important influence on the development of process calculi like CCS, CSP and ACP. In the case of calculi for mobile processes and higher-order calculi, an important heritage from the λ-calculus is static binding, a concept that is understood largely as a result of work on λ-calculus.

Two important features of λ-calculus that distinguish it from π-calculus are *sequentiality* and *confluence*. We discuss these below. First, we briefly compare the basic reduction axioms of the two calculi.

14.2.1 Reduction axioms

The basic reduction axioms of λ-calculus and π-calculus are β and R-INTER:

$$(\lambda x.\, M)N \longrightarrow M\{N/x\} \qquad p(x).\, P \mid \overline{p}a.\, Q \longrightarrow P\{a/x\} \mid Q\,.$$

There are three noteworthy differences:

(1) The λ-terms $\lambda x.\, M$ and N are committed to interacting with each other, even if $(\lambda x.\, M)N$ is part of a larger term; this is so because different λ-redexes act on different parts of a term. In contrast, interference from the environment can prevent the interaction between the π-calculus terms $p(x).\, P$ and $\overline{p}a.\, Q$. For instance, the environment could contain a process $\overline{p}r.\, R$ that is in competition with $\overline{p}a.\, Q$ for access to $p(x).\, P$. For this reason, π-calculus is not confluent, as discussed in Example 1.2.13. Using a terminology from term-rewriting, we may say that the λ-calculus is *orthogonal*, whereas the π-calculus is not.

(2) The λ-calculus reduction requires a term substitution, whereas the π-calculus reduction requires a (simpler) name substitution.

(3) The λ-reduction is asymmetric: the argument N is completely swallowed by the function $\lambda x.\, M$. The π-reduction is more symmetric (and in variants

such as Pπ it *is* symmetric) as both interacting subterms persist after the reduction.

14.2.2 Sequentiality

The λ-calculus captures *sequential* computations. That is, λ-terms express functions that, algorithmically speaking, look at the arguments they need in sequence. If in doing so a function reaches a divergent argument, then the whole computation will diverge. The λ-calculus, in its untyped or typed versions, cannot describe functions whose algorithmic definition requires that some arguments be run in parallel. An enlightening example is the non-definability in PCF (a typed λ-calculus with fixed points, booleans and integers) of a 'parallel or' function `Por`, where for closed terms M and N,

$$\texttt{Por}\ MN \begin{cases} \text{reduces to } \textsf{true}, \text{ if } M \text{ or } N \text{ reduces to } \textsf{true} \\ \text{diverges, otherwise.} \end{cases}$$

With parallelism, this function is algorithmically easy to compute: just let M and N reduce concurrently and return true if and when one of them evaluates to true.[1] There is no PCF term that behaves like `Por`. The sequentiality of the untyped λ-calculus is already clear, at least intuitively, in the *Normalization Theorem*, a corollary of one of the main syntactic theorems of the λ-calculus, the *Standardization Theorem*. The Normalization Theorem asserts that if a term has a normal form, then this will be found by the *leftmost* strategy. This strategy selects the reduction path of a term in which, at each stage, the contracted redex is the one with the leftmost λ-symbol.

The leftmost strategy is clearly sequential: once begun, the evaluation of a subterm continues until a value (a λ-abstraction) is found; only then can control pass to another subterm. Therefore simultaneous or interleaved evaluation of subterms is forbidden.

In contrast, the π-calculus naturally describes parallel computations. The π-calculus 'world' is that of processes, rather than functions. Since functions can be seen as special kinds of processes, parallel functions like `Por` can be described in the π-calculus; we show the encodings of similar functions in Sections 17.3 and 17.4.2.

[1] In the untyped λ-calculus, where there are no ground data types and abstractions are the only closed values, 'parallel or' should probably be defined as the parallel convergence test (Section 17.3, or sensible versions of it such as in [Bar84, p.375]). However, in typed λ-calculi the two operators are different: parallel convergence is usually more powerful (one can derive 'parallel or' from it, but the converse is often false).

14.2.3 Confluence

The reduction relations of both λ-calculus and π-calculus are non-deterministic, because a term may have more than one redex. However, only in the π-calculus is non-determinism semantically significant. Consider the term

$$Q \stackrel{\text{def}}{=} \overline{a}b \mid \overline{a}c \mid a(x).\overline{x}\,.$$

The two outputs are in competition for the input. If $\overline{a}b$ wins, then $\overline{a}c$ may remain without a partner, and conversely if $\overline{a}c$ wins. Indeed, the two immediate derivatives of Q, namely $\mathbf{0} \mid \overline{a}c \mid \overline{b}$ and $\overline{a}b \mid \mathbf{0} \mid \overline{c}$, are behaviourally very different.

This situation cannot happen in the λ-calculus, where contracting a redex never damages other redexes, in the sense of leaving a subterm without a partner. The fact that the non-determinism of the λ-calculus is harmless is expressed by the *confluence* (often called *Church–Rosser*) property, which says that if a term M has two derivatives N_1 and N_2, then we can always find a third term L to close the diamond:

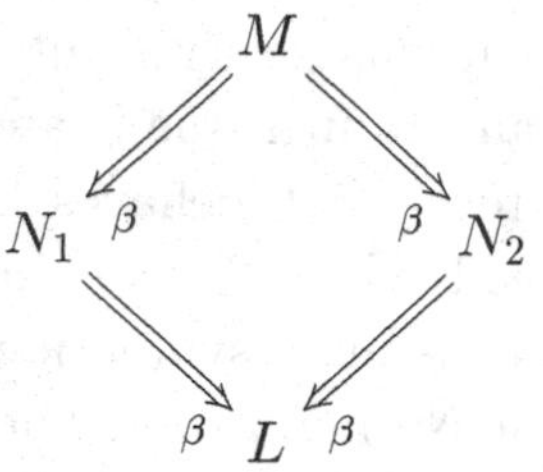

Some consequences of the CR property of the λ-calculus are: (i) the normal form of a term M (if it exists) is unique; (ii) the λ-calculus is consistent, that is, there are terms M and N such that $\lambda\beta \vdash M = N$ does not hold (just take M and N to be different normal forms, for instance $\lambda x.\,x$ and $\lambda x.\,xy$; by point (i) they are not provably equal); (iii) the order in which redexes of a term are reduced is unimportant, in the sense that all finite reduction sequences can be continued to reach a common derivative.

Point (iii) does not imply that all reduction paths must meet. For instance, a term with a normal form may have an infinite reduction sequence that never finds it. An example is the term $(\lambda x.\,I)\Omega$; it has normal form I, obtained by contracting the outermost redex, but it also has the infinite reduction sequence

$$(\lambda x.\,I)\Omega \longrightarrow_\beta (\lambda x.\,I)\Omega \longrightarrow_\beta \cdots$$

obtained by contracting the innermost redex.

14.3 Reduction strategies: call-by-name, call-by-value, call-by-need

The reduction relation $\longrightarrow_\beta$ of the λ-calculus is non-deterministic because a term may have more than one β-redex and therefore several reduction paths. Some of these may lead to a normal form while others may not, as illustrated for the term $(\lambda x. I)\Omega$ above. Different paths from a term to its normal form may have different lengths.

A *reduction strategy* specifies which β-redexes in a term may be contracted. Reduction strategies are useful both for theoretical reasons (for instance, to prove that a term has no normal form), and for practical purposes (for instance, to obtain efficient implementations). Usually a reduction strategy is deterministic. In that case, the one-step reduction relation is a partial function on λ-terms.

Formally, a reduction strategy R is defined by fixing a reduction relation $\longrightarrow_R \subseteq \Lambda \times \Lambda$, which we will usually write in infix notation. The reflexive and transitive closure of $\longrightarrow_R$ is $\Longrightarrow_R$. We say that M *is an R-normal form* (*R-nf*) if there is no N such that $M \longrightarrow_R N$; and that R *has an R-normal form* if there is an R-nf N such that $M \Longrightarrow_R N$. For instance, $\lambda x. M$ is a normal form for any reduction strategy that does not allow the ξ rule. We also write $M \Downarrow_R N$ if $M \Longrightarrow_R N \downarrow$, and $M \Downarrow_R$ if $M \Downarrow_R N$ for some N. A notion of reduction gives rise to a λ-theory, when one adds the rules that turn the reduction relation into a congruence relation.

An example of a strategy is the leftmost strategy mentioned in Section 14.2.2. Important strategies in programming languages are *call-by-name* and *call-by-value*, and variants of them such as *call-by-need*, *parallel call-by-value*, and *strong call-by-name*. There is no 'best' reduction strategy. Different languages, even single languages, adopt different strategies for the evaluation of function or procedure applications. The coding or implementation of different reduction strategies may require different techniques (there are also reduction strategies that are non-computable, and hence impossible to implement!). Below we consider some important reduction strategies; then we show how they can be encoded in π-calculus.

14.3.1 Call-by-name

The idea of the *call-by-name* strategy is that the redex is always the leftmost, but reduction should stop when a constructor is at the top; in the untyped λ-calculus the only constructor is λ-abstraction; in typed λ-calculi there may also be constructors for data, such as '`cons`' for lists. A benefit of not continuing the evaluation underneath an abstraction or a data constructor is that among the call-by-name normal forms are terms representing infinite objects, for instance a term that evaluates to the list of all natural numbers. Therefore one can write meaningful programs for manipulating infinite objects. These programs diverge under other evaluation strategies.

On open terms, the call-by-name strategy also stops on terms with a variable in head position, that is, terms of the form $xM_1 \dots M_n$; this is so because, intuitively, we need to know what the variable is instantiated to in order to decide what reduction to do next. The *one-step call-by-name reduction relation* $\longrightarrow_{\mathrm{N}} \subseteq \Lambda \times \Lambda$ is defined by the two rules

$$\beta \ \frac{}{(\lambda x.\, M)N \longrightarrow_{\mathrm{N}} M\{N/x\}} \qquad\qquad \mu \ \frac{M \longrightarrow_{\mathrm{N}} M'}{MN \longrightarrow_{\mathrm{N}} M'N}$$

Reduction is deterministic: the redex is always at the extreme left of a term. As the ξ rule is absent, evaluation does not continue underneath an abstraction; and as the ν rule is absent, the argument of a function is not evaluated. Examples of call-by-name reductions are

$$(\lambda x.\, I)\Omega \longrightarrow_{\mathrm{N}} I \tag{14.2}$$

$$(\lambda x.\, xx)(II) \longrightarrow_{\mathrm{N}} (II)(II) \longrightarrow_{\mathrm{N}} I(II) \longrightarrow_{\mathrm{N}} II \longrightarrow_{\mathrm{N}} I \tag{14.3}$$

$$(\lambda xy.\, x)z(II) \longrightarrow_{\mathrm{N}} (\lambda y.\, z)(II) \longrightarrow_{\mathrm{N}} z\,. \tag{14.4}$$

Since call-by-name is based on the β rule, the λ-theory induced by call-by-name is the same as $\lambda\beta$. Therefore a correct semantics of call-by-name should validate (at least) the equalities of $\lambda\beta$.

14.3.2 Call-by-value

In the call-by-name strategy, the contraction of a redex $(\lambda x.\, M)N$ is performed without restriction on the form of the argument N. This contrasts with the *call-by-value* (or *eager*) strategy, where the argument N is reduced to a *value* before the redex is contracted. The values of the untyped call-by-value λ-calculus are the functions (that is, the λ-abstractions) and, on open terms, also the variables. It makes sense that variables should be values because, in call-by-value, substitutions replace variables with values – not arbitrary terms – and therefore the closed terms that can be obtained from a variable are closed values.

$$\text{Values} \quad V ::= \lambda x.\, M \mid x \qquad M \in \Lambda$$

The *one-step call-by-value reduction relation* $\longrightarrow_{\mathrm{V}} \subseteq \Lambda \times \Lambda$ is defined by these rules:

$$\beta_{\mathrm{v}} \ \frac{}{(\lambda x.\, M)V \longrightarrow_{\mathrm{V}} M\{V/x\}}$$

$$\mu \ \frac{M \longrightarrow_{\mathrm{V}} M'}{MN \longrightarrow_{\mathrm{V}} M'N} \qquad\qquad \nu_{\mathrm{v}} \ \frac{N \longrightarrow_{\mathrm{V}} N'}{VN \longrightarrow_{\mathrm{V}} VN'}$$

Examples of call-by-value reductions are

$$(\lambda x.\, I)\Omega \longrightarrow_{\mathrm{V}} (\lambda x.\, I)\Omega \longrightarrow_{\mathrm{V}} \cdots \tag{14.5}$$

$$(\lambda x.\, xx)(II) \longrightarrow_{\mathrm{V}} (\lambda x.\, xx)I \longrightarrow_{\mathrm{V}} II \longrightarrow_{\mathrm{V}} I \tag{14.6}$$

$$(\lambda xy.\, x)z(II) \longrightarrow_{\mathrm{V}} (\lambda y.\, z)(II) \longrightarrow_{\mathrm{V}} (\lambda y.\, z)I \longrightarrow_{\mathrm{V}} z\,. \tag{14.7}$$

Call-by-value is based on the β_{V} rule. The λ-theory induced by this rule is the *$\lambda\beta_{\mathrm{V}}$ theory*, also called the *formal theory of β_{V} equality*, defined by the axiom

$$\beta_{\mathrm{V}} \; \frac{}{(\lambda x.\, M)V = M\{V/x\}}$$

plus the inference rules in Table 14.1. A correct semantics of call-by-value should validate (at least) the equalities of $\lambda\beta_{\mathrm{V}}$.

Call-by-value is very common in language implementations. Advantages of call-by-value are: (i) if in $(\lambda x.\, M)N$ the variable x occurs more than once in the body M, then evaluating N before replacing x may avoid having to reduce several copies of N (contrast Example (14.3) with (14.6)); and (ii) in languages with side effects, call-by-value is easier to understand and mathematically more tractable. On the other hand, call-by-name has the advantages that: (i) one does not perform useless reductions of the argument N of a redex $(\lambda x.\, M)N$ if x does not occur in M and therefore N is not used (contrast Example (14.4) with (14.7)); and (ii) on certain terms, the call-by-name strategy terminates whereas call-by-value fails (an example is the term $(\lambda x.\, I)\Omega$, as shown in (14.2) and (14.5)).

A variant of call-by-value is *parallel call-by-value*, which has the ordinary ν rule in place of ν_{V}. Its one-step reduction relation is denoted by $\longrightarrow_{\mathrm{PV}}$. This strategy is not deterministic, because in an application MN both the function and the argument can be reduced. Normal forms are, however, unique (that is, if $M \Longrightarrow_{\mathrm{PV}} M'$ and $M \Longrightarrow_{\mathrm{PV}} M''$ and both M' and M'' are PV-nfs, then $M' = M''$), and if M has a PV-nf, then all reduction sequences from M are finite. Because of these properties, behavioural equivalence under parallel call-by-value is usually the same as that under (sequential) call-by-value; we will talk about behavioural equivalences for λ-calculus in Chapter 17.

14.3.3 Call-by-need

In a language without side effects, where the evaluation of a term always yields the same result, the inefficiency problems of call-by-name arising from repeated evaluation of copies of the argument of a function can be avoided as follows. The first time the argument is evaluated, its value is saved in an environment; if needed subsequently, the value is fetched from the environment. In this way, the evaluation of the argument is shared among all places where the argument is used. This implementation technique is called *call-by-need.* It is usually presented as a reduction strategy on graphs, where *sharing* of subterms is easy to represent. Alternatively, call-by-need can be formalized in a λ-calculus with a `let` construct, to model sharing. The β rule is replaced by the `let` rule

$$\frac{}{(\lambda x.\, M)N \longrightarrow_{\mathrm{NE}} \texttt{let } x = N \texttt{ in } M}\, x \notin \mathsf{fv}(N) \tag{14.8}$$

In the derivative, the evaluation continues on M, and only when the value associated to x is needed is the subterm N evaluated. The value to which N reduces replaces the occurrence of x in question, and all subsequent occurrences of x when their value is needed. There are also some structural rules for manipulating `let` expressions, which usually make use of a notion of *evaluation context* to define the next redex. For instance, in call-by-need we have

$$\begin{array}{rcl} II & = & (\lambda x.\, x)(\lambda y.\, y) \\ & \longrightarrow_{\mathrm{NE}} & \texttt{let } x = \lambda y.\, y \texttt{ in } x \\ & \longrightarrow_{\mathrm{NE}} & \texttt{let } x = \lambda y.\, y \texttt{ in } \lambda z.\, z \\ & \equiv & \lambda z.\, z \\ & = & I \end{array} \tag{14.9}$$

where $\equiv$ indicates application of the garbage-collection rule

$$\texttt{let } x = M \texttt{ in } N \equiv N \qquad x \notin \mathsf{fv}(N)\,. \tag{14.10}$$

(Garbage-collection rules may or may not be present in the definition of a call-by-need reduction; in any case, a rule such as (14.10) can be proved valid for behavioural equivalences.) Similarly, we have

$$Iy \Longrightarrow_{\mathrm{NE}} \equiv y\,. \tag{14.11}$$

Using derivations (14.9) and (14.11) to compress reductions, here is a more interesting call-by-need computation. Note that the work for the evaluation of the argument II is done only once:

$$\begin{array}{lcl} & & (\lambda x.\, (Ix)x)(II) \\ \longrightarrow_{\mathrm{NE}} & & \texttt{let } x = II \texttt{ in } (Ix)x \\ \Longrightarrow_{\mathrm{NE}} & \equiv & \texttt{let } x = II \texttt{ in } xx \\ \Longrightarrow_{\mathrm{NE}} & \equiv & \texttt{let } x = I \texttt{ in } xx \\ \longrightarrow_{\mathrm{NE}} & & \texttt{let } x = I \texttt{ in } Ix \\ \Longrightarrow_{\mathrm{NE}} & \equiv & \texttt{let } x = I \texttt{ in } x \\ \longrightarrow_{\mathrm{NE}} & \equiv & I\,. \end{array}$$

We will not present a formal system for λ-calculus with `let`; the intuitions given above should be enough to understand our uses of call-by-need.

As call-by-need is an implementation technique for call-by-name, its theory is closely related to that of call-by-name. The sets of λ-terms that have a normal form under call-by-need and call-by-name coincide; and two λ-terms are behaviourally equivalent in call-by-need iff they are so in call-by-name.

15

Interpreting λ-calculi

This chapter and the next present various interpretations of λ-calculus strategies into the π-calculus. All the interpretations have two common features:

- Function application is translated as a form of parallel combination of two processes, the function and its argument, and β-reduction is modelled as an interaction between them.
- The encoding of a λ-term is parametric over a name. This name is used by (the translation of) the λ-term to interact with the environment.

In Section 14.2.1 we observed that a redex of the λ-calculus gives rise to a private interaction between two terms. In contrast, a redex of the π-calculus is susceptible to interference from the environment. This interference is avoided if the name used by the two processes to communicate is private to them. Therefore, the appearance of a β-redex in a λ-term should correspond, in the π-calculus translation of that term, to the appearance of two processes that can communicate along a *private* name. We also observed in Section 14.2.1 that the β rule of the λ-calculus is strongly asymmetric. In all encodings, the λ-terms are mapped onto processes of the *Asynchronous* π-calculus, the asymmetry of whose communication rule reflects that of the λ-calculus.

A name parameter is needed in the π-calculus encodings of λ-terms for the following reason. Roughly speaking, in the λ-calculus, λ is the only port; a λ-term receives its argument at λ. In the π-calculus, there are many ports (the names), so one needs to specify at which port (the encoding of) a λ-term interacts with its environment.

15.1 Continuation Passing Style

The parameter of the π-calculus encoding of a function can also be thought of as a *continuation*. In functional languages, a continuation is a parameter of a function that represents the 'rest' of the computation. Functions taking continuations as arguments are called *functions in Continuation Passing Style* (briefly *CPS functions*), and have a special syntactic form: they terminate their computation by passing the result to the continuation. The continuation parameter may also be thought of as an address to which the result of the function is to be delivered. For an informal example, take the following function from integers to integers:

$$f \stackrel{\mathrm{def}}{=} \lambda y.\ \mathtt{let}\ g = \lambda n.\, n+2\ \mathtt{in}\ (g\,y) + (g\,y)\,.$$

Here is a CPS version of f; in the body, g_{CPS} is a CPS version of g, and k is the continuation parameter:

$$\begin{aligned} f_{\mathrm{CPS}} \stackrel{\mathrm{def}}{=} \lambda k\,y.\, &\mathtt{let}\ g_{\mathrm{CPS}} = \lambda k\,n.\ \mathtt{let}\ m = n+2\ \mathtt{in}\ k\,m \\ &\quad \mathtt{in}\ g_{\mathrm{CPS}}\Big(\lambda v.\, g_{\mathrm{CPS}}\Big(\lambda w.\ \mathtt{let}\ u = u+n\ \mathtt{in}\ k\,u\Big)y\Big)y\,. \end{aligned}$$

In programming languages continuations are widely used, for programming, as an implementation technique (to generate an intermediate language that is easier to optimize and manipulate), and for giving denotational semantics. A fairly vast literature of functional programming studies transformations of functions into CPS functions. They are called *CPS transforms*. The best known are the CPS transforms for call-by-name and call-by-value λ-calculus studied by Plotkin in his seminal paper [Plo75].

We will develop the analogy between π-calculus encodings and CPS transforms. We will derive π-calculus encodings of call-by-name and call-by-value λ-calculus via the CPS transforms of [Plo75]. We will observe that the targets of the CPS transforms are essentially subcalculi of HOπ. We will therefore be able to apply compilation $\mathcal{C}$ from HOπ to π-calculus to derive π-calculus encodings ($\mathcal{C}$ is defined in Section 13.2.2). This is the programme for Sections 15.3 and 15.4, and is summarized in Figure 15.1, where: λV and λN are the call-by-value and call-by-name λ-calculi; $\mathcal{C}_{\mathrm{V}}$ and $\mathcal{C}_{\mathrm{N}}$ are the call-by-value and the call-by-name CPS transforms; $\mathrm{CPS}_{\mathrm{V}}$ and $\mathrm{CPS}_{\mathrm{N}}$ are languages of CPS λ-terms, that is, the target languages of the two CPS transforms; $\mathcal{H}$ is the injection of these CPS languages into HOπ; $\mathcal{C}$ is the compilation from HOπ to π-calculus; and $\mathcal{V}$ and $\mathcal{N}$ are the π-calculus encodings of call-by-value and call-by-name. There are many CPS transforms; we have used the transforms that, in our view, yield the simplest and most robust encodings. The schema of Figure 15.1 also applies to *typed* λ-calculi, by extending the translations of terms to translations of types; we consider this in Chapter 16.

Having obtained encodings of call-by-name and call-by-value, in Sections 15.3.3, 15.5, and 15.7 we can then play with them and derive encodings of related strategies, such as call-by-need, parallel call-by-value, and strong call-by-name.

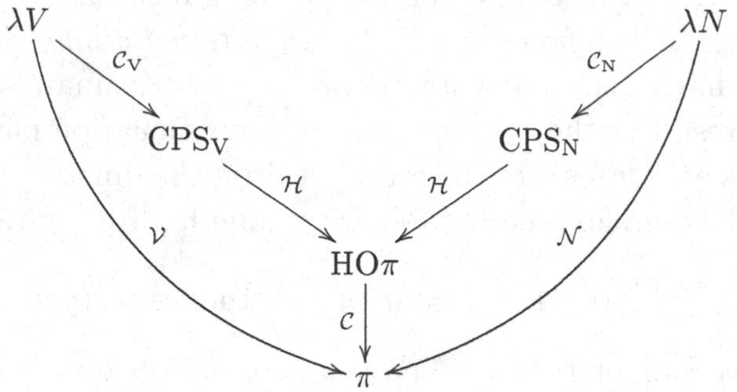

Fig. 15.1. The derivations of the π-calculus encodings of λV and λN.

15.2 Notations and terminology for functions as processes

Below are common notations and terminology for this Part of the book.

Communication of tuples We will use communication of tuples of values extensively. We therefore take the polyadic input, $a(\widetilde{x}).\,P$, as primitive, assuming transition rules (6.4) for it (Section 6.6).

Asynchrony We have mentioned that the λ-terms are translated to processes of the Asynchronous π-calculus. This allows us to exploit certain proof techniques that are available only for processes of the Asynchronous π-calculus. In particular, we will use proof techniques based on ground bisimilarity. We recall that on processes of the Asynchronous π-calculus, both untyped and typed, ground bisimilarity implies full bisimilarity, hence also barbed congruence (see Corollary 5.3.9 and Theorem 5.3.11).

Although the Asynchronous π-calculus would be sufficient, we always consider the target languages of the translations to be the full π-calculus. In principle, the choice of the target language is relevant, because barbed congruence is sensitive to the class of contexts allowed. However, we strongly believe that the choice between full or Asynchronous π-calculus does not affect the results we will present.

In the Asynchronous π-calculus there is no process underneath an output prefix. For convenience, however, we sometimes use output prefixes of the form $\boldsymbol{\nu}\widetilde{b}\,\overline{a}\langle\widetilde{c}, b\rangle.\,\pi.\,P$, where $b \in \widetilde{b}$ and b is the subject of prefix π, to highlight ordering among actions – under those hypotheses, $\boldsymbol{\nu}\widetilde{b}\,\overline{a}\langle\widetilde{c}, b\rangle.\,\pi.\,P$ is semantically the same as $\boldsymbol{\nu}\widetilde{b}\,(\overline{a}\langle\widetilde{c}, b\rangle \mid \pi.\,P)$.

Compilation $\mathcal{C}$ The compilation $\mathcal{C}$ from HOπ to π-calculus is studied in Section 13.2.2. Extensions of the compilation to handle tuple and linear types (which we will sometimes need) are discussed in Section 13.2.3. The results about $\mathcal{C}$ that we will use are Lemma 13.2.3, Theorem 13.2.11, Theorem 13.2.12, and Lemma 13.2.14.

Typed behavioural equivalences We recall that $\Delta \triangleright P \cong^{c} Q$ is barbed congruence at typing Δ. When there is no ambiguity on what Δ is we may drop it. We always omit Δ on the plain polyadic π-calculus ($\pi^{\sharp,\times,\mu}$), which is an extremely simple typed calculus – types are used just to avoid arity mismatches in communications – whereas we keep Δ for calculi with a richer type structure, for instance with i/o types. The same conventions apply to strong barbed congruence. We will use also ground bisimilarity and ground expansion, in typed π-calculi such as $\pi^{\sharp,\times,\mu}$ without basic types (so all atomic values are names); in these calculi the relations are defined as in the untyped π-calculus (Remark 9.4.21).

We write $P \Downarrow$ to mean that $P \Downarrow_a$ or $P \Downarrow_{\overline{a}}$, for some a; that is, process P can perform an input or an output action.

Abstractions As previously mentioned, in all encodings of the λ-calculus into the π-calculus, the encoding of a λ-term is parametric on a name, that is, it is a function from names to π-calculus processes, an ***abstraction***. We use F and G to range over ***abstractions***. We recall some notations for abstractions in the π-calculus, and introduce some new ones. The reader should bear in mind that abstractions in the π-calculus are a notational device, or convenience – they are not part of the syntax. This contrasts with HOπ where abstractions are a key construct in the syntax. An abstraction $(a).\,P$ is a binder for a of the same nature as the input prefix $b(a).\,P$. Indeed, the input $b(a).\,P$ may be seen as constructed by juxtaposition of the name b and the abstraction $(a).\,P$. Accordingly, if F is the abstraction $(a).\,P$, we sometimes write $b\,F$ and $Q\,\{b = F\}$ for the processes $b(a).\,P$ and $Q\,\{b = (a).\,P\}$, respectively. We use the following abbreviations for abstractions: if F is $(a).\,P$ then $b(\widetilde{c})\,F$ and $Q\,\{b = (\widetilde{c})\,F\}$ stand for $b(\widetilde{c}, a).\,P$ and $Q\,\{b = (\widetilde{c}, a).\,P\}$ respectively, $F\,\{b = (\widetilde{c}).\,Q\}$ stands for $(a).\,(P\,\{b = (\widetilde{c}).\,Q\})$, and, as usual, Fc stands for $P\{c/a\}$ – the actual parameter c replaces the formal parameter a in the body P of F.

If $\asymp$ is a behavioural equivalence defined on π-calculus processes, then $F \asymp G$ means that $Fc \asymp Gc$, for all c; in typed π-calculi $\Gamma \triangleright F \asymp G : T \rightarrow \diamond$ means that $\Gamma, c : T \triangleright Fc \asymp Gc$, for all c such that $\Gamma, c : T \vdash Fc, Gc$. As usual: we may omit types in the plain polyadic π-calculus $\pi^{\sharp,\times,\mu}$; and when $\asymp$ is a ground relation, it suffices to check $Fc \asymp Gc$ on a single fresh name c.

λ-calculus variables For simplicity, we assume that λ-calculus variables are also π-calculus names.

Convention on bound names in encodings In the definition of an encoding, all bound names introduced are supposed to be fresh. For instance, in

$$[\![MN]\!] \stackrel{\text{def}}{=} (p).\, \boldsymbol{\nu} q\, ([\![M]\!]q \mid q(v).\, \boldsymbol{\nu} x\, (\overline{v}\langle x, p\rangle.\, !x\, [\![N]\!]))$$

names q, x and v are fresh.

15.3 The interpretation of call-by-value

In this section we develop the left part of the diagram of Figure 15.1. The π-calculus encoding of call-by-value λ-calculus (λV) is obtained in three steps, the first of which is the call-by-value CPS transform of [Plo75]. The reader who is eager to see the π-calculus encoding, and does not want to go through the CPS transform, may go directly to Section 15.3.2. We will not give detailed proofs of results about the CPS transforms, as they are not the subject of the book; see the notes at the end of the Part for references.

15.3.1 The three steps

15.3.1.1 Step 1: the call-by-value CPS transform

The *call-by-value CPS transform*, $\mathcal{C}_{\mathrm{V}}$, transforms functions of λV into CPS functions. In its definition, the translation of values uses the auxiliary translation function $\mathcal{C}^{\star}_{\mathrm{V}}$, which will be particularly useful when considering types. We call a term $\mathcal{C}^{\star}_{\mathrm{V}}[V]$ a *CPS-value*. The transform is presented in Table 15.1. Its definition introduces a new variable, the *continuation variable* k, that represents continuations and that has to be kept separate from the other variables. In the π-calculus encodings, and in typed versions of the CPS transform, the continuation variable and the other variables will have different types. (In the definition of $\mathcal{C}_{\mathrm{V}}$ we also use special symbols v, w for the formal parameters of continuations. The distinction between these variables and ordinary variables is, however, somewhat artificial because the former may be instantiated by the latter.)

We explain informally how the CPS transform works. The CPS image of a λ-term L immediately needs a continuation. When a continuation is provided, L is reduced to a value, and this value (precisely its CPS-value) is passed to the continuation. Therefore if L is itself a value, then it can be passed directly to the continuation. If, however, L is an application MN then the following happens. First M is evaluated with continuation $\lambda v.\, \mathcal{C}_{\mathrm{V}}[\![N]\!](\lambda w.\, vwk)$. When M becomes a function, say $\lambda x.\, M_1$, this function is passed to the continuation, and the body

In this table we abbreviate $\mathcal{C}_{\mathrm{V}}[\![M]\!]$ as $[\![M]\!]$ and $\mathcal{C}^{\star}_{\mathrm{V}}[V]$ as $[V]$.

Call-by-value values $V \quad ::= \quad \lambda x.\, M \mid x$

$$\begin{aligned} [\![V]\!] &\stackrel{\mathrm{def}}{=} \lambda k.\, k[V] \\ [\![MN]\!] &\stackrel{\mathrm{def}}{=} \lambda k.\, [\![M]\!](\lambda v.\, [\![N]\!](\lambda w.\, vwk)) \end{aligned}$$

$$\begin{aligned} [x] &\stackrel{\mathrm{def}}{=} x \\ [\lambda x.\, M] &\stackrel{\mathrm{def}}{=} \lambda x.\, [\![M]\!] \end{aligned}$$

Table 15.1. *The call-by-value CPS transform*

of the continuation is evaluated. This means evaluating N with continuation $\lambda w.\, vwk\{\mathcal{C}^{\star}_{\mathrm{V}}[\lambda x.\, M_1]/v\}$. When N in turn becomes a value V, this value is passed to the continuation, and the body of the continuation is evaluated. This body is the term $(vwk)\{\mathcal{C}^{\star}_{\mathrm{V}}[V]/w\}\{\mathcal{C}^{\star}_{\mathrm{V}}[\lambda x.\, M_1]/v\}$, that is $(\lambda x.\, \mathcal{C}_{\mathrm{V}}[\![M_1]\!])\mathcal{C}^{\star}_{\mathrm{V}}[V]k$. This term reduces to $\mathcal{C}_{\mathrm{V}}[\![M_1]\!]\{\mathcal{C}^{\star}_{\mathrm{V}}[V]/x\}k$, which is the same as $\mathcal{C}_{\mathrm{V}}[\![M_1\{V/x\}]\!]k$. The reduction of $\mathcal{C}_{\mathrm{V}}[\![M_1\{V/x\}]\!]k$ continues and, at the end, the value that $M_1\{V/x\}$ reduces to is passed to k. Note that the flow of control of $\lambda\mathrm{V}$ on application is correctly mimicked: first the operator M of the application is evaluated, then the argument N is evaluated, and finally the two derivatives of M and N are contracted.

To help understanding of the behaviour of application, we report below the details of how a β_{v} reduction

$$(\lambda x.\, M_1)V \longrightarrow_{\mathrm{V}} M_1\{V/x\} \tag{15.1}$$

is simulated. We use the call-by-name reduction $\longrightarrow_{\mathrm{N}}$ for the target CPS terms, but we could just as well have chosen call-by-value, since these strategies coincide on CPS terms (see Remark 15.3.3).

$$\begin{array}{rl} & \mathcal{C}_V[\![(\lambda x.\, M_1)V]\!]k \\ = & \Big(\lambda k.\, \mathcal{C}_V[\![\lambda x.\, M_1]\!](\lambda v.\, \mathcal{C}_V[\![V]\!](\lambda w.\, vwk))\Big)k \\ \longrightarrow_N & \mathcal{C}_V[\![\lambda x.\, M_1]\!](\lambda v.\, \mathcal{C}_V[\![V]\!](\lambda w.\, vwk)) \\ = & \lambda h.\, h\mathcal{C}^\star_V[\lambda x.\, M_1](\lambda v.\, \mathcal{C}_V[\![V]\!](\lambda w.\, vwk)) \\ \longrightarrow_N & (\lambda v.\, \mathcal{C}_V[\![V]\!](\lambda w.\, vwk))\mathcal{C}^\star_V[\lambda x.\, M_1] \\ \longrightarrow_N & \mathcal{C}_V[\![V]\!](\lambda w.\, \mathcal{C}^\star_V[\lambda x.\, M_1]wk) \\ = & \lambda h.\, h\mathcal{C}^\star_V[V](\lambda w.\, \mathcal{C}^\star_V[\lambda x.\, M_1]wk) \\ \longrightarrow_N & (\lambda w.\, \mathcal{C}^\star_V[\lambda x.\, M_1]wk)\mathcal{C}^\star_V[V] \\ \longrightarrow_N & \mathcal{C}^\star_V[\lambda x.\, M_1]\mathcal{C}^\star_V[V]k \\ = & (\lambda x.\, \mathcal{C}_V[\![M_1]\!])\mathcal{C}^\star_V[V]k \\ \longrightarrow_N & \mathcal{C}_V[\![M_1]\!]\{\mathcal{C}^\star_V[V]/x\}k \\ = & \mathcal{C}_V[\![M_1\{V/x\}]\!]k\,. \end{array} \tag{15.2}$$

All but the last reduction can be regarded as *administrative* reductions, because they do not correspond to reductions of the source terms. The last reduction can be regarded as a *proper* reduction, because it directly corresponds to the reduction of the source term.

The call-by-value CPS transform maps λ-terms onto a subset of the λ-terms. The closure of that subset under β-conversion gives the language CPS_V of the call-by-value CPS:

$$\mathrm{CPS}_V \stackrel{\text{def}}{=} \{A \mid \exists M \in \Lambda \text{ with } \mathcal{C}_V[\![M]\!] \Longrightarrow_\beta A\}\,.$$

We call the terms of CPS_V the *CPS terms*. The first theorem shows that on CPS terms, β- and β_v-redexes coincide.

Theorem 15.3.1 (Indifference of CPS_V on reductions) Let $M \in \mathrm{CPS}_V$ and let N be any subterm of M. For all N', we have $N \longrightarrow_N N'$ iff $N \longrightarrow_V N'$.

Proof Below we will give a grammar, Grammar (15.4), that generates all CPS terms. It is immediate to check that on terms generated by that grammar, β-redexes and β_v-redexes coincide, because all arguments of functions are values of λV (abstractions and variables). □

Essentially as a consequence of Theorem 15.3.1, we obtain:

Theorem 15.3.2 (Indifference of CPS_V on λ-theories) Suppose that $M, N \in \mathrm{CPS}_V$. Then we have $\lambda\beta \vdash M = N$ iff $\lambda\beta_v \vdash M = N$.

Proof The implication from right to left holds because a β_v-redex is also a β-redex. We consider the implication from left to right. Since full β-reduction

$\Longrightarrow_\beta$ is confluent, $\lambda\beta \vdash L_1 = L_2$ implies that there is L_3 such that $L_1 \Longrightarrow_\beta L_3$ and $L_2 \Longrightarrow_\beta L_3$. When L_1 and L_2 are CPS terms, L_3 is also a CPS term. By Theorem 15.3.1, all β-redexes contracted in the reductions $L_1 \Longrightarrow_\beta L_3$ and $L_2 \Longrightarrow_\beta L_3$ are also β_v-redexes. Hence $\lambda\beta_\mathrm{v} \vdash L_1 = L_2$. □

Remark 15.3.3 These indifference properties allow us to take either call-by-name or call-by-value as the reduction strategy and the λ-theory on CPS terms. We choose the call-by-name versions, because they are simpler. □

The next two theorems are about the correctness of the CPS transform. The first shows that the computation of a λ-term is correctly mimicked by its CPS image. The second shows that the CPS transform preserves β_v-conversion.

Theorem 15.3.4 (Adequacy of $\mathcal{C}_\mathrm{V}$) Let $M \in \Lambda^0$.

(1) If $M \Longrightarrow_\mathrm{V} V$ then $\mathcal{C}_\mathrm{V}[\![M]\!]k \Longrightarrow_\mathrm{N} k\,\mathcal{C}^\star_\mathrm{V}[V]$ (note that the term $k\,\mathcal{C}^\star_\mathrm{V}[V]$ is a N-nf, that is, a normal form for call-by-name).
(2) The converse: if $\mathcal{C}_\mathrm{V}[\![M]\!]k \Longrightarrow_\mathrm{N} N$ and N is an N-nf, then there is a call-by-value value V such that $M \Longrightarrow_\mathrm{V} V$ and $N = k\,\mathcal{C}^\star_\mathrm{V}[V]$. □

Theorem 15.3.4 can be proved by going through an intermediate CPS transform obtained from the original one by removing some administrative reductions. Doing so is useful because administrative reductions complicate the operational correspondence between source and target terms of the CPS transform. This is clear by considering the open term xx: this term is not reducible (it is a V-nf), but its image $\mathcal{C}_\mathrm{V}[\![xx]\!]k$ has five (administrative) reductions.

Theorem 15.3.5 (Validity of the $\lambda\beta_\mathrm{v}$-theory for $\mathcal{C}_\mathrm{V}$) Let $M, N \in \Lambda$. If $\lambda\beta_\mathrm{v} \vdash M = N$ then $\lambda\beta \vdash \mathcal{C}_\mathrm{V}[\![M]\!] = \mathcal{C}_\mathrm{V}[\![N]\!]$.

Proof (sketch) First one shows that if $M \Longrightarrow_\mathrm{V} N$, then $\lambda\beta \vdash \mathcal{C}_\mathrm{V}[\![M]\!] = \mathcal{C}_\mathrm{V}[\![N]\!]$. Then one concludes using the fact that $\Longrightarrow_\mathrm{V}$ is confluent. □

The converse of Theorem 15.3.5 fails. For instance, if

$$\begin{aligned} M &\stackrel{\mathrm{def}}{=} \Omega y = (\lambda x.\, xx)(\lambda x.\, xx)y \\ N &\stackrel{\mathrm{def}}{=} (\lambda x.\, xy)\Omega = (\lambda x.\, xy)((\lambda x.\, xx)(\lambda x.\, xx)) \end{aligned} \tag{15.3}$$

then $\lambda\beta \vdash \mathcal{C}_\mathrm{V}[\![M]\!] = \mathcal{C}_\mathrm{V}[\![N]\!]$ holds, but $\lambda\beta_\mathrm{v} \vdash M = N$ does not.

The statements on the correctness of the CPS transform complete step 1 of the left-hand part of Figure 15.1.

15.3.1.2 Step 2: from $\mathrm{CPS_V}$ *to* $\mathrm{HO}\pi$

The next step is to show that, modulo the different syntax for abstraction and application, the terms of $\mathrm{CPS_V}$ are also terms of $\mathrm{HO}\pi$. To do this, we present a grammar that generates all $\mathrm{CPS_V}$ terms, and show that the terms generated by this grammar are also terms of $\mathrm{HO}\pi$.

The grammar has four non-terminals, for *principal terms*, *continuations*, *CPS-values*, and *answers*. Principal terms are abstractions on continuations; they describe the images of the λ-terms under the CPS transform. CPS-values correspond, intuitively, to the values of λV; they are used as arguments to continuations. Answers are the results of computations: what we obtain when we evaluate a principal term applied to a continuation. Answers are the terms in which computation (β-reductions) takes place.

$$\begin{array}{rlcl}
\text{continuation variable} & k & & \\
\text{ordinary variables} & x, \ldots & & \\
\text{answers} & P & ::= & KV \mid VVK \mid AK \\
\text{CPS-values} & V & ::= & \lambda x.\, \lambda k.\, P \mid x \\
\text{continuations} & K & ::= & k \mid \lambda x.\, P \\
\text{principal terms} & A & ::= & \lambda k.\, P
\end{array} \tag{15.4}$$

Remark 15.3.6 In the grammar for CPS-values, the production $\lambda x.\, \lambda k.\, P$ can be simplified to $\lambda x.\, A$, but the expanded form is better for the comparison with $\mathrm{HO}\pi$ below. □

Remark 15.3.7 Having only one continuation variable guarantees that the continuation occurs free exactly once in the body of each abstraction $\lambda k.\, P$. (When working up to α-conversion, the continuation variable k may be renamed, but the linearity constraint on continuations remains.) □

The relationships among the four categories of non-terminals in Grammar (15.4) can be expressed using types. Assuming a distinguished type $\diamond$ for answers, the types T_V, T_K, and T_A of CPS-values, continuations, and principal terms are

$$\begin{array}{rcl}
T_V & \stackrel{\text{def}}{=} & \mu X.\, (X \to (X \to \diamond) \to \diamond) \\
T_K & \stackrel{\text{def}}{=} & T_V \to \diamond \\
T_A & \stackrel{\text{def}}{=} & T_K \to \diamond\, .
\end{array} \tag{15.5}$$

The type judgments for the terms M generated by Grammar (15.4) are of the form

$$\Gamma \vdash M : T \tag{15.6}$$

where $T \in \{T_V, T_K, T_A, \diamond\}$ and Γ is either $\widetilde{x} : T_V$ or $\widetilde{x} : T_V, k : T_K$, for some $\widetilde{x}$ with $\widetilde{x} \subseteq \mathsf{fv}(M)$. We will see in Chapter 16 that there is a general schema for translating type judgments on λ-terms to type judgments on the CPS images of the λ-terms, and that the schema applies also to untyped λ-calculus, when this is viewed as a special typed λ-calculus.

Remark 15.3.8 To be precise we should include some linear information in the types (15.5), to show the linear usage of continuations. In the step of encoding into the π-calculus this linear information allows us to avoid some replication operators. We do not show the linear types for these reasons: the linear information is already highlighted in (15.4) by the syntactic separation between continuation and ordinary variables; linearity is not fundamental – the simplification on replications in the π-calculus is pretty straightforward and could anyway be omitted; and linear types are not needed in the final π-calculus encoding – linearity can be 'forgotten' in the step of compilation of HOπ into π-calculus without affecting the results about the compilation that we will need (it suffices to omit some replications in the encoding, as explained in Section 13.2.3). □

All CPS terms are indeed generated by Grammar (15.4):

Lemma 15.3.9 If $M \in \mathrm{CPS}_\mathrm{V}$ then M is a principal term of Grammar (15.4).

Proof One can show that the set of principal terms includes the set $\{\mathcal{C}_\mathrm{V}[\![M]\!] \mid M \in \Lambda\}$ and is closed under β-conversion. □

It is easy to see that the set of terms generated by Grammar (15.4) is, essentially, a subset of HOπ terms. Precisely, answers may be regarded as HOπ processes, and CPS-values, continuations, and principal terms as HOπ higher-order values. In the grammar of HOπ, higher-order values are either variables or parametrized processes (abstractions). CPS-values, continuations, and principal terms of Grammar (15.4) are indeed of this form, if we read P as a 'process', and we uncurry a CPS-value $\lambda x.\,\lambda k.\,P$ to $\lambda(x,k).\,P$ and an answer VVK to $V\langle V, K\rangle$. (Correspondingly, in Table 15.1, $\mathcal{C}^\star_\mathrm{V}[\lambda x.\,M]$ becomes $\lambda(x,k).\,\mathcal{C}_\mathrm{V}[\![M]\!]k$, and in the translation of MN, the term $\lambda w.\,vwk$ becomes $\lambda w.\,v\langle w,k\rangle$.) It is therefore straightforward to define the injection $\mathcal{H}$ from the terms of Grammar (15.4) to HOπ. On terms, modulo this uncurrying, the injection rewrites λ-abstractions into HOπ abstractions, and λ-applications into HOπ applications (with the obvious type annotations, given by (15.5) and the translation of types). The injection is the identity on (uncurried) types; thus

$$\mathcal{H}[\![T_V]\!] \stackrel{\mathrm{def}}{=} \mu X.\,\Big((X \times (X \to \diamond)) \to \diamond\Big)\,. \tag{15.7}$$

We have $\mathcal{H}[\![\diamond]\!] \stackrel{\text{def}}{=} \diamond$, which explains the abuse of notation whereby the same symbol $\diamond$ is used for the type of answers of Grammar (15.4) and for the type of processes of HOπ. The image of $\mathcal{H}$ is HO$\pi^{\times,\mu,\rightarrow\diamond}$, that is, an HO$\pi$ language that has recursive and tuple types. The proofs of the next two lemmas are straightforward.

Lemma 15.3.10 Suppose that M is a term generated by Grammar (15.4), and that $\Gamma \vdash M : T$ for Γ and T as in (15.6). Then $\mathcal{H}[\![\Gamma]\!] \vdash \mathcal{H}[\![M]\!] : \mathcal{H}[\![T]\!]$. □

As a corollary of Lemma 15.3.10, if $M \in \Lambda$ with $\mathsf{fv}(M) \subseteq \widetilde{x}$, then

$$\widetilde{x} : \mathcal{H}[\![T_{\mathrm{V}}]\!] \vdash \mathcal{H}[\![\mathcal{C}_{\mathrm{V}}[\![M]\!]]\!] : \mathcal{H}[\![T_A]\!] = (\mathcal{H}[\![T_{\mathrm{V}}]\!] \rightarrow \diamond) \rightarrow \diamond \ . \tag{15.8}$$

We recall that if P, Q are HOπ processes, then $P \longrightarrow_\beta Q$ and $P =_\beta Q$ denote β-reduction and β-convertibility in HOπ, respectively (Definition 12.1.10).

Lemma 15.3.11 For all terms M of Grammar (15.4), we have: if $M \longrightarrow_{\mathrm{N}} M'$ then $\mathcal{H}[\![M]\!] \longrightarrow_\beta =_\beta \mathcal{H}[\![M']\!]$; and conversely, if $\mathcal{H}[\![M]\!] \longrightarrow_\beta P$ then there is M' such that $M \longrightarrow_{\mathrm{N}} M'$ and $P =_\beta \mathcal{H}[\![M']\!]$. □

(In the lemma above, the use of $=_\beta$ is due to the uncurrying that is used in the injection $\mathcal{H}$.)

Corollary 15.3.12 For all terms M, N generated by Grammar (15.4), $\lambda\beta \vdash M = N$ implies $\mathcal{H}[\![M]\!] =_\beta \mathcal{H}[\![N]\!]$.

Proof Since $\Longrightarrow_\beta$ is confluent, $\lambda\beta \vdash M = N$ holds iff there is some L such that $M \Longrightarrow_\beta L$ and $N \Longrightarrow_\beta L$. Therefore, by Lemma 15.3.11, $\mathcal{H}[\![M]\!] =_\beta \mathcal{H}[\![L]\!] =_\beta \mathcal{H}[\![N]\!]$. □

This concludes the second step of the left part of Figure 15.1.

15.3.1.3 Step 3: from HOπ *to* π*-calculus*

The third and final step for the left part of Figure 15.1 is from HOπ to π-calculus. This step is given by the compilation $\mathcal{C}$ from HOπ to π-calculus of Table 13.3 (we adopt the optimized compilation to get more efficient encodings). Recall that the compilation acts also on types, and that for translating the function types of HOπ we used the i/o types of the π-calculus.

15.3.2 Composing the steps

Composing the three steps, from λV to CPS$_{\mathrm{V}}$, from CPS$_{\mathrm{V}}$ to HOπ, and from HOπ to π-calculus, we obtain the encoding $\mathcal{V}$ of λV into π-calculus in Table 15.2.

$$\mathcal{V}[\![\lambda x.\, M]\!] \stackrel{\text{def}}{=} (p).\, \overline{p}(y).\, !y(x)\, \mathcal{V}[\![M]\!]$$

$$\mathcal{V}[\![x]\!] \stackrel{\text{def}}{=} (p).\, \overline{p}x$$

$$\mathcal{V}[\![MN]\!] \stackrel{\text{def}}{=} (p).\, \nu q \left(\mathcal{V}[\![M]\!]q \mid q(v).\, \nu r\, (\mathcal{V}[\![N]\!]r \mid r(w).\, \overline{v}\langle w, p\rangle)\right)$$

Table 15.2. *The encoding of λV into the π-calculus*

Precisely, the encoding $\mathcal{V}[\![M]\!]$ of a λ-term M is obtained thus (we can omit the type environment index in $\mathcal{C}$, for M is untyped and therefore all free variables are translated in the same way):

$$\mathcal{V}[\![M]\!] \stackrel{\text{def}}{=} \mathcal{C}[\![\, \mathcal{H}[\![\, \mathcal{C}_{\mathrm{V}}[\![M]\!]\,]\!]\,]\!]\,.$$

The encoding $\mathcal{V}$ uses two kinds of name:

- *Location names* (p, q, r), which are used as arguments of the encodings of λ-terms. These names correspond to the continuation variable of the CPS Grammar (15.4).
- *Value names* (x, y), which are used to access values. These names correspond to the ordinary variables of the CPS Grammar (15.4).

(As $\mathcal{V}[\![M]\!]$ is an abstraction, for all M, we recall these notations for abstractions: suppose $\mathcal{V}[\![M]\!]$ is $(q).\, Q$; then $y(x)\, \mathcal{V}[\![M]\!]$ is $y(x, q).\, Q$, and $\mathcal{V}[\![M]\!]r$ is $Q\{^r\!/\!_q\}$. These and other notations for abstractions are discussed in Section 15.2.)

We explain informally how the encoding works. Suppose a λ-term M reduces to a value V. This value represents the result of the λ-term. In the π-calculus encoding, $\mathcal{V}[\![M]\!]p$ reduces to a process that, very roughly, returns the value V at p (this is the analogue of passing the result to the continuation in the CPS transform). The value V can be a variable or a function. If V is a variable then the corresponding π-calculus name is returned at p. If V is a function then it cannot be passed directly at p because π-calculus does not allow communication of terms; instead, a *pointer* to the function is passed. Thus the function sits within the process as a resource that can be accessed arbitrarily many times, via the pointer: when a client sends a value and a return name, the function will answer by sending a result along the return name (if a result exists).

The encoding of an application MN at location p is a process that first runs M at some location q. When M signals that it has become a value v, the argument N is run at some location r; names q and r are private, to avoid interference from the environment. When also N signals that it has become a value w, the application occurs: the pair $\langle w, p\rangle$ is sent at v. This communication is the step that properly simulates the β_{v}-reduction of λV; the previous communications were 'administrative' (exactly as in the CPS transform, see Section 15.3.1.1). The second argument of the pair $\langle w, p\rangle$ is the location where the final result of MN will be delivered.

Remark 15.3.13 In Table 15.2, the inputs at location names (q and r) are not replicated because, in the step of translation from HOπ to π-calculus, we take into account the linearity constraint on continuations (see Remark 15.3.7) and therefore adopt the optimization of Section 13.2.3. As discussed in Remark 15.3.8, linear types are not needed in the π-calculus. □

For the sake of readability, the translation of Table 15.2 is not annotated with types. Types are needed, however, to prove its correctness. The π-calculus translation of type $\mathcal{H}[\![T_V]\!]$ in (15.7) is the recursive type

$$\mathtt{Val} \stackrel{\mathrm{def}}{=} \mu X.\, \mathsf{o}\,(X \times \mathsf{o}\, X) \ .$$

We do not need the i tag on types, because both location and value names that are communicated may only be used by a recipient for sending. Here is the encoding in which names bound by a restriction are annotated with their types (we recall that if T is a π-calculus type then $(T)^{\leftarrow\sharp}$ is the type obtained by replacing the outermost i/o tag in T with $\sharp$, possibly after unfolding T if its outermost construct is recursion; we also recall that $\overline{a}(b:T).\,P$, the typed bound output, stands for $(\boldsymbol{\nu} b:T)\,(\overline{a}b.\,P)$):

$$\begin{aligned}
\mathcal{V}[\![\lambda x.\,M]\!] &\stackrel{\mathrm{def}}{=} (p).\,\overline{p}(y:(\mathtt{Val})^{\leftarrow\sharp}).\,!y(x)\,\mathcal{V}[\![M]\!] \\
\mathcal{V}[\![x]\!] &\stackrel{\mathrm{def}}{=} (p).\,\overline{p}x \\
\mathcal{V}[\![MN]\!] &\stackrel{\mathrm{def}}{=} (p).\ \ (\boldsymbol{\nu} q:\sharp\,(\mathtt{Val})\,) \\
&\qquad \Big(\mathcal{V}[\![M]\!]q \mid q(x).\,(\boldsymbol{\nu} r:\sharp\,(\mathtt{Val})\,)\,(\mathcal{V}[\![N]\!]r \mid r(y).\,\overline{x}\langle y,p\rangle)\Big)\,.
\end{aligned}$$

Types $\mathtt{Val}$ and $\mathsf{o}\,(\mathtt{Val})$ are, respectively, the types of free value names and free location names of a process $\mathcal{V}[\![M]\!]p$. The outermost i/o tag of these types changes to $\sharp$ on names local to $\mathcal{V}[\![M]\!]p$; thus the types become, respectively, $(\mathtt{Val})^{\leftarrow\sharp}$ and $\sharp\,(\mathtt{Val})$. The translation of (15.8) into π-calculus gives:

Lemma 15.3.14 Suppose $\mathsf{fv}(M) \subseteq \widetilde{x}$. Then $\widetilde{x}:\mathtt{Val}, p:\mathsf{o}\,(\mathtt{Val}) \vdash \mathcal{V}[\![M]\!]p$. □

From the correctness of the three steps from which encoding $\mathcal{V}$ has been derived, we get the two corollaries below. Thereafter, we will also derive direct proofs of these corollaries, which do not go through the CPS transform but, instead, appeal to the theory of the π-calculus.

Corollary 15.3.15 (Adequacy of $\mathcal{V}$) Let $M \in \Lambda^0$. It holds that $M \Downarrow_{\mathrm{v}}$ iff $\mathcal{V}[\![M]\!]p \Downarrow$, for any p.

Proof From Theorem 15.3.4, Lemma 15.3.11, and the operational correctness of the encoding of HOπ into the π-calculus (Theorem 13.2.11 and its extensions, Section 13.2.3). $\square$

Corollary 15.3.16 (Validity of $\lambda\beta_{\mathrm{v}}$-theory for $\mathcal{V}$) Suppose $\mathsf{fv}(M, N) \subseteq \widetilde{x}$. If $\lambda\beta_{\mathrm{v}} \vdash M = N$ then $\widetilde{x} : \mathtt{Val} \triangleright \mathcal{V}[\![M]\!] \cong^{\mathrm{c}} \mathcal{V}[\![N]\!] : \mathsf{o}\,(\mathtt{Val}) \rightarrow \diamond$.

Proof From Theorem 15.3.5, Corollary 15.3.12, and (the appropriate extension of) Lemma 13.2.14. $\square$

Remark 15.3.17 (Effect of i/o types on behavioural equivalences) In the barbed congruence of Corollary 15.3.16, the presence of i/o types is important. The result would not hold if each i/o type $I\,T$ (for $I \in \{\mathsf{i}, \mathsf{o}, \sharp\}$) were replaced by the (less informative) connection type $\sharp T$. As a counterexample, take $M \stackrel{\mathrm{def}}{=} (\lambda x.\,(\lambda y.\,x))\lambda z.\,z$ and $N \stackrel{\mathrm{def}}{=} \lambda y.\,(\lambda z.\,z)$. With a β_{v}-conversion, M reduces to N. However, without i/o types $\mathcal{V}[\![M]\!]p$ and $\mathcal{V}[\![N]\!]p$ would not be barbed congruent, as we are going to prove. It suffices to show that M and N are not in the stratification of bisimilarity, that is, $\mathcal{V}[\![M]\!]p \not\approx_n \mathcal{V}[\![N]\!]p$, for some n (without i/o types, barbed congruence implies $\approx_n$, for all n, as we have seen in Part I). Let $R_1 \stackrel{\mathrm{def}}{=} x'(y', r').\,\overline{r'}y'$. By repeated use of the Expansion Lemma and simple application of the structural congruence relation, we get

$$\mathcal{V}[\![M]\!]p \quad \approx \quad \boldsymbol{\nu} x'\,(\overline{p}(x).\,!x(y,r).\,\overline{r}x' \mid !R_1)\,.$$

On the other hand, we have

$$\mathcal{V}[\![N]\!]p \quad = \quad \overline{p}(x).\,!x(y,r).\,\overline{r}(x').\,!R_1\,.$$

Let the processes on the right-hand side of $\approx$ and $=$ be P and Q. We show that $P \not\approx_5 Q$. The different position of the restriction $\boldsymbol{\nu} x'$ will cause a difference in the behaviours of P and Q. Consider the following sequence of transitions from P, where R_2 stands for $x(y,r).\,\overline{r}x'$ and the underlining highlights the source of the action:

$$\begin{array}{rll} P & \xrightarrow{\overline{p}(x)} & \boldsymbol{\nu} x'\,(\underline{!R_2} \mid !R_1) \\ & \xrightarrow{x\langle y,r\rangle} & \boldsymbol{\nu} x'\,(!R_2 \mid \underline{\overline{r}x'} \mid !R_1) \\ & \xrightarrow{\overline{r}(x')} & \underline{!R_2} \mid !R_1 \\ & \xrightarrow{x\langle y,r\rangle} & !R_2 \mid \underline{\overline{r}x'} \mid !R_1 \\ & \xrightarrow{\overline{r}x'} & !R_2 \mid !R_1\,. \end{array}$$

In this sequence, the last action is a *free* output. In the corresponding sequence for Q, however, the last action is a *bound* output. Below, R_3 stands for $x(y,r).\,\overline{r}(x').\,!R_1$:

$$\begin{array}{rll} Q & \xrightarrow{\overline{p}(x)} & \underline{!R_3} \\ & \xrightarrow{x\langle y,r\rangle} & !R_3 \mid \underline{\overline{r}(x').\,!R_1} \\ & \xrightarrow{\overline{r}(x')} & \underline{!R_3} \mid !R_1 \\ & \xrightarrow{x\langle y,r\rangle} & !R_3 \mid \underline{\overline{r}(x').\,!R_1} \mid !R_1 \\ & \xrightarrow{\overline{r}(x'')}\sim & !R_3 \mid !(R_1\{x''/x'\}) \mid !R_1\,. \end{array}$$

□

By Corollary 15.3.16, we know that if $M \longrightarrow_{\mathrm{V}} M'$ then $\mathcal{V}[\![M]\!]$ and $\mathcal{V}[\![M']\!]$ are behaviourally indistinguishable. One might like, however, to see how the reduction of λV is simulated in the π-calculus. This is shown below. We use the local-environment notation $P\{x = (\tilde{z}).\,R\}$, which stands for $\boldsymbol{\nu} x\,(P \mid !x(\tilde{z}).\,R)$ under the hypothesis that P and R possess only the output capability on x (Notation 2.2.27). We write $P \xrightarrow{\tau}{}_{\mathrm{d}}^{n} P'$ if P evolves to P' by performing n *deterministic* reductions (Definition 2.2.19).

Lemma 15.3.18 $\mathcal{V}[\![(\lambda x.\,M)\lambda y.\,N]\!]p \xrightarrow{\tau}{}_{\mathrm{d}}^{3} \sim_{\mathrm{g}} \mathcal{V}[\![M]\!]p\,\{x = (y)\,\mathcal{V}[\![N]\!]\}$.

Proof We apply the laws of structural congruence, which implies $\sim_{\mathrm{g}}$, and law (1) of Lemma 2.2.28, which by Corollary 5.3.10 is also valid for ground bisimilarity, to garbage-collect inaccessible environment entries:

$$\begin{array}{rl} & \mathcal{V}[\![(\lambda x.\, M)\lambda y.\, N]\!]p \\ = & \boldsymbol{\nu} q\left(\overline{q}(z).\, !z(x)\, \mathcal{V}[\![M]\!] \mid q(z).\, \boldsymbol{\nu} r\, (\overline{r}(u).\, !u(y)\, \mathcal{V}[\![N]\!] \mid r(u).\, \overline{z}\langle u, p\rangle)\right) \\ \xrightarrow{\tau}_{\mathrm{d}} \equiv & (\boldsymbol{\nu} r, z\,)\left(!z(x)\, \mathcal{V}[\![M]\!] \mid \overline{r}(u).\, !u(y)\, \mathcal{V}[\![N]\!] \mid r(u).\, \overline{z}\langle u, p\rangle\right) \\ \xrightarrow{\tau}_{\mathrm{d}} \equiv & (\boldsymbol{\nu} u, z\,)\left(!z(x)\, \mathcal{V}[\![M]\!] \mid !u(y)\, \mathcal{V}[\![N]\!] \mid \overline{z}\langle u, p\rangle\right) \\ \xrightarrow{\tau}_{\mathrm{d}} \equiv & (\boldsymbol{\nu} u, z\,)\left(\mathcal{V}[\![M]\!]p\{^{u}\!/\!_{x}\} \mid !z(x)\, \mathcal{V}[\![M]\!] \mid !u(y)\, \mathcal{V}[\![N]\!]\right) \\ \sim_{\mathrm{g}} & (\boldsymbol{\nu} x\,)\left(\mathcal{V}[\![M]\!]p \mid !x(y)\, \mathcal{V}[\![N]\!]\right) \\ = & \mathcal{V}[\![M]\!]p\, \{x = (y)\, \mathcal{V}[\![N]\!]\}\,. \end{array}$$

This proves the lemma, since $\equiv$ and $\sim_{\mathrm{g}}$ commute with $\xrightarrow{\tau}$. □

The reader might like to compare the derivation in the proof of the lemma with that in (15.2), to see the similarities.

Lemma 15.3.19 Suppose $\mathsf{fv}(M, N) \subseteq \widetilde{x}$. We have

$$\widetilde{x} : \mathtt{Val} \triangleright \mathcal{V}[\![M]\!]\, \{x = (y)\, \mathcal{V}[\![N]\!]\} \simeq^{\mathrm{c}} \mathcal{V}[\![M\{^{\lambda y.\, N}\!/\!_{x}\}]\!] : \mathtt{o}\,(\mathtt{Val}) \to \diamond.$$

Proof We proceed by structural induction on M. There are three cases: when M is a variable, an abstraction or an application.

Variable: $M = z$.

Both the case $z = x$ and the case $z \neq x$ are easy.

Abstraction: $M = \lambda z.\, M'$. We have, omitting type annotations also in behavioural equivalences,

$$\begin{array}{rll} & \mathcal{V}[\![M]\!]\, \{x = (y)\, \mathcal{V}[\![N]\!]\} & \\ = & \left(\overline{p}(y).\, !y(z)\, \mathcal{V}[\![M']\!]\right) \{x = (y)\, \mathcal{V}[\![N]\!]\} & \\ \simeq^{\mathrm{c}} & \overline{p}(y).\, \left((!y(z)\, \mathcal{V}[\![M']\!])\, \{x = (y)\, \mathcal{V}[\![N]\!]\}\right) & (15.9) \\ \simeq^{\mathrm{c}} & \overline{p}(y).\, !y(z)\, (\mathcal{V}[\![M']\!]\, \{x = (y)\, \mathcal{V}[\![N]\!]\}) & (15.10) \\ \simeq^{\mathrm{c}} & \overline{p}(y).\, !y(z)\, \mathcal{V}[\![M'\{^{\lambda y.\, N}\!/\!_{x}\}]\!] & (15.11) \\ = & \mathcal{V}[\![M\{^{\lambda y.\, N}\!/\!_{x}\}]\!] & \end{array}$$

where: in (15.9) the scope of the local environment $\{x = (y)\, \mathcal{V}[\![N]\!]\}$ has been reduced, since x does not occur in $\overline{p}(y)$; the equality (15.10) pushes the local environment inside replication and input, and is derived from the Sharpened Replication Theorems 10.5.1 and law (4) of Lemma 2.2.28; and the equality (15.11) follows from the inductive assumption.

Application: $M = M_1 M_2$.

This case is similar to that of abstraction; we leave it as an exercise. □

Exercise 15.3.20 $\mathcal{V}[\![(\lambda x.\, M)y]\!]p \xrightarrow{\tau}_{\mathrm{d}}^{3} \sim_{\mathrm{g}} \mathcal{V}[\![M\{y/x\}]\!]p$. (Hint: it is similar to Lemma 15.3.18.) □

Exercise 15.3.21 Use Lemmas 15.3.18 and 15.3.19 and Exercise 15.3.20 to prove Corollary 15.3.16. □

Lemma 15.3.22 Let $M \in \Lambda^0$. If $M \longrightarrow_{\mathrm{V}} M'$ then there are P, P', and $n \geq 0$ such that $\mathcal{V}[\![M]\!]p \xrightarrow{\tau}_{\mathrm{d}}^{n+3} P$, and $\mathcal{V}[\![M']\!]p \xrightarrow{\tau}_{\mathrm{d}}^{n} P'$, and $p : \mathtt{o}\,(\mathtt{Val}) \triangleright P \simeq^{\mathrm{c}} P'$, for all p.

Proof By transition induction. If the last rule used in the derivation of $M \longrightarrow_{\mathrm{V}} M'$ is β_{V}, then the conclusion follows from Lemmas 15.3.18 and 15.3.19, taking $n = 0$.

Suppose the last rule used is ν_{V}. Then $M = (\lambda x.\, M_1)M_2$ and $M' = (\lambda x.\, M_1)M_2'$, for some M_2' with $M_2 \longrightarrow_{\mathrm{V}} M_2'$. We have

$$\begin{aligned} \mathcal{V}[\![M]\!]p &= \boldsymbol{\nu} q \left(\mathcal{V}[\![\lambda x.\, M_1]\!]q \mid q(v).\, \boldsymbol{\nu} r\, (\mathcal{V}[\![M_2]\!]r \mid r(w).\, \overline{v}\langle w, p\rangle)\right) \\ &= \boldsymbol{\nu} q \left(\overline{q}(y).\, !y(x)\, \mathcal{V}[\![M_1]\!] \mid q(v).\, \boldsymbol{\nu} r\, (\mathcal{V}[\![M_2]\!]r \mid r(w).\, \overline{v}\langle w, p\rangle)\right) \\ &\xrightarrow{\tau}_{\mathrm{d}} (\boldsymbol{\nu} q, y) \left(!y(x)\, \mathcal{V}[\![M_1]\!] \mid \boldsymbol{\nu} r\, (\mathcal{V}[\![M_2]\!]r \mid r(w).\, \overline{y}\langle w, p\rangle)\right). \end{aligned}$$

We write the process so obtained as $C[\mathcal{V}[\![M_2]\!]r]$, where C is the context

$$(\boldsymbol{\nu} q, y) \left(!y(x)\, \mathcal{V}[\![M_1]\!] \mid \boldsymbol{\nu} r\, ([\cdot] \mid r(w).\, \overline{y}\langle w, p\rangle)\right).$$

Proceeding similarly, we derive

$$\mathcal{V}[\![M']\!]p \xrightarrow{\tau}_{\mathrm{d}} C[\mathcal{V}[\![M_2']\!]r].$$

Since $M_2 \longrightarrow_{\mathrm{V}} M_2'$, by induction there are Q, Q', m such that $\mathcal{V}[\![M_2]\!]r \xrightarrow{\tau}_{\mathrm{d}}^{m+3} Q$, and $\mathcal{V}[\![M_2']\!]r \xrightarrow{\tau}_{\mathrm{d}}^{m} Q'$, and $r : \mathtt{o}\,(\mathtt{Val}) \triangleright Q \simeq^{\mathrm{c}} Q'$. Hence, also

$$C[\mathcal{V}[\![M_2]\!]r] \xrightarrow{\tau}_{\mathrm{d}}^{m+3} C[Q]$$

and, similarly,

$$C[\mathcal{V}[\![M_2']\!]r] \xrightarrow{\tau}_{\mathrm{d}}^{m} C[Q'].$$

We can therefore conclude that $\mathcal{V}[\![M]\!]p \xrightarrow{\tau}_{\mathrm{d}}^{m+4} C[Q]$, and that $\mathcal{V}[\![M']\!]p \xrightarrow{\tau}_{\mathrm{d}}^{m+1} C[Q']$, with $p : \mathtt{o}\,(\mathtt{Val}) \triangleright C[Q] \simeq^{\mathrm{c}} C[Q']$, which proves the lemma, taking $n = m + 1$.

Finally, if the last rule used is μ, we simply use induction and the definition of the encoding. □

In Lemma 15.3.22, the number n is given by the position of the redex, precisely the number of λ-abstractions to its left.

Given a process P with $P \Downarrow$, we write $\mathsf{conv}(P)$ for the least n such that $P(\xrightarrow{\tau})^n \downarrow$; that is, the least number of τ-steps that P has to perform before becoming observable. We set $\mathsf{conv}(P) = \omega$ if $P \Downarrow$ does not hold.

Lemma 15.3.23 Let $M \in \Lambda^0$. If $\mathcal{V}[\![M]\!]p \Downarrow$, then also $M \Downarrow_{\mathrm{V}}$.

Proof First note that, by Lemma 15.3.22, if $N \longrightarrow_{\mathrm{V}} N'$, then we have

$$\mathsf{conv}(\mathcal{V}[\![N]\!]p) > \mathsf{conv}(\mathcal{V}[\![N']\!]p)\,. \tag{15.12}$$

Let $n = \mathsf{conv}(\mathcal{V}[\![M]\!]p)$. Suppose, for a contradiction, that not $M \Downarrow_{\mathrm{V}}$. Hence there are $M_1, \ldots, M_{n+1}$ such that

$$M \longrightarrow_{\mathrm{V}} M_1 \longrightarrow_{\mathrm{V}} \cdots \longrightarrow_{\mathrm{V}} M_{n+1}\,.$$

By (15.12), it should be that $\mathsf{conv}(\mathcal{V}[\![M_i]\!]p) > \mathsf{conv}(\mathcal{V}[\![M_{i+1}]\!]p)$ for each $0 \leq i \leq n$ (taking M_0 to be M). We therefore conclude that $\mathsf{conv}(\mathcal{V}[\![M]\!]p) > n$, contradicting the hypothesis. □

Exercise 15.3.24 Use Lemma 15.3.23 and Corollary 15.3.16 to prove Corollary 15.3.15. □

Remark 15.3.25 The results on the CPS transform, notably Theorems 15.3.4 and 15.3.5, have been used to derive results about the correctness of the π-calculus encoding. We may also go in the opposite direction, that is, use the π-calculus encoding to understand, and reason about, the CPS transform. For instance, in Exercise 15.3.24 we have derived a direct proof of Corollary 15.3.15. Using this, Lemma 15.3.11, and Theorem 13.2.11, we can derive the adequacy of the CPS transform (Theorem 15.3.4). Similarly, in Exercise 15.3.21 we have derived Corollary 15.3.16; using this (and Theorem 13.2.12), we can prove a weaker version of Theorem 15.3.5, saying that if $\lambda\beta_{\mathrm{v}} \vdash M = N$ then $\mathcal{C}_{\mathrm{V}}[\![M]\!]$ and $\mathcal{C}_{\mathrm{V}}[\![N]\!]$ are observationally equivalent as terms of λN. (Observational equivalence equates terms that are behaviourally indistinguishable and will be defined and studied in Chapter 17; informally, two λN-terms L_1 and L_2 are observationally indistinguishable if for for all λ-calculus contexts C it holds that $C[L_1] \Downarrow_{\mathrm{N}}$ iff $C[L_2] \Downarrow_{\mathrm{N}}$.) □

15.3.3 Parallel call-by-value

From the call-by-value encoding it is easy to obtain variants with different disciplines for reducing the operator and the operand of an application. One such variant is the *parallel call-by-value* strategy, which has the ordinary ν rule in place of ν_{v}. Here is the definition of application for the parallel call-by-value encoding, denoted by $\mathcal{PV}$:

$$\mathcal{PV}[\![MN]\!] \stackrel{\text{def}}{=} (p).(\boldsymbol{\nu} q, r)\Big(\mathcal{PV}[\![M]\!]q \mid \mathcal{PV}[\![N]\!]r \mid q(x).\, r(y).\, \overline{x}\langle y, p\rangle\Big)\,.$$

The operator and the operand are run in parallel. The clauses for abstractions and values for $\mathcal{PV}$ are the same as for (the sequential) $\mathcal{V}$.

Exercise 15.3.26 Exhibit a term M on which the encodings of sequential and parallel call-by-value do not give the same behaviours, i.e., $\mathcal{V}[\![M]\!] \not\approx_{\mathrm{g}} \mathcal{PV}[\![M]\!]$. □

Exercise 15.3.27

(1) Suppose $\mathsf{fv}(M, V) \subseteq \widetilde{x}$. Prove that

$$\widetilde{x} : \mathtt{Val} \triangleright \mathcal{PV}[\![(\lambda x.\, M)V]\!] \cong^{\mathrm{c}} \mathcal{PV}[\![M\{^{V}\!/\!_{x}\}]\!] : \mathtt{o}\,(\mathtt{Val}) \rightarrow \diamond.$$

(Hint: the argument is similar to that of Exercise 15.3.21.)

(2) Conclude that if $\lambda\beta_{\mathrm{v}} \vdash M = N$ then

$$\widetilde{x} : \mathtt{Val} \triangleright \mathcal{PV}[\![M]\!] \cong^{\mathrm{c}} \mathcal{PV}[\![N]\!] : \mathtt{o}\,(\mathtt{Val}) \rightarrow \diamond.$$

□

15.4 The interpretation of call-by-name

In this section we develop a π-calculus encoding of call-by-name λ-calculus. The approach is similar to that for call-by-value in Section 15.3. The reader not interested in the CPS transform may go directly to the encoding into π-calculus of Section 15.4.2.

15.4.1 The three steps

15.4.1.1 Step 1: the call-by-name CPS

Table 15.3 shows the call-by-name CPS transform of [Plo75] (in fact, a rectified variant of it; see the notes at the of the Part). Here is how a β reduction

$$(\lambda x.\, M)N \longrightarrow_{\mathrm{N}} M\{^{N}\!/\!_{x}\}$$

In this table we abbreviate $\mathcal{C}_N[\![M]\!]$ as $[\![M]\!]$ and $\mathcal{C}^\star_N[V]$ as $[V]$.

$$\text{call-by-name values} \quad V \ ::= \ \lambda x.\, M$$

$$\begin{aligned}
[\![x]\!] &\stackrel{\text{def}}{=} \lambda k.\, xk \\
[\![V]\!] &\stackrel{\text{def}}{=} \lambda k.\, k[V] \\
[\![MN]\!] &\stackrel{\text{def}}{=} \lambda k.\, [\![M]\!](\lambda v.\, v[\![N]\!]k) \\
[\lambda x.\, M] &\stackrel{\text{def}}{=} \lambda x.\, [\![M]\!]
\end{aligned}$$

Table 15.3. *The call-by-name CPS transform*

is simulated in the transform. (As in call-by-value, we choose to take call-by-name for the reduction relation on the images of the CPS, but these terms are evaluation-order independent; see Theorem 15.4.1.)

$$\begin{aligned}
& \mathcal{C}_N[\![(\lambda x.\, M)N]\!]k \\
\longrightarrow_N \ & \mathcal{C}_N[\![\lambda x.\, M]\!](\lambda v.\, v\mathcal{C}_N[\![N]\!]k) \\
= \ & (\lambda k.\, (k\mathcal{C}^\star_N[\lambda x.\, M]))(\lambda v.\, v\mathcal{C}_N[\![N]\!]k) \\
\longrightarrow_N \ & (\lambda v.\, v\mathcal{C}_N[\![N]\!]k)\mathcal{C}^\star_N[\lambda x.\, M] \\
\longrightarrow_N \ & \mathcal{C}^\star_N[\lambda x.\, M]\mathcal{C}_N[\![N]\!]k \\
= \ & (\lambda x.\, \mathcal{C}_N[\![M]\!])\mathcal{C}_N[\![N]\!]k \\
\longrightarrow_N \ & \mathcal{C}_N[\![M]\!]\{\mathcal{C}_N[\![N]\!]/x\}k\,.
\end{aligned}$$

In general, $\mathcal{C}_N[\![M]\!]\{\mathcal{C}_N[\![N]\!]/x\}k$ is not equal to $\mathcal{C}_N[\![M\{N/x\}]\!]k$, because $\mathcal{C}_N$ does not commute with substitution. The two terms are, however, β-convertible; indeed $\mathcal{C}_N[\![M]\!]\{\mathcal{C}_N[\![N]\!]/x\}k \Longrightarrow_\beta \mathcal{C}_N[\![M\{N/x\}]\!]k$.

Closing the image of the transform under β-reduction gives the language CPS_N of the call-by-name CPS:

$$\text{CPS}_N \stackrel{\text{def}}{=} \{A \mid \exists M \in \Lambda \text{ with } \mathcal{C}_N[\![M]\!] \Longrightarrow_\beta A\}.$$

When there is no ambiguity, we call the terms of CPS_N the *CPS terms*.

The theorems below are the call-by-name versions of Theorems 15.3.1–15.3.5. They show the indifference of the CPS terms to the choice between call-by-name and call-by-value, and the correctness of the CPS transform. Theorem 15.4.3 is slightly weaker than the corresponding result for call-by-value. The reason is that, as illustrated above, $\mathcal{C}_N$ commutes with substitution only up to

β-conversion. In contrast, Theorem 15.4.4 is stronger than the corresponding result for call-by-value: it asserts a logical equivalence rather than an implication.

Theorem 15.4.1 (Indifference of $\mathrm{CPS_N}$ **on reductions)** Let $M \in \mathrm{CPS_N}$ and let N be any subterm of M. For all N', we have $N \longrightarrow_{\mathrm{N}} N'$ iff $N \longrightarrow_{\mathrm{V}} N'$. □

Theorem 15.4.2 (Indifference of $\mathrm{CPS_N}$ **on λ-theories)** Suppose that $M, N \in \mathrm{CPS_N}$. Then we have $\lambda\beta \vdash M = N$ iff $\lambda\beta_{\mathrm{v}} \vdash M = N$. □

Theorem 15.4.3 (Adequacy of $\mathcal{C}_{\mathrm{N}}$**)** Let $M \in \Lambda^0$.

(1) If $M \Longrightarrow_{\mathrm{N}} V$ where V is a call-by-name value, then there is an N-nf N such that $\mathcal{C}_{\mathrm{N}}[\![M]\!]k \Longrightarrow_{\mathrm{N}} N$ and $\lambda\beta \vdash N = k\,\mathcal{C}^{\star}_{\mathrm{N}}[V]$.
(2) The converse: if $\mathcal{C}_{\mathrm{N}}[\![M]\!]k \Longrightarrow_{\mathrm{N}} N$ and N is an N-nf, then there is a call-by-name value V such that $M \Longrightarrow_{\mathrm{N}} V$ and $\lambda\beta \vdash N = k\,\mathcal{C}^{\star}_{\mathrm{N}}[V]$. □

Theorem 15.4.4 (Validity of the λβ-theory for $\mathcal{C}_{\mathrm{N}}$**)** Let $M, N \in \Lambda$. Then $\lambda\beta \vdash M = N$ iff $\lambda\beta \vdash \mathcal{C}_{\mathrm{N}}[\![M]\!] = \mathcal{C}_{\mathrm{N}}[\![N]\!]$. □

15.4.1.2 Step 2: from $\mathrm{CPS_N}$ *to* $\mathrm{HO}\pi$

The grammar below generates all terms of $\mathrm{CPS_N}$. The intuitive meaning of the various syntactic categories in the grammar is the same as for the call-by-value Grammar (15.4). The main differences are the addition of the value variable v, representing the parameter of continuations, and the splitting of the set of answers into the sets P_1 and P_2. These modifications are made in order to capture the linear use of the parameters of continuations within the grammar (dropping linearity we would have the CPS language of Table 15.5). As in the call-by-value grammar, there is only one continuation variable k because continuations are used linearly.

$$
\begin{array}{rlll}
\text{continuation variable} & k & & \\
\text{ordinary variables} & x, \ldots & & \\
\text{value variable} & v & & \\
\text{answers} & P & ::= & P_1 \mid P_2 \\
 & P_1 & ::= & KV \mid VAK \mid AK \\
 & P_2 & ::= & vAK \\
\text{CPS-values} & V & ::= & \lambda x.\, \lambda k.\, P_1 \\
\text{continuations} & K & ::= & k \mid \lambda v.\, P_2 \\
\text{principal terms} & A & ::= & \lambda k.\, P_1 \mid x
\end{array}
\qquad (15.13)
$$

Using $\diamond$ as the type of answers, the types T_V, T_K, and T_A of CPS-values, continuations, and principal terms are

$$\begin{aligned} T_V &\stackrel{\text{def}}{=} \mu X. \Big(((X \to \diamond) \to \diamond) \to ((X \to \diamond) \to \diamond) \Big) \\ T_K &\stackrel{\text{def}}{=} T_V \to \diamond \\ T_A &\stackrel{\text{def}}{=} T_K \to \diamond \, . \end{aligned} \tag{15.14}$$

The value variable v has the type T_V of the CPS-values. The typing judgments for the terms generated by the grammar are as expected, given these types.

Proposition 15.4.5 If $M \in \mathrm{CPS_N}$ then M is also a principal term of Grammar (15.13).

Proof One can show that the set of principal terms includes the set $\{\mathcal{C}_\mathrm{N}[\![M]\!] \mid M \in \Lambda\}$ and is closed under β-conversion. □

The injection $\mathcal{H}$, from the terms generated by Grammar (15.13) to HOπ, is defined as for the call-by-value Grammar (15.4), and similar results hold:

Lemma 15.4.6 Suppose M is a term generated by Grammar (15.13), and $\Gamma \vdash M : T$. Then also $\mathcal{H}[\![\Gamma]\!] \vdash \mathcal{H}[\![M]\!] : \mathcal{H}[\![T]\!]$. □

Therefore, if $M \in \Lambda$ with $\mathsf{fv}(M) \subseteq \widetilde{x}$, then

$$\widetilde{x} : \mathcal{H}[\![T_A]\!] \vdash \mathcal{H}[\![\mathcal{C}_\mathrm{N}[\![M]\!]]\!] : \mathcal{H}[\![T_A]\!] = (\mathcal{H}[\![T_V]\!] \to \diamond) \to \diamond \, . \tag{15.15}$$

Lemma 15.4.7 For all terms M of Grammar (15.13), we have: if $M \longrightarrow_\mathrm{N} M'$ then $\mathcal{H}[\![M]\!] \longrightarrow_\beta =_\beta \mathcal{H}[\![M']\!]$; and conversely, if $\mathcal{H}[\![M]\!] \longrightarrow_\beta P$ then there is M' such that $M \longrightarrow_\mathrm{N} M'$ and $P =_\beta \mathcal{H}[\![M']\!]$. □

Corollary 15.4.8 For all terms M, N generated by Grammar (15.13), $\lambda\beta \vdash M = N$ implies $\mathcal{H}[\![M]\!] =_\beta \mathcal{H}[\![N]\!]$. □

15.4.1.3 Step 3: from HOπ *to* π*-calculus*

This step is given by compilation $\mathcal{C}$ of HOπ into π-calculus.

15.4.2 Composing the steps

Composing the three steps, from λN to $\mathrm{CPS_N}$, from $\mathrm{CPS_N}$ to HOπ, and from HOπ to π-calculus, we obtain the encoding of λN into π-calculus in Table 15.4.

The encoding uses three kinds of name: *location names* (p, q), *trigger names* (x), and *value names* (v). Location names are arguments of the encoding, and

$$\begin{aligned}
\mathcal{N}[\![\lambda x.\,M]\!] &\stackrel{\mathrm{def}}{=} (p).\,\overline{p}(v).\,v(x)\,\mathcal{N}[\![M]\!] \\
\mathcal{N}[\![x]\!] &\stackrel{\mathrm{def}}{=} (p).\,\overline{x}p \\
\mathcal{N}[\![MN]\!] &\stackrel{\mathrm{def}}{=} (p).\,\boldsymbol{\nu} q\,\Big(\mathcal{N}[\![M]\!]q \mid q(v).\,\boldsymbol{\nu} x\,(\overline{v}\langle x,p\rangle.\,!x\,\mathcal{N}[\![N]\!])\Big)
\end{aligned}$$

Table 15.4. *The encoding of* λN *into the* π*-calculus*

are the counterpart of the continuation variable of the CPS Grammar (15.13). Trigger names are pointers to λ-terms, and are the counterpart of the ordinary variables of the CPS grammar. Value names are pointers to values (more precisely, to CPS-values, in the terminology of Grammar (15.13)), and are the counterpart of the value variable of the CPS grammar.

We explain briefly how the encoding works. As in the call-by-value encoding, a λ-term M that reduces to a value V is translated as a process $\mathcal{N}[\![M]\!]p$ that, roughly speaking, emits V at p. But, in contrast to call-by-value, in call-by-name a value can only be a function. Moreover, a λ-term that is evaluated may only be the operand – not the argument – of an application. As such, it may not be copied; that is, it may be used only *once*. In the encoding of abstraction in Table 15.4, this linearity is evident in the fact that the input at v is not replicated. Another difference from call-by-value is that in call-by-name the argument passed to a function may be an arbitrary λ-term, which, in the body of the function, has to be evaluated every time its value is needed. This difference is evident in the encoding of a variable x: the corresponding π-calculus name x is used not as a value but as a trigger for activating a term and providing it with a location. In the encoding of an application MN at location p, when M signals that it has become a function, it receives a trigger for the argument N and the location p for interacting with the environment.

Remark 15.4.9 In the table, in the encoding of function and application, the inputs at v and q are not replicated because of the linearity constraint on value variables and on the continuation variable of Grammar (15.13), which, in the compilation of HOπ to the π-calculus, enables us to adopt the optimization of Section 13.2.3; we did similarly in the call-by-value encoding, see Remark 15.3.13. □

Remark 15.4.10 The linearity of the value names of Table 15.4 (and similarly, of the value variables of Grammar (15.13)) may be lost whenever one adds further constructs to the λ-calculus, as we will do in Section 17.4. To support extensions, the definition of abstraction in the table requires a replication in front of the input at v – as in the call-by-value encoding. We derive such an encoding in the next section; we also use it in Exercise 15.4.17. When possible, however, it is good to avoid the replication, to keep the encoding simpler and therefore make it easier to study (which we will do in this section and in Chapters 17 and 18). □

In the encoding of Table 15.4, we have omitted type annotations. Below is the complete encoding including types. The type

$$\mathtt{Trig} \stackrel{\text{def}}{=} \mu X.\, \mathsf{o}\,(\mathsf{o}\,\mathsf{o}\, X \times \mathsf{o}\, X) \tag{15.16}$$

is the translation into π-calculus of the type T_V in (15.14).

$$\begin{aligned}
\mathcal{N}[\![\lambda x.\, M]\!] &\stackrel{\text{def}}{=} (p).\,\overline{p}(v : (\mathtt{Trig})^{-\sharp}).\, v(x)\,\mathcal{N}[\![M]\!] \\
\mathcal{N}[\![x]\!] &\stackrel{\text{def}}{=} (p).\,\overline{x}p \\
\mathcal{N}[\![MN]\!] &\stackrel{\text{def}}{=} (p).\,(\boldsymbol{\nu} q : \sharp\,(\mathtt{Trig})\,) \\
&\quad \Big(\mathcal{N}[\![M]\!]q \mid q(v).\,(\boldsymbol{\nu} x : \sharp\,\mathsf{o}\,(\mathtt{Trig})\,)\,(\overline{v}\langle x, p\rangle.\,!x\,\mathcal{N}[\![N]\!])\Big)
\end{aligned}$$

The translation of (15.15) into π-calculus gives:

Lemma 15.4.11 Suppose $\mathsf{fv}(M) \subseteq \widetilde{x}$. Then

$$\widetilde{x} : \mathsf{o}\,\mathsf{o}\,(\mathtt{Trig})\,, p : \mathsf{o}\,(\mathtt{Trig}) \vdash \mathcal{N}[\![M]\!]p\,.$$

□

We also derive the following two results about the operational correctness of the encoding:

Corollary 15.4.12 (Adequacy of $\mathcal{N}$) Let $M \in \Lambda^0$. Then $M \Downarrow_{\mathrm{N}}$ iff $\mathcal{N}[\![M]\!]p \Downarrow$, for any p.

Proof From Theorem 15.4.3, Lemma 15.4.7, and (the appropriate extension of) Theorem 13.2.11. □

Corollary 15.4.13 (Validity of $\lambda\beta$-theory for $\mathcal{N}$) Suppose $\mathsf{fv}(M, N) \subseteq \widetilde{x}$. If $\lambda\beta \vdash M = N$ then $\widetilde{x} : \mathsf{o}\,\mathsf{o}\,(\mathtt{Trig}) \triangleright \mathcal{N}[\![M]\!] \cong^{\mathrm{c}} \mathcal{N}[\![N]\!] : \mathsf{o}\,(\mathtt{Trig}) \;\rightarrow \diamond$.

Proof From Theorem 15.4.4, Corollary 15.4.8, and (the appropriate extension of) Lemma 13.2.14. □

The encoding $\mathcal{N}$ validates rule β of the λ-calculus. By contrast, as Exercise 15.4.15 below shows, $\mathcal{N}$ does not validate rule η, namely

$$\lambda x.\,(Mx) = M \qquad \text{if } x \notin \mathsf{fv}(M)\,.$$

Neither does the call-by-value encoding $\mathcal{V}$ satisfy η. These failures make sense, as η is not operationally valid in either call-by-name or call-by-value λ-calculus (see Exercise 17.2.4). The η rule is operationally valid, however, if M is a value; indeed the encoding does validate this restricted form of η (Exercise 15.4.16).

Exercise 15.4.14 Show that $\mathcal{N}[\![\Omega]\!]p \approx_{\mathrm{g}} \mathbf{0}$. □

Exercise 15.4.15 (Non-validity of the η rule) Show that there is a λ-term M with $x \notin \mathsf{fv}(M)$ such that if $\mathsf{fv}(M) = \{\widetilde{x}\}$ then

$$\widetilde{x} : \mathsf{o}\,\mathsf{o}\,(\mathtt{Trig}) \rhd \mathcal{N}[\![\lambda x.\,(Mx)]\!] \cong^{\mathrm{c}} \mathcal{N}[\![M]\!] : \mathsf{o}\,(\mathtt{Trig}) \to \diamond$$

does not hold. (Hint: use Exercise 15.4.14.) □

Exercise 15.4.16 (Validity of the conditional η rule) Let $V \in \Lambda$ be a call-by-name value. Show that if $x \notin \mathsf{fv}(V)$ then $\mathcal{N}[\![\lambda x.\,(Vx)]\!] \approx_{\mathrm{g}} \mathcal{N}[\![V]\!]$. □

Exercise 15.4.17 (From call-by-value to call-by-name via thunks) The CPS transform $\mathcal{C}_{\mathrm{N}}$ gives us also an encoding of call-by-name (λN) into call-by-value (λV) λ-calculus. Another way to achieve this goal is by means of *thunks*. A thunk is a parameterless procedure; it may also be thought of as a suspended computation. To represent thunks, we can introduce a constructor $\mathtt{delay}(M)$ and a destructor $\mathtt{force}(M)$. Keeping in mind that they represent parameterless abstraction and application, it is straightforward to add them to λV and to its π-calculus encoding $\mathcal{V}$ (Table 15.2); the additional operational rules are

$$\frac{M \longrightarrow_{\mathrm{V}} M'}{\mathtt{force}(M) \longrightarrow_{\mathrm{V}} \mathtt{force}(M')} \qquad \frac{}{\mathtt{force}(\mathtt{delay}(M)) \longrightarrow_{\mathrm{V}} M}$$

and the additional clauses for $\mathcal{V}$ are

$$\begin{aligned} \mathcal{V}[\![\mathtt{delay}(M)]\!] &\stackrel{\mathrm{def}}{=} (p).\,\overline{p}(v).\,!v\,\mathcal{V}[\![M]\!] \\ \mathcal{V}[\![\mathtt{force}(M)]\!] &\stackrel{\mathrm{def}}{=} (p).\,\boldsymbol{\nu} q\,(\mathcal{V}[\![M]\!]q \mid q(v).\,\overline{v}p)\,. \end{aligned} \tag{15.17}$$

We can now encode λN into this extended λV thus:

$$\begin{aligned} \mathcal{D}[\![x]\!] &\stackrel{\mathrm{def}}{=} \mathtt{force}(x) \\ \mathcal{D}[\![\lambda x.\,M]\!] &\stackrel{\mathrm{def}}{=} \lambda x.\,\mathcal{D}[\![M]\!] \\ \mathcal{D}[\![MN]\!] &\stackrel{\mathrm{def}}{=} \mathcal{D}[\![M]\!](\mathtt{delay}(\mathcal{D}[\![N]\!]))\,. \end{aligned}$$

An adequacy results holds for $\mathcal{D}$ that is similar to the adequacy of the CPS transform $\mathcal{C}_{\mathrm{N}}$ (Theorem 15.4.3).

Let $\mathcal{M}$ be the encoding of λN into π-calculus defined as $\mathcal{N}$ (Table 15.4) but with a replication in the clause of abstraction:

$$\mathcal{M}[\![\lambda x. M]\!] \stackrel{\text{def}}{=} (p).\,\overline{p}(v).\,!v(x)\,\mathcal{M}[\![M]\!]\,.$$

Prove that $\mathcal{M}$ factorizes through the above encoding $\mathcal{D}$ and $\mathcal{V}$ (extended with (15.17)); i.e., for all $M \in \Lambda$

$$\mathcal{V}[\![\mathcal{D}[\![M]\!]]\!] \approx_{\mathrm{g}} \mathcal{M}[\![M]\!]\,.$$

□

We conclude the section by proving some properties of insensitivity to behavioural equivalences for the call-by-name encoding; we will use some of these properties in later chapters.

The next lemma shows that i/o types are not actually necessary in the assertion of Corollary 15.4.13. This is in contrast with the corresponding result for call-by-value, see Remark 15.3.17. (The reason why i/o types are needed for call-by-value but not for call-by-name has to do with the replication theorems: for the proof of Lemma 15.3.19, the Sharpened Replication Theorems 10.5.1 are necessary, and these theorems use i/o types. They are necessary because, in the assertion of Lemma 15.3.19, M may send x, due to the definition of the encoding $\mathcal{V}$ on variables. The same does not happen in the call-by-name encoding $\mathcal{N}$, which uses a different translation of variables and thus can be proved correct from the ordinary Replication Theorems.)

Let us call $\mathcal{N}_\sharp$ the encoding into the polyadic π-calculus ($\pi^{\sharp,\times,\mu}$), without i/o types; omitting types, the definition of $\mathcal{N}_\sharp$ is the same as that of $\mathcal{N}$; the difference is that in $\mathcal{N}_\sharp$ each i/o type $I\,T$ (for $I \in \{\mathsf{i},\mathsf{o},\sharp\}$) is replaced by the less informative connection type $\sharp\,T$. In the polyadic π-calculus we write barbed congruence between processes as $P \cong^{\mathrm{c}} Q$, omitting the type environment index.

Lemma 15.4.18 Suppose $\mathsf{fv}(M, N) \subseteq \widetilde{x}$. Then

$$\widetilde{x} : \mathsf{o}\,\mathsf{o}\,(\mathtt{Trig}) \triangleright \mathcal{N}[\![M]\!] \cong^{\mathrm{c}} \mathcal{N}[\![N]\!] : \mathsf{o}\,(\mathtt{Trig}) \to \diamond \text{ iff } \mathcal{N}_\sharp\,[\![M]\!] \cong^{\mathrm{c}} \mathcal{N}_\sharp\,[\![N]\!].$$

□

The proof of Lemma 15.4.18 is rather complex; rather than giving it, we invite the reader to prove a simpler result, namely the variant of Corollary 15.4.13 without i/o types, through the following four exercises.

Exercise 15.4.19 Show that, for all $M, N \in \Lambda$ with $x \notin \mathsf{fv}(N)$,

$$\mathcal{N}_\sharp\,[\![(\lambda x.\, M)N]\!]p \xrightarrow{\tau}{}^2_{\mathrm{d}} \mathcal{N}_\sharp\,[\![M]\!]p\,\{x = \mathcal{N}_\sharp\,[\![N]\!]\}\,.$$

□

Exercise 15.4.20 Show that, for all $M, N \in \Lambda$ with $x \notin \mathsf{fv}(N)$,

$$\mathcal{N}_\sharp\,[\![M]\!]\,\{x = \mathcal{N}_\sharp\,[\![N]\!]\} \approx_{\mathrm{g}} \mathcal{N}_\sharp\,[\![M\{^N\!/\!_x\}]\!]\,.$$

(Hint: proceed by induction on M, and use the Replication Theorems.) □

Exercise 15.4.21

(1) From the two previous exercises, conclude that if $M \longrightarrow_{\mathrm{N}} N$ then we have $\mathcal{N}_\sharp\,[\![M]\!]p \xrightarrow{\tau}{}^2_{\mathrm{d}} \approx_{\mathrm{g}} \mathcal{N}_\sharp\,[\![N]\!]p$.
(2) Check that in item (1), relation $\approx_{\mathrm{g}}$ can be refined to ${}_{\mathrm{g}}\succeq$ (the ground expansion relation). □

Exercise 15.4.22 Use Exercise 15.4.21 to prove that if $\lambda\beta \vdash M = N$ then $\mathcal{N}_\sharp\,[\![M]\!] \cong^{\mathrm{c}} \mathcal{N}_\sharp\,[\![N]\!]$. □

Exercise 15.4.21 can also be used to get a direct proof of Corollary 15.4.12.

The encoding of call-by-name satisfies some further properties of insensitivity to the behavioural equivalence chosen for the π-calculus. We show one of these (insensitivity to the choice between barbed congruence and ground bisimilarity), that will be useful in the study of full abstraction for this encoding, in Chapters 17 and 18.

Lemma 15.4.23 For all $M, N \in \Lambda$, we have $\mathcal{N}_\sharp\,[\![M]\!] \cong^{\mathrm{c}} \mathcal{N}_\sharp\,[\![N]\!]$ iff $\mathcal{N}_\sharp\,[\![M]\!] \approx_{\mathrm{g}} \mathcal{N}_\sharp\,[\![N]\!]$.

Proof (sketch) On processes of the Asynchronous π-calculus, ground bisimulation implies barbed congruence (Corollary 5.3.9). For the opposite direction, one uses the fact that for all M and p, the process $\mathcal{N}_\sharp\,[\![M]\!]p$ is image-finite, with respect to weak transitions, up to ground bisimilarity (or full bisimilarity, which on processes of the Asynchronous π-calculus coincides with ground bisimilarity). This property follows from the operational correspondence between λ-terms and π-terms analysed in Section 18.3 (in particular Lemma 18.3.9). Then the implication is proved proceeding in a way similar to that used for characterizations of barbed congruence in terms of bisimilarity in Section 2.4. □

In this table we abbeviate $\mathcal{C}_{\mathrm{U}}[\![M]\!]$ as $[\![M]\!]$.

$$[\![x]\!] \stackrel{\text{def}}{=} \lambda k.\, xk$$
$$[\![\lambda x.\, M]\!] \stackrel{\text{def}}{=} \lambda k.\, k(\lambda x.\, [\![M]\!])$$

call-by-name application

$$[\![MN]\!] \stackrel{\text{def}}{=} \lambda k.\, [\![M]\!](\lambda v.\, v[\![N]\!]k)$$

call-by-value application

$$[\![MN]\!] \stackrel{\text{def}}{=} \lambda k.\, [\![M]\!](\lambda v.\, [\![N]\!](\lambda w.\, v(\lambda k.\, kw)k))$$

Table 15.5. *A uniform CPS transform*

15.5 A uniform encoding

The differences between the definitions of application in the π-calculus encodings of call-by-name and call-by-value are inevitable – just because application is precisely where these strategies differ. One may wonder, however, whether the definitions of abstraction and variable need to differ too. In this section, we make some simple modifications to these encodings to obtain new ones that differ *only* in the definitions of application. We will then show that other forms of application, such as call-by-need application, can be easily defined. Having a uniform encoding for a variety of strategies makes it easier to compare them. It also facilitates translation to π-calculus of programming languages that employ different strategies for evaluating arguments of functions.

We obtain the new encodings again by going through a CPS transform, an injection into HOπ, and the compilation of HOπ into π-calculus. We begin with the CPS transform. Starting from the call-by-value and call-by-name transforms examined in the previous sections (Tables 15.1 and 15.3), it is easy to give a CPS transform that is *uniform* for call-by-value and call-by-name, in that it has the same clauses for abstraction and variables. The call-by-value and call-by-name CPS have the same clause for abstractions; to obtain a uniform CPS it suffices to adopt the call-by-name CPS, and modify the definition of application of the call-by-value CPS to compensate for the different clauses for variables. (We cannot adopt the definition of variables of the call-by-value CPS transform because it treats variables as values, and this is correct only when variables are always substituted by values.)

The uniform CPS transform is given in Table 15.5. The associated grammar, which is similar to that for the call-by-name CPS transform but lacks the constraint on linear occurrence of value variables, is this:

$$
\begin{array}{rlcl}
\text{continuation variable} & k & & \\
\text{ordinary variables} & x, \ldots & & \\
\text{value variables} & v, w, \ldots & & \\
\text{answers} & P & ::= & KV \mid VAK \mid AK \\
\text{CPS-values} & V & ::= & \lambda x.\, \lambda k.\, P \mid v \\
\text{continuations} & K & ::= & k \mid \lambda v.\, P \\
\text{principal terms} & A & ::= & \lambda k.\, P \mid x
\end{array}
\tag{15.18}
$$

The types of the non-terminals of the grammar are the same as those of the call-by-name CPS transform. With the usual injection on terms and on types, the terms generated by this grammar and their types become a sublanguage of HOπ. Applying the compilation of HOπ into π-calculus, we obtain the encoding given in Table 15.6. In this table, there is also the code for the call-by-need application. We present call-by-need directly on the π-calculus – without going through HOπ – because, as explained in Section 14.3.3, call-by-need is an implementation technique with an explicit environment in which β-reduction does not require substituting a term for a variable but just substituting a reference to a term for a variable. Therefore for the encoding of call-by-need the process-passing features of HOπ are not so helpful.

We explain the encoding of a call-by-need application MN. When $\mathcal{U}[\![M]\!]q$ becomes a function it signals so on q, and receives a pointer x to the argument N together with the location p for the next interaction. Now the evaluation of M continues. When the argument N is needed for the first time, a request is made on x. Then $\mathcal{U}[\![N]\!]r$ is evaluated and, when it becomes a value, a pointer to this value instantiates w. This pointer is returned to the process that requested N. When further requests for N are made, the pointer is returned immediately. Thus, by contrast with call-by-name, in call-by-need the argument N of the application is evaluated only once. To appreciate this, the reader might like to compare the reductions of the encodings of $(\lambda.\, xx)(II)$ in call-by-name and in call-by-need. In the former, II is evaluated twice, in the latter once.

It is not by chance that the call-by-need encoding is best derived from the uniform encoding of Table 15.6, because call-by-need combines elements of the call-by-name and call-by-value strategies. Indeed it can be defined as call-by-name plus sharing, but can also be seen as a variant of call-by-value where the argument of an application is evaluated at a different point.

We do not prove the correctness of the call-by-need encoding, for it would

$$\mathcal{U}[\![\lambda x.\, M]\!] \stackrel{\text{def}}{=} (p).\,\overline{p}(v).\,!v(x)\,\mathcal{U}[\![M]\!]$$

$$\mathcal{U}[\![x]\!] \stackrel{\text{def}}{=} (p).\,\overline{x}p$$

call-by-value application

$$\mathcal{U}[\![MN]\!] \stackrel{\text{def}}{=} (p).\,(\boldsymbol{\nu} q\,)\Big(\mathcal{U}[\![M]\!]q \mid q(v).\,\boldsymbol{\nu} r\;(\;\mathcal{U}[\![N]\!]r \mid r(w).\,\boldsymbol{\nu} x\,\overline{v}\langle x,p\rangle.\,!x(r').\,\overline{r'}w)\Big)$$

call-by-name application

$$\mathcal{U}[\![MN]\!] \stackrel{\text{def}}{=} (p).\,(\boldsymbol{\nu} q\,)\Big(\mathcal{U}[\![M]\!]q \mid q(v).\,\boldsymbol{\nu} x\,\overline{v}\langle x,p\rangle.\,!x\,\mathcal{U}[\![N]\!]\Big)$$

call-by-need application

$$\mathcal{U}[\![MN]\!] \stackrel{\text{def}}{=} (p).\,(\boldsymbol{\nu} q\,)\Big(\mathcal{U}[\![M]\!]q \mid q(v).\,\boldsymbol{\nu} x\,\overline{v}\langle x,p\rangle.\,x(r).\,\boldsymbol{\nu} q'\;(\;\mathcal{U}[\![N]\!]q' \mid q'(w).\,(\overline{r}w \mid !x(r').\,\overline{r'}w))\Big)$$

Table 15.6. *The uniform encoding of call-by-name, call-by-value, call-by-need*

require formally introducing the call-by-need system. See the notes at the end of the Part for references, and see also Exercise 15.5.3.

Exercise 15.5.1 Add type annotations for the restricted names to the encodings in Table 15.6. What are the types of the free names? Show that these types are correct, by proving the appropriate type judgments on encodings of λ-terms. □

Remark 15.5.2 Proving properties of the encodings of call-by-value λ-calculus and call-by-need in Table 15.6 (for instance, in call-by-value, the validity of β_{V} reduction) may require i/o types. They may be avoided by adopting the modifications proposed in Exercise 15.5.3. □

Exercise 15.5.3 Let $\mathcal{U}^*_{\mathrm{V}}$ be the encoding of call-by-value as defined in Table 15.6 with the exception that in the clause for application the last output $\overline{r'}w$ is replaced by $\overline{r'}(w').\,!w' \twoheadrightarrow w$ (where $w' \twoheadrightarrow w$ is a *wire*, Section 10.3). Similarly, let $\mathcal{U}^*_{\mathrm{Ne}}$ be the encoding of call-by-need as defined in Table 15.6 with the exception that in the clause for application the last output $\overline{r'}w$ is replaced by $\overline{r'}(w').\,!w' \twoheadrightarrow w$. Finally, let $\mathcal{U}_{\mathrm{N}}$ be the encoding of call-by-name in the same table.

Take a λ-term M inside which all applications have the form $N(\lambda x.\, L)$ (i.e.,

$$\mathcal{M}[\![\lambda x.\, M]\!] \stackrel{\text{def}}{=} (p).\, p(x)\, \mathcal{M}[\![M]\!]$$
$$\mathcal{M}[\![x]\!] \stackrel{\text{def}}{=} (p).\, \overline{x}p$$
$$\mathcal{M}[\![MN]\!] \stackrel{\text{def}}{=} (p).\, \boldsymbol{\nu} q\, (\mathcal{M}[\![M]\!]q \mid \boldsymbol{\nu} x\, \overline{q}\langle x, p\rangle.\, !x\, \mathcal{M}[\![N]\!])$$

Table 15.7. *An optimized encoding of* λN

the argument is an abstraction). Show that

$$\mathcal{U}^*_{\mathrm{V}}[\![M]\!] \approx_{\mathrm{g}} \mathcal{U}_{\mathrm{N}}[\![M]\!] \approx_{\mathrm{g}} \mathcal{U}^*_{\mathrm{Ne}}[\![M]\!] \,.$$

(Hint: proceed by structural induction on M.) □

15.6 Optimizations of the call-by-name encoding

We now examine a possible optimization of the encoding $\mathcal{N}$ of λN into π-calculus (Table 15.4). Consider the encoding of abstraction in that table. The name v sent via p is immediately used in an input. Dually, in the definition of application the name received at q is immediately used in output. We can compress the two communications into a single one where an abstraction uses its location in input. The resulting optimized encoding is shown in Table 15.7. This is the simplest encoding of the λ-calculus into π-calculus we are aware of.

The optimization from which the new encoding is obtained is valid in the standard semantics of the π-calculus; but it is not valid in an *asynchronous* semantics. Indeed, the encoding is not quite satisfactory with respect to asynchronous semantics such as asynchronous may testing or (forms of) typed asynchronous barbed congruence. For instance, these semantics equate the processes $\mathcal{M}[\![\lambda x.\, \Omega]\!]p$ and $\mathcal{M}[\![\Omega]\!]p$, but $\lambda x.\, \Omega$ and Ω are not behaviourally equivalent in λN (technically speaking, with these semantics the encoding is not sound). Behavioural equivalence in λN will be discussed in Chapter 17.

In summary, the encoding of Table 15.7 is attractive because it is the shortest of all the λ-calculus encodings presented, but it is less robust than the encoding of Table 15.4. In the remainder of this Part we will prefer the more robust encoding.

An optimization of the encoding $\mathcal{N}$ (and of the other call-by-name encodings in this section and in Section 15.5) is possible using types. The definition of application when the argument is a variable is, including type annotations,

$$\mathcal{N}[\![My]\!] \stackrel{\text{def}}{=} (p).\ (\boldsymbol{\nu} q : \sharp\,\texttt{Trig}) \Big(\mathcal{N}[\![M]\!]q \mid q(v).(\boldsymbol{\nu} x : \sharp\,\mathsf{o}\,\texttt{Trig})\,\overline{v}\langle x,p\rangle.\,!x(r).\,\overline{y}r\Big)\,.$$

It can be rewritten, using wires and removing a semantically useless prefix,

$$(p).\ (\boldsymbol{\nu} q : \sharp\,\texttt{Trig}) \Big(\mathcal{N}[\![M]\!]q \mid q(v).(\boldsymbol{\nu} x : \sharp\,\mathsf{o}\,\texttt{Trig})\,(\overline{v}\langle x,p\rangle \mid !x \rightarrow y)\Big)\,.$$

From the type $\sharp\,\texttt{Trig}$ of q it follows that v is used in the body with type $\texttt{Trig}$. The definition of $\texttt{Trig}$ shows that only the output capability of names may be communicated along v. This means that only the output capability of name x may be communicated; moreover, the input end of x is immediately available, and is replicated. We can conclude that x is an ω-receptive name (Section 8.2.2), so that we can modify the definition of type $\texttt{Trig}$ to be

$$\texttt{Trig} \stackrel{\text{def}}{=} \mu X.\,(\mathsf{o}\,(\omega\mathrm{rec}_{\mathsf{o}}(\mathsf{o}\,X) \times \mathsf{o}\,X)\,)$$

and the type annotation of name x to be $\omega\mathrm{rec}_{\sharp}(\mathsf{o}\,\texttt{Trig})$. We can then apply the law of Lemma 11.2.4(2), for ω-receptiveness, and optimize the above clause to

$$\mathcal{N}[\![My]\!] \stackrel{\text{def}}{=} (p).\,(\boldsymbol{\nu} q : \sharp\,\texttt{Trig})\,\Big(\mathcal{N}[\![M]\!]q \mid\ q(v).\,\overline{v}\langle y,p\rangle\Big)\,. \tag{15.19}$$

(A similar optimization would be possible taking the target language of the encoding to be the Asynchronous π-calculus and applying the law of Lemma 10.3.1.) This optimization is a useful one, because the appearance of variables as arguments of applications is rather frequent. It is the analogue of a very common tail-call optimization of functional languages.

15.7 The interpretation of strong call-by-name

The only rule of the $\lambda\beta$-theory so far totally neglected is the ξ rule, for evaluating underneath the λ. This rule is normally disallowed in implementations of programming languages. Nevertheless, it is interesting to see how the ξ rule can be encoded, for at least two reasons. First, it is a test of expressiveness for the process calculus. Secondly, certain optimizations of compilers of programming languages act on the body of functions and have similarities with the ξ rule.

In this section we show how to add the ξ rule to the call-by-name encodings. Adding ξ to the call-by-value and call-by-need encodings is much harder; we explain why at the end of the section. We will work in the π-calculus only: we have gained enough experience by now with encodings of the λ-calculus in the previous sections so that it is not necessary to go through HOπ again. The strategy defined by the rules of call-by-name plus ξ is called *strong call-by-name.*

We obtain an encoding of strong call-by-name by modifying the definition of abstraction in the call-by-name encoding of Section 15.4. This clause is, expanding the input at v and replacing a prefix by a semantically equivalent parallel composition,

$$\mathcal{N}[\![\lambda x.\, M]\!] \stackrel{\text{def}}{=} (p).\, \boldsymbol{\nu} v\, (\overline{p}v \mid v(x,q).\, \mathcal{N}[\![M]\!]q)\ .$$

Intuitively, to allow the ξ rule, we need to relax the sequentiality imposed by the input prefix $v(x,q)$ that guards the body $\mathcal{N}[\![M]\!]q$ of the function. Precisely, we would like to replace this input with the delayed input introduced in Section 10.4 thus (recall that a delayed input $a(\widetilde{z}):P$ allows reductions in the continuation P):

$$\mathcal{N}_\xi[\![\lambda x.\, M]\!] \stackrel{\text{def}}{=} (p).\, \boldsymbol{\nu} v\, (\overline{p}v \mid v(x,q):\mathcal{N}_\xi[\![M]\!]q)\,. \tag{15.20}$$

The resulting encoding is correct for strong call-by-name, because it is obtained from an encoding that is correct for call-by-name and because the introduction of the delayed input in (15.20) has precisely the effect of the ξ rule of the λ-calculus.

We saw in Section 10.4 that, under certain conditions, a delayed input $a(\widetilde{z}):P$ can be coded up applying transformation (10.4); see (10.5). The conditions are that processes should be asynchronous and the continuation P should have only the output capability[1] on the bound names $\widetilde{z}$. Both conditions hold in (15.20); the output condition holds because the type of v is $(\mathtt{Trig})^{\leftarrow\sharp} = \sharp(\mathrm{o}\,\mathrm{o}\,\mathtt{Trig} \times \mathrm{o}\,\mathtt{Trig})$, as shown in (15.16). We can therefore apply transformation (10.4) to (15.20) to get

$$\mathcal{N}_\xi[\![\lambda x.\, M]\!]p \stackrel{\text{def}}{=} (\boldsymbol{\nu} v, x, q\,)\Big(\overline{p}v \mid v(y,r).\,(!x \multimap y \mid q \multimap r) \mid \mathcal{N}_\xi[\![M]\!]q\Big)\,.$$

(The wires on the location names r, q are not replicated because locations are used linearly.) The correctness of transformation (10.4) (and of its linear variant without replication on wires) guarantees that the result is still a correct encoding of strong call-by-name. Table 15.8 gives the complete encoding, including the unchanged clauses for variable and application.

It is actually possible to eliminate the wire $!x \multimap y$ in the translation of abstraction. The exercise below invites the reader to show this.

Exercise* 15.7.1 A small modification of the encoding of Table 15.8 allows the elimination of the wire $!x \multimap y$. Write down this encoding, and prove a correctness

[1] In Section 10.4 we actually proved the correctness of the transformation (10.4) under the additional hypothesis that names $\widetilde{z}$ occur only in output subject position in P; see the discussion after (10.4).

$$\begin{aligned}
\mathcal{N}_\xi[\![\lambda x.\, M]\!] &\stackrel{\text{def}}{=} (p).(\boldsymbol{\nu} x, q\,)\Big(\overline{p}(v).\, v(y,r).\,(!x \twoheadrightarrow y \mid q \twoheadrightarrow r) \mid \mathcal{N}_\xi[\![M]\!]q\Big)\\
\mathcal{N}_\xi[\![x]\!] &\stackrel{\text{def}}{=} (p).\,\overline{x}p\\
\mathcal{N}_\xi[\![MN]\!] &\stackrel{\text{def}}{=} (p).\,\boldsymbol{\nu} q\,\Big(\mathcal{N}_\xi[\![M]\!]q \mid q(v).\,\boldsymbol{\nu} x\,(\overline{v}\langle x,p\rangle.\,!x\,\mathcal{N}_\xi[\![N]\!])\Big)
\end{aligned}$$

Table 15.8. *The encoding of strong λN into the π-calculus*

result for it analogous to that in Exercise 15.4.21. (Hint: begin from an encoding of call-by-name in which the definition of abstraction is

$$[\![\lambda x.\, M]\!] \stackrel{\text{def}}{=} (\boldsymbol{\nu} x, v\,)(\overline{p}\langle x,v\rangle \mid v\,[\![M]\!])$$

and where the clause for application is changed accordingly.) □

In contrast, encoding call-by-value plus the ξ rule is much more complex. To repeat the trick we used in the call-by-name case, we would need to allow reduction underneath replication, that is to add the rule

$$\frac{P \longrightarrow P'}{!P \longrightarrow\ !P'} \tag{15.21}$$

Section 1.2 explains why this rule is not among the reduction rules of the π-calculus. Rule (15.21) appears necessary to encode in π-calculus any strategy having at least rules β_v, ν_v, and ξ (another such strategy is full β-reduction $\longrightarrow_\beta$). The reason is the following. Suppose the argument N of an application $(\lambda x.\, M)N$ reduces to a function $\lambda y.\, N'$. As this function could be used arbitrarily-many times in M, the π-calculus encoding of N should reduce to a replicated process. But the ξ rule allows reduction within the body N', and then to model this in π-calculus we would need rule (15.21). As a matter of fact, adding the ξ rule to call-by-value does not make much sense anyway, for the notion of value becomes rather complicated.

For similar reasons, rule (15.21) appears necessary for the encoding of any reduction strategy that allows rules β, μ, and ν.

Remark 15.7.2 Reasoning as above, we can also obtain an encoding of strong call-by-name by modifying the definition of abstraction in the optimized call-by-name encoding of Section 15.6. In this case, we need both transformation (10.4) and transformation (10.6). After eliminating a replication in front of a wire because of linearity, we obtain

$$\mathcal{M}_\xi[\![\lambda x.\, M]\!] \stackrel{\text{def}}{=} (\boldsymbol{\nu} x, q\,)\Big(p(y,r).\,(!x \twoheadrightarrow y \mid q \twoheadrightarrow r) \mid \mathcal{M}_\xi[\![M]\!]q\Big)\,.$$

However, we recall from Section 10.4 that the proof of correctness of transformation (10.6) requires some advanced properties of process with i/o types, which we have not examined in the book. The same properties are needed to prove the correctness of the encoding above. □

Exercise 15.7.3 What are the types of the bound and free names of the encoding in Table 15.8? Show that these types are correct, by proving the appropriate type judgments. □

16

Interpreting Typed λ-calculi

In this chapter we show that the encodings of the previous chapter can be extended to encodings of typed λ-calculi. To do this we have to define translations on types to match those on terms. We analyse the case of the *simply-typed λ-calculus* in detail, and discuss subtyping and recursive types. For studies of other type systems, see the notes at the end of the Part.

16.1 Typed λ-calculus

In a core simply-typed λ-calculus, types are built from *basic types*, such as integers and booleans, using the *function type* constructor. The syntax of terms is that of the untyped λ-calculus plus *basic constants*. Each constant has a unique predefined type. We use only constants of basic types: this is sufficient to have a non-empty set of (closed) well-typed terms. This simply-typed λ-calculus is presented in Table 16.1. We write $\Lambda\{c\}$ for the set of terms of the calculus. As usual, function type associates to the right, so $T \to S \to U$ should be read $T \to (S \to U)$. Basic types are ranged over by t, basic constants by c. The reduction relation and the reduction strategies are defined as for the untyped calculus; the only difference is that the set of values for a reduction strategy normally contains the constants. We call the typed versions of λV and λN *simply-typed call-by-value* ($\lambda V^{\to}$) and *simply-typed call-by-name* ($\lambda N^{\to}$), respectively.

We add the same basic constants and basic types to HOπ and π-calculus and repeat the diagram of Figure 15.1, this time for $\lambda V^{\to}$ and $\lambda N^{\to}$. We show how to extend the encodings of λV and λN (from Sections 15.3 and 15.4), and their correctness results, to take account of types. The encodings in Sections 15.5–15.7 can be extended similarly.

Lemma 16.1.1 In the simply-typed λ-calculus, for every Γ and M there is at most one T such that $\Gamma \vdash M : T$. □

Terms	$M \quad ::= \quad x \mid c \mid \lambda x : T.\, M \mid MN$		$c \in$ basic constants
Types	$T \quad ::= \quad T_1 \to T_2 \mid t$		$t \in$ basic types
Type environments	$\Gamma \quad ::= \quad \emptyset \mid \Gamma, x : T$		
Typing rules	$\dfrac{\Gamma, x : S \vdash M : T}{\Gamma \vdash \lambda x : S.\, M : S \to T}$	$\dfrac{\Gamma(x) = T}{\Gamma \vdash x : T}$	
	$\dfrac{\Gamma \vdash M : S \to T \qquad \Gamma \vdash N : S}{\Gamma \vdash MN : T}$		

Table 16.1. *The (core) simpy-typed λ-calculus*

16.2 The interpretation of typed call-by-value

We begin with the left part of Figure 15.1, which concerns $\lambda V^{\to}$. We follow a schema similar to that of Section 15.3, pointing out the main additions. The set of values of $\lambda V^{\to}$ also includes constants:

$$V \quad ::= \quad \lambda x.\, M \mid x \mid c\,.$$

As usual in a translation of typed calculi, the definition of the CPS transform $\mathcal{C}_{\mathrm{V}}$ (Table 15.1) on a term uses the type environment of the term as an index to be able to put the necessary type annotations in the target term. We do not discuss these type annotations any further; they are determined by the definition of $\mathcal{C}_{\mathrm{V}}$ on types, explained below. We have to add a clause for constants:

$$\mathcal{C}^{\star}_{\mathrm{V}}[c]^{\Gamma} \stackrel{\mathrm{def}}{=} c\,.$$

It is important to understand how the CPS transform acts on types. Recalling from Section 15.3 that $\diamond$ is a distinguished type of answers (answers being the 'results' of CPS terms), the call-by-value CPS transform modifies the types of $\lambda V^{\to}$ -terms as follows:

$$\begin{aligned} \mathcal{C}_{\mathrm{V}}[\![T]\!] &\stackrel{\mathrm{def}}{=} (\mathcal{C}^{\star}_{\mathrm{V}}[T] \to \diamond) \to \diamond \\ \mathcal{C}^{\star}_{\mathrm{V}}[t] &\stackrel{\mathrm{def}}{=} t \qquad\qquad \text{if } t \text{ is a basic type} \\ \mathcal{C}^{\star}_{\mathrm{V}}[S \to T] &\stackrel{\mathrm{def}}{=} \mathcal{C}^{\star}_{\mathrm{V}}[S] \to \mathcal{C}_{\mathrm{V}}[\![T]\!]\,. \end{aligned} \tag{16.1}$$

The translation of function types is sometimes called the 'double-negation construction' because, writing $\neg T$ for $T \to \diamond$, we have

$$\mathcal{C}^{\star}_{\mathrm{V}}[S \to T] = \mathcal{C}^{\star}_{\mathrm{V}}[S] \to \neg\neg\mathcal{C}^{\star}_{\mathrm{V}}[T]\,.$$

Type environments are modified accordingly:

$$\begin{aligned}\mathcal{C}_{\mathrm{V}}[\![\emptyset]\!] &\stackrel{\text{def}}{=} \emptyset\\ \mathcal{C}_{\mathrm{V}}[\![\Gamma, x : S]\!] &\stackrel{\text{def}}{=} \mathcal{C}_{\mathrm{V}}[\![\Gamma]\!], x : \mathcal{C}_{\mathrm{V}}[\![S]\!]\end{aligned}$$

and similarly for $\mathcal{C}^{\star}_{\mathrm{V}}$. The correctness of this translation of types is given in:

Theorem 16.2.1 (Correctness of call-by-value CPS on types) Suppose $M \in \Lambda\{c\}$. Then $\Gamma \vdash M : T$ implies $\mathcal{C}^{\star}_{\mathrm{V}}[\Gamma] \vdash \mathcal{C}_{\mathrm{V}}[\![M]\!]^{\Gamma} : \mathcal{C}_{\mathrm{V}}[\![T]\!]$. □

(It follows that for any value V,

$$\Gamma \vdash V : T \quad \text{implies} \quad \mathcal{C}^{\star}_{\mathrm{V}}[\Gamma] \vdash \mathcal{C}^{\star}_{\mathrm{V}}[V]^{\Gamma} : \mathcal{C}^{\star}_{\mathrm{V}}[T]$$

which shows the agreement between the definitions of the auxiliary function $\mathcal{C}^{\star}_{\mathrm{V}}$ on terms and on types.)

Remark 16.2.2 Schema (16.1) is also useful for understanding the types of the CPS images of the untyped λV in (15.5), because the untyped λ-calculus can be described as a typed λ-calculus in which all terms have the recursive type

$$T \stackrel{\text{def}}{=} \mu X.\,(X \to X). \tag{16.2}$$

To apply the type translation to (16.2) we just need to add the clauses for type variables and for recursion to those in (16.1):

$$\mathcal{C}^{\star}_{\mathrm{V}}[X] \stackrel{\text{def}}{=} X \qquad \mathcal{C}^{\star}_{\mathrm{V}}[\mu X.\,T] \stackrel{\text{def}}{=} \mu X.\,\mathcal{C}^{\star}_{\mathrm{V}}[T]\,. \tag{16.3}$$

The translation of type T in (16.2) is then

$$\mathcal{C}^{\star}_{\mathrm{V}}[T] \;=\; \mu X.\,(X \to (X \to \diamond) \to \diamond)$$

which is precisely type T_V in (15.5); moreover

$$\begin{aligned}\mathcal{C}_{\mathrm{V}}[\![T]\!] &= (\mathcal{C}^{\star}_{\mathrm{V}}[T] \to \diamond) \to \diamond\\ &= (T_V \to \diamond) \to \diamond\\ &= T_A\,.\end{aligned}$$

□

The grammar of CPS terms is obtained from Grammar (15.4) by adding a production for constants to those defining CPS-values. The relationship between the CPS grammar and HOπ is as in the untyped case, both on terms and on types. That is, modulo a modification of the syntax and some uncurrying, the

In this table we abbreviate $\mathcal{V}[\![E]\!]$ as $[\![E]\!]$, and $\mathcal{V}^\star[E]$ as $[E]$, for any expression E.

Translation of types

$$[\![T]\!] \stackrel{\text{def}}{=} \mathsf{o}\,\mathsf{o}\,[T]$$

$$\begin{array}{rcll} [t] & \stackrel{\text{def}}{=} & t & t \in \text{basic types} \\ [S \to T] & \stackrel{\text{def}}{=} & \mathsf{o}\,([S] \times \mathsf{o}\,[T]) & \end{array}$$

Translation of type environments

$$[\![\emptyset]\!] = [\emptyset] \stackrel{\text{def}}{=} \emptyset$$

$$[\![\Gamma, x : S]\!] \stackrel{\text{def}}{=} [\![\Gamma]\!], x : [\![S]\!] \qquad [\Gamma, x : S] \stackrel{\text{def}}{=} [\Gamma], x : [S]$$

Translation of terms

$$\begin{array}{rcl} [\![\lambda x : S.\, M]\!]^\Gamma & \stackrel{\text{def}}{=} & (p).\, \overline{p}(y : [S \to T]^{\leftarrow\sharp}).\, !y(x)\, [\![M]\!]^{\Gamma, x:S} \\ [\![x]\!]^\Gamma & \stackrel{\text{def}}{=} & (p).\, \overline{p}x \\ [\![c]\!]^\Gamma & \stackrel{\text{def}}{=} & (p).\, \overline{p}c \\ [\![MN]\!]^\Gamma & \stackrel{\text{def}}{=} & \end{array}$$

$$(p).\, (\boldsymbol{\nu} q : \sharp\, [S \to T]) \Big([\![M]\!]^\Gamma q \mid q(x).\, (\boldsymbol{\nu} r : \sharp\, [S]) \,([\![N]\!]^\Gamma r \mid r(y).\, \overline{x}\langle y, p\rangle)\Big)$$

where in the clause for abstraction, T is the unique type such that $\Gamma \vdash \lambda x : S.\, M : T$ and, similarly, in the clause for application, $S \to T$ is the unique type such that $\Gamma \vdash M : S \to T$ (these types are unique by Lemma 16.1.1).

Table 16.2. *The encoding of $\lambda V^{\to}$ into π-calculus*

CPS grammar generates a sublanguage of HOπ. Thus Theorem 16.2.1 can also be read as a result about the encoding of $\lambda V^{\to}$ into HOπ.

Finally, we apply the compilation $\mathcal{C}$ of HOπ terms and types into π-calculus terms and types, and we obtain the encoding of $\lambda V^{\to}$ into typed π-calculus in Table 16.2, and the results below about its correctness. Apart from type annotations, the translation of terms is the same as for the untyped calculus, with the addition of the clause for translating constants. Writing $(T)^-$ for the type obtained from T by cancelling the outermost i/o tag, so that $(\mathcal{V}[\![T]\!])^-$ is $\mathsf{o}\,\mathcal{V}^\star[T]$, the translation of Theorem 16.2.1 into π-calculus gives:

Corollary 16.2.3 (Correctness of $\mathcal{V}$ on types) Let $M \in \Lambda\{c\}$. Then

$$\Gamma \vdash M : T \quad \text{implies} \quad \mathcal{V}^\star[\Gamma], p : (\mathcal{V}[\![T]\!])^- \vdash \mathcal{V}[\![M]\!]^\Gamma p \ . \qquad \square$$

The results for the encoding of untyped λV, namely validity of $\lambda\beta_v$ theory and adequacy (Corollaries 15.3.16 and 15.3.15), remain valid for the typed calculus, with the necessary modifications to the statements to take account of types. For instance, Corollary 15.3.16 becomes:

Corollary 16.2.4 (Validity of $\lambda\beta_v$-theory) Let $M, N \in \Lambda\{c\}$, and suppose that $\Gamma \vdash M : T$ and $\Gamma \vdash N : T$. If $\lambda\beta_v \vdash M = N$ then $\mathcal{V}^\star[\Gamma] \rhd \mathcal{V}[\![M]\!]^\Gamma \cong^c \mathcal{V}[\![N]\!]^\Gamma : (\mathcal{V}[\![T]\!])^- \to \diamond$. $\square$

Remark 16.2.5 The types of π-calculus names used for the encoding of untyped λV in Section 15.3 agree with those used for $\lambda V^\to$ in this section, when we view the untyped λ-calculus as a typed λ-calculus where the only type is $\mu X.(X \to X)$. From (16.3), the translation of recursive types and type variables of λV into π-calculus is

$$\mathcal{V}^\star[X] \stackrel{\text{def}}{=} X \qquad \mathcal{V}^\star[\mu X.T] \stackrel{\text{def}}{=} \mu X.\mathcal{V}^\star[T] \ .$$

Type `Val` of Section 15.3 is precisely $\mathcal{V}^\star[\mu X.(X \to X)]$, and Lemma 15.3.14 can be presented thus: If $\mathsf{fv}(M) \subseteq \widetilde{x}$, then

$$\widetilde{x} : \mathcal{V}^\star[\mu X.(X \to X)], p : (\mathcal{V}[\![\mu X.(X \to X)]\!])^- \vdash \mathcal{V}[\![M]\!]^{\widetilde{x}:\mu X.(X \to X)} p \ .$$

$\square$

Remark 16.2.6 (Subtyping) In typed λ-calculi with subtyping, the function type is contravariant in the first argument and covariant in the second. Therefore, if $<$ is the subtype relation, then $S \to T < S' \to T'$ if $S' < S$ and $T < T'$. For instance, suppose `Int` and `Real` are the types of integers and real numbers. It holds that `Int` $<$ `Real` (an integer is also a real number) and therefore `Real` $\to$ `Int` $<$ `Int` $\to$ `Real`. This is correct because a function that takes a real and returns an integer may also be used as a function that takes an integer and returns a real (but the converse is false).

The i/o tag o is a contravariant type constructor. In the translation of a function type $S \to T$, component $\mathcal{V}^\star[S]$ is in contravariant position, because it is underneath an odd number of o tags; in contrast $\mathcal{V}^\star[T]$ is in covariant position, because it is underneath an even number of o tags. Therefore the π-calculus translation of types correctly explains the subtyping rule for function type. As a consequence, the translation of this section can be extended to one of $\lambda V^\to$ with subtyping. $\square$

Exercise* 16.2.7 Give a direct proof (i.e., without going through the CPS transform) of Corollary 16.2.3. (Hint: proceed by induction on the structure of M; the hardest case is application, where you will need Lemmas 6.3.4, 6.3.5, and 7.2.5.) □

16.3 The interpretation of typed call-by-name

Constants are also among the values of $\lambda N^{\rightarrow}$:

$$\text{Values} \quad V \quad ::= \quad \lambda x.\, M \mid c\,.$$

Therefore we add a clause for constants to the definition of the call-by-name CPS transform in Table 15.3:

$$\mathcal{C}^{\star}_{\mathrm{N}}[c]^{\Gamma} \stackrel{\text{def}}{=} c\,.$$

The transform modifies types as follows.

$$\begin{aligned} \mathcal{C}_{\mathrm{N}}[\![T]\!] &\stackrel{\text{def}}{=} (\mathcal{C}^{\star}_{\mathrm{N}}[T] \rightarrow \diamond) \rightarrow \diamond \\ \\ \mathcal{C}^{\star}_{\mathrm{N}}[t] &\stackrel{\text{def}}{=} t \qquad\qquad\qquad \text{if } t \text{ is a basic type} \\ \mathcal{C}^{\star}_{\mathrm{N}}[S \rightarrow T] &\stackrel{\text{def}}{=} \mathcal{C}_{\mathrm{N}}[\![S]\!] \rightarrow \mathcal{C}_{\mathrm{N}}[\![T]\!]\,. \end{aligned} \tag{16.4}$$

Type environments are then translated thus:

$$\begin{aligned} \mathcal{C}_{\mathrm{N}}[\![\emptyset]\!] &\stackrel{\text{def}}{=} \emptyset \\ \mathcal{C}_{\mathrm{N}}[\![\Gamma, x : S]\!] &\stackrel{\text{def}}{=} \mathcal{C}_{\mathrm{N}}[\![\Gamma]\!], x : \mathcal{C}_{\mathrm{N}}[\![S]\!] \end{aligned}$$

and similarly for $\mathcal{C}^{\star}_{\mathrm{N}}$.

Theorem 16.3.1 (Correctness of call-by-name CPS on types) Let $M \in \Lambda\{c\}$. Then $\Gamma \vdash M : T$ implies $\mathcal{C}_{\mathrm{N}}[\![\Gamma]\!] \vdash \mathcal{C}_{\mathrm{N}}[\![M]\!]^{\Gamma} : \mathcal{C}_{\mathrm{N}}[\![T]\!]$. □

A corollary is that for every value V of $\lambda N^{\rightarrow}$,

$$\Gamma \vdash V : T \quad \text{implies} \quad \mathcal{C}_{\mathrm{N}}[\![\Gamma]\!] \vdash \mathcal{C}^{\star}_{\mathrm{N}}[V]^{\Gamma} : \mathcal{C}^{\star}_{\mathrm{N}}[T]\,.$$

Remark 16.3.2 Adding clauses for type variables and for recursion as in (16.3), the above translation of types can also be applied to untyped λN. The translation of $T \stackrel{\text{def}}{=} \mu X.\, (X \rightarrow X)$ is

$$\mathcal{C}^{\star}_{\mathrm{N}}[T] = \mu X.\, \Big(((X \rightarrow \diamond) \rightarrow \diamond) \rightarrow ((X \rightarrow \diamond) \rightarrow \diamond)\Big)$$

and

$$\mathcal{C}_{\mathrm{N}}[\![T]\!] = (\mathcal{C}^{\star}_{\mathrm{N}}[T] \rightarrow \diamond) \rightarrow \diamond$$

In this table we abbreviate $\mathcal{N}[\![E]\!]$ as $[\![E]\!]$, and $\mathcal{N}^\star[E]$ as $[E]$, for any expression E.

Translation of types

$$[\![T]\!] \stackrel{\text{def}}{=} \mathsf{o}\,\mathsf{o}\,[T]$$

$$[t] \stackrel{\text{def}}{=} t \qquad\qquad t \in \text{basic types}$$
$$[S \to T] \stackrel{\text{def}}{=} \mathsf{o}\,([\![S]\!] \times \mathsf{o}\,[T])$$

Translation of type environments

$$[\![\emptyset]\!] = [\emptyset] \stackrel{\text{def}}{=} \emptyset$$
$$[\![\Gamma, x : S]\!] \stackrel{\text{def}}{=} [\![\Gamma]\!], x : [\![S]\!] \qquad\qquad [\Gamma, x : S] \stackrel{\text{def}}{=} [\Gamma], x : [S]$$

Translation of terms

$$[\![\lambda x : S.\, M]\!]^\Gamma \stackrel{\text{def}}{=} (p).\, \overline{p}(y : [S \to T]^{\leftarrow\sharp}).\, y(x)\, [\![M]\!]^{\Gamma, x:S}$$
$$[\![x]\!]^\Gamma \stackrel{\text{def}}{=} (p).\, \overline{x}p$$
$$[\![c]\!]^\Gamma \stackrel{\text{def}}{=} (p).\, \overline{p}c$$
$$[\![MN]\!]^\Gamma \stackrel{\text{def}}{=}$$
$$(p).\, (\nu q : \sharp\, [S \to T]) \Big([\![M]\!]^\Gamma q \mid q(y).\, (\nu x : \sharp\, [S \to T])\, (\overline{y}\langle x, p\rangle.\, !x\, [\![N]\!]^\Gamma)\Big)$$

where in the clause for abstraction, T is the unique type such that $\Gamma \vdash \lambda x : S.\, M : T$ and, similarly, in the clause for application, $S \to T$ is the unique type such that $\Gamma \vdash M : S \to T$.

Table 16.3. *The encoding of $\lambda N^{\to}$ into the π-calculus*

which are the types T_V and T_A of (15.14). □

The modifications needed to the CPS grammar for untyped λN, and the injection of the terms generated by the grammar to HOπ, are the same as for call-by-value. The final step of the compilation of HOπ into π-calculus gives us the encoding of types, type environments, and terms of $\lambda N^{\to}$ into π-calculus in Table 16.3. Theorem 16.3.1 then gives:

Corollary 16.3.3 (Correctness of $\mathcal{N}$ on types) Let $M \in \Lambda\{c\}$. Then

$$\Gamma \vdash M : T \quad \text{implies} \quad \mathcal{N}[\![\Gamma]\!], p : (\mathcal{N}[\![T]\!])^- \vdash \mathcal{N}[\![M]\!]^\Gamma p\ . \qquad \square$$

The results on $\mathcal{N}$ from the untyped case, such as Corollaries 15.4.12 and 15.4.13 and Exercise 15.4.22, remain valid, with the expected modifications to the types in the statement of Corollary 15.4.13.

Remark 16.3.4 The types of π-calculus names used for the encoding of untyped λN in Section 15.4 agree with those used for $\lambda N^{\rightarrow}$ in this section, once we add the clauses

$$\mathcal{N}^{\star}[X] \stackrel{\text{def}}{=} X \qquad\qquad \mathcal{N}^{\star}[\mu X.T] \stackrel{\text{def}}{=} \mu X.\mathcal{N}^{\star}[T]\ .$$

The type `Trig` of Section 15.4 is precisely $\mathcal{N}^{\star}[\mu X.(X \rightarrow X)]$, so that Lemma 15.4.11 can be presented thus: Suppose $\mathsf{fv}(M) \subseteq \widetilde{x}$. Then

$$\widetilde{x} : \mathcal{N}[\![\mu X.(X \rightarrow X)]\!], p : (\mathcal{N}[\![\mu X.(X \rightarrow X)]\!])^{-} \vdash \mathcal{N}[\![M]\!]^{\widetilde{x}:\mu X.(X\rightarrow X)}p\ .$$

□

Remark 16.3.5 (Subtyping) As in call-by-value, so in call-by-name the encoding of types agrees with the standard subtyping rule for function types. □

Exercise* 16.3.6 Give a direct proof (i.e., without going through the CPS transform) of Corollary 16.3.3. (Hint: it is similar to Exercise 16.2.7.) □

Exercise* 16.3.7 Prove the analogue of Corollary 16.3.3 in the case that $\mathcal{N}$ is the encoding of Table 15.7. □

17

Full Abstraction

17.1 The full-abstraction problem for the π-interpretation of call-by-name

An interpretation of the λ-calculus into π-calculus, as a translation of one language into another, can be considered a form of denotational semantics. The denotation of a λ-term is an equivalence class of processes. These equivalence classes are the quotient of the π-calculus processes with respect to barbed congruence, the behavioural equivalence of the π-calculus.

In the two previous chapters, we have seen various π-calculus interpretations of λ-calculi and have shown their soundness with respect to the *axiomatic* semantics of the calculi, where equivalence between λ-terms means provable equality from an appropriate set of axioms and inference rules. In this chapter and the next, we go further and compare the π-calculus semantics with the *operational* semantics of the λ-calculus. We study the important case of the untyped call-by-name λ-calculus (λN); the problem is harder in the call-by-value case, and is briefly discussed in Section 18.5. The encoding of λN into π-calculus will be that of Table 15.4, but without i/o types. We can assume that the encoding is into the plain polyadic π-calculus ($\pi^{\sharp,\times,\mu}$), without i/o types, because Lemma 15.4.18 shows that i/o types do not affect behavioural equivalence; in Lemma 15.4.18 we indicated the encoding without i/o types as $\mathcal{N}_\sharp$.

Notation 17.1.1 From now on we omit indices that signify call-by-name; thus the relations $\longrightarrow_{\mathrm{N}}$ and $\Longrightarrow_{\mathrm{N}}$ become $\longrightarrow$ and $\Longrightarrow$, the predicates $\downarrow_{\mathrm{N}}$ and $\Downarrow_{\mathrm{N}}$ become $\downarrow$ and $\Downarrow$, and the encoding $\mathcal{N}_\sharp [\![\cdot]\!]$ becomes $[\![\cdot]\!]$. □

An interpretation of a calculus is said to be *sound* if it equates only operationally equivalent terms, *complete* if it equates all operationally equivalent terms, and *fully abstract* if it is sound and complete. We show in Section 17.3 that the π-calculus interpretation of λN is sound, but not complete.

When an interpretation of a calculus is not fully abstract, one may hope to achieve full abstraction by

(1) enriching the calculus,
(2) choosing a finer notion of operational equivalence for the calculus, or
(3) cutting down the codomain of the interpretation.

In Section 17.4 and Chapter 18 we prove full-abstraction results for the π-interpretation by following (1) and (2), respectively. In the notes at the end of the Part, we will hint that the main theorems are, by and large, independent of the behavioural equivalence chosen for the π-calculus, which suggests that (3) is less interesting. We begin by presenting the standard operational semantics of λN.

Sometimes we simply refer to λN as 'the λ-calculus'; this is partly justified by the fact that the call-by-name strategy is a *weakly normalizing* strategy, that is, a term converges under the full β-reduction of the λ-calculus iff it does so under call-by-name. (Therefore the operational equivalence relation of Definition 17.2.1 below does not change if the convergence predicate is taken to mean convergence under the full β-reduction $\longrightarrow_\beta$.)

17.2 Applicative bisimilarity

In an operational semantics, two terms are deemed equivalent if they have the same observable behaviour in all contexts. What is an appropriate notion of observability for λ-terms? We have adopted the viewpoint that what is observable of a *process* is its interactions with its environment. Regarding functions as processes, it is natural to stipulate that a (closed) λ-term is observable if it is an abstraction, which interacts with its environment by consuming an argument. (In the typed λ-calculus, also constants like integers and booleans would be observable; the integer or the boolean that a term reduces to can be thought of as the output of that term to the environment.)

Having decided what is observable, we can define barbed congruence for any reduction strategy we like, in particular for call-by-name, the strategy that interests us. As call-by-name is confluent (indeed deterministic), the definition of barbed congruence can be simplified, by removing the bisimulation clause on interactions. The definition then becomes the same as that of *Morris's context-equivalence*, sometimes called *observation equivalence* in the literature.

Definition 17.2.1 (Observation equivalence, or barbed congruence, for λN) Let $M, N \in \Lambda^0$. We say that M and N are *observationally equivalent*, or *barbed congruent*, if, in all closed contexts C, it holds that $C[M] \Downarrow$ iff $C[N] \Downarrow$. $\square$

As for the π-calculus, a tractable characterization of barbed congruence on λ-terms is useful.

Definition 17.2.2 *Applicative bisimilarity* is the largest symmetric relation, $\approx_\lambda$, on Λ^0 such that whenever $M \approx_\lambda N$,

$$M \Longrightarrow \lambda x.\, M' \text{ implies } N \Longrightarrow \lambda x.\, N' \text{ with } M'\{L/x\} \approx_\lambda N'\{L/x\} \text{ for all } L \in \Lambda^0.$$

□

Applicative bisimilarity is extended to open terms using closing substitutions: if $M, N \in \Lambda$ with $\mathsf{fv}(M,N) \subseteq \widetilde{x}$, then $M \approx_\lambda N$ if for all $\widetilde{L} \subseteq \Lambda^0$, we have $M\{\widetilde{L}/\widetilde{x}\} \approx_\lambda N\{\widetilde{L}/\widetilde{x}\}$. Observation equivalence can be extended to open terms either in the same way, using closing substitutions, or using closing contexts (that is, testing two terms M and N only in contexts C such that both $C[M]$ and $C[N]$ are closed): the two definitions are equivalent.

Theorem 17.2.3 Applicative bisimilarity and observation equivalence coincide.

Proof The proof in [AO93, page 11] is by Stoughton and uses a variant of Milner's [Mil77] and Berry's [Ber81] Context Lemma. □

Therefore, applicative bisimilarity is a direct characterization of barbed congruence on λN in the same way as labelled equivalences give direct characterizations of barbed congruence on π-calculi. In the light of this characterization, and of the fact that applicative bisimilarity is a mathematically more tractable relation than barbed congruence, we will prefer to use applicative bisimilarity rather than barbed congruence.

Exercise 17.2.4 (η **rule**)

(1) Show that the η rule is not operationally valid in the call-by-name λ-calculus, i.e., show that there is a λ-term M with $x \notin \mathsf{fv}(M)$ such that $\lambda x.\,(Mx) \not\approx_\lambda M$.

(2) Show that the η rule is valid if M is a value, i.e., if $x \notin \mathsf{fv}(\lambda y.\, N)$ then $\lambda x.\,((\lambda y.\, N)x) \approx_\lambda \lambda y.\, N$. □

17.3 Soundness and non-completeness

We now compare applicative bisimilarity with the equivalence on λ-terms induced by the encoding into π-calculus.

Definition 17.3.1 Let $M, N \in \Lambda$. We write $M =_\pi N$ if $[\![M]\!] \cong^c [\![N]\!]$. We call $=_\pi$ the *local structure of the π-interpretation*. □

Because of Lemma 15.4.23, we can work with ground bisimilarity ($\approx_g$) in place of barbed congruence. Ground bisimilarity is easier to work with.

Remark 17.3.2 The terminology in Definition 17.3.1 is consistent with the standard terminology of the λ-calculus. The local structure of a λ-model is the equality on λ-terms induced by that model (two λ-terms are equal if they have the same interpretation in the model). The encoding $[\![\cdot]\!]$ of the λ-calculus into π-calculus gives rise to a λ-model [San00]. This follows from the facts that the encoding is compositional and that it validates the $\lambda\beta$-theory. □

From the adequacy of the interpretation (Corollary 15.4.12), we can prove its operational soundness.

Theorem 17.3.3 Let $M, N \in \Lambda$. If $M =_\pi N$ then $M \approx_\lambda N$.

Proof We have to show that for all $M, N \in \Lambda$ and p, if $[\![M]\!]p \approx_g [\![N]\!]p$ then $M \approx_\lambda N$. We exploit the characterization of $\approx_\lambda$ as observation equivalence (Theorem 17.2.3).

From $[\![M]\!]p \approx_g [\![N]\!]p$ we deduce that $[\![M]\!]p \Downarrow$ iff $[\![N]\!]p \Downarrow$. Therefore since $[\![\cdot]\!]$ is compositional and $\approx_g$ is a congruence on the Asynchronous π-calculus, from $[\![M]\!]p \approx_g [\![N]\!]p$ we also deduce that $[\![C[M]]\!]p \Downarrow$ iff $[\![C[N]]\!]p \Downarrow$, for all λ-calculus contexts C. So by Corollary 15.4.12, $C[M] \Downarrow$ iff $C[N] \Downarrow$, which proves that M and N are observationally equivalent. □

While soundness is a necessary requirement for an interpretation, completeness – the converse of soundness – is a very strong demand, one that often fails. We would not expect the π-calculus semantics of the λ-calculus to be complete: the class of π-calculus contexts is much richer than the class of λ-calculus contexts, and hence potentially more discriminating. In the π-calculus one can express parallelism and non-determinism, which, as discussed in Section 14.2.2, are not expressible in the λ-calculus.

More concretely, there are at least two reasons for not expecting the π-calculus semantics to be complete. The first has to do with the call-by-name CPS transform, from which the π-calculus encoding was derived. This transform, as a translation of λN into λV, is not complete: there are terms of λN that are applicative bisimilar (and therefore operationally indistinguishable) but whose CPS images are distinguishable as terms of λV. It is reasonable to expect that the distinctions made by λV contexts can be exposed by π-calculus contexts. The second concrete reason for not expecting the π-calculus semantics to be complete is some results on the canonical model of λN. This model is defined as the solution to a domain equation [Abr87, Abr89]. The model is sound but not complete. Completeness fails because the model contains the denotations of terms that are not definable in λN, and whose addition to λN increases the discriminating power of the contexts of the language. Examples are *convergence test* and *parallel convergence test*, fairly simple operators (defined below) that one expects to be expressible in π-calculus.

Both the CPS transform and the models of λN offer good candidates for counterexamples to the completeness of the π-calculus encoding. We begin by looking at those from the models as they give insight into what makes the π-calculus more discriminating than the λ-calculus. Convergence test is a unary operator, $\mathtt{C}$, that can detect whether its argument converges; it is defined by these rules:

$$\text{C1}\ \frac{M\downarrow}{\mathtt{C}M \longrightarrow I} \qquad \text{C2}\ \frac{M \longrightarrow N}{\mathtt{C}M \longrightarrow \mathtt{C}N}$$

Parallel convergence test is a binary operator, $\mathtt{P}$, that can detect whether either of its arguments converges; it is defined by these rules:

$$\text{P1}\ \frac{M\downarrow}{\mathtt{P}MN \to I} \qquad \text{P2}\ \frac{M\downarrow}{\mathtt{P}NM \longrightarrow I}$$

$$\text{P3}\ \frac{M \longrightarrow M'}{\mathtt{P}MN \to \mathtt{P}M'N} \qquad \text{P4}\ \frac{M \longrightarrow M'}{\mathtt{P}NM \to \mathtt{P}NM'}$$

Let $\lambda\mathtt{C}$ be λN with the addition of convergence test, and let $\lambda\mathtt{P}$ be λN with the addition of parallel convergence test. In $\lambda\mathtt{P}$, convergence test is definable as $\mathtt{C}M \stackrel{\text{def}}{=} \mathtt{P}M\Omega$. Here are two terms that are operationally indistinguishable in the pure λ-calculus but that are distinguished in $\lambda\mathtt{C}$:

$$\begin{aligned} M &\stackrel{\text{def}}{=} \lambda x.\,(x(\lambda y.\,(x\Xi\Omega y))\Xi) \\ N &\stackrel{\text{def}}{=} \lambda x.\,(x(x\Xi\Omega)\Xi). \end{aligned} \tag{17.1}$$

These terms are further discussed in Remark 18.3.2.

Remark 17.3.4 There are also λ-terms that are indistinguishable in $\lambda\mathtt{C}$ but that can be distinguished in $\lambda\{\mathtt{C},\mathtt{P}\}$, hence also in $\lambda\mathtt{P}$, with the help of the parallel convergence test; see [BL96]. □

Now, to prove that the π-calculus semantics is strictly finer than the operational semantics of the λ-calculus, it suffices to show that convergence test or parallel convergence test is definable in π-calculus. Here are their definitions; as usual, by our convention on bound names in encodings (Section 15.2), names q, r, and a are fresh:

$$[\![\mathtt{C}M]\!] \stackrel{\text{def}}{=} (p).\,\boldsymbol{\nu} q\,(q(x).\,[\![I]\!]p \mid [\![M]\!]q) \tag{17.2}$$

$$[\![\mathtt{P}MN]\!] \stackrel{\text{def}}{=} (p).\,(\boldsymbol{\nu} q, r, a\,)(q(x).\,\overline{a} \mid r(x).\,\overline{a} \mid [\![M]\!]q \mid [\![N]\!]r \mid a.\,[\![I]\!]p)\,. \quad (17.3)$$

Exercise 17.3.5

(1) Show that $[\![\mathtt{C}\lambda x.\, M]\!] \approx_{\mathrm{g}} [\![I]\!]$, whereas $[\![\mathtt{C}\Omega]\!] \;{}_{\mathrm{g}}\!\succeq [\![\Omega]\!]$.

(2) Show that, for all terms M, N of $\lambda\mathtt{P}$:

(a) $[\![\mathtt{P}(\lambda x.\, M)N]\!] \approx_{\mathrm{g}} [\![I]\!]$, and $[\![\mathtt{P}N(\lambda x.\, M)]\!] \approx_{\mathrm{g}} [\![I]\!]$

(b) $[\![\mathtt{P}\Omega\Omega)]\!] \approx_{\mathrm{g}} [\![\Omega]\!]$. □

Corollary 17.3.6 (Non-completeness of the π-interpretation) Suppose $M, N \in \Lambda$. Then $M \approx_\lambda N$ does not imply $M =_\pi N$.

Proof Take the terms M and N in (17.1). These terms are applicative bisimilar (see Remark 18.3.2). However, $M \neq_\pi N$ (Exercise 17.3.7). □

Exercise 17.3.7 Prove that $[\![M]\!] \not\approx_{\mathrm{g}} [\![N]\!]$, for M, N as in (17.1). (Hint: prove that $[\![\mathtt{C}M]\!]p \not\approx_{\mathrm{g}} [\![\mathtt{C}N]\!]p$, and for this use Exercise 17.3.5.) □

We may now ask whether the addition of parallel convergence test to λN is enough to give the same discriminating power as the π-calculus. The canonical domain model of λN mentioned earlier is fully abstract for $\lambda\mathtt{P}$; therefore tackling this question is also comparing the model with the π-calculus interpretation. We will see in the next section that the answer is negative: the π-calculus semantics is strictly finer.

Exercise* 17.3.8 This exercise invites the reader to prove that in the simpler encoding of call-by-name in Table 15.7, convergence test is not definable if we use only the operators of the Asynchronous π-calculus. (To make the exercise simpler, we work with ground bisimilarity instead of barbed congruence.) Let $\mathcal{M}$ be the encoding of Table 15.7. Prove that there are no context C of the Asynchronous π-calculus and names q, p such that

$$\begin{array}{rcl} C[\mathcal{M}[\![\Xi]\!]q] & \approx_{\mathrm{g}} & \mathcal{M}[\![I]\!]p \\ C[\mathcal{M}[\![\Omega]\!]q] & \approx_{\mathrm{g}} & \mathcal{M}[\![\Omega]\!]p\,. \end{array}$$

(Hint: prove, by induction on n, that there are no $n \geq 0$ and context C such that

$$\begin{array}{rcl} C[\mathcal{M}[\![\Xi]\!]q] & (\stackrel{\tau}{\longrightarrow})^n \stackrel{p\langle x,r\rangle}{\longrightarrow}\Longrightarrow\approx_{\mathrm{g}} & \mathcal{M}[\![x]\!]r \\ C[\mathcal{M}[\![\Omega]\!]q] & \approx_{\mathrm{g}} & \mathcal{M}[\![\Omega]\!]p \end{array}$$

for fresh names x, r. For this, reason by contradiction. You might need also the following result: for all $\widetilde{p}$, P, Q, if $\boldsymbol{\nu}\widetilde{p}\,(P \mid Q) \approx_{\mathrm{g}} \mathbf{0}$ then also $\boldsymbol{\nu}\widetilde{p}\,P \approx_{\mathrm{g}} \mathbf{0}$.) □

On the non-completeness of the π-interpretation, see also Remark 18.3.17 and Exercise 18.3.18.

17.4 Extending the λ-calculus

We have seen that the π-interpretation is sound but not fully abstract. We now study how to achieve full abstraction by enriching the λ-calculus. We have already seen extensions of the λ-calculus: $\lambda\mathtt{C}$ obtained by adding convergence test, and $\lambda\mathtt{P}$ obtained by adding parallel convergence test. Another interesting extension is $\lambda\mathtt{U}$, obtained by adding the *internal choice* (or *unconditional choice*) operator U defined by

$$\mathtt{U1}\ \frac{}{\mathtt{U}MN \longrightarrow M} \qquad \mathtt{U2}\ \frac{}{\mathtt{U}MN \longrightarrow N}$$

Exercise 17.4.1 Extend the encoding of Table 15.4 to an encoding of $\lambda\mathtt{U}$. □

By an operator we mean a symbol with reduction rules defining its behaviour:

Definition 17.4.2 A *signature* Σ is a pair $(\mathcal{O}, r)$ where $\mathcal{O}$ is a set of *operator symbols*, disjoint from the set of λ-variables, and r is a *rank function* that assigns an arity to each operator symbol. □

Definition 17.4.3 If $\Sigma = (\mathcal{O}, r)$ is a signature then the set $\Lambda\Sigma$ of *λ-terms extended with operators in* Σ is defined by

$$M ::= pM_1 \dots M_{r(p)} \mid x \mid \lambda x.\, M \mid M_1 M_2, \qquad \text{where } p \in \mathcal{O}. \qquad (17.4)$$

We write $\Lambda\Sigma^0$ for the set of terms in $\Lambda\Sigma$ without free variables (the closed terms). An *extended λ-term* is a member of some $\Lambda\Sigma$. □

To define the behaviour of extended λ-terms, we need operational rules for the operators of the extension. In general, the operational rules of an operator are of two kinds: *evaluation rules* such as C2, P3, P4 for evaluating arguments of an operator, and *δ-rules* such as C1, P1, P2, U1, U2, for manipulating the operator. To give a formal definition of these kinds of rules, we need a metalanguage for talking about terms of a generic extended λ-calculus. The grammar for the metalanguage is just that of the extended λ-calculus, Grammar (17.4), plus metavariables. We have used letters M and N for metavariables so far, so we stick to this convention. We write $A \in \Lambda\Sigma^0(M_1, \dots, M_n)$ if A is a closed metaterm that may contain metavariables among $M_1, \dots, M_n$.

Definition 17.4.4 (Well-formed operators) Let $\Sigma = (\mathcal{O}, r)$ be a signature and $p \in \mathcal{O}$. A *δ-rule for p (in Σ)* is an axiom of the form

$$\frac{\{M_i \downarrow \mid \ i \in I\} \qquad (\text{for } I \subseteq \{1, \dots r(p)\})}{pM_1 \dots M_{r(p)} \longrightarrow A}$$

where $A \in \Lambda\Sigma^0(M_1, \dots, M_{r(p)})$. In this case, we also say that the rule *tests position* i, for all $i \in I$.

An *evaluation rule for p (in Σ)* is an inference rule of the form

$$\frac{M_i \longrightarrow M_i' \qquad (\text{for } i \in \{1, \dots, r(p)\})}{pM_1 \dots M_i \dots M_{r(p)} \longrightarrow pM_1 \dots M_i' \dots M_{r(p)}}$$

We say that the rule *evaluates position* i.

Let R be a set of δ-rules and evaluation rules for the operators in Σ such that for all $p \in \mathcal{O}$ and $1 \le i \le r(p)$, if in R there is a δ-rule for p that tests position i then there is also an evaluation rule for p that evaluates that position. In this case, we say that (Σ, R) is a *specification of well-formed operators.* □

If $\mathcal{S} \stackrel{\text{def}}{=} (\Sigma, R)$ is a specification of well-formed operators, and $M, N \in \Lambda\Sigma$, we write $M \longrightarrow_{\mathcal{S}} N$ if $M \longrightarrow N$ is derivable from the rules in R together with the rules β and μ of λN. The rules in R together with the rules β and μ are *the operational rules of* $\lambda\mathcal{S}$. Further, $\lambda\mathcal{S}$ is the *extended λ-calculus with set of terms $\Lambda\Sigma$ and reduction relation* $\longrightarrow_{\mathcal{S}}$. Relation $\Longrightarrow_{\mathcal{S}}$ is the reflexive and transitive closure of $\longrightarrow_{\mathcal{S}}$, and $M \Downarrow_{\mathcal{S}}$ means $M \Longrightarrow_{\mathcal{S}} N \downarrow$, for some N.

When there is no ambiguity, we drop some indices; thus if $\Sigma = (\mathcal{O}, r)$, we may write $\Lambda\mathcal{O}$ for $\Lambda\Sigma$, and $\Longrightarrow$ for $\Longrightarrow_{\Sigma}$, and $M \Downarrow$ for $M \Downarrow_{\mathcal{S}}$.

The reader might like to check that the rules describing the operators $\mathtt{C}, \mathtt{P}, \mathtt{U}$ in this and in the previous section, fit the format of Definition 17.4.4.

Lemma 17.4.5 Let $\mathcal{S} = (\Sigma, R)$ and $M \in \Lambda\Sigma^0$. If $M \longrightarrow_{\mathcal{S}} N$ then $N \in \Lambda\Sigma^0$. □

Exercise 17.4.6 We can define an operator @ that expresses call-by-value application. Its rules use an auxiliary operator @′:

$$@1\ \frac{M \longrightarrow M'}{@MN \longrightarrow @M'N} \qquad @2\ \frac{M \downarrow}{@MN \longrightarrow @'MN}$$

$$@'1\ \frac{N \longrightarrow N'}{@'MN \longrightarrow @MN'} \qquad @'2\ \frac{N \downarrow}{@'MN \longrightarrow MN}$$

For $M \in \Lambda$ let $\underline{M}$ be the term of $\Lambda\{@, @'\}$ obtained by replacing all subterms of M of the form M_1M_2 with $@M_1M_2$. Show that if $M, N \in \Lambda^0$, then $M \longrightarrow_{\mathrm{V}} N$ iff $\underline{M} \longrightarrow^3 \underline{N}$. □

Definition 17.4.7 Let $\mathcal{S} = (\Sigma, R)$ be a specification of well-formed operators. We say that $\mathcal{S}$ is *Church–Rosser* (*CR*) if $\Longrightarrow_{\mathcal{S}}$ has the Church–Rosser property; that is, for all $M, N, L \in \Lambda\Sigma$, if $M \Longrightarrow_{\mathcal{S}} N$ and $M \Longrightarrow_{\mathcal{S}} L$, then there is M' such that $N \Longrightarrow_{\mathcal{S}} M'$ and $L \Longrightarrow_{\mathcal{S}} M'$. □

We sometimes abbreviate the terminology, saying that $\mathcal{O}$ is a set of well-formed operators or, if $\longrightarrow_{\mathcal{O}}$ is CR, that $\mathcal{O}$ is CR. Observe that if $\longrightarrow_{\mathcal{O}}$ is deterministic then $\mathcal{O}$ is CR.

The sets $\{\mathtt{C}\}$ and $\{\mathtt{P}\}$ are CR. But many operators break the CR property. A simple example is unconditional choice $\mathtt{U}$; for instance, we have both $\mathtt{U}\Omega I \Longrightarrow \Omega$ and $\mathtt{U}\Omega I \Longrightarrow I$, but I and Ω have no common derivative. An even simpler example of a non-CR operator is $\mathtt{U}_\bot$ defined by the rules

$$\mathtt{U}_\bot 1 \ \frac{}{\mathtt{U}_\bot M \longrightarrow M} \qquad \mathtt{U}_\bot 2 \ \frac{}{\mathtt{U}_\bot M \longrightarrow \Omega}$$

This operator is definable from $\mathtt{U}$ thus: $\mathtt{U}_\bot \stackrel{\text{def}}{=} \mathtt{U}\Omega$.

To generalize the definition of applicative bisimilarity to an extended λ-calculus, we add a clause for internal activity (clause (2) of Definition 17.4.8 below). This clause is important if the set of operators is not CR, for detecting the branching structure of terms, as Example 17.4.9 shows. The clause can be omitted when the added operators are CR since then a derivative of a term is bisimilar to that term (Lemma 17.4.12).

Definition 17.4.8 Let $\mathcal{S} = (\Sigma, R)$ be a specification of well-formed operators. *Applicative $\mathcal{S}$-bisimilarity* is the largest symmetric relation, $\approx_{\mathcal{S}}$, on $\Lambda\Sigma^0$ such that whenever $M \approx_{\mathcal{S}} N$:

(1) $M \Longrightarrow_{\mathcal{S}} \lambda x.\, M'$ implies $N \Longrightarrow_{\mathcal{S}} \lambda x.\, N'$ with $M'\{L/x\} \approx_{\mathcal{S}} N'\{L/x\}$ for all $L \in \Lambda\Sigma^0$

(2) $M \Longrightarrow_{\mathcal{S}} M'$ implies $N \Longrightarrow_{\mathcal{S}} \approx_{\mathcal{S}} M'$. □

It is easy to see that $\approx_{\mathcal{S}}$ is an equivalence relation. (Indeed it is a congruence, as can be proved using Howe's technique [How96].) Again, if $\mathcal{S} = ((\mathcal{O}, r), R)$ we sometimes drop indices and write $\approx_{\mathcal{O}}$ for $\approx_{\mathcal{S}}$. Further, when $\mathcal{O}$ is a singleton $\{p\}$, we write $\approx_p$ for $\approx_{\mathcal{S}}$. Relation $\approx_{\mathcal{S}}$ is extended to open terms in the usual way, by means of closing substitutions.

Example 17.4.9 It holds that $I \not\approx_{\mathtt{U}} \mathtt{U}I\Omega$, since the latter has the reduction $\mathtt{U}I\Omega \Longrightarrow \Omega$ which the former cannot match. This distinction is sensible, since I always accepts an input whereas $\mathtt{U}I\Omega$ can also refuse to. The terms I and $\mathtt{U}I\Omega$ would be equated without clause (2) of Definition 17.4.8. □

Remark 17.4.10 The format of the rules that we have used for defining well-formed operators ensures that the operators are well-behaved, in the sense that their behaviour depends only on the semantics – not on the syntax – of their operands. The format captures a large and interesting class of such well-behaved operators, but not all of them. For instance, the format allows the evaluation of the argument of an operator, but does not allow evaluating such an argument in some context. Also, the format does not allow rules with negative premises. The format can be extended in several ways to capture larger classes of well-behaved operators. It is good to realize, however, that the format *cannot be arbitrary*, if we wish the behaviour of operators not to depend on the syntax of their operands. For instance, an operator p with a rule

$$\frac{M \longrightarrow \Omega}{pM \longrightarrow I} \tag{17.5}$$

is disastrous. The rule looks at the syntax of the derivative to which the operand M reduces, by demanding that this derivative shall be syntactically equal to Ω. Using p we can distinguish terms such as Ω and $\Omega\Omega$, since $p\Omega \Longrightarrow I$ whereas $p(\Omega\Omega)$ has no reductions. It is quite unnatural to distinguish between Ω and $\Omega\Omega$, however: both are divergent terms, without any observable behaviour. With rules like (17.5) it would be difficult to define interesting behavioural equivalences that are congruences. □

We base our operational study of $\lambda\mathcal{S}$ on $\approx_{\mathcal{S}}$, because it seems a reasonable notion of behavioural equivalence, and because it is more tractable than barbed congruence (the obvious generalization of Definition 17.2.1). It is not known whether, in general, $\approx_{\mathcal{S}}$ coincides with barbed congruence, although it is known that it does in certain cases and no counterexamples are known.

17.4.1 The discriminating power of extended λ-calculi

We now compare $=_\pi$ (the local structure of the π-interpretation) and the relations $\approx_{\mathcal{S}}$. Since they may be defined on different classes of terms, we compare them on the common core of closed pure λ-terms. We present some of the results without digging into the details of their proofs, which are fairly elaborate.

The first result is that $=_\pi$ is at least as discriminating as any applicative $\mathcal{S}$-bisimilarity. That is, λ-terms that cannot be distinguished as π-calculus processes cannot be distinguished by any extension of the λ-calculus.

Theorem 17.4.11 Let $M, N \in \Lambda$. Then $M =_\pi N$ implies $M \approx_{\mathcal{S}} N$, for any $\mathcal{S}$.

Proof This theorem is proved by going through a characterization of $=_\pi$ similar to that in terms of Lévy–Longo Trees that we will study in Chapter 18. We omit the details; see [San94]. □

The next question is whether there are sets of well-formed operators for which the converse of Theorem 17.4.11 is true and, if so, what is a minimal such set. These are interesting problems, for their solution will tell us what it is necessary to add to the λ-calculus to make it as discriminating as the π-calculus.

We begin by looking at sets of CR operators. We show that sets of CR operators do not give full discriminating power. In the remainder of this section, we write *CR* for an arbitrary set of CR operators.

Lemma 17.4.12 Let $M \in \Lambda CR$. If $M \Longrightarrow N$ then $M \approx_{CR} N$. □

Corollary 17.4.13 In λCR the following conditional η rule holds:

$$M \Downarrow \text{ implies } \lambda y.\,(My) \approx_{CR} M\,.$$

Proof By hypothesis, $M \Longrightarrow \lambda x.\,M'$. By repeated application of Lemma 17.4.12, and since $\approx_{CR}$ is a congruence,

$$\lambda y.\,(My) \approx_{CR} \lambda y.\,((\lambda x.\,M')y) \approx_{CR} \lambda y.\,(M'\{y/x\}) = \lambda x.\,M' \approx_{CR} M.$$

□

Theorem 17.4.14 Let $M, N \in \Lambda$. Then $M \approx_{CR} N$ does not imply $M =_\pi N$.

Proof Take $M = \lambda x.\,(xx)$ and $N = \lambda x.\,(x\lambda y.\,(xy))$. It holds that $M \neq_\pi N$. This can be proved directly, but it is even simpler to derive it from the characterization of $=_\pi$ in terms of Lévy–Longo Trees in Section 18.3.

However, $M \approx_{CR} N$. For this, we have to prove that for each $R \in \Lambda CR$, $RR \approx_{CR} R\lambda y.\,(Ry)$. There are two cases, depending on whether R is convergent or not. If R is convergent, then $RR \approx_{CR} R\lambda y.\,(Ry)$ using Corollary 17.4.13; if it is not then $RR \approx_{CR} \Omega \approx_{CR} R\lambda y.\,(Ry)$. □

Remark 17.4.15 Since the parallel convergence test operator P is Church–Rosser, Theorem 17.4.14 also proves that $=_\pi$ is finer than $\approx_{\mathtt{P}}$. Therefore the local structure of the canonical domain of λN [Abr87, Abr89], which coincides with $\approx_{\mathtt{P}}$, is different from that of the π-interpretation. □

Theorem 17.4.14 shows that we cannot achieve the discriminating power of π-calculus by a confluent extension to the λ-calculus. The next theorem shows that, in contrast, this is possible with non-confluent extensions. For this, it suffices to use one of the simplest forms of non-confluent operator one could think of: the unary operator $\mathtt{U}_\perp$, which when applied to some argument either returns this argument or diverges.

Theorem 17.4.16 Let $M, N \in \Lambda$. Then $M \approx_{\mathtt{U}_\perp} N$ implies $M =_\pi N$. □

This theorem is proved in [San94] using a variant of the Böhm-out technique. This result, together with Theorem 17.4.11, shows that any non-confluent extension of λN in which $\mathtt{U}_\perp$ is expressible can be encoded in π-calculus in a way that is fully abstract on pure λ-terms. (By developing this result further, it should actually be possible to prove that the encoding is fully abstract on all terms of the extended λ-calculus, provided that the operators of the extension can be faithfully encoded.)

17.4.2 Interpreting extended λ-calculi

In this section we show how to encode extended λ-calculi into π-calculus. This should be thought of mainly as an exercise with the π-calculus; the reader may safely skip the section.

We add the following constraint to the definition (17.4.4) of well-formed operators: for each operator p, if p has a rule that evaluates position i, then each of the δ-rules for p either tests position i or has a conclusion $pM_1 \ldots M_{r(p)} \longrightarrow A$ where M_i does not occur in A. This is, pragmatically, a reasonable constraint; it is satisfied by the operators encountered so far, such as $\mathtt{C}$, $\mathtt{P}$, $\mathtt{U}$, and @. Without this constraint the encoding would be very complex. For instance, it is possible to mimic a λ-calculus reduction strategy that has rules β, μ, and ν; as discussed in Section 15.7 this combination of rules is hard to encode.

Fix one such signature Σ and specification of well-formed operators $\mathcal{S} \stackrel{\text{def}}{=} (\Sigma, R)$. To make the encoding of $\lambda\mathcal{S}$ into the π-calculus easier to read, we assume that Σ contains a single operator $\mathtt{Q}$ of arity 2, with δ-rules

$$\mathtt{Q1}\ \frac{N_1 \downarrow \quad N_2 \downarrow}{\mathtt{Q}N_1N_2 \longrightarrow A_1} \qquad \mathtt{Q2}\ \frac{N_1 \downarrow \quad N_2 \downarrow}{\mathtt{Q}N_1N_2 \longrightarrow A_2}$$

(where A_1 and A_2 are some terms in $\Lambda\mathtt{Q}^0(N_1, N_2)$) and evaluation rules

$$\textsc{ev}1\ \frac{N_1 \longrightarrow N_1'}{\mathtt{Q}N_1N_2 \longrightarrow \mathtt{Q}N_1'N_2} \qquad \textsc{ev}2\ \frac{N_2 \longrightarrow N_2'}{\mathtt{Q}N_1N_2 \longrightarrow \mathtt{Q}N_1N_2'}$$

for evaluating the two arguments of $\mathtt{Q}$. We wish to encode this extended λ-calculus $\lambda\mathtt{Q}$ into π-calculus.

The main problem is to define the encoding of a $\Lambda\mathtt{Q}$-term $\mathtt{Q}M_1M_2$. The encoding of the other constructs (abstraction, application, and variable) is as in

Section 15.4, but with the non-linear encoding of abstraction discussed in Remark 15.4.10 and used in the encoding of λN in Table 15.6. (It is necessary to use this encoding as, due to the rules of Q, an argument of Q that reduces to a function may be used more than once.)

Remark 17.4.17 Adding the replication in the definition of abstraction does not affect the local structure of the π-interpretation (see the discussion in Remark 18.3.16). □

We present an encoding that is easy to reason about and is flexible – so that if we modify the rules for Q it is easy to modify the encoding (see Exercises 17.4.19 and 17.4.20). We will consider optimizations of the encoding in Exercises 17.4.21–17.4.25. The enterprising reader might like to try the encoding of $\mathtt{Q}M_1M_2$ before reading further.

We define the encoding of a term $\mathtt{Q}M_1M_2 \in \Lambda\mathtt{Q}$ thus:

$$[\![\mathtt{Q}M_1M_2]\!] \stackrel{\text{def}}{=} (p).\,(\boldsymbol{\nu}\widetilde{h},\widetilde{d},\widetilde{e},a\,)\Big(\begin{array}{l} \;\;!h_1\,[\![M_1]\!] \mid !h_2\,[\![M_2]\!] \\ \mid\; \mathtt{EV}_1\langle h_1,d_1,d_2\rangle \mid \mathtt{EV}_2\langle h_2,e_1,e_2\rangle \\ \mid\; \mathtt{OP}_1\langle d_1,e_1,a\rangle \mid \mathtt{OP}_2\langle d_2,e_2,a\rangle \\ \mid\; \overline{a}p\Big)\end{array} \tag{17.6}$$

where $\widetilde{h}$ stands for h_1, h_2, and similarly for $\widetilde{d}$ and $\widetilde{e}$, and where

$$\mathtt{OP}_1\langle d_1,e_1,a\rangle \stackrel{\text{def}}{=} d_1(x_1).\,e_1(x_2).\,a\,[\![A_1\{x_1,x_2/N_1,N_2\}]\!] \qquad x_1,x_2 \text{ fresh for } A_1$$

$$\mathtt{EV}_1\langle h_1,d_1,d_2\rangle \stackrel{\text{def}}{=} \overline{h_1}(r).\,r(v).\,\boldsymbol{\nu}z\,(\overline{d_1}z \mid \overline{d_2}z \mid !z(r).\,\overline{r}(w).\,!w \rightarrow v)$$

and similarly for $\mathtt{OP}_2\langle d_2,e_2,a\rangle$ and $\mathtt{EV}_2\langle h_2,e_1,e_2\rangle$. We briefly explain these definitions. The process $\mathtt{OP}_1\langle d_1,e_1,a\rangle$ implements the δ-rule Q1. It waits for signals at d_1 and e_1 from $\mathtt{EV}_1\langle h_1,d_1,d_2\rangle$ and $\mathtt{EV}_2\langle h_2,e_1,e_2\rangle$, indicating that the arguments M_1 and M_2 have become values (i.e., functions). Then $\mathtt{OP}_1\langle d_1,e_1,a\rangle$ tries to grab the lock at a; if it succeeds, then the rule may be completed, and A_1 gets evaluated. If the lock cannot be grabbed, $\mathtt{OP}_1\langle d_1,e_1,a\rangle$ is garbage. Only one of $\mathtt{OP}_1\langle d_1,e_1,a\rangle$ and $\mathtt{OP}_2\langle d_2,e_2,a\rangle$ can grab the lock, so only one of the δ-rules can be completed.

$\mathtt{EV}_1\langle h_1,d_1,d_2\rangle$ controls the evaluation of the argument M_1 (and $\mathtt{EV}_2\langle h_2,e_1,e_2\rangle$ that of M_2). First, $\mathtt{EV}_1\langle h_1,d_1,d_2\rangle$ triggers the evaluation of M_1. When M_1 signals that it has reduced to a value, M_1' say, then $\mathtt{EV}_1\langle h_1,d_1,d_2\rangle$ informs $\mathtt{OP}_1\langle d_1,e_1,a\rangle$ and $\mathtt{OP}_2\langle d_2,e_2,a\rangle$, using names d_1 and d_2. In these actions at d_1 and d_2, a pointer z is passed, which the recipient can use to activate copies of M_1'.

Exercise 17.4.18

(1) For all $M_1, M_2 \in \Lambda\mathtt{Q}$, it holds that

$$\mathtt{Q}(\lambda x.\, M_1)(\lambda y.\, M_2) \longrightarrow A_1\{\lambda x.\, M_1, \lambda y.\, M_2/N_1, N_2\}.$$

Prove that

$$\begin{aligned}\llbracket \mathtt{Q}(\lambda x.\, M_1)(\lambda y.\, M_2)\rrbracket p \approx_{\mathrm{g}} \xrightarrow{\tau} \approx_{\mathrm{g}} (\boldsymbol{\nu} z_1, z_2\,)(\ & \llbracket A_1\{z_1, z_2/N_1, N_2\}\rrbracket p \\ & \mid !z_1\, \llbracket \lambda x.\, M_1\rrbracket \\ & \mid !z_2\, \llbracket \lambda y.\, M_2\rrbracket)\,.\end{aligned}$$

(2) Show that, for all $M, N \in \Lambda\mathtt{Q}$ with $x \notin \mathsf{fv}(N)$,

$$\llbracket M\rrbracket\, \{x = \llbracket N\rrbracket\} \approx_{\mathrm{g}} \llbracket M\{N/x\}\rrbracket\,.$$

(Hint: add one case in the inductive proof of Exercise 15.4.20.) □

Exercise 17.4.19 Suppose that rules Q1 and Q2 were not to test position 2 (i.e., their premise were simply $N_1 \downarrow$) and there were no evaluation rule EV2. How should the definition of $\mathtt{EV}_2\langle h_2, e_1, e_2\rangle$ in (17.6) be modified (the other components should remain the same)? □

Exercise 17.4.20 Suppose that the δ-rules of Q are modified so that rule $\mathtt{Q}i$ ($i = 1, 2$) tests only position i (i.e., the premise of $\mathtt{Q}i$ is simply $N_i \downarrow$) and its derivative A_i does not contain metavariable N_j ($j \neq i$). How should the definitions of $\mathtt{EV}_1\langle h_1, d_1, d_2\rangle$ and $\mathtt{EV}_2\langle h_2, e_1, e_2\rangle$ in (17.6) be modified? □

In some cases, the encodings obtained following the schema above can be optimized, as shown in the exercises below.

Exercise* 17.4.21

(1) Prove that, for $\llbracket \mathtt{Q}M_1M_2\rrbracket$ as defined in (17.6), we have, for all $M_1, M_2 \in \Lambda\mathtt{Q}$,

$$\begin{aligned}\llbracket \mathtt{Q}M_1M_2\rrbracket p \approx_{\mathrm{g}} (\boldsymbol{\nu} d, e, q_1, q_2)\Big(\ & \llbracket M_1\rrbracket q_1 \mid \llbracket M_2\rrbracket q_2 \\ & \mid q_1(v).\, \overline{d}(z).\, !z(r).\, \overline{r}(w).\, !w \multimap v \\ & \mid q_2(v).\, \overline{e}(z).\, !z(r).\, \overline{r}(w).\, !w \multimap v \\ & \mid d(x_1).\, e(x_2).\, (\ \tau.\, \llbracket A_1\{x_1, x_2/N_1, N_2\}\rrbracket p \\ & \qquad + \tau.\, \llbracket A_2\{x_1, x_2/N_1, N_2\}\rrbracket p)\Big)\,.\end{aligned}$$

(2) Exhibit two terms $M_1, M_2 \in \Lambda\mathtt{Q}$ such that

$$
\begin{array}{l}
[\![\mathtt{Q} M_1 M_2]\!]p \not\approx_{\mathrm{g}} \\
\quad (\boldsymbol{\nu} d, e, q_1, q_2)\Big([\![M_1]\!]q_1 \mid [\![M_2]\!]q_2 \\
\qquad \mid q_1(v_1).\, q_2(v_2). \\
\qquad\quad (\boldsymbol{\nu} z_1, z_2)(\; !z_1(r).\, \overline{r}(w).\, !w \multimap v_1 \\
\qquad\qquad \mid !z_2(r).\, \overline{r}(w).\, !w \multimap v_2 \\
\qquad\qquad \mid (\; \tau.\, [\![A_1\{^{z_1, z_2}\!/\!_{N_1, N_2}\}]\!]p \\
\qquad\qquad\quad + \tau.\, [\![A_2\{^{z_1, z_2}\!/\!_{N_1, N_2}\}]\!]p))\Big) .
\end{array}
$$

(Hint: M_1 and M_2 can be *open* terms. You may also find item (1) of the exercise useful.) □

Exercise 17.4.22 Write down an encoding $\mathcal{W}$ of $\lambda\mathtt{P}$ (operator $\mathtt{P}$ is parallel convergence test, defined in Section 17.3) following the schema for encoding well-formed operators indicated above.

Prove that if $\mathcal{A}$ is the encoding defined like $\mathcal{W}$ but with clause (17.3) in place of (17.6), then for all $M \in \Lambda\mathtt{P}$, it holds that $\mathcal{W}[\![M]\!] \approx_{\mathrm{g}} \mathcal{A}[\![M]\!]$. □

Exercise 17.4.23 Repeat Exercise 17.4.22 for $\lambda\mathtt{U}$, where the encoding $\mathcal{A}$ uses the clause for $\mathtt{U}$ from Exercise 17.4.1. □

Exercise* 17.4.24 Let @ and @′ be the operators, and $\underline{M}$ the transformation of a λ-term M, defined in Exercise 17.4.6. Define an encoding $\mathcal{W}$ of $\lambda\{@, @'\}$ following the schema above for translating well-formed operators. Prove that, if $\mathcal{U}^*_{\mathrm{V}}$ is the encoding of λV in Exercise 15.5.3 (this encoding is a simple variant of that in Table 15.6), then for all $M \in \Lambda$ it holds that $\mathcal{W}[\![\underline{M}]\!] \approx_{\mathrm{g}} \mathcal{U}^*_{\mathrm{V}}[\![M]\!]$. (Note: in this exercise we are using $\mathcal{U}^*_{\mathrm{V}}$, which is a variant of the encoding in Table 15.6, because in this way the proof does not require i/o types and therefore can be carried out with simpler theory; see also Remark 15.5.2.) □

Exercise 17.4.25 Prove that, using receptive types, the last component in the definition of $\mathtt{EV}_1\langle h_1, d_1, d_2\rangle$, namely $!z(r).\, \overline{r}(w).\, !w \multimap v$, can be simplified to $!z(r).\, \overline{r}v$. (Hint: it is similar to the optimization of (15.19).) □

18

The Local Structure of the Interpretations

The local structure of the π-interpretation, $=_\pi$, is the behavioural equivalence induced on λ-terms by their encoding into π-calculus. In the previous chapter we proved a characterization of $=_\pi$ as the operational equivalence of extended λ-calculi. We continue the study of $=_\pi$ in this chapter, with the purpose of understanding the meaning of function equality when functions are interpreted as processes. We will prove characterizations of $=_\pi$ in terms of tree structures that are an important part of the theory of the λ-calculus. This will show that the equivalence induced by the π-calculus encoding is a natural one. It will also show the utility of some of the π-calculus proof techniques of Section 2.4.3: using techniques such as 'bisimulation up to context' and 'bisimulation up to expansion', the proofs of the main theorems will be much easier than they would have been otherwise.

The main result says that $=_\pi$ coincides with *LT equality*, whereby two λ-terms are equal iff they have the same *Lévy–Longo Trees.* Lévy–Longo Trees are the lazy variant of *Böhm Trees.* We will also discuss modifications of the π-calculus interpretation so that its local structure is the analogous *BT equality.* We begin by recalling what LTs are. A reader familiar with them may go straight to Theorem 18.3.1.

We maintain Notation 17.1.1 throughout the chapter.

18.1 Sensible theories and lazy theories

Böhm Trees (BTs) are the best-known tree structure in the λ-calculus. BTs play a central role in the classical theory of the λ-calculus. The local structure of some of the most influential models of the λ-calculus, like Scott and Plotkin's $P\omega$, Plotkin's T^ω, and Plotkin and Engeler's D_A, is precisely the BT equality; and the local structure of Scott's D_∞ (historically the first mathematical, i.e., non-syntactical, model of the untyped λ-calculus) is the equality of the 'infinite η contraction' of BTs.

BTs naturally give rise to a tree topology that has been used for the proof of some seminal results of the λ-calculus such as Berry's Sequentiality Theorem. BTs were introduced by Barendregt [Bar77], and so called after Böhm's theorem and proof about separability of λ-terms. The proof technique for this theorem, called the *Böhm-out technique*, roughly consists in finding a context capable of isolating a given subtree of a BT; in this way, certain λ-terms that have different BTs may be separated.

BTs are at the heart of the classical theory of the λ-calculus, sometimes referred to as the *sensible theory*. In this theory, a λ-term is meaningful just if it is *solvable*, that is, it has a *head normal form* (*hnf*). The *unsolvable* terms, that is, the terms without hnf, are identified as the 'meaningless terms'. In the mathematical models for this theory, the unsolvable terms are those terms whose image is the least element of the model (the undefined or bottom element). The BT of a term conveys the essential behavioural content of that term under this proposal.

An hnf is a term of the form $\lambda\widetilde{x}.\, y\widetilde{M}$. Examples of terms without an hnf are Ω, $\lambda x.\,\Omega$, and Ξ (recall that Ξ satisfies the equation $\lambda\beta \vdash \Xi = (\lambda x.\,)^n\Xi$, for all n). Finding the hnf of a term requires computing underneath λ, in order to uncover the head variable after a sequence of λ's. Computing underneath λ is a moot decision; for instance it does not reflect the practice of programming language implementations. An alternative proposal for identifying the meaningful terms does not require computing under λ: it uses *weak head normal forms* (*whnf*'s) in place of hnf's. A whnf is a term of the form $\lambda x.\, M$ or $x\widetilde{M}$. This second proposal forms the basis of the *lazy theory*. Its tree structures are the Lévy–Longo Trees. There are interesting mathematical models of the λ-calculus whose local structure is precisely the LT equality; see [Ong88].

As an example, the terms $\lambda x.\,\Omega$ and Ω are distinguished in the lazy theory because only the former has a whnf; but they are identified as meaningless in the sensible theory because neither has an hnf. Similarly, Ξ and $\lambda x.\,\Omega$ are meaningless in a sensible theory, but are meaningful and distinguished in a lazy theory (they are distinguished by feeding an argument since, for all N, ΞN has a whnf, whereas $(\lambda x.\,\Omega)N$ does not).

18.2 Lévy–Longo Trees

To define Lévy–Longo Trees (LTs) we need the notions of the *proper order* of a term, and *head reduction*, which we now introduce. We use n to range over the set of non-negative integers and ω to represent the first limit ordinal.

The *order* of a term M expresses the maximum length of the outermost sequence of λ-abstractions in a term to which M is β-convertible; it says how 'higher-order' M is. More precisely, M has order n if n is the largest i such that $\lambda\beta \vdash M = \lambda x_1 \ldots x_i. N$, for some N. Therefore a term has order 0 if it is not β-convertible to any abstraction. The remaining terms are assigned order ω; they are terms such as Ξ that can reduce to an unbounded number of nested abstractions. A term has *proper order* n if it has order of unsolvability n, i.e., after the initial n λ-abstractions it behaves like Ω. Formally:

- M has *proper order* 0, written $M \in PO_0$, if M has order 0 and there are no $x, \widetilde{N}$ such that $\lambda\beta \vdash M = x\widetilde{N}$;
- M has *proper order* $n+1$, written $M \in PO_{n+1}$, if $\lambda\beta \vdash M = \lambda x. N$ for some $N \in PO_n$;
- M has *proper order* ω, written $M \in PO_\omega$, if M has order ω.

A λ-term is either of the form $\lambda\widetilde{x}. y\widetilde{M}$ or of the form $\lambda\widetilde{x}. (\lambda x. M_0)M_1 \ldots M_n$, $n \geq 1$. In the latter, the redex $(\lambda x. M_0)M_1$ is called the *head redex*. If M has a head redex, then $M \longrightarrow_{\mathrm{h}} N$ holds if N results from M by β-reducing its head redex. *Head reduction*, $\Longrightarrow_{\mathrm{h}}$, is the reflexive and transitive closure of $\longrightarrow_{\mathrm{h}}$. Head reduction is different from the call-by-name reduction ($\Longrightarrow$): a call-by-name redex is also a head redex, but the converse is false as a head redex can also be located underneath an abstraction. We have, however:

Lemma 18.2.1 Let $M \in \Lambda$.

(1) $M \Longrightarrow_{\mathrm{h}} \lambda x. N$ iff $M \Longrightarrow \lambda x. N'$, for some N' such that $N' \Longrightarrow_{\mathrm{h}} N$.
(2) $M \Longrightarrow_{\mathrm{h}} x\widetilde{N}$ iff $M \Longrightarrow x\widetilde{N}$.
(3) $M \Longrightarrow_{\mathrm{h}} \lambda x_1 \ldots x_n. y\widetilde{N}$ iff there are terms M_i, $1 \leq i \leq n$, such that $M \Longrightarrow \lambda x_1. M_1$, $M_i \Longrightarrow \lambda x_{i+1}. M_{i+1}$, $1 \leq i < n$, and $M_n \Longrightarrow y\widetilde{N}$.

Proof (1) and (2) hold because both $\Longrightarrow$ and $\Longrightarrow_{\mathrm{h}}$ progress using the leftmost redex; (3) follows from (1) and (2). □

Also, head reduction is different from strong call-by-name, for only the former is deterministic; however, the normal forms under the two strategies are the same.

The definition of LT below is simple but informal. A precise definition would require formalizing the notion of labelled tree.

Definition 18.2.2 (Lévy–Longo Trees) Let $M \in \Lambda$. The *Lévy–Longo Tree* of M is the labelled tree, LT(M), defined inductively as follows:

(1) $LT(M) = \top$ if $M \in PO_\omega$

(2) $LT(M) = \lambda x_1 \ldots x_n . \bot$ if $M \in PO_n$, $0 \le n < \omega$

(3) $LT(M) =$

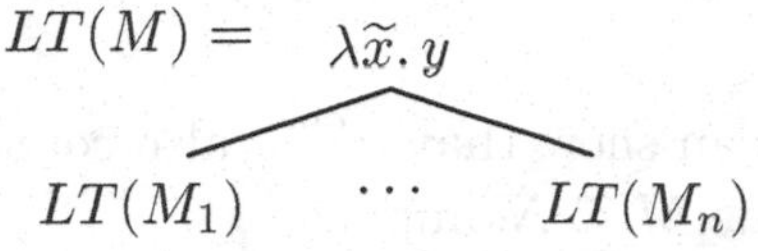

if $M \Longrightarrow_{\mathrm{h}} \lambda \widetilde{x}. yM_1 \ldots M_n$, $n \ge 0$.

Example 18.2.3 Let $M = x(\lambda y. y)\Omega z \Xi(\lambda x_1 x_2 . \Omega)$. Then

$LT(M) =$

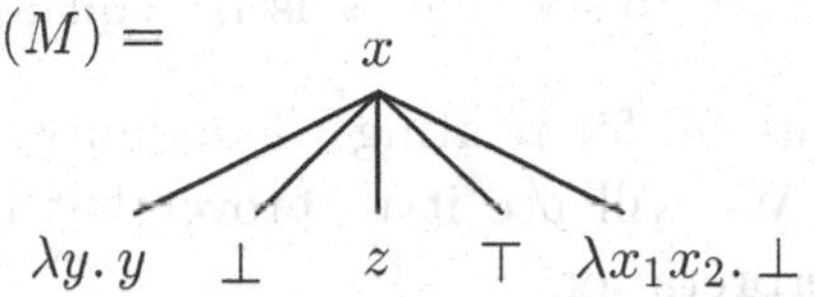

□

We identify α-convertible LTs. LT equality can also be presented as a form of bisimilarity. This bisimilarity, *open applicative bisimilarity*, is a refinement of applicative bisimilarity; indeed it is perhaps the simplest way to extend applicative bisimilarity to open terms.

Definition 18.2.4 *Open applicative bisimilarity* is the largest symmetric relation, $\approx_\lambda^{\text{open}}$, on Λ such that whenever $M \approx_\lambda^{\text{open}} N$,

(1) $M \Longrightarrow \lambda x. M'$ implies $N \Longrightarrow \lambda x. N'$ with $M' \approx_\lambda^{\text{open}} N'$

(2) $M \Longrightarrow xM_1 \ldots M_n$ with $n \ge 0$ implies $N \Longrightarrow xN_1 \ldots N_n$ and $M_i \approx_\lambda^{\text{open}} N_i$ for all $1 \le i \le n$. □

Clause (2), concerning terms with a variable in head position, is absent from the definition of applicative bisimilarity, where all terms are closed. Moreover, in contrast with applicative bisimilarity, in clause (1) no term instantiation on λ-abstractions is required. This simplification is possible because we work on open terms, and is justified by the congruence of $\approx_\lambda^{\text{open}}$. (A straightforward proof that $\approx_\lambda^{\text{open}}$ is a congruence utilizes the full-abstraction Theorems 18.3.13 and 18.3.14 and the congruence of π-calculus bisimilarity $\approx_{\mathrm{g}}$.) Two useful facts are:

Lemma 18.2.5 Let $M \in \Lambda$. If $M \Longrightarrow N$, then $M \approx_\lambda^{\text{open}} N$. □

Lemma 18.2.6 Let $M, N \in \Lambda$, and let ρ be a substitution from λ-variables to λ-variables. If $M \approx_\lambda^{\text{open}} N$ then $M\rho \approx_\lambda^{\text{open}} N\rho$. □

Theorem 18.2.7 Let $M, N \in \Lambda$. It holds that $M \approx_\lambda^{\text{open}} N$ iff $LT(M) = LT(N)$.

Proof Using Lemmas 18.2.1 and 18.2.5, we can show that $\approx_\lambda^{\text{open}}$ also coincides with the largest relation $\mathcal{R}$ on $\Lambda \times \Lambda$ such that $M \mathcal{R} N$ implies

(1) $M \in PO_\omega$ iff $N \in PO_\omega$
(2) $M \in PO_n$ iff $N \in PO_n$
(3) if $x_i \notin \mathsf{fv}(M, N)$, for $1 \le i \le n$, then $M \Longrightarrow_{\text{h}} \lambda x_1 \dots x_n .\, y M_1 \dots M_m$ iff $N \Longrightarrow_{\text{h}} \lambda x_1 \dots x_n .\, y N_1 \dots N_m$ and $M_i \mathcal{R} N_i$, for $1 \le i \le m$.

Finally, it is immediate to see that $\mathcal{R}$ is LT equality. □

Theorem 18.2.7 is useful for relating LT equality to other behavioural equivalences on λ-terms. We will use it to prove that LT equality is the same as equality in the π-interpretation.

18.3 The Local Structure Theorem for call-by-name

We state the Local Structure Theorem and briefly discuss it; most of the section will then be devoted to its proof. We conclude with some further remarks and exercises.

Theorem 18.3.1 (The Local Structure Theorem) Let $M, N \in \Lambda$. It holds that $M =_\pi N$ iff $LT(M) = LT(N)$.

Proof Below. □

Remark 18.3.2 Consider the terms

$$M \stackrel{\text{def}}{=} \lambda x.\, (x(\lambda y.\, (x \Xi \Omega y))\Xi) \qquad\qquad N \stackrel{\text{def}}{=} \lambda x.\, (x(x\Xi\Omega)\Xi).$$

These terms are applicative bisimilar; this can be proved by a case analysis on the order of the λ-term that is given as an input to the two terms. The two terms can be distinguished using the convergence test $\mathtt{C}$, for $M(\lambda x.\, \mathtt{C}x)$ reduces to an abstraction, whereas $N(\lambda x.\, \mathtt{C}x)$ diverges. Since M and N are distinguished using the operator $\mathtt{C}$, by Theorem 17.4.11 they are distinguished by $=_\pi$.

Using Theorem 18.3.1, we can prove $M \neq_\pi N$ simply by observing that their LTs are different:

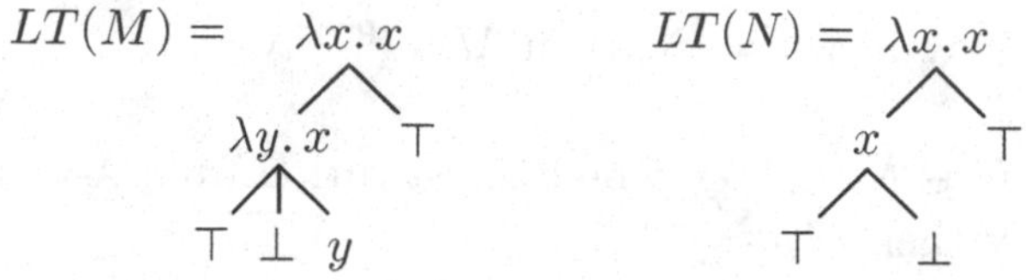

□

In order to prove Theorem 18.3.1, we first need to establish the operational correspondence on weak transitions between functions and their process encodings (Lemmas 18.3.7 and 18.3.9 below).

The encoding of a λ-term is an abstraction, that is, a function from names to processes; abstractions are ranged over by F, G. We introduce a process notation that allows us to give a simpler description of encodings of λ-terms with a variable in head position; this description is expressed by Lemma 18.3.5.

Definition 18.3.3 For $n > 0$ we define

$$\begin{aligned}&\mathcal{O}_n\langle r_0, r_n, F_1, \ldots, F_n\rangle \stackrel{\text{def}}{=} \\ &(\boldsymbol{\nu} r_1, \ldots, r_{n-1}, x_1, \ldots, x_n)\Big(r_0(v_1).\,\overline{v}_1\langle x_1, r_1\rangle \mid \ldots \mid r_{n-1}(v_n).\,\overline{v}_n\langle x_n, r_n\rangle \\ &\qquad \mid !x_1\, F_1 \mid \ldots \mid !x_n\, F_n\Big)\end{aligned}$$

where names $r_1, \ldots, r_{n-1}, x_1 \ldots, x_n$ are fresh. □

The ith process $r_{i-1}(v_i).\,\overline{v}_i\langle x_i, r_i\rangle$ of $\mathcal{O}_n\langle r_0, r_n, F_1, \ldots, F_n\rangle$ liberates the agent $!x_i\, F_i$ and the $(i+1)^{\text{th}}$ process.

Lemma 18.3.4 Suppose $n > 1$.

(1) $\mathcal{O}_n\langle r_0, r_n, F_1, \ldots, F_n\rangle \sim_{\mathrm{g}}$
$(\boldsymbol{\nu} r_{n-1}, x_n\,)\Big(\mathcal{O}_{n-1}\langle r_0, r_{n-1}, F_1, \ldots, F_{n-1}\rangle \mid r_{n-1}(v_n).\,\overline{v}_n\langle x_n, r_n\rangle \mid !x_n\, F_n\Big)$.

(2) If $\mathcal{O}_n\langle r_0, r_n, F_1, \ldots, F_n\rangle \xrightarrow{\alpha_1}\xrightarrow{\alpha_2} P$ then, for some v_1, we have $\alpha_1 = r_0\, v_1$ and $\alpha_2 = (\boldsymbol{\nu} x_1, r_1\,)\overline{v}_1\langle x_1, r_1\rangle$, and $P \sim_{\mathrm{g}} \mathcal{O}_{n-1}\langle r_1, r_n, F_2, \ldots, F_n\rangle \mid !x_1\, F_1$.

□

Lemma 18.3.5 If $n > 0$ then

$$[\![xM_1 \ldots M_n]\!] r_n \sim_{\mathrm{g}} \boldsymbol{\nu} r_0\, (\overline{x} r_0 \mid \mathcal{O}_n\langle r_0, r_n, [\![M_1]\!], \ldots, [\![M_n]\!]\rangle).$$

Proof By induction on n. For $n = 1$,

$$\begin{aligned} & [\![xM_1]\!] r_1 \\ = \;& \boldsymbol{\nu} r_0 \left([\![x]\!] r_0 \mid r_0(v_1).\, \boldsymbol{\nu} x_1\, \overline{v}_1\langle x_1, r_1\rangle.\, !x_1\, [\![M_1]\!] \right) \\ \sim_{\mathrm{g}} \;& \boldsymbol{\nu} r_0 \left([\![x]\!] r_0 \mid \boldsymbol{\nu} x_1\, (r_0(v_1).\, \overline{v}_1\langle x_1, r_1\rangle \mid !x_1\, [\![M_1]\!]) \right) \\ \sim_{\mathrm{g}} \;& \boldsymbol{\nu} r_0\, (\overline{x} r_0 \mid \mathcal{O}_1\langle r_0, r_1, [\![M_1]\!]\rangle)\,. \end{aligned}$$

For $n > 1$, we have, abbreviating $r_{n-1}(v_n).\,\overline{v}_n\langle x_n, r_n\rangle \mid !x_n\, [\![M_n]\!]$ to P,

$$[\![xM_1 \ldots M_n]\!] r_n$$

$$\begin{aligned}
&\sim_{\rm g} \quad (\boldsymbol{\nu} r_{n-1}, x_n)\Big([\![xM_1 \dots M_{n-1}]\!] r_{n-1} \mid P\Big) \\
&\sim_{\rm g} \quad (\boldsymbol{\nu} r_{n-1}, x_n)\Big(\boldsymbol{\nu} r_0\, (\overline{x} r_0 \mid \mathcal{O}_{n-1}\langle r_0, r_{n-1}, M_1, \dots, M_{n-1}\rangle) \mid P\Big) \quad (18.1) \\
&\sim_{\rm g} \quad \boldsymbol{\nu} r_0 \left(\overline{x} r_0 \mid (\boldsymbol{\nu} r_{n-1}, x_n)\Big(\mathcal{O}_{n-1}\langle r_0, r_{n-1}, M_1, \dots, M_{n-1}\rangle \mid P\Big)\right) \\
&\sim_{\rm g} \quad \boldsymbol{\nu} r_0 \left(\overline{x} r_0 \mid \mathcal{O}_n\langle r_0, r_n, M_1, \dots, M_n\rangle\right) \quad (18.2)
\end{aligned}$$

where (18.1) uses induction and (18.2) uses Lemma 18.3.4(1). □

Lemma 18.3.6 Let $M \in \Lambda$.

(1) If $M \longrightarrow N$ then $[\![M]\!]p \;{}_{\rm g}\!\succeq [\![N]\!]p$.
(2) If $M = \lambda x.\, N$ then $[\![M]\!]p \xrightarrow{\overline{p}(v)} v(x)\, [\![N]\!]$.
(3) If $M = x$ then $[\![M]\!]p \xrightarrow{\overline{x}p} \mathbf{0}$.
(4) If $M = xM_1 \dots M_n$ and $n > 0$, then $[\![M]\!]p \xrightarrow{\overline{x}(q)} \sim_{\rm g} \mathcal{O}_n\langle q, p, [\![M_1]\!], \dots, [\![M_n]\!]\rangle$.

Proof (2) and (3) are immediate from the definition of the encoding. (4) follows from Lemma 18.3.5. (1) is an immediate consequence of Exercise 15.4.21 and Lemma 2.2.20. □

Lemma 18.3.7 (Operational correspondence on reductions of M) Let $M \in \Lambda$.

(1) If $M \Longrightarrow N$ then $[\![M]\!]p \;{}_{\rm g}\!\succeq [\![N]\!]p$.
(2) If $M \Longrightarrow \lambda x.\, N$ then $[\![M]\!]p \xRightarrow{\overline{p}(v)} {}_{\rm g}\!\succeq v(x)\, [\![N]\!]$.
(3) If $M \Longrightarrow x$ then $[\![M]\!]p \xRightarrow{\overline{x}q} {}_{\rm g}\!\succeq \mathbf{0}$.
(4) If $M \Longrightarrow xM_1 \dots M_n$ and $n > 0$, then $[\![M]\!]p \xRightarrow{\overline{x}(q)} {}_{\rm g}\!\succeq \mathcal{O}_n\langle q, p, [\![M]\!]_1, \dots, [\![M_n]\!]\rangle$.

Proof (1) is by induction on the number of reductions and Lemma 18.3.6(1). The other assertions are consequences of (1) and Lemma 18.3.6(2)–(4). □

Lemma 18.3.8 Let $M \in \Lambda$, and suppose $[\![M]\!]p \xrightarrow{\alpha} P$.

(1) If $\alpha = \tau$ then there is N such that $M \longrightarrow N$ and $P \;{}_{\rm g}\!\succeq [\![N]\!]p$.
(2) If α is an output at p then $\alpha = \overline{p}(v)$ and there are x, N such that $M = \lambda x.\, N$ and $P = v(x)\, [\![N]\!]$.
(3) If α is a free output then there is x such that $\alpha = \overline{x}p$ and $P = \mathbf{0}$.

(4) Otherwise, there are x and $M_1, \dots, M_n$, $n > 0$, such that $\alpha = \overline{x}(q)$, $M = xM_1 \dots M_n$ and $P \sim_{\mathrm{g}} \mathcal{O}_n\langle q, p, [\![M]\!]_1, \dots, [\![M_n]\!]\rangle$.

Proof For each M and p, $[\![M]\!]p$ has only one possible transition. The assertions then follow from Lemma 18.3.6. □

Lemma 18.3.9 (Operational correspondence on transitions of $[\![M]\!]p$) Let $M \in \Lambda$, and suppose $[\![M]\!]p \overset{\alpha}{\Longrightarrow} P$.

(1) If $\alpha = \tau$ then there is N such that $M \Longrightarrow N$ and $P \ {}_{\mathrm{g}}\!\succeq [\![N]\!]p$.
(2) If α is an output at p then $\alpha = \overline{p}(v)$ and there are x, N such that $M \Longrightarrow \lambda x. N$ and $P \ {}_{\mathrm{g}}\!\succeq v(x)\, [\![N]\!]$.
(3) If α is a free output then there is x such that $\alpha = \overline{x}p$ and $P \ {}_{\mathrm{g}}\!\succeq \mathbf{0}$.
(4) Otherwise, there are x and $M_1, \dots, M_n$, $n > 0$, such that $\alpha = \overline{x}(q)$, $M \Longrightarrow xM_1 \dots M_n$, and $P \ {}_{\mathrm{g}}\!\succeq \mathcal{O}_n\langle q, p, [\![M]\!]_1, \dots, [\![M_n]\!]\rangle$.

Proof By induction on the length of the transition of $[\![M]\!]p$, using Lemma 18.3.8. □

We need a few lemmas before tackling the full-abstraction theorems. Lemma 18.3.10 shows decomposition properties for ground bisimilarity, similar to that in Exercise 2.4.21; Lemmas 18.3.11 and 18.3.12 show properties of the processes $\mathcal{O}_n\langle r_0, r_n, F_1, \dots, F_n\rangle$, introduced in Definition 18.3.3 to represent the encoding of λ-terms with a variable in head position.

For a process P, we let $\mathcal{N}_P$ be the set of names along which P can perform an action, i.e.,

$$\mathcal{N}_P = \{a \mid P \Downarrow_a \text{ or } P \Downarrow_{\overline{a}}\}\,.$$

Lemma 18.3.10

(1) Suppose $\mathsf{fn}(P_1, P_2) \cap (\mathcal{N}_{Q_1} \cup \mathcal{N}_{Q_2}) = \emptyset$. Then $P_1 \mid Q_1 \approx_{\mathrm{g}} P_2 \mid Q_2$ implies $P_1 \approx_{\mathrm{g}} P_2$.
(2) Suppose $x, q \notin \mathsf{fn}(F, G)$. Then $!x\,F \approx_{\mathrm{g}} !x\,G$ implies $Fq \approx_{\mathrm{g}} Gq$.

Proof We first prove (1). The relation

$$\mathcal{R} \overset{\mathrm{def}}{=} \{(P_1, P_2) \mid \text{for some } Q_1, Q_2 \text{ with } \mathsf{fn}(P_1, P_2) \cap (\mathcal{N}_{Q_1} \cup \mathcal{N}_{Q_2}) = \emptyset \text{ it holds that } P_1 \mid Q_1 \approx_{\mathrm{g}} P_2 \mid Q_2 \ \}$$

is a ground bisimulation. The proof is straightforward, for if $\mathsf{fn}(P_1, P_2) \cap (\mathcal{N}_{Q_1} \cup \mathcal{N}_{Q_1}) = \emptyset$, no interaction between P_i and Q_i is possible, $i = 1, 2$. Moreover, if all names received in input actions and all bound names emitted in output actions by P_1 and P_2 are fresh, then the side condition of $\mathcal{R}$ is preserved.

Now assertion (2). We have to show that $Fq \approx_{\mathrm{g}} Gq$. We can assume, without loss of generality, that $q \neq x$. Since $!x\, F \approx_{\mathrm{g}} !x\, G$ and $!x\, F \xrightarrow{xq} Fq \mid !x\, F$, we have, for some P,

$$!x\, G \overset{xq}{\Longrightarrow} P \approx_{\mathrm{g}} Fq \mid !x\, F\,. \tag{18.3}$$

Since x does not occur in Gq, no interaction may occur between Gq and $!x\, G$; therefore P is of the form $P_G \mid !x\, G$, for some P_G such that

$$Gq \Longrightarrow P_G. \tag{18.4}$$

Thus (18.3) can be written $P_G \mid !x\, G \approx_{\mathrm{g}} Fq \mid !x\, F$. From this we get

$$P_G \approx_{\mathrm{g}} Fq \tag{18.5}$$

using the assertion (1) of the lemma, since $\mathcal{N}_{!x\,G} = \mathcal{N}_{!x\,F} = \{x\}$ and x is not free in Fq and P_G. Similarly (exchanging F and G), we can derive, for some P_F,

$$Fq \Longrightarrow P_F\,, \qquad \text{and} \qquad P_F \approx_{\mathrm{g}} Gq\,. \tag{18.6}$$

Now, we exploit (18.4)–(18.6) to show that $Fq \approx_{\mathrm{g}} Gq$. For this, we take

$$\mathcal{R} \overset{\text{def}}{=} \{(Fq, Gq), (Gq, Fq)\} \cup \approx_{\mathrm{g}}$$

and show that $\mathcal{R}$ is a ground bisimulation. Suppose $Fq \xrightarrow{\alpha} Q_F$. We show how Gq can match this move. Since $Fq \approx_{\mathrm{g}} P_G$ we have $P_G \overset{\widehat{\alpha}}{\Longrightarrow} Q_G \approx_{\mathrm{g}} Q_F$. Therefore, using (18.4), $Gq \Longrightarrow P_G \overset{\widehat{\alpha}}{\Longrightarrow} Q_G \approx_{\mathrm{g}} Q_F$, which closes the bisimulation. Similarly Fq can match an action of Gq. □

Lemma 18.3.11 If $\mathcal{O}_n\langle r_0, r_n, F_1, \ldots, F_n\rangle \approx_{\mathrm{g}} \mathcal{O}_m\langle r_0, r_m, G_1, \ldots, G_m\rangle$ then $n = m$. □

Lemma 18.3.12 $\mathcal{O}_n\langle r_0, r_n, F_1, \ldots, F_n\rangle \approx_{\mathrm{g}} \mathcal{O}_n\langle r_0, r_n, G_1, \ldots, G_n\rangle$ iff $(F_i)q \approx_{\mathrm{g}} (G_i)q$ for all $1 \leq i \leq n$ and for some fresh q.

Proof The implication from right to left follows from congruence properties of $\approx_{\mathrm{g}}$. For the converse we proceed by induction on n. We consider only the inductive case. Let

$$P \overset{\text{def}}{=} \mathcal{O}_n\langle r_0, r_n, F_1, \ldots, F_n\rangle, \qquad Q \overset{\text{def}}{=} \mathcal{O}_n\langle r_0, r_n, G_1, \ldots, G_n\rangle.$$

By Lemma 18.3.4(2), their first two transitions are

$$P \xrightarrow{r_0\,v_1} \xrightarrow{(\boldsymbol{\nu} x_1, r_1)\overline{v_1}\langle x_1, r_1\rangle} \sim_{\mathrm{g}} \mathcal{O}_{n-1}\langle r_1, r_n, F_2, \ldots, F_n\rangle \mid !x_1\, F_1$$

$$Q \xrightarrow{r_0\,v_1} \xrightarrow{(\boldsymbol{\nu} x_1, r_1)\overline{v_1}\langle x_1, r_1\rangle} \sim_{\mathrm{g}} \mathcal{O}_{n-1}\langle r_1, r_n, G_2, \ldots, G_n\rangle \mid !x_1\, G_1.$$

From this, we can derive $P \approx_{\mathrm{g}} Q$ implies $\mathcal{O}_{n-1}\langle r_1, r_n, F_2, \ldots, F_n\rangle \mid !x_1\, F_1 \approx_{\mathrm{g}} \mathcal{O}_{n-1}\langle r_1, r_n, G_2, \ldots, G_n\rangle \mid !x_1\, G_1$; we omit the details, which are simple. Let $P_1 \stackrel{\mathrm{def}}{=} \mathcal{O}_{n-1}\langle r_1, r_n, F_2, \ldots, F_n\rangle$ and $Q_1 \stackrel{\mathrm{def}}{=} \mathcal{O}_{n-1}\langle r_1, r_n, G_2, \ldots, G_n\rangle$. The only actions that $!x_1\, F_1$ and $!x_1\, G_1$ can perform are at x_1 and, by Lemma 18.3.4(2), the only actions that P_1 and Q_1 can perform are at r_1. Since r_1 is not free in $!x_1\, F_1$ and $!x_1\, G_1$, and x_1 is not free in P_1 and Q_1, using Lemma 18.3.10(1) twice we infer

$$!x_1\, F_1 \approx_{\mathrm{g}} !x_1\, G_1 \text{ and } P_1 \approx_{\mathrm{g}} Q_1 \quad .$$

From the first, by Lemma 18.3.10(2), we get $(F_1)q \approx_{\mathrm{g}} (G_1)q$. From the second, by the induction hypothesis, we get $(F_i)q \approx_{\mathrm{g}} (G_i)q$, for $2 \leq i \leq n$. □

We now ready to prove that open applicative bisimilarity is the same as the local structure of the π-interpretation.

Theorem 18.3.13 (Soundness w.r.t. $\approx_\lambda^{\mathrm{open}}$) Let $M, N \in \Lambda$. If $M =_\pi N$ then $M \approx_\lambda^{\mathrm{open}} N$.

Proof By Definition 17.3.1 and Lemma 15.4.23, we have to prove that $[\![M]\!] \approx_{\mathrm{g}} [\![N]\!]$ implies $M \approx_\lambda^{\mathrm{open}} N$. We prove that

$$\mathcal{R} \stackrel{\mathrm{def}}{=} \{(M, N) \mid [\![M]\!] \approx_{\mathrm{g}} [\![N]\!]\,\}$$

is an open applicative bisimulation. First, suppose $M \Longrightarrow \lambda x.\, M'$. We have to find N' such that $N \Longrightarrow \lambda x.\, N'$ and $(M', N') \in \mathcal{R}$. From $M \Longrightarrow \lambda x.\, M'$ and Lemma 18.3.7(2), we get, for arbitrary names p and q,

$$[\![M]\!]p \xRightarrow{\overline{p}(v)} \xRightarrow{v\langle x, q\rangle} {}_{\mathrm{g}}\!\succeq [\![M']\!]q\,.$$

Since $[\![M]\!]p \approx_{\mathrm{g}} [\![N]\!]p$, there is P'' such that

$$[\![N]\!]p \xRightarrow{\overline{p}(v)} \xRightarrow{v\langle x, q\rangle} P'' \approx_{\mathrm{g}} [\![M']\!]q\,. \tag{18.7}$$

We can decompose $[\![N]\!]p \xRightarrow{\overline{p}(v)} \xRightarrow{v\langle x, q\rangle} P''$ into $[\![N]\!]p \Longrightarrow \xrightarrow{\overline{p}(v)} P' \xRightarrow{v\langle x, q\rangle} P''$, for some P'. Then, using Lemma 18.3.9(1)–(2), we infer that there are N' and N'' such that $N \Longrightarrow \lambda x.\, N'$ and $N' \Longrightarrow N''$ with $P' \;{}_{\mathrm{g}}\!\succeq v(x)\, [\![N']\!]$ and

$$P'' \;{}_{\mathrm{g}}\!\succeq [\![N'']\!]q\,. \tag{18.8}$$

Moreover, by Lemma 18.3.7(1),

$$[\![N']\!]p \;{}_{\mathrm{g}}\!\succeq [\![N'']\!]p\,. \tag{18.9}$$

Since $\preceq_{\mathrm{g}}$ implies $\approx_{\mathrm{g}}$, we can combine (18.7), (18.8) and (18.9) to derive $[\![M']\!]q \approx_{\mathrm{g}} [\![N']\!]q$; hence $(M', N') \in \mathcal{R}$, as required.

Now suppose $M \Longrightarrow xM_1 \ldots M_n$. We suppose $n > 0$; the case $n = 0$ is simpler. We have to find $N_1, \ldots, N_n$ such that $N \Longrightarrow xN_1 \ldots N_n$ and $M_i \mathrel{\mathcal{R}} N_i$, for all i.

From Lemma 18.3.7(4), we get

$$[\![M]\!]p \stackrel{\overline{x}(q)}{\Longrightarrow}{}_{\mathrm{g}}\!\succeq \mathcal{O}_n\langle q, p, [\![M_1]\!], \ldots, [\![M_n]\!]\rangle$$

and, from $[\![M]\!]p \approx_{\mathrm{g}} [\![N]\!]p$ and Lemma 18.3.9(4), for some m and $N_1, \ldots, N_m$,

$$[\![N]\!]p \stackrel{\overline{x}(q)}{\Longrightarrow}{}_{\mathrm{g}}\!\succeq \mathcal{O}_m\langle q, p, [\![N_1]\!], \ldots, [\![N_m]\!]\rangle \tag{18.10}$$

with $\mathcal{O}_n\langle q, p, [\![M_1]\!], \ldots, [\![M_n]\!]\rangle \approx_{\mathrm{g}} \mathcal{O}_m\langle q, p, [\![N_1]\!], \ldots, [\![N_m]\!]\rangle$. From this and Lemmas 18.3.11 and 18.3.12 we infer that $m = n$ and that $[\![M_i]\!] \approx_{\mathrm{g}} [\![N_i]\!]$, for all i. Hence $(M_i, N_i) \in \mathcal{R}$. Moreover, from (18.10) and Lemma 18.3.9(4) we infer that

$$N \Longrightarrow xN_1 \ldots N_n\,.$$

This closes the bisimulation. □

Theorem 18.3.14 (Completeness w.r.t. $\approx_\lambda^{\mathrm{open}}$) Let $M, N \in \Lambda$. If $M \approx_\lambda^{\mathrm{open}} N$ then $M =_\pi N$.

Proof We show that

$$\mathcal{R} \stackrel{\mathrm{def}}{=} \bigcup_p \{([\![M]\!]p, [\![N]\!]p) \mid M \approx_\lambda^{\mathrm{open}} N\}$$

is a ground bisimulation up to context and up to ${}_{\mathrm{g}}\!\succeq$. By Lemma 5.3.13, this implies $\mathcal{R} \subseteq \approx_{\mathrm{g}}$.

First, we show that $\mathcal{R}$ is closed under substitution, which guarantees the condition on substitutions required in the definition of 'bisimulation up to context'. The free names of a process $[\![M]\!]p$ are $\{p\} \cup \mathsf{fv}(M)$. Therefore, for each name substitution σ there is a variable substitution ρ such that

$$([\![M]\!]p)\sigma = [\![M\rho]\!](\sigma(p))\,.$$

Since, by Lemma 18.2.6, $\approx_\lambda^{\mathrm{open}}$ is closed under variable substitution, $\mathcal{R}$ is closed under name substitution.

Now we show that $\mathcal{R}$ is a ground bisimulation up to context and up to ${}_{\mathrm{g}}\succeq$. Let $([\![M]\!]p, [\![N]\!]p) \in \mathcal{R}$ and suppose that $[\![M]\!]p \xrightarrow{\alpha} P$. By Lemma 18.3.9, there are four cases to consider, according to the form of α. We show only the argument for the case when α is a bound output $\overline{x}(q)$ (this case needs both up to context and up to ${}_{\mathrm{g}}\succeq$; the other cases are simpler because they need only up to ${}_{\mathrm{g}}\succeq$).

By Lemma 18.3.9(4), there are x and $M_1, \ldots, M_n$ such that $M = xM_1 \ldots M_n$ and $P \;{}_{\mathrm{g}}\succeq\; \mathcal{O}_n\langle q, p, [\![M_1]\!], \ldots, [\![M_n]\!]\rangle$. Since $M \approx_{\lambda}^{\mathrm{open}} N$, there are $N_1, \ldots, N_n$ such that

$$N \Longrightarrow xN_1 \ldots N_n \tag{18.11}$$

and

$$M_i \approx_{\lambda}^{\mathrm{open}} N_i, \text{ for all } 1 \leq i \leq n. \tag{18.12}$$

Now, from (18.11), by Lemma 18.3.7(4) we get

$$[\![N]\!]p \stackrel{\overline{x}(q)}{\Longrightarrow}{}_{\mathrm{g}}\succeq \mathcal{O}_n\langle q, p, [\![N_1]\!], \ldots, [\![N_n]\!]\rangle$$

and from (18.12) we get

$$([\![M_i]\!]r, [\![N_i]\!]r) \in \mathcal{R}$$

for all i and r. Summarizing, we have obtained that

$$\begin{aligned} &[\![M]\!]p \xrightarrow{\overline{x}(q)}{}_{\mathrm{g}}\succeq \mathcal{O}_n\langle q, p, [\![M_1]\!], \ldots, [\![M_n]\!]\rangle, \\ &[\![N]\!]p \stackrel{\overline{x}(q)}{\Longrightarrow}{}_{\mathrm{g}}\succeq \mathcal{O}_n\langle q, p, [\![N_1]\!], \ldots, [\![N_n]\!]\rangle, \\ &([\![M_i]\!]r, [\![N_i]\!]r) \in \mathcal{R}, \quad \text{ for all } r \text{ and } 1 \leq i \leq n, \end{aligned}$$

as required, appealing to up to context and up to ${}_{\mathrm{g}}\succeq$. □

It is worth stressing that without the 'up to context and up to ${}_{\mathrm{g}}\succeq$' technique the proof of Theorem 18.3.14 would be much longer. Also important is the fact that we can work with ground relations (bisimilarity, expansion).

Theorems 18.2.7, 18.3.13 and 18.3.14 prove Theorem 18.3.1. We summarize the results of Theorems 18.2.7 and 18.3.1:

Corollary 18.3.15 For all $M, N \in \Lambda$, it holds that

$$M =_{\pi} N \text{ iff } M \approx_{\lambda}^{\mathrm{open}} N \text{ iff } LT(M) = LT(N).$$

□

Remark 18.3.16 (Encodings of strategies related to call-by-name) The local structure of the π-interpretation (Corollary 18.3.15) does not change if the call-by-name encoding is taken to be that in Table 15.6 (which has a replication in front of the abstraction) or that in Table 15.7. The proofs are similar to those given in this section. It is likely that the local structure also does not change under the strong call-by-name and call-by-need encodings of Sections 15.7 and 15.5. □

Remark 18.3.17 (On the discriminating power of π) The encoding of the convergence test, in Section 17.3, shows that the π-calculus can detect whether a λ-term reduces to a λ-abstraction. Using operational correspondence results between λ-terms and π-terms such as Lemma 18.3.9, we can go further, and prove that the π-calculus can detect whether a λ-term has a head normal form (which means that the label of the root of the LT of the term has the form $\lambda\widetilde{x}.\, y\widetilde{M}$), or a normal form (which means that the LT of the term is finite and has no occurrences of $\bot$ and $\top$); more generally, it can detect whether the LT of a term has a certain shape (although occurrences of $\bot$ and $\top$ in the tree are not directly observable). These properties are not observable within the λ-calculus, which, once more, explains the greater discriminating power of the π-calculus. Exercise 18.3.18 gives an example. □

Exercise 18.3.18 Write a π-calculus context C such that for all terms $M \in \Lambda$ with $\mathsf{fv}(M) \subseteq \widetilde{x}$, it holds that $C[[\![M]\!]p] \Downarrow$ iff M has a head normal form. □

Exercise 18.3.19 (Undecidability of π-calculus equivalences) This exercise invites the reader to discover that behavioural equivalences in the π-calculus, both in their strong and in their weak versions, are not semi-decidable (which implies that they are undecidable). This is done by exploiting known properties of the λ-calculus. We consider ground bisimilarity and barbed congruence, but other behavioural equivalences could be used as well.

In any of the λ-calculus reduction strategies we have considered, it is not semi-decidable whether a term reduces to a value. In particular this holds for call-by-name. Let $M \in \Lambda^0$. Write $M \Uparrow$ (pronounced 'M diverges') if M has an infinite reduction sequence

$$M \longrightarrow M_1 \longrightarrow M_2 \longrightarrow \dots$$

under the call-by-name strategy.

(1) Prove that $M \Uparrow$ iff it is not the case that $[\![M]\!]p \Downarrow$.
(2) Conclude that both strong and weak ground bisimilarity are not semi-decidable.
(3) Conclude the same for strong and weak barbed congruence.

(Hint: bear in mind Exercise 15.4.21(1) and the operational correspondence results Lemmas 18.3.9 and 18.3.7.) □

Exercise 18.3.20 Prove that the property that a process leaks (Section 9.3) is undecidable. For this, work in the polyadic π-calculus, and use Exercise 18.3.19(1) and Lemmas 18.3.9 and 18.3.7. $\square$

18.4 Böhm Trees

The definition of Böhm Tree (BT) is obtained from that of LT by replacing clauses (1) and (2) of Definition 18.2.2 with the clause

$$BT(M) = \bot \qquad \text{if } M \in PO_n,\ 0 \leq n \leq \omega.$$

We briefly discuss how to obtain BTs from an encoding of the λ-calculus into π-calculus. The definition of BT is based on the notion of head normal form, rather than on weak head normal form as in the case of LTs, since only the terms with head normal forms have BTs different from $\bot$. To define a π-calculus semantics that captures BT equality we therefore need the following two modifications:

(1) The π-calculus encoding of a λ-term should allow reductions under λ (rule ξ).
(2) The behavioural equivalence chosen for the π-calculus should be divergence-sensitive. This is necessary because the computation under the 'λ' may never terminate (this happens in terms that have a whnf but no hnf, such as $\lambda x.\,\Omega$ and Ξ).

To satisfy (1), we can take the π-calculus encoding of strong call-by-name, in Section 15.7. For (2), we can take a divergence-sensitive bisimilarity [Wal90], or must-testing [Hen88]. In this way, the π-interpretation validates equations such as $\lambda x.\,\Omega = \Omega$ and $\Xi = \Omega$, that are at the basis of the difference between LTs and BTs.

18.5 Local structure of the call-by-value interpretation

Proceeding as for the call-by-name encoding, one can show that also the call-by-value encoding of Table 15.2 is sound, but not complete, with respect to the operational equivalence of λV. For closed λ-terms M, N, if $\mathcal{V}[\![M]\!]$ and $\mathcal{V}[\![N]\!]$ are behaviourally indistinguishable as π-calculus processes, then M and N are operationally equivalent in λV (defined as for call-by-name, Definition 17.2.1). But the converse may fail. For a counterexample, take $M \stackrel{\text{def}}{=} \lambda x.\,x$ and $N \stackrel{\text{def}}{=} \lambda x.\,\lambda y.\,(xy)$. (Note: this counterexample is again obtained using the η rule.) Behavioural equivalence in call-by-value is different from call-by-name: for instance in call-by-name $(\lambda x.\,I)\Omega$ and I are semantically the same, whereas in call-by-value

$(\lambda x.\, I)\Omega$ is the same as Ω. No characterization is known of the equivalence on λ-terms induced by the call-by-value encoding $\mathcal{V}$ or other call-by-value encodings.

Notes and References for Part VI

The λ-calculus was introduced by Church [Chu32, Chu41], who was hoping to use it, on the one hand, to produce a foundation for logic and mathematics and, on the other, to understand mathematically the notion of function. While the first endeavour failed, the second one has been a remarkable success. Church (and Kleene, who proved important results on λ-definability) realized that the λ-calculus captures the notion of function that is 'effectively computable', and conjectured that the class of effectively computable functions should coincide with the class of λ-definable functions. This proposal, referred to as *Church's thesis*, is now generally accepted.

The λ-calculus was rediscovered by computer scientists in the 1960s, mainly thanks to Böhm, McCarthy, Scott, and especially Landin, as a basis for programming languages. It has been important for understanding essential programming constructs such as parametrization mechanisms – those, for instance, of procedures – and types. In particular, it has served as a mathematical foundation for the class of *functional languages*.

The standard references on the classical theory of the λ-calculus (the sensible theory) are [Bar84, HS86]. The textbooks by Gunter [Gun92], Hindley [Hin97], and Mitchell [Mit96] contain detailed presentations of typed λ-calculi and PCF. PCF was introduced by Plotkin [Plo77]. In the same paper, he showed a sequentiality lemma for PCF from which the non-definability of parallel operators, such as forms of 'parallel-or' and 'parallel-if-then-else', can be derived. The classical sequentiality theorem for the untyped λ-calculus is due to Berry [Ber78]. A recent treatise on sequentiality in the λ-calculus is by Bethke and Klop [BK98]. The standardization and normalization theorems of the λ-calculus were proved in [CF58].

Call-by-need was proposed by Wadsworth [Wad71] as an implementation technique. Formalizations of call-by-need on a λ-calculus with a `let` construct or with environments include Ariola et al. [AFM$^+$95], Launchbury [Lau93], Purushothaman and Seaman [PS92], and Yoshida [Yos93].

Continuations were so named by Strachey and Wadsworth [SW74], who used them to give semantics to control jumps. See Reynolds [Rey93] for a history of the discovery of continuations and CPS transforms. For continuations in denotational semantics, see Gordon [Gor79], Schmidt [Sch86], or Tennent [Ten91]. For continuations as a programming technique, see [FWH92]. For the use of CPS transforms in compilers, see Appel [App92], where the language is ML, or [FWH92], where the language is Scheme. Hatcliff and Danvy [HD94] presented a unifying account of various CPS transforms based on Moggi's computational metalanguage [Mog91]. The encoding of λN into λV using thunks in Exercise 15.4.17, and its relationship to the CPS transform $\mathcal{C}_{\mathrm{N}}$, were studied by Danvy and Hatcliff [DH92, HD97]. The idea of using thunks for implementing call-by-name dates back to Ingerman [Ing61].

The call-by-value CPS transform of Table 15.1 is due to Fischer [Fis72] (of which a more complete version is [Fis93]). The call-by-name CPS transform of Table 15.3 is that of Plotkin [Plo75], based on work by Reynolds (such as [Rey72]); however, we have adopted the rectification in the clause for variables due to Hatcliff and Danvy [HD97]. (Plotkin's translation for variables was $\mathcal{C}_{\mathrm{N}}[\![x]\!] \stackrel{\text{def}}{=} x$; the rectification is necessary for the left-to-right implication of Theorem 15.4.4 to hold.)

Theorems 15.3.1–15.3.4 and 15.4.1–15.4.3, on CPS terms and CPS transforms, were proved by Plotkin [Plo75]. (The assertions of these theorems are actually slightly different from Plotkin's, but the content and the proofs are similar.) Plotkin also presented counterexample (15.3) to the converse of Theorem 15.3.5. The terms M and N used in the proof of Theorem 17.4.14 – non-completeness of the call-by-name encoding – are those used by Plotkin [Plo75] to prove the non-completeness of the call-by-name CPS transform (Table 15.3) as a transformation of λN into λV. A CPS transform for call-by-need was studied by Okasaki, Lee and Tarditi [OLT94], using a λ-calculus extended with reference cells as target language. We have not found in the literature grammars for the terms of the CPS transforms (Grammars (15.4), (15.13), (15.18)); but related to our grammars are Ogata's [Oga98], who compared cut elimination of certain logics and CPS transforms, and Sabry and Felleisen's [SF93], who gave the language of an optimized version of Fischer's call-by-value CPS. We also have not found in the literature the uniform CPS transform of Table 15.5.

The relationship between types of λ-terms and types of their CPS images was first noticed by Meyer and Wand [MW85]. Other important papers on types and CPS are [Mur92, HL93, HDM93]. Theorem 16.2.1 is due to Meyer and

Wand. The transformation of types for the call-by-name CPS in (16.4), and Theorem 16.3.1, are by Harper and Lillibridge [HL93], who followed what Meyer and Wand had done for call-by-value.

Connections among functions, continuations and message-passing were already clear, though (as far as we know) not formally stated, in Hewitt's works on *Actors* [Hew77, HBG$^+$73, HB77]. A function was represented as an actor that accepts messages containing an argument for the function and a continuation to which the result of the function should be sent. This is the same idea that we have used for representing functions as π-calculus processes in this Part.

The analogy between Milner's encodings of λ-calculus into π-calculus and the CPS transforms was noticed by several people, and was first partly formalized by Boudol [Bou97a] and Thielecke [Thi97]. Boudol compared encodings of call-by-name and call-by-value λ-calculus into, respectively, the Blue Calculus and the π-calculus. He noticed that, for either strategy, if the CPS transform is composed with the encoding of (call-by-name) λ-calculus into the Blue Calculus, then the results can be read as the standard encoding of that λ-calculus strategy into the π-calculus. Thielecke introduced a CPS calculus, similar to the intermediate language in Appel's compiler [App92]. He showed that this CPS calculus has a simple translation into the π-calculus and that, if Plotkin's CPS transforms are formulated in the CPS calculus, then their translations into the π-calculus yield an encoding similar to Milner's [Mil92]. In this Part we go further, in that the encodings of both call-by-name and call-by-value λ-calculus into the π-calculus are *factorized* using the CPS transforms and the compilation $\mathcal{C}$ of HOπ into π-calculus, for both untyped *and* typed λ-calculi. One of the reasons for working out the factorizations in detail is to be able to *derive* the correctness of the π-calculus encodings (on terms as well as on types) from those of the CPS transforms and of the compilation of HOπ into π-calculus. The presentation of the factorizations is based on [San99a].

Translations of functions into process calculi were given by Kennaway and Sleep [KS82], Leth [Let91], Thomsen [Tho90], and Boudol [Bou89]. Milner's work on functions as π-calculus processes [Mil92] is a landmark in the area. Milner considered the call-by-name and parallel call-by-value strategies (his encodings were, respectively, that in Table 15.7 and a variant of that in Table 15.2). Milner proved the operational correspondence between reductions in the λ-terms and in their process encodings (the analogue of Lemma 15.3.18 and Exercise 15.4.19); he also proved that, in both cases, the encoding is operationally sound but not complete.

Regarding the call-by-value encoding, (variants of) Corollary 15.3.15 and Lemma 15.3.18 were proved by Milner [Mil92]; Corollary 15.3.16 by Pierce and Sangiorgi [PS96]; Remark 15.3.17 is from [San92]. Vasconcelos [Vas01] studied an optimization of the encoding of call-by-value; the price is that the compositionality of the encoding is partially lost. Regarding the call-by-name encoding, Corollaries 15.4.12 and 15.4.13 are by Milner [Mil92, Mil93]. The remainder of Section 15.4 is from [San99a]. The uniform encoding in Section 15.5 is from [OD93]. A study of the correctness of the call-by-need encoding in Table 15.6 is in [BO95]. Encodings of graph reductions, related to call-by-need, into π-calculus were given in [Bou94, Jef93] but their correctness was not studied. Niehren [Nie96] used encodings of call-by-name, call-by-value and call-by-need λ-calculi into π-calculus to compare the time complexity of the strategies. The encoding of Table 15.7 is precisely Milner's original encoding of λN. The optimization (15.19) is from [San99b] (using receptive types) and [MS98] (using asynchrony). An encoding of the ξ rule into π-calculus was given in [San96c], where the target calculus is Pπ; the encoding presented in Section 15.7 is from [MS98].

Turner first established a relationship between the types of λ-calculus terms and those of their encodings into π-calculus [Tur96]. He took (variants of) Milner's encodings of the λ-calculus into the π-calculus and proved that for some of these encodings there is a correspondence between principal types of the λ-terms and principal types of the encoding π-calculus terms. Turner also extended Milner's encodings to the polymorphic λ-calculus. Turner's type system has the connection type $\sharp T$ as the only link type. Using i/o types (and types based on them, such as linearity and receptiveness), as we have done in this Part, the relationship between λ-calculus and π-calculus types is clearer and sharper, and can be more easily extended to other type systems. The work presented in Chapter 16 follows the schema of the interpretation of Abadi and Cardelli's typed Object Calculi [AC96] into π-calculus [San98a, KS98]. Encodings of simply-typed λ-calculi were also given by Kobayashi [Kob98], to illustrate the use of a type system guaranteeing absence of deadlocks. The encodings of reduction strategies in this Part can be combined with those of higher-order calculi in Chapter 13, to obtain π-calculus representations of higher-order languages equipped with reduction strategies for value expressions (that is, expressions that are not necessarily in normal form; see Remark 12.1.5). Examples of such combinations were studied in [ALT95] and [Röc01].

Applicative bisimilarity was introduced by Abramsky [Abr89], inspired by the work of Milner and Park in concurrency [Par81, Mil89]. Since Abramsky's work, the idea of applicative bisimilarity has been applied to a variety of higher-order sequential languages; see [Gor95, Pit97] for surveys. Open applicative bisimilarity coincides with the equivalence induced by Ong's *lazy PSE ordering* [Ong88]; however, a conceptual difference between the two is the emphasis that Ong's preorder places on η-expansion.

The operational and denotational theory of λN was extensively studied by Abramsky and Ong (they call λN the *lazy λ-calculus*). The canonical model of λN mentioned in Section 17.3 was defined by Abramsky, as the solution to a certain domain equation [Abr87, Abr89]. He and Ong then proved that this model is sound but not complete [Abr87, Ong88, AO93]. The *internal choice* operator in Section 17.4 is inspired by the CSP operator with the same name [Hoa85]. Studies of formats of operators in concurrency include [DS85, BIM95, ABV94, GV92], and in functional languages [Blo90, How96, San94]. The Lévy–Longo Trees were introduced by Longo [Lon83] – where they were simply called trees – developing an original idea by Levy [Lév76]. They were called Lévy–Longo Trees by Ong [Ong88]. Böhm Trees are studied in depth in [Bar84]. For models of the λ-calculus, such as $P\omega$, T^ω, D_A, D_∞, and free lazy models, see [Bar84, HS86, Ong88]. Most of the results in Chapters 17 and 18 are from [San94, San00]. The grammar of well-formed operators in [San94] is however more generous. Section 18.4 is from [San95].

The equivalence on λ-terms induced by their encoding into the π-calculus (Definition 17.3.1) is largely independent of the choice of the behavioural equivalence on π-calculus processes. We have adopted bisimilarity, which is widely accepted as the finest extensional behavioural equivalence one would like to impose on processes. At the opposite extreme, as the coarsest equivalence, one normally places Morris's context-equivalence, which is defined as barbed congruence but without the clause on τ moves [Mor68]. On processes encoding λ-terms, the main forms of π-calculus labelled bisimilarity (bisimilarity, and its ground, late, and open variants, as well as their asynchronous variants) coincide (Corollary 5.3.10). They also coincide with Morris's context-equivalence. The latter fact intuitively holds because the encoded lazy λ-terms are deterministic; it is formally proved in [BL00]. Other characterizations of Lévy–Longo Trees as Morris's context-equivalence of extended λ-terms include: Boudol and Laneve [BL96], who use *lambda calculus with multiplicities*, a form of λN where arguments of functions have a multiplicity and reduction, although deterministic, may introduce deadlock; and Dezani-Ciancaglini, Tiuryn and Urzyczyn [DCTU97], who use the *concurrent λ-calculus*, an extension of λN with a form of call-by-value application and operators for nondeterminism and parallelism. Boudol [Bou00] showed that the Lévy–Longo Trees are also the semantics induced on λN by the call-by-name CPS tranform $\mathcal{C}_{\mathrm{N}}$; that is, two λ-terms M and N have the same Lévy–Longo Tree iff $\mathcal{C}_{\mathrm{N}}[\![M]\!]$ and $\mathcal{C}_{\mathrm{N}}[\![N]\!]$ are barbed congruent in λN (or applicative bisimilar, as the two coincide, Theorem 17.2.3). Bearing in mind the factorization of the π-calculus encoding of λN through the CPS transform and HOπ, this result shows that the lack of full abstraction of the encoding (Corollary 17.3.6) may be blamed on the first step, namely the CPS transform, if we see this step as a transformation of λN to itself.

Part VII

Objects and π-calculus

Introduction to Part VII

Object-oriented programming is widely practised. It is based on an analogy between concrete physical models, built from real objects, and abstract software models, whose components are intangible computational entities – an example being a physical model of an aircraft wing, for testing in a wind tunnel, and a software model of the wing, for testing by computer simulation. Following the analogy, the intangible entities that comprise the software models are themselves called *objects*. In general, as an object-oriented system evolves, objects are created and the interconnection structure among objects changes. Although some implementations of object-oriented programming languages are sequential, activity within a system of objects is naturally thought of as concurrent.

This final Part of the book is about how π-calculus can be useful in object-oriented design and programming. The most important point is an indirect one. It is that a good theory offers a conceptual framework, a way of thinking about design and analysis of systems that helps one see the wood as well as the trees. The π-calculus captures in a tractable mathematical form a particular conception of mobile system. That conception is closely related to ideas that are important in object-orientation, especially its behavioural aspects. It may also be that particular concepts from π-calculus can usefully be transferred to objects, for instance ways of understanding behaviour, analytical techniques, type constructs, and process operators.

The π-calculus can be used to express systems of objects mathematically. This modelling can be carried out at all points on the spectrum from design-sketch to implementation in a programming language. And π-calculus techniques can be used to reason about object systems, both their static aspects, for instance types, and their dynamic properties.

Part VII illustrates some of these points by giving a semantic definition for a simple object-oriented language by translation to the π-calculus, and using techniques from earlier in the book to show some properties of the language and programs written in it.

The requirements placed on π-calculus descriptions may vary from one region of the design-implementation spectrum to another. At the design-sketch end, an informal understanding of the notation or language used may be sufficient to grasp the accuracy of π-calculus descriptions. Indeed, the act of modelling may help to sharpen understanding. At the other end of the spectrum, depending on the programming language in question and on the uses to which the π-calculus descriptions are to be put, one may wish to give an operational-semantic definition for the language, and establish operational correspondence and soundness results for the π-calculus translation, like those we have seen in Part V and Part VI. For the language and purposes considered here, an informal understanding of the programming language is sufficient, and we therefore take the translation to be the semantic definition.

This Part is of a different character from the others in the book, notably Part VI. The main reason for this is that the world of objects is multifarious. There is no single reference model for objects, in the way that the λ-calculus is a reference model for functions, for instance. The π-calculus description that we give can, however, be modified to accommodate object features that are absent from the language we consider. On this, see the notes at the end. An interesting point is whether there are conceptions of objects or language features that cannot be expressed adequately in the π-calculus. A discovery that this were so might suggest fruitful directions to develop the general theory of mobile processes. One point deserves special mention. The language we consider has a very simple type structure, and in that respect is not typical of object-oriented languages. It is possible to treat languages with more complicated type structures, in particular languages featuring subtyping. Indeed, an aspect of the treatment of subtyping was mentioned in Section 7.4, where an operation was added to the the priority queues considered in Section 3.3. Such treatments are inevitably more complicated, however, and draw more deeply on the theory of typed calculi than we will need to do to handle the language considered here.

Structure of the Part The first of Part VII's two chapters, Chapter 19, is concerned with describing object systems in π-calculus. Section 19.1 introduces the object-oriented language and explains its meaning informally. Section 19.2 explains via examples how to represent systems of objects expressed in the language in the π-calculus. Section 19.3 then gives a formal semantic definition for the language by translation to the calculus. The four sections in Chapter 20 contain several examples of using π-calculus techniques to reason about the behaviour of object systems.

19

Semantic Definition

19.1 A programming language

A central issue in object-oriented programming is how objects are described. Broadly, object-oriented languages fall into two groups. One comprises the *object-based* languages, such as Emerald and Self. In a program of an object-based language, one finds phrases that express individual objects, and objects are created by performing operations on existing objects. The other, larger, group comprises the *class-based* languages. Among its members are Simula, Smalltalk, C++, and Java. A program of a class-based language contains definitions of *classes*, which serve as blueprints for objects that share a common structure and behaviour. The language we will consider is class-based. The ideas and techniques illustrated can also be applied to object-based languages, however.

A key idea in object-oriented design and programming is *encapsulation*: each object has private data that are not directly accessible to other objects. These are typically simple data, such as integers, and references to objects. An object a can interact with an object b only if a has a reference to b. An interaction typically consists in a asking b to carry out one of its repertoire of actions – that is, in a *invoking* one of b's *methods* – and b returning the result of the invocation, in due course. The arguments and results of method invocations can contain references to objects, and it is in this way, and via creation of objects, that the interconnection structure among objects changes as a system evolves.

We call the language we consider OOL. Its main syntactic categories are declarations, commands, and expressions. A program comprises some class declarations and an expression, whose evaluation serves to trigger the system's activity. A class declaration consists of some variable declarations, the *instance* variables of the class, and some method declarations, which describe the actions that objects of the class can perform. A method declaration comprises type information and the *body* of the method, a command that describes the activity to be carried out when the method is invoked. A variable declaration states the names and types of variables.

The syntax of OOL is given in Table 19.1. We use X to range over identifiers for variables, m for methods, and A for classes. We use T, C, and E as metavariables over type expressions, commands, and expressions, respectively. We use op as a metavariable over the *operators*. These are the constant $\star$ of `unit` type, the constants for the truth-values and the integers, the terms $\mathsf{nil}(A)$, which represent null references, and the other operators: negation, addition, equality, etc. Each operator has the obvious type.

The only type expressions that appear in OOL programs are `unit`, `Int`, and `ref` (A) with A a class identifier. The implicit language of types is richer, however, as we will see in detail later. Typing in OOL is by structure. So, for instance, if in an OOL program classes A and A' are declared with the same interface, and a variable X is declared with type `ref` (A), then the command $X := \mathsf{new}(A')$ *is* well typed. In OOL, a name such as A is both a class name and a type name. We could have used a by-name typing in OOL and, correspondingly, a by-name typing in the π-calculus. We consider the question of by-name or by-structure typing to be orthogonal to the issues we wish mainly to address in this Part. The emphasis is on reasoning about the behaviour of objects, not typing of objects. Moreover, typing for object-oriented languages remains an active area of research. We use a by-structure typing because this is the kind we have developed most in the book.

We give an informal explanation of the intended meanings of language phrases using the example program declaration $Pdec_0$ in Table 19.2. In general, an OOL program interacts with its environment by consuming integers from an input stream and emitting integers to an output stream. The program $Pdec_0$ consumes ten integers, and then emits them in decreasing order.

Execution of $Pdec_0$ begins with evaluation of the expression `new(A)!sort(10)`. This starts with evaluation of `new(A)`, which results in an object of class `A` being created. The value of `new(A)` is a reference to that object. Next, the argument `10` is evaluated (it is in fact already a value), and then the method `sort` is invoked in the object of class `A`, with argument `10`.

This invocation results in the body of the method `sort` being executed, with its formal parameter `n` replaced by `10`. This involves creation of an object of class `PQ` and an object of class `IO`, and assignment of references to those objects to the instance variables `p` and `i`. Those objects can then be accessed using `p` and `i`. For ease of reading, we use `p` and `i` as names for the objects in what follows.

Each object has its own private instance variables, of the types given in the declaration of its class. When an object is created, each variable has an initial

			Type expressions
T	::=	`unit`	unit
	|	`Int`	integers
	|	`ref` (A)	references to objects
			Expressions
E	::=	X	variable
	|	$op(E_1, \ldots, E_n)$	operator
	|	new(A)	object creation
	|	$E!m(E_1, \ldots, E_n)$	method invocation
	|	input	input
			Commands
C	::=	E	expression
	|	$X := E$	assignment
	|	$C; C'$	sequence
	|	if E then C else C'	conditional
	|	while E do C	iteration
	|	return E	return
	|	output E	output
			Declarations
$Vdec$	::=	var $X_1 : T_1, \ldots, X_n : T_n$	variables
$Mdec$	::=	method m $(X_1 : T_1, \ldots, X_n : T_n) : T,\ C$	method
$Cdec$	::=	class $A,\ Vdec,\ Mdec_1, \ldots, Mdec_n$	class
$Pdec$	::=	$Cdec_1, \ldots, Cdec_n,\ E$	program

Table 19.1. *Syntax of OOL*

value: $\star$, 0, or nil(A). Thus, in particular, when the first iteration command in the body of method `sort` is reached, the variable `c` has value 0. The first substantial step in evaluating the expression `p!insert(i!get())` is invocation of the method `get` in the object `i`. And the effect of this is to consume an integer from the input stream and return it as the result of the invocation. The value of `i!get()` is the integer that is returned. Evaluation of `p!insert(i!get())` then continues with the invocation of the method `insert` in the object `p`, with argument the integer that was consumed.

The class `PQ` implements a priority-queue datatype. It is similar to the second implementation described using the π-calculus in Section 3.3. For convenience,

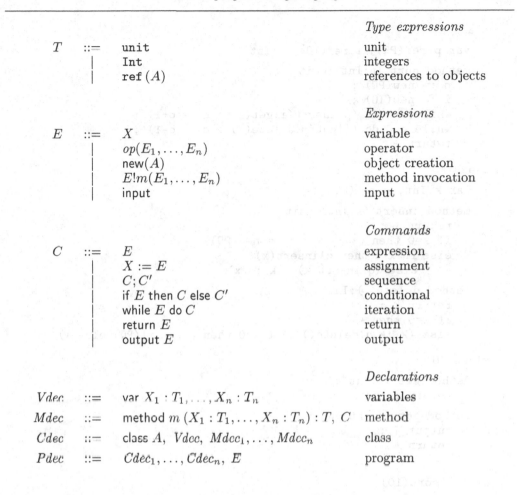

```
class A

   var p:ref(PQ), i:ref(IO), c:Int

   method sort (n:Int):unit
      p := new(PQ) ;
      i := new(IO) ;
      while c<n do (p!insert(i!get()) ; c := c+1) ;
      while c>0 do (i!put(p!delete()) ; c := c-1) ;
      return ⋆

class PQ

   var k:Int, q:ref(PQ)

   method insert (x:Int):unit
      return ⋆ ;
      if k=0 then (k := x ; q := new(PQ))
      else if x<k then q!insert(x)
           else (q!insert(k) ; k := x)

   method delete ():Int
      return k ;
      if k=0 then ⋆
      else (k := q!delete() ; if k=0 then q := nil(PQ) else ⋆)

class IO

   method get ():Int
      return input

   method put (j:Int):unit
      output j ;
      return ⋆

new(A)!sort(10)
```

Table 19.2. *The OOL program* $Pdec_0$

we assume that the integers in the input stream are positive. This allows us to use the value 0 (which is the initial value of the instance variable k) as a mark of the end cell in a chain; so, the end cell is distinguished by the values of its instance variables k and q being 0 and nil(PQ). The integer consumed from the input stream is accepted by the queue, and the value of unit type returned to indicate that it has been inserted into the queue, or more precisely, that the queue undertakes *to* insert it.

This process is repeated until 10 positive integers have been consumed from the input stream and inserted into the queue. Those integers are then removed from the queue, in decreasing order by virtue of the way the queue behaves, and placed in the output stream by repeated invocation of the method `put` in the object of type `IO`.

Finally, the value of `unit` type is returned as the result of the invocation of method `sort`. This completes evaluation of the expression `new(A)!sort(10)` – its value is $\star$ – and hence execution of the program.

In general, when an object is created during execution of an OOL program, the object assumes a quiescent state in which any of its methods can be invoked. When a method is invoked, its body is executed, and when the invocation is complete, the object returns to its quiescent state, ready to accept another method call. When an object a invokes a method m in an object b, the activity of a is suspended until b returns the result of the method invocation to it, by executing a command of the form `return` E. The object a can then continue. And if the `return` command is not the last in the body of m, then b can continue too. It is in this way that concurrent activity is possible within a system of OOL-objects. For instance, in the example program $Pdec_0$, when the object of class `A` invokes the method `insert` in the object of class `PQ` that is at the head of the chain, the `PQ`-object returns the value of `unit` type immediately, and then continues with the insertion. Consequently, the `A`-object may ask the object of class `IO` to consume another integer from the input stream while that insertion – indeed several insertions – are rippling along the chain of `PQ`-objects.

We consider only OOL programs that are statically well typed. Well-typing means in particular that the argument and result of any invocation of any method have the types specified in the relevant declaration. Further, if C is the body of a method, then in each path through C there must be exactly one `return` command: whenever the method is invoked, the object should not complete execution of the body without returning a result, and it should not attempt to return more than one result.

It is fairly straightforward to separate out the well-typed programs by means of a type-inference system. We briefly discuss this below; as it is not essential for understanding what follows, the reader may prefer to go straight to Section 19.2. Consider a program declaration $Pdec$. Phrases are assigned types of the language given by

$$\begin{aligned} S \ ::= \ & Z \mid \texttt{unit} \mid \texttt{Bool} \mid \texttt{Int} \mid \texttt{ref}\,(S) \mid S_1 \times \ldots \times S_n \mid \\ & S \to S' \mid \{m_1 : S_1, \ldots, m_n : S_n\} \mid \mu Z.\, S\,, \end{aligned}$$

where Z ranges over type variables. We have `Bool` to type truth-valued expressions, tuple types for typing multi-argument methods, and function types, record types, and recursive types for assigning types to objects. Roughly, the idea is that an object has a record type whose fields are of the form $m : (S_m \to S'_m)$, where m is the name of one of the object's methods, and S_m and S'_m are the argument type and result type of m. Recursion comes in because the argument and result types may contain the type of the object, or a type recursively related to that type: the methods may take references as arguments and return references as results. (In fact, only a subset of the types in the grammar is needed to type OOL-phrases. For instance, in $\{m_1 : S_1, \ldots, m_n : S_n\}$, each S_i should be a function type.)

As an example, suppose *Pdec* contains the declaration of a class A that has methods m_1 and m_2. Suppose that m_1 has two parameters, one an integer and the other a reference to an object of class A, and that it returns the `unit` value. Suppose also that m_2 has no parameters, and that it returns a reference to an object of class A. Then the expression $\mathsf{new}(A)$, indeed any expression whose value is a reference to an object of class A, is assigned the type

$$\mu Z.\mathtt{ref}\,(\{m_1 : (\mathtt{Int} \times Z) \to \mathtt{unit}, m_2 : \mathtt{unit} \to Z\})\ .$$

Given *Pdec*, let Γ be the type environment that associates the appropriate type with each class name and with each variable. The judgments of the inference system can then take the forms:

(1) $\Gamma \vdash E : S$, read: expression E is well typed and has type S
(2) $\Gamma \vdash C$, read: command C is well typed and contains no return command
(3) $\Gamma \vdash C \succ S$, read: command C is well typed and can return a value of type S
(4) $\Gamma \vdash \mathit{Mdec}$, read: method declaration *Mdec* is well typed
(5) $\Gamma \vdash \mathit{Cdec}$, read: class declaration *Cdec* is well typed
(6) $\Gamma \vdash \mathit{Pdec}$, read: program declaration *Pdec* is well typed.

It holds in particular that if $\Gamma \vdash E : \mathsf{unit}$ then $\Gamma \vdash E$, that is, an expression of unit type can serve as a command. For instance, Pdec_0 has the expressions `p!insert(i!get())`, `i!put(p!delete())`, `q!insert(x)`, `q!insert(k)`, and $\star$ in places where commands are needed.

Exercise 19.1.1 Give a suitable family of inference rules for separating out the well-typed OOL programs. □

19.2 Modelling examples

The formal semantic definition for OOL will take the form of a translation into a typed π-calculus. The calculus will have basic types, tuples and variants, recursive types, $\mathsf{i/o}$ types, and linear-receptive types. The basic types will be unit and the types of truth-values and integers. The calculus will have the same operators on basic values (negation, addition, equality, etc.) as OOL. We will not go into the details of how these operators are evaluated, which are straightforward: we just mirror in the calculus this aspect of the programming language, and to achieve this we assume a call-by-value evaluation strategy for terms of the calculus, as discussed in Remark 6.2.2. The calculus will also have the conditional process form from Section 3.3, to make possible a clear treatment of conditional and iterative commands.

We first explain the main ideas that underlie the translation via three examples. To best achieve this explanatory aim, the examples will not follow the translation of expressions and commands exactly, though they will show its salient features. Also for clarity, the examples will use process constants as well as replication. Moreover, we will not give types explicitly, but will rather draw attention to interesting points about typing.

Notation 19.2.1 Throughout this chapter and the next:

(1) We use pattern matching in input of tuples and variants as in Section 6.6, and similarly for abstractions.
(2) The name z is used only as a placeholder for the value of type unit.
(3) In all of the examples except for the one in Section 20.4, in asserting behavioural equalities between typed terms, we omit the type environment because the type information is not needed for understanding the equalities.
(4) We continue to use the notations $K\lfloor v \rfloor$ for constant application and $F\,v$ for pseudo-application of an abstraction. □

Example 19.2.2 This first example illustrates how the objects of a simple class are represented. The program $Pdec_1$ is given in Table 19.3. When run, it emits 3 to the output stream and then stops. The translation of $Pdec_1$ is

$$[\![Pdec_1]\!] \stackrel{\text{def}}{=} (in, out).\\ (\boldsymbol{\nu} n_{\mathtt{IO}})\,([\![\mathtt{class\ IO}]\!]\langle n_{\mathtt{IO}}, in, out\rangle \mid [\![\mathtt{new(IO)!put(3)}]\!]\, n_{\mathtt{IO}})$$

where

$$[\![\mathtt{class\ IO}]\!] \stackrel{\text{def}}{=} (n_{\mathtt{IO}}, in, out).\,!(\boldsymbol{\nu} i)\,\overline{n_{\mathtt{IO}}}\,i.\,\mathcal{O}_{\mathtt{IO}}\lfloor\langle i, in, out\rangle\rfloor$$

$$\mathcal{O}_{\mathtt{IO}} \triangleq (i, in, out).\,i\,[\ \mathtt{get\_}(z,g) \ \rhd\ in(x).\,\overline{g}x.\,\mathcal{O}_{\mathtt{IO}}\lfloor\langle i, in, out\rangle\rfloor,\\ \mathtt{put\_}(v,p) \ \rhd\ \overline{out}\,v.\,\overline{p}\star.\,\mathcal{O}_{\mathtt{IO}}\lfloor\langle i, in, out\rangle\rfloor\,]$$

$$[\![\mathtt{new(IO)!put(3)}]\!] \stackrel{\text{def}}{=} (n_{\mathtt{IO}}).\,n_{\mathtt{IO}}(i).\,(\boldsymbol{\nu} p)\ (\overline{i}\,\mathtt{put\_}\langle 3, p\rangle \mid p(z).\,\mathbf{0})\,.$$

```
class IO {as before}
   method get ():Int
      return input
   method put (j:Int):unit
      output j ;
      return ⋆

new(IO)!put(3)
```

Table 19.3. *The program* $Pdec_1$

$[\![Pdec_1]\!]$, like the translation of any OOL program, is abstracted on the two names that represent its interface, that is, the input and output streams. In typing $[\![Pdec_1]\!]$, the name *in* can be given type $\mathsf{i}\,\mathtt{Int}$ and the name *out* type $\mathsf{o}\,\mathtt{Int}$.

In general, the translation of a program will be the composition of the encodings of the classes declared in it and of the initial expression, restricted on the names of the class-encodings. For $Pdec_1$, this is the composition of the encoding of the class `IO` and the translation of the expression `new(IO)!put(3)`, restricted on the name $n_{\mathtt{IO}}$.

The process $[\![\mathtt{class\ IO}]\!]\langle n_{\mathtt{IO}}, in, out\rangle$ can send a fresh name i at $n_{\mathtt{IO}}$ and produce $\mathcal{O}_{\mathtt{IO}}\lfloor\langle i, in, out\rangle\rfloor$, which represents an object of class `IO`, named i, in its initial, quiescent state. The replication allows the class-encoding to do this repeatedly. The fact that *fresh* names are sent guarantees that no two objects come to have the same name. The class-encoding sends only the output capability of the name i. This ensures that only the new object-process can receive requests for method invocations addressed to i. For this reason, i can really be thought of as the name of the object.

In typing $[\![\mathtt{class\ IO}]\!]$, the restricted name i can be given the type $\sharp\, T_{\mathtt{IO}}$ where

$$T_{\mathtt{IO}} \stackrel{\mathrm{def}}{=} [\,\mathsf{get\_}(\mathtt{unit} \times \ell\mathsf{rec}_{\mathsf{o}}\,\mathtt{Int}), \mathsf{put\_}(\mathtt{Int} \times \ell\mathsf{rec}_{\mathsf{o}}\,\mathtt{unit})\,],$$

and the name $n_{\mathtt{IO}}$ the type $\mathsf{o}\,\mathsf{o}\,T_{\mathtt{IO}}$. If we were to admit ω-receptive types then $n_{\mathtt{IO}}$ could be given the type $\omega\mathsf{rec}_{\mathsf{o}}\ \mathsf{o}\,T_{\mathtt{IO}}$. (We omit ω-receptive types, which add complexity, to avoid putting too much emphasis on typing.) The labels (get and put) of the variant type $T_{\mathtt{IO}}$ are the names of the methods of class `IO`, and the associated types correspond to the argument and result types of the methods. We hinted at aspects of this representation of objects when we discussed priority queues in Section 7.4. The appearance of the linear-receptive type constructor captures that in any execution of a method, at most one result will be returned

```
class A

   method go ():unit
      new(B)!print(new(IO),3) ;
      return ⋆

class B

   method print (i:ref(IO),k:Int):unit
      i!put(k) ;
      return ⋆

class IO ...   {as before}

new(A)!go()
```

Table 19.4. *The program $Pdec_2$*

(linearity), and that when an object invokes a method, it waits for the result to be returned to it (receptiveness).

The only source of input actions with subject $n_{\mathtt{IO}}$ is the translation of the expression new(IO). In typing $[\![\mathtt{new(IO)!put(3)}]\!]$, the name i can be assigned the type $\mathsf{o}\, T_{\mathtt{IO}}$. The process $[\![\mathtt{new(IO)!put(3)}]\!]\, n_{\mathtt{IO}}$ first receives a name i via $n_{\mathtt{IO}}$. Its continuation uses i to invoke the method put by sending the argument 3, paired with a fresh name p to be used to return the result, and tagged with put to indicate the method that is requested. The restricted name p can be given the linear-receptive type $\ell\mathtt{rec}_\sharp\ \mathtt{unit}$ (corresponding to the subexpression $\ell\mathtt{rec}_\mathsf{o}\ \mathtt{unit}$ in $T_{\mathtt{IO}}$). When the value $\star$ is returned via p, the $\mathcal{O}_{\mathtt{IO}}$-process resumes its quiescent state, and the expression-process becomes inactive. Indeed, the whole system becomes inactive, because after the actions $\tau, \tau, \overline{out}\, 3, \tau$, it is structurally congruent to

$$(\boldsymbol{\nu} n_{\mathtt{IO}})\ ([\![\mathtt{class\ IO}]\!]\langle n_{\mathtt{IO}}, in, out\rangle \mid (\boldsymbol{\nu} i)\ \mathcal{O}_{\mathtt{IO}} \lfloor\langle i, in, out\rangle\rfloor)\ .$$

Thus, $[\![Pdec_1]\!]\langle in, out\rangle \cong^{\mathrm{c}} \overline{out}\, 3.\, \mathbf{0}$. □

Example 19.2.3 The second example illustrates how passing of references is represented. The program $Pdec_2$ is given in Table 19.4. Like $Pdec_1$, the program $Pdec_2$ emits 3 to the output stream (but by different means) and stops. The translation of $Pdec_2$ is

$$[\![Pdec_2]\!] \stackrel{\text{def}}{=} (in, out).\,(\boldsymbol{\nu} n_{\mathtt{A}}, n_{\mathtt{B}}, n_{\mathtt{IO}}) \quad \begin{array}{ll} (& [\![\mathtt{class\,A}]\!]\langle n_{\mathtt{A}}, n_{\mathtt{B}}, n_{\mathtt{IO}}\rangle \\ | & [\![\mathtt{class\,B}]\!]\, n_{\mathtt{B}} \\ | & [\![\mathtt{class\,IO}]\!]\langle n_{\mathtt{IO}}, in, out\rangle \\ | & [\![\mathtt{new(A)!go()}]\!]\, n_{\mathtt{A}}\,) \end{array}$$

where

$$[\![\mathtt{class\,A}]\!] \stackrel{\text{def}}{=} (n_{\mathtt{A}}, n_{\mathtt{B}}, n_{\mathtt{IO}}).\,!(\boldsymbol{\nu} a)\, \overline{n_{\mathtt{A}}}\, a.\, \mathcal{O}_{\mathtt{A}}\lfloor\langle a, n_{\mathtt{B}}, n_{\mathtt{IO}}\rangle\rfloor$$

$$\begin{array}{llll} \mathcal{O}_{\mathtt{A}} \triangleq (a, n_{\mathtt{B}}, n_{\mathtt{IO}}).\, a\,[\mathsf{go\_}(z,g) & \rhd & n_{\mathtt{B}}(b).\, n_{\mathtt{IO}}(i). & (1) \\ & & (\boldsymbol{\nu} p)\, \bar{b}\,\mathsf{print\_}\langle i, 3, p\rangle. & (2) \\ & & p(z).\, \bar{g}\star.\, \mathcal{O}_{\mathtt{A}}\lfloor\langle a, n_{\mathtt{B}}, n_{\mathtt{IO}}\rangle\rfloor\,] & \end{array}$$

$$[\![\mathtt{class\,B}]\!] \stackrel{\text{def}}{=} (n_{\mathtt{B}}).\,!(\boldsymbol{\nu} b)\, \overline{n_{\mathtt{B}}}\, b.\, \mathcal{O}_{\mathtt{B}}\lfloor b\rfloor$$

$$\mathcal{O}_{\mathtt{B}} \triangleq (b).\, b\,[\mathsf{print\_}(i,k,p) \;\rhd\; (\boldsymbol{\nu} q)\, \bar{i}\,\mathsf{put\_}\langle k, q\rangle.\, q(z).\, \bar{p}\star.\, \mathcal{O}_{\mathtt{B}}\lfloor b\rfloor\,]$$

$$[\![\mathtt{new(A)!go()}]\!] \stackrel{\text{def}}{=} (n_{\mathtt{A}}).\, n_{\mathtt{A}}(a).\, (\boldsymbol{\nu} g)\, \bar{a}\,\mathsf{go\_}\langle\star, g\rangle.\, g(z).\, \mathbf{0}\ .$$

The most significant new point is in the definitions of $\mathcal{O}_{\mathtt{A}}$ and $\mathcal{O}_{\mathtt{B}}$. When the method go is invoked, the continuation of $\mathcal{O}_{\mathtt{A}}\lfloor\langle a, n_{\mathtt{B}}, n_{\mathtt{IO}}\rangle\rfloor$ interacts with $[\![\mathtt{class\,B}]\!]\, n_{\mathtt{B}}$ and $[\![\mathtt{class\,IO}]\!]\langle n_{\mathtt{IO}}, in, out\rangle$ to produce new components $\mathcal{O}_{\mathtt{B}}\lfloor b\rfloor$ and $\mathcal{O}_{\mathtt{IO}}\lfloor\langle i, in, out\rangle\rfloor$ – see (1). The continuation of $\mathcal{O}_{\mathtt{A}}\lfloor a\rfloor$ then invokes `print` in $\mathcal{O}_{\mathtt{B}}\lfloor b\rfloor$, with parameters the name i of the object-process $\mathcal{O}_{\mathtt{IO}}\lfloor\langle i, in, out\rangle\rfloor$ and the integer 3 – see (2). On receiving these parameters and the return name p, the process $\mathcal{O}_{\mathtt{B}}\lfloor b\rfloor$ uses i to invoke put in $\mathcal{O}_{\mathtt{IO}}\lfloor\langle i, in, out\rangle\rfloor$. This illustrates how a reference can be passed and used. On receiving the value $\star$ of the invocation of put, the continuation of $\mathcal{O}_{\mathtt{B}}\lfloor b\rfloor$ itself returns $\star$ via p, and the continuation of $\mathcal{O}_{\mathtt{A}}\lfloor\langle a, n_{\mathtt{B}}, n_{\mathtt{IO}}\rangle\rfloor$ returns $\star$ via g to the continuation of $[\![\mathtt{new(A)!go()}]\!]\, n_{\mathtt{A}}$.

In summary, any complete computation of the system involves ten transitions, one of which is labelled $\overline{out}\,3$ and the others τ, and leads to a configuration in which each of the three object-processes is in its quiescent state. Since the final configuration is inactive, $[\![Pdec_2]\!]\langle in, out\rangle \cong^{c} \overline{out}\,3.\,\mathbf{0}$. □

Example 19.2.4 The third example illustrates how encapsulation of instance variables is achieved. The program $Pdec_3$ is given in Table 19.5. When run, the program consumes two integers from the input stream, emits their sum to the output stream, and then stops. The translation of $Pdec_3$ is

$$[\![Pdec_3]\!] \stackrel{\text{def}}{=} (in, out).\,(\boldsymbol{\nu} n_{\mathtt{C}}, n_{\mathtt{IO}}) \quad \begin{array}{ll} (& [\![\mathtt{class\,C}]\!]\langle n_{\mathtt{C}}, n_{\mathtt{IO}}\rangle \\ | & [\![\mathtt{class\,IO}]\!]\langle n_{\mathtt{IO}}, in, out\rangle \\ | & [\![\mathtt{new(C)!sum()}]\!]\, n_{\mathtt{C}}\,) \end{array}$$

```
class C

  var x:Int, y:Int
  method sum ():unit
     x := new(IO)!get() ;
     y := new(IO)!get() ;
     new(IO)!put(x+y) ;
     return ⋆

class IO ...  {as before}

new(C)!sum()
```

Table 19.5. *The program Pdec₃*

where

$$[\![\texttt{class C}]\!] \stackrel{\text{def}}{=} (n_{\mathtt{C}}, n_{\mathtt{IO}}).\,!(\boldsymbol{\nu} c)\,\overline{n_{\mathtt{C}}}\,c.\,\mathcal{O}_{\mathtt{C}}\langle c, n_{\mathtt{IO}}\rangle$$

$$\mathcal{O}_{\mathtt{C}} \stackrel{\text{def}}{=} (c, n_{\mathtt{IO}}).\,(\boldsymbol{\nu}\widetilde{g}, \widetilde{p})\,(U_{\mathtt{C}}\langle \widetilde{g}, \widetilde{p}, 0, 0\rangle \mid M_{\mathtt{C}}\lfloor\langle c, \widetilde{g}, \widetilde{p}, n_{\mathtt{IO}}\rangle\rfloor)$$

$$U_{\mathtt{C}} \stackrel{\text{def}}{=} (\widetilde{g}, \widetilde{p}, v_{\mathtt{X}}, v_{\mathtt{Y}}).\,(V\lfloor\langle g_{\mathtt{X}}, p_{\mathtt{X}}, v_{\mathtt{X}}\rangle\rfloor \mid V\lfloor\langle g_{\mathtt{Y}}, p_{\mathtt{Y}}, v_{\mathtt{Y}}\rangle\rfloor)$$

$$V \triangleq (g, p, u).\,(g(r).\,\overline{r}u.\,V\lfloor\langle g, p, u\rangle\rfloor + p(v, w).\,\overline{w}\star.\,V\lfloor\langle g, p, v\rangle\rfloor)$$

$$\begin{aligned}
M_{\mathtt{C}} \triangleq (c, g, p, n_{\mathtt{IO}}).\,c\,[\mathsf{sum_}(z, s) \quad \rhd \quad & n_{\mathtt{IO}}(i).\,(\boldsymbol{\nu} g)\,\overline{i}\,\mathsf{get_}\langle\star, g\rangle.\,g(a). && (1)\\
& (\boldsymbol{\nu} w)\,\overline{p_{\mathtt{X}}}\,\langle a, w\rangle.\,w(z). && (2)\\
& n_{\mathtt{IO}}(i).\,(\boldsymbol{\nu} g)\,\overline{i}\,\mathsf{get_}\langle\star, g\rangle.\,g(b). &&\\
& (\boldsymbol{\nu} w)\,\overline{p_{\mathtt{Y}}}\,\langle b, w\rangle.\,w(z). &&\\
& n_{\mathtt{IO}}(i). &&\\
& (\boldsymbol{\nu} r)\,\overline{g_{\mathtt{X}}}\,r.\,r(c).\,(\boldsymbol{\nu} r)\,\overline{g_{\mathtt{Y}}}\,r.\,r(d). && (3)\\
& (\boldsymbol{\nu} p)\,\overline{i}\,\mathsf{put_}\langle c + d, p\rangle.\,p(z). && (4)\\
& \overline{s}\star.\,M_{\mathtt{C}}\lfloor\langle c, \widetilde{g}, \widetilde{p}, n_{\mathtt{IO}}\rangle\rfloor\,]
\end{aligned}$$

where $\widetilde{g}$ is $g_{\mathtt{X}}, g_{\mathtt{Y}}$ and $\widetilde{p}$ is $p_{\mathtt{X}}, p_{\mathtt{Y}}$, and

$$[\![\texttt{new(C)!sum()}]\!] \stackrel{\text{def}}{=} (n_{\mathtt{C}}).\,n_{\mathtt{C}}(c).\,(\boldsymbol{\nu} s)\,\overline{c}\,\mathsf{sum\_}\langle\star, s\rangle.\,s(z).\,\mathbf{0}\;.$$

The components of $\mathcal{O}_{\mathtt{C}}\langle c, n_{\mathtt{IO}}\rangle$ are $U_{\mathtt{C}}\langle \widetilde{g}, \widetilde{p}, 0, 0\rangle$, which represents the object's private store, and $M_{\mathtt{C}}\lfloor\langle c, \widetilde{g}, \widetilde{p}, n_{\mathtt{IO}}\rangle\rfloor$, which represents its method-handler. These two processes interact via the private names $\widetilde{g}, \widetilde{p}$, using the kind of dialogue we have seen many times, most recently in modelling method invocation and return. The name $g_{\mathtt{X}}$ is used to get the value of the variable X, and $p_{\mathtt{X}}$ to put a value to

X. The abstraction $U_{\mathtt{C}}$ also has as parameters the values of the variables, initially both 0.

When `sum` is invoked in $M_{\mathtt{C}}$, it interacts with $[\![\mathtt{class\ IO}]\!]\langle n_{\mathtt{IO}}, in, out\rangle$ and then with the $\mathcal{O}_{\mathtt{IO}}$-process produced to consume an integer from the input stream – see (1). The continuation then writes that value to the variable X – see (2). The next two lines are similar, for the variable Y. The two variables are then read – see (3) – and the sum of the values is emitted to the output stream – see (4). The method-handler then returns the result $\star$ of `sum`, and restores itself. In the translation proper, the name $p_{\mathtt{X}}$ can be given the type $\mathsf{i}\,(\mathtt{Int} \times \ell\mathsf{rec}_\mathsf{o}\, \mathtt{unit})$ in typing $U_{\mathtt{C}}$, and the type $\mathsf{o}\,(\mathtt{Int} \times \ell\mathsf{rec}_\mathsf{o}\, \mathtt{unit})$ in typing $M_{\mathtt{C}}$. In (2) in the definition of $M_{\mathtt{C}}$, the name $p_{\mathtt{X}}$ does *not* carry a linear-receptive type, because the occurrence of w in the input prefix is itself underneath a prefix. In the translation proper, however, the form will instead be $(\boldsymbol{\nu} w)\,(\overline{p_{\mathtt{X}}}\,\langle a, w\rangle \mid w(z).\cdots)$, and then the linear-receptive typing is valid. □

19.3 Formal definition

Having seen the main features of the translation in these three examples, we are now ready for the formal semantic definition. Fix a well-typed program *Pdec*. For notational simplicity, we assume that each method of each class in *Pdec* has a single formal parameter.

The translation is defined inductively on the phrases of *Pdec* and on the types that are assigned to them. Taking types first, the translation is the identity on basic types and type variables, and it acts as a homomorphism on tuple types and recursive types. On reference types, record types, and function types we have

$$\begin{aligned}
[\![\mathtt{ref}\,(S)]\!] &\stackrel{\mathrm{def}}{=} \sharp\,[\![S]\!] \\
[\![\{_{i\in 1,\ldots,k}\ m_i : S_i\}]\!] &\stackrel{\mathrm{def}}{=} [_{i\in 1,\ldots,k}\ \mathsf{m}_i_[\![S_i]\!]\,] \\
[\![S \rightarrow S']\!] &\stackrel{\mathrm{def}}{=} [\![S]\!] \times \ell\mathsf{rec}_\mathsf{o}\, [\![S']\!]\,.
\end{aligned}$$

So, for example, applying the translation to the type

$$\mu Z.\mathtt{ref}\,(\{m_1 : (\mathtt{Int} \times Z) \rightarrow \mathtt{unit}, m_2 : \mathtt{unit} \rightarrow Z\}) \tag{19.1}$$

considered at the end of Section 19.1 yields the π-calculus type

$$\mu Z.\sharp\,[\mathsf{m}_1\_(\mathtt{Int} \times Z \times \ell\mathsf{rec}_\mathsf{o}\, \mathtt{unit}), \mathsf{m}_2\_(\mathtt{unit} \times \ell\mathsf{rec}_\mathsf{o}\, Z)]\,.$$

A π-calculus name a that represents a reference that has the type in (19.1) can carry values of the forms $\mathsf{m}_1\_\langle 3, a', r\rangle$ and $\mathsf{m}_2\_\langle\star, r'\rangle$, where a' has the same type as a, and r and r' have the appropriate linear-receptive types.

$$
\begin{aligned}
[\![X]\!] &\stackrel{\text{def}}{=} (h,\ldots).\,(\nu r)\,(\overline{g_X}\,r \mid r(v).\,\overline{h}v)\\
[\![E_1 + E_2]\!] &\stackrel{\text{def}}{=} (h,\ldots).\,(\nu h_1, h_2, w)\,([\![E_1]\!]\langle h_1,\ldots\rangle \mid w(z).\,[\![E_2]\!]\langle h_2,\ldots\rangle\\
&\qquad \mid h_1(v_1).\,(\overline{w}\star \mid h_2(v_2).\,\overline{h}\,(v_1+v_2)))\\
[\![\mathsf{new}(A)]\!] &\stackrel{\text{def}}{=} (h,\ldots).\,n_A(a).\,\overline{h}a\\
[\![E_1!m(E_2)]\!] &\stackrel{\text{def}}{=} (h,\ldots).\,(\nu h_1, h_2, w)\,([\![E_1]\!]\langle h_1,\ldots\rangle \mid w(z).\,[\![E_2]\!]\langle h_2,\ldots\rangle\\
&\qquad \mid h_1(v_1).\,(\overline{w}\star \mid h_2(v_2).\,(\nu r)\,(\overline{v_1}\,\mathsf{m\_}\langle v_2, r\rangle \mid r(v).\,\overline{h}v)))\\
[\![\mathsf{input}]\!] &\stackrel{\text{def}}{=} (h,\ldots).\,in(v).\,\overline{h}v
\end{aligned}
$$

Table 19.6. *The translation of expressions*

Now we consider the translation of expressions. It is defined inductively, each clause being of the form

$$[\![E]\!] \stackrel{\text{def}}{=} (h, \widetilde{g}, in, \widetilde{n}).\, P_E$$

for some process P_E. The process $[\![E]\!]\langle h, \widetilde{g}, in, \widetilde{n}\rangle$ will 'evaluate' E and, as its last act, hand on the resulting value via h. The process can use the names $\widetilde{g}$ to get the values of variables that occur in E, by interacting with the appropriate store-process; cf. U_{C} in Example 19.2.4. (No expression can write to a variable.) When E is the expression input, the name in is used to consume an integer from the input stream. The names $\widetilde{n}$ are the names of the encodings of *Pdec*'s classes, such as n_{IO} in Example 19.2.2. Although, depending on what E actually is, $[\![E]\!]\langle h, \widetilde{g}, in, \widetilde{n}\rangle$ may not use in or some of the names in $\widetilde{g}, \widetilde{n}$, it is notationally convenient to include them all as parameters. We will often elide parameters to highlight important points, however. The translation, omitting type annotations and eliding $\widetilde{g}, in, \widetilde{n}$, is given in Table 19.6. In the second line of the table, we give the clause for addition to illustrate the translation of operator expressions. We briefly draw attention to how the correct flow of control is achieved. It is intended that evaluation of $E_1!m(E_2)$ should begin with evaluation of E_1, continue with evaluation of E_2, and conclude with invocation of the method m and receipt of the result, the result being the value of the composite expression. In $[\![E_1!m(E_2)]\!]$, the third component is responsible for coordinating the activity of the two expression-processes, and for invoking the method and receiving and handing on the result. On receiving the value of E_1 via h_1, this component activates $[\![E_2]\!]$ via w. Then, on receiving the value of E_2 via h_2, it invokes the method m by using the name that is the value of E_1. Finally, on receiving the

$$
\begin{aligned}
[\![X := E]\!] &\stackrel{\text{def}}{=} (h,\ldots).\,(\boldsymbol{\nu} h')\,([\![E]\!]\langle h',\ldots\rangle \\
&\qquad \mid h'(v).\,(\boldsymbol{\nu} w)\,(\overline{p_X}\langle v,w\rangle \mid w(z).\,\overline{h}\star)) \\
[\![C_1;C_2]\!] &\stackrel{\text{def}}{=} (h,\ldots).\,(\boldsymbol{\nu} h')\,([\![C_1]\!]\langle h',\ldots\rangle \mid h'(z).\,[\![C_2]\!]\langle h,\ldots\rangle) \\
[\![\mathsf{if}\ E\ \mathsf{then}\ C_1\ \mathsf{else}\ C_2]\!] &\stackrel{\text{def}}{=} (h,\ldots).\,(\boldsymbol{\nu} h')\,([\![E]\!]\langle h',\ldots\rangle \\
&\qquad \mid h'(v).\,\mathsf{IF}(v \hookrightarrow [\![C_1]\!]\langle h,\ldots\rangle, \neg v \hookrightarrow [\![C_2]\!]\langle h,\ldots\rangle)) \\
[\![\mathsf{while}\ E\ \mathsf{do}\ C]\!] &\stackrel{\text{def}}{=} (h,\ldots).\,(\boldsymbol{\nu} h',h'',g)\,(\overline{g}\star \mid !g(z).\,([\![E]\!]\langle h',\ldots\rangle \\
&\qquad \mid h'(v).\,\mathsf{IF}(v \hookrightarrow [\![C]\!]\langle h'',\ldots\rangle, \neg v \hookrightarrow \overline{h}\star) \mid h''(z).\,\overline{g}\star)) \\
[\![\mathsf{return}\ E]\!] &\stackrel{\text{def}}{=} (h,\ldots).\,(\boldsymbol{\nu} h')\,([\![E]\!]\langle h',\ldots\rangle \mid h'(v).\,\overline{r}v.\,\overline{h}\star) \\
[\![\mathsf{output}\ E]\!] &\stackrel{\text{def}}{=} (h,\ldots).\,(\boldsymbol{\nu} h')\,([\![E]\!]\langle h',\ldots\rangle \mid h'(v).\,\overline{out}\,v.\,\overline{h}\star)
\end{aligned}
$$

Table 19.7. *The translation of commands*

result of the invocation via the fresh name r, it hands the result on via h as the final value.

We now consider the translation of commands. It too is defined inductively, each clause being of the form

$$[\![C]\!] \stackrel{\text{def}}{=} (h, r, \widetilde{g}, \widetilde{p}, in, out, \widetilde{n}).\, P_C$$

for some process P_C. The process $[\![C]\!]\langle h, r, \widetilde{g}, \widetilde{p}, in, out, \widetilde{n}\rangle$ will 'execute' C and, as its last act, hand on via h the value $\star$ to indicate to the appropriate process that it has finished. It can use the name r to return a result to some object, and the names $\widetilde{p}$ to put values to variables. Similarly to the case with expressions, although $[\![C]\!]\langle h, r, \widetilde{g}, \widetilde{p}, in, out, \widetilde{n}\rangle$ may not use r or in or out or some of the names in $\widetilde{g}, \widetilde{p}, \widetilde{n}$, it is notationally convenient to include them all as parameters. The translation, again omitting type annotations and eliding $r, \widetilde{g}, \widetilde{p}, in, out, \widetilde{n}$, is given in Table 19.7.

The translation of commands uses similar ideas to the translation of expressions. For instance, in $[\![X := E]\!]$, the second component receives the value of E via h', writes it to the variable X in the way we saw in Example 19.2.4, and then signals via h that it has finished. When $[\![\mathsf{while}\ E\ \mathsf{do}\ C]\!]$ is executed, a copy of the replicated process is activated via the private name g. The value of E is delivered via h'. If that value is false then the activated process signals via h that the while command has finished. If the value is true then a copy of $[\![C]\!]$ is activated, and when this process has finished, it signals via h'', and another copy of the replicated process is activated.

Now suppose that the class declaration *Cdec* appears in *Pdec*. Suppose that the name of the class is A, and its methods are $Mdec_1, \ldots, Mdec_k$ where $Mdec_i$ is

$$\mathsf{method}\, m_i(X_i : T_i) : T_i',\ C_i\ .$$

Suppose also that its instance variables are

$$\mathsf{var}\, X_{k+1} : T_{k+1}, \ldots, X_{k+j} : T_{k+j}\ .$$

Then

$$[\![Cdec]\!] \stackrel{\mathrm{def}}{=} (\widetilde{n}, in, out).\,!(\boldsymbol{\nu} a)\, \overline{n}a.\, \mathcal{O}_A\langle a, \widetilde{n}, in, out\rangle$$

where n is the appropriate member of $\widetilde{n}$ and

$$\mathcal{O}_A \stackrel{\mathrm{def}}{=} (a, \widetilde{n}, in, out).\,(\boldsymbol{\nu}\widetilde{g}, \widetilde{p}, \widetilde{a})\,(U_A\langle \widetilde{g}, \widetilde{p}, \widetilde{v_0}\rangle \mid M_A\langle a, \widetilde{g}, \widetilde{p}, \widetilde{n}, in, out\rangle)$$

where the members of $\widetilde{v_0}$ represent the initial values of the variables, that is, each is (according to type) $\star$, 0, or a link. The links in $\widetilde{v_0}$ are the names $\widetilde{a}$ that are restricted in $\mathcal{O}_A$, and hence represent null references. The process $\mathcal{O}_A$, which represents an object, has two components: U_A, which represents the object's store, and M_A, which represents its method-handler. These components are defined as follows. First,

$$U_A \stackrel{\mathrm{def}}{=} (\widetilde{g}, \widetilde{p}, \widetilde{v}).\, \Pi_{i=1}^{k+j}\, V\langle g_i, p_i, v_i\rangle$$

where $\widetilde{g}$ is $g_1, \ldots, g_{k+j}$ and $\widetilde{p}$ is $p_1, \ldots, p_{k+j}$ (where we write g_i and p_i for g_{X_i} and p_{X_i}) and $\widetilde{v}$ is $v_1, \ldots, v_{k+j}$, and V is a cell very similar to one we considered in Section 5.2:

$$V \stackrel{\mathrm{def}}{=} (g, p, u).\,(\boldsymbol{\nu}\ell)\,(\overline{\ell}u \mid !\ell(u).\,(g(r).\,(\overline{r}u \mid \overline{\ell}u) + p(v, w).\,(\overline{w}\star \mid \overline{\ell}v)))\ .$$

The composition in U_A is indexed from 1 to $k + j$ because method parameters are treated in the same way as instance variables. Second,

$$\begin{aligned} M_A \stackrel{\mathrm{def}}{=} (a, \widetilde{g}, \widetilde{p}, \widetilde{n}, in, out).\,(\boldsymbol{\nu} g)\,(\overline{g}\star \\ \mid !g(z).\, a\,[_{i\in 1,\ldots,k}\, \mathsf{m_i}\_(v, r) \rhd (\boldsymbol{\nu} w)\,(\,\overline{p_i}\,\langle v, w\rangle \mid \\ w(z).\,(\boldsymbol{\nu} h)\ \ ([\![C_i]\!]\langle h, \ldots\rangle \\ \mid h(z).\,\overline{g}\star))\,])\ . \end{aligned}$$

(Note that $(\boldsymbol{\nu} h)\,([\![C_i]\!]\langle h, \ldots\rangle \mid h(z).\,\overline{g}\star)$ could be abbreviated to $[\![C_i]\!]\langle g, \ldots\rangle$; the longer form is clearer, however.)

These definitions are similar to what we have seen in the three examples, except that they use replication rather than process constants (to make typing slightly simpler). When the method-handler M_A receives a method invocation, it writes the argument to the appropriate variable, activates the appropriate command-process, and restores itself when that process signals that it has finished.

Finally, suppose *Pdec* is $Cdec_1, \ldots, Cdec_p,\ E_0$. Then

$$\begin{aligned}[\![Pdec]\!] \stackrel{\text{def}}{=} (in, out).\,(\boldsymbol{\nu}\widetilde{n})\,(\;& [\![Cdec_1]\!]\langle n_1, \ldots\rangle \\ |\; & \ldots \\ |\; & [\![Cdec_p]\!]\langle n_p, \ldots\rangle \\ |\; & (\boldsymbol{\nu}h)\ [\![E_0]\!]\langle h, \ldots\rangle)\end{aligned}$$

where $\widetilde{n} = n_1, \ldots, n_p$. This too is essentially as in the examples, the only refinement being that the name h is restricted as $[\![E_0]\!]\langle h, \ldots\rangle$ need not hand on its value.

The reader may care to revisit Examples 19.2.2–19.2.4 with the formal definition to hand. The reader may also care to check that the remarks in the three examples about typing are justified on the basis of the definition.

Exercise 19.3.1 Extend the definition to accommodate the additional command form repeat C until E. □

Exercise 19.3.2 Extend the definition to accommodate the additional expression form $E_1!!m(E_2)$, which has the following intended meaning. To evaluate the expression, first evaluate E_1 to v_1, then evaluate E_2 to v_2, and then invoke m in v_1 with v_2 as argument, but do not wait for a result: the value of the expression $E_1!!m(E_2)$ is $\star$. □

Exercise 19.3.3 Extend the definition to accommodate the additional command form delegate $E_1!m(E_2)$, which has the following intended meaning. Suppose an object a invokes a method m' in an object b, and that the body of m' contains the delegate command. Suppose E_1 evaluates to a reference to an object c. Then, when b invokes m in c, it transfers to c the obligation to return a result to a. Thus, b is free to proceed, and c should return the result of m not to b but to a. (Note: the body of m may itself contain a delegate command.) □

20

Applications

This chapter illustrates some uses of the kind of semantic definition given in Chapter 19 via a series of examples. We continue to use the notations in Notation 19.2.1.

20.1 Some properties of declarations and commands

Example 20.1.1 (Eliminating an unused variable) Consider the skeleton class declaration in Table 20.1. If none of $\mathtt{C}_1, \ldots, \mathtt{C}_k$ contains either the expression `X` or a command of the form `X := E`, then deleting the declaration of `X` should not change the behaviour of objects of the class, and hence should not affect the behaviour of any program in which the class appears. To prove this, we use the straightforward equivalence

$$(\nu x, y)\,((x(w).\,P + y(v).\,Q) \mid R) \cong^{c} R \tag{20.1}$$

provided $x, y \notin \mathsf{fn}(R)$. (For notational convenience, in what follows we assume that `T` is `Int`.)

Now suppose that `X` is the jth variable of `A`, and write V_j for $V\langle g_j, p_j, 0\rangle$ and abbreviate g_j to g and p_j to p. Then there are processes G and P such that

$$V_j \cong^{c} g(r).\,G + p(v, w).\,P\ . \tag{20.2}$$

Let `A'` be the class obtained from `A` by deleting the declaration of `X`. Then, since none of the method bodies contains the expression `X` or an assignment to `X`,

$$M_{\mathtt{A}'} = M_{\mathtt{A}}\ . \tag{20.3}$$

Hence

```
class A
   var ...  X:T ...
   method m₁ (X₁:T₁):T'₁
      C₁
   ...
   method mₖ (Xₖ:Tₖ):T'ₖ
      Cₖ
```

Table 20.1. *A skeleton class declaration*

$$\begin{aligned}
\mathcal{O}_{\mathtt{A}} &\equiv (\boldsymbol{\nu} g, \widetilde{g}, p, \widetilde{p})\,(U_{\mathtt{A}} \mid M_{\mathtt{A}}) \\
&\equiv (\boldsymbol{\nu} g, p)\,(V_j \mid (\boldsymbol{\nu} \widetilde{g}, \widetilde{p})\,(\Pi_{i \neq j} V_i \mid M_{\mathtt{A}})) \\
&\cong^{c} (\boldsymbol{\nu} g, p)\,((g(r).\, G + p(v, w).\, P) \mid (\boldsymbol{\nu} \widetilde{g}, \widetilde{p})\,(\Pi_{i \neq j} V_i \mid M_{\mathtt{A}})) \\
&\cong^{c} (\boldsymbol{\nu} \widetilde{g}, \widetilde{p})\,(\Pi_{i \neq j} V_i \mid M_{\mathtt{A}}) \\
&= (\boldsymbol{\nu} \widetilde{g}, \widetilde{p})\,(\Pi_{i \neq j} V_i \mid M_{\mathtt{A'}}) \\
&= \mathcal{O}_{\mathtt{A'}}\,,
\end{aligned}$$

using (20.2), the equivalence in (20.1), and the observation in (20.3). This completes Example 20.1.1. □

Example 20.1.2 (Replacing a variable by a constant) Consider again the skeleton class declaration in Table 20.1. If none of $\mathtt{C}_1, \ldots, \mathtt{C}_k$ contains a command of the form `X := E`, then replacing each occurrence of the expression `X` in $\mathtt{C}_1, \ldots, \mathtt{C}_k$ by `0` (the initial value of `X`) and deleting the declaration of `X` should not change the behaviour of objects of the class, and hence should not affect the behaviour of any program in which the class appears.

Let us reuse the notations V_j, $M_{\mathtt{A}}$, etc. from Example 20.1.1, and write $\mathtt{A}''$ for the class obtained from `A` by applying the transformation. So,

$$\mathcal{O}_{\mathtt{A}} \equiv (\boldsymbol{\nu} g, p)\,(V_j \mid (\boldsymbol{\nu} \widetilde{g}, \widetilde{p})\,(\Pi_{i \neq j} V_i \mid M_{\mathtt{A}}))$$

and

$$\mathcal{O}_{\mathtt{A''}} \equiv (\boldsymbol{\nu} \widetilde{g}, \widetilde{p})\,(\Pi_{i \neq j} V_i \mid M_{\mathtt{A''}})\,.$$

Suppose there are n occurrences of `X` in the method bodies. Then there exists an n-ary context D such that $g, p \notin \mathsf{fn}(D)$ and

$$M_{\mathtt{A}} = D[[\![\mathtt{X}]\!]\langle h_1, g, \ldots\rangle, \ldots, [\![\mathtt{X}]\!]\langle h_n, g, \ldots\rangle]$$

and

$$M_{\mathtt{A}''} = D[[\![\mathtt{O}]\!]\langle h_1, \ldots\rangle, \ldots, [\![\mathtt{O}]\!]\langle h_n, \ldots\rangle]$$

for some names $h_1, \ldots, h_n$.

Exercise 20.1.3

(1) Show that if $p \notin \mathsf{fn}(Q)$ then

$$(\boldsymbol{\nu} g, p)\,(V_j \mid Q) \cong^{\mathrm{c}} (\boldsymbol{\nu} g)\,(!g(r).\,\overline{r}0 \mid Q)\ .$$

(2) Show that if $p, g, \notin \mathsf{fn}(D)$ then

$$\begin{aligned} &(\boldsymbol{\nu} g)\,(!g(r).\,\overline{r}0 \mid D[[\![\mathtt{X}]\!]\langle h_1, g\rangle, \ldots, [\![\mathtt{X}]\!]\langle h_n, g\rangle]) \\ \cong^{\mathrm{c}}\ & D[[\![\mathtt{O}]\!]\langle h_1, \ldots\rangle, \ldots, [\![\mathtt{O}]\!]\langle h_n, \ldots\rangle]\ . \end{aligned}$$

(Hint: argue by induction on D, using the Replication Theorems.)

(3) Deduce that $\mathcal{O}_{\mathtt{A}} \cong^{\mathrm{c}} \mathcal{O}_{\mathtt{A}''}$. □

This completes Example 20.1.2. □

Example 20.1.4 (Equivalence of two commands) Exercise 19.3.1 invited the reader to extend the semantic definition to accommodate the command form $\mathsf{repeat}\ C\ \mathsf{until}\ E$.

Exercise 20.1.5 Show that for any command C and expression E,

$$\mathsf{repeat}\ C\ \mathsf{until}\ E \qquad \text{and} \qquad C; \mathsf{while\ not}\ E\ \mathsf{do}\ C$$

are interchangeable, that is, whenever one occurs in a program, it can be replaced by the other without altering the observable behaviour of the system. □

This completes Example 20.1.4. □

20.2 Proxies

In OOL, when an object a invokes a method m in an object b, the object a waits for b to return a result to it. In some cases, however, a may not require the result: it may simply wish the action to be carried out. In such a case, the result type of m would most likely be `unit`. We saw in the program $Pdec_{\mathrm{O}}$ in Table 19.2 involving the priority queue that the return of $\star$ can sometimes be anticipated so that the calling object is not delayed unnecessarily. This is not always possible, however.

A *proxy* can sometimes provide a way round the difficulty. Suppose that a is of class A, that b is of class B, that m has argument type T, and that `E!m(E')` is the expression whose evaluation by a produces the call to b. The idea is that if

```
class P
   method pm (t:ref(B),x:T):unit
      return ⋆ ;
      t!m(x)
```

Table 20.2. *A proxy class*

```
class A
   var b:ref(B)
   method go ():unit
      b := new(B) ;
      b!m(0) ;
      new(IO)!put(3) ;
      return ⋆
class B
   var q:ref(B)
   method m (k:Int):unit
      if k=0 then return ⋆
      else (q := new(B) ; q!m(k-1) ; return ⋆)
class IO ...  {as before}
new(A)!go()
```

Table 20.3. *The program* $Pdec_4$

we add the class in Table 20.2 to the program, then we can achieve the desired effect by replacing the expression `E!m(E′)` by `new(P)!pm(E,E′)` in the declaration of A. When a invokes `pm` in the proxy, that is, the new object of class `P`, that object immediately returns $\star$ to a, and then invokes m in b and waits for the result. When the result is returned, no object has a reference to the proxy. A garbage-collector can therefore reclaim the storage that the proxy occupies.

There is some subtlety to this transformation, however. Using the semantic definition, it is possible to explore this with precision. First, consider applying the transformation to the program $Pdec_4$ in Table 20.3. This involves adding the declaration of `P` to the program, and replacing the expression `b!m(0)` in the body of go by `new(P)!pm(b,0)`. In very rough π-calculus terms, the essence of the transformation is to replace a process of the form

$$R \stackrel{\text{def}}{=} (\boldsymbol{\nu} r)\, \overline{b}\, \langle v, r\rangle.\, r(z).\, R^*$$

by the process

$$R' \stackrel{\text{def}}{=} (\boldsymbol{\nu} p)\, ((\boldsymbol{\nu} r)\, \overline{p}\, \langle b, v, r\rangle.\, r(z).\, R^* \mid p(b, v, r).\, \overline{r}\star.\, (\boldsymbol{\nu} r')\, \overline{b}\, \langle v, r'\rangle.\, r'(z).\, \mathbf{0})\, .$$

In general, R and R' are *not* behaviourally equivalent. To see this, suppose that R'' is a process that can receive via b. Then, in $R \mid R''$ the subterm R^* cannot proceed without a response from R'' via the private name r that is sent via b; but this it not so in $R' \mid R''$. A second difference has to do with sharing. Suppose that R^* and R'' share access to some process R''', and that before responding via r, R'' should interact with R'''. In $R \mid R'' \mid R'''$, this interaction cannot be interfered with by R^*; but in $R' \mid R'' \mid R'''$, it is possible that R^* may interact with R''' before R'' does. This is explored in detail in Exercise 20.2.1.

In certain contexts, however, R and R' are indistinguishable, as we now see. In this example, we appeal to typed bisimilarity, and therefore coerce linear-receptive types to connection types; see Remark 9.4.11. The first step makes explicit the sequentiality of processes representing OOL-objects. This involves transforming object-processes into a form similar to that used in Examples 19.2.2–19.2.4. For readability, we use process constants rather than replication.

Applying the semantic definition and carrying out some calculation, possibly applying the Unique-Solution Theorem, we have that $\mathcal{O}_{\mathtt{A}}\langle a, \ldots\rangle \approx Q_{\mathtt{A}}$ and $\mathcal{O}_{\mathtt{B}}\langle b, \ldots\rangle \approx Q_{\mathtt{B}}$ and $\mathcal{O}_{\mathtt{P}}\langle p, \ldots\rangle \approx Q_{\mathtt{P}}$, where, eliding for readability the parameters in the constant definitions, which are fixed:

$$\begin{aligned}
Q_{\mathtt{A}} &\triangleq a\, [\mathsf{go_}(z, g) && \rhd\ \ n_{\mathtt{B}}(b).\, (\boldsymbol{\nu} r)\, \overline{b}\, \mathsf{m_}\langle 0, r\rangle.\, r(z). \\
& && \quad\ n_{\mathtt{IO}}(i).\, (\boldsymbol{\nu} p)\, \overline{i}\, \mathsf{put_}\langle 3, p\rangle.\, p(z).\, \overline{g}\star.\, Q_{\mathtt{A}}\,] \\
Q_{\mathtt{B}} &\triangleq b\, [\, \mathsf{m_}(k, r) && \rhd\ \ \mathsf{IF}(k = 0 \hookrightarrow \overline{r}\star.\, Q_{\mathtt{B}},\ k \neq 0 \hookrightarrow n_{\mathtt{B}}(b). \\
& && \quad\ (\boldsymbol{\nu} r')\, \overline{b}\, \mathsf{m_}\langle k-1, r'\rangle.\, r'(z).\, \overline{r}\star.\, Q_{\mathtt{B}})\,] \\
Q_{\mathtt{P}} &\triangleq p\, [\, \mathsf{pm_}(b, k, r) && \rhd\ \ \overline{r}\star.\, (\boldsymbol{\nu} r')\, \overline{b}\, \mathsf{m_}\langle k, r'\rangle.\, r'(z).\, Q_{\mathtt{P}}\,]\, .
\end{aligned}$$

Also, $[\![\mathtt{new(A)!go()}]\!]\langle n_{\mathtt{A}}, \ldots\rangle \approx Q_E$ where

$$Q_E \stackrel{\text{def}}{=} n_{\mathtt{A}}(a).\, (\boldsymbol{\nu} g)\, \overline{a}\, \mathsf{go\_}\langle \star, g\rangle.\, g(z).\, \mathbf{0}\, .$$

For the transformed object of class A, the analogue of process $Q_{\mathtt{A}}$ is

$$\begin{aligned}
Q^*_{\mathtt{A}} \triangleq a\, [\mathsf{go_}(z, g)\ \ \rhd\ \ & n_{\mathtt{B}}(b).\, n_{\mathtt{P}}(p).\, (\boldsymbol{\nu} r)\, \overline{p}\, \mathsf{pm_}\langle b, 0, r\rangle.\, r(z). \\
& n_{\mathtt{IO}}(i).\, (\boldsymbol{\nu} p)\, \overline{i}\, \mathsf{put_}\langle 3, p\rangle.\, p(z).\, \overline{g}\star.\, Q^*_{\mathtt{A}}\,]\, .
\end{aligned}$$

Let also $C_{\mathtt{A}} \stackrel{\text{def}}{=} !(\nu a)\, \overline{n_{\mathtt{A}}}\, a.\, Q_{\mathtt{A}}$ and $C^*_{\mathtt{A}} \stackrel{\text{def}}{=} !(\nu a)\, \overline{n_{\mathtt{A}}}\, a.\, Q^*_{\mathtt{A}}$, where again we elide the fixed parameters, and define $C_{\mathtt{B}}$ and $C_{\mathtt{P}}$ and $C_{\mathtt{IO}}$ analogously.

Then, the correctness of the transformation in this case can be established by proving that

$$(\nu\tilde{n})\,(C_{\mathtt{A}} \mid C_{\mathtt{B}} \mid C_{\mathtt{IO}} \mid Q_E) \approx (\nu\tilde{n})\,(C^*_{\mathtt{A}} \mid C_{\mathtt{P}} \mid C_{\mathtt{B}} \mid C_{\mathtt{IO}} \mid Q_E)\,.$$

The proof is straightforward but tedious. By expanding the behaviour we see that the process on the left has a single computation consisting of seven τ transitions, followed by the action $\overline{out}\,3$, followed by two more τ transitions, after which it can do nothing more. The process on the right can only perform six τ transitions and reach a state from which the remaining actions will be two τ transitions (representing the interaction between the proxy and the object of class B) interleaved with two τ transitions, the action $\overline{out}\,3$, and two more τ transitions (the remaining actions of the object of class A and the object of class IO). Thus both processes are equivalent to $\overline{out}\,3.\,\mathbf{0}$. The calculation shows clearly that after the proxy has played its part, it can be garbage-collected. In π-calculus terms, this is expressed by the familiar equivalence

$$(\nu p)\,(p\,[\,\mathsf{pm\_}(b,k,r) \rhd \ldots] \mid Q) \sim^{\mathrm{c}} Q \quad \text{if } p \notin \mathsf{fn}(Q)\,,$$

where the first component represents the quiescent proxy after the result has been returned to it, and Q represents the rest of the system. A similar result could be obtained if the argument 0 in the invocation of m were replaced by any positive integer.

One can also see, however, that the transformation cannot be applied arbitrarily without affecting the observable behaviour of the system.

Exercise 20.2.1 Give an example program *Pdec* such that if *Pdec** is the program obtained by applying the proxy transformation, then $[\![Pdec]\!] \not\approx [\![Pdec^*]\!]$. (Hint: consider again the argument in the invocation of m in the program above; or consider a *Pdec* that produces objects a and b that share a reference to some object as in the discussion at the beginning of this section.) □

The semantic definition gives us a way of expressing precisely conditions under which the transformation can be correctly applied, and of justifying rigorously that this is so. We do not go into this here, however.

A variation of the above scenario is when a *does* require the result of its invocation of m in b, but not immediately. Suppose the result is of type T', and y is a variable where the result is to be found when needed. Then one possibility is to add the class in Table 20.4 to the program, and to change the body of the method, of A, in question from

```
class P
   var r:T′
   method pm (t:ref(B),x:T):unit
      return ⋆ ;
      r := t!m(x)
   method pget ():T′
      return r
```

Table 20.4. *A second proxy class*

```
... ; y := E!m(E′) ; ... ; C ; ...
```

where C is the first subsequent command that involves y, to

```
... ; p := new(P) ; p!pm(E,E′) ; ... ; y := p!pget() ; C ; ...
```

where p is a new variable of type P. Note that the method pget cannot be invoked until the proxy has returned to its quiescent state, and that the proxy becomes quiescent only when it receives the result of m from the B-object.

A similar subtlety attends the relationship between the original and transformed programs. Using the semantic definition, however, it is possible to prove that under certain conditions, this kind of proxy does indeed do what is intended and then vanishes. Again we do not go into this here.

20.3 An implementation technique

We introduced objects by saying that they are often explained informally as persistent entities that have some private data, stored in instance variables, and a repertoire of actions, or methods, that they can perform. The semantic definition elaborates that informal account faithfully. In particular, an object is expressed as the composition of a process representing the object's private store and a process that handles method requests.

In implementations of object-oriented languages, however, it is common for the code of methods to be shared among all the objects of a given class. Thus, an object is rather thought of as made up of a private store and a process that is able to activate the shared code as appropriate. Indeed, often there is a tree whose nodes contain (pointers to) method codes, the structure of the tree being determined by *inheritance* among classes within the program. (Inheritance allows methods declared in one class to be used in another.) Using the semantic definition, we can establish rigorously the harmony between these two views of objects.

An object-process, according to the semantic definition in Section 19.3, has the form

$$\mathcal{O} \stackrel{\text{def}}{=} (a, \ldots).\,(\boldsymbol{\nu} s, \ldots)\;(U\langle s\rangle \mid M\langle a, s, \ldots\rangle)\,,$$

where U is the store and M is the method-handler, and we elide some parameters and write s for $\widetilde{g}, \widetilde{p}$. Using the Replication Theorems and some other simple properties, it can be transformed into the form

$$\mathcal{O}^* \stackrel{\text{def}}{=} (a, \ldots).\,(\boldsymbol{\nu} s, \widetilde{u})\;(U\langle s\rangle \mid H\langle a, s, \widetilde{u}\rangle \mid \Pi_i\, !u_i(h, r, s).\,[\![C_i]\!]\langle h, r, s, \ldots\rangle)\,,$$

where again we elide some parameters. The method-handler, M, is split into two: a coordinating process H, defined by

$$\begin{aligned} H \stackrel{\text{def}}{=}\; & (a, s, \widetilde{u}).\,(\boldsymbol{\nu} g)\;(\overline{g}\star \\ & \mid !g(z).\,a\,[_i\ \mathsf{m_i\_}(v, r)\ \rhd\ (\boldsymbol{\nu} w)\;(\,\overline{p_i}\,\langle v, w\rangle \mid \\ & \qquad\qquad w(z).\,(\boldsymbol{\nu} h)\;(\overline{u_i}\,\langle h, r, s\rangle \mid h(z).\,\overline{g}\star))\,])\,, \end{aligned}$$

and a composition of processes derived from the translations of the method bodies, the C_i. When H receives an invocation of method m_i via a, it writes the argument v to the appropriate variable via p_i, and then activates via u_i a copy of the appropriate method-body process, supplying it with access to the store, the return name r, and a name h to signal when it has finished. A class is then represented by

$$(n, \ldots).\,!(\boldsymbol{\nu} a)\,\overline{n}a.\,\mathcal{O}^*\langle a, \ldots\rangle\,.$$

Exercise 20.3.1 Show that $\mathcal{O} \cong^{\mathrm{c}} \mathcal{O}^*$. □

Let us now consider the view of objects as sharers of method codes. Then a class is represented by

$$(n, \ldots).\,(\boldsymbol{\nu}\widetilde{u})\;(!(\boldsymbol{\nu} a)\,\overline{n}a.\,\mathcal{O}^{**}\langle a, \widetilde{u}\rangle \mid \Pi_i\, !u_i(h, r, s).\,[\![C_i]\!]\langle h, r, s, \ldots\rangle)$$

where

$$\mathcal{O}^{**} \stackrel{\text{def}}{=} (a, \widetilde{u}).\,(\boldsymbol{\nu} s)\;(U\langle s\rangle \mid H\langle a, s, \widetilde{u}\rangle)\,.$$

That is, an object comprises a private store and a process H to deal with method invocations. The method codes, however, are shared among the objects of the class – and replicated so that as many concurrent invocations as are needed are possible.

The harmony between the two views is then expressed formally as the assertion

```
class PQ
   var k:Int, q:ref(PQ)
   method insert (x:Int):unit
      return ⋆ ;
      if k=0 then (k := x ; q := new(PQ))
      else if x<k then q!insert(x)
           else (q!insert(k) ; k := x)
   method delete ():Int
      return k ;
      if k=0 then ⋆
      else (k := q!delete() ; if k=0 then q := nil(PQ) else ⋆)
   method search (y:Int):Bool
      if (k=0 or y>k) then return false
      else if y=k then return true
           else delegate q!search(k)
```

Table 20.5. *A priority-queue class*

$$
\begin{aligned}
& !(\boldsymbol{\nu} a)\, \overline{n}a.\, \mathcal{O}^*\langle a, \ldots \rangle \\
\cong^{\mathrm{c}} \quad & (\boldsymbol{\nu} \widetilde{u})\, (!(\boldsymbol{\nu} a)\, \overline{n}a.\, \mathcal{O}^{**}\langle a, \widetilde{u} \rangle \mid \Pi_i\, !u_i(h, r, s).\, [\![C_i]\!]\langle h, r, s, \ldots \rangle)\, .
\end{aligned}
$$

Exercise 20.3.2 Prove this equivalence. □

20.4 A program transformation

This final example shows the interchangeability of two class definitions. An interesting feature of the example is that the processes that are the translations of the two classes are behaviourally very different: they do not even perform the same sequences of actions. No π-context that is the translation of a program context can distinguish them, however.

The first class extends the priority-queue class PQ in the program $Pdec_0$ in Table 19.2 with a method search. The class is given in Table 20.5 (we reuse the class name). When the new method search is invoked in a cell, the value false is returned if the cell is the end of the chain (k=0) or the argument cannot be in the chain (y>k), while if the argument is found (y=k), then the value true is returned. In the remaining case, the delegate command introduced in Exercise 19.3.3 is used to pass on to the next cell in the chain the responsibility for returning the result of the search to the invoking object.

An alternative implementation, which allows less concurrency and is therefore

```
method search (y:Int):Bool
   if (k=0 or y>k) then return false
   else if y=k then return true
        else return q!search(k)
```

Table 20.6. *A modified method declaration*

easier to understand, is for the cell to wait for the result from the next cell and itself return it to the invoking object, as in Table 20.6, where `delegate` is replaced by `return`. We refer to this modified class as PQ′.

In Section 3.3 we proved the equivalence of two π-calculus implementations of a priority queue. The second, concurrent, implementation can be obtained by easy simplification of the process that is the translation of the class PQ (without `search`). The first, sequential, implementation can be derived similarly from the class obtained from PQ (without `search`) when the `return` commands are moved to the ends of the bodies of the `insert` and `delete` methods. The strategy for the proof in Section 3.3 was to show that the two processes are solutions of the same guarded equation.

When the `search` method is added, however, we cannot hope to follow a similar strategy. For consider a quiescent queue of PQ cells. If a `search` is invoked in the head object and delegated to the next object, then the head object is ready to receive another method invocation. This is not possible for a queue of PQ′ cells, however, because the head cell waits until the result of the search reaches it, and then returns the result to the invoking object. More formally, the translation of PQ can perform, for example, the sequence of non-τ actions

$$(\boldsymbol{\nu} p)\,\overline{n_{\mathsf{PQ}}}\,p,\quad p\,\mathsf{insert\_}\langle 2,r\rangle,\quad \overline{r}\star,\quad p\,\mathsf{search\_}\langle 1,r'\rangle,\quad p\,\mathsf{insert\_}\langle 3,r''\rangle\,,$$

but the translation of PQ′ cannot: it cannot perform $p\,\mathsf{insert\_}\langle 3,r''\rangle$ before performing $\overline{r'}\,\mathsf{false}$.

Replacing one class by the other in a program would not change the system's behaviour, however, for the following reasons. First, the linear structure ensures that there can be no 'overtaking' within a chain; the result of a method invocation in the head cell is therefore determined at the moment the invocation occurs, even though it may not be possible to return the result of the invocation until other results are returned. And secondly, when an object invokes a method, it waits for the result; so, for instance, there is no possibility of the return of one result being blocked by failure to return another.

Therefore, for every π-calculus context D that is the translation of a suitable program context, that is, a context obtained from a program by removing the declaration of the class PQ,

$$in : \mathsf{i}\ \mathtt{Int}, out : \mathsf{o}\ \mathtt{Int} \rhd D[[\![\mathtt{class\,PQ}]\!]] \cong^{c} D[[\![\mathtt{class\,PQ'}]\!]] \ . \qquad (20.4)$$

We will outline a proof of this, inviting the reader to fill in some of the details. The proof will provide another illustration of the usefulness of types, in this case receptive types, for reasoning about the behaviour of mobile processes.

To begin, we simplify the processes $[\![\mathtt{class\,PQ}]\!]$ and $[\![\mathtt{class\,PQ'}]\!]$. Since the classes differ only in their search methods, and we have already considered insert and delete in Section 3.3, we elide some details. We abbreviate insert to i and delete to d and search to s. For the class PQ we obtain

$$\begin{aligned}\mathcal{O}_{\mathtt{PQ}} \stackrel{\text{def}}{=} (p,k,q).\,(\boldsymbol{\nu} g)\,(\,\overline{g}\star \mid\, !g(z).\\ &p[\,\mathsf{i\_}(x,r) \rhd \ \ldots,\\ &\quad \mathsf{d\_}(z,r) \rhd \ldots,\\ &\quad \mathsf{s\_}(y,r) \rhd \mathsf{IF}(\ k=0 \text{ or } y>k \hookrightarrow \overline{r}\,\mathsf{false}.\,\overline{g}\star,\\ &\qquad\qquad y=k \qquad\qquad \hookrightarrow \overline{r}\,\mathsf{true}.\,\overline{g}\star,\\ &\qquad\qquad 0<y<k \qquad \hookrightarrow \overline{q}\,\mathsf{s\_}\langle y,r\rangle.\,\overline{g}\star)]) \,,\end{aligned}$$

and for the class PQ$'$ we have

$$\begin{aligned}\mathcal{O}_{\mathtt{PQ'}} \stackrel{\text{def}}{=} (p,k,q).\,(\boldsymbol{\nu} g)\,(\,\overline{g}\star \mid\, !g(z).\\ &p[\,\mathsf{i\_}(x,r) \rhd \ \ldots,\\ &\quad \mathsf{d\_}(z,r) \rhd \ \ldots,\\ &\quad \mathsf{s\_}(y,r) \rhd \mathsf{IF}(\ k=0 \text{ or } y>k \hookrightarrow \overline{r}\,\mathsf{false}.\,\overline{g}\star,\\ &\qquad\qquad y=k \qquad\qquad \hookrightarrow \overline{r}\,\mathsf{true}.\,\overline{g}\star,\\ &\qquad\qquad 0<y<k \qquad \hookrightarrow (\boldsymbol{\nu} r')\,(\overline{q}\,\mathsf{s\_}\langle y,r'\rangle\\ &\qquad\qquad\qquad\qquad\qquad \mid r'(v).\,\overline{r}v.\,\overline{g}\star))]) \,.\end{aligned}$$

Set

$$\mathcal{K}_{\mathtt{PQ}} \stackrel{\text{def}}{=} (a,\ldots).\,!(\boldsymbol{\nu} p)\,\overline{a}p.\,(\boldsymbol{\nu} q)\,\mathcal{O}_{\mathtt{PQ}}\langle p,0,q\rangle$$

and

$$\mathcal{K}_{\mathtt{PQ'}} \stackrel{\text{def}}{=} (a,\ldots).\,!(\boldsymbol{\nu} p)\,\overline{a}p.\,(\boldsymbol{\nu} q)\,\mathcal{O}_{\mathtt{PQ'}}\langle p,0,q\rangle \,.$$

Then, as the reader may care to check by examining the definition, for the appropriate Γ,

$$\Gamma \rhd [\![\mathtt{class\,PQ}]\!]\langle a,\ldots\rangle \cong^{c} \mathcal{K}_{\mathtt{PQ}}\langle a,\ldots\rangle \qquad (20.5)$$

and

$$\Gamma \rhd [\![\mathtt{class\,PQ'}]\!]\langle a,\ldots\rangle \cong^{c} \mathcal{K}_{\mathtt{PQ'}}\langle a,\ldots\rangle \,. \qquad (20.6)$$

Let $\mathcal{O}^*_{\mathsf{PQ}}$ be defined like $\mathcal{O}_{\mathsf{PQ}}$, but replacing $\overline{q}\,\mathsf{s\_}\langle y,r\rangle.\,\overline{g}\star$ by

$$(\boldsymbol{\nu} r')\,(\overline{q}\,\mathsf{s\_}\langle y,r'\rangle.\,\overline{g}\star \mid r'(v).\,\overline{r}v)\,. \tag{20.7}$$

Define $\mathcal{K}^*_{\mathsf{PQ}}$ from $\mathcal{O}^*_{\mathsf{PQ}}$ as $\mathcal{K}_{\mathsf{PQ}}$ is defined from $\mathcal{O}_{\mathsf{PQ}}$. Then, using Lemma 11.2.1(2) for linear receptiveness,

$$\Gamma \triangleright \mathcal{K}^*_{\mathsf{PQ}}\langle a,\ldots\rangle \cong^{\mathrm{c}} \mathcal{K}_{\mathsf{PQ}}\langle a,\ldots\rangle\,.$$

Now let $\mathcal{O}^*_{\mathsf{PQ'}}$ be defined like $\mathcal{O}_{\mathsf{PQ'}}$, but replacing

$$(\boldsymbol{\nu} r')\,(\overline{q}\,\mathsf{s\_}\langle y,r'\rangle \mid r'(v).\,\overline{r}v.\,\overline{g}\star)$$

by

$$(\boldsymbol{\nu} r')\,(\overline{q}\,\mathsf{s\_}\langle y,r'\rangle \mid r'(v).\,(\overline{r}v \mid \overline{g}\star))\,.$$

Define $\mathcal{K}^*_{\mathsf{PQ'}}$ from $\mathcal{O}^*_{\mathsf{PQ'}}$ as $\mathcal{K}_{\mathsf{PQ'}}$ is defined from $\mathcal{O}_{\mathsf{PQ'}}$. Then, using Lemma 11.2.1(1),

$$\Gamma \triangleright \mathcal{K}^*_{\mathsf{PQ'}}\langle a,\ldots\rangle \cong^{\mathrm{c}} \mathcal{K}_{\mathsf{PQ'}}\langle a,\ldots\rangle\,.$$

From now on, we use typed bisimilarity, omitting the type environment and again coercing linear-receptive types to connection types as in Section 20.2.

Let $\mathcal{O}^{**}_{\mathsf{PQ}}$ be defined like $\mathcal{O}^*_{\mathsf{PQ}}$, but replacing (20.7) by

$$(\boldsymbol{\nu} r')\,(\overline{q}\,\mathsf{s\_}\langle y,r'\rangle.\,(\overline{g}\star \mid r'(v).\,\overline{r}v))\,.$$

Also, define $\mathcal{K}^{**}_{\mathsf{PQ}}$ from $\mathcal{O}^{**}_{\mathsf{PQ}}$ as $\mathcal{K}_{\mathsf{PQ}}$ is defined from $\mathcal{O}_{\mathsf{PQ}}$.

Exercise 20.4.1 Show that $\mathcal{K}^{**}_{\mathsf{PQ}}\langle a,\ldots\rangle \approx \mathcal{K}^*_{\mathsf{PQ}}\langle a,\ldots\rangle$. □

Now, the difference between $\mathcal{O}^{**}_{\mathsf{PQ}}$ and $\mathcal{O}^*_{\mathsf{PQ'}}$ is just that the former has

$$(\boldsymbol{\nu} r')\,(\overline{q}\,\mathsf{s\_}\langle y,r'\rangle.\,(\overline{g}\star \mid r'(v).\,\overline{r}v))$$

where the latter has

$$(\boldsymbol{\nu} r')\,(\overline{q}\,\mathsf{s\_}\langle y,r'\rangle \mid r'(v).\,(\overline{r}v \mid \overline{g}\star))\,.$$

Using reasoning similar to that employed to prove QUEUE $\approx$ QUEUE* in Section 3.3:

Exercise 20.4.2 Show that $\mathcal{K}^{**}_{\mathsf{PQ}}\langle a,\ldots\rangle \approx \mathcal{K}^*_{\mathsf{PQ'}}\langle a,\ldots\rangle$. □

Using these results:

Exercise 20.4.3 Complete the proof that $\Gamma \triangleright \mathcal{K}_{\mathsf{PQ}}\langle a,\ldots\rangle \cong^{\mathrm{c}} \mathcal{K}_{\mathsf{PQ'}}\langle a,\ldots\rangle$, and hence the proof of (20.4). □

This example, in conjunction with the argument in Section 3.3, illustrates how a formal semantic definition by translation to a typed π-calculus can be used to prove soundness of program transformations that increase the scope for concurrent activity within systems of objects. The arguments show that the sequential class, where each **return** is at the end of the method body, is interchangeable with the class where the **return** commands are anticipated in the `insert` and `delete` methods, and the **return** command in `search` is replaced by **delegate**.

Notes and References for Part VII

In [Mil80], Milner gave a formal semantic definition for a concurrent programming language with shared variables by translation to CCS. The formal semantic definition for OOL by translation to a typed π-calculus is similar in nature. The π-calculus semantics goes beyond the CCS semantics by giving a formal account of naming and reference-passing in object-oriented languages. The π-calculus types express program structure, and the disciplines of name use that they capture are hepful in reasoning about object-oriented systems.

The language OOL is derived from the POOL family of languages studied by America et al. [Ame89]. Semantics for POOL-like languages by translation to π-calculus were given by Walker in [Wal91, Wal95]. The π-calculus translation given in Section 19.3 can be modified to accommodate other object features. For this, one may find it useful to start from the definition of object-process in Section 20.3, which separates the process handling the requests to an object from the processes representing the object's methods. A similar translation scheme was used by Kleist and Sangiorgi [KS98, San98a] and by Dal-Zilio [DZ99] to interpret some of the functional and imperative Object Calculi of Abadi and Cardelli [AC96], and by Merro, Kleist, and Nestmann [MKN00] to interpret the language Obliq [Car95]. The Object Calculi are object-based, and incorporate constructs for overriding a method and for cloning an object. Obliq is a distributed object language; it has constructs for concurrency and distribution, for serializing the activities of objects, for protecting certain methods from overriding, and a forwarding operator, whose effect is to make one object an alias for another object. Pierce and Turner [PT95] explored how programming languages for concurrent objects can be built on an asynchronous polyadic π-calculus with records. Fournet, Laneve, Maranget, and Rémy [FLMR00] used a typed variant of the Join Calculus to model concurrent objects, and in particular studied operators for expressing various kinds of inheritance.

The examples of proofs of program transformations using a π-calculus semantics given in Chapter 20 follow Liu, Philippou, and Walker [LW98, PW98], and [San99c]. The works [San98a, KS98, DZ99] used the π-calculus semantics of object calculi to show the soundness of the typing and subtyping rules of the source calculi, and to validate basic algebraic laws for objects. [MKN00, Mer00] used the π-calculus semantics of Obliq to study the transparency of object migration, that is, the property that a change of site of an object is not observable.

List of Tables

List of Notations

We report here the main notations under the following headings: Metavariables, Miscellaneous symbols, Process syntax, Reduction and transitions, Calculi, Relations on processes, Up-to techniques, Typing, Encodings between first-order and higher-order calculi, λ-calculus, Metavariables for objects.

The page number refers to the first occurrence of the notation.

Metavariables

$x, y, z, \ldots$	names	11
π	prefixes	11
P, Q, R	processes	11
M, N	summations	11
σ	substitutions	14
C	contexts	19
$\mathcal{R}, \mathcal{S}$	relations	19
α	actions	36
μ	names and co-names	56
κ, λ	prefixes including bound outputs	72
$\mathcal{F}, \mathcal{G}$	functions on relations	83
F, G	abstractions	105
Σ	sortings	128
γ	sorts	128
K	process constants	132
D	distinctions	155
φ	conditions	180

Metavariables for typed calculi

Γ, Δ	type environments	236
E	processes and values	237
S, T	types	239
L	link types	239
V	value types	239
B	basic types	240
basval	values of basic types	240
v, w	values	240
χ	type substitutions	303

Miscellaneous symbols

$\stackrel{\text{def}}{=}$	definitional equality	16
$\widetilde{E}$	tuple of entities	23
$\mathcal{R}^{=}$	symmetric closure of a relation	156
$D\backslash x$	operation on distinctions	156
$D\lceil M$	operation on distinctions	156

Process syntax

$\mathbf{0}$	inaction	12
$\pi. P$	prefix	12
$\overline{x}y. P$	output prefix	12
$x(z). P$	input prefix	12
$\tau. P$	unobservable prefix	12
$[x = y]\pi. P$	match prefix	12
$P + Q$	sum	12
$P \mid Q$	composition	12
$\boldsymbol{\nu} z\, P$	restriction	12
$!P$	replication	13
$[x \neq y]$	mismatching	13
$[\cdot]$	context hole	19
$C[P]$	instantiation of context	19
$(\boldsymbol{\nu} x_1, \ldots, x_n)$	abbreviation for $\boldsymbol{\nu} x_1 \ldots \boldsymbol{\nu} x_n$	23
$C[P_1, \ldots, P_n]$	instantiation of n-hole context	29

$x.\,P$	input prefix	59
$\overline{x}.\,P$	output prefix	59
π, μ	short for $\pi.\,\mathbf{0}$, $\mu.\,\mathbf{0}$	59
$\Sigma_{i\in I}\, P_i$	indexed summation	70
$\overline{x}(z).\,P$	bound output prefix	72
$\mathsf{subj}(\pi)$	subject of prefix	73
$P\,\{x = (z).\,R\}$	process with local environment	79
$\Sigma_{i\in I} M_i$	infinite summation	103
$(x_1, \ldots, x_n).\,P$	polyadic abstraction	105
$F\langle\widetilde{y}\rangle$	pseudo-application for polyadic abstractions	105
$\mathsf{IF}(b_1 \hookrightarrow P_1, \ldots)$	conditional process	139
$\Pi_{i\in I}\, P_i$	indexed composition	147
$x \hookrightarrow y$	process abbreviation	212
$a(x) : P$	delayed input prefix	337

Syntax for polyadic π-calculi and sorting

$\overline{x}\langle\widetilde{y}\rangle.\,P$	polyadic output prefix	127
$x(\widetilde{z}).\,P$	polyadic input prefix	127
$x : \gamma$	sorting information	128
$x : y$	sorting information	128
$K \triangleq (\widetilde{x}).\,P$	recursive definition of constant	132
$K\lfloor\widetilde{a}\rfloor$	constant application	132
$\mathsf{const}(P)$	constants on which process depends	133

Syntax for typed calculi

$(\boldsymbol{\nu} a : T)\, P$	typed restriction	237
$\overline{b}(a : T).\,P$	typed bound output prefix	237
$P\,\{a : T = (x).\,Q\}$	process with typed local environment	237
`wrong`	process with a run-time error	240
$\star$	unit value	240
$\langle v_1, \ldots, v_n\rangle$	tuple value	250
$\mathsf{with} \ldots \mathsf{do}\ P$	destructor for tuples and records	250
$\mathsf{inl\_}v$, $\mathsf{inr\_}v$	union values	252
$\{\ell_1 = v_1, \ldots, \ell_n = v_n\}$	record value	252
$\{_{j\in 1,\ldots,n}\, \ell_j = v_j\}$	shorthand for $\{\ell_1 = v_1, \ldots, \ell_n = v_n\}$	252
$\mathsf{case}[\ldots]$	destructor for unions and variants	253
$[_{j\in 1,\ldots,n}\, \ell_j\_(y_j) \rhd P_j]$	shorthand for $[\,\ell_1\_(y_1) \rhd P_1\,;\ \ldots]$	254

ℓ_v	variant value	255
$a(x_1, \ldots, x_n).\, P$	pattern matching on tuples in input	255
$z[_{j\in 1,\ldots,n}\, \ell_j\_(y_j) \rhd P_j]$	pattern matching on variants in input	256
$(x).\, P$	abstraction	273
$F v$	pseudo-application	273
$\langle V; v\rangle$	polymorphic value	300
$\overline{a}.\, P$, $a.\, P$	prefixes in which the object has type `unit`	312
(Γ/Δ)-context	typed context	320
$x \multimap y$	wire process	335
$a \twoheadrightarrow b$	dynamic wire process	349
$v\lfloor w : T\rfloor$	application in HOπ	373
$v\lfloor w\rfloor$	shorthand for $v\lfloor w : T\rfloor$	375
$@P$	process value	375
$a\, F$, $b(\widetilde{c})\, F$	input prefix, using an abstraction	375
$(\Gamma/\Delta/\!\!/T)$-context	typed value context	380
$Q\,\{b = F\}$, $Q\,\{b = (\widetilde{c})\, F\}$	process with local environment, using an abstraction	437

Free names and substitutions

$\mathsf{fn}(\ldots)$	free names of specified entities	13
$\{\widetilde{y}/\widetilde{x}\}$	substitution	14
$\mathsf{supp}(\sigma)$	support of substitution	15
$\mathsf{cosupp}(\sigma)$	co-support of substitution	15
$\mathsf{n}(\sigma)$	names of substitution	15
$x\sigma$, $\sigma(x)$	application of a substitution to a name	15
$E\sigma$	application of a substitution to an expression	16
$\mathsf{tvar}(E)$	free type variables of an expression	300
$\{\widetilde{T}/\widetilde{X}\}$	type substitution	301

Reduction and transitions

$P \longrightarrow Q$	reduction	23
Act	set of actions	36
$\overline{x}y$	free output action	37
xy	input action	37
$\overline{x}(z)$	bound output action	37
τ	internal action	37
$\mathsf{subj}(\alpha)$	subject of action	37

Calculi

$P \;{}^{c}\!\succeq Q$	expansion precongruence	114
$P \;{}_{g}\!\succeq Q$	ground expansion relation	172

Ground relations

$P \sim_{g} Q$	strong ground bisimilarity	162
$P \approx_{g} Q$	ground bisimilarity	172
$P \approx_{g}^{c} Q$	ground congruence	173

Late relations

$P \sim_{\ell} Q$	strong late bisimilarity	164
$P \sim_{\ell}^{c} Q$	strong late congruence	165
$P \sim_{\ell}^{D} Q$	strong late D-congruence	168
$P \approx_{\ell} Q$	late bisimilarity	173
$P \approx_{\ell}^{c} Q$	late congruence	173

Open relations

$P \sim_{o}^{D} Q$	strong open D-bisimilarity	167
$P \approx_{o} Q$	open bisimilarity	173
$P \simeq_{o}^{D} Q$	symbolic open D-bisimilarity	169

Asynchronous relations

$P \overset{\centerdot}{\approx}_{a} Q$	asynchronous barbed bisimilarity	199
$P \cong_{a}^{c} Q$	asynchronous barbed congruence	199
$P \approx_{a} Q$	asynchronous bisimilarity	199
$P \approx_{ag} Q$	asynchronous ground bisimilarity	201
$P \sim_{a} Q$	strong asynchronous bisimilarity	200
$P \simeq_{a}^{c} Q$	strong asynchronous barbed congruence	202
$P \sim_{ag} Q$	strong asynchronous ground bisimilarity	202
$P \cong_{a} Q$	asynchronous barbed equivalence	202

Sorted relations

$\Sigma \triangleright P \cong^{c} Q$	barbed congruence with respect to a sorting	129
$\Sigma \triangleright P \approx^{c} Q$	full bisimilarity with respect to a sorting	129

Typed (weak) relations

Up-to techniques

Typing

Type environments and type judgments

$\Gamma \vdash E_1, E_2 : T$	$\Gamma \vdash E_1 : T$ and $\Gamma \vdash E_2 : T$	237
$\mathcal{L} \triangleright \Gamma \vdash E : T$	type judgment of the calculus $\mathcal{L}$	237
Δ-to-Γ substitution	substitution relating Δ to Γ	324

Types

$\diamond$	behaviour type	237
$\sharp T$	connection type	239
`unit`	unit type	240
$T_1 \times \ldots \times T_n$	tuple type	250
$\times(T_1, \ldots, T_n)$	other notation for tuple type	250
$T_1 \oplus T_2$	union type	252
$\{\ell_1 : T_1, \ldots, \ell_n : T_n\}$	record type	252
$\{_{j \in 1,\ldots,n}\, \ell_j : T_j\}$	shorthand for $\{\ell_1 : T_1, \ldots, \ell_n : T_n\}$	252
$[_{j \in 1,\ldots,n}\, \ell_j\_T_j]$	shorthand for $[\ell_1\_T_1, \ldots, \ell_n\_T_n]$	254
$[\ell_1\_T_1, \ldots, \ell_n\_T_n]$	variant type	255
$\mu X . T$	recursive type	257
X	type variable	257
$\mathsf{i}\,T$, $\mathsf{o}\,T$	input and output capability type	262
$\sharp$, i, o	i/o tags	262
$\ell_{\mathsf{o}}\,T$, $\ell_{\mathsf{i}}\,T$, $\ell_{\sharp}\,T$	linear types	281
$\ell\mathrm{rec}_{\mathsf{i}}\,T, \ell\mathrm{rec}_{\mathsf{o}}\,T, \ell\mathrm{rec}_{\sharp}\,T$	linear receptive types	290
$\omega\mathrm{rec}_{\mathsf{i}}\,T, \omega\mathrm{rec}_{\mathsf{o}}\,T, \omega\mathrm{rec}_{\sharp}\,T$	ω-receptive types	293
$\langle X; V \rangle$	polymorphic type	300

Functions and relations on types

$\mathcal{O}(T)$	type of values that names of type T can carry	238
$T_1 \sim_{\text{type}} T_2$	type equivalence	257
$S \leq T$	subtype relation	261
$\mathsf{varpart}(\Gamma)$	variables in the support of Γ	301
$(T)^{\leftarrow\sharp}$	replace the outermost i/o tag in T with $\sharp$	385
$(T)^{-}$	delete the outermost i/o tag from T	472

Encodings between first-order and higher-order calculi

$\mathcal{D}$	first compilation of HOπ into the π-calculus	386
$\mathcal{C}^{+}$	first optimization of the compilation of HOπ	399
$\mathcal{C}$	final compilation of HOπ	403

λ-calculus

Term syntax

Reductions and strategies

Metavariables for objects

Bibliography

[Aba99] M. Abadi. Secrecy by typing in security protocols. *Journal of the ACM*, 46(5):749–786, 1999.

[ABL99] R. Amadio, G. Boudol, and C. Lhoussaine. The receptive distributed pi-calculus. In *5th ECOOP Workshop on Mobile Object Systems*, volume 1738 of *Lecture Notes in Computer Science*. Springer-Verlag, 1999.

[Abr87] S. Abramsky. *Domain Theory and the Logic of Observable Properties.* PhD thesis, University of London, 1987.

[Abr89] S. Abramsky. The lazy lambda calculus. In *Research Topics in Functional Programming*. Addison-Wesley, 1989.

[Abr91] S. Abramsky. A domain equation for bisimulation. *Information and Computation*, 92:161–218, 1991.

[Abr93] S. Abramsky. Computational interpretations of linear logic. *Theoretical Computer Science*, 111(1–2):3–57, 1993.

[ABV94] L. Aceto, B. Bloom, and F. Vaandrager. Turning SOS rules into equations. *Information and Computation*, 111(1):1–52, 1994.

[AC93] R. Amadio and L. Cardelli. Subtyping recursive types. *ACM Transactions on Programming Languages and Systems*, 15(4):575–631, 1993.

[AC96] M. Abadi and L. Cardelli. *A Theory of Objects.* Springer-Verlag, 1996.

[ACS98] R. Amadio, I. Castellani, and D. Sangiorgi. On bisimulations for the asynchronous π-calculus. *Theoretical Computer Science*, 195(2):291–324, 1998.

[Acz88] P. Aczel. *Non-well-founded Sets.* CSLI lecture notes; no. 14, 1988.

[AD95] R. Amadio and M. Dam. Reasoning about higher-order processes. In *TAPSOFT'95: Theory and Practice of Software Development*, volume 915 of *Lecture Notes in Computer Science*. Springer-Verlag, 1995.

[AFM$^+$95] Z. Ariola, M. Felleisen, J. Maraist, M. Odersky, and P. Wadler. A call-by-need λ-calculus. In *22nd Annual ACM Symposium on Principles of Programming Languages*. ACM Press, 1995.

[AG97] M. Abadi and A. Gordon. A calculus for cryptographic protocols: The Spi calculus. In *Fourth ACM Conference on Computer and Communications Security*. ACM Press, 1997.

[AGN95] S. Abramsky, S. Gay, and R. Nagarajan. Interaction categories and the foundations of typed concurrent programming. In *Deductive Program Design: Proceedings of the 1994 Marktoberdorf Summer School.* Springer-Verlag, 1995.

[AGR88] E. Astesiano, A. Giovini, and G. Reggio. Generalized bisimulation in relational specifications. In *STACS'88: 5th Annual Symposium on Theoretical Aspects of Computer Science*, volume 294 of *Lecture Notes in Computer Science.* Springer-Verlag, 1988.

[AGR92] E. Astesiano, A. Giovini, and G. Reggio. Observational structures and their logic. *Theoretical Computer Science*, 96:249–283, 1992.

[AKH92] S. Arun-Kumar and M. Hennessy. An efficiency preorder for processes. *Acta Informatica*, 29:737–760, 1992.

[ALT95] R. Amadio, L. Leth, and B. Thomsen. From a concurrent λ-calculus to the π-calculus. In *FCT'95: Foundations of Computation Theory*, volume 965 of *Lecture Notes in Computer Science.* Springer-Verlag, 1995.

[Ame89] P. America. Issues in the design of a parallel object-oriented language. *Formal Aspects of Computing*, 1(4):366–411, 1989.

[ANN99] T. Amtoft, F. Nielson, and H.R. Nielson. *Type and Effect Systems: Behaviours for Concurrency.* Imperial College Press, 1999.

[AO93] S. Abramsky and L. Ong. Full abstraction in the lazy lambda calculus. *Information and Computation*, 105:159–267, 1993.

[AP94] R. Amadio and S. Prasad. Localities and failures. In *FSTTCS'94: Foundations of Software Technology and Theoretical Computer Science*, volume 880 of *Lecture Notes in Computer Science.* Springer-Verlag, 1994.

[App92] A. Appel. *Compiling with Continuations.* Cambridge University Press, 1992.

[AWO$^+$99] K. Arnold, A. Wollrath, B. O'Sullivan, R. Scheifler, and J. Waldo. *The Jini specification.* Addison-Wesley, 1999.

[AZ84] E. Astesiano and E. Zucca. Parametric channels via label expressions in CCS. *Theoretical Computer Science*, 33:45–64, 1984.

[Bak92] H. Baker. Lively linear lisp — 'Look Ma, no garbage!'. *ACM Sigplan Notices*, 27(8):89–98, 1992.

[Bal98] M. Baldamus. *Semantics and Logic of Higher-order Processes: Characterizing Late Context Bisimulation.* PhD thesis, Berlin University of Technology, 1998.

[Bar77] H. Barendregt. The type free lambda calculus. In *Handbook of Mathematical Logic.* North Holland, 1977.

[Bar84] H. Barendregt. *The Lambda Calculus: Its Syntax and Semantics.* North Holland, 1984.

[BB89] T. Bolognesi and E. Brinksma. Introduction to the ISO specification language LOTOS. In *The Formal Description Technique LOTOS.* North Holland, 1989.

[BB92] G. Berry and G. Boudol. The chemical abstract machine. *Theoretical Computer Science*, 96:217–248, 1992.

[BD95] M. Boreale and R. De Nicola. Testing equivalence for mobile processes. *Information and Computation*, 120:279–303, 1995.

[BD96] M. Boreale and R. De Nicola. A symbolic semantics for the π-calculus. *Information and Computation*, 126:34–52, 1996.

[BDNN98] C. Bodei, P. Degano, F. Nielson, and H.R. Nielson. Control flow analysis for the pi-calculus. In *CONCUR'98: Concurrency Theory*, volume 1466 of *Lecture Notes in Computer Science.* Springer-Verlag, 1998.

[Ber78] G. Berry. Séquentialité de l'évaluation formelle des λ-expressions. In B. Robinet, editor, *Program Transformations, 3rd International Colloquium on Programming*, 1978.

[Ber81] G. Berry. Some syntactic and categorical constructions of lambda calculus models. Rapport de Recherche 80, Institut National de Recherche en Informatique et en Automatique (INRIA), 1981.

[BIM95] B. Bloom, S. Istrail, and A. Meyer. Bisimulation can't be traced. *Journal of the ACM*, 42(1):232–268, 1995.

[BK98] I. Bethke and J.W. Klop. Sequentiality in the lambda-calculus and combinatory logic. Unpublished note, 1998.

[BL96] G. Boudol and C. Laneve. The discriminating power of the λ-calculus with multiplicities. *Information and Computation*, 126(1):83–102, 1996.

[BL00] G. Boudol and C. Laneve. λ-calculus, multiplicities and the π-calculus. In *Proof, Language, and Interaction*. MIT Press, 2000.

[Blo90] B. Bloom. Can LCF be topped? Flat lattice models of typed λ-calculus. *Information and Computation*, 87(1/2):263–300, 1990.

[BO95] S. Brock and G. Ostheimer. Process semantics of graph reduction. In *CONCUR'95: Concurrency Theory*, volume 962 of *Lecture Notes in Computer Science*. Springer-Verlag, 1995.

[Bor98] M. Boreale. On the expressiveness of internal mobility in name-passing calculi. *Theoretical Computer Science*, 195(2):205–226, 1998.

[Bou89] G. Boudol. Towards a lambda calculus for concurrent and communicating systems. In *TAPSOFT'89: Theory and Practice of Software Development*, volume 351 of *Lecture Notes in Computer Science*, 1989.

[Bou92] G. Boudol. Asynchrony and the π-calculus. Rapport de Recherche RR-1702, INRIA Sophia Antipolis, 1992.

[Bou94] G. Boudol. Some chemical abstract machines. In *A Decade of Concurrency*, volume 803 of *Lecture Notes in Computer Science*. Springer-Verlag, 1994.

[Bou97a] G. Boudol. The pi-calculus in direct style. In *24th Annual ACM Symposium on Principles of Programming Languages*. ACM Press, 1997.

[Bou97b] G. Boudol. Typing the use of resources in a concurrent calculus. In *ASIAN'97: Advances in Computing Science*, volume 1345 of *Lecture Notes in Computer Science*. Springer-Verlag, 1997.

[Bou00] G. Boudol. On the semantics of the call-by-name CPS transform. *Theoretical Computer Science*, 234:309–321, 2000.

[Bro96] S. Brookes. The essence of Parallel Algol. In *11th Annual IEEE Symposium on Logic in Computer Science*. IEEE Computer Society Press, 1996.

[BS98a] M. Boreale and D. Sangiorgi. Bisimulation in name-passing calculi without matching. In *13th Annual IEEE Symposium on Logic in Computer Science*. IEEE Computer Society Press, 1998.

[BS98b] M. Boreale and D. Sangiorgi. Some congruence properties for π-calculus bisimilarities. *Theoretical Computer Science*, 198:159–176, 1998.

[Car95] L. Cardelli. A language with distributed scope. *Computing Systems*, 8(1):27–59, 1995.

[Car96] L. Cardelli. Type systems. In *Handbook of Computer Science and Engineering*. CRC Press, 1996.

[Cat99] G.L. Cattani. *Presheaf Models for Concurrency*. PhD thesis, University of

Aarhus, 1999.

[CF58] H. Curry and R. Feys. *Combinatory Logic (Vol I)*. North Holland, 1958.

[CG98] L. Cardelli and A. Gordon. Mobile ambients. In *FOSSACS'98: Foundations of Software Science and Computational Structures*, volume 1378 of *Lecture Notes in Computer Science*. Springer-Verlag, 1998.

[CG99] L. Cardelli and A. Gordon. Types for mobile ambients. In *26th Annual ACM Symposium on Principles of Programming Languages*. ACM Press, 1999.

[CGG00] L. Cardelli, A. Gordon, and G. Ghelli. Group creation and secrecy. In *CONCUR'00: Concurrency Theory*, Lecture Notes in Computer Science. Springer-Verlag, 2000.

[Chu32] A. Church. A set of postulates for the foundations of logic. *Annals of Mathematics*, 33:346–366, 1932. Second part in Vol. 34, pages 839–864.

[Chu41] A. Church. *The Calculi of Lambda Conversion*. Princeton University Press, 1941.

[Cli81] W. Clinger. Foundations of Actor Semantics. Technical Report AI-TR-633, MIT Artificial Intelligence Laboratory, 1981.

[DCTU97] M. Dezani-Ciancaglini, J. Tiuryn, and P. Urzyczyn. Discrimination by parallel observers. In *12th Annual IEEE Symposium on Logic in Computer Science*. IEEE Computer Society Press, 1997.

[DH84] R. De Nicola and M. Hennessy. Testing equivalences for processes. *Theoretical Computer Science*, 34:83–133, 1984.

[DH92] O. Danvy and J. Hatcliff. Thunks (continued). In *Workshop on Static Analysis*, Bordeaux, 1992.

[DNFP98] R. De Nicola, G. Ferrari, and R. Pugliese. KLAIM: A kernel language for agents interaction and mobility. *IEEE Transactions on Software Engineering*, 24(5):315–330, 1998.

[DS85] R. De Simone. Higher level synchronising devices in MEIJE-SCCS. *Theoretical Computer Science*, 37:245–267, 1985.

[DZ97] S. Dal-Zilio. Implicit polymorphic type system for the Blue Calculus. Rapport de Recherche RR-3244, INRIA, 1997.

[DZ99] S. Dal-Zilio. *Le Calcul Bleu: Types et Objets*. PhD thesis, Université de Nice – Sophia Antipolis, 1999.

[EG99] J. Engelfreit and T. Gelsema. Multisets and structural congruence of the pi-calculus with replication. *Theoretical Computer Science*, 211:311–337, 1999.

[EN86] U. Engberg and M. Nielsen. A calculus of communicating systems with label-passing. Report DAIMI PB-208, Computer Science Department, University of Aarhus, 1986.

[EN00] U. Engberg and M. Nielsen. A calculus of communicating systems with label passing – ten years after. In *Proof, Language, and Interaction*. MIT Press, 2000.

[FG96] C. Fournet and G. Gonthier. The reflexive chemical abstract machine and the join calculus. In *23rd Annual ACM Symposium on Principles of Programming Languages*. ACM Press, 1996.

[FG98] C. Fournet and G. Gonthier. A hierarchy of equivalences for asynchronous calculi. In *ICALP'98: Automata, Languages and Programming*, volume 1443 of *Lecture Notes in Computer Science*. Springer-Verlag, 1998.

[FGL+96] C. Fournet, G. Gonthier, J.-J. Lévy, L. Maranget, and D. Rémy. A calculus of mobile processes. In *CONCUR'96: Concurrency Theory*, volume 1119 of *Lecture Notes in Computer Science*. Springer-Verlag, 1996.

[FGM+98] G. Ferrari, S. Gnesi, U. Montanari, M. Pistore, and G. Ristori. Verifying mobile processes in the HAL environment. In *CAV'98: Computer-Aided Verification*, volume 1427 of *Lecture Notes in Computer Science*. Springer-Verlag, 1998.

[FHJ95] W. Ferreira, M. Hennessy, and A. Jeffrey. A theory of weak bisimulation for core CML. Technical Report TR 95:05, School of Cognitive and Computing Sciences, University of Sussex, 1995.

[Fis72] M. Fischer. Lambda-calculus schemata. In *ACM Conference on Proving Assertions about Programs*. ACM Press, 1972.

[Fis93] M. Fischer. Lambda-calculus schemata. *Lisp and Symbolic Computation*, 6:259–288, 1993.

[FLMR97] C. Fournet, C. Laneve, L. Maranget, and D. Rémy. Implict typing à la ML for the Join-Calculus. In *CONCUR'97: Concurrency Theory*, volume 1119 of *Lecture Notes in Computer Science*. Springer-Verlag, 1997.

[FLMR00] C. Fournet, C. Laneve, L. Maranget, and D. Rémy. Inheritance in the join calculus. In *FSTTCS'00: Foundations of Software Technology and Theoretical Computer Science*, volume 1974 of *Lecture Notes in Computer Science*. Springer-Verlag, 2000.

[FMQ96] G. Ferrari, U. Montanari, and P. Quaglia. A π-calculus with explicit substitutions. *Theoretical Computer Science*, 168(1):53–103, 1996.

[Fou98] C. Fournet. *The Join Calculus: a Calculus for Distributed Mobile Programming*. PhD thesis, Ecole Polytechnique, 1998.

[FT01] M. Fiore and D. Turi. Semantics of name and value passing. In *16th Annual IEEE Symposium on Logic in Computer Science*. IEEE Computer Society Press, 2001.

[Fu97] Y. Fu. A proof theoretical approach to communication. In *ICALP'97: Automata, Languages and Programming*, volume 1256 of *Lecture Notes in Computer Science*. Springer-Verlag, 1997.

[Fu99] Y. Fu. Open bisimulations on chi processes. In *CONCUR'99: Concurrency Theory*, volume 1664 of *Lecture Notes in Computer Science*. Springer-Verlag, 1999.

[FWH92] D. Friedman, M. Wand, and C. Haynes. *Essentials of Programming Languages*. McGraw-Hill, 1992.

[Gay93] S. Gay. A sort inference algorithm for the polyadic π-calculus. In *20th Annual ACM Symposium on Principles of Programming Languages*. ACM Press, 1993.

[Gir72] J.-Y. Girard. *Interprétation Fonctionelle et Elimination des Coupures de l'Arithmétique d'Ordre Supérieur*. PhD thesis, Université Paris VII, 1972.

[Gir87] J.-Y. Girard. Linear logic. *Theoretical Computer Science*, 50:1–102, 1987.

[GLT88] J.-Y. Girard, Y. Lafont, and P. Taylor. *Proofs and Types*. Cambridge University Press, 1988.

[GMP89] A. Giacalone, P. Mishra, and S. Prasad. FACILE, a symmetric integration of concurrent and functional programming. In *TAPSOFT'89: Theory and Practice of Software Development*, volume 352 of *Lecture Notes in Computer Science*. Springer-Verlag, 1989.

[GN95] S. Gay and R. Nagarajan. A typed calculus of synchronous processes. In *10th Annual IEEE Symposium on Logic in Computer Science*. IEEE Computer Society

Press, 1995.

[Gor79] M. Gordon. *The Denotational Description of Programming Languages.* Springer-Verlag, 1979.

[Gor95] A. Gordon. Bisimilarity as a theory of functional programming. Notes Series BRICS-NS-95-3, University of Aarhus, 1995.

[Gun92] C. Gunter. *Semantics of Programming Languages.* MIT Press, 1992.

[GV92] J.F. Groote and F. Vaandrager. Structured operational semantics and bisimulation as a congruence. *Information and Computation*, 100:202–260, 1992.

[HB77] C. Hewitt and H. Baker. Laws for communicating parallel processes. In *IFIP Congress.* IFIP, 1977.

[HBG$^+$73] C. Hewitt, P. Bishop, I. Greif, B. Smith, T. Matson, and R. Steiger. Actor induction and meta-evaluation. In *ACM Symposium on Principles of Programming Languages.* ACM Press, 1973.

[HD94] J. Hatcliff and O. Danvy. A generic account of continuation-passing styles. In *21st Annual ACM Symposium on Principles of Programming Languages.* ACM Press, 1994.

[HD97] J. Hatcliff and O. Danvy. Thunks and the λ-calculus. *Journal of Functional Programming*, 7(3):303–319, 1997.

[HDM93] R. Harper, F. Duba, and D. MacQueen. Typing first-class continuations in ML. *Journal of Functional Programming*, 3(4):465–484, 1993.

[Hen88] M. Hennessy. Observing processes. In *Linear Time, Branching Time and Partial Order in Logics and Models for Concurrency*, volume 354 of *Lecture Notes in Computer Science.* Springer-Verlag, 1988.

[Hen91] M. Hennessy. A model for the π-calculus. Technical Report 91/08, Department of Computer Science, University of Sussex, 1991.

[Hen93] M. Hennessy. A fully abstract denotational model for higher-order processes. In *8th Annual IEEE Symposium on Logic in Computer Science.* IEEE Computer Society Press, 1993.

[Hew77] C. Hewitt. Viewing control structures as patterns of passing messages. *Journal of Artificial Intelligence*, 8(3):323–364, 1977.

[HH98] C. Hartonas and M. Hennessy. Full abstractness for a functional/concurrent language with higher-order value-passing. *Information and Computation*, 145(1):64–106, 1998.

[HHK96] M. Hansen, H. Hüttel, and J. Kleist. Bisimulations for asynchronous mobile processes. In *Tbilisi Symposium on Language, Logic, and Computation*, 1996.

[Hin97] J.R. Hindley. *Basic Simple Type Theory.* Cambridge University Press, 1997.

[Hir99] D. Hirschkoff. *Mise en Oeuvre de Preuves de Bisimulation.* PhD thesis, L'Ecole Nationale des Ponts et Chaussées, 1999.

[HK94] M. Hansen and J. Kleist. Process calculi with asynchronous communication. Master's thesis, Aalborg University, 1994.

[HL93] R. Harper and M. Lillibridge. Polymorphic type assignment and CPS conversion. *Lisp and Symbolic Computation*, 6:361–380, 1993.

[HL95] M. Hennessy and H. Lin. Symbolic bisimulations. *Theoretical Computer Science*, 138:353–389, 1995.

[HLMP98] F. Honsell, M. Lenisa, U. Montanari, and M. Pistore. Final semantics for the pi-calculus. In *PROCOMET'98: Programming Concepts and Methods.* Chapman &

Hall, 1998.

[HM85] M. Hennessy and R. Milner. Algebraic laws for nondeterminism and concurrency. *Journal of the ACM*, 32:137–161, 1985.

[HMS01] F. Honsell, M. Miculan, and I. Scagnetto. Pi calculus in (co)inductive type theories. *Theoretical Computer Science*, 253(2):239–285, 2001.

[Hoa85] C.A.R. Hoare. *Communicating Sequential Processes.* Prentice Hall, 1985.

[How96] D. Howe. Proving congruence of bisimulation in functional programming languages. *Information and Computation*, 124(2):103–112, 1996.

[HR98a] N. Heintze and J. Riecke. The SLam calculus: Programming with security and integrity. In *25th Annual ACM Symposium on Principles of Programming Languages.* ACM Press, 1998.

[HR98b] M. Hennessy and J. Riely. Resource access control in systems of mobile agents. In *HLCL'98: High-Level Concurrent Languages*, volume 16.3 of *ENTCS*. Elsevier, 1998.

[HR98c] M. Hennessy and J. Riely. A typed language for distributed mobile processes. In *25th Annual ACM Symposium on Principles of Programming Languages.* ACM Press, 1998.

[HS86] J.R. Hindley and J. Seldin. *Introduction to Combinators and λ-calculus.* Cambridge University Press, 1986.

[HT91] K. Honda and M. Tokoro. An object calculus for asynchronous communications. In *ECOOP'91: Workshop on Object Based Concurrent Programming*, volume 512 of *Lecture Notes in Computer Science.* Springer-Verlag, 1991.

[HT92] K. Honda and M. Tokoro. On asynchronous communication semantics. In *Object-based Concurrent Computing*, volume 612 of *Lecture Notes in Computer Science.* Springer-Verlag, 1992.

[HVK98] K. Honda, V. Vasconcelos, and M. Kubo. Language primitives and type discipline for structured communication-based programming. In *ESOP'98: European Symposium on Programming*, volume 1381 of *Lecture Notes in Computer Science.* Springer-Verlag, 1998.

[HY95] K. Honda and N. Yoshida. On reduction-based process semantics. *Theoretical Computer Science*, 152(2):437–486, 1995.

[IK01] A. Igarashi and N. Kobayashi. A generic type system for the pi-calculus. In *28th Annual ACM Symposium on Principles of Programming Languages.* ACM Press, 2001.

[Ing61] P. Ingerman. Thunks, a way of compiling procedure statements with some comments on procedure declarations. *Communications of the ACM*, 4(1):55–58, 1961.

[INR] INRIA Rocquencourt, projet Moscova, `http://pauillac.inria.fr/join/`. *The join calculus language.*

[Jef93] A. Jeffrey. A chemical abstract machine for graph reduction. In *MFPS'93: Mathematical Foundations of Programming Semantics*, volume 802 of *Lecture Notes in Computer Science.* Springer-Verlag, 1993.

[JNW96] A. Joyal, M. Nielsen, and G. Winskel. Bisimulation from open maps. *Information and Computation*, 127(2):164–185, 1996.

[JP93] B. Jonsson and J. Parrow. Deciding bisimulation equivalences for a class of non-finite-state programs. *Information and Computation*, 107:272–302, 1993.

[JR00] A. Jeffrey and J. Rathke. A theory of bisimulation for a fragment of Concurrent

ML with local names. In *15th Annual IEEE Symposium on Logic in Computer Science*. IEEE Computer Society Press, 2000.

[KNY95] N. Kobayashi, M. Nakade, and A. Yonezawa. Static analysis of communication for asynchronous concurrent programming languages. In *SAS'95: Static Analysis Symposium*, volume 983 of *Lecture Notes in Computer Science*. Springer-Verlag, 1995.

[Kob98] N. Kobayashi. A partially deadlock-free typed process calculus. *ACM Transactions on Programming Languages and Systems*, 20(2):436–482, 1998.

[Kön00] B. König. Analysing input/output capabilities of mobile processes with a generic type system. In *ICALP'00: Automata, Languages and Programming*, volume 1853 of *Lecture Notes in Computer Science*. Springer-Verlag, 2000.

[KPT99] N. Kobayashi, B Pierce, and D. Turner. Linearity and the pi-calculus. *ACM Transactions on Programming Languages and Systems*, 21(5):914–947, 1999.

[Kri93] J. L. Krivine. *Lambda-Calculus, Types and Models*. Ellis Horwood, 1993.

[KS82] J. Kennaway and M.R. Sleep. Expressions as processes. In *ACM Conference on LISP and Functional Programming*. ACM Press, 1982.

[KS98] J. Kleist and D. Sangiorgi. Imperative objects and mobile processes. In *PROCOMET'98: Programming Concepts and Methods*. Chapman & Hall, 1998.

[Lau93] J. Launchbury. A natural semantics for lazy evaluation. In *20th Annual ACM Symposium on Principles of Programming Languages*. ACM Press, 1993.

[Laz99] R. Lazic. *A Semantic Study of Data Independence with Applications to Model Checking*. PhD thesis, University of Oxford, 1999.

[Let91] L. Leth. *Functional Programs as Reconfigurable Networks of Communicating Processes*. PhD thesis, University of London, 1991.

[Lév76] J.-J. Lévy. An algebraic interpretation of the $\lambda\beta\kappa$-calculus; and an application of a labelled λ-calculus. *Theoretical Computer Science*, 2(1):97–114, 1976.

[LG88] J. Lucassen and D. Gifford. Polymorphic effect systems. In *15th Annual ACM Symposium on Principles of Programming Languages*. ACM Press, 1988.

[Lin94] H. Lin. Symbolic bisimulation and proof systems for the π-calculus. Technical Report 7/94, University of Sussex, 1994.

[Lin95] H. Lin. Complete inference systems for weak bisimulation equivalences in the π-calculus. In *TAPSOFT'95: Theory and Practice of Software Development*, volume 915 of *Lecture Notes in Computer Science*. Springer-Verlag, 1995.

[Lon83] G. Longo. Set theoretical models of lambda calculus: Theory, expansions and isomorphisms. *Annals of Pure and Applied Logic*, 24:153–188, 1983.

[LR98] X. Leroy and F. Rouaix. Security properties of typed applets. In *25th Annual ACM Symposium on Principles of Programming Languages*. ACM Press, 1998.

[LW95] X. Liu and D. Walker. A polymorphic type system for the polyadic-calculus. In *CONCUR'95: Concurrency Theory*, volume 962 of *Lecture Notes in Computer Science*. Springer-Verlag, 1995.

[LW98] X. Liu and D. Walker. Partial confluence of processes and systems of objects. *Theoretical Computer Science*, 206:127–162, 1998.

[Lyn96] N. Lynch. *Distributed Algorithms*. Morgan Kaufmann, 1996.

[Mac94] I. Mackie. Lilac: A functional programming language based on linear logic. *Journal of Functional Programming*, 4(4):1–39, 1994.

[Mer00] M. Merro. *Locality in the π-calculus and Applications to Object-Oriented Languages*. PhD thesis, Ecole des Mines de Paris, 2000.

[Mil77] R. Milner. Fully abstract models of typed lambda calculus. *Theoretical Computer Science*, 4:1–22, 1977.

[Mil80] R. Milner. *A Calculus of Communicating Systems*, volume 92 of *Lecture Notes in Computer Science*. Springer-Verlag, 1980.

[Mil89] R. Milner. *Communication and Concurrency.* Prentice Hall, 1989.

[Mil92] R. Milner. Functions as processes. *Journal of Mathematical Structures in Computer Science*, 2(2):119–141, 1992.

[Mil93] R. Milner. The polyadic π-calculus: a tutorial. In *Logic and Algebra of Specification.* Springer-Verlag, 1993.

[Mil99] R. Milner. *Communicating and Mobile Systems: the π-Calculus.* Cambridge University Press, 1999.

[Mit96] J. Mitchell. *Foundations for Programming Languages.* MIT Press, 1996.

[MKN00] M. Merro, J. Kleist, and U. Nestmann. Local π-calculus at work: Mobile objects as mobile processes. In *IFIP International Conference on Theoretical Computer Science*, 2000.

[Mog91] E. Moggi. Notions of computation and monads. *Information and Computation*, 93(1):55–92, 1991.

[Mor68] J. Morris. *Lambda-Calculus Models of Programming Languages.* PhD thesis, Massachusetts Institute of Technology, 1968.

[MP88] J. Mitchell and G. Plotkin. Abstract types have existential type. *ACM Transactions on Programming Languages and Systems*, 10(3):470–502, 1988.

[MPW89] R. Milner, J. Parrow, and D. Walker. A calculus of mobile processes, parts I and II. Technical Report ECS-LFCS-89-85 and -86, University of Edinburgh, 1989.

[MPW92] R. Milner, J. Parrow, and D. Walker. A calculus of mobile processes, parts I and II. *Information and Computation*, 100(1):1–77, 1992.

[MPW93] R. Milner, J. Parrow, and D. Walker. Modal logics for mobile processes. *Theoretical Computer Science*, 114:149–171, 1993.

[MS92a] R. Milner and D. Sangiorgi. Barbed bisimulation. In *ICALP'92: Automata, Languages and Programming*, volume 623 of *Lecture Notes in Computer Science.* Springer-Verlag, 1992.

[MS92b] U. Montanari and V. Sassone. Dynamic congruence vs. progressing bisimulation for CCS. *Fundamenta Informaticae*, XVI(2):171–199, 1992.

[MS98] M. Merro and D. Sangiorgi. On asynchrony in name-passing calculi. In *ICALP'98: Automata, Languages and Programming*, volume 1443 of *Lecture Notes in Computer Science.* Springer-Verlag, 1998.

[Mur92] C. Murthy. A computational analysis of Girard's translation and LC. In *7th Annual IEEE Symposium on Logic in Computer Science.* IEEE Computer Society Press, 1992.

[MW85] A. Meyer and M. Wand. Continuation semantics in typed lambda-calculi. In *Logic of Programs*, volume 193 of *Lecture Notes in Computer Science.* Springer-Verlag, 1985.

[Nes00] U. Nestmann. What is a 'good' encoding of guarded choice? *Information and Computation*, 156:287–319, 2000.

[Nie95] O. Nierstrasz. Regular types for active objects. In *Object-Oriented Software Composition.* Prentice Hall, 1995.

[Nie96] J. Niehren. Functional computation as concurrent computation. In *23rd Annual*

ACM Symposium on Principles of Programming Languages. ACM Press, 1996.

[Nie00] J. Niehren. Uniform confluence in concurrent computation. *Journal of Functional Programming*, 10(3):1–47, 2000.

[NN94] H.R. Nielson and F. Nielson. Higher-order concurrent programs with finite communications topology. In *21st Annual ACM Symposium on Principles of Programming Languages.* ACM Press, 1994.

[NNH99] F. Nielson, H.R. Nielson, and C. Hankin. *Principles of Program Analysis.* Springer-Verlag, 1999.

[NP96] U. Nestmann and B. Pierce. Decoding choice encodings. In *CONCUR'96: Concurrency Theory*, volume 1119 of *Lecture Notes in Computer Science.* Springer-Verlag, 1996.

[OD93] G. Ostheimer and A. Davie. Pi-calculus characterizations of some practical lambda-calculus reduction strategies. Technical Report 93/14, Department of Computer Science, University of St Andrews, 1993.

[Oga98] I. Ogata. Cut elimination for classical proofs as continuation passing style computation. In *ASIAN'98: Advances in Computing Science*, volume 1538 of *Lecture Notes in Computer Science.* Springer-Verlag, 1998.

[OLT94] C. Okasaki, P. Lee, and D. Tarditi. Call-by-need and continuation-passing style. *Lisp and Symbolic Computation*, 7(1):57–82, 1994.

[Ong88] L. Ong. *The Lazy Lambda Calculus: an Investigation into the Foundations of Functional Programming.* PhD thesis, University of London, 1988.

[Pal97] C. Palamidessi. Comparing the expressive power of the synchronous and the asynchronous pi-calculus. In *24th Annual ACM Symposium on Principles of Programming Languages.* ACM Press, 1997.

[Par81] D. Park. Concurrency on automata and infinite sequences. In *Theoretical Computer Science*, volume 104 of *Lecture Notes in Computer Science.* Springer-Verlag, 1981.

[Par99] J. Parrow. On the relationship between two proof systems for the pi-calculus. Unpublished note, 1999.

[Par01] J. Parrow. An introduction to the π-calculus. In *Handbook of Process Algebra.* Elsevier, 2001.

[Phi87] I. Phillips. Refusal testing. *Theoretical Computer Science*, 50:241–284, 1987.

[Pit97] A. Pitts. Operationally-based theories of program equivalence. In *Semantics and Logics of Computation.* Cambridge University Press, 1997.

[Plo75] G. Plotkin. Call by name, call by value and the λ-calculus. *Theoretical Computer Science*, 1:125–159, 1975.

[Plo77] G. Plotkin. LCF as a programming language. *Theoretical Computer Science*, 5:223–255, 1977.

[PS92] S. Purushothaman and J. Seaman. An adequate operational semantics for sharing in lazy evaluation. In *ESOP'92: European Symposium on Programming*, volume 582 of *Lecture Notes in Computer Science.* Springer-Verlag, 1992.

[PS95] J. Parrow and D. Sangiorgi. Algebraic theories for name-passing calculi. *Information and Computation*, 120(2):174–197, 1995.

[PS96] B. Pierce and D. Sangiorgi. Typing and subtyping for mobile processes. *Journal of Mathematical Structures in Computer Science*, 6(5):409–454, 1996.

[PS00] B. Pierce and D. Sangiorgi. Behavioral equivalence in the polymorphic pi-calculus. *Journal of the ACM*, 47(5):531–584, 2000.

[PT95] B. Pierce and D. Turner. Concurrent objects in a process calculus. In *Theory and Practice of Parallel Programming*, volume 907 of *Lecture Notes in Computer Science*. Springer-Verlag, 1995.

[PT00] B. Pierce and D. Turner. Pict: A programming language based on the Pi-calculus. In *Proof, Language, and Interaction*. MIT Press, 2000.

[PV98] J. Parrow and B. Victor. The fusion calculus: Expressiveness and symmetry in mobile processes. In *13th Annual IEEE Symposium on Logic in Computer Science*. IEEE Computer Society Press, 1998.

[PW98] A. Philippou and D. Walker. On transformations of concurrent-object programs. *Theoretical Computer Science*, 195:259–289, 1998.

[QW98] P. Quaglia and D. Walker. On encoding pπ in mπ. In *FSTTCS'98: Foundations of Software Technology and Theoretical Computer Science*, volume 1530 of *Lecture Notes in Computer Science*. Springer-Verlag, 1998.

[QW00] P. Quaglia and D. Walker. On synchronous and asynchronous mobile processes. In *FOSSACS'00: Foundations of Software Science and Computational Structures*, volume 1784 of *Lecture Notes in Computer Science*. Springer-Verlag, 2000.

[Rep99] J. Reppy. *Concurrent Programming in ML*. Cambridge University Press, 1999.

[Rey72] J. Reynolds. Definitional interpreters for higher order programming languages. *ACM Conference Proceedings*, 1972.

[Rey88] J. Reynolds. Preliminary design of the programming language Forsythe. Technical Report CMU-CS-88-159, Carnegie Mellon University, 1988.

[Rey93] J. Reynolds. The discoveries of continuations. *Lisp and Symbolic Computation*, 6:233–248, 1993.

[Röc01] C. Röckl. *On the Mechanised Validation of Infinite-State and Parametrised Reactive and Mobile Systems*. Ph.D. thesis, Technische Universität München, 2001.

[RT94] J. Rutten and D. Turi. Initial algebra and final coalgebra semantics for concurrency. In *A Decade of Concurrency*, volume 803 of *Lecture Notes in Computer Science*. Springer-Verlag, 1994.

[RV97] A. Ravara and V. Vasconcelos. Behavioural types for a calculus of concurrent objects. In *Euro-Par'97: Parallel Processing*, volume 1300 of *Lecture Notes in Computer Science*. Springer-Verlag, 1997.

[San92] D. Sangiorgi. *Expressing Mobility in Process Algebras: First-Order and Higher-Order Paradigms*. PhD thesis, Department of Computer Science, University of Edinburgh, 1992.

[San94] D. Sangiorgi. The lazy lambda calculus in a concurrency scenario. *Information and Computation*, 111(1):120–153, 1994.

[San95] D. Sangiorgi. Lévy-Longo Trees and Böhm Trees from encodings of λ-calculus into π-calculus. Unpublished note, 1995.

[San96a] D. Sangiorgi. Bisimulation for higher-order process calculi. *Information and Computation*, 131(2):141–178, 1996.

[San96b] D. Sangiorgi. Locality and non-interleaving semantics in calculi for mobile processes. *Theoretical Computer Science*, 155:39–83, 1996.

[San96c] D. Sangiorgi. π-calculus, internal mobility and agent-passing calculi. *Theoretical Computer Science*, 167(2):235–274, 1996.

[San96d] D. Sangiorgi. A theory of bisimulation for the π-calculus. *Acta Informatica*,

33:69–97, 1996.

[San98a] D. Sangiorgi. An interpretation of typed objects into typed π-calculus. *Information and Computation*, 143(1):34–73, 1998.

[San98b] D. Sangiorgi. On the bisimulation proof method. *Journal of Mathematical Structures in Computer Science*, 8:447–479, 1998.

[San99a] D Sangiorgi. From λ to π, or: Rediscovering continuations. *Journal of Mathematical Structures in Computer Science*, 9(4), 1999.

[San99b] D. Sangiorgi. The name discipline of uniform receptiveness. *Theoretical Computer Science*, 221:457–493, 1999.

[San99c] D. Sangiorgi. Typed π-calculus at work: a correctness proof of Jones's parallelisation transformation on concurrent objects. *Theory and Practice of Object Systems*, 5(1):25–34, 1999.

[San00] D. Sangiorgi. Lazy functions and mobile processes. In *Proof, Language, and Interaction.* MIT Press, 2000.

[San01a] D. Sangiorgi. Asynchronous process calculi: the first-order and higher-order paradigms (tutorial). *Theoretical Computer Science*, 253:311–350, 2001.

[San01b] D. Sangiorgi. Some results on barbed congruence. Unpublished note, 2001.

[Sch86] D. Schmidt. *Denotational Semantics – A methodology for language development.* Allyn and Bacon, 1986.

[Sel97] P. Selinger. First-order axioms for asynchrony. In *CONCUR'97: Concurrency Theory*, volume 1243 of *Lecture Notes in Computer Science.* Springer-Verlag, 1997.

[Sew98] P. Sewell. Global/local subtyping and capability inference for a distributed π-calculus. In *ICALP'98: Automata, Languages and Programming*, volume 1443 of *Lecture Notes in Computer Science.* Springer-Verlag, 1998.

[SF93] A. Sabry and M. Felleisen. Reasoning about programs in continuation-passing style. *Lisp and Symbolic Computation*, 6:289–360, 1993.

[SK98] E. Sumii and N. Kobayashi. A generalized deadlock-free process calculus. In *HLCL'98: High-Level Concurrent Languages*, volume 16.3 of *ENTCS*. Elsevier, 1998.

[SM92] D. Sangiorgi and R. Milner. The problem of "weak bisimulation up to". In *CONCUR'92: Concurrency Theory*, volume 630 of *Lecture Notes in Computer Science.* Springer-Verlag, 1992.

[Smo95] G. Smolka. The Oz programming model. In *Computer Science Today.* Springer-Verlag, 1995.

[SN97] M. Steffen and U. Nestmann. Typing confluence. In *Second International ERCIM Workshop on Formal Methods in Industrial Critical Systems.* Consiglio Nazionale Ricerche di Pisa, 1997.

[Sti96] C. Stirling. Modal and temporal logics for processes. In *Logics for Concurrency: Structure versus Automata*, volume 1043 of *Lecture Notes in Computer Science.* Springer-Verlag, 1996.

[SV98] G. Smith and D. Volpano. Secure information flow in a multi-threaded imperative language. In *25th Annual ACM Symposium on Principles of Programming Languages.* ACM Press, 1998.

[SW74] C. Strachey and C. Wadsworth. Continuations: A mathematical semantics for handling full jumps. Technical Monograph PRG-11, Oxford University Computing Laboratory, 1974.

[Ten91] R. Tennent. *Semantics of Programming Languages.* Prentice Hall, 1991.

[Thi97] H. Thielecke. *Categorical Structure of Continuation Passing Style*. PhD thesis, Department of Computer Science, University of Edinburgh, 1997.

[Tho90] B. Thomsen. *Calculi for Higher Order Communicating Systems*. PhD thesis, University of London, 1990.

[Tho94] B. Thomsen. Polymorphic sorts and types for concurrent functional programs. In *6th Workshop on the Implementation of Functional Languages*. University of East Anglia, 1994.

[TJ94] J.-P. Talpin and P. Jouvelot. The type and effect discipline. *Information and Computation*, 111(2):245–296, 1994.

[TLK96] B. Thomsen, L. Leth, and T.-M. Kuo. A Facile tutorial. In *CONCUR'96: Concurrency Theory*, volume 1119 of *Lecture Notes in Computer Science*. Springer-Verlag, 1996.

[Tur96] D. Turner. *The Polymorphic pi-calculus: Theory and Implementation*. PhD thesis, Department of Computer Science, University of Edinburgh, 1996.

[TWM95] D. Turner, P. Wadler, and C. Mossin. Once upon a type. In *Functional Programming and Computer Architecture*. ACM Press, 1995.

[Vas94] V. Vasconcelos. Predicative polymorphism in π-calculus. In *PARLE'94: Parallel Architectures and Languages Europe*, volume 817 of *Lecture Notes in Computer Science*. Springer-Verlag, 1994.

[Vas01] V. Vasconcelos. An efficient encoding of call-by-value λ-calculus into the π-calculus. Unpublished note, 2001.

[VB98] V. Vasconcelos and R. Bastos. Core-TyCO, the language definition, version 0.1. DI/FCUL TR 98–3, Department of Computer Science, University of Lisbon, 1998. See also `http://www.di.fc.ul.pt/~vv/tyco.html`.

[VD98] J.-L. Vivas and M. Dam. From higher-order pi-calculus to pi-calculus in the presence of static operators. In *CONCUR'98: Concurrency Theory*, volume 1466 of *Lecture Notes in Computer Science*. Springer-Verlag, 1998.

[VH93] V. Vasconcelos and K. Honda. Principal typing schemes in a polyadic π-calculus. In *CONCUR'93: Concurrency Theory*, volume 715 of *Lecture Notes in Computer Science*. Springer-Verlag, 1993.

[Vic98] B. Victor. *The Fusion Calculus: Expressiveness and Symmetry in Mobile Processes*. PhD thesis, Uppsala University, 1998.

[VM94] B. Victor and F. Moller. The Mobility Workbench: A tool for the pi-calculus. In *CAV'94: Computer-Aided Verification*, volume 818 of *Lecture Notes in Computer Science*. Springer-Verlag, 1994.

[VP98] B. Victor and J. Parrow. Concurrent constraints in the Fusion Calculus. In *ICALP'98: Automata, Languages and Programming*, volume 1443 of *Lecture Notes in Computer Science*. Springer-Verlag, 1998.

[Wad71] C. Wadsworth. *Semantics and Pragmatics of the Lambda Calculus*. PhD thesis, University of Oxford, 1971.

[Wal90] D. Walker. Bisimulation and divergence. *Information and Computation*, 85(2):202–241, 1990.

[Wal91] D. Walker. π-calculus semantics of object-oriented programming languages. In *TACS'91: Theoretical Aspects of Computer Software*, volume 526 of *Lecture Notes in Computer Science*. Springer-Verlag, 1991.

[Wal94] D. Walker. Algebraic proofs of properties of objects. In *ESOP'94: European*

Symposium on Programming, volume 788 of *Lecture Notes in Computer Science*. Springer-Verlag, 1994.

[Wal95] D. Walker. Objects in the π-calculus. *Information and Computation*, 116(2):253–271, 1995.

[Wri92] A. Wright. Typing references by effect inference. In *ESOP'92: European Symposium on Programming*, volume 582 of *Lecture Notes in Computer Science*. Springer-Verlag, 1992.

[YH99] N. Yoshida and M. Hennessy. Subtyping and locality in distributed higher order processes. In *CONCUR'99: Concurrency Theory*, volume 1664 of *Lecture Notes in Computer Science*. Springer-Verlag, 1999.

[Yos93] N. Yoshida. Optimal reduction in weak lambda-calculus with shared environments. In *Functional Programming Languages and Computer Architecture*, 1993.

[Yos96] N. Yoshida. Graph types for monadic mobile processes. In *FSTTCS'96: Foundations of Software Technology and Theoretical Computer Science*, volume 1180 of *Lecture Notes in Computer Science*. Springer-Verlag, 1996.

[Yos98] N. Yoshida. Minimality and separation results on asynchronous mobile processes. In *CONCUR'98: Concurrency Theory*, volume 1466 of *Lecture Notes in Computer Science*. Springer-Verlag, 1998.

Index